The rise, race, and royalty of the kingdom of God in the soul of man opened in several sermons upon Matthew 18.3: as also the loveliness & love of Christ set forth in several other sermons upon Psal. 45. v. 1, 2 (1683)

Peter Sterry

The rise, race, and royalty of the kingdom of God in the soul of man opened in several sermons upon Matthew 18.3 : as also the loveliness & love of Christ set forth in several other sermons upon Psal. 45. v. 1, 2

Sterry, Peter, 1613-1672.
"The publisher to the reader" signed: J. White.
[26], 515, [1] p.
London : Printed for Thomas Cockerill ..., 1683.
McAlpin Coll. / IV 151
Wing / S5482
English
Reproduction of the original in the Bristol (England) Public Libraries

Early English Books Online (EEBO) Editions

Imagine holding history in your hands.

Now you can. Digitally preserved and previously accessible only through libraries as Early English Books Online, this rare material is now available in single print editions. Thousands of books written between 1475 and 1700 and ranging from religion to astronomy, medicine to music, can be delivered to your doorstep in individual volumes of high-quality historical reproductions.

We have been compiling these historic treasures for more than 70 years. Long before such a thing as "digital" even existed, ProQuest founder Eugene Power began the noble task of preserving the British Museum's collection on microfilm. He then sought out other rare and endangered titles, providing unparalleled access to these works and collaborating with the world's top academic institutions to make them widely available for the first time. This project furthers that original vision.

These texts have now made the full journey -- from their original printing-press versions available only in rare-book rooms to online library access to new single volumes made possible by the partnership between artifact preservation and modern printing technology. A portion of the proceeds from every book sold supports the libraries and institutions that made this collection possible, and that still work to preserve these invaluable treasures passed down through time.

This is history, traveling through time since the dawn of printing to your own personal library.

Initial Proquest EEBO Print Editions collections include:

Early Literature

This comprehensive collection begins with the famous Elizabethan Era that saw such literary giants as Chaucer, Shakespeare and Marlowe, as well as the introduction of the sonnet. Traveling through Jacobean and Restoration literature, the highlight of this series is the Pollard and Redgrave 1475-1640 selection of the rarest works from the English Renaissance.

Early Documents of World History

This collection combines early English perspectives on world history with documentation of Parliament records, royal decrees and military documents that reveal the delicate balance of Church and State in early English government. For social historians, almanacs and calendars offer insight into daily life of common citizens. This exhaustively complete series presents a thorough picture of history through the English Civil War.

Historical Almanacs

Historically, almanacs served a variety of purposes from the more practical, such as planting and harvesting crops and plotting nautical routes, to predicting the future through the movements of the stars. This collection provides a wide range of consecutive years of "almanacks" and calendars that depict a vast array of everyday life as it was several hundred years ago.

Early History of Astronomy & Space

Humankind has studied the skies for centuries, seeking to find our place in the universe. Some of the most important discoveries in the field of astronomy were made in these texts recorded by ancient stargazers, but almost as impactful were the perspectives of those who considered their discoveries to be heresy. Any independent astronomer will find this an invaluable collection of titles arguing the truth of the cosmic system.

Early History of Industry & Science

Acting as a kind of historical Wall Street, this collection of industry manuals and records explores the thriving industries of construction; textile, especially wool and linen; salt; livestock; and many more.

Early English Wit, Poetry & Satire

The power of literary device was never more in its prime than during this period of history, where a wide array of political and religious satire mocked the status quo and poetry called humankind to transcend the rigors of daily life through love, God or principle. This series comments on historical patterns of the human condition that are still visible today.

Early English Drama & Theatre

This collection needs no introduction, combining the works of some of the greatest canonical writers of all time, including many plays composed for royalty such as Queen Elizabeth I and King Edward VI. In addition, this series includes history and criticism of drama, as well as examinations of technique.

Early History of Travel & Geography

Offering a fascinating view into the perception of the world during the sixteenth and seventeenth centuries, this collection includes accounts of Columbus's discovery of the Americas and encompasses most of the Age of Discovery, during which Europeans and their descendants intensively explored and mapped the world. This series is a wealth of information from some the most groundbreaking explorers.

Early Fables & Fairy Tales

This series includes many translations, some illustrated, of some of the most well-known mythologies of today, including Aesop's Fables and English fairy tales, as well as many Greek, Latin and even Oriental parables and criticism and interpretation on the subject.

Early Documents of Language & Linguistics

The evolution of English and foreign languages is documented in these original texts studying and recording early philology from the study of a variety of languages including Greek, Latin and Chinese, as well as multilingual volumes, to current slang and obscure words. Translations from Latin, Hebrew and Aramaic, grammar treatises and even dictionaries and guides to translation make this collection rich in cultures from around the world.

Early History of the Law

With extensive collections of land tenure and business law "forms" in Great Britain, this is a comprehensive resource for all kinds of early English legal precedents from feudal to constitutional law, Jewish and Jesuit law, laws about public finance to food supply and forestry, and even "immoral conditions." An abundance of law dictionaries, philosophy and history and criticism completes this series.

Early History of Kings, Queens and Royalty

This collection includes debates on the divine right of kings, royal statutes and proclamations, and political ballads and songs as related to a number of English kings and queens, with notable concentrations on foreign rulers King Louis IX and King Louis XIV of France, and King Philip II of Spain. Writings on ancient rulers and royal tradition focus on Scottish and Roman kings, Cleopatra and the Biblical kings Nebuchadnezzar and Solomon.

Early History of Love, Marriage & Sex

Human relationships intrigued and baffled thinkers and writers well before the postmodern age of psychology and self-help. Now readers can access the insights and intricacies of Anglo-Saxon interactions in sex and love, marriage and politics, and the truth that lies somewhere in between action and thought.

Early History of Medicine, Health & Disease

This series includes fascinating studies on the human brain from as early as the 16th century, as well as early studies on the physiological effects of tobacco use. Anatomy texts, medical treatises and wound treatment are also discussed, revealing the exponential development of medical theory and practice over more than two hundred years.

Early History of Logic, Science and Math

The "hard sciences" developed exponentially during the 16th and 17th centuries, both relying upon centuries of tradition and adding to the foundation of modern application, as is evidenced by this extensive collection. This is a rich collection of practical mathematics as applied to business, carpentry and geography as well as explorations of mathematical instruments and arithmetic; logic and logicians such as Aristotle and Socrates; and a number of scientific disciplines from natural history to physics.

Early History of Military, War and Weaponry

Any professional or amateur student of war will thrill at the untold riches in this collection of war theory and practice in the early Western World. The Age of Discovery and Enlightenment was also a time of great political and religious unrest, revealed in accounts of conflicts such as the Wars of the Roses.

Early History of Food

This collection combines the commercial aspects of food handling, preservation and supply to the more specific aspects of canning and preserving, meat carving, brewing beer and even candy-making with fruits and flowers, with a large resource of cookery and recipe books. Not to be forgotten is a "the great eater of Kent," a study in food habits.

Early History of Religion

From the beginning of recorded history we have looked to the heavens for inspiration and guidance. In these early religious documents, sermons, and pamphlets, we see the spiritual impact on the lives of both royalty and the commoner. We also get insights into a clergy that was growing ever more powerful as a political force. This is one of the world's largest collections of religious works of this type, revealing much about our interpretation of the modern church and spirituality.

Early Social Customs

Social customs, human interaction and leisure are the driving force of any culture. These unique and quirky works give us a glimpse of interesting aspects of day-to-day life as it existed in an earlier time. With books on games, sports, traditions, festivals, and hobbies it is one of the most fascinating collections in the series.

H: y ..a...

THE

Riſe, Race, and Royalty

OF THE

Kingdom of God

IN THE

Soul of MAN.

OPENED

In ſeveral Sermons upon *Matthew* 18. 3.

AS ALSO

The Lovelineſs & Love of Chriſt

Set forth

In ſeveral other Sermons upon *Pſal.* 45. *v.* 1, 2.

Together with

An Account of the State of a Saint's Soul and Body in Death.

By PETER STERRY, ſometimes Fellow of *Emanuel* Colledge in *Cambridge*, and Late Preacher of the Goſpel in *London*.

Matthew 11. 19. *But Wiſdom is juſtified of her Children.*

LONDON,

Printed for *Thomas Cockerill*, at the Three Leggs over againſt the *Stocks-Market* in the *Poultry*. 1683.

THE

PUBLISHER

TO THE

READER.

Reader,

IF *thou knew'st the* Author *of these following Discourses, it is needless to say any thing to thee concerning* him *or* them. *And if thou art still a stranger to him, it is pity to detain thee from so profitable an Acquaintance as thou may'st yet most happily redeem with* him, *by these his* Excellent Works, *in which he has given us a much better Account of himself, than it is possible now to receive from any other hand.*

However, the Publisher professes so great a Love and Veneration for his Person, and is so great an Admirer of these, and all other Discourses of his, which he has yet seen, that he dare not venture to tell thee his own thoughts of either, *lest he should offend against the* Spring, *whilst he commends the* Stream. *Upon this and some other considerations, which are to him of much weight, he declines doing any thing that may pretend to look like a* Preface; *and believes upon thy due perusal of what is here presented to thee, thou wilt easily justifie his Modesty and Prudence herein. Nor wilt thou then wonder that our* Author, *and this* his Book *addresses thee so directly, and without the* recommendations *of some of the* Greater Lights *and* Rabbies *of our present Times. It would indeed be a new thing for a Person, and Discourses so very heavenly and spiritual, to receive such a* complement; and eſpecially in an Age which has all along diſcovered ſuch a watchful jealouſie over, and oppoſition to all the encreaſes and growths of Truth above the pitch and ſtature of Opinions and Principles commonly received among us. An Age, which inſtead of forgetting thoſe things which are behind, and reaching forth unto thoſe things which are before, as the Apoſtle ſpeaks, Phil. 3. 13. has taken up its reſt and ſatisfaction in preſent meaſures and attainments, making them the Rule, the Law, the Teſt, and the Standard to all the further diſcoveries and breakings forth of God in the midſt of us. It has ſtill been the Lot of the Divineſt Births, and Appearances of God in this lower World, to be moſt ſolitary and neglected as to an outward pomp and attendance. They are reſerved for the Glory and Triumph of another day. We read indeed of a Ruler, who came to Chriſt by night, being drawn by the fame of his Miracles; and of the Multitude following him for the Loaves: but upon that moſt ſpiritual Sermon of our Saviour's in the 6th chap. of John, the Text tells us, Many of the Diſciples went back, and walked no more with him: And that the Twelve were themſelves ſo ſtagger'd, that our Lord ſaies unto them, Will ye alſo go away?

Leaving then our Author, and his Book among thoſe excellent and beſt things, which have alwaies ſtood alone in this World, and been contented ſo to do; I now apply my ſelf to the proper ſervice of theſe Lines, which is to acquaint thee, that theſe Diſcourſes are poſthumous, and not deſigned for the Preſs, when they were firſt Preached; but are now made publick, to anſwer the importunities of particular Friends, and the requiring of a more univerſal Charity, that ſo much Goodneſs ſhould be communicative.

This is the reaſon, why in the diligent peruſal of this Book, thou wilt find an omiſſion of ſome few Heads of Diſcourſe, as to the particular enlargement upon them, both in the Sermons upon Matth. 18. and thoſe upon the 45th Pſalm: As alſo why neither of thoſe Diſcourſes are compleatly finiſhed: Thoſe few particular Heads being forgotten by our Author in his Original Copy, which

is

's *here exactly observed; and he by his death prevented bringing* *f either Discourse to their desired and designed perfection.*

I must also acquaint thee, that the State of a Saint's Soul and Body in death, *which makes the* last part *of this Book, was in-* *tended by our Author, as an Introduction only to several* Sermons *which he afterwards Preached upon that* Argument, *from those* *two* Scriptures, 1 Thes. 4 14. *and* Heb. 2. 14, 15. *in which he* *dispatch'd the several* Heads *enumerated in the* beginning, *as al-* *so those which are wanting at the* end *of that Discourse, belong-* *ing to the* first *consolation and joy of death to a Saint; which* *Sermons, to the Reader's great satisfaction had been here publish-* *ed as the Author's* finishing strokes *to his excellent* representa- tion *of Death, had they not proved his* own Funeral Discourses; *for before he could give us a* Copy *of them, or correct* one, *which* *was imperfectly taken from his mouth,* he died; *confirming to us* *his* Belief *of what he had deliver'd upon that* Subject, *by his* *hastening to the highest* proof *thereof, which is* enjoyment. *However, it is judg'd worth the Reader's while, to make what* *our Author design'd for the* beginning *of several other Discourses,* *to be the* conclusion *of these, it being so sweet a* strain *in his* Dying Song, *and so admirable an expression of his* Victory *and* Triumph *over the* King of Terrors.

I must also tell thee, that some few Errata's have escaped the *Press, which the more intelligent may rectifie as they read;* *although for the sake of the more ordinary Readers they are care-* *fully corrected in the end of the Book. 'Tis hoped the Reader* *will not think it* one, *that these Discourses are Printed in no* *bigger a* Letter, *and that we have left him no fairer a* Margent, *because we have herein consulted his Purse, and taken care he* *should buy as little waste Paper as was possible in the purchase of* *this Book. Nor will the understanding Reader complain it wants* *the Ornament of a large empty Margent, or the ostentation of one* *filled with Learned Quotations, whilst in the reading of it he will* *find our Author has given him throughout his Book all manner* *of* Humane, *and* Divine *learning, after the best sort; Well di-* *gested, and converted into an excellent* habit, strength, *and acti-* *vity of mind.*

And

And now Reader, *I have only some few requests to present to* thee *for* thy own sake, *rather then our* Authours.

First, *It is probable thou maist here meet with some things which not onely from the* manner *of the expression, but chiefly from the* matter *of them, may be* difficult, *and* hard *to be understood. My request here is, Thou would'st take great care not to* Judge *and* condemn *what thou art not able first to* hear *and* understand, *lest by thy rash Censures thou should'st blindly rush upon* the hiding of power, *which the Prophet* Habakkuk *speaking of* Christ in the Spirit, *tells us*, Chap. 3. ver. 4. is in his hand. *That is*, "*In the spiritual discoveries* "*of Christ, which are as hands of light, by which he puts forth himself, and taks hold of the World. As our Author some where expresses himself upon those words. Who among us is yet able to comprehend all the distinct* ages *and* growths *of good minds; To understand the various* Improvements, measures *and* attainments, *the several* capacities, languages *and* operations, *which are peculiar to those* ages *and* growths? *It is impossible for us to set the* bounds *to spiritual things; To stint* that *S*pirit *in our selves or others which is a* fountain *of Divine Light and Life in all regenerated Souls, continually sending forth new streams, and running along with a fresh succession of Waters without any stop or limit. We are too* proud *to understand the* condescentions, *too* low *to take the* height, *too* shallow *to fathom the* depth, *too* narrow *to measure the* breadth, *too* short *to reach the* length *of the Divine truth and goodness, and the various communications of themselves to us. We cannot assign the* highest *or the* lowest *state of Saints, whilst they are here below. We cannot say all above* this *is* fancy, whimsie, dream, *and* delusion; *all below* that, *is* common, carnal, formal *and* superstitious. *As we ought not then to despise, and contemn that which is* below; *So let us not censure and condemn that which is* above *us. Blessed be* God all Good *S*ouls *in the midst of their greatest distances from one another here below do all* meet *in the* Divine Comprehension *above. We are all enfolded in the Divine Arms, we are all encircled in the Divine Love. That has* breadth, *and* length, *and* depth, *and* height

height *enough to reach, and hold us all. And if we cannot yet receive and embrace each other in our several ages, growths measures, and attainments, it is because we have little, low, dark, narrow and contracted hearts, feel but little of the love of Christ, and are no more fill'd with that Spirit which is the* spring, *the* center, *the* circle, *the* band *to all good Spirits in heaven, and on Earth. There is as great a difference in the* statures *of* Souls, *as of* bodies; *In the* growths *of* Christians, *as of* men *and all other things.* St. John, Joh. 12. &c. *distinguishes these* growths *into* little Children, Young men, Fathers, *twice together; That we might take the more distinct notice of them. Our* Author *was in the* highest *of these* ranks; *Was indeed one of the* tallest *among his* Brethren, *whether we consider the* height *of his own spiritual discoveries and enjoyments, or the* depth *of his condescentions to the* lowest *and* least *of* them. *For the* true stature *of any thing cannot be exactly taken without measuring from* both ends. That *is not truly* tall *or* great *which seems to stand high, and look big, but* that *which reaches* furthest, *which is most* extensive, comprehending *and* Universal. *Our Author was indeed a* true Father in Christ, *and so esteemed by all who knew him For his own great* understanding, *and* experience *in Divine things, for the* excellency *of his* Ministery, *whereby he did* in Jesus Christ thorow the Gospel *beget and edifie many; As also for the great* tenderness, *and* Father like bowels *which throughout his whole Ministry, and in all his other converses, he delighted to be still expressing towards all the* weak *and* little ones. *Nor was his* skill *herein less considerable than his* Naturalness. *This Character thou wilt find eminently due to him as thou perusest these* discourses, *in which he is still careful to provide* Milk *for the* Babes, *whilst he sets* stronger *Meat before the* men; *Those who are* Spiritual, *and by being so, are able* spiritually to discern spiritual things, *to* compare them with themselves, *and to feed* on them *not only as they are brought down to us in* fleshly Images, *and* resemblances; *But as they express and manifest themselves in us in their own spiritual* forms *and glories. Sure I am if thou art truly come within the compass of the* lowest *of those* growths *before mentioned*

ed

ed, if thou art become ſo much as a little Child in Chriſt, if thou haſt but that genuine inſtinct, and naturalneſs of Soul towards God and all Divine things, which is eſſential to, and inſeparable from the New birth in its moſt infant ſtate, if thou haſt but the leaſt degree of a Spiritual mind, any ſpiritual ſenſe and ſavour, there are a great many things in this Book which thy Soul muſt of neceſſity underſtand, eccho to, relliſh, and acknowledge to be exceeding good. Let then the goodneſs of what thou doſt underſtand, encourage thy Charity to think that which is above thy reach, may be better; At leaſt let it prevail with thy reaſon not to judge, ſentence, and condemn it.

It is every where eſteemed an high and difficult Office to be a Judge in the Affairs of this lower World. The Wiſdom of our Nation has provided (as a Noble Author obſerves) that ſo great a Work ſhould not depend upon One Perſon, every Court of Judicature having a certain number of Judges or Aſſiſtants belonging to it. Nor can a Judge depute his Authority to another, it being an Office and Work of greateſt Confidence, Truſt and Skill, and therefore perſonal and inherent And with what warineſs and caution do the Rules of all our Courts direct their own proceeding to a Judgment in every little caſe here below. It is certainly a much higher and harder work to be a Judge in the matters of another World, in things not obvious to Senſe, and tranſcendent to Reaſon, in things above all the natural Principles of Wiſdom or Truth in any creature. The Jews ſpeak of it as one of the firſt things delivered by God to Moſes, by him to Joſhua, and ſo down to all their Elders and Wiſe men in all Ages, To be ſlow in judging. St. Paul cautions us, 1 Cor. 4. 5. To judge nothing before the time, until the Lord come. To paſs a Judgment, to pronounce a Sentence upon Perſons and Principles in ſpiritual matters, is in its own nature, and in the conſequences thereof, the greateſt, the weightieſt act our Souls can put forth; and therefore not to be haſtily executed; nor indeed at all, without his preſence, from whom all the Authority, Power and Capacity of Spiritual Judgment is derived. God has committed all this Judgment in a more eſpecial manner to Jeſus Chriſt, and there can be

no

no true, right, authentick, valid, and final Judgment, without him, *and where he is not* present. *He has no where so deputed this Office and Work to any* Person *or* Company *of persons, as to* alienate *the dignity and glory of it from himself. And whether he dispence it* immediately *or* mediately, *he cannot be excluded. It is his Presence, and Power, the Appearances of Christ, and the manifestations of his Spirit, which do give to any Society of men the Distinction and Authority of a Church; to every Church or Person, the right, the ability of Spiritual Judgment. No man, no Church has here any other Spiritual Power and Capacity, besides that of* Christ, *and his* Spirit *in them. And how rich, full and sufficient soever the several Churches of Christ may at this day esteem themselves to be without him; yet sure I am, there is nothing more speaks the absence of Christ, and his spirit; And their poverty, emptiness, and weakness, then that* hasty, rash, sleight, partial, blind, *and* bold *judging and censuring one another which every where abounds in the present Christian Churches: Whilst* in some of them, *the greatest acts of spiritual judgment that can be done on Earth,* (as a great man long since complained,) *are made to* lackey *up and down for* Fees, *and become the most* ordinary process *that is. And* in others *which pretend to be more refin'd, to* attend *upon* outward forms, inward Opinions, *our own* parties, interests, *and* passions. *As if instead of* judging nothing before the time, until the Lord comes; *The Spirit of man would so determine every thing, that no* knot *should be left for him to* unty, *nothing remain for him to judge. But blessed be God* the causeless curse shall not come. *All the judgments which are fondly and proudly made in* mans day *shall be* cancell'd *in the* day *of* Christ. Your Brethren (*as God speaks by the* evangelical Prophet *to those that tremble at his Word*) That hated you, that cast you out for my name sake, said, Let the Lord be glorified: But he shall appear to your joy, and they shall be ashamed.

Be perswaded then to do *as God has* done: *Leave all judgment to the* Son, *to his* manner *and* measure *of appearing in thee. Wait still for his coming who is to set judgment in the*

Earth, to bring it forth in thy Spirit. Be first able to say, Thou art full of Power by the Spirit of the Lord, and of Judgment, *before thou takest upon thee to declare unto thy Brethren their transgressions, mistakes, follies, and errours. Do not venture to step into the Throne of Judicature, till he, whose place it is, lead thee up, lest thou find thy self ere thou art aware, in the* Chair of Scorners, *instead of the* Seat *of* Judgment. Judge nothing till Christ comes, *lest thou shouldest then be judged by him, as an* evil doer, *and a* busie body. *'Tis true, the* Spiritual Man *is said to* judge all things. *But that* Word, *that* State, *that* Work, *do all of them import a* distinct *and* critical discerning *of things: such must thine be of all things before they can be rightly judg'd by thee. Thou mayest indeed speak evil of what thou knowest not, but thou canst not* fairly *judge it, till thou doest thoroughly understand it. As a spiritual man read these following Discourses, and as such give thy judgment of them. Remember still, that every Truth is not spoken at* once *to every good man, nor any Truth opened to him in its full glory at the* first sight; *but as* Luther *speaks, we are enlightened by* Beam after Beam. *It is said of some things* our Saviour *did, and which were done unto him,* Joh. 12. *That* his Disciples understood them not at the first, but when Christ was glorified, *when he took away his fleshly presence, and came in more spirit,* then they were acquainted with them. What I do, *says* Christ *to* Peter, Joh. 13. 7. thou knowest not now, but thou shalt know hereafter. *And in* Joh. 16. 12, 13. *He tells his Disciples,* he had yet many things to say unto them, but they could not bear them then; *howbeit,* when the Spirit of Truth was come, he should guide them into all Truth. *When St.* Paul *was a little beforehand caught up into the World to come, the Text says,* 2 Cor. 12. 4. *that he* heard unspeakable words, which it is not lawful for a man to utter; *that* could not, *that* might not *be spoken. Such things as would no doubt have offended the best men then alive, if he had declared them. Good Souls have their several Orbs and Spheats of Spiritual Light and Life; all* below *are comprehended by them* above, *and lie in their Bosoms; but the* lesser Circle *can by no*

means

means contain *the* greater. *A Soul got no further than the* first Heavens, *cannot* hear, *cannot* receive *the discoveries and enjoyments of* one *in the* third. *If a Truth be very* raised *and* spiritual, *it is not the* first Beam of Christ himself *can shew us that Truth: And if I by my glimmering light shall go about to examine and judge things spoken in a clearer day, I shall be subject to many mistakes, and in great danger of rejecting the Truth, because I do not understand it.* In my Father's house, *saies Christ*, are many Mansions. *'Tis true of his* house *of* grace *here* below; *as well as* that *of* glory above. *Let every Christian then say of his present* state *and* measure, *This is my* present Heaven, *my* present Mansion; *here my God is pleased to meet me, thus he dispenseth himself to me; here I will wait, until I am called up higher; and if another comes and speaks things beyond my present understanding and experience, I will judge no man's* Light, Life *and* Liberty *in the Lord; being constant to this, that as* Christ *in the* flesh *came to his* own, *and his* own *received him not; so also may Christ in the* Spirit. *Instead then of judging and censuring what thou doest not yet understand, be faithful to that which thou already knowest; answer thy present light with a suitable life, so shalt thou* grow up, *not only into all the* Discoveries, Truths *and* Mysteries *which are in* this, *and* all other *spiritual Books, but* into him *also* in all things who is thy Head. *Hast thou received any one* ray, *any one* glimpse *of spiritual Light into thy Soul*, watch *it*, cherish *it*, walk *according to the* direction *and* instinct *of it; and* this Beam *shall quickly, swiftly grow up into a* glorious day *in thy spirit. For*, the path of the Just is as the shining Light that shineth more and more unto the perfect day.

Secondly; *It is possible thou mayest here meet with some few things very different from some of thy beloved Sentiments; for our* Author *intended in these Discourses, to tell thee his* own thoughts, *not to guess at* thine. *My* Requests *in this case, are such as these; not* to make thy self overwise; *not* to think thou knowest any thing; *not* to abound in thy own sense; *not to lay* too much *weight upon thy own Judgment, nor too little*

upon

upon thy Brother's; not to overvalue *thy own Notions and Opinions, nor to* undervalue *his; not to forget that* modesty *and* sobriety *of mind which every good man ought still to preserve towards himself; nor that* moderation, forbearance, indulgence, allowance *and* respect *which not only* charity, *but* reason *and* interest *oblige thee alwaies to express towards all good men that differ from thee. For we all stand in need of, and have a right to such a* tender behaviour *from one another. To impress a little such Requests as these upon thy mind, let me briefly offer to thy larger thoughts upon them, these few Considerations.*

1. *It is possible for us then to have* wrong *Notions and Opinions of Spiritual Truth, when we think we have the* rightest. *How easily do we mistake an* Object, *and the* true colour *of it, when we see it through a dyed and colour'd* Medium? *The Staff that is streight in the Air, seems crooked when it is seen under Water, through the grossness and inconstancy of that Element. Such are all our views, our reports of Divine Truths, whilst we take in, and give forth the Copies of them through the thick, colour'd, and spotted Glass of our Natural Understanding. Thou confessest thy self to bee a poor fallible creature; thou bemoanest daily thy Ignorance before the Lord, and beggest of him that thou mayest* understand thy own Errours: *Be not then too hasty in charging thy Brother with false Notions, whilst thou thy self art not exempted from mistakes: Do not think thy self an Infallible Judge of his Errours, whilst thou art but a Fallible Discerner of Truth for thy self.*

2. *It is impossible for us to have* clear *Notions and Opinions of Spiritual Truth, whilst we are in this* dark *and* distant *World.* We now see but through a Glass darkly. *We are in a* confused state. *We can better make a shift to puzzle and perplex the Notions of* another, *than we know how to disintangle and extricate our* own. *The Sun appears not to us in his true brightness and glory, but as a red bunning fire, when we see him in the mornings and evenings through those earthly vapours and mists which interpose. Such Fogs are still gathering between the God of Truth and our Understandings, whilest they dwell below. We are as yet but*

but like the blind man *in the* Gospel, *who upon the first touching of his Eyes, saw* Men *like* Trees. *How fond and obstinate should we think that man, who going forth in the* twilight, *when it is impossible clearly to discover and distinguish any thing, is however very confident he sees, and reports all things* aright? *All our Notions of Spiritual Truths here below, are at best but as a* Twilight, *in which* Light *and* Darkness *meet. How unreasonable is it whilst thy own Light is shaded with so much Darkness, to think there is no mixture of Light in thy Brother's Darkness?*

3. *It is impossible for us to have* full *and* comprehensive *Notions and Opinions of* Spiritual *Truth, whilst we are in this* separated *and* divided *state. Our knowledge here below is not only* dark (*as was said before*) *but* partial. *St.* Paul *with excellent reason puts these two together,* 1 Cor. 13. 12. We now see through a Glass darkly; we know but in part; *or*, in division. *It is indeed the* partiality *of our knowledge, which causes and encreases the* darkness *and* difficulty *of it, and turns it into a* Riddle. That *will be plain, easie, and pleasant to us, when we come at* once *to see the whole body of Divine Truth; when we shall in* one view *behold the entire frame, and universal harmony of it; the connexion, proportion, consent and sympathy of* one *Truth with* another, *and of* each *Truth with* every *Truth; which being now seen* alone, *puzzles, perplexes, intangles, and labyrinths us. Spiritual Truths are now* Ænigma's *to us, because we know but in* part, *in* division. *All our Notions and Opinions here can be but broken things, but little pieces of Truth. We are all running away with scattered bits and scraps of Spiritual Truth; every one fondly calling his own* share *the* entire Purchase: *But we know not how to put things together.* Some *are zealous for* one; others *for* another *part of Divine Truth; whilst we contend for* one, *we are apt to let go* another; *whilst we are seeking after* one, *we lose* another: *We continually mistake one another, and the Truth in each other, through our partial discovery of things: We have so much light, so much knowledge, as through the darkness and ignorance mingled with it, and prevailing over it, serves us.*

us to wrangle, dispute, and quarrel with our Brethren; but not enough to receive and comprehend them. We have indeed a Notion of the Indivisibility *of Truth, and are sure of it in the* Theory, *but we know not how to make it out in our* practice. *It is true, that is not Truth which cannot dwell with* any, *with every Truth; but all Truth is not yet thus reconciled in the head of any Good man on Earth, although it be so in every Good man's heart; he is in love with all Truth, but has not yet found out all its Alliances, the whole compass and circle of it. Truth is* one *in it self, but it is broken into I know not how many* pieces *as it is in us; and those pieces through the darkness mixt with them in our spirits, fighting one against another. The next state will give us a clear and comprehensive view of things; all the divisions of* Truths *and of* Spirits, *will then be at an end. Those Truths, those Spirits shall then be reconciled, and run into the Embraces of one another, that seem now to stand at the greatest distance and defiance: Then the Darkness shall no more predominate over the Light, nor employ it thus unnaturally to contend against it self; but the Light running together from all parts, and every where mingling with it self, shall swallow up all the Darkness. But we have now only a glimmering prospect of this happiness. It is impossible to attain here to a full view of the whole face of Truth, which is* great *and* glorious *as* God. *All our present Notions and Opinions are too narrow, too contracted to take in those innumerable Raies and Beams of Divine Truth, which are every where scattered and dispersed among all the Children of Light. Thou hast but one little part of it in all thy Notions and Opinions; thy Brother has another part in his. Instead of undervaluing* his *share, it becomes us much better to acknowledge the shortness of our* own; *and to say of* God (*with* Job *upon another occasion not much different*) Job 26. 14 Lo, these *are* parts of his waies, but how little a portion is heard of him!

4. *The* same *Spiritual Truth may communicate it self to us in* various, different, *and* contrary *Notions and Opinions. The whole state of things all along throughout the Christian World, is a sufficient proof of this matter. It is somewhere well observ'd by* our

our Author *to this purpose, as they say in Philosophy*, The Essences, and kinds of things, are unmoveable, and ever the same; *However there be an infiniteness of uncertainty and change in the* Individuals *by the variety and change of outward accidents: So if you compare one good man with all other good men in all ages, you will every where find the* same New Nature, the same inward savour *and* rellish, *the* same Divine Principle *and* God-like life *in them all*; *Whilst the* inward forms *of truth and goodness upon their understandings, and the* outward expressions *of them in their conversations, and practices, do exceedingly vary and differ, from the different degrees and waies of their light* within *and their educations, and customs* without. *The* Apostle *tells us, Rom.* 14. One *Christian* believeth that he may eat all things: Another who is weak eateth herbs. Let not him that eateth despise him that eateth not; And let not him which eateth not, judge him which eateth: For God hath received him. One man esteemeth one day above another: Another esteemeth every day alike. Let every man be fully assured in his own mind. He that regardeth the day, regardeth it unto the Lord; And he that regardeth not the day, to the Lord he doth not regard it. He that eateth, eateth to the Lord, for he giveth God thanks; And he that eateth not, to the Lord he eateth not, and giveth God thanks. *Both these are different, and contrary in their Notions, Opinions, and practices; And yet in that difference, and contrariety, do both serve the same Lord, and are accepted by him, They both in their several opinions, Notions, and practices, have the same apprehensions of the glory of God, the same reference and regard to it, the same aim and intention of* Soul *to make themselves a Spiritual sacrifice to him. Nor does this hold only in the* lesser *matters of Religion, but in the* greater *also. Besides that* Babel *and confusion of languages, that variety and contrariety of opinions which are in the Christian World, about things of a lower consideration; What disputes, what controversies, what contradictions, do we see at this day among good men concerning the most substantial, and vital truths of the Gospel? How even among the best Christians themselves, are some of the greatest points of Christianity, darkened and perplexed with Clouds of disputes, with diversity, and uncertainty of opinions, with different and contrary explications? What Principle of Christianity (how clearly and expresly soever it has been revealed to us in the letter of the Scriptures) has been universally received and explained alike by all good men? Do we not every where see those very Persons, who have (as we have reason to judge) entertained the same Divine Truths in the inward power, life, and Spirit of them, do yet discourse, interpret, and preach them in Notions, Opinions, and Forms, very different and contrary to one another? Do we not every where see good men puzling, and confounding each other with their own explanations of those very things, in the life and power of which they are all agreed? Have we not upon this accompt seen some of the best of men such strangers to, and so jealous of one another, that they have been unable to bear one another. Look abroad, lay aside all thy prejudice, fondness, and partiality; And then tell me if thou dost not every where meet with the same* ingenuity, modesty, humility, *and* meekness *of Soul; The same* desire *and diligence in the search after truth; the same* goodness, holiness *of* heart *and* life; *The same* Love *to God, and his waies; the same* sincerity, *and* integrity, *the same* purity *of* intention, aim *and* end; *in* persons *that appear to thee, and to one another, of very different, and contrary minds, and practices, in matters of Religion. Their Souls are vitally quickened, and informed, their conversations beautified, and adorned, with the same Spiritual truths; Which by their explications of them, they seem not to* understand, *yea to* contradict.

I have some where read a story of a blind man *who could distinguish and judge of all metals, or pretious stones, by* weighing *them in his hand. I am perswaded if we had learnt thus to judge of Spiritual things, not by the* beauty *of some outward form and appearance, or an* agreeableness *to our own Notions and Opinions; But by the* weight *of an inward Principle, and the Power of a Divine life; We should discover a most harmonious agreement in the* Essential *and* radical *Principles of Divine* truth *and* goodness, *among*

mong those who seem most of all to oppose one another, in their Notions, and Opinions. If we did but know how to get into, *to* open, *and* interpret *each others Souls; How to weigh not only* words, *and* phrases, *but* Spirits, *as God is said to do*, Prov. 16. 2. *We should quickly find, that we differ more in* words, *then in* thoughts, *and in the* Notions *of* things, *then in the* things themselves.

Our Spiritual wisdom, holiness, strength, *and* happiness, *do not lye in our Notions, and Opinions of Spiritual truth, but in the truth itself.* St. Paul *excellently distinguishes, and explains this matter*, 2 Cor. 4. 6, 7. *Where speaking of the* light of the knowledge of the Glory of God in the face of Jesus Christ, *he tells us*, we have this treasure in Earthen Vessels, that the excellency of the power may be of God, and not of us. That Spiritual truth *which is the shining forth of the glory of God in the* Person *of Christ, the* first, *the* supream, *the* universal truth, *is the* heavenly treasure; *The* several Notions, *and* forms *in our understandings, by which this truth appears to us, are but a part of the* Earthen Vessel *which holds this* treasure. *How weak is it, to lay the* weight *of such a* treasure, *upon such a* Vessel, *subject to so many frailties, flaws, and cracks? How unworthy is it, to ascribe the excellency of* that power *to our* selves, *which belongs wholly to* God? *Sure I am, it is not the* Vessel *that makes us* rich, *but the* treasure *which is in the* Vessel. *Thus again, The same* Apostle *speaking of the same thing in another expression, tells us*, 1 Cor. 4. 20. The Kingdom of God is not in word, but in power. *This Kingdom consists not in the excellency of our notions and apprehensions, of our* words, *and* expressions *concerning Spiritual things; But in the inward* Vertue, Vigour, Life, Power, *and* Spirit *that is in the Nature of them, to change the whole man into one image of glory with themselves. Spiritual knowledge is not a* notional, verbal, *and* talking; *but a* real, living, *and* practical *thing. Divine truth is better understood, as it opens and unfolds itself in the* holy, *and* heavenly mind, *and* life *of a good man, then by all the* Systems *of Divinity, and* good Books *in the World.*

Thy Brother *has (it may be) several Notions and opinions of Spiritual Truth, very different from thine; But he is really* sanctified

ctified through the same truth; He has purified his Soul in obeying the truth through the Spirit. *He is become a* living Edition *of the truth, it is* written *in his* heart, *it* shines forth *in his* life, *he has* so learned the truth, *that* he knows it as it is *in* Jesus; *although he cannot yet receive it*, as it is in thee, *nor thy notions and representations of it. His* Soul, *his* life, *is* dyed, coloured *and* figured *with it; the truth is transforming his whole being into one beautiful and blessed image* with, *framing, fashioning, his whole man* according to, *itself. This must needs be a better proof that he is truly* one *with thee in the same truth, then the highest complement he can pay to thy own notions and Opinions concerning it, can possibly be;* Holiness *is the* Character, *and* seal *of the Spirit of Truth. The result of this consideration is plainly this, That we should not lay too great a stress upon our own notions and Opinions, nor despise our Brothers; That we should make the* image of God, *and not our* own likeness, *the* reason, rule, *and* measure *of our Brotherly Love; Observing still in all our Christian converses, that excellent* League *which our* Saviour himself *has established.* He that is not against us, is with us. *Whilst we see the same truth vitally influencing, and quickening the* Souls *and spreading itself throughout the* lives *of good men of different and contrary sentiments, let us no longer judge another by his comprimising with our own sense of things, but his agreement with us in the substance, power, efficacy, and Spirit of the truth.*

Thus the primitive Christians judged, before the iniquity of the times, and a worldly interest corrupted the simplicity, and quenched the first and purer warmths of Religion. No man was then censured for his Opinion, that lived well, *although there were very strange notions then commenced. So much and so justly did those better ages of Christianity, prefer a* God like life, *to the* rightest notions *and* Opinions. *Nor did they want the highest Example, Authority, and Reason in this matter, God himself having told them, and us.* He is no respecter of Persons, but in every Nation, he that feareth him, and worketh righteousness is accepted with him, Act. 10. 34. *And again, Rom.* 14. 17. The Kingdom of God is not meat and Drink, but righteousness

ousness and peace, and joy in the Holy Ghost, and he that in these things serveth Christ, is acceptable to God, and approved of men: *That is, shall be justified in the* day *of all* Divine, *and* humane Principles. *Whatever his* outward form, *or* inward Opinion *be*; *Whether he eat, or eat not*; *Keep a day, or keep it not*; *So it be to the* Lord, *to* Charity, *and to Ædification.*

5. *All the truest and best notions, and Opinions we can have of Spiritual truth here* below, *are to be* done away, *when we arrive at that state* above, *So the* Apostle *expresly tells us*, 1 *Cor.* 13. 9. 10. We know in part, and we Prophesy in part. *But when that which is* perfect is come, then that which is in part shall be done away. *We shall* then *lose all our present Notions and Opinions of Spiritual things, not in a blackness of Darkness and Death, violently breaking in upon, and overspreading them*; *But in the brightness of an unmixt, and eternal light arising upon, and comprehending them in it self. They shall all be blotted out, not as water quenches the fire*; *But after such a manner as the Beams of the Sun do* put *it out, by drawing up the finer, and more fiery parts into themselves. They shall be* put *out, not as a Candle is by the* Extinguisher ; *But as the darknesses, and shadows of the night are swallowed up by the light of the morning: Or rather, as the several colours of light in the first dawning of the day, are afterwards drunk up into the pure and perfect light of the encreasing day. It is yet but a morning light with the most enlightned Souls here on Earth. In the first breaking of the day, the Light (you know) appears to us in a variety of colours, one after another*; *Till at last as the day comes on, all those colours are changed into an unstained and pure light. Such are the discoveries of Spiritual things to our understandings, whilst our* true day *is yet but* Springing. *All our Notions and Opinions of them are as so many colours of light, growing clearer and clearer, unto a Noon day brightness. Now all these colours vanish; Now all our mistaken, dark, mixt, short, and disproportioned notions and apprehensions, break up into a light which has nothing of privation, mixture, imperfection, or shadow in it. But till then it is impossible for us, to have such Notions & Opinions of* Spiritual *truth as can admit of no change*,

or

or emprovement.We are here in a growing *& travelling state. And whilst we are so, motion is better then rest. We can now no more stint, and fix our sense of things, then we can hinder and stop our own growth; Or keep day out of the World, when the Sun arises. It is not here, our* reproach, *but our* praise, *to be still changing our minds, to be still* transformed in the renewing of them, *that* we may prove what the good and acceptable will of God is. *To change for emprovement, to alter our minds for the better, is not our* inconstancy, *but our* virtue. *This is only to change, as all things do, when they encrease; nothing speaks us more* rooted, fixt, *and* established, *then such a* change. *Thou art not (it may be) of the same mind, at this instant, thou wert in, a few daies past, neither dost thou know what mind thou shalt have to morrow. The* spirit *of man changes Opinion every moment; And what one reason brings in this hour, a stronger may carry out the next. Nor will the* good Spirit *(if thou art indeed acted, and informed by it) suffer thee to rest in thy present light, and much less in thy remaining darkness. Thou art not yet so knowing, so good as thou shouldst be, if thou canst be satisfied with thy self, and thy present Notions of things. Art thou not waiting for Christ to* touch thine Eyes a second time? *Dost thou not pray for his Spirit to lead thee into all truth? Can'st thou be contented to lose thy share in the riches of that glory, thou art yet a stranger to? Thou thinkest (it may be) that thou* understandest all mysteries, *and hast all knowledge, but still all thou canst attain to here below, is but a* little part *of what is yet to come; And will be* done away, when that which is perfect appears. *Why then dost thou lay so great a weight upon those Notions and Opinions, which thou hadst not the other day, which thou mayst lose to morrow, and which are finally to be swallowed up? Why should an obscure, dark, intricate, curious, unnecessary, uncertain, and fading Notion and Opinion, be imploy'd to the prejudice of that* Charity *that shall never fail? All our Notions and Opinions are* changeable, temporary, transient, *and* perishing *things; They pass away, and confute themselves, whilst we are contending for them. but* Love *is a* lasting, permanent, *and* Eternal Duty, *and* perfection. *This shall remain, when all our Noti-*

ons

ons and Opinions of one sort and another, shall for ever cease to be ; Shall either sink down *into their* first darkness *out of which they sprung ; Or* rise up *into, and happily* lose *themselves in their* Original Light.

6. *Let us seriously consider how* mischievous *the want of that* moderation, *I am pleading for, has all along been to Christians and to* Christianity *it self. What depths of* inward filthinesses *have the* differences *and* animosities *of good men about Opinions, discovered* in them, *and drawn forth* from them ? *What floods of* outward *miseries have they brought* upon them ? *It is this has given such a scope, and power to our lusts, to our pride, ambition, covetousness, anger, wrath, bitterness of Spirit and revenge, as has been more* wounding *to Religion, then the malice of all the wicked men in the World can possibly be. It is* this *has set us to rake into the Infirmities, Weaknesses, and Miscarriages of our* mistaken Brother ; *And whilst men have been thus employed, what heaps of dirt, and folly have they poured out of their* own Spirits, *to the greater scandal of* themselves, *and their* profession ? *It is* this, *has for several ages delivered up the Christian World to disorder, bloud, and desolation. It is* this, *has rendred a great part of* it unhabitable *to a man that asserts the just liberty of his mind. It is* this *has made* Christians (*who should be the best of men*) *much worse to each other, than* wild Bears *and* Beasts of prey, *for they devour not one another of the same kind. It is* this *has raised so many suspitions, jealousies, fears, heart-burnings, evil surmises, mutual provocations to wrath, and thoughts of revenge, and ruine, among our selves, that we are almost become an* easy prey *to our common enemies ; And if we should escape* them, *are in danger to be* consumed one of another. *We have laid the stress, and weight of our Religion upon Notions, Opinions, outward modes and forms, and some of those subservient only to a secular interest, and* reasons of state, *and not upon the* truth *and* substance *it self, which is* Jesus Christ, *and* his Spirit. *For this reason the Righteous God seems to have given up the whole frame of Nature to confusion and destruction, and to be drowning the face of the Earth in bloud.*

St-

St. *Paul*, 2 Thess. 2. 1. *puts these* two *together*: The coming of our Lord Jesus Christ; *and*, our gathering together to him. *And we often read in the Scripture of* his coming with all his Saints. Lines *are at their greatest distance in the* circumference; *the* nearer *they come to their* center, *the* nearer *still they are to one another. As we are drawn forth from all those things which we have set up in the room of* Christ, *and are made to unite in his* Person *alone, so shall we also draw near to, and be at peace* with *one another. It is he alone who is our* King of Righteousness, and Prince of Peace, the true *Shiloe. Unto him shall the* gathering *of the People be, and unto each other in him. Nothing more proves him to be so* far off *from us, as our being so miserably scattered, divided, and driven away from one another, When he shall again return, and appear to us in his own Person, when we shall for* his sake *cast away all our* Idols, *and unanimously running into his Bosom, cry out with an universal shout*, None but Christ, *he alone is that* eternal image *it self of all* truth, *and* goodness, *which we have been every where seeking, our* center *and* rest *for ever: When we shall no more place our wisdom, righteousness, sanctification, and redemption, our* Religion *in those forms and Opinions, which are but the outsides, and dresses of* it, *and must* pass away with the fashion of this World; *Which are but the leaves and husks that shall fall to the ground; But* in him *who is that Truth, Life, Power, and Substance which* endures for ever. Then shall a peace which is to encrease without end, bless the World; All our Swords shall then be beaten into Plow-shares, our spears turned into pruning-hooks, and nothing be left to hurt, and destroy in Gods holy Mountain.

A mutual forbearance, indulgence, allowance, and kindness among all honest hearts *of different perswasions, and practices, has not only thy* own interest, *but the* concern *of all thy Brethren, and the* welfare *of the whole Christian World after the highest manner contained in it. For it is the* safety, stability, security, strength, *and* subsistence *of a* good interest, *and of all* good men, *in the midst of a very* unkind, angry *and* wicked *World; Whose rage doth not terminate in the extirpation of any one particular*

sect,

sect, or party of good men, *but would by degrees, and as fast as it can, blot out* goodness *itself. St. Paul with admirable reason joins these* two *together, Eph.* 4. 2, 3. Our walking with all lowliness and meekness, with long suffering, forbearing one another in love; *And*, our endeavouring to keep the unity of the *Spirit* in the bond of peace. *It is most plain from this* Scripture, *That the* unity *of the Church of God, is not an* agreement *in inward Opinions. and outward forms; But an* Unity *of Spirit; an* Unity *in* that Spirit, *which is the common Soul of the Church, the specificating form, the constituting and conserving Principle of all true Christianity. We are not united to* Christ, *and to* one another, *by the same Opinions, and Forms; but by one and the same Spirit, nor can any Opinions and Forms divide us from Christ, (and therefore ought not to separate us from each other) if they have not in their own nature an* enmity *to the* heavenly image *of* Christ, *which is* Spirituality; *Or to the* natural image *of* him *which is* morality. *It is* again *expresly told us in the* connexion *of this Sciptu re. That the way to preserve this Unity of the Spirit in the Body of Christ, is by walking towards one another* with all lowliness and meekness, with long-suffering, forbearing one another in love; *And not by a* proud, haughty, impatient, peevish *and* angry, *imposing of our own Notions, and modes of Religion upon them. This may indeed be a mistaken piece of humane policy to serve our own Worldly interest upon Christianity; but I am very sure, there is nothing of the true Spirit of Christ in this temper, nor of a right endeavouring to keep the Unity of his Spirit in such a proceeding.*

How clear is it again *from this Scripture, That the* bond of peace *has its* strength, *and* root, *not in an* Unity *of* knowledge *and* uniformity *of* worship, *but in the* Unity *of a* Divine Spirit; *As the sympathy, and Union of all the members in the body arise from, and is preserved by the Unity of the Soul.*

Whilst there is as great a difference in the Original make *of* Souls *as of* faces; *in the* complexions *of* minds, *as of* bodies; *whilst the* variety *of humane understandings is so great; Whilst we are under the* power *of different* tempers, educations, *and* interests, *several* measures *and* degrees *of* light; *Whilst there is* imperfection *in our state*, negligence *in our searchings after truth*; & *an* envious one *alwaies ready* to sow Tares; *It is unreasonable to expect a proportion, and analogy of Notions and Opinions among good men. Whilst we are thus circumstanced, there will be some o*therwise minded; *Nor do I know any remedy in such a case, but a* mutual forbearance, *till* God cleares *up the* matter of difference. *This* forbearance *cannot be more our* Duty, *then it is our* interest, *and* necessity; *for it is our* preservation *in the midst of powerful lusts* within, *and potent Enemies* without. *If all good men could but make a shift to* tollerate one another, *this wicked World must be bound to* endure them all. *Could they but hold together and love one another; No forreign violence could* break them. Goodness *is stronger then* Evil; *and therefore the* good *thus* united, *and in an* Association; *Must be too powerful for the* Evil, *with all its* Plots, Conspiracies, *and* Force. *What a* root *of mischiefs have the* Divisions *of good men been in all ages to* themselves. *From hence we may derive all the* Evils *we* feel, *and those also we fear. When the* sheep push, *and* run heads *against one another, the* Shepheard *saies, we shall have* foul weather. *We have already seen the truth of this* observation, *and I am affraid must feel it once again. 'Tis easy to* presage *a* storm *when so much* ill weather *appeares in the Spirits, faces, and actions of men. God grant it may prove but a* storm, *for from the animosities that are yet between good men, and an* implacableness *of Spirit which is started among us, we have cause to fear a* Deluge.

These Reader, *are some few* General considerations *to impress a little upon thy mind*, that moderation *which is thy* Duty, *and every good mans* Right, *how different soever his Notions, and Opinions may be from thine. I might now add some* others, *which more* particularly *relate to our* excellent Author, *but I have already too much exceeded the bounds of my own intentions, and thy patience; nor would I willingly depart from the Modesty of my first Resolution, which was to do nothing in this service, that might pretend to pass for a* Preface *to these* following Discourses. *I therefore*

therefore leave the Book itself *to open to thee its own unspeakable worth, as thou readest it. And I perswade my self, when thou hast duly perused it, and well observed those* excellent rules *by which our* Author *governs himself throughout these discourses; That admirable* temper, *and* Spirit; *That pleasant, and powerful* tendency *to* holiness, *and* spirituality, *that is every where to be found in them?* *Whatever thy thoughts may be concerning some of his* sentiments, *thou must needs have a great love for his* memory.

There is not in the universal Nature *of things a more intimate* Sympathy, *then* that *of* Truth, *and* Gooodness; *they are really* one; *They are for ever* inseparable: *They differ only as the* seal *and the* stamp; Goodness *being but the* Impression *of* Truth.

This consideration (I must confess) has so far prevailed with me, that I cannot defend my self from thinking, there must be something *of* truth *in* all *our* Author *has here delivered to us, whilst I find there is so much* goodness *in it* all.

And now Reader, *according to* custom, *I should spend a great deal more of thy* time *in a* long Apology, *for having already taken up so much of* it. *But in my Opinion to excuse this matter, is at once to abuse my* self, *and* thee. *For it was in my power not to have given* thee *all this trouble, if for the sake at least of some Readers, I had not judged it reasonable so to do; and if thou thinkest otherwise, it is still in thy power to escape as much of it as thou pleasest. I chuse rather to take my leave of* thee *with* this serious Request to the, *That thou wouldst read these* Heavenly Discourses *with the same* Divine Love *which first brought them forth from the* fountain *of all Loves. It is not by the* sagacity *of our own* Natural understandings, *but by being* rooted *and* grounded *in* Love *that we come* to comprehend *S*piritual truths. *That this* Love may abound in thee *yet* more and more in knowledge, and in all judgment, *or* sense, that thou mayst approve things that are excellent, *Is the hearty prayer of*

Thy Well-wisher and *S*ervant.

J. WHITE.

MAT. XVIII. 3.

Except ye be converted, and become as little Children, ye cannot enter into the Kingdom of Heaven.

IN the *First Verse*, the Disciples of our Lord measuring the State of Things above, by the Principles of Reason, and the Fashion of this World; make this Inquiry; *Who should be Greatest in the Kingdom of God*; as if *Ambition* must follow us into *Heaven*, there also to make a *Hell*.

Our Savior would undeceive those, whom He lov'd, by answering not so much to their Proposals, as their Principles. Therefore He gives them a full *Description* of the Christian Mystery, which is exprest in the words of my Text: *Except ye be Converted, and become as little Children, ye cannot enter into the Kingdom of Heaven.*

This *Description* hath *Three Parts*.

1. *A Rise to a Kingdom.*
2. *The Race towards it.*
3. *The Royalty it self.*

1. *The Rise to the Kingdom* lyes in these words: *Except ye be converted*: The Greek word signifies a *Turn* or *Change* from the present *Principles*, and *Forms* of things to another *vertue* and *view*.

2. *The Race to the Kingdom* is thus set forth: *and become as little Children*: *Diminutives* are signs of *Affection, Delight*, and *Dependence*; as that; *One of those little Ones, that believeth on Me*: Mar. 18. 6.

3. *The Royalty it self*, is magnificently describ'd: *Ye cannot enter into the Kingdom of Heaven. The Kingdom of Heaven* hath a *Twofold* Signification. Sometimes it is *generally* taken for both States of *Grace* and *Glory*: one being the *Incheation*; the other the *Consummation*: Man in one, being as a King *Elect*: in the other a King *Crown'd*. Sometimes it hath a *particular* sense, and points out one peculiar State of Liberty, and Spiritual Glory; as Rom. 14. 17. *The Kingdom of God consisteth not in Meats and Drinks: but in Righteousness, Peace, and Joy in the Holy Ghost.* So again, 2 Pet. 1. 8, 11. *If these things be in you, and abound, a large entrance shall be made for you into the Kingdom of Heaven.* The *Reason* of the Expression in both senses is; because God is both the *King* of Believers, and their *Kingdom*, either in *Fleshly Types*, or in his own *Spiritual Appearance.*

These *three Parts* thus opened, afford us *three Doctrines* for our Discourse.

Doct. 1. *The first Rise to true Religion is a Conversion or Change.*

Doct. 2. *The second Course of things in Christianity, is a Childhood or Sonship.*

Doct. 3. *The third Degree in Christianity is, an entrance into the Kingdom of Heaven, or the Royalty begun.*

Doct. 1. *The first Rise to true Religion, is a Conversion or Change.* This is he *first Doctrine*; and I begin with it.

David's language makes it good, *Psa.* 51. 13. *Then will I teach transgres-ours thy ways, and sinners shall be converted unto thee.* He that will pass from he dismal Depths of sin and Woe, to those Heights of Strength, Holiness and sweetness in God, must make his *first Motion* a *Conversion*, a *Change* from a *Descent* to an *Ascent*; from going *Outward* to the *Circle*, to go *Inward* to-vards the *Center* of things, which comprehends and casts forth all the *Circles*.

The *Explication* of the *Point* will be its fullest *Confirmation*. I will open it n *three Parts*.

1. *The Change.* 2. *The Circumstances.* 3. *The Cause of this Change.*

Part 1. *The Change.* There are *two States* to be considered in this *Part*.

1. *The State of Man before this Change.*

2. *The State, to which this Change is made.*

1. *State.* That of Man *before this Change*. Man before his *Conversion* valks in a *threefold Image*.

1. *The Image of Nature.* 2. *The Image of the Devil.* 3. *The Image of Divine Vrath.*

1, *Image of Nature.* St. *Paul* tells us, 1 *Cor.* 15. 49. *As we have born the mage of the Earthy, we shall also bear the Image of the Heavenly Man. Earth* and *leaven* are here opposed, not as *Men* and *Angels*, *Visible* and *Invisible* things; ut as the State of things *in the Creature*, and *in Christ*. So it appears mani-estly by the *Context* of that place, that the *first Adam*, the *Earthly Man*, the *st Creation*, *Nature* in the Visible and Invisible things of it, are all the same ing, and *One Image*. Into this *Image* Man is born of his Natural Parents. In is he lives *Naturally*.

This *Image* hath *three things* in it.

1. 'Tis a *Representation*. 2. 'Tis a *Meer* Representation. 3. 'Tis a *Mixt* One.

1. The *Image* of *Nature* is a *Representation*. The *Earthly* Man is an Image God, as well as the *Heavenly*. St. *Paul* teacheth us, *Rom.* 5. 14. in the latter art of it, that the *first Adam is a figure of him, who is to come*; that is, Jesus hrist. Whatever *Rich* workings, and *various* forms are in him, who is the *isdom* of God. Whatever *Depth* of *Life*. *Heighth* of *Activity*, *Store* of *Virtues* e in him, who is the *Power* of God: Whatever ravishing *Beauties* are in m, who is the *Brightness* of the Father's *Glory*: Whatever endless *Sweet-sses* of *Love*, *Loveliness*, mutual *Relations* are in him, who is the *first*, the *Only*

begotten

begotten of the Father; All these are *figured* out, and represented to us in the *Earthly Image*. This is the *first thing*.

2. The *Image* of *Nature* is a *Meer* Representation: It hath a *show* of things, but not the *very* things themselves. We read *Psal.* 39. 5. *Man at his best Estate is altogether vanity*. Take the *first* Man at his *Best*; as he was crown'd with the whole Quire of *Angels* when they were the first and freshest *Rayes* of Divinity among the Creatures; as he was cloath'd with the heavenly *Bodies*, *Sun*, *Moon* and *Stars*, while yet they were the near and transparent *Images* of Angels *living* in them; as he hath spread about his *Feet*, all the Delicacies of *Air*, *Earth* and Sea, when they were Pure and Chrystalline, *Reflections* of the heavenly *Bodies*: The *first* Man in this State was a meer *Phantome*, a fleeting Fancy, a Bubble, *Vanity* quite thorow, and so he vanisht in his Fall.

Gen. 1. 27. *God made Man in his own Image*, *Psal.* 39. 6. *Surely Man walketh in a vain show*. Those two expressions; *Image*, *vain Show*, are both the same in Hebrew, *TSelem*. If you translate the same word in *Genesis*, as it is translated in the *Psalm*, you will then read thus; *God made Man in a vain show of himself*.

Obj. But you may object thus against this; If God be *Omnipresent*, and fill All, how can any thing be a Representation *of him*, *without him*? He is at the bottom of the Sea, in the shades of Death and Hell, *Psal.* 139. 8, 9, 10. Can any thing be a *meer Show*, when he who is *All*, is *every where*, and *fills* each Show of things.

Ans. 'Tis true, as *Euthydemus* the Heathen taught of old; *All things are in each thing*: Or as St. *Paul* since him hath Preacht upon clearer grounds: God is *a Fulness filling all in All*, *Eph.* 1. 23. But this also is true, that All things are in each thing *according to the Manner* of that in which they are. God is as truly in the *Froward*, as in the *Gentle* Spirit. But we learn the *Differences* of his Presence from *David*, *Psal.* 18. 26. *With the Pure thou wilt shew thy self Pure*; *with the Froward thou wilt shew thy self Froward*.

God is not only on *Mount Sion*, but on *Mount Sinai*; yet so, that on *Mount Sinai* he is a flame of *fire*; on *Mount Sion* a calm and clear *Light*. So God is *in Himself*, and *in the Creature*: *In Himself* he is *Himself*; the Eternal *Rock* and *Substance* of things. He is *in the Creature*, only as *his own Shadow*.

This is the *Infiniteness* and *Unsearchableness* of God. He comprehends the thinnest *Shadows in Himself*, and makes them there *Substantial*. Again, he casts *Himself* into every *Shadow* or *Show*, and *Himself* there becomes but *shadowy*. Thus he is *All in All*. Thus much for the *second thing* in the *Natural Image*.

3. The *Image* of *Nature* is a *Mixt* Representation. The Making of the World was divided into so many *Parts*, as *Days*; each *Day* had its *Night*; a *Morning* and an *Evening* made the *Day*. This was to signifie that the Funda-

mental Conſtitution of this frame of things, was laid in a commixture of *Light* and *Darkneſs*. Theſe two mutually *catch* and *enfold* one another.

The *Light diſcovers* God: The *Darkneſs obſcures* that Diſcovery; ſo that *ſeeing, we do not ſee*. The *Light pleaſeth* us; the *Darkneſs perplexeth* thoſe pleaſures; ſo that this Life is as a *Shady Valley*, as a *Shadow* of *Life* and *Death*, *Heaven* and *Hell* both in one. The *Light* invites and allures us to thoſe Immortal Seats above, pointing out a ſhining Path to them. The *Darkneſs affrights* us, and drives us back, caſting a miſt of *Doubt* upon thoſe beautiful Beings, preſenting it ſelf between them and us, as a *Dreadful Gulf* to be paſs'd,

Nature is by this means an *Image* of the *Perfections*, which are beyond Nature; but an *Imperfect* one. God ſpeaks it, *Iſa*. 55. 9. *As the Heavens are higher than the Earth; ſo are my waies higher than your waies, and my thoughts than your thoughts.* The *waies* of God are the unchang'd workings of Glory, perpetually caſting it ſelf into all Changes in the Divine Nature. The *Thoughts* of God are the deepeſt *Roots*, the moſt ſpatious *Expanſion* and *Putting forth*, the fixt and glorious *Platforms* or *Figures* of things, in the Godhead. The *Waies* and *Thoughts* of Man, are the *figurings* of things in *Nature*, or *according to the Forms* of Nature. This is a certain Rule: The *firſt* thing in every kind is the *Original* and *Subſtance*; all *ſecond things* are *Images* of that. The *firſt thoughts* and *waies* are thoſe in God. The *Waies* of *Nature*, the *Thoughts* in *Man*, are *ſecond* to thoſe, and ſo *Images* of them; but with as vaſt a *Difference*, as the *Diſtance* is between *Heaven* and *Earth*. Thus *Imperfect* and *Mixt* is *Nature*, yet an *Image* of Divine Perfections and Purity.

We have now taken a view of the *firſt Image*, in which Man walks before his *Change*.

Uſe 1. *Excitation*. The *firſt Uſe* is to awaken in us a *Senſe* of our *State*, as we are *Men*. This would very advantagiouſly direct, ſweeten, aſſiſt our *Converſion*. Let us then to this end conſider theſe *four Queſtions*.

1. *What we are*. 3. *Whence we come*.
2. *Where we are*. 4. *How we came hither*.

Queſt. 1. *What are we?* *David* anſwers for us, *Pſal*. 39. 6. *Surely Man walketh in a vain ſhow, and diſquieteth himſelf in vain.* Man is a *Shadowy Show*. *Deſcend* O Man! into thine own Being: Enter into the ſecreteſt Retirement of thine own Spirit; there ſit, look round about thee and ſay, *Can I comprehend my ſelf? Can I tell into what form my will would grow up? or into what ſhapes I ſhall paſs after this moment, while I live, or when I am dead? If I cannot tell this, then ſure I am not my own Original.*

Vain Main! why doſt thou exalt thy ſelf by Pride, as if thou wert *ſomething*, ſeeing thou art not the *Beauty*, but the *Face* in the *Glaſs*; too *ſlight* a thing for thy ſelf to *take hold* of; too weak a thing to *reflect* upon it ſelf?

Fooliſh Man! What doſt thou, feeding upon thy Spirit ſuch a numerous

ſlock

flock of *Cares*, *Contrivances*, *Confidences*, *Plots* and *Paſſions* ? Haſt thou no ſenſe of this, that, *it is not in Man, that walks, to guide his own ſteps ?* There is ſome *Eternal thing* above thy reach, paſt thy underſtanding, which *faſhions* thee, and *carries* thee on in *its own Image*.

Look upward then, and ſay, O *thou hidden and ſupreme Subſtance ! which haſt caſt me, as thy Shadow, upon this Earth* ; *comprehend me. O thou ſupreme Pattern ! which haſt ſent me forth to paſs thorow this world in thy Image ; Guide me.*

Q. 2. *Where are we ?* I ſhall give a twofold Anſwer to this Queſtion.

Anſ. 1. We are *in a world of Images*. This world is a *Type* of God, inſomuch that ſome Heathens call'd the world, the *Great God*. *Solomon* ſaith, *Wiſdom lifts up her voice, and cryes in the corner of every ſtreet. Wiſdom* is the *Brightneſs* of *Eternal Beauties* ; the *Streets* are the *Outward Forms*, on which all the Creatures walk forth ; the *Corner* or *Head* of the *Street* is the *Power* or *Principle* in theſe Forms thorow which, as by ſeveral *Tongues of Fire*, the *Forms above* ſparkle and proclaim themſelves. *Their ſound*, ſaith St. *Paul*, *is gone forth into the whole Earth.*

Canſt thou ſleep, be ſlothful or ſad here ? *Hear* and *ſee*. O Man ! thou art in this world, as *at a Show*. A *Noiſe* of Diving Glories deſcending thorow the Clouds : *Apparitions* of heavenly Eſſences, or Excellencies coming forth ſhadowed ; theſe fill the empty ſpace. A *Repetition* of Bleſſed *Sounds* ; a *Reflection* of Holy *Images* falling from above ; *This* is the *World* in which thou liveſt.

Doſt thou not feel *Deſire* awakened in thee ? Haſt thou not a ſecret ſenſe of high Joys infus'd into thy Soul ? then ſpread thy Spirit thorow this world ; take it into thy Spirit, as the *Noiſe* of a Harmony ſounding from far. Take in *thy ſelf*, as a *Part* of this Noiſe. Paſs thorow this world, as a *Throng* of *Apparitions*, thy ſelf being *One* among the reſt. Aſcend now with theſe ; for if thou ſlide *downward*, thou *ſinkeſt* out of them into a *waſte Deſert* : But if thou be carried *upward* in them, they will ſtill grow ſweeter, brighter, and fuller to thee, till they bring thee to their *firſt Fountain*, where thou and they together ſhall drink and be wrapt up into an *Immortal Fulneſs*.

Thus this *Shallow* world will have a *Depth* in it, ſtill to *content* thee, and ſtill to *carry* thee on farther ; while it ſhall ſtill have a *Relative Delight*, as in a *Repreſentative Beauty*. Jeſus Chriſt is brought in ſpeaking after this manner, *Iſa.* 8. 18. I *and the Children which thou haſt given me, are for ſigns and wonders.* So let my Soul ſay to my God. *Higheſt Beauty ! Greateſt Love ! I and this World, into which thou haſt brought me, are for ſigns of thee, ſo to move wonder and delight. O ! that I might be in the midſt of them ; that they might be unto me, as figures only of thee, ſubſiſting only in thee.* So *theſe ſlight things would have a Divine Fulneſs ; for even they would be thy Pleaſures, thy Glories, O God ! as in a figure.*

Anſ. 2.

Anſ. 2. *We are in a World of Meer Images.* The multitude of Creatures is often in *Scripture* compar'd to *Waters*; for as *Water* they receive the *Images* of heavenly things without the *Subſtance* into their thin paſſing ſtreams. Look then on *Theſe*, and immediately caſt thy Eye upward to the *Subſtances* which ſhine fixt above, and ſhed theſe *Glimpſes* of *themſelves*. O Men! why do you caſt your ſelves ſo ardently on the *Faces* of Beauty in theſe *unſtable Waters?* You can embrace *Nothing*; you can meet *Nothing* to *ſuſtain* you. You ſink and periſh in the midſt of theſe *wavy Sun-ſhines.*

The firſt Creation is often call'd a *Sea*. The *Sea* is *unfruitful*; nothing can take *Root* in the *floods*; *untam'd*, devouring all things. We are launcht forth upon this *Sea* of Appearances, in this Veſſel, the *Body*, not to *Dwell* or *Grow* upon it, much leſs to *Throw* our ſelves into it; but to *Glide* ſwiftly over the *Face* of it, to a firm Land of Bliſs. But, alas! what throngs of people are there on every ſide caſting themſelves with a furious Delight into this *Gulf*, where every *Wave* is a *Grave*, when it once receives thee? *Moſt*, the *Wiſeſt*, *linger* and *dally* on this rolling, roaring Deep, till their *Veſſel* worn out, or ſplit upon ſome Rock, they be ſwallowed up in the midſt of the *Floods*, and never reach the wiſhed Shoar of *Immortality*.

Angels ſignifie *Meſſengers*. The Beſt things of this world are *Invitations* only, *Meſſengers* ſent forth to *call* the *Gueſts*: They cannot *Feaſt* us: They have not *for us*. All cry *Wiſdom*; That which we *ſhow*, and you *ſeek*, is not *in us*. *I am not He*. We are not *The Life*, *Beauty*, *Joy*, but a *Voice crying in the Wilderneſs*, in a vaſt *Emptineſs*. *Come, taſte and ſee how good the Lord is*; *what ſatisfactory ſweetneſſes are in the Godhead.*

Joſeph ſent Aſſes laden with proviſions, and Waggons, to bring his Father *Jacob* with his Family into *Egypt*. Our *Younger Brother*, the *New Man*, the *Lord Jeſus*, hath ſent forth the Contents of this Life, as *Waggons* and *Aſſes*, to bring the *Old Man* out of the Fleſh, into the Boſom of the Father, the Pallace of Eternity, there to rejoyce for ever with our Brethren, all the Children of the Great King. How fooliſh a thing is it for us to miſtake the *Waggon* for the *Court*, which is only the *Convoy*? How brutiſh a thing is it to forget the Glories of our *Father's Houſe*, that we may run, feed, lie down with the *Aſſes*?

Q. 3. *Whence came we?* Whence are *Shadows* caſt? from their *Subſtances*. Whence do *Images* flow? from their *Original*. From an Immutable *Subſtance*, from an Eternal *Original* are we then come forth into this world. Then ſhall we never have *Reſt*, till we *Return* thither again. Our *firſt Seed* will be moſt *Inward* with us, and *Inſeparable* from us; it will travel with us thorow all Forms ſtill working in us, ſtill wearing out, and caſting off all Forms, in which it *ſojourns* with us, until it bring us back into *it ſelf*, and become our only *Clothing*, our only *Content*.

Hagar was flying from the face of her Miſtreſs *Sarah*; but ſhe meets an

Angel

Angel that sweetly sends her back thither, where God would provide for her. *Sarah* is the *Divine Form* in the Spirit; *Hagar*, this *Fleshly Being*, the *Bond-woman.* This *Earthly Nature* is unable to bear the frowns and severity of her *Heavenly Mistress*; she flies from *her Face*, *her Appearances*, which oppress the Flesh with their Glory. But the bright Images of this Beauty, as *Angels*, meet the *Natural Man* in the way of his flight, in the *Principles* of Nature. By the flashes and breakings forth of these, Man is persuaded to return, and submit himself to the supreme Beauty, his *Mistress* and *Parent*; so only shall he have provisions of *Joy* and *Rest* from his wandrings.

Our *Saviour* takes a sweet farewel of the Earth in this language, *Joh.* 16. *v.* 28. *I came forth from the Father into the world; again I leave the world, and go to the Father.* Happy is that Soul, that after all her weary steps thorow the world, to seek Content, now tyred, thinks of Returning to her Father, her first Husband; and breaths forth such sighs as these towards him: *O my God! Thy Fulness is the womb, out of which I was brought forth into this world: Thy Sweetness is the Bosom, in which I must eternally rest. How long shall I linger here? O when shall I once leave this world, and come again to thee?*

Q. 4. *How came we hither?* Thorow a *Darkness.* You shall in the first of *Genesis* see, that *Darkness* is the *Ground* of this Creation, and all *Light-Colours* are laid upon that Ground. *Darkness* is the *Bound* between *God* and the *Creature*, thorow which all things pass out of one into the other.

This *Darkness* holds forth to us the *Light* of a *Twofold Rule.*

Rule 1. *Let us not think to know eternal things by the Light of this World, or any Creature.* When we come into this life, we come well drencht, drawn thorow a Sea of Darkness. There is no more any *Remembrance* of former things. We know not where we were, when God laid the Foundations of the Earth; or, what we were before that, when all our *Bones* were first *written* by God, in *his Book*; when first those *Eternal Forms*, which were to *frame* and *sustain* every shape or state, into which we should pass, were brought forth in the *Divine Wisdom.*

We are of *Yesterday*, and know nothing. We are started up into this Life thorow a Darkness behind us, which lies upon all things which are beyond this Image before us, and swallows up this into it self, as it passeth along. *Vain Man would be wise, though he be born, as the wild Asses Colt.* Why should Man undertake to bring forth from himself the Beauties of Wisdom, when he comes upon the face of the Earth out of the same Darkness with the Asses Colt, as void, as that, of all Eternal Images?

Rule 2. *Care not to cloath your selves with the Contents of this World*, all which you must put off, so soon as you touch the Brim of this Darkness, into which you must return. Care not for the Cares or Sorrows of this Life. Those waters of Forgetfulness, into which we must all descend, will wash them all

away.

away. Imagine this Life, as an *Iſland,* ſurrrounded with a *Sea* of Darkneſs; beyond which lies the *main Land* of Eternity. Bleſſed is he, that can raiſe himſelf to ſuch a Pitch, as to look off this Iſland, beyond that Darkneſs, to the utmoſt bound of things. He ſees his *way before,* and *behind* him. What ſhall trouble him, on this *Twig* of Life, on which he is like a Bird but now *alighted* from a far Region, from whence again he ſhall immediately take his *Flight*?

Thou cam'ſt through a darkneſs hither,but *Yeſterday* when thou wer't born. Why then ſhouldſt thou not more readily, and cheerfully return thorough the ſame darkneſs back again to thoſe everlaſting Hills?

Let us then ever be in Tune to ſing, that ſadly ſweet Song of Far-ſeeing, and *ſo* much-ſuffering, *Job,* Job. 1. 21. *Naked came I out of my Mother's womb; Naked ſhall I return thither again.The Lord giveth, and the Lord taketh. Bleſſed be the name of the Lo d.* Naked cameſt thou, my Soul, thorough a Darkneſs into this World, ſtrip't of all the Glories above. Naked muſt thou return again out of this World, quite ſtrip't of all the Glories; and Griefs here. The Lord gives thee forth thorough this Darkneſs into this *Life*: the Lord takes thee in thorough the Darkneſs out of this Life to Himſelf. Bleſſed is the Name of the Lord. Reſt thou in the Bleſſed and Glorious Workings of the High God, while thou art in that Darkneſs. Thou ſhalt ſuddenly be paſs'd beyond it; where thou ſhalt in an open Light enjoy the Hidden workings there; where thou ſhall ſee the Higheſt Beatitudes and Glories,*Eye to Eye,Heart in Heart*; They and Thou, being made One Life, One Spirit, and without *Partition* or *Vail.*

Uſe 2. *The endearment of the Lord Jeſus to us.* If this Face of *Nature,* which now preſents it ſelf to us, have ſuch Beauties, Greatneſſes, Varieties; as raviſh us from all ſenſe of our ſelves, our preſent ſafety, our ſouls, our God; from the Love and Delight, which from them flow into our Spirits: what *Sights,* what *Things* above *Words* are there then *in Jeſus Chriſt*? what *Raviſhments* would ſurprize us, and ſnatch us out of *Fleſh,* if we ſaw *Him*? For *Nature* and this World is but the *Earthly, Inferiour, Imperfect Image* of God, and of the Perſon of Chriſt, which is the *Heavenly,* and *Supream Image.*

Now we under-value and neglect the ſweetneſſes of our *Saviour* for this *World's* joyes. But if we ſaw *Him,* we ſhould much more deſpiſe, Ten thouſand Worlds, ten thouſand times heightned in Glory; as a heap of *Dunghills,* in Compariſon of *Him.*

Our *Blindneſs,* our *Blindneſs* clips the wings of Deſire, clogs the Spirit of Delight in us. O *Jeſus*! caſt thou but *one Glimpſe* of thy ſelf into our ſouls, and we ſhall run from all things after thee,fly beyond all things towards Thee. How *Dark* and *cold* things are theſe *Shadows* to him, that hath ſeen the *Light* of Beauty in thy Perſon, and felt the warm *Life* of Love in Thine Embraces? Shew thy ſelf to me, and ſet many Worlds, many Deaths more between

me

me and thy self; my Spirit shall shoot it self, like an *Arrow*, thorow them all into thine Arms. A *Look* of thine, can *Translate* me; as *Enoch*, or *Eliah*, of old.

I have thus Finish'd the *First Image*, in which man lives before his *Conversion*; The *Image of Nature*.

2. *Image of the Devil.* The State of man before his Change is in a *Three-fold Image.* The *First* was that of *Nature*; the *Second*, this of the *Devil*, which we now are to take a view of. But what can we see or say of this; Who can draw a *Picture* of, or describe *Darkness*, and *Confusion*?

The Power of Darkness, and Division, prevailing over the Powers of Light, and Love, in the Creature; This is the *Devil.* If you will pourtray a *Devil*; *Darkness* must be the *Ground*, *Division*, the *Work* upon it.

There are then *two Powers, as two Parts* in this *Image.*

1. *Power, of Darkness.* 2. *Power, of Division.*

1. *Power of Darkness. This* is the *Form*, and *Division* the *Figure* of this Black Spirit. *Darkness* is made his Character; *The Power of Darkness* his Princely Title: *Colos.* 1. 13. *Who hath delivered us out of the Power of Darkness into the Kingdom of his Dear Son.* It is read thus in *Greek*: *out of the Principality of Darkness, into the Kingdom of the Son of his Love,* The *Devil*, as the Prince of *Darkness*, which implies *Division*, is opposed to *Jesus Christ*, the King of *Love*, which is *unity*, and lives only in *Light.*

Again: *Ephes.* 6. 12. *We fight against the Rulers of the Darkness of this World.* You may thus translate it more to the words: *against the World-comprehending Powers of the Darkness of this State.* As God is *One and Many*, by a *grateful Distinction in the Unity*, so is the *Devil*, *One and Many* by a *grating Division without Unity*: many Powers of Darkness in one Power.

The Devil in this *Darkness* lies, as a *Stain* upon the *Beauties* of the whole Creation; defacing the Image, dimming the Glory of God in them. He lies, as a *Cloud* upon all the *Contents* of the Creature; spreading a melancholy Shade over them, infusing a Poyson of Fears, Falshoods, Deceits, Mistakes, Dangers, Death into them. He is a *Prison*, and a *Chain* Shutting up, holding down the Spirits of men, when they would break forth, and raise themselves into that Light of Divinity, which faintly glimmers in this Darkness. Such is the *First Part* of the *Image*, the *Power of Darkness.*

2. *Power of Division.* The Name, *Devil*, comes from the Greek Word, Διάβολος, which signifies most properly one, that casts in Principles, or Seeds of *Division.* So he is described by our *Saviour*, in the *Parable*: *The Envious man, the Enemy hath sown Tares.* Our Lord with a Divine depth defines this Spirit in those words: *A Kingdom divided against it self cannot stand.* Whatever stands, must be founded upon a *Unity.* The Devil is a *divided Kingdom*, a *Duality*, a *Ruinous Thing.*

This *Power of Division* divides itself into a *Seven-fold Power*, which is known by these Names.

1. *Self-love.* 2. *Lust.* 3. *Covetousness.* 4. *Pride.*
5. *Envy.* 6. *Passion.* 7. *Enmity, or Despair.*

1. *Power, Self-love,* 1 John 4. 8. *God is Love: Love* in the *Abstract*; *Love Absolute, Unlimited, Infinite*, a Universal Sweetness. The Devil is *Self-love*; a particular Being cutting off itself from the rest of things; from Him, who is the Great, *I am*; in whom all things have their Being. These are the *Circlings* of the *Serpent*, by which he folds, and wraps up himself in himself.

This Serpent, before he spake to the Woman, tempted himself with this glittering language. Es. 14. 14. *I will be like the most High.* The first word in this aspiring speech is that, which first made him a *Devil* of an *Angel*: *I*: The establishing of a *Proper Interest* divided from the *general Interest* of things in the God-head. This *Self-love* is the *Horned head*; into which he then sprouted forth; the *Cloven Foot*, in which he ended; when he first with-drew himself from the all-comprehending Unity, into a Circle, and Center of his own.

2. *Power, Lust.* This is a prægnancy to multiply *himself*; to bring forth *himself* in strange, and diverse forms; upon strange and diverse Images. *God is One*, *Gal.* 3. 20. God brings forth himself *in One Image*, Jesus Christ is his *Only-begotten Son*: *Joh.* 1. 14. God brings forth all things *by* this One Image, and *in* it: *Coloss.* 1. 16. *In him were all things Created.* The Devil is contrary to God in all this. He is that *Son of God*, which broken, and deform'd by his Fall from the First Unity; goes full of monstrous Lust after the *Daughters of Men*, dark, divided, fleshly Images of the Creature. With these he mingles himself; so he brings forth himself and them into *Gyantly shapes*, and in a Brood of Gyants. *Gyants*, in *Hebrew*, signifie, *Dead, Distracted; Prodigious* Forms, as appearing from the shades below; or faln, and sunk thither.

Our *Saviour* calls this Spirit of *Lust*: Joh. 8. 45. *The Father of Lyes*: because he begets himself upon all things in base, spurious, and various Shapes. *Solomon* represents the Image of the Devil in Flesh, and this World, by a *Whorish Woman*; because she lusts after, and wanders thorow all the diversity of divided Forms in the Devil.

3. *Power, Covetousness.* Pro. 30. 16. *There are two things, that never say, enough: the Grave, and the Barren Womb.* This Invisible Power is a *Womb* of Darkness, which takes in all things; but brings forth nothing. So the Darkness is never enlightned, but ever increas'd, made deeper and more devouring. This Spirit is the *Invisible Grave*, which draws all things into it. But then it crumbles them into *Dust*; it divides them from themselves. So the Principle of *Division* is sharpned, not satisfied: fretted to a greater wideness, not fill'd.

This is the Serpent *feeding upon Dust*; ever encompassing the Earth. This is the *Bottomless Pit.*

4. *Power, Pride.* The Devil under this *property* is call'd Is. 14. 12. Lucifer, *the Son of the Morning*. He saith, *v.* 13. *I will exalt my Throne above*

the Stars of God. His ambition is to shine *alone*; and as he riseth to put out all other Lights by the Malignity of his appearance. He goes on: v. 13. *I will sit upon the Mount of the Congregation, in the sides of the North.* The appearance of our Lord Jesus in the double flame of Terror and Triumph; Consuming, and Crowning; is from the *North*: Ezek. 1. 4. *The Mount of the Congregation* is Mount *Sion*, where the *General Assembly, and Church or Congregation of the First-born are,* Hebr, 12. 22, 23. This is the Mount lifted up above every Mountain: The Spirit exalted above every Spirit.

The Devil would seat himself upon this Mount in the place of Jesus Christ; to be, as he is, the *Onely One.* Yet he would have it with this difference; to be the top of the Mount, while the great Congregation sit, as the Clouds, under his Feet: to be a consuming Fire to all others; a Crowning Glory, only to himself.

God is the Heavenly *Hierusalem,* where all things are *Fellow-citizens.* The Devil is that *Babel,* which saith; *I sit alone as a Queen,* Revel. 18. She thinks her self never Great, till she have swallowed up all her Companions; never Great enough, till she be Great alone. This is the difference between *Pride,* and *Plenty.*

5. *Power, Envy.* This *Power* is a *Reflection of Darkness and Division upon it self, from the Sense of Beauty and Unity else-where.* It is Mystically describ'd, Revel. 20. 1. *An Angel came down from Heaven with a Chain in one hand, a Key in the other,* v. 2. *He took hold of the Dragon, the old Serpent, and bound him up in the Bottomless Pit.* Divine Wisdom is that *Chain* which reacheth from the Top of Heaven to the Center of the Earth; where at both ends, it meets, and is fastned in God. The several Ranks of things, the distinct Orders of Causes and effects are the *Links* of this Chain mutually enwrapping each other. The *Key* is a Divine Light, and Spiritual Power, which fastneth, or looseth, draws up, or lets down; waves this Chain, and every Link of it, at pleasure. The *Angel* represents our *Lord Jesus.*

When he brings forth this Glory from God to men; He by it takes such hold of that Power of envy in the Devil; that he makes him to sink himself deeper, lock himself up fast, into the Bottomless Pit, into his own dark and dividing Principle.

6. *Power, Passion. Passion* is a *Rage kindled, and heightned by Resistance.* It is said of the Devil, *He hath great wrath, because he hath a short time,* Revel. 12. 12. He is in that *Chapter* set before us, as a *Dragon.* A *Dragon* hath his upper part *winged,*, like a *Bird,* that flies in the air: his lower parts *Snaky,* like a *Serpent* crawling on the Earth. So is *Passion,* partly rais'd to its own pitch, and height, there breathing flames, and sparkling fury: partly kept down, laid low in the Dust by opposition.

The Devil in this Power is, as Fire shut up in close matter, Earth, or Iron; where it burns with a Fierce and dismal Rednes. C 2 7. *Power*

7. *Power, Enmity, or Deſpair.* God is *Eternal Life*: The Devil is *Eternal Death* and Ruine: *Apollyon, Abaddon*: Revel. 9. 11. The Myſtery of God is *a Fellowſhip*, Epheſ. 3. 9. The Myſtery of the Devil is *a Deſolation*: Eſ. 66. 24.

Jeſus Chriſt is a *Braſen Serpent*, lifted up; a Glorious, Eternal Principle of *Diſtinction*, dividing between the neareſt Forms, bringing each one forth to a naked Diſcovery in its own Property; and all in his own Divine Light. The Devil is a *Fiery Serpent* below on the Earth; a Dark, Furious Principle of *Diviſion*, ſeparating all Forms of things, ſetting each apart in its full Power, in the midſt of his Helliſh Flames.

Theſe are the *Seven Heads* of that monſtrous *Half* of the Devil's *Image*, *the Power of Diviſion.*

The Man in the *Goſpel* poſſeſs'd by the Devil was a ſhadow of the Devil in this *Twofold Shape* of *Darkneſs* and *Diviſion*. *He was ever among the Tombs, tearing and rending his own fleſh.* So this Diſtracted *Spirit* dwels in himſelf, as in a *Living Tomb*, into which he labours to draw all other things. He is perpetually dividing, and Tearing all things, but moſt of all himſelf.

Qu. I cannot paſs from this *Image*, till I enquire how *Man* was brought forth in it. Our Saviour fully ſets forth the Truth, and manner of this in one word: *Ye are of your Father the Devil*, Joh. 8. 44.

We read in the Third of *Geneſis*, of *Two Seeds*: *The Seed of the Woman*, who was the Image given by God to Man, out of himſelf, through Man; in which Image Man was to enjoy, and bring forth himſelf: *The Seed of the Serpent.* When God had brought forth Man from a Divine Seed into a beautiful, and bleſſed Image: the *Serpent* ſows his dark, and dividing ſeed in this Fair Field. He brings forth man the ſecond time from this poyſonous Seed into his own Image, in which he captivates the Image of God. Thus the Son of God is become the Son of the Devil.

The Spirit of lies and murthers by the *Forbidden Tree*, as by his own Image, begets the Woman into the Form of ſin, and death: through the Woman he begets Man in the ſame Principle and State.

Thus we ſee *Man* before his *Converſion* in the *Image of the Devil.*

3. *Image of Divine Wrath.* This is *God* in a *Twofold appearance*:

1. *Fire.* 2. *Smoak.*

1. *Appearance, Fire. Who ſhall dwell with Everlaſting Burnings*: Eſ. 33. 14. The Nature of *Fire* is to work upon *Confuſed* things, to *Separate* them in their *Diſtinctions*; to *gather* them together in their *Affinities.* So the *Fire* in a *Stick*, makes the *Fiery* part to take its way by it ſelf; while the *Airy* part vapours into Smoke; the *Earthy* falls down-ward into Duſt; the *Water* weeps out at the ends of the Stick.

The Forms of things in *Fleſh* lie hudled, and impriſon'd one in another. God comes down upon the Creature in his *Wrath*, as in a Fire; to Conſume that

dark

dark *Band* of Confusion, that *Bar* of division, the *Flesh*; to *Dispose* all things into their several *Varieties*; to *Collect* all things into their proper *Unities*, both the *Vailing*, and the *Vailed* Forms.

2. *Appearance, Smoak.* So the *Wrath* of God is describ'd : Psal. 18. 8. *A Smoak went up out of his Nostrils.* Fuel by *Smoak* passeth into a *Flame*: the *Flame* again works itself into a *Smoak*, and so vanisheth. God, as a *Smoak* darkens the Glory of the Creature, and so draws it into the Fire. Again he carries it out of the Fire into a fine cloud of *white Smoak*, which disappears to appear again in the God-head. Thus the *Smoak* is God's clothing, as he goes into the Fire, as he comes out of it; both *Ascending*, and *Descending*. Yet withal the Smoak, and the Fire are mingled too.

Man stands *Naturally* in this *Image of Wrath*, as in his deepest Root, next the God-head in its naked being. Out of this he Springs, into this he Sinks. So *St. Paul* signifies, *Ephes.* 2. 3. *And were by Nature the Children of Wrath, as well as others.* We are the Children of this *Three-fold Image*; *Nature*; *Devil*; *Wrath*; *Subordinately.*

God comes forth in an Image of *Wrath*. This brings forth *Devils*. These wrap themselves up in the *Natural Seed*, which first brings forth the *Natural Image*, then thorow that breaks forth into a *Devil*, out of which it grows up into a Form of *Divine Anger*. So the most *Radical Principle* puts forth itself last into appearance; as the Rational life in Man.

Thus much of the *Three Images.*

Application.

Use. Admonition. Let us take heed of *Sin*, for its *Father's sake the Devil*; and for *its own*. This *Admonition* will make its way into your Spirits; if from that, which hath been said, you seriously consider *Two Things.*

1. *The Nature of the Devil.* 2. *The Nature of Sin.*

1. *The Nature of the Devil.* Behold in this, as in a Glass, *Four* unlovely *Spectacles:*

1. *Solitude.* 3. *Torture.*
2. *Horrour.* 4. *Ugliness.*

1. *Spectacle, Solitude.* As a high and dreadful Cliff upon some dangerous Shoar: such a *Solitude* is the Devil. I, *saith he will be like the most High*: as high as he; but with this difference: God is *above* all, and *in* all: The Devil would be *above* all, and *without* all: God is such a *Height*, as is *all in all*: The Devil would be *all alone*: God is *alone*, but so, as that he is *One* with *all* Things: The Devil would be *alone*, but as a *Precipice* broken off *from* all things.

As the Mouth of a Burning Mountain, which wasts all things round about it, and makes the neighbouring Circuit a wide Desolation: such a *Solitude* is the Devil, Revel. 12. He is represented, as a *Dragon ready to devour the Man-child, so soon, as he is born.* As a Dragon in his lonely Den, the Country a Wilderness all about: So is this Fiery Spirit eager to consume all appearances of Life, and God upon their first discovery. As

As the *Night*, which entombs all things in it self, and makes the richest variety of Shapes, but one Lonely shade: such a *Solitude* is the Devil.

Consider this, all ye who cleave to the Noise, Glories, Pleasures of this world, and leave your God, least you should be *Melancholy*. See, and tremble to see into what a Melancholy Shade, what a solitude your souls pass, when you die.

2. *Spectacle, Horrour.* Imagine a *world*, where *over your head* instead of a *Sky*, black, pitchy Clouds perpetually roul, not suffering any Glimpse of Light, or Day ever to appear: *under your feet*, instead of Land, or Sea, a vast, amazing depth, which no where by nothing bounds your sight, or thought: *round about you*, a Desolate Darkness, presenting near, and at furthest distance, all those Forms, which are bred in the womb of darkness, and carry an astonishing darkness with them to the Senses, and Spirits of Men; like apparitions, Lightnings, Shrieks, dying Groans, roaring Tempests, Howling of wild Beasts; to a man alone in a Forrest at Midnight. Such a world of Horrours is this *Evil Spirit*. Therefore he is set forth by the *Outward Darkness, where the Worm dies not*: a Darkness without *Light* or *Limit*, in which all gnawing Forms of Horrour live. Let him, that hates not that world of Curses, love this world of Vanities, For the Vanities of one are the *Porch* to the Vexations of the other.

3. *Spectacle, Torture.* Every Wound is a *Division*. What are *Fears, Pains, Griefs, Death? Separations* of *Desires* from their *Delights, Faculties* from their *Objects, Principles* from their *Act, End, Perfection*; in a word, *Things* from *Themselves*. All Deaths and Tortures then are in the Devil, at their heighth, in their fullest Power. For he is the *Principle*, and *Power* of Division.

The Life of this Mighty Creature is a *Two-edged, Flaming Sword* in the midst of it self. Each Act, and Motion of life is the *Brandishing* of this Sword, Cutting and Burning in every Part, and point of life with ten thousand Anguishes.

4. *Spectacle, Ugliness. Deformity* is *Darkness* with a *Disproportion*. Darkness in harmony with Light makes a Beauty. So the Evening and the Morning make a Day. So the Night, and sleep are the shade of an Angel's wing, dropping sweet sleep, and rest on Men.

Proportion is a *Kind*, and *Image* of *Unity*. *Disproportion* is a *Division* without any form of *Unity*. Where this Division, and Darkness first meet, there is the *Center* of Ugliness, the Fountain of ugly things. This is the *Babel*, where *Ziim* and *Ijim* dwell, *Unclean Birds*; Forms dry without any beautiful Water; desolate, no pleasant plant of Life, putting forth it self there; irksome, and hateful, being surrounded with a rude Darkness, like rocky, uncouth Islands in a Tempestuous Sea; or *Screech-Owles* in a Melancholy Night.

These are the *Four Spectacles* of dread, & death, in the Nature of the Devil: *Solitude, Horrour: Torture*, and *Ugliness*. Now make up these *Four* into *One*, let that *One* be a *Living Spirit* of greatest *Activity*, and *Capacity*: This

is

is the *Devil*, the *Bottomless Pit* of Things; the *Unpassable Gulf*, which divides Heaven from Hell. This is the *Father* of *Sin*, and *Sinners*.

Now before you commit a Sin, propound this *Question* to your selves: Can I eternally wander in a Darkness, where I shall never meet Companion or Comfort? Can I make everlasting Clouds my Canopy? Can I lie under these at Rest? Can I sleep sweetly over an unknown, roaring Deep? Can I imbrace Fire, feed on Poysons, drink down Tortures, like Water? Can I make those hateful Shapes, at which, when they appear, the stoutest men grow stiff with horrour, and feel their hair to stand on end upon their heads? Can I make these ghastly, dismal things my *Play-fellows*?

If you can do all this, then go, sin freely. But if these be Terrours above Man, to bear: take heed, and start at a *Lust*, more than you would at a *Ghost*, for these are but weak *Types* of those Tormenting *Truths*, which Sinners must try below. For, as *God* makes *Heaven*; so the *Devil* is the *Hell*, into him do all polluted Souls descend; they dwell, not only *with*, but *in* Him.

Obj. Why should any doubt, whether there be a Devil. But alass! who believes him to be any thing besides a Scar-crow; except Children, or weak and superstitious Spirits?

Answ. Yet, you that thus reason, ask those *Principles*, that govern you: Do not *Sense* and *Reason* shew, that all things have their *Roots*, out of which they rise? Are there not such things, as *Follies*, *Filths*, and *Furies* spread through the World? Are they not, if not the *All*, yet the *Greatest part* of the word? Can these be, and no *Spring* be, in which they are *United*, and at their *Height*? This *Spring* is this *Spirit*, which we call the *Devil*. This is that untam'd *Sea*, of which *Job* speaks. Job. 7. 12. *Am I a Sea, or Whale, that thou thus breakest me?*

What pity then is it to see Millions of men go with merry dalliance down the streams of fleshly delights; and at the same time to see that Cloudy Sea of Horrours, into which they are within a few moments delivered by these streams?

If every thing make hast to its own *Principle*, and *Element*; *Fire* to the upper Circle; *Earth* to its Center below: If it be Natural for every *Plant* to bring forth its own *Seed*: then sure, it cannot be, but that each guilty Soul should sink downward to the Element of Woe, and Horrours, the Center of Darkness: then sure, every *Sin* must at last bring forth a *Devil*.

You that love your *lusts*, more than your *God*, learn from your *Bodies*, the state determin'd upon your *Souls*. Your *Bodies* are *Dust*, and to *Dust* they must return. Your defiled *Spirits* are of their Father the *Devil*, and to him they must again go, when they leave this World. This is the first consideration to preserve us from Sin: *The Nature of the Devil.*

2. *The Nature of Sin.* We read no where of *Mary Magdalen*, that she was *Possess'd* according to the common acceptation of that word. We read, that she was a *Sinner*, *eminently*, *absolutely*, without restraint, as if she, who is

said

said to have been an *Hostess*, had been an *Inne* to all Sins. Yet she is thus describ'd: Mark. 16. 9. *Mary Magdalen, out of whom he had cast Seven Devils.* All *Sins* are rankt under *Seven Heads.* These are the *Seven Powers* of *Evil*, in the *Devil*; which are, as so many *Devils* there. These are the *Unclean Spirits*, which go forth from the Mouth of the *Dragon* into the breasts of all the Sons and Daughters of *Adam.* Fly then from a *Sin*; for 'tis a *Devil.* Fly from the sweetest Temptations. They may look like Angels: but they are the *Devil's Angels*, the most immediate *Emanations* or Images from that foul Principle.

Qu. But you will say; *What is Sin? How shall I know it?* That I may fly from it.

Ans. You may know it by the *Image*, it bears. Whatever you meet with like a *Devil* any where, that's a *Sin.* Wherever you see the Cloven Foot of *Division*, or the Horned head of *Darkness*; fly, and cry: an *Apparition* from Hell.

Take then *Two Rules*, which measure out every Sin.

Rule 1. *Every choice of an Act or Object, that draws you down, out of the Light of God*; is *Sin.* In the *Light* of God, we worship and love the Supream Beauty; we possess the most perfect, and purest Pleasures; we grow up into the Divine Image, which continually appears to us; we have all our Faculties fill'd, enlarg'd to a Freedom, an Infiniteness. When we leave this *Light*, we fall down before Idols, empty Shows of Beauty; so we become *Idolaters*, and *Adulterers*; we mingle our selves with mixt Pleasures, Dark Delights; so we *pollute* our selves: we are *transform'd* into every base, inferiour Image, with which we converse: Our Souls are *imprison'd* in low, and narrow Objects, where they beat themselves against the walls of their Prison into perpetual vexations.

Such are the *Loves*, *Lusts*, *Ambitions*, *Entertainments* of this World. *The Love of the World is Enmity with the Father*: Ja. 4. 4. He that casts his eye down upon the Earth, must necessarily take it off from Heaven. He that sets his Face, as if he would go into the Embraces of Vanity; must have his back upon the Eternal Glory.

Rule 2. *The Divided enjoyment of any particular Image apart from the Image of God*; is *Sin. God is one.* The *Image* of God is that, in which all things are *United.* He that takes any Piece out of this *Image*, he breaks the *Unity*, he makes a *Wound*, to let in Death, and Ruine.

This makes *Fleshly Lusts, Sins.* Man and woman are each to other, the *Image* of God, which is *One.* When therefore they rest not in the bosom of *One Another*, they commit the Sin of the Devil, in a *Type*.

St. *Jude* makes the Lustful Sin of *Sodom* an exemplar Copy of the Sin of Angels: *Jude* 6. 7. *The Angels kept not their first state, but left their own habitation*, &c. *Even as* Sodom *and* Gomorrah, *in like manner, giving themselves* over

over to Fornication, and going after strange (divers, ἑτέρας *Flesh, &c.* The Sin of *Devils* was a *Spiritual Whoredom,* in which *they* dissolv'd the *Unity* of the Divine Image, and fell into a *Diversity* of divided Images, as into a deep Pit.

Both are join'd together in *Solomon.* At once he multiplyed *Wives,* and *Idols.* A Converse with the Creatures in Diverse Principles and Images is, as the Familiarity of a Man with many Women. *Fleshly Lust* is the proper *Image,* and *Fruitfulness* of the *Devil;* by which he brings forth himself into this Visible World most *Naturally,* and therefore most *Potently,* most *Plentifully.*

Obj. But you will say; may we not enjoy the delights of the Creature, which is an Inferiour Image?

Ans. Yes, as a Man may have a Conversation with many Women, so that he break not the *Marriage-Union.* Thy *Fountain* must be thine own. All delights abroad must be, as *Streams* of this Fountain, not divided *Springs.* All other Images must be onely *Reflections* of this One, & *concentred* in it.

Please thy self to the full with every Content. Only let it be no *Cloud* to cut off: but a *Christal* to take in the Divine Glory, that this may shine, and flame in them.

Use 2. *Consolation.* Wretched Man! What wilt thou do? *Hell* is sown in thy Nature. This is the Paradise, which is planted in thee; all manner of loathsom, bitter, venemous deadly Plants. The *Sap* of these is the *Life* of thy Spirit: the *Fruit* of these the *Food* of thy Life. What shall deliver thee? Shall *Time?* No: As Nature puts forth itself in thee, so these Trees of baleful Woe grow up. What shall reskue thee from them? Shall *Death?* No: When thou puttest off this Natural Image, thou must then be transform'd into these Invisible Plants, to be everlastingly inclos'd in them, to have one Root, one Stock, one Sap, one Fruit for ever with them, that is, with Devils.

Is there then no *Help?* There is. behold, *God* descends to be thy *Saviour.* He comes by a *Two-fold Step,* and brings Salvation into thy Bosom.

1. *Step.* God comes into our *Nature,* as the *Root* of each single Person. Here he becomes our *Jesus,* making himself a *New Seed.* Out of this *Seed,* he brings forth a *New Image* of Divinity, by which he breaks thorow the *Image* of the *Devil,* and *Nature,* brings forth *Man* out of them, brings them into subjection to this growing Beauty. As the *Fuel* is dissolv'd into *Smoak,* and the *Smoak* again breaks up into *Flame:* So the Image of the *Devil* riseth up out of the Image of *Nature,* shaking that to Dust, as it riseth: The Image of *God* again, sprouts forth in the midst of the *Devils Image,* First spoiling, then Triumphing *over,* and *in both.*

2. *Step.* God thorow *Nature,* as the *Root,* grows up into *single Persons,* as the *Branches.* Then, as the shades of Night flie away before the Ascending Day; so, as this Divine Seed our Jesus sends forth itself in an Image of Beauty

thorow our Souls; the Image of Darkneſs and Death ſinks down into its own Place, and Principle.

Love this Jeſus then. You will love Him, when He ſhall do this. And He that *ſhall* do it, *will* do it. He is the *Root* and *Branch.* He is a *Root*, which holds every other Root of Pollution and Perplexity, *&c.* He will grow up thorow them the *Laſt* of All. He is the *Branch*, that is impriſon'd in every other Branch of Death, and Hell, which will at laſt ſpread forth itſelf over All; if thou wait for it. As the *Head* of the *Devil* is *Enmity* and *Deſpair*: ſo the *Lord Jeſus* is an *Eternal Root* of *Hope*, and *Love.*

2. *State, That to which the Change is made in our Converſion.* This is *Three-fold.* 1. *The Inward State in Nature.* 2. *The Spiritual State, in Chriſt.* 3. *The Divine State, in God.*

1. *The Inward State, in Nature.* The *Change* is for the moſt part, at firſt, a *Converſion*, or *Introverſion* into this *State.* This needs a *Three-fold Explication.*

1. *Explication. The Inward State, in Nature as it is in itſelf.* Man is naturally the Off-ſpring of God, *Act.* 17. 28. *We are all his Off-ſpring.* God hath an *Inward Glory*, and *Outward Cloathing.* The Scripture ſpeaks of both theſe, *Hebr.* 1. It ſaith of *One*, v. 8. *Thy Throne, O God, is for ever, and ever.* It ſaith of the *Other*, v. 10. *Thou haſt laid the Foundations of the Earth: the Heavens are the Work of thine hands*, v. 12. *Thou foldeſt them up, as a Garment, and they are changed.* God over-ſpread his *Outward Cloathing* with his *Inward Glory.* he poſſeſſeth *both* his *Perſon*, and his *Veſture* in One Fountain of Life. So *both* become to him *One* Life and Beauty.

Man is in *Nature* the Off-Spring, and Reſemblance of God. So Man alſo in his *Natural State* is compoſed of a *Twofold Image*, the one *Inward*, the other *Outward*; the one the Image of *God* in Man, the other of the *Creature.* While man ſtood in Innocency, he abode in the *Inward Image*, as his *Center*: in that he Comprehended, and Commanded the *Image* of the *Creature.* The Image of *God* was *Eden*, the Fountain of pleaſures within, from thence a *River* went forth watering the Image of the *Creature*, and making that a *Paradiſe.* All things were *Trees* in this *Paradiſe, good for food, and pleaſant to the Eye*: Trees of perpetual *Youth, Beauty, Pleaſure* to Man, Man was ſeated in this *Inward Image*, as on his *Throne*, from which he commanded, and changed all the Creatures into divers Shapes of Delight, at pleaſure. This is the *Firſt Explication.*

2. *Explication: The Departure of Man out of this Inward State.* When Man fell, he went forth from his *Inward* Glory, into the *Outward* Image, this is ſignified, *Gen.* 3. by the *Woman* yielding her ſelf over to the Will of the *Serpent*: and the *Man* giving himſelf up to the Will of the *Woman.* So it was true of *Man*, what is ſaid of the *Devils*, Jude 6. He left his *Firſt Eſtate*, and his *Proper Habitation.* Now he lived wholly in the *Out-forms* of things which he

he broke off from the *Inward Image*, and so made them all an *Image* of Vanity, Darkness, and Death; keeping the Image of God *imprisoned* in this Outward Image, which suffered it not to put forth itself, or appear.

St. *Paul* expresseth this *Departure*, as the Root of all Sin, *Rom.* 1. 18. All wickedness is there sum'd up in this; *Detaining the Truth of God in Unrighteousness.* That is, keeping down the Image of God, and True Glory, in a corrupt, and false Image.

3. *Explication. The return of Man into this Image*, Man hunting, and hunted thorow the exteriour face of things, finds neither his desired Prey, nor Rest, Poor Man! oppressed with cares and sorrows, he sinks down by a sad Retirement to the bottom of his own Spirit. There he happily falls into the bosom of the *Divine Image*, which lay buried under the Ruines of his Soul. Here he catcheth some Glimpses of Immortal beauty, some Tasts of a high delight, some sense of a true Rest. Now he loaths the Empty, Tedious, Tormenting Follies of this Outer World.

David experimented this in himself, *Psal.* 16. 7. *My Reins instruct me in the Night-season.* When a Night of *nature*, or *melancholy* takes away these sensual forms of things from us, or makes them a Torture to us: then this *Hidden Image* from the retired Principles of Nature, from the secret of our souls, puts up itself before us, draws us down into itself, makes its own Impressions upon us; Impressions which have another manner of Light, Strength, Sweetness in them.

Now the Soul cries out in the language of *Cain*, to a sweeter purpose: *How have I been a Fugitive, and a Vagabond upon the Earth, while I have been driven out from thy Face, and Presence, and thou beautiful Image of things! Come, lock me up in thine Embraces, that I may never go forth more into that Outward Court of things, which is troden down by the Feet of Lusts, and Confusions. Or if I must go forth again; O that I might carry thee forth with me, as my Brother, that suckt the breasts of my Mother-Nature. I would kiss thee, and I should not be despised. I would enjoy perpetual pleasures in thee; and no shame, but strength, and glory should rest upon me.*

This is the *First Change* into the *Inward State, in Nature.*

2. *The Spiritual State, in Christ.* The Change to this State we are to consider in *Three Parts.*

1. *The Preparation* in Man. 2. *The Spiritual State.* 3. *The Passage of Man into it.*

1. *Part. The Prepararion in Man to this Spiritual State.* Man pursued by Griefs from without, retired into the Inward Image, the Recess of Nature, as *David* into his Cave, meeteth with a fresh, unexpected view of Beauties here. Now he is refresh't, now he comes to himself. Now he begins to raise himself, and say, as *Samuel* did, when the eldest Son of *Jesse* was presented to him:

D 2 *Behold*

Behold the Annointed of God is before me. Surely this is no other, than the *Gate of Heaven.*

But after a little Tryal, Man finds this to be, but a *Natural Image* of God, an *Earthly Paradise* only, which so soon as it puts forth is ready so soon to dis-appear again. He finds it too weak to raise itself clearly from the bottom of those Waters of Vanity, Sin and Trouble, which have over-flown, and over-whelm'd it. He perceives it too slight to satisfie him. 'Tis an *Intimation* of true joys, rather than the *Joys* themselves. 'Tis a fair *Invitation*, no full *Entertainment.*

Mans joys and hopes here prove to him like the *Seed* sown in *Rocky* Ground; which springs up suddenly, but suddenly withers, when once the Sun, the Tempting Glories, or Scorching Furies of this World beat upon it.

Now the Soul is, as *Mary Magdalen* at the Grave of her Saviour; She looks into her Heart for this Image but finds that gone, and her heart, as an empty Grave. Then she cries; *O my God; who hath taken these Comforts away? I thought, that these should have delivered me, and dwelt for ever with me.* But wipe away thy Tears, distressed Soul. As Jesus carryed away his *Natural body* from *Mary*, to bring it again a *Spiritual body*: So thy God hath withdrawn this *Natural Image* of divine joyes in thy Spirit; but he will restore, and bring it into thy soul again a *Spiritual Image.*

St. *Paul* gives thee this *Consolation*, Rom. 8. 3, 4. *What the Law could not do, being weak thorow the flesh.* &c. *That the Righteousness of the Law might be fulfill'd in us, who walk not after the flesh, but after the Spirit.* The weakness of *Natures Inward Image* prepares the Spirit of Man for the *Spiritual State* of things.

2. *Part*: *The Spiritual State itself.* The *Prophet* represents this in a *Promise.* Joel 2. 28. *I will pour forth my Spirit upon all Flesh. Three things* are here to be explained.

1. *The Spirit.* 2. *Flesh.* 3. *Effusion, or Pouring forth of Spirit upon Flesh.*

1. *The Spirit* is the *Unity* of things: *Ephes.* 4. 3. *The Unity of the Spirit. Unity* is appropriated to the *Spirit.* This *Spirit* is the most High God. For he is the First, Supream, only *Unity*: Gal. 3. 20. *God is One.* God, *eminently*, and *exclusively*, is *One.* This *Spirit*, the *Unity* is the Fountain, and Life of Things. All sorts of Life, all Beauty every where are *Images* of this *Self-comprehending, All-comprehending* Unity. This is the *Spirit.*

2. *Flesh. Flesh*, and *Spirit* differ, as *Unity*, and *Division*; or which is the same, as *Life*, and *Death*: Rom. 8. 6. *To be Carnally-minded is Death: to be Spiritually-minded is Life, and Peace. Life* is the *Unity* of Things, in which they Contain themselves. *Death* is the *Division* of Things from themselves.

Flesh is all Divided Forms of things in the Creature according to the language of the *Scripture.* The *Scripture* in this sense reckons *Angels*, and *Souls* of Men, as *Fleshly* things. Though *Angels* are the most United Things, the

First

First *Unities, or Springs* in the Creature ; and so *Spirits.* Yet they compared with *God* are *Compounded,* and *Divided* Things, and so *fleshly.*

St. *Peter* thus sums up under the name of *Flesh,* all things, that have a *Principle* of *Division* in them, by which they are cut off from their own *Beauty* or *Being* ; by which they fade, and fall away. This is *Flesh.*

3. The *Effusion, or Pouring forth of the Spirit upon Flesh.* This signifies *Three things.*

1. *The Spirit nakedly sustaining the Creature, as its Immediate Root, and Principle.* So the Spirit is a *Spring* pouring itself forth into *Flesh,* as it's *Channel.*

2. *The Spirit filling the Fleshly form with its Waters,* with its clear and fresh Streams, the workings of its own Life.

3. *The Spirit planting its own Image upon each Created Image* ; clothing and overflowing it with its own Appearances.

Thus St. *Paul* expresseth the *Effusions,* the *Overflowings* of the Spirit, *Rom.* 8. 6. *To be Spiritually-minded is Life, and Peace.* To be *Spiritually-minded* is to see Things, as they are in their *Spiritual State.* In this *State* all things have a *Twofold Representation.*

1. *Represen. Life,* true Life, without any mixture of Death. Every Sight here is Life. For all things are seen ; as growing up out of this *Life-Principle,* the *Spirit* ; and *Themselves,* as *Powers* of this *Life* displaying themselves, and working in themselves.

2. *Represen. Peace.* This is the *Efficacy* of that Life, in the *Harmony* of an *Inward Sweetness,* an *Outward Beauty.*

Thus this *Spiritual State* brings forth to Light again in itself, the *Inward Image* of God, in *Nature,* For it shews all *Fleshly Forms,* being yet *Fleshly,* and *yet* Harmonious Images of the Supream Unity, or Beauty. But it brings forth this *Natural Image* with this *Twofold Advantage.* 1. It formerly grew upon a *Natural Principle,* and so was subject to Decay. Now it is rooted in this *Immortal Spirit,* and so becomes Immortal. 2. It was in Nature an *Image only* Now it is an *Image,* and a *Glass.* It doth not only *Represent* the Glories of the *Spirit* by an empty *Show* : but it sets them before you as *Present* in their proper substances, and so shining thorow it.

Thus we have gone thorow the *Second Part* in this *Head,* and seen *the Spiritual State in itself.*

3. *Part* : *The Passage of Man into this Spiritual State.* When the Soul is taught by her Experience, and her God ; that the Secret Delights of the Natural Image are for a *Repast* only, not a *Repose* ; that in the strength of these ; as *Eliah's* food, brought by Angels, she is to travel thorow a Wilderness, the Ruines of Nature, with all its *Principles,* and *Images* ; till she comes to the *Mount of God* : Then she takes up a resolution ; to stay no longer in this Field of Swine with the Swine ; but to make hast to her Fathers House, where every

Counte-

Servant hath *Bread* enough; each *Fleshly Form* is fill'd with a *Substantial Glory*.

When God hath secretly instructed the Soul thus to resolve, he as a tender-hearted Father meets her in the beginning of *these resolutions*, falls upon her neck, and kisseth her. God shews himself in the Soul, gives her sweet Testimonies of his Love, carries her further off from the Outward Image, carries her thorow the most retired Principles of Nature *beyond*, and *above* them, into this *Spiritual Principle*, and State, which is the *Spirit* of Christ; where God and the Creature are United; where the *Spirit* is, as *Water*; the *Flesh* as a flourishing *Earth* standing *in* that *Water*, and *out* of it; being continually *fed*, continually made *Fruitful*, and *Beautiful* by it.

As *Jacob* at the sight of the *Waggons*, which came from *Joseph*; so this Soul now revives, she begins to be *her self*, and to live again, as after a long Trance, or Death. She looks about, and sees her self at *home*, she perceives her self in that Spirit; in which she came forth from God; in which she sees the Face of God again; by which she is assured to be carryed on to the full and eternal enjoyment of her God, and Father.

Now, saith the Soul; *I have enough; I have not only seen the Face of my God; but He hath made me to see His Seeds also; the Face of each Object, as the Face of an Angel of God. Now let me die; that I entirely in my Body, and whole Soul may be call'd home from my Banishment into this remote part of Things, the Out-side of Nature. Now let me die in Peace, with this Spiritual Image in my Embraces, this Sense of Joys, and Glories in my Heart. Let me ever abide here, O my God! never to go forth more from this Inner Chamber of the Great King into the Tumultuous street of my senses, or sensual Reason. O that this Spiritual State so full of ravishing Sights, which like the Sheet full of all living Creatures before* Peter, *is now let down out of Heaven into my Soul; O! that it might never be drawn up again; until it take me also up with it into Heaven.*

I have finisht the *Second State* of our Change at our *Conversion*: The *Spiritual State, in Christ*, I pass to the *Third*,

3. *The Divine State of things, in God.* As *Christ* is the *way* to *God*. So the *Divine State* is the Spiritual State made *Perfect*. The Soul having been a while taught in the Bosom of Christ, begins to grow up to a fuller sense of God, in a more *naked, abstracted, absolute, and comprehensive* manner. Now she begins to *put off* all, that ever she *put on*, that God may be her *only Clothing*. She begins to think it not enough *to live and walk in the Spirit of God*; except she *be One Spirit with Christ, and God.* She perceives some dark glimpse of that, which is meant, 1 *Cor.* 13. 12. To *Know, as we are Known*; that is, *in patria*, at home *in God, Comprehensively*, by being Comprehended in God, and so Comprehending him again.

The Soul in the glimmering Light of this State brought forth in her Flesh, as a small Candle in a dark Lanthorn, or faint twinklings of a Star in a Cloud;

the

the Soul rudely descries a difference between making the *Creature* the *Glass*, thorow which we see *God*, and having the *Godhead* for the *Glass*, placing itself next our *Eye*, and discovering all the *Creatures in itself*, this the Soul climbs up towards, this makes her long for *Heaven*, that she may enjoy this *Beatifical Vision* clearly, *uncas'd* of *Flesh*.

The imperfectest Beginnings, and rudest Hints of this State in the Soul are to the other State; as *Honey*, and *Wine*, to Milk. They melt the Spirit of Man to a Transcendent Sweetness, and heighten it to a Triumphant Strength. As *Jesus Christ* saith of God out of the *Psalmist*, Psal. 82. 16. *He saith of those to whom the word of God came: I have said: Ye are Gods.* Joh. 10. 35. So saith the Soul to all things, as she looks upon them in this *Divine State*. *Ye are God-like Appearances, rising up out of God, and abiding in him.*

Saul cries, 1 *Sam.* 28. 13. *I see Gods ascending up out of the Earth.* But this Soul in this *Divine Principle* sees God Himself with the whole Troop of the Sons of God, *God-like Forms* ascending out of every Point of the Earth, and the lowest parts of things.

Use. Conviction. Consider with thy self after this manner, *Am I Chang'd?* If I be not, I stand in the Circle of Vanity, Darkness, and Woe. I am gone forth from my Center, outward, into a Waste Wilderness, whither no clear Line of Light, or Life stretcheth itself; where are no Sparks of peace, or joy, which are not scattered into wild Distractions, torn in pieces and devoured by Confusion.

Am I still wandering in this World? I am already upon the very Brink, and Precipice of Things. Whither do I wander? Whither shall I fall, when I die? Is there yet any thing beyond this World, further from God, and Goodness, besides the Place of Devils.

There are *Four Discoveries* of a Chang'd, or Unchang'd State.

1. *Discovery. Have I seen a Resurrection in my self.* Our *Conversion* is made the same thing with the *Resurrection* of our Saviour, *Colos.* 3. 1. *If ye be risen with Christ.* When Jesus *rose again, He returned* to that Glory, which He had with God, before he was in Flesh. His *Resurrection* was a *Return* not to that Life, which he had in the World; this was part of his Death: but to that Life, which he had before This among Earthly Men. So when we *Turn* to God, we *Return* truly to our selves. We perceive our Selves now to be our Selves, and all below this, to have been a *Shadow of* us, or a *Disguise upon* us.

The *Conversion* of Man is call'd an *Awakening*, Ephes. 5. 14. *Awake thou, that sleepest: stand up from the Dead.* My God is a Light, in which all Things are seen ever, as they were from the Beginning. My Jesus is a Life, in which all things are the same Yesterday, before the World, as they shall be to Morrow, and for ever. My Soul! Art thou awakened into the Light, the Life of thy God, thy Jesus? If thou art, what seest thou? Thou seest thy true, and

substantial

am I climbs? *

ſubſtantial Being, thy *proper Perſon* appearing; thou ſeeſt all things in their *firſt Principle*, in their *right ſtate*; thou ſeeſt every *Inferiour Perſon*, which thou haſt been cloth'd with, and each *Lower State* of Things, in which thou haſt acted any Part, as *Dreams* of a ſleeping Man in the Night, out of which he awakens the *ſame*, that he was, when firſt he lay down, and they vaniſh, as *Airy Images*.

The *Goſpel* declares the *Myſtery, that was hid in God from the beginning of the World*, Epheſ. 3. 9. If you have not beheld *preſent things*, *things to come*, *Heaven, Glory, your future State*; as it was *in the Myſtery of God* from *Eternity*: you are ſtill buried under the Ruines of this Confuſed *World*, beneath which that *Myſtery* lies hid.

2. *Diſcovery*. *Can I tell the Difference between Fleſh, and Spirit?* A Converted, and a Regenerate Condition are thus diſtinguiſht by *Walking in Fleſh, or Spirit*, Rom. 8. 4. The *Eye* guides the *Feet*. How can I walk after *One*, and not the *Other*, if I know not, how *One* differs from the *Other*. *The Light ſhined in Darkneſs, but the Darkneſs comprehended it not*. The *Fleſh* is the *Darkneſs*, which underſtands neither the *Spirit*, nor *itſelf*, The *Spirit* is the *Light*, in which *both* are underſtood, and diſcern'd.

Say thus to thy Heart: *My Heart!* Canſt thou tell a way to poſſeſs all Things in one point, in a *Unity* of Life? Haſt thou lookt on all Things *at once*, and ſeen them in a *Harmony* of Beauty? Haſt thou taken in the Tunes and Motions of all Things Created and Uncreated in a *Concent* of Pleaſures? Didſt thou ever yet deſcry a glorious *Eternity* in each winged *Moment* of Time; a Bright *Infiniteneſs* in the narrow *points* of every dark Object? Then thou knoweſt what the *Spirit* means, that *Spire-top* of Things, whither all aſcend harmoniouſly, where they meet, and ſit together *recollected*, and *concentred* in an Unfathom'd Depth of Glorious Life. From hence thou lookeſt down, and ſeeſt all *Fleſh*, as a heap of *Single Duſts*; *Dark*, though falling from the midſt of a bright Flame; *Divided*, though laid together.

He that knows no *Spirit*, but that which breaths thorow Fleſh, and feeds on the Air. He that underſtands the higheſt *Spirit*, but as a Fleſhly *Fancy* exalted; is yet *Fleſh*, condemn'd like *Nebucchadnezzar* to graze on the fading Field of Fleſh, till he know, this *Fleſh* to be that *Darkneſs*, which covers all Truth; and the moſt high *Spirit*, to be the only Light, which diſcovers all things, and itſelf.

3. *Diſcovery*. *Have I ſeen a Night upon this World?* One *Day* paſſeth not away for another to ſucceed, except a *Night* come between. My ſoul is not yet born again out of the Light of this World into the *Day* of Chriſt, if ſhe hath not gone thorow a *Night*, a Night of Eternal Darkneſs upon all Earthly Contents. Thou canſt not look down upon Fleſhly Things with a Delight, from the *Throne* of Chriſt; except thou haſt lookt upon them, as a *Proſpect* of Horreur; from the *Croſs* of Chriſt.

Jeſus

Jesus Christ threatens *Jezabel*, and her Companions, to throw her into a *Bed*, and great *Tribulation*: Revel. 2. 22. He never comes into the *Bed of Eternal Repose* with *Jesus Christ*, as his *Spouse*; that hath not been in a *Bed of afflictions*, and Flames, with his *Jezabel* the *Flesh*.

4. *Discovery. Have I tasted the Sweetness of a Life within, in my own Spirit?* Hast thou not made a *Retreat* into thine own Depths? Hast thou not seen the Beauties, that shine in *this Glass?* Then art thou far from the Depths of the Divine Spirit, and the Glories that disclose themselves in *that Glass*.

Solomon tells us, *Prov.* 20. 27. *That the Spirit of Man is the Candle of the Lord in his Bowels*: if the *Spirit* of Man within be but a *Candle*; what then is this *Sensual State* without? Neither Life, nor Death; nor Light, nor Darkness: but *Shadows* of Life, and Death between both. But who can think he hath receiv'd the *Beams* of the *Sun*, when yet he hath not seen a *Candles Light*?

We read of a *Strumpet*, Prov. 7. 11, 12. *That her Feet abide not in the house; but she loves to be abroad.* While the Feet, the Affections of our Souls are ever gadding and our eyes gazing in the broad ways of *Sense*; while they love not to dwell in the *Habitation* of their *own Spirits*: they make themselves *Strumpets* to every unclean Spirit.

I have ended the *First Head* of this Doctrine, the *Conversion*, or *Change* it self. I am now to pass to the *Second*, the *Circumstances* of this Change.

2. *Part*: *The Circumstances of the Change*. These are *Two*.

1. *Circumstance*: *A Universal Motion in all the Passions.*

2. *Circumstance*: *A General Alteration in Practice*.

1. *Circumstance*: *A Universal Motion in all the Passions.* These are moved at the time of our *Conversion*, for the most part, in this *Threefold Order*.

1. *Order.*	2. *Order.*	3. *Order.*
1. *Grief.*	1. *Hope.*	1. *Love.*
2. *Shame.*	2. *Desire.*	2. *Hatred.*
3. *Fear.*	3. *Rage.*	

1. *Order of Passions* in our Change.

1. *Passion*: *Grief.* John 12. 32, 33. *And I, if I be lifted up, will draw up all men after me. This he spake, signifying, by what Death he should die.* The Explication of the *Exaltation*, the *lifting up*, the *drawing up*, is *Death*. The Lord *Jesus* was lifted up to Glory *by Death*. He draws up all men to himself, and Immortality, *by Death*. *Grief* is the Souls Death. God by this for the most part begins to draw us up, out of Sin, and Flesh to himself, and eternal joys.

Grief naturally is the *Sense of some Great, and Present Evil oppressing the Soul*. Grief *Spiritually* is the Sense of some Great, and Present Evil *oppressing* the Soul, and *pressing* it thorow itself into the lap of the Godhead.

Psal. 119. 67. *David* communicates his Experience: *Before I was afflicted,*

flicted, I went astray : but now I keep thy Commandments. The word *afflicted* signifies to be *brought low*, or *down*. When the Soul gone forth into the midst of the Creatures is arrived at the utmost point of one *Contrary*, then it begins to return towards the other : as the Sun first turns itself towards us again at Midnight. The utmost Point of a worldly life in Sin, and Vanity, is *Grief*, or Torment taking away all our Rest. The Soul hurried hither by the Torrent of her lusts, here begins to look, and move towards God. So the *Grave* of our joys, our *Grief* becomes a *Womb* bringing us forth to a Spiritual life.

Psal. 40. 2. David speaks of God, and himself : *He hath drawn me up out of the Horrible Pit, and Dirty Clay.* This world hath a *Root* of Darkness, which bears for a *Flower* the *Images of Light.* When the Spirit of Man lives upon, and makes itself One with these *Imaginary* Pleasures ; they quickly fade : So both together sink down into their *Root*, where they are swallowed up in a melancholy darkness. Here the Vanities, which before were Light, now grow heavy, weighing down the Soul. Here all her former Contents meet her again, as *Parts*, and *Powers* of this Darkness. That, which was before *beautiful Clay, soft Clay*, easie to any Impression of Desire, is now *stiff, and dirty Clay*, holding the feet of the Soul fast in the bottom of this *Horrible Pit.*

Now God takes hold of us thus low, thus lost, and draws us upward. So our Change begins in *Grief.*

2. *Passion : Shame.* Es. 6. 11, 12, 13. *Shame* ariseth from a *Mixt sense* of Light, and Darkness ; Good, and Evil ; Beauty, and Deformity. It is a *mixt Passion* of Grief, Anger, Fear. As when the Light, and Day first sink into Night, and Darkness in the Evening ; or first ascend out of these in the Morning, the Sky looks red: So the Soul blusheth in the midst of her Sins, and is *ashamed*, when God first *dawnes* upon her, and begins to draw near to her.

Ezek. 43. 10. *Son of man, shew them the House that they may be ashamed of all their Iniquities, and let them measure the Pattern. Shame is a Reflection of foul, and hateful Deformities, made upon our Spirits by the Light of Beauty, Goodness, God shining forth upon them. Shame* is the Divine Glory glowing thorow our Darkness, and Filth ; before yet it is broken forth into a clear Flame to scatter, and consume them.

God saith to *Jesus Christ*, of man : *Son, go and shew thy self to him, as the Image, in which he was made, in which he should have lived. So let him be ashamed of that dark, narrow, vile, brutish Image, in which he walks. Let him take measure by Thee, as his Original and Pattern.*

3. *Passion* : *Fear.* As *Grief* awakens *Shame*, so *Shame* rowseth *Fear* out of its Den. *Psal.* 119. 120. *David* cries out : *My Flesh trembleth because of Thee : I am afraid of thy Judgments. Fear* is the *Commotion of the Soul, upon the sense of some approaching Evil.* As the Sea trembles before a Storm : So at

the

the ſign of God's breaking forth upon the Soul, the fleſhly part trembles, and ſhakes before its fall.

The Man himſelf is afraid of the *Judgments* of God; the ways of God with the Creature. The Devils at the Preſence of Chriſt feared *two Things*: 1. A *Baniſhment* from off the Face of the Earth. 2. A *Confinement* to the Lower-moſt parts of the Earth. Such now is the Fear of a Man, leſt he ſhould be *call'd off* from his Carnal Contents, and *caſt down* into the Straitneſs, and Horrour of his Carnal Principles.

He diſcourſeth with himſelf thus: *Muſt not I, who have lived in Fleſh, now be ſeparated from all the delights of Fleſh, and be ſhut up in the Darkneſs of it? Muſt I not abide there, till I have paſs'd thorow the Fire, and endur'd the Conſumption of all that which is Corruptible in me? The longer I live in the Fleſh, will not the Fire be the ſtronger?*

Thus *Fear* becomes a *Spur* in the ſide of the Spirit to increaſe her ſpeed out of the World, to God. This is the *Firſt Order of Paſſions: Grief, Shame, Fear.*

2. *Order of Paſſions.*

1. *Paſſion: Hope.* Lament. 3. 21, 22. *This I call to mind, therefore have I hope: It is the mercies of the Lord, that we are not conſumed. Hope* is the *Springing of the Soul towards good, or God, firſt dawning upon it, and diſpenſing Himſelf to it. Jeremy*, was all before wrapt up in Sorrows, Deſpairs, Death: Now one ſingle Beam of *Hope*, and that a ſmall one, glimmers in his Soul: *It is the mercies of the Lord, that we are not conſumed.* Yet this lights him into freſh Fields of Contemplations, and Conſolations in God.

There is Mercy with thee, that thou mayſt be feared: ſaith the *Scripture* to God. When *Fear* affrights the fainting Soul from God: *Hope* invites it to entertain that *Fear. Fear* ſaith: *The Preſence of God will take away thy Natural Strength, and Joy. Hope* anſwers: *I ſhall find a better Strength, and Joy in God. Fear* goes on: *The Glory of God will be, as a Fire in thee. Hope* replies: *This Fire will be a Glory to me. Fear* ſtill urgeth: *Canſt thou ly down with Everlaſting Burnings? Hope* concludes: *I ſhall have everlaſting Arms beneath me.* So the Soul caſts her ſelf into theſe *Arms* to be *carried*, whitherſoever they will *bear* her.

2. *Paſſion: Deſire.* 2 Sam. 7. 27. David thus conveys his *Deſires* to God: *Becauſe thou O Lord, haſt revealed it to thy Servant concerning his Houſe: therefore hath he found in his heart to pray this prayer. Hope* is the *Conception* of Bleſſedneſs. *Deſire* is the *Teeming*, the Breeding, Bearing, and Growing big with it, till it be brought forth. The Veſtal Virgins firſt kindled their Spark by a Beam: then they from that Spark kept a continual Flame upon their Altar. So the *Revelation* of God in Man is the Foundation of *Hope*: *Hope* the Fountain of *Deſires*, which grow into great Streams, and ſo pour forth themſelves into their Sea, into God again.

 The

The *Desires* of a New Convert, when once they are kindled, increase suddenly to a mighty Flame. For they are *proportion'd* by *Two things* : The *Good*, at which he aims: The *Evil*, from which he flies. *Desires* here are the *Attractions* of the highest Good, the most high God : backed by the *Impressions* of the greatest Evils, Sin, Death, Devils. As *one* draws ; the *Other* drive. The Soul sees God *before* her opening a World of new Hopes, and Delights. She sees Lusts and Furies *behind* her, labouring to overtake her, and hold her back from those fresh Glories, which are now in her eye. This makes her *Desires*, as swift feet, as strong Wings to her.

Now the newly-converted Spirit begins to discover her self by continual, violent Breathings, and cries towards Heaven : *How long Lord* ? Now she speaks in *Davids* tune, and tone *Psal.* 84. 2. *My soul longeth, yea even fainteth for the Courts of the Lord : my Heart, and my Flesh cry out for the Living God.* Grones are now the constant beatings of the Heart ; Longings and Faintings become the Language of all parts inward, and outward : Longings after, Faintings for, the Life of God, the Living God.

3. *Passion* : *Rage.* 2 Corin. 7. 11. The *Corinthians* had slept secure in a foul Sin. They now awakened by St. *Paul*, give those Testimonies of their *Change*, which he reckons up in this place : *What vehement Desire* : *yea, what Zeal? yea, what Revenge?* As a Flood foaming, and roaring, when it is streightned : or swelling, and over-bearing all, when it is stopt in its Course : So are Anger, or *Rage*, *Desires multiplied, and growing Mighty by Resistance.*

There are *Three*, that resist the Soul in her *Conversion* : the *Flesh*, the *World*, the *Devil*. *The Flesh lusteth against the Spirit* : Gal. 5. 17. The Inclinations of the *Flesh* cross, and quench the Motions of the *Spirit*. The *World* infuseth a poyson of Desires and Delights into the Heart, which kill Heavenly Loves, which infect the Heart with hatred, and enmity against God and his Glory, *James* 4. 4. *The Friendship of the World is enmity with God.* The *Devil* is *like a Lyon, seeking whom he may devour.* 1 Pet. 5. 8. He would draw down our Souls into himself out of the Arms of our Saviour.

The *World* works upon us thorow the *Flesh* in our selves. For this is the *Property*, and the Birth of the *World* in us, *John* 8. 23. *Ye are of the World* : *Ye*, that is they that are Fleshly. The *Devil* prevaileth upon us by the *World*. This is the *Body* with which he cloaths himself, when he comes, he is *Prince of this World.* This world is his *Power.*

As *God*, *Christ*, and a *Saint* are all united in the *Spiritual part* of a Christian : So the *Devil*, the *World*, the *Flesh* are all in one, in the *Natural part.* These the Soul at her *Conversion* now understands to be, the Enemies of her Hope, the Tyrants over her joy, the Rubs in the way of her Desires. She riseth to a brave heat of Rage, and height of Revenge against these. Thus she vents her Rage, thus she takes Revenge. By fastning her own *Flesh* to the Cross of her Lord, She Crucifies Spoils, Triumphs over, them all. *Gal.* 6. 14. *I Glory* saith Paul, *in the Cross of Christ, by which the World is crucified to me, and I to the World.*

Nothing now is so sweet, nothing so Glorious to this Soul, as the *Cross* of her Jesus. By this she revengeth her self upon her Spiritual Enemy, as they treated her Lord, her Life; that is with Scorn, and Despight.

First she puts them to open Shame. She uncloaths them of all their fair Appearances. In the face of Heav'n, in the eye of her Sun, her God, she displays them naked in their ugly monstrous Shapes; in their loathsom, and hateful Uncleannesses.

Then she nails them by a constant force to their Pains, and Sufferance; till they languish to Death.

I have gone thorow the *Second Order of Passions: Hope, Desire, Rage.*

3. *Order of Passions.*

1. *Passion: Love. Love is a Conjunction with, a Complacency in Goodness, God.* Gal. 2. 20. *I am, saith St. Paul, Crucified with Christ, and now I live, yet not I, but Christ liveth in me,* &c. The Holy Soul having strugled thorow the *Streights* of Grief, and Shame; thorow the *Cross-tides* of Hope, and Fear; having wrestled with the Principles of Nature, the Principalities, and Powers of this world; Fleshly Honours, and heights: now comes to tast the Freedom, and Sweetness of life; which is *Love*; now she knows what 'tis to Live *indeed*, to live in the Embraces, and mutual Twinings of the Lord Jesus. Now she hath no *Life*, but his *Love*: now her *Love* hath no *Object*, but *His Life*.

By this time our *Convert* is grown up out of a *Servant*, to a *Spouse-like* temper: like her in the *Canticles*: She grows *Sick of Love*. Her Love to God consumes her strength, wasts her Life, dispossesseth her of her self. Nothing can be *Strength, Life, Self* to her, save her *Saviour* only. She is strong, *only* when he is present. She is happy when he is pleased.

A man in this State breaths nothing, but Affection to *God*. He cries continually, as *David* doth: *Psal.* 18. 1. *I love Thee.* The word signifies: *I love thee dearly, tenderly, inwardly: I twist thy love upon my inwardest, and tenderest bowels, O my Jesus.*

2. *Passion*: *Hatred.* Psal. 139. 22. *I hate them, that hate thee with a perfect Hatred. Hatred* is the *Life of Contrariety, Casting out* from itself, yet *Comprehending in* it self, as in a Chain, *Conquering to* it self, its Contrary. God promiseth *Christ* thus much: *Psal.* 110. 1, *Sit thou at my right hand, till I make thine enemies thy Foot-stool.* We hold our *Foot-stool near* us, but *under* us. We hold it *down*, yet we hold *up*, and raise our selves by it.

There is a *Twofold Hatred.*

1. *Hatred before Love.* 2. *Hatred from Love.*

Hatred before Love is weak, and imperfect, rellishing much, of *self-love*, Darkness, and Hell.

Hatred

Hatred from Love is Perfect, it springs from the Heart of sweetness, it subordinates itself to it, it ends in it. The Life of this Hatred is Love.

As the soul at her first Conversion is strong in Love, so is she sweet in her Hatred. She hates *perfectly* like a *God*, not a *Devil*, every thing, which brings not the Loveliness of her Saviour along with it, as a Pass-port: She turns away her face from it, she sets her feet upon it: not suffering it to rise up against the Life of the Lord Jesus within her: forcing it to serve his *Glory*.

So much for the *Third Order of Passions, Love, Hatred.* So much for the *First Circumstance* in our Conversion: *The Universal Motion in our Passions.*

2. *Circumstance*: *A General Alteration in Practice.* This *Alteration is Twofold:*

1. *A Manifest withdrawing from all Companies, and Contents, that draw the Soul outward, or downward.*

2. *An eminent Delight in all Persons, and Paths, that draw the Spirit inward, or upward.*

David expresseth both these in himself: *Psal. 16. My delight is in the Excellent of the Earth. As for them, that go after other Gods, I will not make mention of their Name.*

1. *Use*: For *Discovery. Religion* is no *empty Name*, but a *Real Thing. Two Things* make a *Reality* in the Soul.

1. *The Object.* 2. *The Inward Affections.* *

1. *The Object.* As the *Woman* is to the *Man* his *Image*, his Glory in the Image: So is the *Soul* to her *Object*. If she espouse her self to the Lying Vanities of this World, she makes her self one with them, both *Vanity*, and a *Lye*. If she cleave to the Rock of Ages, the Rock of the Godhead, growing to that, growing up out of that, she becomes a *Living Stone*, a *Rock* of Eternity in her self.

This is the *First Motion* in Religion, the winding of the Soul about the utmost point of the Creature, and turning in towards God again. This is the Discriminating, Dividing Temper; between Religious and unregenerate Persons; the *Touching* of the Soul with God, as the *Needle* is touch't with the Load-stone; when it may have various agitations, yet it feels the Impressions of God in the midst of all: when it can never establish, or quiet itself in any posture, save then only, when it is pointed on God. *My Soul hath said to the Lord, thou art my Portion*: Lamen. 3.

Psal. 16. 8. *I have set the Lord always before me: He is at my Right hand: I shall not be moved. God is our Assistant there, where he is our Object*: at our *Hand*, if he be in our *Eye*. This is the Life and Essence of Religion; the exaltation of God in our Spirits, as our *Chief Object, to* which, and *by* which we are directed.

Examine thy self, by this. If the world be all to thee, and God a Fancy: then art thou like that world, a *Fancy*, and a *Bubble*. If God be all to thee,

and

and the world a Dream: then thou hast Strength, Life, and Substance. For thou art one with him, who is the *Life, Strength, Substance, Being* of all things.

Is thy Heart, as a *Hearth*, on which Thorns only blaze? Are the workings of thy Spirit like thin, and fine Smoak, slight and vanishing? Can then there be any *Religion*, where there is no *Reality*? He is the Religious man who graspes *Substance*; who digs thorow all things, till he meets with a sure *Foundation*; who hath taken hold of something Solid, Satisfactory, Everlasting at which his Soul stops, on which she stays her self. *I hate them, saith* David, *that look to lying Vanities: but my trust is in the Lord.*

There is a *Three-fold Sense* of things, which makes a *Religious* man *Real*: 1. *Sense, of this World's sorrows.* 2. *Sense, of Divine Wrath.* 3. *Sense, of Divine Love.*

1. *Sense, of this World's sorrows.* No man is in the Spirit of Christ, who hath not been at the Cross, in the Grave of Christ, and there seen the end of all this world's Glories. Who beholds things in the Eternal Light? He, that hath first seen this world in a Fire, out of which it falls into blackness of Darkness? *By the Cross of Christ, the World is crucified to me*; saith St. *Paul*. *I come to kindle a Fire in the World*, saith our Saviour, *and what will I, if it be already Kindled.*

They that go down into the Deep, see the Wonders of the Lord: saith the Psalmist. Whoever is gone up to Heights of Grace, hath gone down into the Deep of the First Creation, and seen Wonders of Darkness there.

Jonah tells us of himself: *Jon.* 2, 6. *I went down to the bottom of the Mountains, the bars of the Earth were about me for ever.* Hast thou descended with thy Saviour to the *Bottom* of this Creation, hast thou seen about thee those everlasting *Bars* of Darkness, which bear up, and bound this Creation? Then shew us the effect, which *Solomon* mentions in *Ecclesiastes*: *A sad Countenance makes a good Heart.* As Darkness contracts the Eye, unites the Fancy, and makes it strong: So a sad Face of things makes the Spirit gather up itself into itself, live serious, and Recollected.

2. *Sense, of Divine Wrath. We*, saith St. *Paul*, *knowing the Terrours of the Lord, persuade men*: 2 Cor. 5. 11, If we know God, we know his *Terrours*, and what the *Power of his Wrath* is; can we not then persuade our selves to be serious? Have you seen the Treasures of wrath laid up with God for those that harden their Hearts in Sloth, and Sense, to an *insensibleness* of Spiritual, and Eternal things? Have you heard those seven-times-seven fold increases of Fury upon those, who go on in Vanity; and yet say, it shall not be so, it shall be well with them? Cannot these things make you *Real*, and *Sober*?

If still vanity be your Life, your Food, your Joy; if still Lightness be your Air, and Shadows the Game, which you hunt with your Reason, and Senses; then fear, lest you have seen Shadows only of these Objects, lest your *Religion* too be *vain*.

3. *Sense*,

3. *Sense of Divine Love.* The Scripture saith in one place to good men: *The Joy of the Lord shall be your Strength.* Such as the *Nourishment* of our Spirit is, such will its *Constitution*, and our Conversation be. If our Food, our Joy be Divine, and we eat the Bread of Angels, our Lives will be Divine, and our Faces shine with Angelical Beams. If our Delights be Vanity, and we feed on wind; our Spirits, and Conversation will be windy.

The same *Solomon, that said of Mirth, what dost thou? And of Laughter, it is Madness*: Eccles. 2. 2. He saith *Prov.* 3. *The ways of Wisdom are ways of Peace, and all her Paths are pleasantness.* Spiritual Pleasures are Serious ones, as Grave, as Wisdom itself: for they are *her Walks. The Love of Christ constrains us*: saith St. Paul, 2 *Cor.* 5. The Love of Christ *holds in, binds up*, and *unites* the Spirit, not suffering it to pour forth itself loosely.

That *Liberty*, which is Daughter to Divine Love, what a Stranger is it to *Licentiousness*? Those Sweetnesses, which flow from God and his Glories how do they look down upon, and despise *Empty Mirths*, and mad Laughters? A Bride, made a Woman of a Cat, and set among the Guests in the bridal Chambear, on a sudden runs after a Mouse which stir'd in a Corner of the Room. If thy Soul be still ready to fly at every vanity, which is at any time started in the eye of it: thou maist be cloth'd with the Form of a Heavenly Bride; but sure thou hast still a Brutish Spirit.

Thus you see, how the *Object* of a *Religious* man makes him *Real*. The *Second Reality* in Religion is that of *Inward Affections.*

2. *The Inward Affections. My Son*, saith Wisdom in the *Proverbs, give me thy Heart.* Perhaps you give to God your *Feet* to carry you to Sermons; you give him your *Hands* to work, or fight for him; you give him your *Tongue* to discourse of Him: but have you given him your *Heart*? Doth that cleave to him, long and pant after him, sigh for him, live only in Him? *David* saith to God: *Psal* 51. *Thou lovest Uprightness in the Inward parts.* The more *Inward* any thing is, the more *Upright* it is. Are thy frequentest Groans such, as thou dost not express, thou canst not express; such, as thy Spirit only feels, God's Spirit only hears?

It is the Counsel of our Lord Jesus: *Pray to thy Father in Secret, and He shall reward thee openly.* The most *Secret* things are the most *Serious.* Dost thou commune with thine own Heart upon thy Bed about the things of God, and Eternity? Do the workings and Labourings of thy Soul after thy Saviour hold thine eyes waking, while others are sleeping?

Solomon tells us: *The Heart knoweth its own Sorrow, and a stranger intermeddles not with its Joys.* Blessed is he who hath a sense of a Sorrow for Sin, and the absence of God, which his own Heart only is conscious to. Blessed is he, who lives on hidden Manna, who hath his Bosom still warmed with a secret Flame of Divine Love, and Joy, to which all others are Strangers.

Man

Man hath, as St. *Paul* teacheth, a *Spirit*, a *Soul*, a *Body*. So hath *Religion*. *God* the Eternal Object and Spring of our Religion is the *Spirit*: our *Inward Affections* are the *Soul*; our *outward Actions*, *the Body*. *Outward* Actions most glorious, if they go alone, make but a *Dead Religion*, are a *Body* without a Soul. *Inward Affections* without God make but a *Brutish Religion*, a Soul in a Body without the Immortal Spirit. I now conclude this Application.

2. *Use*: *For Direction*, I will divide this into a *Threefold Direction*.

1. *Direction*. *Entertain mournful Tempers as Angels; Improve them as Treasures*. When *Jonah* was in the bottom of the Sea, and belly of the Fish, his Soul fainting within him; then he remembred the Lord; *Jonah* 2. 7. As Pearls are found at the bottom of the Sea: so, frequently do the Beauties of the Lord Jesus disclose themselves to us in the depths of Grief, when we are sunk below the waters of this world, and are swallowed up into a Spirit of Darkness. It is St. *James*'s advice, *Jam*. 1 4. *Let Patience have its perfect work, and it shall make you perfect*. As one Element stretcht to the utmost passeth into another, Water into Air, Air into Fire: as a Cloud big, and swelling dissolves it self upon the Earth: so thy Griefs, if thou wait calmly upon them, as they swell, and grow, will at length dissolve themselves into God. As Snow and Frost cherish the Seed in the ground: so do biting and binding Sorrows both kill the weeds of Vanity, and ripen the Seed of Divinity in Man. I can no more want Sorrows for my Soul, than the Husband-man can want *Winter seasons* for his Corn fields. As natural Melancholy draws the Soul deeply into her self, and her Divinest Principles; whence she issues forth again, with the most great and glorious Lights: so do sad things work upon a holy Spirit sinking her thorow her self into the Depths of the Godhead, out of which she riseth renewed to a fresh Spring of Life and Joy.

2. *Direction*. *Look stedfastly to the end of all Flesh*. In every Pleasure, Strength, Glory, see the Worm, and the Fire which is bred in all fleshly things, the one never to go out, the other never to die till Flesh be no more. *The belly for meats, and meat for the belly*; *but God shall destroy them both*; *and I will be in bondage to neither*, saith St. *Paul*. If thou engage thy Soul in any earthly Content, thou puttest thy self into a Prison, whence you must come by Death, or where Death will find you. Why should I *put on* that, which I must *keep on* with lasting vexations, or *put off* with present Pains? The world and my senses were made one for another. The Devil hath defiled, and disordered both: God distracts, and will destroy both: The Joy of my Life, and my Life shall depend on neither.

3. *Direction*. *Preserve Hope towards God ever alive in thy self*, Hos. 2. 15. We read of the *Door of Hope*. *Hope* is the *Door* of Happiness. This admits us into the Godhead. He that suffers *Hope* to sink under Despair in his Spirit, locks and bars up the *Door* of Heaven against himself. *Prov*. 13. 12. *Hope*

desirr'd makes the heart sick. But *Hope* cut off *kills* the Heart, and makes it lie dead in Sin, and Flesh. *He will lay his mouth in the Dust, if there may be Hope,* Give a man *Hope*, and you cast the Seed of a New Soul, of God into him. *What?* saith one, *May I, the vilest of men, the lowest of creatures, hope to be pardoned? Nay more, to be loved? to be made partaker of a Divine Spirit, and Glory? May I thus lost, hope this? Then will I fear, worship, serve God, do, suffer any thing for him, or from him; I will lay my mouth in the Dust at his feet, if I may have Hope.* Hope declares the most right, and most sweet thoughts of God. It sets the Soul in the rightest and sweetest frame towards God. He exalts God, and gives him the highest Glory, that dares at *worst*, to *hope* for the *best* things from him. *He that praiseth me, he honoureth me*, saith God, *Psal.* 50. There are *Two Grounds* for *Hope*, which never fail.

1. *God is nigh thee, Acts* 15. Thou hast *thy Being in him.* Thou wer't made by Jesus Christ, thou subsistest in him, as in thy *Root.* Thou art the work of his hand; the Son of his *Handmaid, Nature.* Thy *Natural Being* is a putting forth, a manifestation of Christ. Wait alwaies in Hope, for his highest, and divinest manifestations, which come after this. Thine eyes shall see them, if thou let not go thy *Hope*, but wait confidently to the end.

2. *God is Infinite.* He is All: All that thou canst *think* or *wish.* For thou couldst not *think*, or *wish* any thing, if it were not first in him. He is beyond thy *Distresses* or *Desires.* Hope then ever in this God, who is already *in thee*, who is *Infinite*, whose *Power* is above all thy *Pressures*, whose *Love* is above his own *Wrath. Christ* is called *our Hope: Christ in you the Hope of Glory*: to signifie, that *Hope* is the Son of God, and his Image growing in us; that Hope should have no *Ground*, but Christ; and then be as its Ground; *Immortal, Infinite.* Thus much for the *Second Part* in this Point of *Conversion*; *The Circumstances.* There is yet remaining the *Third Part*; the *Causes* of this Change.

3. *Part. The Cause of our Change or Conversion.* This is *manifold.* Some *Causes* are *essential*, some only *Occasional.* Some *remote*, some *near.* Yet all are as *Links* in a Chain, one depending on another. St. *Paul* scatters all these *Causes* within the compass of a *few verses*; 1 Tim. 2. 1. *I will therefore that prayers be made for all men.* 3. *For God will have all to be saved, and come to the knowledge of the Truth.* 4. *For there is one God, and one Mediator, the man Christ Jesus.* 5. *Who hath given himself a ransom for all to be revealed in due time.* All the *Causes* of our *Conversion* are in these words comprehended under *Five Heads.*

1. *Cause: The Relation of God to Man.*
2. *Cause: The Mediation of Jesus Christ.*
3. *Cause: The Manifestation of the Truth.*
4. *Cause: The Ministry of Man to Man.*
5. *Cause: The Manages of Providence.*

1. *Cause:*

1. *Cause: The Relation of God to Man.* 1 Tim. 2. 5. *There is one God.* All Mankind, all creatures are gathered up into one point of Life, which is *Love*, the *Unity* of Life, *in God. There is one God, the Father of all*, Ephes. 4. 6.

God is a *Father* in *Fulness*, in *Sweetness*.

1. *God is a Father in Fulness*, Luk. 20. 38. Our Saviour speaks thus of God: *He is not the God of the Dead, but of the Living. For all live to God*: πάντα; *All things live to* God. After the same manner, with the same force you may reason thus: God is not the God of the *Dead*, but the living; of the *unclean*, but the *pure*; of the *imperfect*, but the *perfect*; of the *miserable*, but the *happy*; of the *fading*, but the *eternal*. For all things are *living, pure, perfect, happy, eternal*, to God. So all things have *pure, happy, eternal lives* in God. These are the *Original* and *Radical Lives*; the *First*, the *Fairest Seeds* of all things in the Divine Nature. Thus God is *All*. This is the *Fulness* of God.

2. *God is a Father in Sweetness. God is* Love, 1 Joh. 4. 16. God is *Love* in the *Fountain*. As waters in their Spring, so is *Love* in God. It makes him flow *into* creatures, it makes him flow forth in Love *upon* the creatures; and still he pursues, he chaseth one Love with another in a *Stream*, till all return to their Original. Thus, as St. *Paul* speaketh, *Rom.* 11. 36. *All things are from him, thorow him, and to him. From* him, as the *Fountain* of Love; *thorow* him, as the *Stream* of Love; *to* him, as the *Sea* of Love. *All Cattel are mine upon a thousand hills*, saith God, *Psal.* 50. 10. As a Father looks upon his Children, as his own, as Images, parts of himself, himself multiplied: So is God a *Father* in *Sweetness*.

These two, the *Fulness*, the *Sweetness* of God, as a *Father*, are the *First Ground* of *Hope*, and *Root* of *Happiness* to the creature. The *Fulness* is that which we call the *All-sufficiency* of God; the *Sweetness* is that which we call *Free Grace*. These are the *Two Pillars* in the Temple of Glory: *Booz* (*strength*) Jakin, (*He will prepare.*) The *Fulness* of God is one, *Sweetness* the other.

2. *Cause: The Mediation of Jesus Christ: There is one Mediator, the Man Jesus Christ*, 1 Tim. 2. 5. Our Lord Jesus is *Mediator two waies*: He is

1. *A Divine Head to the Soul.* 2. *A Divine Seed in the Soul.*

1. *Our Lord Jesus is a Divine Head to the Soul*, 1 Cor. 11. 3. *The Head of every man is Christ*. This is the difference between *God*, and *Christ*; *God* contains eternally all the creatures in one *Nature* and *Person* in himself. *God is One. Jesus Christ* comprehends the creature in one *Person*, not *Nature*, together with himself. Therefore as in one place he is said to be the *Head of Man*, 1 Cor. 11. 3. So in another place he is called the *Man*, 1 *Tim.* 2. 5.

Our Blessed Saviour is God uniting the different *Natures* of *God*, and the *Creature* in One *Person*, and that his *Own* Person. From this *Person* he communicates the Being of the creature, and streams forth immediately into it, in a different *Nature* and *Person*. In this *Person* he holds the creature in its proper and distinct Being, by being annext and united to himself. Thus the Lord is a *Head to Man.* And as the *Head* puts a beauty upon the whole Body, so doth Jesus Christ upon the whole Creation, by making himself a Head to it.

2. *Our Lord Jesus is a Divine Seed in the Soul.* He is called *the Seed*: Gen. 3. 16. 19. *till the Seed came*: He is *the Seed of the Woman*, Gen. 3. 15. But what *Woman* is this? He is the Seed of the *Earthly Woman, Eve.* For he lies hid in her, as in a Womb. He groweth up out of her in the Virgin *Mary*, clothing himself with her Flesh. But there is another *Woman* besides this, which is a *Mother*, and hath her *Seed*; a *heavenly Mother* of a heavenly Seed. St. *Paul* makes mention of her, *Gal.* 4. 26. *The* Hierusalem *above is free, which is the Mother of us all.* Jesus Christ is a *Seed.* God is the *Father*, this heavenly Woman is the *Mother*, the Spiritual State of the creature. He derives himself from *both these.* He unites *both these* in himself. So he lies in the earthly *Woman*, the fleshly Image, and becomes *her Seed* in the second place; *Seed thrice over, bearing her, abiding in her, bringing her forth the second* time.

As every creature hath this *Seed* in it, so it hath lying hid in it the Eternal Beauty of the Divine Nature, the Immortal Beauty of the Spiritual Creature, which both are wrapt up together, in this *Seed*, to grow up together out o it *in their Season.* Thus our Saviour is a *Divine Seed in the Soul.*

These two, *Christ* the *Head of* Man, the *Seed in* Man expound that of St. *Paul*, Ephes. 1. 4. *He hath elected us in him.* We are elected in Christ by *double meaning*:

1. We are made the *Desire*, and *Delight* of God, in *Christ*, as in ou *Head.*

2. We are *design'd* to be *saved* by *Christ*, as the *Seed* of Grace and Glory.

3. *Cause*: *The manifestation of the Truth*, 1 Tim. 2 3. *God will have all t be saved, and come to the knowledge of the Truth.* As in *Hebrew*, so in the Gree of the New Testament, *and* hath various significations. Sometimes it shew a *Cause*, sometimes an *Instrument*, sometimes a *Means*, or *Way*; so *Joh.* 17. 3 *This is eternal Life, to know thee the only true God, and* (*that is*, in, *or* by) *him whom thou hast sent Jesus Christ.* So 'tis here: *God will have all men to b saved, and come* (that is, *by coming*) *to the knowledge of the Truth. The mani festation of the Truth* is One *Cause* of our *Conversion* to Holiness and Happiness

But *what is Truth?* said *Pilate* to *Christ. Christ* had often said of *himself I am the Truth.* We read of *him, Rev.* 1. 5. that he is the *Faithful Witness* And he is said to *reveal the Father*: *No man knows who the Son is, but th Father. No man knows who the Father is, but the Son, and he to whom the So will reveal him.*

The *First Truth* in *General* and *Particular*, is the *Life of God*, and the *Li of the Creature in God.* Jesus Christ is *Truth*, as he is a *True Discovery* of thi *Truth.* He *reveals the Father*, that is, he opens the bosom of God; he mani fests the Life of God, as it enfolds the Life of the Creature in it self; he mani

fe

fects the Life of the Creature, as it abides in the Life of God, and grows upon the same Root with it. This is Truth, But what is the *Manifestation* of this Truth in Man? *No man can come unto me, except the Father draw him*, saith Jesus Christ, *Joh.*6. 44. *To come to the Truth*; to *have the Truth manifested in us* are both the same thing. The *Coming* is not *Natural*, nor the *Manifestation Moral*; both are *Supernatural* and *Spiritual*; the *Drawing* of the *Father*. A *Seed* hath a *Power* or *Principle*, which *sent* it forth, *abides* in it, and *works* thorow it. It hath also an *Image*, which grows up out of it. Jesus Christ is the *Seed* in the Soul of Man; the *Father* is the *Power*; the *Son* is the *Image* in this Seed.

When a *Corn* is cast into the ground, a *Power* goes forth from it into the *Earth* round about, which attracts, and draws it; which unites, and incorporates it with the *Seed*, which sends it forth again in the *Form* of that *Plant*, first in the *Herb*, then in the *Blade*, last in the *Ear*. So the *Father* thorow *Jesus Christ* diffuseth himself into the whole *Soul*, *draws* it into *Christ*, who lies there as a *Seed*, makes it *One* with him, who *brings* it forth again into his own *Form* and *Fruit*. St. *James* saith, *Jam.* 1. 18. *Of his own Will begat he us by the Word of Truth.* The *Word* is the *Seed* of Truth, *Christ Jesus* in us.

The *Will* of God is composed of those *two* forementioned; *A Supream Fulness, a Soveraign Sweetness*: These powerfully and pleasantly stir up the *Godhead* to bring forth the creatures, and to bring forth it self in the creatures: These delightfully and effectually move God to propagate himself endlesly and infinitely. These heats of love, the delights of fruitfulness are the inward and only Motives which put on our heavenly Father to quicken his Seed in us, to make it grow up by degrees, till it hath perfectly brought forth it self into its own form and fulness.

Thus St. *Paul* tells us, *Gal.* 1. 16. *It pleased the Father to reveal his Son in him.* As the Sun draws up the Plants out of their Roots, and discovers them to the open Air; so the Father reveals and discloseth Jesus Christ in the Soul.

4. *Cause*: The Ministry of Man to Man; *Heb.* 1. 14. We read that Angels are made *Ministring Spirits for the good of those that are to inherit Salvation.* So it pleaseth God often to make men as Angels, to minister Spiritual things to their Brethren.

It is one of the Mysteries of Godliness, 1 *Tim.* 3. 16. *God manifested in the Flesh, justified in the Spirit.* The great God is pleased by the *Fleshly* waies of man's *doing, speaking, writing, reading, living*, to express and convey himself.

A Learned man admires it, as having a Height of Wonder in it, that so low, so narrow; so dark, dead, divided things, as *words*, and *letters* should carry into our Souls the *highest Images* of the divinest Life, Truth, and Glory. This is the *Infiniteness* of the Godhead, which brings forth itself in the greatest *Variety* of Shapes, yet still keeps the *Unity*, preserves it self entire, and full in every one. Thus the Divine Nature imprints it self upon the thoughts of

Earthly

Earthly man, as *scattered Dust*, and by the *Motions* of this Dust in words implants it self by one Man upon the Soul of another.

There is a *Three-fold Ministry* of Man by which God works in the *Conversion* of men :

1. *Elevation of the heart in Prayer to God.* 2. *Exhortation by words to men.* 3. *Example of life before men.*

1. *Elevation of the heart in* Prayer *to God for men.* St. *Paul* describes Prayer, *Rom.* 8. 27. *God heareth His Spirit, for it makes intercessions in us, according to his will. Prayer* is the *Conception* of the Soul, when it hath taken in from Heaven the *Spirit* in the *Form* of some Divine *Blessing* : Then it grows big with this *Blessing* ; it travels with it ; it labours to raise it self into God, that by the *clearness* of his Light, by the *fulness* of his Life, it may bring it forth to perfection. A Spiritual man is like *Abraham*, who had in himself that *Seed*, in which all the Nations of the Earth were to be blessed. He hath conceived with a Seed of Blessedness to all Creatures. Therefore as *Paul* travelled in birth with the *Galatians*, till *Christ was formed in them* : so doth a good man travel in birth by *Prayer*, having many *Pangs*, and *Throws* in the *Spirit*, till this Blessedness be formed in each Soul.

St. *Paul* tells the *Corinthians*, 1 Cor. 3. 22. *All things are yours*, &c. A Heavenly Spirit is an *Universal Father* ; it looks upon all Creatures, as its own *Off-spring*, or *Bowels*. As *Job sacrificed* constantly for his Children, while they were *feasting* in their course : So is this Spirit *praying* for the Souls of men, while they are *playing* away themselves in Vanity. This is the *First Ministry*.

2. *Exhortation by words to men. David* promiseth, and prophesieth, *Psal.* 51. 13. *I will teach transgressours thy ways, and Sinners shall be converted unto thee.* Before in the former verse he had prayed ; *Restore thy Joy, and establish thy free Spirit in me.* Then he adds ; *I will teach transgressours thy ways*, (the ways of thy Love and Wisdom with man) *Sinners shall be converted unto thee*, that is, by the report of thy sweet *Contrivances* upon me, and *Compassions* towards me. When the *Heart* feels the Waters of Divine Life and Joy bubling up warm from the bosom of the Godhead, then the *Tongue* becomes the Pen of a ready Writer, labouring to imprint the Form of the same Life and Joys upon other hearts also.

If you will have me weep when you speak, weep your self, you that speak, said a Wise man. When a man utters those heavenly Loves, Truths, Delights of Jesus Christ, in which his own Soul lies melting and bathing her self, while he reports them : Then he often hath his *Tongue* made the *Quill* of the Godhead, by which he toucheth other Souls, and makes the same *Musick* upon them.

David calls his *Tongue*, his *Glory*, because by it he displayed that Glory of God, which was treasured up in *his* heart, to the view of *many* Hearts.

St.

St. *Paul* tells us, that God hath chosen the *Foolishness of Preaching* to make it *His Power* unto Salvation. God sends down the highest Glory into inferiour Forms, in which they descend by degrees; then in the lowest they become a *Seed*, out of which they grow and rise again by degrees to their first Height. So the *Divinity* puts its self into *our Saviour*, then into *our Hearts*, then into *our Tongues*, so into *Words* hovering in the *Air*, thus *low* it is become. Now by *Words*, as a *Seed* it is cast into the *Ear* of another, so it passeth into the *Heart*, where it springeth up into the *Fairness of Christ*, and from that into the *Fulness of God*.

3. *Example of Life before Men*. St. *Paul* tells the Saints! *Philip*. 2. 15. *They should be blameless, and harmless, in the midst of a crooked generation, in which they shine, as Lights*. When one *Candle* is lighted, we light many by that. When God hath kindled the Life of his Glory in one man's *Heart*, he often enlightens many by the Flame of that spread thorow his Conversation. Philosophers tell us; that, every thing hath *Beams*, by which it *manifests*, and *multiplies* itself. Sure nothing hath so piercing, so plentiful *Beams*, as the *Divine Nature*. When this is brought forth in any Spirit, it cannot but manifest itself by beautiful *Beams of Love*, and *Holiness*; as it *manifests*, so it often *multiplies* itself upon other Spirits.

When thou art Converted, saith Christ to *Peter strengthen thy Brethren*. It is the Perfection of *Life* to bring forth its *Like*. When a man is himself made partaker of the life of God: The Perfection of this life displays itself with such *power*, and *luster* thorow the whole man; that it many times draws strangers, first into the *Love*, then into the *Likeness* of it.

5. *Cause: Manages of Providence*, These are often *Moral Helps* to Man, *Outward Hints*, which God is pleased to make, and take for the Inward, and Spiritual work of our Conversion. But as they say of *Stars*: they do not *operate*, but *indicate* only; not *produce*, but *point* out effects, and events in Earthly things: So outward Providences, when they are most, are *Concurrencies* only, not *Causes* in a proper sense: not *Living Hands* to *do* any thing in the Truth of this Change; but as *Hands in a Margin*, to *declare* sometimes, what *God* is doing.

These Workings of *Providence*, by *Natural effects* in our Bodies; *civil accidents* in our Life; *Moral Impressions* on our Hearts are as the motion of the Waters, when the Angel descended into the Pool, which motion *accompanied*, but *contributed* nothing to the Healing Vertue. *It is not of him, that wills, nor of him, that runs; but of God, that hath mercy*.

Sometimes God brings forth this *Change*; when the Waters of outward *Providence* are quite calm; as when the *Apostles* were called from their *Nets*; *Matthew* from the *Custom*; *Gideon* from the *Flail*; *Elisha* from the *Plow*.

Sometimes God spreadeth this healing, and enlivening vertue thorow the Soul, when the Waters of the Natural man work high a contrary way; as

when

when *Saul* was chang'd into *Paul*, he was *then ſurprized* with the Love, and appearance of Jeſus Chriſt, *when* he was *perſecuting* him.

Yet it pleaſeth our Father very often to manage, and *forelay* outward things ſo; that he takes hold of them, as *occaſions*, or *opportunities* to make his way into our Souls.

There are *Two things* in *outward Providence*, which God eſpecially makes uſe of to this purpoſe:

1. *Natural Affections.* 2. *Temporal Afflictions.*

1. *Natural Affections.* As we ſeaſon Veſſels for the Liquor, with which we mean to fill them; and as the Threſhers of old had the *Staff* for the more tender Corn, and the *Wheel* for the Harder: So God made *John* the Evangeliſt of a gentle Heart, ſeaſoned with *ſtill*, but *ſtrong* affections; like a River, that runs quiet, but ſwift and deep. This *John* Jeſus Chriſt takes into his boſom, makes him his *Lute*, on which he ſounds forth his ſofteſt, ſweeteſt Loves, Beauty, Delights: So he lives, ſo he dies.

St. *Peter* was naturally more of the *Rock*, and *Flint*; ſharp, hard, and fiery, Jeſus Chriſt brings the *Wheel* over him, and breaks him ſorely, while he firſt forſwears his Saviour near his Croſs; then afterwards is forc'd to follow his Saviour to the Croſs.

St. *Paul* had a vigorous, profound Spirit by Nature, and Education; Jeſus Chriſt flaſhes upon him a with Glory from Heaven; fills him with the deep, and high Diſcoveries of Divine Glory; makes him to fill the world with the loud reports of them; as the *Trumpet* of Chriſt.

Our Lord found ſome of his Apoſtles *Fiſhing*. He takes hold of them by this, which was their Employment, and Enjoyment; their Inclination, or Education: *Come*, ſaith he, *follow me, and I will make you Fiſhers of Men.*

One Man is caught and carried by *ſenſual* Beauties, and Pleaſures: Jeſus Chriſt covers the Golden Hook of His Love, and Spirit with a Bait of Beauty, and Pleaſure to take this Man: *come*, ſaith Chriſt, *and follow me. I am fairer than the Sons of Men. I have a Beauty beyond that of any Creature. I am the Brightneſs of the Eternal Glory; the Lively Image of the Inviſible God. I am the Light and Life of all Lovelineſs in all the Creatures, They, when they ſhine ſweeteſt, are but ſhadows to me, ſhadows of me. I am all Pleaſant altogether; all Pleaſantneſſes, and Delights together.* As Jeſus Chriſt whiſpers this to the Soul, he lets fall upon it a Glimpſe, a Touch, a Taſt of Himſelf, which makes all this Real. So he raviſheth the Soul of this Man from the midſt of his Vanities, Senſualities, Luſts, into his own Embraces, by the ſtrength of a higher, though purer Delight.

Another man is *Rational*, and Philoſophical, led, by inclination, and ſtudy to trace the hidden ways of Nature, to ſearch the firſt Springs, and continued courſe of Things. The Lord Jeſus works Himſelf into the Reaſon, and ſpecu-

sation of this Man: *Come*, saith our Saviour, *and follow me. I am the Wisdom of God, by which the whole Creation was contrived, came forth, and is carried on. I am the beginning, the way, the end of all things. Time draws out its Line, and runs its Race, in me. Eternity comprehends itself, in its Center, and Circle, in me. All the Treasures of Knowledge are in my Love. You shall see all Mysteries, all Forms, and Motions of God, and the Creature, bare and naked in my Light.* As He speaks this, He opens something of Himself upon the Soul, which gives it a Glance of this Light, and Sight. Now He, that sat before at *Gamaliels* feet, like *Paul*, sets his feet upon the head of all that learning, and sits with *Mary*, at the feet of Christ. Now Jesus Christ is the *Reason of* his *Reason*, and the only *Reason to* it. Now *Jesus Christ* is all his *Philosophy*, and *Study*. Thus God makes use of *Natural Affections*.

2. *Temporal Afflictions.* You have a Platform of Gods working by these, from the mouth of *Elihu*: Job. 33. 19. *He is chastned with pain upon his bed, the multitude of his bones with strong pain.* The place of a mans Rest, and Pleasure, is made the place of his Torment. All the several Principles, and Strengths of Life are several Springs, Seats, and Strengths of Pain, and Misery,

20. v. *His Life abhorreth Bread, and his Soul dainty Meat.* The Nourishment of Life is tedious, and becomes a Burthen. The most pleasant Entertainments, the sweetest delicacies of Nature, and the Creature are now loath'd.

21. v. *His Flesh is consumed away, that it cannot be seen, his bones that were not seen, stick out.* All the cloathings, all the Beauties of his Being wither, and wear away. Those *Forms* in which he walked, disappear. The *Foundations*, the lowest Principles of being in him, are discovered, and left naked; like the *Sea* without waters, a *Deep* having no Face, but that of Darkness; an *Earth*, void, and without Form.

22. v. *His Soul draweth near unto the Grave; and his Life to the Destroyers.* The Life of the Spirit in the Body is now sinking into a Silent Darkness. The Life of the Spirit in itself is almost swallowed up into those Spirits, which are the *Principles* of a dark, a dying Life; or a living Darkness, and Death.

23. v. *If there be a Messenger with him, an Interpreter, one among a Thousand, to shew to man his Uprightness.* Now in this *Evening-close* of life, and joy; in this *rushing approach* of a dreadful, eternal Night; Jesus Christ steps forth, as a *Messenger*, an *Interpreter* between God, and Man. He opens upon him *his own* Beauty, the *mans own*, proper, and true Beauty; which was *his own*, in Eternity.

24. v. *Then he is gracious to him, and saith: Deliver him from going into the Pit. I have found a Ransom.* Then the Father smiles upon the Soul. Then He gives a command in the Ears of the Soul to all the *Invisible Ministers* of Darkness, and Death; to let him go: To all the Spirits of Life, and Light; to take charge of him, to hold him in their Arms, that his Life come not into the Prison of Spirits.

25. v. *His Flesh shall be fresher than a Childs*; *he shall return to the days of his Youth.* He shall be translated into the Kingdom of Christ, into that Paradise of God, out of which he came. There he shall flourish with a *Flesh* more beautiful, more heavenly, than that of *Adam* in Innocency. There he shall see those *Youthful Days*, which were before this World.

Thus God takes hold of *Temporal Afflictions*, in them to convert us to *Eternal Affections*, and Objects.

1. *Use. Instruction. See how absolute, and universal thy dependence is on thy God for Happiness.* His *Fulness* is the only *Treasury*, in which every *minute* of thy Life, every *moment* of thy Grief, or Joy is laid up. *My times* saith David, *are at the Right hand of the most High* Psal. 31. 15. His *Sweetness* is the only *Port*, or *Gate*, by which this *Fulness* issues forth on thee, and brings thee home to its own Place. These *Two* are the *Mine*, and *Mint* of thy *Natural*, and *Spiritual* Life.

Jesus Christ is the *Way* of both these. A man can receive nothing from God, can never come to God; but *thorow* Jesus Christ. Thus nothing comes to us, or from us; nothing comes to pass round about us; which is not first pass'd through a *Double Strainer*, the *Heart* of the *Father*, and of *Christ*.

Not a *Sparrow* falls to the Ground; much less a *Soul*, without both these our Heavenly *Father*, and *Saviour*. Not a *Hair* falls from our Heads; much less a *Thought* from our Hearts without this *Divine Pair. The Father works, and I work*: Saith Christ. Every thing of *Man*, and the *Creature* is *distill'd*, or dropt thorow this *Double Heaven* of the Father, and Christ.

We have our Being in these *Two*. Nothing then can *be* without them. *We live in* these *Two*. Our Life then, and each article of it, is *Their Life* in us. *We move in* Them. Each *Motion* then would be none, if it did not run upon this *greater*, and *less Wheel. We* lie still, when *they* move not.

Thus, *thou knowest, O God, that it is not in him, that walks, to order his own steps*, Jere. 10. 23.

What then shall we cast our selves into a Gulf of Ryot or sensual Pleasures; because we cannot *resist* His Will, nor *rule* our own? Unhappy he, on whose mind the Almighty God stamps this Image of His Will in the Wrathful, and Dark Part of it? Yet he also shall go, as it is written of him, upon the Heart of God, but in *Fiery Letters. God hath made all things for Himself, even the wicked for the Day of Wrath*: Prov. 16. 4.

But how can we abide in the Dark, or bitter Part of things; in Flesh, and Sin: If we know, that the *Will* of God is the *Rule* of all things, and an *Infinite* Light, Love, Goodness, the *Rule* of this *Will? He, that saith, he hath seen God, and walks in Darkness, lies, and the Truth is not in him*: 1 John 1. 6. He that saith, he sees the Will of God to act all things, and yet is himself acted by a Contrary Will, checks and contradicts himself, while he speaks, and acts.

How

How can we, that are dead to sin, live any longer in it? Rom. 6. 2. If the Divine *Fulness* and *Sweetness* have discovered themselves to us; they have overshadowed us; darkning by an Eternal Death the Light of our own Life in Vanity, and Flesh. They have drunk up our Spirits into themselves, and infused their Spirit into us. Thus they themselves are become the *Death* and *Resurrection* of Christ in us; that *we* live no longer, but *Christ* liveth in us, and the *Father* in *Christ*.

Obj. But you will say, *If I be wicked, what can I do?* I have no power upon my own Spirit, but am over ruled by a Power above me, which commands All. Must I then still sin, still be forlorn without any hope, or help in my self? Must I sit down with Despair, and make that my only comfort to hope for no comfort?

Ans. No, No! Let this be not my *Despair*, but my surest *Hope*, and sweetest; that I am no more in my *own power*, who am a foolish, weak, inconstant Creature; but form'd fashion'd, commanded, managed entirely by *Him*, who is the *Greatest* and *Best* of all things.

Let me draw from this *Consideration*, these holy, and happy Resolutions.

1. I will *resign* my self to my God. I will give up the *rudder* of my Spirit to him, who alone guides it, and guides it by a *Sweetness unclouded*, a *Wisdom unquestioned*, a *Power uncheck't*.

2. I will *repose* my self in my God. What the bad King said foolishly, I desire ever to say upon a holy and divine Principle: *This also is of the Lord: Therefore will I wait upon him.* 2 Kings ch. 6. v. last. He hath a *Glory* in *this*; He will make *this* a *Glory to me*, if I wait stedfastly to the end. For he doth this, who doth *all*, and doth all *well*; who hath no *Principle*, but *Love*; no *act*, but *Power*; no *end*, but *Glory*.

I have finish'd the *First Part* of my *Text*, which was, The *Rise to the Kingdom.* I have concluded the *Doctrine*, which was propounded from that *Part*: *The first Rise to Religion, is a Change, or Conversion.*

Part 2. The Race to the Kingdom: and become as little Children.

These Words afford this *Second Doctrine.*

Doctr. 2. *The second Step in Religion is to a state of Childhood.* Read *Gal.* 4. 1. *The Heir, while he is a child, differeth not from a Servant, though he be Lord of all.* We have here a *Child*, a Regenerate person, one born a *Son* of God, made a Saint; yet at *first*, nothing differing from a *Servant*, coming afterwards in the *second place*, to the quality of a *Son* and *Heir*.

The Person of a man, in the Non-age, till *Reason*, which is the *Principle* of a man, puts forth itself in him, is but as a *Plant*, or at best a *Brute*, a *sensitive Creature.* So that Soul which hath the *Seed* of the Divine Nature sown in it, until that *Seed* be grown up, is as a *Servant*, not as a *Son*.

These are the *Two states in Religion*:

1. *A Servile State*. 2. *A Son-like State*.

As St. *Paul* saith in another case: *First is that which is Natural, then that which is Spiritual*: so it is true in this: *First* is the *Servile State* in Religion, *then* the *Son-like*. So we read, *Gal.* 4. 7. *Now are ye no more Servants, but Sons*.

Thus the Son-like *State* is the *second step*, or *Remove* in Religion.

But it will be necessary for me to open the *Servile* State first, that the *Son-like* may be the better understood.

1. *State, Servile*. This *State* hath *Four Signs*.

1. *Sign*: *Fear*.	3. *Sign*: *Forms*.
2. *Sign*: *Dependencies*.	4. *Sign*: *Solicitude*.

1. *Sign*: *Fear*. *A Saint in a Servile State serves God chiefly from a Principle of Fear*.

Rom. 8. 15. *Ye have not received the Spirit of Bondage again to fear*. St. *Paul* doth not speak here of a *Sinful State in Nature*, but of a *Servile State in Grace*. This will appear clearly, if you compare this place with the *fourth Chapter* of the *Epistle* to the *Galatians*. You shall see in both Places, the *Twofold State* of a *Servant*, and a *Son* in Religion described alike, almost in the same terms. *Rom.* 8. 15. *Ye have not received the Spirit of Bondage again*. *Galat.* 4. 1. *The Heir, while a Child, differeth nothing from a Servant*. v. 3. *Ye were in bondage to worldly Elements*. v. 7. *Now are ye no longer Servants*. Rom. 8. 15, 17. *But the Spirit of Adoption, whereby ye cry Abba Father. Now are ye Sons, if Sons, then Heirs*. Galat. 4. 6. *He hath sent forth the Spirit of his Son into our Hearts, whereby we cry, Abba Father*. 7. *Sons and Heirs* &c.

Thus the Spirit of Bondage is a Spirit sent forth from God in the ministry of the Law. Therefore the *Apostle* saith, *Ye have not received the Spirit of Bondage*. This Spirit begets men to God, but it is in a *Servile-State*, by, and to Fear. *Fear* is the *Seed* and *Fruit* of this Spirit; So a man by it becomes a *Son* to God, but *by* the *Bond-woman*. So he is partly a *Son*, partly a *Servant*; or rather a *Son* in the State of a *Servant*.

But I must further explain this *Fear* by,

1. *The Distinction of Fear*. 2. *The Object*.

1. *The Distinction of Fear*. There is a *Twofold Fear*.

1. *Fear, Slavish*. 2. *Fear, Filial*.

1. *Fear, Slavish*. This *Fear* comes before *Love*, and is cast out, when *Love* comes: 1 *John*. 4. 18. *Perfect Love casteth out Fear*. But what *Fear* is this? That, which is *Slavish*. So it is added: *Fear hath Torment*. A *Slavish Fear* is to the Heart, as *Fire* is to Gold. Gold is wrought by the Fire to a

softness

softness, and fitness, to receive the King's Image: then it is taken out of the Fire. So this Fear subdues the Heart to a yielding temper, to receive the Impressions, and Image of God in Love. Then it is cast out.

2. *Fear, Filial.* This follows after *Love*, flows from it, is as sweet, and desirable, as *Love* it self. The *Scripture* saith in one Place: *Who would not fear thee?* This *Fear* is a *Plyantness* of the Soul to God, yielding to him, from a near sense of his *Greatness*, and *Goodness*, *both* in *one*. It is like the *Bowing* of some Flowers towards the Sun, being toucht with his Influences, and Beams.

Revel. 14. 6. *An Angel in the midst of Heaven preacheth the Everlasting Gospel.* What is the *Everlasting Gospel?* The glad Tidings of Eternal Love in God to the Creature. This Angel at the seventh v. cries aloud: *Fear God.* This *Fear* answers *Love*, and *Ecchos* to it in the Heart: *Love* saith: *God is thine. Fear* saith: *I will no more be mine own. Love* saith: God *will come down into thee, and fill thee*, Fear saith: *I will sink down out of my self, and give way to God.*

The *Filial Fear* is proper to the *Son-like* State. It is the *Slavish Fear*, which is the *Sign* of that *Servile State* of which we now speak.

A *Son-like State* hath *Love* for its *Eldest* Child; *Fear* for its *Youngest*. A *Servile State* hath *Fear* for its *First-born*: *Love* here is a *Younger Brother*.

In the *Son Fear* is the *Motion of* Love. In the *Servant* it is the *Motive to* Love.

The *Servant* is the *Son* of the *Bond-woman*. The *Son* is born of the *Free-woman*. The Soul in a *Servile* State of Religion *ascends* out of *Flesh* towards God. So *Fear* is First, and *Love* riseth out of Fear, as *Fire* out of *Smoak*. The Soul in a *Son-like state descends*, comes down from God, as a *Bride* ready trim'd. So *L ve* is First, and brings forth *Fear*, as a pure *Flame* breaths from it a fine *Air*.

This is the *Distinction* of Fear. This the Sign of a *Servile* State, a *Slavish* Fear.

2. *The Object of* Fear. This is exprest *by* the Holy Ghost: *Heb.* 2. 15 *Those, that were held in bondage, by the* Fear *of Death.* The Jews were under the Law, in a *Servile State*, under a *Slavish Fear*. This *Fear* had *Death* in its Eye, for its *Object*. *Death* hath two things in it, *Loss*, and *Pain*; *Loss* of Life, with all the Sweets, and Comforts of Life: *Pain* in the Labours, and Pangs at the parting of Soul, and Body,

Thus a *Slavish Fear* hath a *Twofold Object*:

1: *Object, Loss.* 2. *Object, Pain.*

1. *Object, Loss.* A Christian in a *Servile State* fears the *Loss* of God, more than *God*. The *Fear of God* makes a man sink out of himself into God. *Fear* of *Loss* of him makes a man apt to sink into himself in Despair. A Servile Christian fears the loss of *Gods Favour*, more than the loss of *God*: the loss of the *Fruits* of his Favour, which are Peace within, Prosperity without; more than the loss of his *Favour*.

2. *Object*:

2. *Object :Pain.* A Spiritual, *Son-like* Saint fears the Departures of God, the loss of Divine Enjoyments, more then all Pains or Tortures. But the *Servant* in Religion is not any thing so much sensible of the loss of all the joys in Heaven; as he is struck with, trembles at the pains of Hell.

John the Baptist was a Figure of the *Servile State.* He presseth his *Exhortation* with such *Reasons*, as these: *The Axe is laid to the Root of the Tree. Save your selves from that wrath, which is to come.*

Jesus Christ was the *Head*, and *Figure* of the *Son-like State.* He moveth by other *Arguments: The Kingdom of God is at hand. Light is come into the World. Come to me, and have life in abundance.*

I have done with the *First*, and most apparent *Sign* of a *Servile State: Fear.*

2. *Sign: Dependencies. A Servile Christian seeks God chiefly by outward Assistances.* Gal. 3. 24. *The Law was a School-master to bring us to Christ.* A School-master ties Children to their set Times, Rules, Exercises ;till they can speak a Language, judge of Truth, converse with wisdom naturally, from inward, and free Principles. So the Law, which is the Mistris, under whom we are in bondage, teacheth us, to seek Communion with God at peculiar Times: The Forming of our Spirits according to God, by particular Rules: The Deriving of Truths, Strengths Comforts from God, by several Performances. This is our way of Life, till the Seed of Life be come up in us, which makes Divine Love, as our Pulse: Faith, our Breath: Holiness, our Constitution.

Galat. 3. 23. *We were kept under the Law,shut up unto the Faith,that should be revealed.* A Legal Christian having a perpetual Alarm of Fears within him, entrencheth himself strongly in Promises and Threatnings, Ordinances and Duties in the outward Letter, as a Wall, or Mount of Earth. He plants a Guard about his Spirit,of Resolutions, Vows,and such like Fleshly obligations. He takes care for a constant supply of Provision from without, from the Gifts, and Parts of men, for a maintenance of these Forces.

Angels, saith Christ, *Marry not, nor are given in Marriage.* Angels are ever strong, ever feasted, yet have no Meals: They are always refresh't,and at rest, yet have no season for Sleep: They marry not to any thing without themselves, yet they multiply themselves, their Images, and Fruits to Eternity.Earthly man must have his Meals,and Sleeps in their appointed time,or else he dies.He must joyn himself in marriage to another without himself, or else he remains barren. Such is a Christian under the Law, if he have not his Duties, Ordinances, Rules, and Retirements, to which he is true, and constant; he falls down into *Dust* and *Deadness*; or runs out into *Lust*, and *Profaness.* Therefore saith St. *Paul, we were shut up.*

A Saint is now like an *Ivy*, which cannot bear itself up, or bring forth fruit upon its own *Root*, or Stock; but must twine about some outward *Prop*; else it lies on the ground, and withers.

I defer

I defer the other *Two Signs*, that I may now divert my self to some *Application* of these.

1. *Use.* *Exhortation.* This is *Double*:

1. *Exhorta.* *Serve God from a Principle of Fear, till you know why to serve him, from the Freedom of a Natural Life.*

2. *Exhorta. Serve God by outward Rules, till you know how to serve Him, by the Regulation of an Inward Light.*

1. *Exhorta. Serve God from a Principle of Fear, till you know why to serve Him from the Freedom of a Natural Life.* We read, 2 *Pet.* 1. 4. of *a Divine Nature.* Nothing is so skilful, sweet, strong, lasting, as that which is *Natural*: as the Sun shines, God is kind, a man truly Spiritual is holy, and heavenly. But where is that man among the whole race of men, who loves God, lives in God, as his *Element*, lives to God, as his Joy, and Glory; and all this, because it is *his Nature*?

Are not these the times of which our *Saviour* spake, when he said: *Shall the Son of Man find Faith upon the Earth?* In what heart can we find such a *Faith*, such a *Union* between God, and Man, as that these Two shall have but *one Life*; that the Man may say, as Saint *Paul* did: *Now Christ liveth in me*?

In this universal Dis-appearance of the Divine Nature, it were happy, if men would serve God from the Force of *Fear*, when they cannot do it from a natural *Freedom*: If men would be wrought by an awe to a *Compliance* with God, while yet they have no *Complacency* in him.

O that men would *fear*, if they cannot *love* that Omni-present, Omni-potent God, in whom we all live, by whom we breath!

I shall urge this *Exhortation by Four Persuasives.*

1: *Persuasive. Fear the Loss of the Divine Presence here on Earth. Job* expresseth a great sense of this, *Job.* 29, He sighs out his complaints: v. 2. *O that it were with me, as in the days of old, when God preserved me!* v. 3. *When his Candle shined upon my Head, when by his Light I walked thorow Darkness.* The *Candle* is the Image of God in Nature, which burns in the Seven-fold Candlestick of the Angelical Nature. This Glory rested upon the Spirit of *Job's* Natural Man, as a Light upon his Head, leading him thorow the Darkness of his Fleshly Being. *v.* 4. *As I was in the days of my Youth, when the Secret of God was upon my Tabernacle.* The *Secret* of God is the Invisible Glory of the Divine Image among the Angels, which before he express'd by the Candle. The *Angels* seem to be the *Secret*. For they are the Chambers, the Pavilions of God. God was in the midst of them in the Dark at *Mount Sinai.* The *Tabernacle* is the Body, or outward Man.

To this place agrees that in the *Psalm.* Psal. 34. 7. *The Angel of the Lord pitcheth his Camp round about them, that fear him. The Angel of the Lord, or the Angel the Lord*, is the Divine Image in Nature, and the Law. The *Camp*,

the

the Host, or Armies of Angels. In the Gospel, instead of this *Image* is Jesus Christ; instead of *Angels* in their *Natural Glory*, are Angels in a *Spiritual State*, residing upon the *Head*, the Spirit; the *Tabernacle*, the visible Frame, the Bodily Being of a Saint.

V. 5. *When the Almighty was yet with me: When my Children were yet about me.* *Job* in his first days was a *Type* of man in Innocency. The Presence of the Almighty in the Angelical Nature on the *top* of his Spirit was, as the *Head* of his Being. The *Angelical Lives* putting themselves forth in the rest of bodily things, as *Souls* to them, were as the *Children*, Images, and Dependencies of the Soul of Man. But at the Fall, the Almighty withdrew from man: These *Lives* were drawn in from the rest of the Creatures.

V. 6. When I washt my steps in Butter; When the Rock poured me out Rivers of Oil. The *steps* of *Job* were his wayes below in the visible part of things; which were wash'd with the Peace and Plenty of Inferiour Contents, raised from these Inferiour Creatures, as *Butter*, *Rivers of Oyl.* The Spirit of Angelical, Divine Life, among invisible, Superiour Glories did flow forth abundantly upon him, from that *Rock*, which was the Almighty.

These Words of *Job* afford us a *Twofold Principle of Policy* for Natural things.

1. Principle. *The Divine Presence is the spring of all Earthly Comforts.*

2. Principle. *The Removal of this Presence is the Root of all Bitterness in this Life.*

1. Principle. *The Divine Presence is the spring of all earthly Comforts.* Tell me, O Man! what hath kept thee thy Peace, and Plenty, all thy Dayes, Months, and Years? *Thy God hath preserved thee.* When thou hast been in a doubtful, difficult, dangerous State of things; what then hath pointed out a clear and shining path to thee in that darkness? When thou hast had trouble in thine Affairs, calamities in thy Person, confusion in thy Soul; what then hath sent forth a Beam of Comfort, and Council through thy Spirit, to light thee out of all these; *The Candle of God hath been upon thy head*: God hath look'd sweetly forth from the top of thy Spirit, through the Principles of Nature, and this hath been thy Light. When thou hast wash'd thy Feet as thou hast walk'd, in smooth, soft, flowing streams of Peace, and Plenty: when thou hast seen thy Children playing about thee, like lively Lambs in pleasant Pastures; while thou hast been as their Sheepherd, feeding thy Spirit from invisible Spirits, and then feeding their Spirit from thine; who gave thee all these? *The secret of the Almighty was with thee.*

2. Principle. *The Removal of the Divine Presence is the Root of all Bitterness in this Life.* When God *withdraws*, he *draws* in all his Blessings, as the Sun often goes in, and gives up the Sky, and Day to dark Clouds. What wilt thou do, when like wretched *Saul*, *The Philistines are upon thee, and God hath*

hath forsaken thee? When Perplexity shall take hold of thy Spirit, when there shall be no Counsel or Comfort left, because God hath forsaken thee? What then can all thy Pleasures or Honours do? Will they not be as miserable Comforters, as the *Witch* of *Endor* to *Saul*; presenting thee with Devils under God-like forms; ill-boding, foretelling thy death and Ruine?

When our dear Saviour was on the Cross, he did not cry out, *O my Disciples! why do ye fly from me, or deny me? O ye Jews, my Brethren! why do ye wound so bloodily my Feet, Hands, and Head?* No, but he cries out; *My God, my God, why hast thou forsaken me*; This broke his heart.

David complains in *Psal.* 30. 7. *Thou hast made my Mountain strong*; *but thou didst turn away thy face, and I was troubled.* Place a man in a Wilderness of Horrours, in a Sea of Flames, let the *Secret* of God be with him, and he will fear, he will feel no Evil. Plant a man on a Mountain, where he may not only with Christ see, but possess all the Delights and Glories of this World; let God be gone, and you may call them all *Ichabod*; *where's the Glory? Where's the Delight?* The whole Mountain will moulder into Melancholy, and crumble away into Griefs.

O! Fear to estrange this God from you by a neglect of him, on whose Presence all your present Joyes depend. Fear to put out his Light in your Souls, by your Lusts: fear to chase away by your hardnesses and Rebellions, that God; who, when he removes his Glory from off any Person, or Place; gives up all to ruine, and leaves a Hell behind him.

This is the first *Persuasive.*

2. Persuasive. *Fear the loss of Divine Enjoyments after Death.* Is there any thing, any where, more moving, more full of sweetness, than the language of the Apostle: 1 *Thes.* 4. 18. *Then we shall be for ever with the Lord. Comfort ye one another with these words.*

I will present your Spirits with the force of this place, in *three* short *Propositions.*

1. Proposition. *There is a Lord over all*; a supream *Principle*, or Power, which makes, maintains, manages all the Creatures; a *Spirit* of Strength and Wisdom, which governs the affairs of the whole World. Thus St. *Paul* speaks, 1. *Cor.* 8. 6. *To us there is one God, the Father, of whom are All*; *one Lord Jesus, by whom are All.*

2. Proposition. *This Lord is the best of all things.* As he is *over*, so he is *above* all. 1 *Cor.* 2. 8. St. *Paul* calls him, *the Lord of Glory.* The *Heathens* teach us, that the God of the Sun, is the God of Musick; because he *tempers* with his Beams, and tunes all the visible world. This Lord, our Lord is the God of Light, Beauty, Musick, the God of all Sweetnesses, Glories, Blessednesses. For he *tunes* both the visible, and invisible World, to a happy *Harmony.*

3. Propoſition. *All good Spirits are the Friends; all evil Spirits the Enemies of this Lord.* Each pure, lightſome, peaceful Spirit comes from this Jeſus, and goes to him again, when it goes off the Stage of this Earth; as a Beam darted from his Glory, and drawn up to him again. Each dark, unclean, diſorderly Spirit is cut off, and caſt out from him. One is every where in Scripture ſtiled, *His Child, His Brother*: The other is thus ſpoken to by him; *Depart from me, ye curſed.*

Now what joy is it, when a man in all the troubles of Life, can comfort himſelf with theſe words, and ſay: *This Life will quickly end; then ſhall I be ever with the Lord, my Lord, the Lord of Bleſſedneſs?* Who can expreſs the Peace and Pleaſure of that Soul within, which lies upon its Death-bed, and in the laſt moment of its abode in the World, comforts itſelf with theſe words, *Now I muſt be uncloath'd of all Being, or Appearance among men on Earth for ever: But it is, that I may be for ever in the naked Embraces of the Eternal Spirit of Life, and Beauty. I go from hence for ever, but I go to be for ever with the Lord.*

I had fainted ſaith David, *if I had not hoped to ſee the Goodneſs of the Lord in the land of the Living.* Who can tell thoſe fainting fits in the midſt of higheſt Pleaſures, thoſe bitter, Soul-turning Qualmes in fulleſt Glories; which thoſe men have, that have no hope to ſee the Goodneſs of the Lord after this Life? Many pangs, many pangs of remorſe, and anguiſh, pangs far beyond the pangs of a natural Death, hath that dying Soul, which hath no hope to live with God after Death.

Fear then this *Loſs* ſo great, ſo irreparable. Fear to be prophane, like *Eſau*; to ſell your *Birth-right* for a Meſs of *Pottage*, to ſell your hopes of Heaven for a ſhort Satisfaction to your ſenſual Appetite.

3. Perſwaſive. *Fear, what God can do.* What cannot he do to make you miſerable, who is the *God of the Spirits of all Fleſh*? He can let forth *Five Spirits* upon you:

1. *Spirit of Diſeaſes.*
2. *Spirit of Folly, and Falſhood.*
3. *Spirit of Melancholy.*
4. *Spirit of Ruine.*
5. *His own Spirit.*

1. *Spirit of Diſeaſes.* God can ſend a *Spirit of Diſeaſes* into thy Body, to ſtrike thee with *Worms*, with ſome foul and ſharp ſickneſs, till thou dye a loath'd, and horrid Death. Thus he did to King *Herod* in the *Acts.* Can all thy Phyſicians then cure thee?

2. *Spirit of Folly and Falſhood.* God can ſend into thy Breaſt a Lying *Spirit*, that ſhall carry the on to fooliſh Counſels; that thou mayſt periſh. Thus he did with King *Ahab.* Can thy Wiſdom foreſee, or prevent this?

3. *Spirit of Melancholy.* God can let forth upon thee a *Spirit*, that ſhall ſit upon thy Brain and Heart like a black Cloud, diſtilling poyſon upon both. This ſhall be thy inſeparable Companion at Table, and Bed; in ſociety, in ſolitude; to vex thee perpetually. This ſhall make thy ſweeteſt Delights, thy deareſt

Rela-

Relations a Burthen and a disease to thee. This shall make thy surest Strengths, and firmest aids a matter of continual Suspicion, and mortal Jealousy to thee. Thus he did with King *Saul*. What delights or businesses can now divert thee?

4. *Spirit, of Ruine.* God can let upon thee, as upon *Job*, a *Spirit*, like a devouring Sea, or Storm. This shall take away from thee, thy whole Estate; from thy Children, their Life; from thy Wife, and wisest Friends, their Affection, and Tenderness. This will fill thy Skin with Noysomness; thy veins with Fire; thy Bones with Pains; thy Head with black vapours. This shall take away all rest from thy Sleeps, filling them with affrighting Dreams; all peace from thy waking hours, filling them with Tumult, and Sorrow; till Life become more hateful to thee, than the most hateful Death *I chose Strangling, rather than Life*; saith *Job*, Chap. 7. 15. What can help, or comfort thee, at such a time as this? When an evil *Spirit* over-whelms all the Creatures to a man; what can the Creatures do?

5. *Spirit of God.* I cannot express, I tremble to think this; God can make his *own Spirit* a *stream of Fire and Brimstone* in thy Spirit, *Is.* 30. 33. *The breath* (the Spirit) *of the Lord, a stream of Brimstone.* God can himself be an *everlasting Burning* upon thy Immortal part. *Who can lie down with everlasting Burnings*? Can all thy Tears, or Pleasures quench these Burnings?

Well might *Moses* cry out: *Psal.* 90. 11. *Who knows the Power of his Wrath. According to thy Fear, so is thy Wrath.* You may read the latter Clause thus: *As is thy Wrath, so should the Fear of thee be.* There is an unsearchableness, an Incomprehensibleness in the Wrath of God. No Creature can take it in, but is swallowed up by it.

Let men *fear* God, according to his *Wrath.* Let men fear to make him their Enemy, or if they do, let them meet so potent an Enemy betimes, while he is yet on the way, that they may cast themselves at his Feet, with Submission, Repentance; Fears, and Tears.

If you harden your Heart by Insensibleness, or sensuality, he can multiply the Stroak of Sorrow upon thy Heart seven times, seven times more, still seven times, nay seventy times seven, endlesly, till thy Heart be ground to the smallest Dust, and so lie under his Feet.

If thy Soul be as high, rough, untractable, as a *Whale*, or *Sea*; He can tame, and calm thee by Griefs.

If thy Soul were a *Leviathan*, arm'd with impenetrable Scales over-looking every lofty thing: God can make his *Sword*, which is his *Spirit*, to approach thee: he can put his Hook into thy Nostrils, draw thee forth out of thy swelling Seas of Lust, and Pride, lay thee Panting, and Languishing upon the dry Shore before him.

Thus ends the *Third Persuasive.*

4. *Persuasive. Fear what God will certainly do, to punish, and purge Sinners.*

1 Cor. 3. 13. *The Fire shall try every man's work*. Mark. 9. 49. *Every one shall be salted with Fire*. That, which is the highest *Principle*, the Supreamest Power in every kind, will subdue all other Powers, and Parts of things to itself. So it is said of Christ: *Philip*. 3. 21. *According to that working, whereby he is able even to subdue all things to himself*.

If this *Principle* of power meet with any thing *suitable* to itself, it cherisheth, and heightens that till it be perfectly *like*, perfectly *one* with itself. Thus every Sacrifice is seasoned with the Salt of Divinity.

But where it meets with a *Contrariety*, it conflicts, and contests with it, making the Conflict as fierce, and lasting; as the Contrariety; till it have consumed it. Thus every man shall be Salted with Fire.

Thus is *Fire* among the Elements. Thus is *God* among the Creatures, as a *Fire* Salting every man's Person, trying every man's Work. If he meet with any holy work, he rests upon it in the Secret of his Glory, as a Fountain of Beauty, and Blessings If he meet with any pure, and sweet Spirit, like himself; he closeth with it, in all manner of gentleness, and softness, as *Two Flames* embrace one another.

But where he meets with opposition he rageth. He burns upon dark, unclean, untractable Hearts, as *Fire* in the *Iron-works*; till he hath poured them forth into the Temper, and Mold of his Spirit, and Image.

Take heed then of feeding upon fleshly Pleasures *without Fear*, as St. *Jude* speaks. O men, and women, what do you, while you live upon the World, and in Sin?

As the Woman said of her self in the story of the Kings, 1 *King*. 17. 12. *I am gathering sticks to bake a Cake for me and my Son, that we may eat it, and die*. This is your posture. You are every where wandring, and busied to gather the Greatnesses and Pleasures of this world, that you may feed with these your Fleshly part fat, and strong, as a Sacrifice, that the Fire of Divine wrath may come down upon you, and devour you.

I shall conclude this whole *use* thus: If there be a *God*, which hath brought forth all the Sweet, and good things, which are before us here, which now move Desire, or Delight in us: sure this God is Almighty, and can yet heighten this Goodness, this Sweetness, to an *Infiniteness*, as well, as an *Endlesness*. Fear then for a *Drop* to lose the *Sea* for a *Tast*, the *Feast*; thy share in such Delights, for the short temptation of a Darling-Sin.

If there be a *God* which hath contrived, and sent abroad all the Evils, which now afflict, affright, amaze mortal men: sure this *God* is this way too *Almighty*, and can extend these Sufferings, till there be no Bound to them in our sense, no end of them in our Eye. Fear then to dare this God by your Dalliances in Fleshly vanities.

If there be a *God*, who is pure, just, true, sweet, meek: sure he loves such things

things as these, and hates the contrary: sure he will set himself against all proud, impure, false, fiery Ways, and Spirits; till he have *confounded* them, or *consumed* these things in them. Fear then, to be found before the Eyes of this God without the Righteousness, and Spirit of your Saviour as a Garment fast, and close girt to you. Fear to be seen by him in your Nakedness. For his Eyes are a bright and hot Flame, which will discover thy Shame, and burn thy *Flesh*, as the *Whore's* in the *Revelation*, with Fire.

I have spoken of *Two Signs* of a *Servile State* in Religion: *Fear*; and *Dependencies*. There Remain *Two* more: *Forms*; *Solicitude*.

3. *Sign*: *Forms*. There are *Two Sorts of Forms*, which the Holy Ghost mentions, in the *Scripture*:

1. *Eternal Forms*. 2. *Temporary Forms*.

1. *Eternal Forms*. *Philip*. 2. 6. Jesus Christ, is said to be *In the Form of God*, ἐν μορφῇ and in that *Form* He *thought it no Robbery to be equal with God*.

This *Form* is the *Substance* itself; *Spirit*, and *Truth*. This is the *Essential Form*, which is no *Shadow*, but One with the Substance; no *Appearance* Separable from Truth, but that Appearance, which is Truth; no *Letter* or Outside, but One Spirit with the Spirit, having Life in itself.

St. *Paul* speaks of this *Form*: Rom. 12. 2. *Be ye transformed in the Renewing of your Mind*: Μεταμορφοῦσθε Again: *Rom*. 8. 29. *He hath predestinated us to be conformed to the Image of his Son*: Συμμόρφους. This is an *Inward*, and *Spiritual Form*. It is the *Evangelical Form*, which is seen by Evangelical Eyes; which is felt, as well as seen; being *Power*, as well as *Form*: 1 *John* 1. 2.

2. *Temporary Forms*. The *Apostle* speaks of these *Forms*: 1 Cor. 7. 31. *The Fashion of this World passeth away*. St. *Paul* useth the Word Σχῆμα, which signifieth the *Outward Figure*, and *Shape* in Bodily Things, which is a meer *Accident*, varying often, while the *Substance* remains the same, not reaching to the *Spirit*, but Inhering in the Outward *Body*, and Perishing with it.

He makes use of the same word: *Rom*. 12. 2. *Be not ye Conformed to the World*: Συσχηματίζεσθε And this is opposed to Μεταμορφοῦσθε *but be ye Transformed*.

Temporary Forms are *Empty Figures*; Accidental Out-side Shapes. But *Divine Forms* are *Substantial*, Spiritual, Essential.

We speak now of such *Forms*, as these, under the *Law*; which are not the Life, and Power of God; but may be *without* these, and yet *as Fair* in themselves.

The *Scripture* makes use of this Word, *Form*, in this Sense frequently: *Rom*. 2. 21. St. *Paul* saith of the *Jew*, who is One *Outwardly*, not *Inwardly*, as he concludes in the *last Verse* of that *Chapter*; that he hath a *Form of Knowledge*; Μόρφωσιν. The Word is Elegant, and seems to signify a *Form* not *Natural*, springing forth from the Life, or Substance; but a *Form Affectate*, Artificially made.

2 *Tim*

2 *Tim.* [illegible]. 5. St. *Paul* ſpeaks of the ſame thing, and uſeth the ſame Word: *Having a Form of Godlineſs*: Μόρφωσιν: *but denying the Power of it.*

Thus much for the *Explication*, and *Juſtification* of the Word: *Forms*; as they are a *Sign* of *Legality*.

The *Thing*, which I underſtand by *Forms*, is the *Image* of God, and Godlineſs taken in, or held forth according to the Principles, and Appearances of *This Creation*.

St. *Paul* ſaith: *Galat.* 4. v. 3. *When we were Children, we were in Bondage under the Elements of the World.* v. 4. *But when the Fulneſs of Time came, God ſent forth His Son.* v. 9. *After that ye have known* God, *or rather are known of God*, (or, are made to know by God) *how turn ye again to weak and Beggerly Elements, to which ye deſire again to be in Bondage.*

Mark, what *Oppoſitions* the *Apoſtle* maketh.

1. *Oppoſition*: Between the *Elements of the World*: and the *Son ſent forth.* When Jeſus Chriſt the *Heavenly Image* of God is revealed in our Spirits, then we are free from that Slavery of *Spelling* the Name of God out of the *Elements* of *this Creation.* We no more go to the *Ægyptians* for their Learning; that is, to the *Principles of Nature* for the knowledge of God.

2. *Oppoſition*: Between the *Knowing of God*, ſo as *being known*, or *made to know by God*, and the *Elements of the World.* We know God by *Divine Principles*, when we know him by an *Immediate Union* with Him, which gives us the Naked Appearance of God in our Spirits, by the Mutual Comprehenſion of our Spirits in that Appearance, and Spirit.

Till we thus know God, we know Him not. We have no *Image*, but *Shadows* only of Him. We know Him by Worldly Principles, which are Dark, and Beggerly.

The Scripture often links together *theſe*, as in a Chain: The *Law*, the *Letter*, the *Fleſh*, *Man*, the *World*, the *Outward Man*, the *Jew*, *Forms*, —

Rom. 2. 28. 29. You have a *Jew*, *Outwardly*, in the *Letter*, *Outward* in the *Fleſh*, whoſe Praiſe is of *Men*.

Rom. 8. 3. The *Law* is weak thorow the *Fleſh*.

2 *Cor.* 3. 6. 7. There are Coupled; The *Letter*, which kills: and the *Miniſtration* of Death engraven in Stone.

Gal. 4. 3. 5. Thoſe that are under the *Elements of the World*, are the ſame with thoſe, that are under the *Law*.

Rom. 2. 17. There is a *Jew* reſting in the *Law*: v. 18. He is inſtructed out of the Law, and approves the things, that are Excellent: v. 20. He hath a *Form* of knowledge, and of Truth in the Law.

All theſe, and the Particular *Sign* of a *Servile State* now in hand, which is *Forms*, will be clearly underſtood by the Opening of *Three* of the Fore-mentioned *Terms*.

1. *The*

1. *The Flesh.* 2. *The Spirit.* 3. *The Law.*

1. *The Flesh. Flesh*, and *Spirit*; Carnal, and Spiritual are opposed, as *Time*, and *Eternity*; the *First*, and the *Second Creation*. All the Empty, and Temporary Things of this World are *Flesh. Joh.* 6. 63. 1 *Pet.* 1. 24. *Joh.* 17. 2.

Sometimes Flesh is taken for the *Corrupt State* of Things: as *Jude* 23. *The Garment spotted with the Flesh.*

Sometimes it is taken for the *Visible Part* of *Natural* Things: as 2 *Cor.* 7. 1. *All Filthiness of Flesh and Spirit.* In the Former place *Flesh* was the Filth, that defiled the Garment of Nature. Here it is *Natures upper*, and *Outward Garment*, which is in danger of being defiled.

Thirdly, *Flesh* is taken for the *whole Frame* of *Nature* in the *Visible*, and *Invisible* Part of it. So *Mat.* 26. 41. *The Spirit is willing, but the Flesh is weak.* The *Spirit* there is the *Spiritual*; the *Flesh* the *Natural Man.* So *Luke* 3. 6. *All Flesh shall see the Salvation of the Lord.* This place is cited from *Es.* 40. 5. *The Glory of the Lord shall be revealed, and all Flesh shall see it together.* Compare this with 1 *Tim.* 3. 16. *God manifest in the Flesh, justified in the Spirit, seen of Angels. Angels* are Part of that *Flesh*, which sees the Glory of God, and hath it revealed in them.

Lastly, *Flesh* is taken for *Created Nature*, both Body, and Spirit; as it is *spiritualized.* Jesus Christ spake in this sense: *John* 6. 55. *My flesh is meat indeed.* He expounds himself afterwards: *v.* 63. *It is the Spirit, that quickeneth; the Flesh profiteth nothing.* Our Saviour means thus much: *The Creature in me, as it is a meer Creature, is uncapable of so near an Union with you, or so great a vertue in itself, as to be the food, or Conveyance of Eternal Life to you. But as it is become a New Creature, and is made One in Person, and Spirit with the Divine Nature: So you may feed upon it after a Spiritual manner, and be nourished up by it to Eternal Life.* For so the Lord adds; *The Words that I speak, are Spirit and Life.* So we read of the *Fleshly Tables of the Heart.*

But the Common Acceptation of *Flesh*, when it is opposed to Spiritual Things, and joyned with the *Law*, is the *Third*: that is, the *first Creation*, or *this World.*

This is manifest from the seventh of the *Epistle* to the *Romans.* v. 2. *The Woman is bound by the Law to her Husband, while he liveth*; saith St. *Paul* v. 4. *Ye are dead to the Law by the Body of Christ, that ye may be married to another, even to him who is raised from the Dead.* He goes on, v. 5. *When we were in the Flesh, the Motions of Sin, which were by the Law.* Then, v. 6. *But now we are delivered from the Law, that being dead, wherein we were held.*

The Principles and Frame of Nature in the Invisible Powers, and visible Parts of it are our *Husband* by the first Creation. For we were made subject to Angels in that State, as in the New Creation we are to Jesus Christ. And we were made by Nature a little Lower than Angels, in the next degree of Inferiority to them: as the *Woman* to the *Man.* This is plain by comparing those Two Places: *Psal.* 8. 5. *Thou hast made him* (that is, man) *a little lower than the Angels:* Heb. 2. 5. *Unto Angels he hath not put in subjection the World, which is to come:* But unto Jesus Christ, That is implyed in the Place.

The *Law* is the Law of the Husband. Now the *Law* was administred by *Angels,* the Ministring Spirits, which are Principalities. and Powers of this Creation, as the Vice-Gerents of God.

Now St. *Paul* saith; that by the Body of Christ that Husband died, which held us in Subjection to the Law. The whole Frame of Nature was shaken by the Death of Christ, and must fall by the Power of it.

Then St. *Paul* adds, that we were subject to the *Law* while we were in the *Flesh.*

All these things make it plain, that by the Flesh he understands the *State of Nature* in its highest *Principles,* and utmost *Extent.*

Thus much for the First *Term, Flesh.*

2. *Letter.* This is the *Image of God in Flesh.* *Letter* and *Spirit* are opposed by St. *Paul,* as *Old,* and *New*: *Rom.* 7. 4. And he teacheth us, that by the Death of the *Flesh* in the Body of Christ, we are freed from our Service to God in the *Oldness of the Letter.*

St. *Paul* opposeth *Spirit,* and *Letter,* as *Inward* and *Outward.* He calleth that the *Letter,* which is *Outward* in the *Flesh*: *Rom.* 2. 28, 29.

The *Spirit* is Jesus Christ, as He is the Heavenly Image of God within in the Heart of God; 2. *Cor.* 3. 15. This is that which is *Inward,* under the *Vail of Flesh.*

The *Letter* is the Image of God in the outward *Man,* as it is drawn forth from, and discovered in the Principles of the first Creation, which is the *Vail.*

3. The *Law.* This is the State of the Soul, while she lives in the *Letter,* and hath Communion with God only by the Letter.

St. *Paul* thus describes a *Legal State*: *Gal.* 4. 3. *When we were Children,* (νήπιοι, Infants) *we were in Bondage under the Elements of the World.*

While we are under the *Law,* we are *Infants,* we have neither the *Ear,* nor the *Heart,* nor the *Mouth* of the *Spirit,* and the Spiritual man, in our Souls. We are Uncapable of Taking in, or making out God in his own Divine Image, according to Spiritual Principles, or the Elements of the New Creation. Therefore we are in *Bondage* to Natural Principles, and Reasonings.

We are bound up within the Compass of this Creation, as in a Prison. We are unskill'd in, unacquainted with any Principles, or Appearances of things; besides those of this Creation. We compare Spiritual Things by these Things of of Nature. We hear God with the Ear, we ſpeak of him with the Tongue, of this Creation, We receive, and cheriſh ſuch Notions of God, as are agreeable with this Frame.

The Manifeſtations of God, which ſpring from Spiritual Principles, from the Face of God himſelf, are *Barbarians* to us, while we are under the Law.

To the Law of Nature, to the Teſtimony of Reaſon, to the Elements of this World; whatſoever ſpeaketh not acccording to theſe, whatſoever caſteth off, or doth not cloth its Speakings with theſe Forms, though it be the Spirit Himſelf; hath no Light in it to our Underſtandings, while we are under the Law.

Theſe *Elements*, or *Forms* in which we are tied up, while we are under the Law, are,

1. *Weak.*	3. *Beggarly.*
2. *Dark.*	4. *Old.*

1. *Forms are weak Things.* They have only the *Shadows* of Good Things to come. They have not the *Subſtance.* They cannot give us the Good Things *Themſelves.*

Forms ſet the *Picture* of our Beloved before our Eyes; but they cannot lay the *Perſon* Himſelf in our Arms. They are but a *Letter* from our Husband. They have not the *Spirit* of our Husband in them.

2. *Forms* in the knowledge of God are *Dark* Things. They can give us no clear, or certain Diſcoveries.

The greateſt Light of Communion or Comfort, that can come, while we are ſhut up in *Forms*, is but like a Spark from a Flint at Midnight. It hath much Doubt, Diffidence, and Fear mingled with it.

3. *Forms* are *Beggerly* Things. They cannot lay open before us the Unſearchable Riches of Chriſt.

Jeſus Chriſt is Rich in Glory. He can fill all Appearances. He can bring forth Innumerable Appearances. He hath Glory above all appearances, which the Creature is capable of. He can bring forth more Glory into thy Heart, than can be made out in thy Heart itſelf by any Appearance, The *Power* of Glory which thy Spirit feels, ſhall be above the *Appearance*, which it ſees, 1 *Corin.* 14. 14. *Epheſ.* 3. 19.

How poor then, and Beggarly muſt that Spirit be in the knowledge of the Glory of God, which is ſhut up in any one Form, in any one Sort, or Degree of Manifeſtations?

While thou canſt not part with any Particular Form of Appearance while thy Spirit is not indifferent, and univerſal, extending itſelf to all Forms in the Manifeſtation of God: while thou art not above the Forms of this World: Thou wilt be but a *Beggar* in thy Divine Diſcoveries or Enjoyments.

He muſt be above, the *Letter*, in the *Spirit*; above and out of all Created

Images in the Light of Life itself, that will attain to those *Riches of assurance of a full understanding in the Mystery of God, and Christ*, which St. *Paul* speaks of : *Coloss.* 2. 2.

4. *Forms* are *Old.* God hath blasted all Forms and Ways of his Appearing by the Principles, and Elements of the Creature. If they have had any Beauty, yet now they are *Blear-eyed.* If they have been Fruitful, yet now they are become a Barren Womb, which is as the Grave.

The Cross of Christ, and the Glory of his Appearance in the Spirit have taken away the Life, and Glory of all Manifestations, or Administrations in the Flesh.

They are Old, Withered, Decayed, and Dying. The more our Saviour shines out in the Glory of his Father, the more will they Droop till they drop quite into the Dust,

4. *Sign : Solicitude.* *Rest*, and *want of Rest* are the distinguishing Notes of a *Legal*, or *Evangelical* State. *His Rest shall be Glorious*; saith the Prophet of the Lord Jesus in the Times of the Gospel, *Esa.* 11. 10. *Come to me*, saith our Saviour to those under the Law, *You that labour, and are heavy laden, and I will give you Rest*, Mat. 11. 28.

A Legal Spirit hath a *Four-fold Solicitude.*

1. *Solicitude, for Acceptance of the Person.*
2. *Solicitude, for Assiance in Perplexities.*
3. *Solicitude, for Light in the way.*
4. *Solicitude, for Life in the work of Grace.*

1. *Solicitude, for Acceptance of the Person.* While the Soul is under the *Law*, the *Seed* of God, Jesus Christ is not yet come up, nor revealed within her. She sits therefore trembling in the Dark, sometimes Confident, that it is a *Seed* of *Love* ; sometimes as Peremptory, that it is a Seed of *Wrath*, which lies hid in her. So she is perplexed, and anxious in herself.

St. *Paul* teacheth us, *Coloss.* 2. 2. that *Assurance* ariseth from the *Acknowledgment* of God in the *Mystery* even of the Father, and of Christ.

The Mystery of the Gospel lies hid under the Law, the *Heavenly Image* is covered, and kept out of Sight by the *Earthly*. All this while a Saint is apt to be looking down into himself, and to judge of *Love*, or *Hatred*, by those Appearances, which he finds of either in himself. But still he finds those Appearances Mixt, Unconstant, Doubtful. So he is ever tost from one thing to another with much Unstableness, and Unquietness.

If he look up to God, he sees Him in a Cloud, thorow the Principles of the Creature, in which he judgeth of God after the manner of Man ; and so one while he believes him to be a Sweet Friend ; another while, an Irreconcileable Enemy.

But he that is truly *Evangelical*, looks upward still, like *Stephen.* He sees with the

the Eye of his Spirit *Heaven*, that Divine Image, and State of things, opened to him. He seeth the *Father*, and *Jesus Christ* standing at the Right Hand of the Father, and *himself* in the Arms of Jesus Christ, as *Lazarus* was seen lying in *Abraham's* Bosom.

This Discovery of the Mystery of God above, gives him a full Assurance concerning the Acceptance of his Person in the Beloved One.

2. *Solicitude, for Affiance in Perplexities.* The Temper of a *Legal Spirit* in this Point is fitly express'd, *Psal.* 116. 10. 11. *I was greatly afflicted, I said in my hast: All men are Lyars.*

While our Comforts depend upon the *Forms* of our Saviour's Appearing to us, either *Inwardly*, or *Outwardly*: we are, as cast off, and at a Loss upon every Change. When a Temptation, or unexpected Trouble ariseth, we are like a Ship in a Storm, that hath lost its Anchor. We are carried away with the violence of the Tempest.

Then we cry: *All our Signs for Good have deceived us. All the Marks of Divine Love, which men have given us, all the Encouragements, and Comforts, with which they have carried us on: All the Manifestations, and Workings, which we discovered, as Grounds of Assurance, in our own Hearts; All these have deceived us. Good God whom, or what shall we trust? What shall we do, that we may have rest in the Time of Trouble?*

This is the uncertainty of his Comforts, who is under the Law, who hath not all his Comforts, and Confidence wrapt up in One Spirit with Jesus Christ, who is the *Same*, without Change, in the midst of all Changes; *Yesterday, and to Day*. It is this alone, which can make us sweetly to Rejoyce in our Infirmities, and Tribulations.

3. *Solicitude: for Light in the way.* While the *Law* is our *School-master*, the *Letter* is our *Way*, and *Guide*. The *Letter* hath a *Twofold Inconvenience* in it.

First, the *Way* of the *Letter* is cut out into great *Diversity of Paths*. It is full of Windings, and Turnings. It hath manifold Rites, and Observations in it.

Secondly, the *Letter* itself is *Old, and Dim.* So the Directions, which it gives us are very Dark, and uncertain to us.

These Two Inconveniences make us perpetually full of Disputes, and Doubts in our selves, every step, that we take, whether we be in a right way, or no.

We never can be delivered from this Solicitude, till we be brought into the High, and Plain way of the Spirit, in which the wayfaring Man, though a Fool, cannot erre.

4. *Solicitude: For Life in the Work of Grace*, Rom. 8. 3. *The Law being weak thorow the Flesh*, Heb. 7. 16. *Jesus Christ is made a Priest, not after the Law of a Carnal Command; but after the Power of an Endless Life.*

The Life of Grace under the Law is very Weak. For the way of its Working is by Fleshly Principles. It is so conveyed thorow them, as if it were wrought out of them altogether.

In this State the Soul eats the Bread of Life, with the Sweat of her Brows. She is fain to till an Earth full of Bryars, and Thorns. She carries on the Working of Grace with much Difficulty for the present, and Anxiety for the Future. For the Life of Grace is weak, and it puts forth itself after the Way of the Life of Reason, by Parts, Affections, Passions, Resolution, Industry. This way of Working by these Powers naturally carrieth along with it much Care, and Vexation. Whereas under the Gospel the New Earth bringeth forth the Fruit of the Spirit of its own accord, according to the several Seasons, and Growths of it. And this is done, while the Husbandman sleepeth, while the Spirit lies sweetly at Rest in the Bosom of her Saviour without any Care, or Toil.

The Life of Grace in the Law, is as Water drawn up out of a Deep Well by Buckets-full at a time. But in the Gospel it is a Living Fountain springing up Freely, Plentifully, Uncessantly.

So much for the *Signs* of a *Servile*, or *Legal State* in Religion.

I will conclude this *Head* with one *Use* of *Consolation*.

Application.

Use. Consolation. You, who feel not your selves carried up into the Glory of God by the Spirit, as upon the Wing of an Eagle; but are creeping towards Heaven, like Worms upon the Ground: you have great *Priviledges* belonging to you, and a great Portion of Comfort.

Your *Priviledges*, in which you that are under the *Law*, may Glory, and take *Comfort*, are these:

You have an *Adoption*, or *Son-ship*; a *Protection*; a *Presence of Glory*; a *Peculiar Worship*; a *Pledge, and Type*, you may have a *Precious Seed* in you.

1. *Priviledge*: *Adoption*, or *Son-ship. Rom.* 9. 4. You are the *Israelites* in the *Letter*, or *Flesh*, *to whom pertaineth the Adoption*. God is your Father in a more especial way, than to the Rest of Men, in a nearer Relation, than that of Creation. You are Sons, though by the Bond-woman. You are begotten again of God into a New Image of Himself: though this Image be in the Flesh, and of the Flesh, as the Mother.

2. *Priviledge*: *Protection*. God was with all his Thousands of Angels on Mount *Sinai* in the midst of the Fire, and Thick Darkness. This was an *Allegory*, and signified thy Heart with its Fears and Agonies under the Law; in the midst of which God, and His Angels dwell, as a Defence over thee. *The Law was added because of Transgressions*: to Protect thee from the Power of the Devil in thy Lusts, and Corruptions.

3] *Priviledge: the Presence of Glory*. This is reckoned up, *Rom.* 9. 4. *The Glory*. The Glory is some Manifestation above the Work of Nature, sent forth from God, and having God present in it, conversing with us by it. Such was the *Pillar* in the Wilderness; such the Smoak in the Temple; the *Appeapearance* at the *Oracle*.

Thou

Thou also who fearest God, and workest Righteousness, though under the Law; yet hast a Glorious Work of God upon thy Heart, a Divine Appearance of God in thy Spirit, a near Presence of God with it; by which thou hast Access to Him, and Communion with him.

We read of those that are *near*, and those, that are *far off.* Thou in the State of *Nature* wast *far* off from God. Now being brought under the *Law*, thou art *near* to Him. When thou shalt be brought up into the Light of the *Gospel*, thou wilt see thy self *in Him.*

4. *Priviledge: Peculiar Worship. The Covenants; the giving of the Law; The Service of God pertained to the Israelites:* Rom. 9. 3. Thou art an Israelite, a Kinsman of Christ, and all the Saints, nay a Brother according to the Flesh: if thou hast the Work of the Law upon thy Heart. The Covenant, nay both Covenants, in the Letter, in the Outward Dispensation, and Administration belong to thee. Thou hast a Right to all the Ordinances, and to every Instituted Service of God. The Promises in the Proposal of them concern thee in the First Place.

Go then to the Sacraments; Pray; Read the Word; Hearken to the Promises; whatever thy Troubles, or Terrours be. These are appointed for thee to keep, to Comfort, to carry thee on, till Christ be revealed in thee.

5. *Priviledge: The Pledge, and Type* of Spiritual and Eternal things, *Rom.* 9. 4. The *Promises*; The *Fathers*; *Christ according to the Flesh.*

When thou feelest the Bondage of the Law to lie heaviest upon thee, thou hast this to comfort thy self with: All the Saints of old, in whose Loyns, the Life, and Heirs of all Grace, and Glory lay; lived in this State, and were subject to the Law, even until death: Jesus Christ Himself was born of Legal Parents, and made under the Law.

Besides; The Law is a Fleshly Image of all the Joys of the Gospel, and the Spirit, and Heaven. The Law holds them forth all, not in the *Type*, or Image only; but in the *Prophecy* of them, as being certainly *to come.*

Moses, and the *Prophets* go together, and Moses himself is One of the Chief of the Prophets.

As Christ according to the Flesh was an Israelite, so the Law is the Beauty, and Glory of Christ in the Flesh, testifying of itself, and its own coming in the Spirit.

Sit down then under thy *Fig-tree*, under the Shadow of the Law, with good *Nathaniel*, till thy Vine be grown up. There look on Him, who seeth thee. Behold that Glory, which looks forth in the Law, as in a Fleshly Image of itself. Feed thy self with the Expectations of his Shining out, whom this Image prophesies of to thee. When he discovers himself, thou shalt know, that He was in Covenant, and Communion with thee, even when thou wert under the *Fig-tree.*

6. *Privi-*

6. *Priviledge* : You may have a *Precious Seed* in you. While you are Legal you are in Bondage to many Fears, and Terrours: You weep, for you ſay ; you can diſcover nothing of Chriſt in you. It is true the Seed is not come up yet; but it may be Sown. You come not Rejoycing, and bearing your Sheafs with you: yet you may be thoſe, who go forth weeping, and carrying your Precious Seed with you.

When Darkneſs would drive you to Deſpair, then take to your ſelves the words of St. *Paul*, *Gal.* 3. 23. *Before Faith* (that is, the Revelation of Chriſt in my Fleſh) *I am kept under the Law*, under Terrours, and Rigours; *Shut up in Darkneſs* and Fear, from all Comforts, or Confidence *unto the Faith*, (that Appearance of Chriſt) *which ſhall be revealed* ; but now is hid, as a Seed only in me.

Though thou canſt not yet with good old *Simeon*, ſing over Jeſus Chriſt in thine Arms, a Song of Peace, and Reſt to thy Soul: yet thou mayſt with *Mary* have him in thy Womb. This *Burthen*, which thou beareſt, and goeſt with ſo heavily, may be the *Burthen* of the Lord, the Immortal Word in thee.

Theſe *Pangs*, which thou feeleſt may be, not to the Death of thy Soul, but the Birth of a *Son*, a Saviour, whoſe coming forth ſhall make thee to forget all thy Sorrows, and Rejoyce; becauſe a *Son* is born unto thee, by which Birth thou art no more a *Servant*, but a *Son*.

I have now done ſpeaking of the *Servile*, and come to the *Son-like State* in Religion.

2. *The Son-like State.* This is known by a *Four-fold Property.*

1. *Love.* 3. *Spirituality.*
2. *Life.* 4. *Reſignation.*

1. *Property* : *Love.* I ſhall ſhew this in *two places* of *Scripture.*

1. *Scripture* : Galat. 4. 6. *Becauſe ye are Sons, he hath ſent forth the Spirit of his Son into your hearts, crying, Abba, Father.* St. *Paul* in theſe words toucheth *four Things*, which will much open this *Point*, and this Particular.

1. *The Sonſhip of a Saint.* 3. *The Diſcovery of it.*
2. *The Concealment of this Sonſhip* 4. *The Effect of this Diſcovery.*

1. *The Sonſhip of a Saint.* This is the Union of a Saint in one Spirit with him, who is the only begotten Son of the Father, Jeſus Chriſt. It is the Fellowſhip of the Perſon of a Saint in one Life, one Image with the Perſon of his bleſſed Saviour. The *Apoſtle* unites theſe *two*: *our being Sons* ; and *our having the Spirit of his Son.* And that which St. *Paul* in this place calls *The Spirit of His Son* : he calls *the Spirit of Adoption*, Rom. 8. 15. That Spirit, which is the Spirit of all the Sons of God.

2. *The Concealment of this Sonſhip.* The coming of the Spirit into our Souls doth not *make* us Sons, but *manifeſts* us to be ſuch. We are *Firſt* Sons, and *then* the Spirit of his Son is ſent forth into our Spirits. So we read plainly : *Becauſe*

ye

ye are Sons, he hath sent forth the Spirit of his Son into your Hearts.

While we live in sin and slavery, we are in truth Sons, though we be, as *Princes in disguise.* Yet ever God retains in himself, the *Root*, and *Image* of our Persons, as of Sons.

So our State of Sonship is *twice hid: once* in the *Secret* of divine Glory; *again* under the *Shadow* of our Flesh.

3. *The Discovery of this Sonship.* This is by the *sending of the Spirit into our Hearts.* This Spirit is *manifold.* Ephes. 4. 3. *Keeping the unity of the Spirit in the bond of peace.* Where the *Unity* is kept by a *Bond*, there a *Multiplicity* is clearly signified.

1 Cor. 12. 13. *We are all baptized by one Spirit into one Body.* Christ and his Saints are there spoken of. All these together are one *Body* of Divinity, and Glory. Each particular Saint is a Member of this Glory, a Son, or Child of this Divinity. Each one hath the same *Spirit*, which comprehends all the Persons of our Saviour, and his Brethren.

God in his own time sends down this Spirit upon every one of his Sons. When it comes, it discovereth in itself, thy Saviours Person, and thine, in one Light, Life, and Form; in one Relation to God, as being both *Sons.*

The *Spirit* shining forth in thy Spirit, shews itself at once, One with God, and One with Thee. So it becomes both the *Witness*, and the *Evidence* of thy Relation to God, as of a Son to a Father.

Therefore St. *Paul* teacheth us: *Rom.* 8. 16. *The Spirit beareth witness with our Spirits, that we are the Sons of God.* The Spirit is the *Brightness* of the Godhead; which, as it descends into our bosoms, opens the Godhead to us, there discovers us to our selves, as we were Eternally *comprehended* in that *Root*, as we *grow* up out of it, as we *abide*, and flourish in it.

This Spirit being immediately united to God, immediately united to our Spirits, is an immediate Testimony of our Sonship.

4, *The Effect of this Discovery. He hath sent forth the Spirit of his Son into our Hearts, crying; Abba, Father.* The natural *Effect* of our Sonship made manifest in us is a natural *Affection* to our Father. While we are in the State of Nature we know not whence we come, nor whither we go, when once we have received the Spirit of Sons, we then see God to be the Father, who did bear us in his Loyns from Eternity, who brought us forth into this World; who can never forget us, though a Woman should forget her only Child; who hath ever Bowels of a Father, care, tenderness, sweetness towards us; who cannot always hold, but He must discover himself to us.

When a Saint feels these Workings of the Spirit of God in his own Spirit, then his Bowels turn within him, then he melts, then he casts himself into the Embraces of his God, and cries; *My Father: Abba, Father.*

Thus God gives a Check to our Lusts, changing them into a divine Love, *by Discovery.*

This

This is the *First place* of *Scripture.*

2. *Scripture.* 1 Joh. 4. 16. 17. *He that dwells in Love, dwells in God, and God dwells in him. For God is Love. In this is Love made perfect, that we may have Boldness before him in the day of Judgment. Because, as He is, so are we in this World.*

Two things are taught us in these words:

1. *The Relation between God, and a Saint in an Evangelical State.*
2. *The Affection of such a Saint towards God.*

1. *The Relation between God, and a Saint in an Evangelical State.* The Relation between a Father, and a Son in *Nature* hath *three Parts.*

1. *Part.* The Nature of the Father is in the Person of the Son. It is one in both, as the Sap, and Seminal Power is the same thorow the whole Tree.

2. *Part.* The Person of the Son subsists in the Nature of the Father; as the Body of the Tree in the Root.

3. *Part.* The Person of the Father propagates and multiplies itself in the Person of the Son; as the Body of a Tree runs out into Branches.

Such a Relation with so many Parts is there between God, and a Saint, as between Father and Son.

1. *Part.* The Divine nature is in the Person of a Saint, as the *Fountain* of his Being, the *Fulness* of his Person. Thus St. *John* saith: *We dwell in God*; not in the *Fleshly Image* of God, as a Servile Christian; but in the *Spiritual Image*, the naked Bosom of the Godhead.

2. *Part.* The Person of a Saint is in the Divine Nature, as in his Root, in his Element, in his proper *Principle*; as that, which *comprehends* him, *communicates* itself to him, *sustains* him, *flows* in upon him, *shows* itself in all things, *possesseth*, *acts* him entirely. Thus saith St. *John*: *We dwell in God*: that is, as a Worldly Spirit dwells in the Spirit of this World.

3. *Part.* God propagates himself in a Saint. Both are one Life, one Spirit multiplying itself into various Forms: Both unitedly, and in One, pass thorow all Forms. So St. *John* again teacheth: *As He is, so are we in this World.*

This is the *Relation* between God, and a Saint in an Evangelical State, as that between a Father and a Son.

2. *The Affection of a Son-like Saint towards God.* To dwell in *God*, and dwell in *Love*: to have *God*, and to have *Love* dwelling in us, are both One thing. For *God is Love.*

God is an Infinite Sweetness, which is both *Fountain*, and *Sea* in one: a Fountain sending forth many Streams, many Sons: a Sea drawing all into its own Bosom again by a Natural course.

He then that is a Son of *God* is a Son of *Love*: Love of that first Love, coming forth from it, and returning thither, whence it first came.

This Son-like or *Filial Love* hath *Two Characters*,

1. *Character*:

1. *Character: The Degree.* 2. *Character: The Extent.*

1. *Character: The Degree of Love. Love* in a Son-like Saint riseth to a Confidence, a Boldness in the presence of God, even then, when he puts on the most terrible Appearance in the day of Judgment.

The *Ground* of this Boldness in a Filial love is *Three-fold.*

1. *Reason.* A Saint, that is, a Son, knows, and feels God to be *Love.*

2. *Reason.* He knows himself to be in this *Love,* to be One with God in his Heavenly Glory.

3. *Reason.* He knows this *Love* to be in him, God to be one with him in his worldly Disguise: *We have boldness;because as he is, so are we* in this World. All these *Three Reasons* are wrapt up in this *One Clause.*

As he is in the World; *Love itself:* so are we with Him, sensible of Him.

As He is in the World, and at once *above the World, in Glory:* so are we in Him.

As he is in the World, *clothing his Divine Substance with Fleshly Appearances:* so are we, because he is in us. This is the *first Character* of a Filial Love.

2. *Character: Extent of Love.* A Saint, that is a Son, hath not a *particular* Love to God,or any Object. He is,as his Father is,Love in its full Latitude. *He dwells in Love.* Love is the *Air,* in which he breaths, in which he receives all Shapes of things, in which he communicates himself to them.

A Son of God is like his Father in *Two Things:*

1. He is a beautiful Light shining upon all things equally, stamping its own bright Form upon them, so beholding them.

2. He is a Cloud of Sweetness, like gentle and soft Rain falling upon every thing, till it have sweetned it by degrees to the same height; and enjoying it in that Sweetness:

Exhortation. Make *God* your only *Mark,* and Aim. What is it, which you seek for? *Love?* God is *Love.* What is it, which makes every Action, or suffering sweet? This, if *Love* be the beginning. What gives you Rest in every End of things? *Love.* Then seek *God* above all things. Make him the *Beginning,* and the *End* of your way. So you shall have a sweet Rest in all. For He is *Love.*

How strange is that perverseness, which is in the Nature of man! When man was first made, he was placed in a Garden, where he had liberty to eat of all the Trees, excepting one Tree only, which bare all manner of Curses for Fruit, the *Forbidden Tree.* Yet then man eats of this one Tree, and lets the rest alone. Now all the Trees in the same Garden, which are all Creatures in the World, have wo, and death growing upon them. There is one Tree only in the midst of the Garden bringing forth Glory,and Immortality. This Tree is *God.* Now man will feed plentifully on all the other Trees; but will not touch this *Tree of Life.*

We all have *Notions* in our heads, and *Expressions* upon our Tongues concerning *God*; that, if we ſpeak of Wiſdom, *He* is *Wiſe*; if we ſpeak of Strength, He hath *power*; if we ſpeak of Glory, He is *beautiful*; if we ſpeak of Joy, and Delights, He is *ſweet*. But oh that there were ſuch Hearts in us to ſet up this *God* in our Spirits for the ſupream *Wiſdom*, *Power*, *Beauty*, *Sweetneſs*!

I will divide this *Exhortation* into *Three*.

1. *Exhortation. Seek the Knowledge of God.* As our Saviour once ſpake paſſionately over the Jews: *O Hieruſalem, Hieruſalem, if thou hadſt known the things of thy peace!* In like paſſion doth my Spirit breath forth this over you, that now read it: *O Man! O Woman! If thou knewest the One thing of thy Peace, the Knowledge of thy God.* This is the Chief, the only thing, the All-things of thy Peace. For when thou knoweſt him, thou knoweſt *Love* in truth, the Life of Love; and this is Eternal Life. *John* 17. 4. *This is Eternal Life to know thee.*

Preſs the knowledge of God upon thy Spirit by theſe *Three Motives*.

1. *Motive*: *The Knowledge of God is the Inlet of all Grace, and Comfort*, Rom. 10. 14. *How ſhall they believe in him, of whom they have not heard?* If Faith be the mother, and nurſe of a Spiritual Life; the knowledge of God is the Father, and the Food of Faith, and of that. If Faith be the Fountain, that ſends forth the Streams of Divine Strengths, and Conſolations; the Knowledge of God is the Sea that ſupplies this Spring.

Rom. 10. 17. *Faith cometh by Hearing, and Hearing by the Word of God.* The *Word* of God is the *Image* of God, which is Jeſus Chriſt. This *Word* repreſents itſelf *Three ways*: *Eternally*: *Internally*: *Externally*.

1. *Eternally* the Word of God repreſents itſelf to Glorified Spirits. That *Knowledge* of God, which is begotten upon the Spirit by this Repreſentation is call'd *Seeing*. For it is a Repreſentation in a clear Light, as before a man, as face to face. 1 *Tim*. 3. laſt, *Seen of Angels*.

2. *Internally* to men on Earth by the Principles of *Natural Reaſon*, or by *Supernatural Principles* from the *Spirit*, or from the *Written Word*.

3. *Externally* by the outward Creatures, by the Senſes, and Objects of Senſe. Theſe two laſt ways of Repreſentation are call'd; *Hearing* or *Report*. For they are Repreſentations of God conveyed thorow the darkneſs of our Natures, as a Voice ſpeaking from behind us, from behind the *wall* of our *Fleſh*.

When God is pleaſed thus to give his Word, to put forth a Diſcovery of himſelf thorow our dark Principles, as by the Hearing of the Ear, in our Souls; then God, in all that he appears to *be*, appears to be *Love*. This Senſe of God thus impreſt upon the Heart, *unites* it to God, makes it to *believe* him, truſt itſelf to him, repoſe itſelf on him, reſt in him, leave its deſires, and hopes with him; that as He lives, ſo this Heart may live; as he works, and carries on his own Deſire, ſo he may work on this Heart, and advance the Happineſs of it. Thus *Faith cometh by Hearing*.

Hear then what *Nature* without you, ſpeaks aloud of God: that He is good, true, juſt, full and free. Liſten to that report, which is made of God by all your *Senſes*, by all the things of Senſe, in the ſeveral Languages of their Beauty, Power, Plenty, Pleaſure, Variety.

Liſten to the inbred voice of your own *Reaſon*. Hear the clear report, which that makes of God; that there muſt be *One*, the *Firſt*, and ſo the *Beſt* of all; *above* All, *in* All, gathering up all into himſelf; the *Beginning*, and the *End* of All.

Liſten to *Supernatural Principles*. If you cannot hear, or underſtand the language of the *Spirit*; yet hearken to the ſound of the *Written Word*, which cries in your Ears: *God gave his Love, and Glory to man, before he gave a Being to the World. When man had made himſelf Miſerable, God gave Himſelf to miſery, and death for man: God all along quite thorow Time to Eternity carries on this work of making himſelf wonderful in man, and Man a wonder of Bleſſedneſs in Him.*

He that ſtops not his Ears againſt theſe ſweet Reports of ſuch a *God*, a God of *Love*, cannot but be charmed by them. A man that *hears* this, will *beleive*, he will at leaſt caſt himſelf on *God*, and ſay: *Whither-ever thou goeſt, carry me with thee: Where-ever thou ſtayeſt, be thou my Reſt. To thee only, O my God; to thee entirely, O my Love, do I truſt my ſelf.* This is the *firſt Motive* to the knowledge of God.

2. *Motive: The Knowledge of God emproves, and exalts the Soul.* Pſal. 90. 14. *I*, ſaith God, *will ſet him up on high, becauſe he hath known my name.* None can tell, but they, who have taſted, what a Divine Height, what a Height of Divine Strength, and ſweetneſs there is in the *Knowledge* of God. *I will ſet him on high*: the word in *Hebrew* ſignifies: *I will ſeat him in a ſtrong Caſtle ſituate on a high Rock.* Such a Caſtle is the Knowledge of God for *Air, Proſpect*, and *Strength.* As a man grows in the Knowledge of God; he feels himſelf lifted up into a Divine *air*, in which purity, peace, pleaſure, Angels breath; he perceives himſelf *walled* in with an aſſured ſafety, and reſt, which nothing can reach, nothing can ſhake.

The *Knowledge* of God opens a man's Eyes, to *ſee* Fields of Glory, and Rivers of Pleaſure, in the midſt of which he is every where; together with Horſes of Fire, and Chariots of Fire, which continually plant themſelves between him, and every Enemy.

3. *Motive: The Knowledge of God preſerves a man from Evil.* Gal. 4. 9. *After that ye have Known God, or rather are known of him, how come ye to turn back to thoſe weak, and beggarly Principles, to which ye deſire to be in bondage.*

Theſe *Beggarly Principles* are the Principles of this world, in which we lye by nature, as in a *Priſon*, In a Houſe of Bondage, where Sin binds us, Shame

 covers

covers us, Death feeds upon us. What ſhall deliver us from this Priſon, this Slavery? The *Knowledge* of God will do it, and that alone can do it.

When God puts forth his own Image in us, he then owns us, and makes us to know, and own him. Thus we know, and are known by this Image of God living in our Spirits. As the *Serpent* of *Moſes* devoured the *Serpents* of the *Magicians*: So this *Image* of God in our Spirits ſwallows up all the *Images* and *Shapes* of this inchanting World, which are as *Serpents* tempting, and ſtinging us, caſting forth the Poyſon of Sin, and death upon us. This *Image preſents* us with Heavenly Forms; *plants* us in itſelf; *cloths* us with itſelf; ſo furniſheth us with *Treaſure*, and *Armour*. Now having thus known God, and the ſweet Freedom of his Love; how can we deſire, or bear to be again in bondage to our former Vanities.

4. *Motive: the Diſcovery of God ſhews us, all, that our hearts can wiſh to ſee.* Pſal. 37. 4. You have this Counſel given you: *Delight thy ſelf in the Lord, and he ſhall give thee thy hearts deſire.* Acquaint thy ſelf with the Lord, and he ſhall ſhew thee thy hearts deſire, in ſhewing thee himſelf.

What is God? Eſa. 57. 15. *He is the High and Holy One, that inhabits Eternity.* What then ſhalt thou *ſee* in the Diſcovery of God? Thou ſhalt *ſee* Excellency, and Joy at their Height, and fixt there, unchangeable, Eternal, as Eternity itſelf; without any *Change*, which is the *cauſe* of all Loſs, and Death; without any *Shadow* of Change, which makes all Fear and Melancholy.

What is God? See by Jeſus Chriſt, who is the Image of God. You read of him: *Epheſ.* 1. 10. *God hath gathered up all things into One, in Him.* What then ſhalt thou *ſee* in the Appearance of God? Thou ſhalt *ſee* all thoſe Forms of things, which affrighted, and oppreſt thee in *Shapes* as Delightful, as Delight itſelf. For thou ſhalt *ſee* all things *in One, in Chriſt.* Thou ſhalt *ſee* all Varieties of things in *One Beauty*, as the various *Mixtures* of that with itſelf, or *Multiplications* in itſelf. Thou ſhalt *ſee* thy ſelf immortal in a State of full Glory: according to that, which St. *Paul* ſpeaks: 2 *Tim.* 1. 9. *The Grace, which was given us in Chriſt, before the World was.* Thou ſhalt *ſee* thoſe dear Relations, thoſe ſweet Contents, which thou haſt loſt, and over which thou bitterly mourneſt, breaking thine Heart; or which thou feareſt to loſe, and ſo liveſt ever trembling in this Fear: Thou ſhalt *ſee* all theſe living together in one Bleſſedneſs; preſent before thee in one view, never to die, never to be loſt, when once thou ſeeſt God in thy Soul. *For all things live to God.* Thy dead Joys are ſtill living in him; *Death* itſelf, which kill'd them, and threatens thee, lives a *lovely life* there.

What is God? God is Love. What then ſhalt thou *ſee*, when thou ſeeſt God? Thou ſhalt *ſee* a pure, unmixt, abſolute, unconfin'd *Love.* Thou ſhalt *ſee* all things having their Being in *Love*, becauſe they have their Being in *God.* Thou ſhalt *ſee* all things animated by a Life of *Love*, inſpired by a Spirit of *Love*:

becauſe

because *God* is the *Quickning Spirit* of all. O *Sweet Sight*! To see every thing *quickned* by *Love*, and so made perfectly *Loving*; every thing *clothed* with *Love*, and so made perfectly *Lovely*. This he *sees*, that *sees* God made manifest to him.

Now, as the *Woman* said of our *Saviour*: *Behold a man, that hath told me all, that ever was in my heart*: may not we say this of the *Knowledge* of God: *Behold a* Light, *in which you shall see all, that ever was in your heart to hope, wish, or imagine?*

Is not this the *Wisdom*, which is sweeter than Honey? Richer than Pearl? Better for traffick than fine Gold? Even the *Knowledge of God*, in the opening of which, all delights flow forth, all Beauties sparkle, all wares of Blessedness offer themselves, and press in upon your Spirits. Seek then the *Knowledge of God* in the *first*, and *last* place, in all places, for it is in the *place* of all things.

This is the first Exhortation.

2. *Exhortation*: *Let nothing keep you at a distance from God?* Where can you be so well, as in the Bosom of Him, who *loves* you? Nay, who is *Love*? Nay who is *Love* to you if you will receive Him? For he is *all Love*.

Whatever departs from *God*, departs from *Love*, and goes towards *Wrath*, Enmity, Hatred, take heed how you trust your self to any thing, that tempts you from *God*, whatever it pretends: It cannot come from *Love*, or bring *Love* with it. It is an *Enemy*, and seeks to betray you by winning you from your sweetest Strength. The *Blossom* of a Vanity, or Sin may be fair to the Eye. But *Hatred* is the *Root*, and will be the *Fruit*.

Every thing of *Love* is of *God*, and carries the heart to God. *Hatred*, saith *Solomon breeds strife*. Canst thou look for *Peace*, I say not, *Pleasure*, in that Temptation, which draws thee down from *Love* into *Hatred*.

3. *Exhortation*: *Walk worthy of God*; If you be *His Sons*, you are Sons of *Love*; a *Love* which is untainted with Particular respects; a *Love*, which is Invincible by any unsuitableness, or opposition, a Divine Love. Cherish such a *Love* in your selves, shew it to others.

Let your *Love* be your *Selves*, as it is in *God*, that you may as soon cease to *be*, as cease to *Love*. Let *Love* appear, wherever you appear like your Selves. Let your *Love* be as Universal, as your Conversation. Let it be your *Nature*.

Let your *Love* be like *Aarons Ointment* poured forth upon the *Head* of things, the *Godhead*, and running down thorow all the *Creatures*, to the very lowest *Skirts*, the *least* of Things.

Be you *Love*, as *God* is. *Love exalteth not itself*. For it dwelleth with all things as *One*, in *One*. *Love thinketh no Evil*. For it looketh upon all things *thorow* One, and judgeth of them, as they appear *in that One*. *Love is not angry*. For *Union* is its Life, and all its Streams are sent forth from that sweet Spring. *Love is not suspicious*. For it makes itself *One* with All, and gathers

up

up all into *One Principle* with itself. *Love worketh no ill.* For it possesseth, converseth with, enjoys each several thing *in One.* So every thing to *Love* is *Love's Self.* Thus *God is Love.* Thus be *you*, if you be *Sons* of *God.* This is to be *Perfect, as your heavenly Father is.*

2. *Property : Life,* Heb. 7. 16. *Who,* (that is, Christ) *was not made according to the Law of a carnal command, but the power of an Endless Life.* A Comparison is made in this Scripture between the Priesthood of *Aaron,* and our blessed *Saviour. Aaron* was a Priest of the first Covenant, the Law: The Lord *Jesus* was the Priest of the New Covenant, the Gospel. He that lives under the Priesthood of the One, is a *Servant.* He that lives under the Priesthood of the Other, is a *Son.*

We have a *Threefold Opposition* between these *Two States,* the *Servile,* and the *Son-like.*

The *First Opposition* is between *Law* and *Life.* A *Law* is something *imposed,* a *Compact,* a Treaty between Two. *Life* is something *Inbred.* A *Principle,* a Spring, a Unity.

The *Second Opposition* is between a *Law-command,* and a *Life-power,* A *Command* works by violence, and force, from without, uncertainly : A *Power* of Life works kindly, constantly, inwardly, and sweetly.

The *Third Opposition* is between *Time,* and *Eternity. The Law of a Carnal Command,* a carnal, or *Fleshly* Command decays, and dies, it begins, and ends in *Time,* as every thing of *Flesh* doth. But the *Gospel* is the *Power of an Endless life.*

He, that lives, as a *Servant* under the Law, lives in *Fleshly* Principles, which are frail, false, and fading. The *impressions,* which he hath of goodness are made by terrour, and work unkindly. They are like Images in *water,* dark ; ever vanishing, if they be not maintained by outward objects, Ordinances, Duties, Sermons, Books, Men.

He, that lives, as a *Son,* under the Gospel, lives in a *Divine Principle,* is naturally good. If you ask, why this man is good against the stream of all earthly things, which are evil. It is his *Nature* to be so. For he is *made partaker of the Divine Nature,* 2 Pet. 1. 4. If you ask, how he comes to love, imitate, grow up into an unseen Glory, the Eternal Spirit. It is his *Life* to do so. As every Plant hath its proper *Life,* by which it is formed, and grows. So to this man his God, his Jesus is his *Life.* You may wonder, that a Son of God should continually flow forth into Spiritual Discourses; continually bath himself, in high, hidden, heavenly Joys ; continually be mastering Lusts, and Passions, in despight of Temptations without, and within him ; continually maintain a Lowly, and Lovely temper in this froward world. But all this is no wonder, for he is carried on by *the Power of an Endless* (indissoluble, invincible) *life.*

This is the *Second Property* of a *Son-like State.*

3. *Pro-*

3. *Property* : *Spirituality*, 1 Corin. 3. 1. *I could not ſpeak to you, as unto Spiritual, but as unto Carnal, Babes in Chriſt.* Galat. 4. 1. *The Heir, while he is a Child, differs nothing at all from a Servant, though he be Lord of all.* Theſe *two places* laid together ſhew, that a *Babe* in Chriſt, and *Servant* in religion are both the ſamething ; as alſo, that a *Servant* and a *Son* are diſtinguiſhed by their *Spirituality*, and *Carnality*. He is a *Son*, that is *Spiritual*.

St. *Paul* giveth *Two Deſcriptions* of *Spirituality* in this *Chapter* to the *Corinthians*.

1. *Deſcription* : *Spirituality feeds itſelf on Meat, not on Milk.* v. 2. *I could not feed you with Meat, but with Milk.* A *Spiritual* Perſon feeds, and lives on *Divine things* ; not only, as they are *repreſented* in *Fleſhly Types*, and Images ; but as they are *preſented* in their *own Shape*, and Figures.

Our *Saviour* complains of *Nicodemus* : John 3. 12. *If I have ſpoken to you of Earthly things, and you receive them not : how would you underſtand them, if I ſhould ſpeak of Heavenly.* If now you do not underſtand me, when I ſpeak of Heavenly things in an *Earthly manner*, by reſemblances taken from below : how would you take in, or bear Heavenly things expreſs'd in their *own language*, ſet before you in their own form, and Glories.

The *Heathens* have a Fable of *Semele*, a Lady, who had the chief God for her Lover. She deſired that ſhe might ſee him in the Form, and Majeſty of a God. She had her deſire, and dyed, *oppreſt* by the weight of Glory. In like manner, if you ſhould ſhew the myſteries of God, and the Goſpel to low, and legal Spirits by *their own Light*, without the *Shadowings* of *Fleſhly* Similitudes, and Parables ; you would undo their Religion, confound their underſtandings, drive them to *deſpair*, *deadneſs*, or *profaneneſs*.

This is the *Firſt Deſcription* of *Spirituality*.

2. *Deſcription* : *Spirituality keeps the Unity of things*, 1 Cor. 3. 7. *While there are diviſions among you, are you not carnal ?* Every thing is *Carnal*, which makes *Diviſion* ; that alone is *Spiritual* which maintains the *Unity*.

1 *Gen.* 28. *Man* was made in the Image of God, and to have dominion over all the Fowl, Fiſh, and Beaſts. *Man* was the *Harmony*, and *Unity* of this lower World. He knits up into one Frame of Life, and Beauty the divers Natures of all the ſeveral Creatures. Thus he was the Image of God. This *Firſt*, *Earthly* man was the *Type* only of the Second, the *Spiritual* man.

Coloſs. 2. 18. Many are blamed, not ſo much for looking into the Nature of *Angels*, as for not looking upon them by a right *Light*, in a right *Poſture*: *Not holding the Head*: Not beholding the various glories of Angels in the Divine *Unity* of Chriſt's Perſon.

A *Spiritual* man takes not away the Differences of things, he allows, owns them in their utmoſt variety, latitude, and diſtance. But he tunes them, and attones them, 1 *Cor.* 12. 23, 25. St. *Paul* makes the Body of man a Figure

of

of this truth. *There are many Members. The greater Comelineß is put upon the more uncomely parts. So there is no ſchiſm in the Body.* Thus the *Son* of God knows, that there are divers *Parts* of things: the *pleaſant*, and the *painful* Part: the *dark*, and the *light* Part: the *comely*, and the *uncomely*, He knows alſo, that the higheſt *Pleaſures* are put upon the moſt *painful* Part: that the eternal *ligh:* reſts upon the greateſt *darkneß*, that the moſt *uncomely* Things are cloathed with a divine *Comelineß*, as the *Death* of Chriſt. So there is no *Schiſm* in the *Body* of things to him. He makes, or finds a *Unity* every where.

St. *Paul* ſets out *Spirituality at large*: 1. Cor. 2. 10, 11. *No man knows the things of a man, ſave the Spirit of man. No man knows the things of God, but the Spirit of God. The Spirit ſearcheth out the deep things of God.* A Saint, while he is *Carnal*, knows thoſe things only, which lie within the Compaſs of a humane Spirit: and divine things only ſo far as they are ſhadowed out in the Spirit of man. But he that is *Spiritual*, knows all things, the things of God, as they ſhine out in the Spirit of God. He ſees the great Deep of the Godhead diſcovered in the Spirit; and all things, as forms floating upon this Deep, as the waters of this *Abyſs*.

This is an eminent difference between a *Carnal*, and *Spiritual* Chriſtian. A Carnal Chriſtian ſees Heavenly things only, as *Images* ſtamp'd upon an earthly *Subſtance*, repreſented in an earthly *Principle*. A Spiritual Chriſtian ſees earthly things, as *Images* in a Heavenly *Subſtance*, and *Principle*.

1. Cor. 2. 13. *Spiritual things are ſpiritually diſcerned: Comparing ſpiritual things with ſpiritual.* A *Servile* Saint is in the Fleſhly Principle, as in his own Place. He therefore meaſures every thing by Fleſhly Grounds, and Objects. He receives each thing, as it is proportion'd to fleſhly Appearances, and Notions; or prompted by fleſhly Apprehenſions, and Impreſſions. A *Son-like* Saint is in the Spirit, as in his *Element*. He therefore receives things according to the Suggeſtions and Infuſions of the Spirit: he compares them with the Appearances, and Workings of the Spirit: ſo he tryes, and judges them.

This is the *Third Property* of a Son-like Saint, *Spirituality*.

4. Property: *Reſignation*. The *Son* of God practiſeth this *Reſignation* in *Three Caſes*: in

1. *Wants*. 2. *Woes*. 3. *Works*.

1. *Reſignation* in *Wants*. Matth. 6. 31, 32. Our Saviour takes off his Diſciples from a *Solicitude* concerning Worldly Supplies, by putting them in mind of the *Relation* between their God, and them: *After all theſe things the Heathen take care: Your Heavenly Father knows, that you have need of theſe things.* A Son-like Chriſtian, thus diſputes it in himſelf: *The little Child plays freely before his Father. He takes no thought, what he ſhall eat at Supper, what he ſhall put on to morrow. He leaves all that to his Father to provide. I alſo will caſt off all care from me upon my Father. He knows what is neceſſary for the maintenance*

tenance of my Being, of the Beauty, Comfort of my Being, every moment. Let those be troubled with these anxieties, who know no God, or know not that God to be their Father. It is my Fathers Pleasure to take care of me. It shall be my only care to please him. If I be careful for any outward thing, my care shall be not a Solicitude for my self, but Obedience to Him. Yet the care of this also shall be upon him. For if my Father cloath the Flowers, and my Flesh, will he not much more cloath my Soul: if He feed the Birds, and my Body, will He not much more feed my immortal Part with food convenient for it.

2. *Resignation*: in *Woes.* When our dear Lord saw a black Sea of Horrours ready to break upon him, when he heard the Tempest of Divine wrath now roar about him: in the midst of all this he maintains a Calm upon his Spirit by a *Resignation* of himself, and all things to his Father: *Father, not my Will, but Thine be done.*

There is nothing so natural, as for a Child to run to the lap of its Parents in extremities, and to have a Confidence in them. It is as natural for a Child of God in pains, or griefs to cast itself into the arms of God, and there to breath forth its sorrows after such a manner as this: *My God, thou art my Father; thou hast a greater share in me, than I have in my self. I was thine, before I was mine own. Thou gavest my Being to me, and me to my self. O how great is thy Dearness towards me thine own! How great is thy Delight in me! Thou art far nearer to me, than my Self to my Self. I have my Being not in my Self, but in Thee. I am the Branch, thou art the Sap, the Spirit that runs thorow this Branch, and quickens it. How much more quick, more deep, more full a Sense hast thou, my God, of all my Sufferings, than I can have? Thou canst do all things. Thou hast Strength, I have none. Thou knowest all things. Thou hast Wisdom, I have none. I then give over my whole Being unto thee. Bear me, as thou dost always, in thine Arms, and carry me, whither thou wilt. Comprehend me, as One with Thee. Let me be Thine, be Thou mine; and do, what thou wilt with me. I can fall no lower than thou fallest with me. When I am at lowest, I shall have thy Power, and Wisdom beneath me. As thou risest; thou shalt raise me together with thy self by These.*

Application.

Use. 1. A *Conviction of the Evil in Sin.* Can I *think*, and not think, that I have a *Being*? Can I think that I have a *Being*, and not think, that I have it from *God*, the Fountain of Being? Can I think, that I have my Being from *Him*, and not think of Him, as my *Father*? Can I think of Him, as of a *Father*, and oppose *my* Will to *His* Will, and cherish in my Breast an Enmity against him? This I do, as often as I *Sin.* Is there any thing so *Unnatural*, as *Sin*?

I will press this *Dissuasion* from Sin by a Two-fold *Aggravation* of the Evil in it.

1. *Aggravation.* There is no *Obligation* like to that of a Child to its Father. A Mans Wife is his *Glory*, 1 *Corin.* 11. 8. But it is the Glory of an

L. *Image*

Image. For the Man is the *Head* of the Woman, who is *of* the Man. But the Father is the First, the Fountain Glory of the Child, its *Head.* For the Child is *of* the Father.

God is the *Father* of us all, our Head, our Glory. Do we then refuse to be guided by him? Do we chuse our *Shame* instead of him? Can we cut our selves off from him, to unite our selves to vanity, and make our Lusts our *Head?*

A Man should love his Wife, as his own Body; saith St. *Paul*: *Ephes.* 5. 28. A Man's *Wife*, is as *Himself*. But a Father is *more.* The Lord *Jesus* said: *It is more Blessed to give, than to receive.* The Child is to honour, to love its Father above itself as a greater, a more *Blessed* Thing; as that which *gives* itself to itself.

Our God is our Father. How unnatural then, is it to prefer our *Self*; nay the Brutish, the sensual part of our selves, nay the Disorders of that part before Him? The *Apostle* fitly joyned these *Two*: *Lovers of Pleasure more than Lovers of God*: *without natural Affection.*

2. *Aggravation*: There is no *such* Father, as God is. God is *twice* our Father: once *by Nature*: another time *by Grace.* When we Sin against him, we are his Enemies *four* times over. 1. *We* deface his Image in our Natural man. 2. *We* obscure, and oppose his Heavenly Image. 3. *We* grieve the Spirit of His Grace. 4. *We* crucifie his Son. Shall we be less than Men to him, because he is more than a Friend to us? Shall we be worse than Single Enemies to him, because he is better than a Single Father to us?

O Let us take heed, how we refuse the *Commands* of our God, as a Father; lest we receive not from him the *Comforts* of a Father in our Confusions, and Desolations, when we shall most need them; lest we be not received by Him into the Bosom of a Father, when Death shall take away all other Refuges.

Use. 2. *Exhortation*; *Consolation* to the Children of God. Maintain the *Affections*, and *Obedience* of Children towards God. Have the *Confidence*, and *Comfort* of Children in God. Remember this always, that God is your Father. It was this, that carryed on *Jesus Christ* with so much Integrity, and Industry, thorow Life, thorow Death: *John* 17 4. *Father, I have finished the Work, which thou gavest me to do.* It was this comforted *Jesus Christ* in the Darkest Night of Affliction, when he was forsaken by all his followers, and Friends: *John* 16. 24. *Yet I am not alone, for my Father is with me.*

Would you have Oyl for the Wheels of your Spirit to make it run swiftly, smoothly, and sweetly thorow the hardest, and roughest Employments? Say this over often to your Spirits: *This is the Work of my Father.* Would you have Oyl for the Lamp of your Hearts, to make it burn with a bright, and chearful Flame in the greatest Trouble: Say this over often to your Hearts: *This is the Will of my Father.*

Enforce this double *Use* upon thy self by *Three Considerations.*

1. *Con-*

1. *Consider. God is by Nature more than a Natural Father to thee.* Thou hast thy Being not only *of*, but *in* Him. *In Him we live, and move, and have our Being:* Acts 17. 28.

Can then thy God *forget* thee, or thou *neglect* Him, while thou art in his Power, his Presence, his Arms, his Bosom? *There* thou art *ever.* Canst thou lie in his Embraces, grow up out of his Heart, and see him frown at Sin, and yet Sin, and yet not melt under his Frown? Can he hold thee in his Spirit, as one Spirit with him, and hear thee groan, and feel thy heart beat, and yet not melt over thee?

2. *Consider. God is by nature many Fathers to thee:* The *Continuation* of thy Being is a *continued Creation.* For it flows forth from God fresh every moment. So many moments as there are in thy life; so many times over is thy God thy Father. *Gen.* 2. 7. *God breathed into Man the Breath of life, and he became a Living Soul.* The issuing forth of our Life, and Being from God is compared to *Breathing.* 'Tis as perpetual.

Can God cast off all affection, and care for me, in the same moment, in which He brings me forth? Or can I in that very moment, in which I receive my *Being* from Him, rob Him of *it*, pollute *it*, turn *it* against Him. This I do every moment in which I sin. For but now came I forth from God; *that Appearance*, which fill'd the last minute, being vanisht, and giving way to *this.* A Mother forgets her Sorrows so soon, as a Man-child is born into the World. Sure then God cannot forget his Delights in me, his Loves to me, so soon as He hath brought me out from Himself into this world: and this he doth freshly each minute of Time.

3. *Consider.* God is my *Father*, a *sweeter*, and *nearer* way, than *by Nature*; *by Grace* too. The relation of a Father is the Top of all Sweetness, and Nearness in Nature. But as much as Heaven is above the Earth; Time above Eternity; God above the Creature: so much is a Father by *Grace* sweeter, and nearer than a Father by *Nature.*

If a Natural Father plant his Image, and place his Affection, his Care upon his Son: shall not thy Heavenly Father much more love thee, make thee like Himself, make all Provisions of life, and joy for thee? It is the rule of God, *He that provides not for his Family* (in Nature) *hath denyed the Faith, and is worse than an Infidel.* Can Himself then ever deny *Himself* so far, as to prove unfaithful, or unnatural towards his Family of Grace, his own Children that way? He will certainly take all care of them with all tenderness.

He that blasphemed, or disobeyed his Parents under the Law, was to die. What deaths then is he worthy of, who doth not think sweetly, speak sweetly of, obey chearfully this Father of his Spirit?

Use. 3. *Direction.* If you would attain to the State of *Sons*, and know God, as your Father: feed well upon this *Four-fold Meditation.*

1. *Medita. I lay Eternally in the Fulneſs of the God-Head, as in the Loyns of my Father.* Epheſ. 1. 5. *Having predeſtinated us to the Adoption of Children by Jeſus Chriſt to Himſelf, according to the Pleaſure of His Will.*

When God had his Firſt and moſt retired thoughts before the World; then was I in his thoughts, as a Son of Delights, all lovely, without a ſpot. When no other thing yet was, when no Creature was yet made, when God lived alone in the higheſt, and pureſt Joys of his own Nature; then in the midſt of all thoſe Joys was I in the Fulneſs of the Divine Nature preſented to him, as an Image of Himſelf ſpringing up in him, to be ſent forth into this world, again to grow up out of this world into that Eternal Image of His Pleaſure, and Will. Thus was I *Predeſtinated* a Son.

2. *Medita. God hath made me his Son a ſecond time by Purchaſe.* He hath given his *Son*, his *Beloved*, his *Only* Son for me, that I might be his Son, 2 *Cor.* 5. 21. *He was made Sin for us; that we might be made the Righteouſneſs of God in Him.* God hath given the Body of his Son to reproaches, and pains; his Soul to Guilt, and Horrours; His Perſon in both parts to Death; his Name to Infamy. Thus he was made Sin for us. And all this that we might be made the *Righteouſneſs of God*, Images of his full Beauty, Sons of his higheſt Glory, *in Him, as He is*, who is the Subſtantial Image, the Eſſential Son.

As the *Seed* is by Nature placed loweſt in the Earth, at the bottom of the Plant, that by the Diſſolution of itſelf, it may bring forth its kind: So was the *Son* of God laid below, at the bottom of the Creature, in the depth of Darkneſs; that by his Diſſolution he might reſolve himſelf into us, and as by an Exchange bring forth his *Son-ſhip* in our Perſons.

3. *Medita. God hath made me his Son yet once more by Deſign.* He hath joyned me in *Affinity* with his only-begotten Son. Marriage on Earth is a *Type* of that True Marriage between my Saviour, and my Spirit, *Epheſ.* 5. 30.

He hath joyned me with Him in *Conſanguinity*, Heb. 2. 12. *He that Sanctifies*, (which is Jeſus) *and they that are Sanctified are both of One.*

He hath made me One with his Eternal Son *Myſtically*. The Myſtical Union is a Myſterious one, hidden, Divine, the higheſt Union, ſuch as is among Divine things; not to be *reſembled* by any thing among the Creatures, not to be *comprehended* by any meer Creature. *I in them, and they in me; that all may be made perfect in One*, John 17. 21. 23.

4. *Medita. God hath made me his Son finally by Generation*, 1 Pet. 1. 3. *He hath begotten us again to a lively hope by the Reſurrection from the dead.* As the Eternal Spirit lay like a Seed in the dead body of our Lord Jeſus, which putting forth itſelf, brought forth Eternal Life, and Glory in it: So God the Father ſends forth the ſame Spirit into our Spirits by which the Divine Life, and Image of His Glorified Son ſpring up in us, making us alſo Sons to Him in the ſame manner.

Thus

Thus if you would lead *Son-like* lives with God, consider him as your Father. There is no Earthly Relation, or Form, which more sets out the Spiritual, Evangelical, Eternal Union between God, and Man, than this of a *Father*. Trace it, apply it from the beginning to the end, and it will lead you into all the *Mysteries* of Eternity. Only remember these *two Cautions*. 1. *Take* away all the *Imperfection*, which this Relation hath in the Creature. 2. *Add* to it all *Perfection*, that it is capable of, or can be imagined. So apply it to God, and a Saint. For the Brightest Beauty in Nature, is but a *Shadow* of Spiritual Glories.

I have finish't the *SecondPart* of my Text, which is the *Race to the Kingdom*.

3. *Part. The Royalty, or Kingly State itself: Enter into the Kingdom of God.*

Doct. 3. The *Third Doctrine* from this *Third Part* is this: *The Third, and last State in Christianity is a State of Royalty, or a Kingly State.*

This *Kingly State* is described by St. *Paul*, Rom. 14. 17. *The Kingdom of God is Righteousness, Peace, and Joy in the Holy Ghost.*

The Kingly *State* or *Royalty* of a Saint hath *Four Properties.*

1. *Righteousness.* 3. *Joy.*
2. *Peace.* 4. *The Holy Ghost.*

1. *Property. Righteousness.* This is the Conformity of a Saint to *God*, as to his *Rule*, Genes. 17. 1. *Walk thou before me, and be perfect*: Saith God to *Abraham*. To be *Perfect*, and to be *Righteous* are the same thing. Set thy God, the Supream Glory, continually in thine Eye, as thy *Pattern*, and thine *Aim*: So shalt thou be perfectly Righteous.

I will endeavour further to unfold the Nature of this *Righteousness* by *two Illustrations, and one Distinction.*

1. *Illustr.* Then a thing is truly *Right*, when it answereth to its *Idea*, that is, to its *First Principle*, and *Pattern* in God. God himself in the Fulness of his Person is the Principle, and Pattern of Man.

Righteousness is the Image of God in Man. *Coloss.* 3. 10. The *New man*, which is the Righteous man, and the Righteousness of man is said to be *Created in Knowledge, after the Image of Him, who hath created Him.* There is a *Twofold Image* of God, one *Earthly*: the other *Heavenly*: The *Earthly Image* of God in Man, is the Righteousness of *Nature*: The *Heavenly Image* is the Righteousness *of* the *Spirit*, or *in* the Spirit.

2. *Illustr.* Then a thing is truly Right, when it answereth its *End* in God. God is the *End* of all things: *Prov.* 16. 4. *God made all things for Himself.* The End of Man is the *Possession*, and *Fruition* of God as his only *Portion* of Being, Beauty, Blessedness, *Psal.* 16. 5. *The Lord is my Portion, saith my Soul.*

This then is the Righteousness of man, his *Union*, and *Communion* with God, to live *in* Him, *by* Him, *with* Him, *to* Him. For this reason is Christ said to be *made of God Righteousness, and Sanctification to us*, 1 Cor. 1. 30. Because

in

in the Person of Christ it is, that God and Man are made One, one *Love*, one *Life*, one *Likeness*.

Distinct. There are two sorts of Righteousness.

1. *Imputed.* 2. *Inherent.*

1. *Righteousness imputed.* You may read of this: *Philip.* 3.9. *That I may be found in Him, not having mine own righteousness, which is of the Law, but that which is of God, by Jesus Christ.* There is a Righteousness of the *First*, and of the *Second* Adam. That of the *First* Adam, is our own, the Righteousness of the Law. It riseth out of the Earth, it is but a Shadow, at best, the *Gilding* of an Earthen Vessel, a Reflection upon a Brick Wall. That of the *Second* Adam comes down from Heaven, is of God, is the true *Gold*, the sure, substantial, everlasting Righteousness.

As when a Cloud is placed in that part of the Sky, on which the Sun shoots forth his Beams, the Cloud is over-spread by those Beams, and made Glorious in their Glories: So are there four Things in this *Imputed Righteousness*.

1. *The* Person of *Christ*, as the Sky, or Heaven.

2. *The God-head*, as the Sun shining in this Sky.

3. *The Cloud*, poor man drawn up from the Earth into the bosom of his Saviour, by his Union with Him.

4. *The Glory* of the God-Head falling upon him, encompassing, and clothing his whole Person in Jesus Christ. This is that Righteousness, which is *of God by Jesus Christ.*

1 Cor. 12. 26. St. *Paul* teacheth us, that if one member be honoured, all the members rejoyce together with it. When a Crown is set upon the Head of a King, it puts a Royalty, and Majesty upon his whole Person. The Head of *Man* is *Christ*, the Head of *Christ* is *God.* The *Glory* of the God-Head in Christ is the *Crown* upon the Head of the Heavenly man; this puts a Royal Beauty of Holiness, the Majesty of that Divine Righteousness upon every mystical member upon each Soul, how mean soever, that is united to Jesus Christ in one Spirit thorow believing.

The Beauty of the God-head shining thorow the Humane Nature of Christ, thorow his active, and passive Obedience, thorow his Wounds, and so falling upon that Soul, which hath cast herself into the Arms of her Saviour: this is the *Imputed Righteousness* of man.

Take this *Caution* concerning this Righteousness. It is said to be *imputed*, not because it is not truly *Ours*, and *in us*: but because it is not *Primarily* Ours, but *by our Union* with another Person.

The Colours in the Rain-bow are said to be *Apparent*, not *Real*; because the Rain-bow is not their *Spring*, though it be their *Seat*; but they are reflected from the Sun shining on the watry Cloud. So this *Righteousness* is said to be *imputed* to us, because it is *First* seated in Jesus Christ, and *then* reflected from Him

Him on us. Yet it is a true Righteousness, it is *truly, immediately on our Persons, in our Persons, as Jesus Christ is.*

It is therefore said to be *imputed*, because it is not ours *Primitively*, but *Consequently*; because *Christ* is *ours*; yet not as *Absent* from us, but *Present in us, possess'd by us.*

2. *Righteousness Inherent*, 2 Cor. 3. last. *We all as in a Glass beholding the Glory of the Lord, are Translated into the likeness of the same Image from glory to glory, as by the Lord the Spirit.* The Lord Jesus at once enters into a *Two-fold Relation* to man: *one* of a *Sun shining* all over him: the other of a *Root growing* up in him. We see his Glory in our *selves*, as in a *Glass*, we bring the face of Glory with us. We have *the Glory* in our selves, and are our selves the *Glass*. There is the *Sun* shining, which beautifies, and *justifies* a St. We grow up into that Image, by the Lord, the Spirit of that Glory, planting itself in us. There is the *Root* growing, which purifies, and *sanctifies* us.

Our Saviour, when he discovers Himself, appears at once, *without* us, and *within* us. *Without* us he riseth upon us, as a *Light of Loveliness*. Es. 60. 1. *Rise out of the Dust, and shine, for thy Light is come, the glory of the Lord is risen upon thee. Within us* He riseth, as a *Light of Life*, Galat. 1. 16. *When it pleased the Father to reveal his Son within me.*

This is our Righteousness, *Imputed*, and *Inherent*.

This Righteousness is the *Crown, Robe, Scepter* of Royalty in the Kingdom of God.

1. *The Crown.* So St. *Paul* stiles it, 2 *Tim.* 4. 8. *Henceforth is laid up for me a Crown of Righteousness, which God, the righteous Judge shall give me in that day.* The Righteousness, the Glory of God resting on Man, is that Crown, which both entitles him *to*, and enstates him *in* the Kingdom of God.

As a King ever possesseth his *Crown*, though he wear it only on high days, at solemn meetings of the people: so a Christian may *have* this *Crown*, though laid up, while he is on Earth. But he doth not *appear* with it openly, till that great day, the Resurrection, when the whole world shall meet.

2. *The Robe.* The Righteousness of God, and Man is the Imperial Robe, which both, as Kings, are cloth'd with, *Es.* 61. 10 *He hath covered me with a Robe of Righteousness, as a Bridegroom decketh himself with Ornaments.* Behold, a *Royal*, and a *Bridal* Robe! It is *Righteousness* which puts upon the Spirit the beauty of a *Bridegroom*; the Majesty of a *King*. That Soul, which shines forth in *Righteousness* makes itself a *King* not by *Right* only, but *Choice* too; by *Love*, as well as *Law*.

Psal. 45. 4. 5. *In thy Majesty ride prosperously, because of Truth, Meekness, and Righteousness,* &c. *Thine Arrows stick in the hearts of thine Enemies, the people fall under thee.* This was sung of the Lord *Jesus*; *Righteousness* cloth'd him with so sweet a Majesty, that he pierc'd the Hearts of His Enemies with Arrows of *Love*. Such a *King* is every Spirit, which is Brother to this Jesus. *Righteousness* sits upon him, and shines from him, as a Garment of Light, Truth, and Wisdom; it shews, as wrought into a Harmony of Courage, Justice, Temperance; it sparkles with Tempers of Goodness, Gentleness, Meekness, Humility. These things, like *Arrows*, wound the stubbornest Hearts with a *Liking*, and a *Love*; that a man's bitterest Enemies bow to him.

3. *The Scepter. Psal.* 45. 6. It is said to our Saviour: *The Scepter of thy Kingdom is a Righteous Scepter.* Righteousness is the Scepter of Strength in the Kingdom of Christ, by which all things are swayed, and governed, *Psal.* 16. 7. *If a mans ways please the Lord, his Enemies shall be at peace with him.* Holiness, or Righteousness is such a *Harmony*, such a Musick between God and Man, as all things hear, and obey.

They that make use of hellish Charms, make the Picture of a Person in Wax, and as they work the Wax by the Fire, so they work upon the Person. Goodness hath a Heavenly Charm in it. For a Righteous man hath in himself the Heavenly Image of God, which is the *First*, and *radical* Image of all things. By this *Image*, he hath a power upon all things.

Thus *Righteousness* is the *Crown, Robe, Scepter* in the Kingdom of God.

1. *Use. Learn to hate Sin by the Rule of Contraries.* For, if Righteousness cloath you with the highest Honour, Worth, Strength of Kings; if it crown you with the Glory of God, if it carry you up to the Life of God: then what doth *Sin*? Sin by the Rule of *Contraries* puts upon you the *Baseness, Badness, Weakness* of Slaves; Sin wraps you up in the *Shape*, sows in you the *Seeds* of Devils.

Let us then look on Sin in this *Five-fold View*: As it puts on us. 1. *Weakness.* 2. *Badness.* 3. *Baseness of Slaves.* 4. *Shapes of Devils.* 5. As it plants in us *Seeds of Devils.*

1. *Sin puts upon us the Weakness of Slaves.* Gen. 49. 3. 4. *Reuben, thou art my First born, the Beginning of my Strength, Excellency of power.* O Man! O my Soul! consider what thou wert in thy Beginning. A Divine Flame shot forth from an Angels Bosom into this lump of Clay, not to abide imprisoned in it, but to feed upon it, as fuel, so to return, and make its way upward, making all things that resist, its prey, and nourishment, What is it, that hath thus enfeebled, and cool'd thee, and chang'd thee from *Fire* into *Water*? *Sin* hath done this. Now thou lyest spread upon the Earth, swayed by every weak Breath, or Spirit, that blows upon thee; unable to contain thy self; casting thy self into the Figure, and Shape of every Object, on which thou touchest. Thy Sin hath thus weakned thee.

Man was the *Reuben* of God, the *First-born* in the first Creation, the Excellency of Dignity, and Power; the Head of Strength. He was the Chief Image of the Divine Nature, made to be the Spouse, and Queen of the God-

Head

Head, the Onely One of her Mother. The Rest of the Creatures were to be, as *Concubines* only, particular, inferiour Images of God, The Soul foolishly forsakes the Bosom of her God, to throw herself into the Embraces of these Concubines; so she defileth herself, and them; so she dishonoureth her King, and Husband in both; so pours forth her self loosely upon the Ground as *spilt Water*.

2. *Sin puts a Badness into men.* It puts into us a *Three-fold Badness*; of *Folly, Filth, Fury*.

1. *Sin fills us with folly.* Sin so far befools thee, O vain Man, as to despise, deny Blessedness, Beauty, Eternity *there, where* they are, *in God*, the First, the Fountain, the Substance of all Beings: and to seek them *there, where* they are not, in Fleshly, shadowy, fleeting Trifles.

This is that *Folly*, the Head-Spring of all Sin, which St. *Paul* complains of, *Rom.* 1. 21. *They became vain in their Imaginations, their foolish Heart being darkned.* This was the *Folly*, The Eternal Substance, and Fulness was darkned and disappeared in their Spirits, which brought forth instead thereof empty Images. So St. *Paul* explains it at the 23. *v. Changing the glory of the Incorruptible God into an Image made like to Corruptible Man, and Birds* &c.

What degree of *Folly* is this, to refuse to acknowledge, or own the *true God*, who is Eternal Life: and to make each painted, perishing *Vanity* a *God* to us, while we make it the *Object*, and *Spring* of our Hopes, and Happiness?

But thus it is most just, that they to whom the true God, is but as an Idol, an empty name; to them each Idol, each empty Appearance should be their God. This is the *First Badness* in Sin, *Folly*.

2. *Sin fills a Man with Filth.* Carnality, and Corruption signify both the same thing in Scripture. To be Spiritual is to be Holy; to be Fleshly, Sinful, *To be Carnally minded*, (that is, to be Fleshly-minded) *is Death: but to be Spiritually minded is Life, and Peace*: Rom. 8. 6.

Is there any thing more *foul* than this; for a Soul, which was made, as a *Spirit*, for Spiritual Joys, and Glories; so to mingle itself with *Flesh*, as to see, receive, rellish nothing but by Senses of Flesh; so to drown itself in Flesh, as to be uncapable of conversing with, taking content in any, but Fleshly objects? This is the State of a Sinful Soul: Thus is she over-spread with *Flesh*, as one great *Spot*.

The Interpreters of the *Proverbs* teach us, that the *Young Man* there, is the *Soul*, which is naturally Immortal, ever young, ever flourishing: the *Matron*, the chast Spouse, that woes this Young Man, *Divine Wisdom*, the Heavenly Image of the Divine Nature: The *Strumpet* this *Worldly Image* of things. O say now, when thou Sinnest; *Alass! How do I dishonour, and defile my self? I, who should, who might live chastly, constantly, sweetly with the Eternal Image of Glory, my God, my Spouse, mine own: I pour forth my self into the lap of Strangers*

gers, of Unconſtant, Whoriſh, Flattering, Fading Beauties in Fleſh.

O Filth! O Shame! That Spirit, that ſhould tread upon the Stars, ride upon the Angels, rejoyce with God everlaſtingly; that Soul labours and ſweats in Duſt, and Death, as a Slave; rowls in the Mire of Fleſh, like a Beaſt; rakes in the unſavory ſinks of all various Luſts, as an unclean Spirit.

3. *Sin fills a man with Fury. Solomon* in his *Proverbs* tells us of One, *that throws about Fire-brands and Swords, and ſaith, Am I not in jeſt?* Prov. 26. 18. 19. This is *Solomon*'s *Fool*, which is a *Sinner.* Can it be, that any ſhould make Ruines, and Reproaches their *Delight*, nay their *Devotion* too? *Jonah* ſaid once. *He did well to be angry even unto Death.* Can it be, that any ſhould cheriſh a Rage to the Death, Deſtruction of Men, Kingdoms, and Souls; and then think ſuch a *Rage, Religion*; ſuch a *Fury, Zeal*; and that theſe things they ought to do? Can it be that any ſhould draw Tears, and blood from others, from Millions, from ſuch as do them no harm; and then ſay, *With ſuch Sacrifices God is well pleaſed; that God,* who is *Love?*

O take heed of *Sin*, it blows up in a mans Breaſt, the Fire of Hell; it ſtrangely corrupts *Nature* itſelf conſumes all *good Nature* in Man. There is no *Notion* ſo common, no *Principle* ſo plain in the minds of men, which it will not darken, and deprave. It will make you believe that Helliſh Paſſions, are Heavenly Motions; and that there is Fury, and Fire in the Boſom of Sweetneſs itſelf, of God.

This is the *Second Evil* in Sin, *Filth.*

3. *Sin puts upon a man the Baſeneſs of a Slave.* Prov. 28. 1. *The wicked fleeth, when none purſues.* Sin makes a man the verieſt Coward in the World, the object of the greateſt Pity and Scorn. When thou haſt committed a ſin, how art thou aſham'd to ſee the light, to look up in the Eyes of God or any man, to behold thine own Face in a Glaſs? How doſt thou ſtart at every Motion, tremble at thine own Shadow, fly from the Reflection of thy ſelf in the thoughts of another? How doſt thou wiſh to be tranſported into ſome Wilderneſs, where thou might'ſt be a Stranger to all things, and eſpecially to thy ſelf?

Gen. 4. 14. *Cain* complains: *I am driven from thy Face, and from the Face of the Earth; a Fugitive and a vagabond ſhall I be in the Earth.* Behold the weight of Shame, with which Sin oppreſſeth a Guilty Soul. Who would buy all the pleaſures, and profits of Sin at ſuch a rate, as this? To be driven by Shame from the Face of God, and every Creature? To be hunted by the wretched Senſe of Guilt, as a Deer with the Arrow ſticking in his ſide? To run reſtleſs thorow all Companies, and Conditions, as a Fugitive, and Vagabond in them all?

Gen. 3. 7. It is ſaid of our firſt Parents, when they had eaten the forbidden Fruit, *their eyes were opened, and they ſaw, that they were naked,* and now they were aſhamed. Do you ask, *what is Sin?* There is an inſeparable Peace, and Pleaſure goes along with every good deed; There is an unavoidable ſting

of

of Shame, and Horrour in the tail of every evil Act. He that doth evil, hath his Eyes immediately opened by that, which he feels in himself; and now he knows what he hath done.

What is that, which when you have done it, takes away your sweet Peace, and Rest from you? which makes you wish for a thick Darkness to fall upon you, that may hide you from every eye? This is *Sin*, hate it, and fly from it. This is the *Third Evil* in Sin.

4. *Sin wraps up a man in the Shape of a Devil. Man being in Honour continues not, but becomes like the Beast, that perisheth.* What doth the *Body* of a *Man* now differ from that of a *Beast*, more than the Body of one Beast differs from that of another? Nay the *Bodies* of many Brute Creatures excel it in Beauty, Strength, Vertue, Sense.

What hath thus chang'd Man, and put upon his *Body* the form of a Beast? *Sin* hath done it. But if we could see the *Soul* of man, as plainly, as we see his *Body*; we should see that far more like to *Devils*, than this is to *Beasts*. The Evil Powers, and Spirits might well say of Man, when he had sinn'd; *He is become as one of us.*

What reason hath man to abhor this Poysonous, this Potent Evil, which transforms him into this monstrous Shape, that he appears, as a *Beast* among the Beasts, in his Body; as a *Devil* among the Devils, in his Soul?

5. *Sin plants the Seeds of Devils in Man. Daniel* teacheth us in his Prophesy, that the Messiah should come *to take away Sin, and Iniquity. Dan.* 9.24. We read in the Promise, *Gen.* 3. That there should be Enmity between the Seed of the Woman, and the Seed of the Serpent. The Seed of the Woman is the Messias: Then the Seed of the Serpent must be Sin. Each *Sin* is the *Seed* of a *Devil* in us, which as it grows up, becomes a perfect Devil. A Lying Spirit entred into Ahab's Prophets, and possest them when they became Lyars.

Happy were we, if as often, as we feel motions to Lust, Covetousness, Falshood, Ambition in us; we would then say: Now a Lustful, Covetous, False, Ambitious *Devil* enters into me; if I yield to him, he will carry me away into the Waters, and Fires, of Confusion, and Torment, he will be still growing into me, till I become *one Devil* with him.

2. *Property: Peace.* This is the *Second Property* in the *Kingdom of God*, that is, in the *Royal State* of a Saint on Earth.

The name of *Peace* in the three Learned Languages signifieth *Three things*: a *Cessation*: a *Combination*: a *Perfection*; a *Cessation* from trouble: a *Combination*, or league with all things: *Perfection* of excellency, and joy to give Rest.

There is a *Three-fold Peace.*

1. *Natural*: the *Peace* of the Elements in the great World, and the little World of Man's Body.

2. *Civil*: the *Peace* of men among themselves in their outward Conversation.

3. *Religious*:

3. *Religious*: this is the *Peace* of the Soul in relation to God. This *Religious Peace* is *Two-fold*.

1. *Rational*: that which is built upon the Principle of *Reason*.

2. *Spiritual*: that which is sprung from a *Divine* Light. This is the union of mans Spirit with the Spirit of God, which is the *Band of peace*.

It is a *Spiritual Peace*, which I now speak of: This hath *Two Parts*.

1. *Part*: *Silence*. 2. *Part*: *Satisfaction*.

He, (that is, God) makes me to lye down in green pastures, and leads me by still waters.

1. *Part*: *Silence*. *Psal.* 23. 2. In this *Psalm* God is brought in, as a *Shepherd*; the Soul as a *Sheep*. In this *verse Three Things* are put together.

1. The *Prosperity* of the Soul. 2. The *Repose* of the Soul. 3. The *Stilness* of all things about the Soul.

1. The *Prosperity* of the Soul is express'd by *green pastures*. The Lord Jesus makes the Soul to feed on the green Pastures of the Fresh, and Flourishing discoveries of his Person, and Excellencies. That this is the Souls *Pasture* appears by that place of *Scripture*, John 6. 57. *As the living Father hath sent me; and I live by the Father: So he that eateth me, shall live by me.* As the Father is the *Pasture-ground* of the Son, on which he feeds, and out of which he is taken into this World, to be made a Sacrifice: So the *Pasture-ground* of the Soul is *Jesus Christ*.

2. The *Repose* of the Soul is signified: *He makes me to lye down* in green pastures. Jesus Christ, as a *Shepherd* makes the Soul to lay herself down to rest with security in the midst of his appearances springing up round about her.

3. The *Stilness* and *Silence* of all things about the Soul is set down: *He leads me by still Waters.*

Waters are often used by the *Scriptures* to represent the nature of *Spirits*, John 7. 38. 39. *He that believeth on me, as the Scripture saith, out of his belly shall flow Rivers of living waters. This he spake of the Holy Ghost, which they, that beleive in him, should receive.*

The *Scripture* maketh two *resemblances* between *Waters*, and *Spirits*. 1. As the Springs of *water* nourish the Earth, and make it fruitful: So every fleshly thing hath a *Spirit*, which sends forth its streams upon it, to refresh it. *Psal.* 46. 4. *There is a River, that makes glad the City of our God.* The Holy Spirit is the *River*, that maintains, and renews the life, and *appearances* of God in the Flesh, which make the *City* of God on Earth. 2. The *Second Resemblance* is this, 2 *Pet.* 3. 5. We read of the *Earth standing in the Water, and out of the Water*. In like manner we learn, *Heb.* 11. 3. that *the things which are seen, were not made of things, that do appear*. Some read it thus: *the things which are seen, were made of things, that do not appear*

As the *Earth* stands in the *Water*, and out of the Water: So every *Visible Thing* stands in a *Spirit*, and stands up out of a *Spirit*. The

The Tumultuous workings, and agitations of these *Spirits* in us are the cause of all unquietness in our Spirits. But when Jesus Christ leads forth our Souls into the Fields of his Excellencies, and gives us of his *Love*: He calms all; so that every *Spirit* by which we pass along, as by a *River* side, is still, and silent.

The *Peace* of the Soul dependeth upon the *Silencing* of a *Three-fold Spirit* in her.

1. *The Spirit of Wrath from God.* 2. *The Spirit of the Devil.* 3. *Her own Spirit.*

1. *The Spirit of Wrath from God* must be silenc'd in us, that we may have peace, *Jere.* 25. 30. You may read of this *Spirit of Wrath. The Lord shall roar from above, and send forth his voice from his holy habitation: He shall roar upon his habitation, and cry aloud, as they that press the Grapes, against all the Inhabitants of the Earth.*

The terrours, and troubles of the Soul do not always come *from*, or *by* some *Secundary cause*; but sometimes they come *immediately from* God Himself. God comes forth into the Soul, like a *Lyon*: He sends forth his voice quite thorow the Soul, as the roaring of an enraged Lyon: He presseth, and squeezeth the Souls with his own weight, with a cry of Wrath; as *Grapes* are troden. This may be the case of any Soul, even the most *Holy Habitation* of the Lord, while she is the Inhabitant of an *Earthly* body.

What shall the Soul now do, that is in this case? To what Creature shall she call to help her against the mighty God? What course will you take to find rest to this Soul? No creature, no course can give any rest, till it please God to change Himself from a roaring *Lyon*, to a still, and quiet *Lamb* in the Soul. He can make this change in a moment, and by this change make the Soul, though she were but just before, as a dreadful *Forest* to herself, now to become a safe, and silent *Fold*, that she may lye down quietly, and take her rest.

See, what *Job* complains of, and what he prays for, *Job* 10. 16. *Thou huntest me, as a fierce Lyon: Thou shewest thy self marvellous upon me:* v. 17. *Thou renewest thy witnesses against me: Changes, and War are upon me.* v. 20. *Cease, and let me alone, that I may take a little comfort.*

Oft-times God pursues a Soul fiercely, and swiftly, as if she were some great, and mighty creature. He hunts her from thought to thought, from place to place, from creature to creature; not suffering her to take her breath. *He reneweth his Witnesses against her*; He maketh her guilt, her miseries, her fears, his wrath, eternal horrours to appear continually before her in fresh, and new Shapes, as *witnesses* against her. So he makes himself *marvellous* upon her in those various, and heart-shaking *Forms* of darkness, with which he clothes himself in the midst of her. He brings *Changes*: He suffers her not to abide in any temper or state, but tosseth and changeth the whole appearance of things to her; till she be quite lost in confusion, and amazement.

And

And poor Soul, whither shall she go? What shall she do, that she may have ease, that she may have some comfort, though never so little? She can have no ease, no comfort at all, till Gods time be come, till his will be, to cease, and take his plague away from her, and silence the Spirit of his wrath within her. All that the Soul can do in the mean time is; and that by his Strength alone, to wait, and cry: *Cease thou from me*, O *God*. There is a Time to break in pieces: and a Time to bind up, that which is broken.

Obj. But some one may say: How can God trouble or disquiet a Soul, *immediately, and by Himself, Fury is not in Him*, Es. 24. 4. There is no Principle of Evil or Torment in the Person of God. There is no Spirit of anguish, or vexation in the *Divine nature.* We read of him, *Psal.* 16. 11. *In thy presence is fulness of joy.* When God brings forth his own presence into the Soul; he brings along with it all peace, and pleasantness, a *Fulness of Joy.*

Ans. You must distinguish upon the *Appearances*, and the *Person* of God.

Distinct. You must distinguish upon the *Appearances* of God. God puts forth *Himself immediately two ways*, either in *his own Appearance*, or in *a strange Appearance.*

1. *First*, God puts forth *Himself immediately*, sometimes in *his own Appearance*: and then he ever makes peace. This Apppearance of God calms, quiets, and sweetens all in the Soul, *Es.* 4. 5. *Upon all the Glory shall be a Defence.* The Presence of God in his proper Glory, the naked Face of God looking forth in the Soul is a *Defence* from trouble, and terrour. This is the *Holy Mount*, on which nothing can hurt, or spoil. This Discovery of God is a *Light*, which hath no darkness in it, no trembling, or fear.

Therefore, when the *Holy Ghost* had said, *Psal.* 16. 11. *In thy presence is the fulness of Joy:* He adds for explication: *At thy right hand are pleasures for evermore.* The presence of God at the *right hand* of his own proper Sweetness, and Glory; which is his Strength: this is ever accompanied in the Soul, with a *Fulness of Joy, and everlasting pleasures.*

2. *Secondly*, God can put forth *Himself immediately* in a *strange Appearance*, without the interposal of any *Created Substance* between God, and that Appearance; between that appearance, and the Soul, *Joh.* 20. 15. *Jesus Christ* appeared to *Mary*, and conversed immediately with her in the *likeness* of a Gardiner, which made her weep for fear, that she had lost her Saviour, who was his under this strange Shape; which drew forth her tears.

So God can set his own Person, and presence in our Souls in the Shape of a *Stranger*, of an *Enemy*, of a devouring *Tempest*, of a burning *Fire*, *Psal.* 18. 11. It is written of God: *He maketh Darkness his Secret place: and thick Clouds of the Sky his pavilion.* God can make *Darkness* in thy Soul *His Secret place*, out of which he shoots his invenomed arrows into thy heart. He can make *thick Clouds* upon thy Soul, his *Pavilion*, from whence he will make

war

war upon thee. Thus we must distinguish upon the *Appearances* of God.

2. *Distinct.* Secondly, we must distinguish upon the *Person* of God, as *He is in Himself*; and as *He is in Jesus Christ*.

1. *First*, God as *He is in Himself* is *One*, One rest, and blessedness in every State? Thus God is *All in All*, all that sweetness, peace, joy in *every* Appearance, which he is in *any* Appearance.

It is said in *Job* of the Earth, as it was in its first State: *No stranger passed thorow it.* So it is true of the God-Head in its first State, in its simplicity; that there is no *Strange Appearance* there. This Throne of God wherever it is set up, is a *Circle*; and every hand is the *Right Hand* there, every *Shape*, in which God puts forth Himself is *Love*.

2. *Secondly*, God, as He is *in Jesus Christ*, hath his *Right*, and his *Left Hand*; his *Sweet*, and *Strange* Appearances; *Light*, and *Darkness*; *Love*, and *Wrath*: *Revel.* 6. 16. They cry *to the Rocks, and the Mountains to fall upon them, to hide them from the wrath of the Lamb.*

Jesus Christ witnesseth: *John* 5. 22. *The Father judgeth no man, but hath committed all judgment to the Son.* This distinguishing, and dividing Judgment, by which God puts forth Himself in *Love* upon some, in *Wrath* upon others, is not exercised by the *Father*, that is, by God, as He is *in Himself*; but by the *Son*, that is, by God, as He is *in Jesus Christ*.

This is the *Kingdom of God*, the shining forth of the God-Head from the right hand of the Lord Jesus, in its own proper Glory, calming, and clearing up all in the Soul; scattering, like Clouds, those strange Appearances of Darkness, and Terrour, into which God had before put himself.

This is Christ *shewing us the Father*, discovering God in his *First Light*, as He is the Fountain of Love, where there is neither Fear, nor Torment.

Use. 1. For *Tryal*. By this we may try our selves, whether we be *in the Kingdom of God*, or no. *The Kingdom of God is Peace.* If you be truly in *Peace*, you are of a truth in the Kingdom of God.

I will enlarge this *Tryal* by *Three Instances*, which are the *Glory*, the *Grace*, the *Blessing* of God.

1. *Glory*: *First* the *Glory* of God, and the *Peace* of God ever go together, *Luk.* 2. 14. In the Angels Song these two are united: *Glory to God on high, Peace on Earth. Jesus Christ*, when he came down from Heaven, and was incarnate: *Angels* in their Praises, and Prayers at the Incarnation, joyn these two, Spiritual *Glory*, and Spiritual *Peace*, as undivided in their Life, and Death, in their *absence*, and *presence*.

The Soul, that is without Peace, is indeed *without* in that Darkness, which is *without*; whither nothing of the Glory of God comes, whence no Glory is given to God. If thou canst live without *Peace*; thou livest in a true *Hell*, where there is nothing of the Light of the Glory of God; nor any desire of it.

If

If thou hadst any taste or glympse of the *Glory* of God in thy Soul; thou wouldst feel a sweet *peace* within thee, with thy God, with thy self, and with all things.

The *Glory* of God is a *Healing*, a *Uniting*, a Perfecting thing: it makes all perfect in One, *Mal.* 4. 2. *A Sun of Righteousness shall arise with healing in his Wings.* The Sun-shine of *Glory* falling from the Face of God upon the Soul in any degree, sweetly and soundly closeth up wounds, maketh up breaches, and divisions in the Spirit. The *Wings* of the Sun are his Beams. Each touch of any one Beam of the *Glory* of God upon the Soul, carries a healing, lenifying, appeasing vertue.

2. *Grace.* Secondly the *Grace*, and the *Peace* of God ever go together. St. *Paul*, when he prays for the Saints at the beginning of all his *Epistles*, joyns *these Two*: *Grace, and peace from God our Father, and from our Lord Jesus Christ.* So much of the *Grace* of God, as goes forth into the Soul; so much of *Peace* goes along with it. Where there is no *Peace*, there is no *Grace.*

There is a *Two-fold Grace* of God, the *Love* of God towards the Soul; the *Loveliness*, or *Image* of God in the Soul.

1. Where there is nothing of *Peace*, there is nothing of the *Grace* of God, that is, of the *Love* of God, yet appearing to that Soul. Where the *Love* of God is poured forth, it is an overflowing *Sweetness*, 1 *Corin.* 13. 5. *Charity thinketh no ill.* This *Charity*, which is said in the same Chapter to be *perfect*, to remain *for ever*, can be no other, than the *Love of God* let down from Heaven into the Soul, and revealed there, gathering the Soul up into itself, to dwell in this *Love.*

The Soul, that dwells in this *Love*, *thinks no evil* of God, of itself, of any thing: but is *at peace* with all, hath *sweet thoughts* of all. For the Love of God is its *Eye*, by which it sees, and its *Heart* by which it thinks. It sees *God*, *itself*, and *all things* by the *Light* of this *Love*: it thinks of all things by the *Strength* of this *Love.*

2. Where there is nothing of *Peace*, there is nothing of the *Grace* of God, that is of the *loveliness* of God, of the Beauty of Holiness in that Soul. So much of *Peace*, so much of *Holiness*, and Spirituality: So much of Distraction, and Disquiet, so much of Corruption, and Carnality.

Where things begin to *descend*, there begins *Flesh*, and *Division.* As things descend, and go lower, so these things increase. Where things begin to *ascend*, there begins *Spirit*, *Spirituality*, Unity, and Peace. The more we ascend, and go upward, the more we increase in these.

3. *Blessing.* Thirdly, the *Blessing*, and the *Peace* of God ever go together, *Prov.* 15. 17. *Better is a Dinner of Herbs with Love, than a stalled Ox with hatred. Love* is the *Womb* of *Peace*, and *Hatred* is the *Mother* of *Unquietness*; as appears by that place, *Prov.* 10. 12. *Hatred stirreth up strife: but Love covereth a multitude of Sins.* Didst

Didst thou live at the highest rate of all content in thine outward man, and hadst no *peace* in thy Soul ; thou couldst have nothing *blest* to thee. All thy delicacies would have a *bitterness* on thy palate, and a venom in thy bowels, that will never suffer thee to have a true joy in any thing, which thou enjoyest.

Hadst thou but a *Dinner of Herbs* the lowest fare, such as the Cattel may have together with thee; and hadst Spiritual *peace* with it : these Herbs would have such a *blessing* in them, that they would be, as the food of *Paradise* was to man, when he had Herbs, and all Green things given him for meat.

If thine inward man had a *stalled Ox*, those *Oxen*, which *Wisdom* slays, *Prov.* 9. 2. prepared for it ; the *strongest notions*, the highest *Mysteries* set before thine understanding : if thou hadst not the *peace* of God in these, these could be no *Blessing* ; thy Soul with them would not thrive, it would be but as *Pharoah's lean Kine*, that devoured the *fat* ones, and were still, as lean : All thy *notions*, and *Mysteries* would be but a tinkling *noise*, an empty *sound* vanishing without any profit, or lasting pleasure.

But *Herbs*, the *lowest administrations*, the darkest discoveries of Christ together with *peace*, is a *Feast of fat things*, and *Wine upon the Lees*, which though it have not so *clear manifestations*, yet may have, as *sweet*, and *strong consolations*.

Obj. But now some good Soul may cry out : Alass ! this shuts me quite out of the Kingdom of God : by this I have nothing of the *Glory* of God, or of His *Grace* in me, or of his *Blessing* going along with me, for I have no *peace*. My Tears are my Drink, Day, and Night.

Ans. Thou art no *good Judge* in this cause. For thou mayst be deceived two ways, and this is the *Two-fold Answer*, which thou art to make to thine own Soul.

1. The *Kingdom*, and the *Peace* of God may both be grown up to a good degree in thee, though thou discern them not.

2. The *Kingdom*, and the *Peace* of God may be *sown*, though they be not *grown* up in thy Soul.

Ans. 1. *First*, the *Kingdom*, and the *Peace* of God may be grown up to a good degree in thy Soul, though thou discern them not.

Mar. 4. 27. The *Kingdom of God* is compared to *Corn*, which while a man *Sleeps* and *Rises*, *Night and Day*, *Springs and Grows up*, *he knows not how*. The *Image* and *Peace* of the Lord Jesus may be springing, and well sprung up in thy Spirit, while thou *sleepest* in the Darkness of some Temptation, and hast no sense at all of this Spring, and Growth, though it be continual, and flourishing within thee. This is hard to believe, or understand, *how* it should be. Yet thus the Lord tells thee, that his *Kingdom*, which is *Peace* puts forth itself in the Ground of thine Heart, and prospers, and grows a *tall plant* there, while thou hast *no sense* of it, but *sleepest* ; though *thou knowest not how*.

Our *Saviour* distinguisheth this growth of the Kingdom of God in the Soul into a *Three-fold State* : v. 28. *The Earth bringeth forth fruit of herself* ; *First*

the

the blade; then the Ear; after that the full Corn in the Ear. The *Earth* is the Lord Jesus in his *Earthly*, or *Fleshly* Image; as he is the *Ground* out of which we all Spring forth in our First *State*, or *Image*. He in us *of Himself* sends forth and shoots up his Kingdom *naturally* in our *Souls*, as *Trees* set or planted *in Him*.

The full *Corn in the Ear*; the *Ear*; the *Blade* signify a *Three-fold Evangelical State* of a Saint on Earth, in the Body.

The *First* is the *Royal*, or *Kingly State*, of which I am now speaking. The other *Two* are distinct *degrees* of the State of *Sonship*, or *Child-hood*, as it is different from the State of a *Servant*, which hath the *Kingdom of God* only *Sown*, not yet *grown* up in him.

1. *First*, the *full Corn in the Ear*. This is the *Royal State*, in which the *Mysteries* of the Gospel are displaid, the *Spiritual Person* of the Lord Jesus in all his *Proportions* is form'd, and puts forth himself in the Soul with a *fulness*, a fulness of Spiritual *Light*, *Peace*, *Strength*, and joy. Yet all this *clearness*, and *fulness* is under a *vail*, in the *Husk* still of *Flesh*. It is the full Corn *in the Ear*, not *thresh't* out by Death, and *winnow'd* by a Resurrection; but still standing in *this World*.

Thou mayst have this *State* in thee, and yet not see the *Corn* for the *Husk*: but mistake, and mis-interpret Christ in thee; because thou seest the *Flesh* still; and feelest thy self shaken with Winds, and beaten with Storms, as being still in the *open Field* of this world.

2. The *Second State* is the *Ear*. Thou mayst have the *Blessing*, *Grace*, and *Glory* of the Lord Jesus running up in thy Spirit to a good height, with great store of *Sap*: thou mayst be now near to a kind of perfection in *Spirituality*. Yet all this may be in a form of *Darkness*, *Emptiness*, and *Confusion*.

Take heed of judging the *State*, in which thou art; the *power*, and *vertue* in thee, by the *appearance*. For so doing thou mayst call *Light*, *Darkness*; because it *shines in the Dark*. Be not like a foolish Husbandman, that should look upon his Corn in the Field, when it were new *Eared*, and should complain, that all his hopes were cast away; that he had *Straw* or *Grass*, instead of *Wheat*; because he yet sees not the *Corn* formed in the *Ear*.

3. The *Third State* is the *Blade*. Do not deny the *Kingdom of God* with the *Peace* thereof to be come up in thee; because thou canst not *discern* it. It may be truly come up in thee; but perhaps 'tis yet in the *Blade*, in tender, weak, low appearances; hardly shewing it self above the *Clods* of the plowed Earth, the trouble of thy broken heart; hardly distinguish't from *weeds*, the workings of the Flesh in thee.

Now take this *Three-fold Caution*.

1. *Caut. First*, take heed of over-seeing or undervaluing the *full Corn*, because it is still in the *Ear* or *Husk*. Do not cast away from your self the Praise of Christ, and Joy of Spirit, which belong to a *strong*, and *reigning* Christian

because

because you have *Strong*, and *raging* Temptations, as being still in the *Flesh*.

2. *Caut.* *Secondly*: Refuse not to acknowledge Jesus Christ in the *Ear*; because you have not yet the *full Corn*.

3. *Caut.* Thirdly: Deny not Jesus Christ to have appeared in you; because he is as yet only in the *Blade* or tender Herb.

Thus I have discours'd upon the *First Answer* to a Doubting Soul.

Ans. 2. *The Second Answer* is this: *The Kingdom, and Peace of God may be sown, though they be not grown up in thy Soul.* You must distinguish between the *Devil's Madmen*, and *God's Mourners*.

1. The *Devil's Madmen* are such, as throw abroad Swords, and Fire-brands in the midst of their own Spirits, and say; *Are we not in Jest?* They toss Vanity up and down in their Souls, and Lives; they brandish, and blaze their Pride, Passion, and Lusts. These are their *Peace*, and *Kingdom*; their *Pleasures*, and *Glories*. But they have no sense of the *Peace of God*, and his Kingdom. They understand not how they drive these far from their Souls, and kindle the Fire of Hell-torments in their Hearts, while they roul themselves in carnal security, and Fleshly Pleasures. Against these *this use* is directed, and the Terrours of God are discovered.

2. But *Secondly*, there are *God's Mourners*, holy Souls, which can take no Joy in any Worldly thing, because they have no sense of the Peace of God in their Spirits. These good Hearts are cloth'd with a Garment of Heaviness; but that Garment is as a vail only upon the Beauty of Jesus Christ, which is of a Truth in their *Hearts*, though as yet it be hid from their *Eyes*. And therefore their Eyes are full of Tears, they go on weeping; but they carry their *precious Seed* with them in the Secret of their Souls.

These are *Gods Mourners*, and these are to apply to themselves, that sweet Promise, *Es.* 57. 18. *I have seen his ways, I will heal him; I will lead him also, and I will restore Peace to him, and to his Mourners*, the verse before was: *For the iniquities of his Covetousness I was Wroth with him, and smote him: I hid me, and was Wroth, and he went on frowardly in the way of his Heart.*

How absolute, how sweet, how full is this Promise? What objection canst thou make against thy self, which the Lord doth not here punctually answer?

1. *Object.* *Thou sayest*: I have been very sinful, and still continue so. Mercies, Judgments do me no good; but make me more wanton, or more froward in an evil way. *Ans.* Hark, the Lord tells thee, that he knows all this, He *hath seen thy ways*, the *Evil* of thy ways, and every *Aggravation* of the Evil in them: yet he saith: *I will heal thee.* He undertakes to be Himself thy Physician.

2. *Object.* *But thou cryest out*: I am Sick with my Lusts; I am wounded with miseries, I am broken with horrours. And I have no Strength to recover my self out of any of these. *Ans.* But the Lord Jesus saith: *I will heal thee of all these Evils, of thy Sins, thy Sorrows, and thy Fears. I will do it for thee, by mine own Right Hand, and for mine own Sake.*

3. *Obj.* Still *thou objectest* against thine own Mercies, and complainest; that thou knowest not Jesus Christ, nor the way to Him: Or if thou didst; thou hast neither Will, nor Power to come to him, that thou mayst be healed by Him. *Ans.* But what saith the Lord to thee? *I will lead thee also*: I will first come to thee, I will stretch out my Hand towards thee, and take hold of thy Spirit, I will draw thee towards my self, I will direct thee in the right Paths of my Love, I will bear thee up in the way, that thou shalt not fall *in* it, nor fall *from* it.

4. *Obj.* But thy Melancholy, Dark, and Sullen thoughts still abound in thee, and suffer thee to have no Peace. These fill thee with Fears, and Tremblings, that thou canst not take comfort in any thing. *Ans.* But God will *restore comfort* to thee, and *to thy Mourners*. He will bring again, that Comfort, which thou hadst once in thy Spirit, which thou hadst in Paradise. It is now but laid aside, hid, *sown* in thee. God will bring it forth to Light, and set it before thee, and make it to grow up out of thine own Spirit, in the sight of thy Spirit, and in the sight of all *thy Mourners*; all those melancholy thoughts, which now fill thee with so much heaviness.

I will restore Comfort: Saith God. The Comfort, the Joy, for the want of which thou Mournest, is *thine already*, it was *thine Eternally*, it was the *Grace given to thee before all times in Jesus Christ*, as St. *Paul* speaks to *Timothy*. But as the *Trees* were first in the Creation, and then the *Seed*, and then again the *Trees* are restored to themselves out of their Seed. So thy Comforts have been hid in thine Heart, in which they lye in their proper Seed, and out of which God will make them to grow up, and so restore them to thee, and thee to thy Spiritual, and Heavenly self.

Thus much for the *Second Answer*: The *Peace*, and the *Kingdom of God* may be *sown* though they be not *grown* up in thee.

So I have done with the *First Spirit* to be *silenc'd* in the Soul that she may have *Peace*; which is the *Spirit of Wrath from God*.

2. *The Spirit of the Devil.* This is the *Second Spirit* to be *silenced* in the Soul for her Spiritual Peace. Read those *Verses*, Psal. 46. 2. 3. *Therefore we will not fear, though the Earth be removed: and though the Mountains be carryed into the midst of the Sea. Though the Waters thereof roar, and the Mountains shake with the swelling thereof. Selah.* In the verse following you read of a *River, whose streams refresh the City of God.* This *River* is clearly the *Spirit of God.* This *Sea* then, which troubles the *Earth*, must be the *Spirit of the Devil*, the Natural Power of Darkness in the Creature, which, while it kept its own place, and order, had a *Beauty* in it; but *forsaking its own habitation*, as St. *Jude* speaketh, it brings *Confusion*.

You may confirm that sense of the *Sea* in this place, by comparing Two, or Three places of Scripture more, one with another.

Gen. 1. 2. That Darkness, out of which the Light, and Strength of the

Crea-

Creature was first raised, is expreſs'd by a *Sea*: *Darkneſs was upon the Face of the Deep, and the Spirit of God moved upon the Face of the Waters.*

Revel. 20. 3. *The Angel casts the Devil into the Bottomleſs Pit.* The Word here, which is tranſlated *Bottomleſs Pit*, ἄβυσσος answers in *Greek*, to that in *Hebrew*, *Tehôm*; which is expounded, the *Deep*, in that *First* of *Geneſis*. And the *Sea* is frequently called by this Name thorough the Scriptures; *Tehôm*; Ἄβυσσος; The *Deep*. The Devil was caſt down into the great *Deep* of his own Darkneſs, and ſhut up there.

Revel. 21. 1. *I ſaw a new Heaven, and a new Earth, and there was no more Sea.* The *Spirit of the Devil*, and the Power of Darkneſs was now ſhut up in itſelf, and no more troubled the Peace and Beauty of the *Creature*. Though there was ſtill *Night*, and *Day*; *Darkneſs*, and *Light*; yet there was no more *Sea*, the *Darkneſs*, was as a ſweet Calm Stream refreſhing the *Earth*, and mingled with the *Light* of Life.

This *Sea* of Darkneſs, and confuſion lies at the bottom of the Spirit of every man *naturally*. It encompaſſeth us on every ſide. This often opens itſelf upon us, and the *Mountains* of all our Strength, Joy or Glory are ſwallowed up in the midſt of it.

When the *Waters* of this *Sea*, evil Spirits roar upon our Souls; they fill them with Fear, amazement, and Horrour.

The *Sea* is accounted the Cauſe of *Earth-quakes*. The Earth in a Man, all the *Foundations* of his Life, and Joy are violently ſhaken in him, when this *Sea* ſwells beneath them.

What Peace, what Eſtabliſhment can there be to the Soul, while this Power of Darkneſs rageth? As the World ſhall have no Peace, till it be bound up in its own Deep, ſo neither can the Soul.

This is the *Second Spirit to be ſilenced.*

3. *The Spirit of a Man in Himſelf.* Before the Soul can have Peace, her own Spirit muſt be ſilent in the midſt of her.

Pſal. 4. 4. We have this advice given us: *Commune with your own Heart upon your Bed, and be ſtill.* This ſeems to be a Contradiction *Commune*, and *be ſtill*. But the *Selah* added, points out a more hidden ſenſe.

Here are *Two Terms* in this *Scripture*, which have a various Senſe. *Heart*, and *Bed*.

1. *Heart. Commune with your Hearts.* What is the Heart? The Heart is the *Inward Principle*, the *Life-Principle*.

1. *The Heart is the Inward Principle.* So you read of the *Heart of the Sea*, Exod. 15. 8. and the *Heart of the Earth*, Mat. 12. 40.

Mark 7. 18. *Whatſoever thing cometh from without, defileth not the Man.* v. 19. *Becauſe it entreth not into thy Heart, but into thy Belly; and paſſeth into the Draughts.* v. 21. *From within, from the Heart of men proceed Evil thoughts, Adulteries*, &c.

The

The *Meats*, which we take in from without, reach the *Body* in all the parts of it; and they reach the *Soul*, as it lives in the Body, working upon it, and making changes in it. Both these then are the *Belly*, the *Outward Man*, which is maintained from an *Outward Principle*, and passeth away into the *Dust*, and *Darkness*.

But the *Heart* is more *Inward*, and Immutable. It is that, which abides in the *Invisible* part of things, and is that *Hidden Spring*, the *Principle* both of Soul, and Body.

This *Heart* in the *Natural Man* is the Spirit of Man, in the *Spirit of the Devil*, or in the *Spirit of Divine Wrath*; or rather *in both*. So from the *Heart come evil thoughts*. So St. *John* saith, 1 *John*. 3. 20. *If our Hearts condemn us, God is greater than our Hearts and knoweth all things. But if our Hearts condemn us not, then have we confidence before God.* Every man hath in him a *Principle* more *Inward*, than the *Spirit of the Devil*, which is *the Spirit of God*, as it comes forth into his Spirit, and gives his Spirit, a Created Invisible, Immortal Being in itself among Angels.

This is that *Heart* of man, with which he is to *commune*, this is the Seat of *Justification*, or *Condemnation*: The *Spirit* of *Man*, as it lives above in the *Spirit* of *God*, according to his *Wrath*, or his *Love*: Or the *Spirit* of *God*, as it becomes the *Principle of Nature*, a *Principle* in the Spirit of Man.

If this *Heart condemn us*; that is, the Spirit of God, as it is the Principle of our Spirits: *God is greater than our Hearts*: that is, the Spirit of God, as it is *in itself*, above our Spirits, hath a greater Fulness of Majesty, and Light in itself, where it is, as the Light in the *Sun*; when as in our Spirits, it is, but as the Light in the *Star*. If therefore it testifie *Wrath* to us in this *relation*, in which it is, but as a *Glance*; it shall more fully testify wrath against us in that State in which it is the *Full Glory*. As it is a *Principle* in our Spirits it opens itself *truly*, but *imperfectly*: in a *right Sense*; but in a *part* only of *its own Sense*. But as it is *in itself*, it *knows all things*; it opens itself to the utmost of its own sense, and eternal purpose.

A man should neither *comfort*, nor *condemn* himself from the language of his own Spirit, as it lives in the Outward Soul, or Body, and speaks of *its own*. This Spirit should be *silent*, and still.

But we are to *commune* with the *Divine Principle* in us, with our Spirits, as they dwell *within*, in the Spirit of God. For so the Spirit of God, and our Spirits, are twisted in One, make *One Heart*, testify One thing, and that truly, whether it be for Life, or for Death; from *Wrath* or from *Love*.

For the Spirit of God, and of Man in this Principle, are an *Image* of the Spirit of God, as it is *absolute*, and supream in the God-Head.

But there is a *Heart, within this Heart*. This Heart is a *Principle* of *Life* or *Death*, Love or Wrath. There is within this a Heart, which is the *Life-Principle*, and the *Love-Principle*.

2. *The*

2. *The Heart is the Life-Principle.* Prov. 4. 23. *Keep thy Heart with all Diligence: for out of it are the Issues of Life.* What is this *Heart*, which we are to *keep*, when we are to *deny our selves*? We are to keep it, not with *Caution* to preserve our selves *from* it; but with *Confidence*, to preserve our selves *by* it.

This place of *Scripture* is like that before it, *Prov.* 4. 13. Where *Solomon* speaking of *Wisdom*, or *Instruction*, saith: *Keep her, for she is thy Life.*

Jesus Christ, as he is in the Spirit, is our *Life-Principle*, Colos. 3. 4. *When Christ, who is our Life shall appear.*

He is the *Treasure* of our Hearts, and our truest *Heart*. For *from Him*, as He is in the Spirituality of his own Person, are the *Issues*, the Out-goings, *of our Life*, Mat. 6. 21. *Where your Treasure is, there will your Hearts be also.* Our *Treasure*, and our *Hearts* are both with Jesus Christ in Heaven, *Colos.* 3. 1.

The *Heart*, is the *Treasury* of all good things. *A good man out of the good Treasury of his Heart bringeth forth good things*, *Mat.* 12. 35. Jesus Christ is this *Heart*, which hath the *Treasure* in it. *For in him are all the Treasures of Wisdom, and Knowledge hid*, *Colos.* 2. 3.

Jesus Christ is the *Heart*, as he is the *Head* of Man, 1 *Corin.* 11. 3. *The Head of every Man is Christ: The Head of Christ is God.*

The Lord Jesus, as he is the *Heavenly Man*, is the most proper *Head*, and *Heart* of man: the *First Principle* before all others, the most *inward Principle* lying within, and beneath all other Principles; the *Life-Principle.*

Thus we see, what the Heart is.

1. Jesus Christ, as He puts forth Himself in the Natural Spirit of Man, to be the *Principle of Nature* either, in a Power of *Wrath*, or *Love.*

2. Jesus Christ, as He is in his own Heavenly Spirit, and Person, comprehending the Life, Perfection, and Blessedness of Man in Himself, as in a Divine Root, or Treasury.

2. *The Bed.* This is the *Second* thing, of which we are to seek the meaning. We read of a *Bed of Tribulation, Revel.* 2. 22. This *Bed* is a *Spirit* of Darkness, Weakness, Woe, and Torment.

We read of a *Bed in Tribulation*, which *God* prepares for those, whom he loves, *Psal.* 41. 3. *Thou wilt make all his Bed in his Sickness*, or, *Thou wilt turn it*, the *Inside* of Peace, Love, and Glory, for the *Outside* of Pain, and Trouble: or thou wilt *change* it from a *Bed of Languishings*, into a *Bed of Rest*, or a *Bed of Love.*

We read of *Beds of Joy, and Glory*, Psal. 149. 5. *Let the Saints be joyful in Glory, let them Sing aloud on their Beds.*

In the *Canticles* there is mention made of the *Bed of Christ, and His Spouse*: Can. 1. 16. *Our bed is Green.* There is also *Solomons Bed*, who was a Type of the Heavenly Bridegroom, *Cant.* 3. 7. *Behold his Bed, which is Solomons, threescore valiant men are about it, of the valiant men of Israel.*

This *Bed* is the *Spirit* of the Lord Jesus, which shines forth, and buds with

Sweet-

Sweetneſs, and Beauty, which goes forth in the midſt of the *Angels*, cloathing itſelf with thoſe Mighty, and Glorious Spirits. This *Spirit* draws the Soul forth from the Tumults of the Fleſh, takes her off from her own Strength, and caſts her upon itſelf, as upon a *Bed* of Reſt.

By this time we ſee, what the Holy Ghoſt means by the *Heart*, and the *Bed*.

Let us now return to that place of that *Pſalmiſt*, for the *opening* of which we have brought in all theſe Scriptures, *Pſal.* 4. 4. *Commune with your own Heart upon your Bed, and be ſtill*: that is, diſcourſe not with your Spirit, as it lives in this Body, upon theſe Outward Appearances. For ſo it is one with the *Strange Woman*, it is a *Strange Heart*: it is a Fountain, that makes itſelf common, and defiles itſelf; it is not *your own Fountain alone*, your *own Heart*; but a *wandring*, *falſe*, *lying* Heart.

Retire your ſelf into your *Chamber*, in which the *Candle* of the Lord ſhines; that is, into your *Spirit*, as it hath the Spirit of God, for the Spring of *Natural* Light, and Life in it. Here wait quietly, and ſilently for the *openings* of the Spirit of God in the ſecret Voice of *Nature* within you.

But, ſtay not here, *Silence* this Spirit too, draw your ſelf yet more *inward*, into the *Spirit* of the Lord Jeſus, as He is the *Inward Man*, within, the more inward than, the ſecreteſt Retirements of the Natural Spirit.

Here caſt thy ſelf upon thy *Bed* in thy *Heart*, and commune with thy *Heart* upon thy *Bed*. This is thy *Bed*, and thy *Heart* both in one. Here lay thy ſelf at Reſt, upon this Spirit, which is the *Comforter*; adviſe with this Spirit, which is the only *Counſellor*, the *Spirit of Truth*. So be *thou ſtill*, let thine own Spirit, the Spirit of *this World*, and *Nature* in thee be *ſilent*.

He that thus hearkens in *Silence*, what the Lord will ſay, ſhall certainly hear him ſpeak *Peace* to his Saints.

The Spirit of God in thy *Natural Man* may ſpeak of *Wrath* to thee; and God will confirm that voice of Wrath in the Spirit of thy Natural Man. And ſo here thou canſt find no *Bed* to comfort thee. But go a little beyond thy *Natural Man*, and thou ſhalt meet with the Spirit of God, as it is in its own Freedom, and Fulneſs in the Lord Jeſus. Here is a *Bed* ready prepared for thee. Now ſilence thine own Spirit for ever; and hear no more, what the Spirit in thine own Spirit ſpeaks; but, what this Spirit ſpeaks, as it is here, *in Jeſus Chriſt*; and this Spirit will certainly make thee to hear the voice of Joy, and Gladneſs. Thus *the Lord giveth his Beloved Reſt*: not *in themſelves*, but *in Himſelf*.

I have now finiſhed the *Firſt Part* of *Spiritual Peace*, which is *Silence*; the *Silencing* of a *Three-fold Spirit*; the *Spirit* of *Wrath* from God; the *Spirit* of the *Devil*; the *Spirit* of *Man*.

2. *Part*: *Satisfaction*. The *Second* Part of *Spiritual* Peace is *Satisfaction*. This conſiſts in *Two Things*.

1. *A Sweet League with all things.*
2. *A Satisfactory Reſt in this League.*

1. A

1. *A Sweet League with all things.* There can be no *Satisfaction*, where there is any thing *wanting*, and *not made up*; or any thing *Crooked*, and *not made straight* : as *Solomon* speaks, *Eccl.* 1. 15. There is no *Satisfaction*, where there is Division, or Contention.

Jobs Friends promiseth this *Satisfaction* to *Job*, *Job* 5. 23. *Thou shalt be in League with the Stones of the Field, and the Beasts of the Field shall be at Peace with thee.* v. 24. *And thou shalt know, that thy Tabernacle shall be in Peace.* Behold a *League* with all things below thee, *Beasts*, and Stones: Principles, and Appearances of Life descending are the *Beasts*: The *Stones* are the Principles and Appearances of Darkness descended to the lowest, the Dead Images of things. Behold a *League* here with all things above thee; *thy Tabernacle shall be in Peace.* The *Powers* above thee are thy Tabernacle: The *Angels* are thy *Tabernacle*, *God* is thy *Tabernacle.* Thou shalt dwell peaceably in these. These shall be in *Peace*, not in stormy or fiery Appearances upon thee.

Behold a *League* with all *Times*, with *Eternity*: *Thou shalt know, that thy Tabernacle shall be in Peace.* Thou shalt not fear, what is to come; because all Times to come shall be in Covenant with thee. Whatever Times come to others, still thy Tabernacle, thy Angel, thy God shall be peace upon thee; and this thou shalt know before hand.

This is that *League* with all things, which *Jobs* Friend promiseth to him, without which there can be no *Satisfaction* or *Peace.*

Quest. But you will perhaps ask me, how this *League* is made.

Ans. I *answer*, that it is made by living in the Spirit of Jesus Christ. This *Spirit* in you is this *League* or Covenant. For the *Spirit* is the *Unity*, and hath the *Band of Peace* in itself, *Ephes.* 4. 3.

The Lord, who is the Spirit, is call'd, the *God of the Spirits of all Flesh*, *Num.* 16. 12. and 27. 16. This place agrees with that, *Luk.* 20. 38. *God is the God of the Living, not of the Dead, for all things live to Him.*

As our Saviour said; *that Little Children had their Angels, which beheld the Face of God in Heaven*: So it is most true, that each *Fleshly* Appearance hath its *Spirit* in which it lives *with*, and *to* God. Every *Beast*, or *Stone* hath its *Angel*, *in* which it is *comprehended* after a *living* manner, and *by* which it is *governed.* Every *Angel* hath its *Spirit* in Jesus Christ, *in* which itself is again *comprehended* after a *Divine* manner, and *by* which it is *entirely managed.*

Thus the *Spirits* of all things are in the *Spirit* of Jesus Christ. The *Spirit* of every Creature, which is the *Scepter*, that sways it, the *Law-giver* to it, is in the *hand* of the *Spirit* of Christ, and goes forth from between his Feet.

If then thou wouldst be in *League* with all things, and at Peace with them: be thou *One Spirit* with Jesus Christ; so all Things, and Times shall be *One Spirit* with thee; and this *Unity of Spirit* is the *Bond of Peace.*

To be Spiritually-minded is Life, and Peace, *Rom.* 8. 6. If thou wouldst live comfortably, take heed of dwelling in the *Fleshly Tabernacle*, in the Fleshly Savour, and rellish of things. Let thy understanding, and Soul abide in the Spirit of God. So thou shalt converse always, every where with *lively*, and *lovely* Objects. All things round about thee, within thee, without thee, shall have Life, and a Harmony, a Tuneableness with themselves, and with thy Spirit, a Peace-fulness in their Life. All things shall have an *Angelical Life* and Sweetness to *thee* as they have to the *Elect Angels*. All things shall have a *Divine Life* and Sweetness to *thee*, as they have to *God*.

This is the *First thing*, in which *Satisfaction* consists, a *Sweet League with all things*.

2. *A Satisfactory Rest in this League*. This is the *Second* Thing, in which the *Satisfaction* of *Spiritual Peace* consists.

Es. 14. 3. *And it shall come to pass in that day; the Lord shall give thee Rest from thy Sorrow, and from thy Fear, and from thy hard Bondage, wherein thou wast made to serve.*

Poor Soul! while thou livest in the Darkness of Fleshly things, thou hast *Sorrow* breaking thee by the Oppression of *present* Evils, thou hast *Fear* pursuing thee with the expectation of more Evils yet to *come*, thou hast thy Desires carried forth uncessantly, and violently toward those Objects which cannot satisfy, but divide, disappoint, and distract them, making them to labour under a hard Bondage, to work in the *Fire*, and feed on the *Wind*.

But when the *Day* of the *Lord*, the *Day* of the *Spirit* comes; then the Soul is *in Covenant* with all things; she hath all Evils subdued to her, so her *Passionate* part is Satisfied, and calm; she hath all good things freely to enjoy, so her *Desires* are at rest in the bosom of their proper Objects; thus the whole Soul hath Peace, all her Faculties *acquiesce* in their several Perfections, all her Powers move with a full Complacency in their several Operations.

Thus that is made good which is prophesied in another place, *Es.* 32. 17. *The work of Righteousness shall be Peace, and the Effect of Righteousness, Quietness, and Assurance for ever.* When thou hast the Lord Jesus in the Spirit, then thou hast *Righteousness* brought forth to *victory* in thee. For all things are then gathered up into *One Body*, or Fulness of Divine Glory in thy Soul. Now thou hast *Peace* with *Quietness*, and *Assurance* for ever. This is the *Satisfactory Rest*, when no *Passion* hath any thing, to *disturb* it, no *Desire* wants any thing to *distract* it. But all is *quiet* in the Soul for *present*, and *assured* to *Eternity*. This God doth, when he brings us into his *Kingdom*, which is the *Unity of the Spirit*.

Thus much for the *Second Property* of the *Kingdom of God*, which is *Peace* in the *Two Parts* of it, *Silence*, and *Satisfaction*.

Application.

Use. 1. *Direction*. If you would have *Peace*, understand, and distinguish rightly the *Grounds* of your trouble. As they are *Three*, so you shall know them by their several ways of *working*.

1. *Ground*. The *Spirit of Wrath* from God hath its way of Working in the

the Soul peculiar to itself. It makes *present Impressions* of Trouble, and Terrour. But it doth it with an *Absoluteness*, an *Arbitrariness*, laying no *Premises*, drawing no *Conclusions*.

This was the great *Dispute* between *Job*, and his *Friends*. *Job* complained that *God set a Watch over him*; a Spirit of trouble, that should suffer him to take no Rest, no way, on no side: that *He scar'd him with Visions, and frighted him with Dreams*; God appointed a Spirit over him, which fill'd him sleeping and waking with dreadful Appearances, *Job* 7. 12. 14.

Jobs Friends charge him to have Iniquity in his Hand, *Job* 11. 14. And Hypocrisy in his Heart, *Job* 8. 13. otherwise say they: *Thou shouldst have prosper'd still; thy hopes should not thus have perished*. So they laid *Premises* to the *Wrath* of God, which fell upon *Job*.

On the other side *Job* maintains; the *Vanity* of this Life, where *all things fall alike to all*: the *Absoluteness* of God, who deals alike with all, *at Pleasure*: the *Slightness*, and *Shadowiness* of Man in this Fleshly State, where God alike sweeps away the Lives, and Glories of all sorts of men, as *Shadows*: The *Excellency* of Afflictions in the Saints: the *Propriety* of this State of things, which is properly subject to the Principalities, and Powers of Darkness, *Job* 9. 22. 23. 24. *He destroyeth the Perfect, and the Wicked*. None therefore can say, that any Sufferings are a *Sign* of a Reprobate Man, or of Hatred in God. *If the Scourge slay suddenly, he will laugh at the Tryal of the Innocent*. God will laugh at the miseries of a Good man, as being, but a *Melancholy Dream*, when the Man is asleep, which wakes him, and he finds himself well in Glory. *The Earth is given into the Hand of the Wicked, and hath covered the face of the Judges of it*. It is *improper* to expect any thing right in *this State*, which is the *Season* for Darkness, and the time of the Reign of those Spirits which are the Powers of Darkness, under whom the good Angels are vailed, and imprisoned.

Thus *Job* shews his Friends how they *plead deceitfully for God*. And *Job* hath this Testimony given him by God, that *his Friends had not spoken right things of God, as he had done*.

Job would grant, that he had sinn'd. But the Lord could forgive him all his Sins, and he knew, *His Redeemer liv'd, his Record was on High*. He would never grant that his *Sufferings* were any Argument of his Sinfulness, or want of Sincerity in him.

Jeremy complains, *Lamen.* 3. 6. *He hath set me in dark places, as they that be dead of old*. The *Spirit of Wrath* from God can make itself a Prison of Darkness to thee, depriving thee of all the Sweet, Comfortable, Lightsom Appearances of things; leaving thee only Shady, Frightful, Empty, Melancholy Shapes hovering about thee, as they that are Dead. This Spirit can keep thee in this Darkness, that thou shalt find no way out of it, by Friends, Ordinances, Prayers, Endeavours of thy Spirit within thee. This Spirit can bind thee fast up in itself, sit heavy upon thee, sink thee still lower, as a *Chain*. So he goes on complaining, v. 7. *He hath hedg'd me about; he hath made my Chain heavy.*

But the *Spirit of Wrath* from God never draws forth any uncomfortable *Conclusions* for *Eternity*. No when such thoughts as these arise: *I am cast away for ever: I shall be eternally damn'd in Hell.* These thoughts are not from the Spirit of God, but from some other Spirit. And so *Jeremy* brings them in. v. 18. *I said; my Hope, and my Strength is perished from the Lord.* It is not: *He, the Lord said,* though he were *in His Wrath*: but, *I said.*

Thus we see, how we may know, when the *Spirit of Wrath from God* is the *Ground* of our Inward Trouble.

There is a *Four-fold Remedy* against this *Trouble.*

1. *Remedy*: *Resignation.* Say in the midst of this Darkness, and Fear: *It is the Lord, let him do, whatsoever pleaseth him.* I am in *His arms,* these are *His ways* with me. Can the same Fountain bring forth Bitter, and Sweet Waters? Be not deceived, be not disturbed O my Soul, but leave thy self with God, as a *Faithful Creator*; let him make, what He will of thee. *The Word of the Lord,* every Appearance, in which God comes forth unto thee, *is good.* Fear not to receive him, and to sit down, though it be in Darkness: for then thou sittest under *his Shadow.* Only neither *take from,* nor *add* to his Words, or Appearances in thee; by the Suggestions of any other Spirit.

2. *Remedy*: *Retirement.* Withdraw from the Fleshly Man, together with this P*illar* of Clouds and Fire; which sits upon that. Draw thy Spirit up to the Unchangeable Spirit of Glory, and the State of thy Spiritual Man in that Glory. So did *Job*: *My Record is on* High. Appeal from that Testimony, or Discovery, which God gives of Himself below in thy Earthly Man; to that Testimony, or Discovery, which God gives of thee, above, in the Simplicity, and Nakedness of His Divine Nature. So did P*aul*: *Of such a man I will boast; a man caught up into the Third* Heavens, *into* P*aradise.* Though thou canst see nothing but anger, and frowns in the Face of Jesus Christ, as thou seest that in thy Flesh below: yet thou mayst see Joys and Glories in thy self, as thou seest thy Person in the Heavenly Person of the Lord Jesus above.

3. *Remedy*: P*rayer.* Cry to God continually for Two Things: *First,* that He *would take his* Hand *off from you.* No means, or Power can remove your Trouble, till the Hand of God be removed. 'Tis that, holds down your Eyes, that you cannot see the Light of Comfort. No art, or force, can remove the Hand of God, till Himself please to do it: The Second is, that He *would turn unto thee.*

4. *Remedy*: *Waiting. Submit,* and *Wait. I waited patiently for the Lord, and he inclined unto me*: Saith *David.* Give the Lord leave first to sit down Himself, and Feast on his own Will, and thy Comforts; while thou waitest, and ministrest all thy Peace, and Strength to Him: then will God say to thee: Sit thou down, and Feast upon thy Will in mine, upon thy Joys together with mine.

So much for the *Discovery,* and *Remedies* of the *First Ground* of Inward Trouble.

2. *Ground*:

2. *Ground*: *The Spirit of the Devil*, when he is the cause of Trouble, manifests himself by his *Lying Arts*; and *Murthering Aims.* He increaseth thy Feelings by *Fears*, and thy Darkness by *false Reasonings.* He would teach thee, to argue against thy self from the *present Anger* of the Lord towards thee that he *eternally hates* thee. He would teach thee to dispute against thy self; that no *Sufferings* are like unto thine, and therefore never any *Sinner* like unto thee. What clear Falshoods are these, when God plainly affirms in his word: that *All things come alike to all, and no man can know either Love, or Hatred by any thing under the Sun?*

The *Devil* is ever drawing *Inferences* of *Despair* from *Desertions*, prompting thee to such Language, as this in thy Spirit: *This Evil is from the Lord*; *why should I wait any longer upon him? There is no hope for me in God.*

Thus the *Devil* is known by *Lies* leading to *Despair*, which leads to *Death*, and *Destruction.*

There is one Remedy against this Ground of Trouble besides those mentioned before, and that is this: Resist the Devil, and he will fly from you.

Beat back his Suggestions, by stopping your Ears against them. Answer him, that *he is the Accuser of the Father, and the Brethren one to another.* When he puts into you Dark thoughts of God; Despairing thoughts towards God; that he is a *Lyar*, and a *Murtherer*. But God is *Light*, and there is no Darkness in Him: God is *Love*, aad Fury is not in Him. All these *Fears* are *thy weakness*, and thy Low Estate, in which thou sufferest with Jesus Christ.

3. *Property*. The *Third Property* in the *Kingdom of God* is *Joy*. St. *Paul* in 1 *Thes.* 2. 19, 20. joyns these Two, *Joy*, and a *Crown*: *Ye are my Joy, and my Crown.*

Spiritual Joy hath *Three Parts.*

1. The *Exaltation* of the Soul. 2. The *Enlargement.* 3. The *Activity* of the Soul *in God.*

1. *Part*: The *Exaltation of the Soul in God* is *Two-fold.*

1, There is a Spiritual *Exaltation* of the Soul *over* her Spiritual Enemies. 2. *Chron.* 20.27, It is said of *Jehoshaphat*, and *all Israel*, that, *they returned to Jerusalem with joy. For God had made them to rejoyce over all their Enemies.* This is a *Figure* of the Souls Joy over her Spiritual Enemies; when Jesus Christ brings her, as a Conqueror into the *Spirit*, which is the *Jerusalem above.*

This *Exaltation*, and *Joy* is described in the Person of our Lord Jesus: *Colos.* 2. 15. *He spoyled Principalities and Powers, making a shew of them openly triumphing over them.* Thus is her Royal State, set above the *Principalities* of Hell, the *Powers* of Darkness; Corruptions, *Temptations*, Death, and Devils. She sees them set under her *Feet*, that is, beneath her lowest Appearance; She sees them *spoyled* of all *power* to hurt, and *glory* to tempt her. She *shews* them, and makes them manifest in the Light of God. She *Triumphs* over them, exalts herself, and rejoyceth over them; raising a Joy, and a Praise to herself, and her Saviour out of them.

This

This is the *First Exaltation* of the Soul in her *Spiritual Joy*.

2. The *Second* is the *Exaltation* of the Soul *to* the *Spiritual State* of Jesus Christ. This is set forth in a *Parable*, by our Lord *Jesus* : *Mat.* 25. 23. The Lord saith to him that had emproved, and multiplyed his *Talents* : *Well done, thou good, and Faithful Servant* ; *thou hast been Faithful in a few things, I will make thee ruler over many : enter thou into the Joy of thy Lord.* Here is a *Rule*, and a *Joy* : the *Kingdom*, and the *Joy* of the Lord. To both these the Soul is at once exalted with her Lord.

This *Parable* is worth our stay upon it for a while. The *Opening* of it will add much Light to this *Particular* of *Spiritual Joy*.

A Christian hath a *Two-fold State* on Earth.

1. *State of sad Employment.* 2. *State of sweet Enjoyment.*

1. A Christian hath a *State* of *sad Employment* in a *Two-fold Season* ; while he is a *Servant* ; and while he is a *Son*, before he is yet past the growth of a *Young Man*.

1. *Season.* The *First Season* of a Christians *sad Employment* is, while he is a *Servant*. He then lives under *Legal Administrations*, which are the Manifestations of God in the *Earthly Image*. These are the *Two Talents*, with which the Soul is now to Trade. When *Adam* was driven out of *Paradise*, he was to till the Ground, and to *eat his Bread in the Sweat of his Brows*. So a Saint in this *Season* is put to dig into the *Earthly Image*, and to feed upon the Bread of Heaven in the toil, and labour of his *Natural Principles*.

2. *Season.* The *other Season* of a Saints *sad Employment* is, when he is a *Son*, but not yet grown up out of the Age of a *Young Man*, to that of a *Father*, or a *King*. Now he hath in his Soul the *Evangelical Appearances* of God, and Jesus Christ. But he hath them after a *Fleshly* manner, and in a Fleshly way. These Appearances are the *Five Talents*. The Lord Jesus, while he was in the *Flesh*, had not, *where to lay his Head*. So it is with the Soul in this *Season*. She hath not yet attain'd to her State of *Rest*. She is not yet come to her *sweet Enjoyments*. As her Saviour, so she hath *a Baptism to be baptized with, and she is straightned, till it be over*. She is in difficulty, pain, and travel, till these *Talents* be multiplyed. Then comes the *sweet Enjoyment*, which is the *Second State* of a Christian on Earth.

2. A Christian hath his *State of sweet Enjoyment*, when the *Talents* are *multiplyed*. But what is the *multiplying* of the *Talents* ? What is the casting of them into the *Bank* to receive them again with *increase*? Our Saviour teacheth us, what all this means by another, a plainer *Parable*, John 12. 24. *If the Corn dye not, it abides alone. But if it dye; it brings forth much fruit.*

The *Fleshly Appearances* of Christ are the *Talents* un-multiplyed, the *Corn* abiding alone. While they so continue, they are solitary, melancholy, bearing little fruit of Glory to God, or Joy to the Soul. But then the Soul casts these *Talents* into the *Bank*, then she sows this *Corn*, when she resigns them to God,

when

when she crucifies them, and dies to them by the power of the Death of the Lord Jesus in her.

Now the Soul hath them within her *rising again* in the *Spirit*, after a Spiritual manner. Now she receives them again with an *increase* of Holiness, Peace, and Joy.

Now the Lord Jesus saith to the Soul: *Well done, good, and faithful Servant; thou hast been faithful in a few things, in poor, low, and dark manifestations. Thou hast submitted them to my will, and yielded them up to the power of my Death. I therefore will make thee ruler over many. Thou shalt no more be subject to low, and single Appearances. Thou shalt reign in the power, plenty, and variety of more Glorious Manifestations. Enter thou into these high, and Spiritual Discoveries of God, in which thy Lord and Saviour now enjoys Himself. So the Kingdom, and Joy of the Lord shall be thy Kingdom, and Joy.*

Application.

Use. 1. *Examination.* There is nothing of more concernment to us, than to *distinguish*, and discern aright our *Joys*. *Sensual*, and carnal *Joys* are apt to make us sensual, and fleshly, ignorant, and brutish, as the *Beasts*. *Delusive Joys* make our Souls, as *Devils* in the form of Angels of Light. *Spiritual Joys*, when they are truly such, make us most like to God.

The Delights of *Nature*, and sense are *indifferent* things, *lawful*, *if they be lawfully used.* They are therefore to be taken with much moderation, and caution, as the *Wine*, that St. *Paul* speaks of to *Timothy*: *Drink not alwaies Water: but drink a little Wine for thy healths sake.*

Delusions, and false Raptures of Spirit are a *sweet* Poyson, which are taken in greedily, and kill so much the more speedily. The Soul is naked, open, free, simple in her joys, she mingles herself inwardly, and deeply with the Spirit of her joys: As *Herod* offered to the half of his Kingdom to *Herodias*, when she pleased him, with dancing before him.

It is then a thing of great moment to understand the nature of our Joys that we may know, *when* to admit, and to reject them; *How*, and to what height, to cherish, or check them;

I will propound *Four Tryals* of our Joy.

1. *Tryal.* The First Tryal is this. *Spiritual Joys ever spring from a Spiritual sense of the Love of God towards us. Rom.* 5. St. *Paul* speaks of his *Joy.* v. 5. *Rejoycing in the hope of the Glory of God.* He goes on discoursing of the growth, strength, effects of this Joy. Then v. 5. He shews you the Ground of his Joy: *The Love of God is shed abroad in our hearts by the Holy Ghost that he hath given us.*

Spiritual Joys can give an account, and a reason of themselves. There are *Three things*, which go to make up the *Reason* of Spiritual Joy, when it is Right.

1. *The Love of God*, not any Loveliness of our own, or the Sweetness of any Creature.

2. The

2. The *Discovery* of this Love in an open, manifest way, with a *Fulness*, and *Clearness*; like a *Liquor* that is poured forth, and spread abroad.

3. The *Holy Ghost* making this Discovery, and evidencing it by his own presence, and power in the Soul. This is the *Reason*, which Spiritual Rejoycings, and Gloryings give of themselves: *The Love of God shed abroad in our Hearts, by the Holy Ghost, which he hath given us.*

Are your *Joys* ignorant, sudden, and violent, such, as spring from no appearing cause, and can give no account of themselves?

Whence do your Joys arise from a Sense of the Love of God, or from a Reflection upon your Selves, upon any thing, *of*, or *in* the Creature?

Whence have you your *Sense* of the Love of God? Is it wrought upon you by *Fancy*, by the strength, and frequency of Imagination; or by the *Perswasions* of your own Souls; or by the *Reasonings* of your own Hearts consulting with themselves, and with the Letter of the Scriptures, without the Holy Ghost; by any of the Words, or ways of mans Wisdom, or Power, without you or within you?

If your *Joys* be such, as these, you have reason to suspect, and fear them, least they be from the *Father of Lies*, and not from the *Father of Lights*; from the Fountain of bitterness, and enmity, not of sweetness, and Love.

2. *Tryal.* The Second Tryal of your Joy *is* the *Effect* of it. *Spiritual Joys increase Spiritual Strength in the Soul as they increase themselves.*

Nehem. 8. 10. *Go your ways*, saith *Nehemiah* to the People, *Eat the Fat, and Drink the Sweet, and send portions to them, for whom nothing is prepared. For this day is holy to the Lord. Be ye not sorry: for the Joy of the Lord is your Strength.* Thus the Lord *Jesus* speaks to the Soul in the Ministry of the Gospel: *Go your ways, Feed upon the Fat of my Glory, Drink the Sweet of my Love. Send forth Portions, and Manifestations of this Glory, and Love to them, who have nothing of it yet prepared, and set forth in their own Spirits. This day is holy to me; in it you are to live altogether to me, and in the Light of my Appearances. Then let not your Hearts be heavy, nor your countenances sad, For my Joy shall not weaken, or betray you. My Joy shall be a Preservative against Corruptions, a Strength against Temptations, the Power of a new life carrying you up on high into further Communion with God, and Conformity to him.*

There is a *Threefold Joy* that takes to itself often the name of being *Spiritual.*

1. A *Joy* flowing from our *natural temper*, and Complexion, from sparklings of Blood, or Flashings of melancholy is many times mistaken for a Spiritual Joy. But this Joy *dissolves*, it makes the Soul airy, light, and loose: it exposeth the Soul to Vanity, and Sin.

2. A *Joy* brought forth by an *Evil Spirit* of *Delusion* carries the Appearance of a Spiritual Joy. This *swells* the Soul, makes it vain-glorious, confident, secure in itself. In this State the Soul easily falls *into* Temptation, easily falls *in* the Temptation.

3. *Spiri-*

3. *Spiritual Joy* truly so called. This *Knits* the Union between Christ and the Soul more close, and strong: It gathers up the Soul more fully into the Spirit of the Lord Jesus.

St. *John* saith: *He that dwells in Love, dwells in God.* It is as true: He that dwells in Spiritual Joys, dwells of a Truth in the Lord Jesus.

Vanity, Lust, Passion, Pride come to the Soul in other Joys, and find her fittest for them. But, when they come to the Soul in her Spiritual Joy, so far, as she is in that Joy, they find nothing in her, nothing to comply with them.

This is the *Second Tryal.*

3. *Tryal.* The *Third Tryal* of *Spiritual Joy* is the *Quality* of it. *Spiritual Joy is a Glorious Joy,* 1 Pet. 1. 8. *You Rejoyce with Joy Glorious, and unspeakable.* *Spiritual Joy* hath a Spiritual Glory resting upon it, and puts a Spiritual Glory upon the Spirit, and Person of that man, in whom it is.

Spiritual Joy ariseth from a sight of the Glory of God. Therefore it holdeth forth the Image of this Glory in the Spirit, and in all its workings.

Try your Joys by this: What of the Glory of God? What of the Mysteries of the Gospel? What of the Heavenly Man? What of the Spiritual manifestations of the Lord Jesus have you seen, or known? St. *James* saith, that; *Faith is dead without works,* that is, without the life, and power of God working in you. So *Joy* without the *Spiritual Discoveries* of God in it, is carnal, dead and empty.

Tell me not, that your Heart is full of *Joy*. But unfold to me those *Discoveries*, those Shinings out of God, which you have met with in your Spirits. So shew me your *Joy*.

Obj. But you will say perhaps: *I see a Glory, but it is unexpressible, and you are uncapable of it.*

Ans. I answer to that *Four Things.*

1. A *Spiritual Glory* cannot be exprest by any *inferiour Principle*, or Power, by any abilities of the Natural man. But it can express itself. As it can *be*, so it can be *manifested* in the Soul. Spiritual things give a *Subsistance* to themselves in the Natural man: So they can give an *Expression* to themselves there.

Rom. 10. 8. *The Word is nigh thee in thy Heart, and in thy Mouth.* v. 10. *With the Heart man believeth unto Righteousness, with the Mouth man confesseth unto Salvation.* The Life of Christ, who is the Glory of God, hath a *Mouth* as well as a *Heart* in the Soul of man.

The *Glory* of God unites itself to the *Spirit*, and *Principle* of man, for the adopting of him, and entituling of him to Heaven; for his *Justification.* It puts forth itself by the *Mouth*, thorow the whole *Image* of the man, for the Change, and Transfiguration of that; for his *Glorification.*

Ans. 2. Secondly; it is true, that the Glory of God in the Soul cannot express itself, in its *own Form*, thorow the natural man. But it can express itself by *Earthly Images*, by Types, and Figures; so as to convince even Carnal Hearts.

Jesus Christ so shewed forth the Glory of his Father, while he lived in Flesh, that the very Officers which came to apprehend him, confessed, and said: *Never man spake like this man*: *John* 7. 46. He spake to their sense, *as having Authority*; ἐξουσίαν He put forth thorow his Flesh, Declarations, of that Power of Light, and Divine Glory, which dwelt in him, beyond all that any other Spirit, or Principle could send forth.

Ans. 3. *Thirdly*, though a Spiritual Glory cannot evidence, or testifie it self to *Natural* men, yet it may to such as are *Spiritual*. *As Face answers Face in a Glass, so doth the Heart of man*: Saith *Solomon*. *Prov.* 27. 19. So doth the Spiritual Heart of man. There is a *Proportion* between Spiritual men, and Spiritual things. The Glory of God in one Heart shews it self to the Glory of God in another Heart, thorow the *Natural man*, as a Face shews it self to it self in a *Glass*.

He that hath an Ear to hear, let him hear, what the Spirit saith to the Churches, Revel. 2. 7. A Spiritual man hath an *Ear* in his Heart by which he can hear, and take in thorow the outward Ear, the things spoken by the Spirit, even as they are inwardly spoken by the Spirit in its own Language.

The Spirit of the Prophets is subject to the Prophets, saith St. *Paul*, 1 *Corin.* 14. 32. *Spiritual men* can judge of the Workings, the Appearances, the Joys, the Glories of the *Spirit* in another man; as *Rational men* can judge of *Reason*.

Ans. 4. Spiritual *Joy* is as unexpressible, as Spiritual *Glory*. You may hold forth, as much of one, as of the other. If you can declare nothing of either distinctly, and clearly; then both are at the best, but confused and uncertain in your Souls.

Spiritual *Love*, and Spiritual *Joy* have both this *Property*; they set the Heart on work, to be ever *enditing a good matter*, sweet matter, *touching the King*, the Glory of the Lord Jesus. They make the *Tongue* of a man *like the Pen of a ready writer*, *Psal.* 45. 1. sweetly, swiftly, forming, and warbling forth distinct Expressions of the Divine Glory.

Thus much for the *Third Tryal*.

4. *Tryal*. The Fourth Tryal of Spiritual Joy is this: *Spiritual Joy is above the Natural man*, 1 Pet. 1. 8. *Joy Glorious, and Unspeakable.* 1 *Cor.* 2. 9. The *Eye* sees not; the *Ear* hears not; the *Heart* takes not in the Spiritual Joys of a Christian. Sense, Fancy, Reason, all the Faculties, and Powers of the Rational man are too low to reach, too narrow to receive these Joys.

Obj. If it be thus, how can any man have these *Joys*, or have any *sense* of of them, while he is on the *Earth*?

Ans. I answer to that by *Two places of Scripture*. 1. The *First place of Scripture* is, 2 Corin. 4. 7. *We have this Treasure in Earthly Vessels, that the Excellency of the Power may be of God, and not of us.* The *Spiritual man* possesseth the Treasure of Spiritual Joys in it self. But the *Natural man* holdeth in it self this *Joy*; because it holdeth the *Spiritual man* in it self, as the *Water* of

life

life in a *Vessel.* So the Excellency of the Power, which takes in Spiritual Joy, is *of* the Spiritual man, though it be *in* the Natural man, who is united with the Spiritual man *in One Person.*

2. The *Second Place* of *Scripture* is, 2 *Cor.* 4. *last. We as in a Glass beholding the Glory of the Lord,* &c. The *Natural man* is the *Glass,* the *Spiritual man* is the living *Face.* As a living Face makes an Image of itself in a Glass, and then sees, enjoys itself in that Image. So the Spiritual man makes an Image of its Joys in the Natural man; and hath a living, substantial Enjoyment of them that way: while the Natural man holds the Image only. After the same manner the Soul in the Body contemplates, enjoys itself, and all immaterial things, in the imagination only, which is a Material Glass.

Examine your Joys; do they admit a Stranger, the outward man into their Fellowship, to intermeddle with them? Do they flow alike thorow the *Regenerate,* and the *Unregenerate* part, as upon a Level? I would then question, though I would not condemn them.

Those Spiritual Joys have the greatest Doubtfulness, and Danger in them, which make the greatest Impressions, Motions, and Discoveries of themselves in the Natural man.

St. Paul speaketh of the Spirits putting up from the Heart of a Saint, *Unexpressible Groans, Rom.* 8. Those Griefs, and Joys are most likely to come from the Spirit, which make the least Sound, Noise, or Alteration in the Fleshly part.

I have done with this *Use of Examination.*

Use. 2. *Conviction.* Do not think Religion, or Holiness a *Melancholy thing.* Do not fear to be Religious, as if then you must part with all your Delights, and put your self into the perpetual *Desert* of a solitary, sad sou r Conversation. Holiness, and Religion have their *own Joy,* and will take none of *yours.*

1 Tim. 6. 6. *Godliness is great gain with Contentment.* Let me commend *Holiness* to you in *Three Particulars.*

1. *Particular.* The *First Particular* is this: *Holiness is a Kingdom in itself:* It is *Godliness,* εὐσέβεια, the Right way of *taking in,* and *holding forth the* Majesty of God.

Holiness, is the *Uniting* of the Soul, by a *vital,* and *conjugal* Union to God, who is the *Lord of All,* who is *All in All. Thy Maker is thy Husband. Es.* 54. 5.

Religion is a *Discovery* in the Soul, of God, as the *Eternal Spirit,* the *Quickning Spirit;* as bringing forth Himself, as working his own works, as fulfilling his Joy, as setting up his Kingdom in the Soul. *He hath shined into our Hearts the Glory of the Knowledge of God,* 2 *Corin.* 4. 6.

Religion is a *Drawing* of the Soul up to God, into the Glory of God: as the *Sheet,* which St. *Peter* saw, was drawn up into Heaven. *Brethren, partakers of the Heavenly Call, Heb.* 3. 1.

Can this be a *Melancholy* thing, where there is so much of Heaven, so much of the Love, Life, Glory of God himself ? Can there want Content, where there is a Kingdom, the Kingdom of God ? Or Delights, where the Immortal King Jesus Christ keeps his Court ?

Why shouldst thou think it strange, when all things in Nature are united to their Head, and in that have their Perfection ; that thy Soul should be re-united to her God, and partake of his Fulness, and there possess a Fulness of Joy ? *Thou art our Father*: Say they in the Prophet, *I will return to my Father* ; saith the *Prodigal Son, Luke* 15. 18.

This is the *First Particular*.

2. *Particular: Godliness, or true Religion is Gain*. It is so far from making you loosers in any point ; that it gives you your own again with Usury and Increase. It will not divorce your Spirit from any of your Joys ; but it will make the Marriage-bed of your Delights, *Honourable*, and *Undefiled* : *Green*, and *Flourishing*.

There is a *double Gain* of Joy in Holiness.

1. There is a *Gainful Change* made upon your Joys, when you come to be truly Religious. Your former Joys are transfigured like the Garments of Jesus Christ. They are changed from a *Vile* to a *Glorious* State, from a *Corruptible* to an *Immortal* State.

2. There is a *Gainful Addition* made to your Joys, by being Holy. Holiness brings in upon your Spirits higher, greater, and more Heavenly Joys, such as you were never acquainted with before.

Godliness hath the Promises of this Life, and that, which is to come, 1 Tim. 4. 8. Gen. 49. 26. *Jacob* blesseth his Son *Joseph* after this manner: *The Almighty shall bless thee with the Blessings of Heaven above, and with the Blessings of the Deep, that lieth under*. v. 27. He adds: *The Blessings of thy Father hath prevailed above the Blessings of my Progenitors*. Come, taste, and see, what Sweetness, what a Blessing there is in being *Holy*. The Blessing of a Holy and Spiritual *Principle* in your Hearts will prevail above the Blessings, and Joys of all your Natural, and Worldly *Principles*. You shall have the Delights of *Heaven* above, and the Delights that are in the *Deep* of *Nature* which lies below.

All these you shall enjoy, while you are on Earth ; 'tis true indeed you shall enjoy them in the Promises, which is, as a *Spring* in the Earth ; which is by the Life of Faith as under a vail of Contradiction ; in a hidden way ; but a sweet, sure, substantial way.

Do not thou *Doubt*, but that God can make *Abrahams* dead Body a Father to an *Isaac* ; even *thee* in this Earthly State, which is dark, and dead to possess, as thine own all mirth of Angels, men ; all the Precious things of the *Sun*, and *Moon*, the Creature, and the Creator, if thou put thy trust in him.

Do not *fear* to give up, and Sacrifice thy *Isaac*, thy Natural Joys to thy God, by devoting thy self to Him in a Religious way. It shall be no loss or Death

to

to thy Joys. He shall give thee thy *Isaac*, thy Joys again, in the *Figure*, and *Fellowship*, as a *Seed* of Eternal Joys.

3. *Particular*: *Religion gives you Joy with Contentment*; with Assurance, and Rest. When you come to God, and have your Joys in him, you are at home, at your End, in your Center: So all the Workings, Desires, Inclinations of your Soul are satisfied, they acquiesce, and are still.

God is your *Beginning*, and your *End*: When you live to him, he gives you assurance in your *Joys*, he seals them to you; because he is the *Beginning*, the first of all. He gives you *Rest* in your Joys, that you care for, you are capable of nothing more; because he is the *End*, the close, the fulness of all.

Happy, and Blessed is he, to whom the Kingdom of God is come: God giveth that man *Joy*, and no trouble; no Stain, no Shame, no Sting with it.

Happy, and Blessed is he, who hath share in this *Joy*, for to him the Bitterness of Death, and every evil is already past.

2. *Part*: *Enlargement*. The *Enlargement* of the Soul in God is the *Second Part* of Spiritual *Joy*. This is fitly exprest by the *Prophet*. Esa. 52. 9. *Break forth into Joy, Sing together, ye wast places of Jerusalem: For the Lord hath comforted his people, he hath redeemed Jerusalem*. The Lord first *Redeems* the Soul, delivers her from the State of Servitude, and Subjection; then she *breaks forth into Joy*.

Natural Joy is the Dilatation, or Enlargement of the *Heart*. Spiritual Joy is the Dilatation, or Enlargement of the *Holy Spirit* in man. When the Divine Principle in the Soul breaks out of the Darkness of our Nature, when it breaks forth from the Bonds of Flesh into its own Liberty, and Freedom: this is the *Kingdom of God*, and the *Joy* thereof in the Soul.

You have this *Joy* of the Kingdom fitly, and fully described in a *Parable*, by our Lord Jesus: *Mat.* 13. 44. *The Kingdom of Heaven is like unto a Treasure hid in a Field: the which, when a man hath found, he hideth, and for Joy thereof goeth, and selleth all that he hath, and buyeth that Field*. The opening of this Parable will tend very much to the Explaining of this *Particular*, of which I am now speaking.

There are *Five Things* to be opened in the *Parable*. 1. The *Field*. 2. The *Treasure* in the Field. 3. The *Concealment* of this Treasure. 4. The *Discovery* of the Treasure. 5. The *Purchase* of the Field.

1. The *Field*. This is the First Thing. *The Kingdom of God is like unto a Treasure hid in a Field*. What should this *Field* be? Can it be any other thing, than the *Natural Image of God* in Man? This is that in which the *Heavenly Image* lies hid, as the *Substance* in the *Shadow*, as the *Child* in the *Mother*, as the *Seed* in the *Field*. This is that, which is not quite *hid*, but is quite *lost* in us; and to be recovered, and re purchased by an Exchange of our *Selves*, and all that *we have*.

As the *Sea* in the Creation expresseth the *Darkness* of the Creature: So the *Earth*

Earth represents the Contrary *Principle* of *Light*, and Beauty in the Creature, which stands up out of that Darkness: *He hath founded it upon*, (*or above*) *the Waters*: *Psal.* 24. 2. God hath given to the *Earth*, a *Principle* of *Strength*, and *Eminency*, by which it appears *out of*, and *above* the *Darkness*, Therefore the *Psalmist* adds in the same place: *He*, (that is, God) *hath established it*, (that is, prepared, adorned, and fixed it, he hath put a Beauty and Strength into it) *above the Floods*, (that is, all Dark, confused, and wandring Principles.) Then he goes on. v. 3. *Who shall go up into the Holy Hill?* (that is, out of the *Waters* of the Darkness of the Creature, which now have over-flown all, into this *Hill*, this *Habitable Earth*, which is above the *Waters*; the *Principle* of Beauty in the Creature, as it is in its *Flower*.) This is the *Earth*, of *which Christ* speaks in a *Parable*, Mark 4. 28. *The Earth of its own accord sends forth the Fruit.*

The *Field* now is the *Natural Image of God* springing up out of the *Principle* of Light in the Creature, and clothing that with itself; as a *Field* doth the *Earth*. This *Field* in its Flourishing State was the *Garden of Eden*, or *Paradise*, which Paradise, though *outwardly*, and in the letter, it was a real *Garden* yet was it also, and principally *Inward*, and in the *Spirit*, the Natural Image of God shining forth with a peculiar Glory upon the Beauty of the Creature.

It is very observable, that *Adam*, when he fell, was cast out of the *Garden*, out of *Paradise* only: *Gen.* 3. 23. *Therefore the Lord God sent him forth from the Garden of Eden.* But *Cain*, when he had killed his Brother, was cast off from the *Face of the Earth*. For so he complains, *Gen.* 4. 14. *Behold I am driven away from the Face of the Earth, and from thy Face shall I be hid.*

There is the *Earth*, the *Face of the Earth*, the *Field*, which is the Natural Image of God; the *Garden*, which is the Glory of the *Field*, the *Face of God* in this Image.

Man fallen from God in *Adam* is banished out of the *Garden*. He hath lost the pleasant, and glorious Appearances of God in him, by the *Natural Image*. Yet he hath the *Field* left in him still, the *Natural Image* itself: which though it be beset, over-grown, shut up with Bryers, and Thorns from the Earth, corruptions, cares, miseries from the Image of the Creature; yet it affords us some low, weak Strength, and Sweetness for man to feed upon. So you shall read, *Gen.* 3. 18. *Bryars, and Thorns shall it bring forth to thee*, (*that is, the Ground*) *and thou shalt eat the Herb of the Field.* Though thou, O man seest no more the *Trees of the Garden*, the high Appearances of God in the Glory of his Image; yet thou shalt have the *Herb* of the *Field* still left thee.

Man, like *Cain* falling into the depth of Sin, murthering in *Abel*, the Image of God remaining in him, hath a Darkness brought upon him, which takes away from him, all the Discoveries of God, with every thing of the Beauty, and Sweetness of his Image. He also hath withdrawn from him all the Comfort, Chearfulness, Vigour, and Life of the *Light-Principle* in the Creature.

Though

Though that *Light-Principle* remains still in him, yet he is restless in it, and as a Stranger to it, rejected by it. Thus *he is driven from the Face of the Earth, he is hid from the Face of God, he is a Vagabond in the Earth.*

We see now, what the *Field* is.

2. *The Treasure.* This is the *Second Thing* in the *Parable*, the *Treasure* hid in the Field. This is *Jesus Christ, Eph.* 3. 8. *Paul* saith of himself, that he was *to make known among the Gentiles, the Unsearchable Riches of Christ.* Jesus Christ is the *Treasure* of *Unsearchable Riches.*

The Lord is the *Seed*, in which all the Vertue, or Powers of God, or the Creature lie wrapt up. He is the *Root*, which bears the variety of all Divine, and Humane Excellencies.

Coloss. 1. 29. *It pleased ~~the Father,~~ that all Fulness should dwell in him:* namely, in Jesus Christ, as in its *Principle.*

Coloss. 2. 9. All the Fulness of the God-Head dwelleth in him Bodily: that is, *fully, flourishingly,* shot forth into all its distinct Branches, and Fruits.

This *Jesus* the Treasure of Heaven lies hid in the Natural Image of God in Man, as the *Seed* lies hid in the *Field*, or as the *Plant* lies hid in its *Seed*, or as the *New Creation* lies hid in the *First Creation.* So St. *Paul* tells us, the *Mystery* of the Gospel *was hid from the Beginning of the World, Ephes.* 3. 9.

Jesus Christ is called the Seed of the Woman in this sense. As *Jesus Christ* is to *God*, his Image, in which he beholds himself: So the *Woman* was to be to the *Man*, who was made in the Image of God. She was to be, as that *Image of God*, drawn forth from *Man*, set continually before the Man, that he might bring forth Children in that Image.

Gen. 2. 23. It is said: *Adam* called her name *Woman, because she was taken out of Man.* Woman in *Hebrew* is *Ishah*, Which is the Name of *God*, and the Name of *Man*, joyned in one, to signify, that the *Woman* was as the Image of God in Nature, sprung forth from Man, and united to him.

Jesus Christ is the *Seed* of this *Woman*, the Natural Image of God in the Creature. This is the *Treasure* in this *Field*, as in a Womb.

3. *Concealment.* The *Third Thing* is the *Concealment* of this Treasure. There is a great deal of difference between the State of *Innocency* in *Nature*; and the State of *Grace* in *Christ.* The *First Adam* had only the *Natural Image* of God appearing and flourishing in him. But a *Saint* under the Gospel hath the Lord Jesus revealed in him, who is the Super-natural, and Heavenly Image, which lay undiscovered in the Perfection of Nature, and did not as yet put forth itself thorow that Inferiour Appearance of God in the first Creation.

The Scripture tells us of *Two Paradises*: an *Earthly*, and a *Heavenly Paradise.*

The Glory of *Nature* before the Fall, was but an *Earthly Paradise*, Gen. 2. 9. *God planted a Garden Eastward in Eden. And out of the Ground the Lord God made to grow every Plant, that was pleasant,* &c. Here you have a *Paradise* made to grow up out of the *Earth.*

The

The Glory of the Gospel in Christ, to which a Saint is to be advanced is a *Heavenly* Paradise, 2 Cor. 12. 2. *I knew a man*, saith St. *Paul, caught up into the Third Heavens.* v. 4. *caught up into Paradise.* Here you have a Paradise *in*, or *above* the Third Heavens.

We read, that the most Holy place was not yet opened while the *First Tabernacle* stood: *Heb.*9.8.*The way into the most Holy place was not yet made manifest, while the First Tabernacle was standing.* So the *Heavenly* Paradise was not discovered, while the *Earthly* Paradise flourished in the Creature, but there was a vail between them. Jesus Christ lay hid in the Image of the Earthly man.

Thus the *Treasure* was *hid* in the *Field, before* the Fall of Man.

But *by* the Fall, the Field itself was lost. The Natural Image of God withdrew, and disappeared in all the *Glory* of it, when man sinned. So far, as it remained; it remains captived, imprisoned by the Devil, under Darkness, Lusts, monstrous Images, *Rom.* 1. 23. Sinful men are said to *change the Glory of the incorruptible God* (in the Natural Image) *into the Image of a Corruptible Man, of four-footed Beasts*, &c. The Fall of Man brought in this Corruptible Image in which Man, and all the Creatures now are, which detains the Image of God, as a Prisoner in itself.

Thus now the *Treasure* is doubly *hid*, in the *Field*, and in the *Bryars*, which over-grow, and hide the *Field* itself.

4. *Discovery*: *Which, when a man finds*, saith Christ.

When Jesus Christ was to come in the Flesh, he sent *John* Baptist to *prepare his way*. This *Preparation* was to be made by a *restoring* of the Divine Image in Nature, which is the *First Restitution* of all things, that was to be made by *Eliah*; and this *Eliah* was *John* the Baptist. He was also *to point out Jesus Christ*; to shew how he was figured out in that First Image, and now ready to break forth thorow this Image.

So, when the Season comes in the Soul, Jesus Christ, the Eternal Image puts up the Natural Image of God in the Soul; and puts forth himself thorow it: as the Seed of Corn first comes up in the tender Blade, like a low *Herb*, an ordinary Grass before it comes forth into the shape of *Corn*.

So the Redemption, and the Discovery begins in the Soul, which makes way for the *Joy* of the Kingdom of God.

5. The *Purchase*. *He hides it, and goes with joy. and sells all that he hath, and buys this Field.* Here the Purchase of the *Field* for the *Treasures* sake is exprest. About this the Soul goes with Joy.

But what means this *Second Concealment*? This *Hiding* of the Treasure again, after that it is once found? This *Hiding* of it is, the *laying it up* in a Mans Heart: The hiding of it in a Mans inward Spirit; and the hiding of a mans self in it, according to his Inward Spirit. A man now draws this Treasure of Glory out of that Fleshly Darkness, under which it lay, into his *inward Principle*; and withdraws his inward Principle out of the Flesh, and the Lusts of it into this Treasure.

Then

Then a Man for the love of this Treaſure, and in the Strength of it, ſells all that *he hath*, caſts away his Corruptions, the Creatures, his own Being, as they are *his own*, as he hath them *in himſelf*, that he may have his own Being, and all the Creatures, in the Natural Image of God; and that Image, in Jeſus Chriſt: And this the Soul doth with Joy. For this is that *Enlargement*, that *Liberty*, which is the *Kingdom of God*, and the *Joy* thereof in the Soul.

Now the *Firſt Image* of God is brought out of its Priſon; now Jeſus Chriſt is brought out of his hidden, ſtreightned State to Freedom in the Soul. Now thoſe Diſcoveries of God, which lay ſhut up in Jeſus Chriſt, as in a Seed, thruſt forth themſelves into Liberty in the Spirit of Man. The Spirit of a man is brought forth from the darkneſs, narrowneſs of Luſts, and the Fleſh, into the Liberty of theſe divine Appearances, into the Spirit of the Lord Jeſus, where the Spirit of man is in a Depth, Height, Breadth, Length, without any Limit, or Confinement. This *Liberty* is the *Divine Joy* of the Spirit.

I will conclude this *Particular* with that place of *Scripture*, Pſal. 96. 12. *Let the Field be joyful, and all that is therein: then ſhall all the Trees of the Wood Rejoyce.*

This *Pſalm* is a *Propheſy* of the State, and times of the Goſpel, as appears by the *Firſt Verſe*, which calls this *Pſalm* a *New Song*. This is the Name, by which the Goſpel is frequently expreſſed in Scripture. The Senſe then of this *Pſalm* is chiefly Spiritual.

In the *Verſe* before this *Twelfth Verſe* we read thus. v. 11. *Let the Heavens rejoyce, and let the Earth be glad, let the Sea roar with the fulneſs thereof.* The Natural Image of God, as it is above the Creature, and the Head of the Creature, is the *Heavens*: The *Earth*, the Light-part: the *Sea*, the Dark part; which both make *One Creature*, as Earth, and Sea make *One Globe*. Then follows. v. 12. *Let the Field rejoyce.* The *Field* is the Image of God, as it grows up out of the Creature, and is the Life of that.

While a man is in a Sinful State, the *Field* languiſheth; the Vertues, and Excellencies of God are withdrawn, and hid in it. But when a man is *New-born*, then this *Field* rejoyceth, and breaks forth into *Singing*. The Diſcoveries of God grow up high, full, and thick, as *Trees* of the Wood, and *Sing* together in the Soul; which is now at *Liberty*, and in *Joy*, in the midſt of them; as in her *Paradiſe* reſtored.

Application.

Uſe. 1. *Information.* That which hath been ſpoken on this Particular inſtructs us in *Three Things* of very great Concernment.

1. *Inſtr. What Man is.* 2. *Inſtr. What a Sinner.* 3. *Inſtr. What a Saint.*

1. *Inſtr. What Man is.* That, which makes a *Man*, is the Natural Image of God. *Firſt is, that which is Natural, then that which is Spiritual,* 1 Corin. 15. 46.

Three Things go to make up the *Being* of a *Man.* To be a *Man* is,

1. To be the *Image of another.* 2. To be the *Image of God.* 3. To be the *Image only, and no more.*

1. *To be a Man, is to be the Image of another. Gen.* 1. 26. God made Man *in an Image, in a Likeness.* He that is a *Man* is to have no *Principle, Form, Activity, Appearance* of his own. But in all he is to answer the *Principle, Forms, Actings, Appearances* of another, in that manner, of which *Solomon* speaks, *Prov.* 27. 19. *As in the Water, Face answers Face: so is the Heart of Man.* Man in this Creation is the *Face* in the *Water,* which answers to another *Face* above the *Water.*

All Creatures are *Representations. Man,* the chief Creature is the chief *Representation.* The Philosopher called Man, ζῷον μιμητικὸν, a Creature made for *Imitation*; to hold forth something *before,* and *above* himself.

St. *Paul* calls the *First Adam* a *Figure* or *Type: Rom.* 5. 14. St. *Paul* in one place tells the *Corinthians,* that he transferred things to himself, and to *Apollos,* as in a *Type,* or *Figure,* for their sakes. Man is to possess his Being, and all things, that appertain to it, as *in a Figure,* as a *Type* of some higher thing.

With what Humility, and Peace? In what Silence, and Satisfaction would Man live, if he did but know himself; that he *walkt in a Figure*; that his whole *Being,* and *Life* is altogether a *Figure* of something above him, something to come, which is to be revealed in him?

What would become of all our Pride, Plots, Passions; if we knew; that Man is as the *Reflection* of the Light of the Sun from a Glass upon a wall. That *reflection,* that Light upon the wall *danceth,* and *trembleth,* as the Glass moveth, from which it is cast? The *Sun* is *God*: the *Light Jesus Christ*: the *Glass,* the *Angelical Nature*: the *Reflection,* or Light on the Wall, the *Earthly Man.*

This is the *First Thing* in the *Being* of a *Man.*

2. *To be a Man, is to be the Image of God, Gen.* 1. 26. God made man *in his own Image, and Likeness,* Rom. 5. 14. *The First Man was the Figure of him, who was to come*: that is, of Jesus Christ.

Man is the *Supream,* and *Universal* Image of God in the *First Creation*; as Jesus Christ is in the *Second,* Eccles. 6. 10. *That which hath been, it is named already, that it is man: and he may not contend with him, who is mightier than he. Man* is *all* in this *First Creation* which is that, which hath been already, and is now faded, passing away, but this *Man* must yield to *Jesus Christ,* who is coming, and bringing with him a New Creation.

So far thou art a *Man,* as thou comprehendest, sustainest, subduest, possessest enjoyest all Images of things among the *Creatures, in thy self,* as the *Universal Image*; and *thy self,* as an *Image,* in the *Appearance of God.*

He indeed is a *Man,* and lives, as the *Image* of God, who lives at a Height above the Creatures, *in himself*; and at a Height above himself, *in God.*

That

That, by which we ſee a Building, a Wood, a large Proſpect, or the Body of Heaven, is a very *little thing*, and lies in a little compaſs in the *Apple* of the Eye, as *one* with it. But it ſhews not the Eye, to the Eye; nor itſelf to the Eye; but only thoſe things, which it repreſents. Man is the great *Repreſentative* of God. He ceaſeth to be a *Man*, ſo far, as he ſees any thing, beſides *himſelf*, in the Creatures; and any thing beſides *God*, in himſelf.

As God in Divine things: ſo Man, as the Image of God in Natural things, is to be *All in All*. This is the *Natural Righteouſneſs*, and Perfection of Man, thus to ſtand in the Image of God.

This is the *Second Thing*.

3. *To be a Man, is to be the Image only, and no more. David* ſaith, *Pſal.* 39. 6. *Man walks in a vain ſhow*: an empty Image. And leaſt you ſhould think, that this is ſpoken of Man only ſince his Fall: when man was firſt made in a State of Perfection, *Gen.* 1. 26. it is ſaid, that *God made man in his own Image, and Likeneſs*: the very ſame word is uſed there by *Moſes*, which is uſed here by *David*: TSELEM. The Word ſignifies a *Dying Shadow*.

Man is only a *Shadow* of God without the *Subſtance*: a *Shadowy* Image, not a *Subſtantial* one: an *Image*, which ſubſiſts by the *Subſtance*, and hath the *Likeneſs* of it: but poſſeſſeth not the *Subſtance* with the *Life* in itſelf.

The Difference between *Man*, as he was created at firſt, and the *Lord Jeſus*, is expreſſed by *St. Paul*, 1 Corin. 15. 49. *As we have born the Image of the Earthly, ſo ſhall we bear the Image of the Heavenly alſo.* Man is an *Earthly Image*: Jeſus Chriſt is the *Heavenly Image* of God.

Earth is an Image of Heaven in a baſer Subſtance, or Kind. *Man* is an *Image* of God in a Principle of Darkneſs, which hides, and vails the *Subſtance*. Jeſus Chriſt is a *Perfect Image*, which holds forth the *Subſtance* clearly, and is *One* with it.

Thus *Man at his beſt Eſtate is altogether Vanity*, as *David* ſpeaks.

So we have ſeen, *what Man is*: by which we ſee, from whence we are fallen: How little of *Man* there is left in *Man*. When Man was perfect, Humility, Submiſſion, Obedience was the Perfection of man, as being an Image only. What little reaſon then hath empty, wretched man *now* for Pride, Vainglory, Confidence, Self-love?

I have done with the *Firſt Inſtruction*.

2. *Inſtr. What a Sinner is.* A Sinner *un-mans* himſelf. He puts himſelf out of the Image of God into ſome low, inferiour Image of a Creature. God complains of ſinful men, *Pſal.* 4. 2. *How long will ye turn my Glory into Shame?* Man is the *Glory of God*, Saith *St. Paul*; that is, the Image of God. Man by by Sin exchangeth this Glorious Image for ſome baſe Image among the Creatures, which becomes an Idol, and a Reproach, when it is not held in the Image of God, as in its Head. Thus Man *turns the Glory of God into Shame*.

O! That we did underſtand, how Glorious an Image *Man* is by his Creation; what a change *Sin* hath made in him! We should then hate *Sin* to purpose, and tremble at every Act of it.

A *Sinner* is. { 1. *The Ape of a Man*, and not a *Man*.
2. *A Monster*.
3. *A Devil*. }

1. *A Sinner is the Ape of a Man*, and not a *Man*: He is a Beast in the Likeness of a Man: or the Image of Man shut up, and imprisoned in a Brutish Principle, and Image.

Psal. 49. 12. *Man being in Honour continueth not, but becomes like the Beast that perisheth.* By each act of Lust, Passion, any inordinate Inclination toward any Created Appearance, thou un-clothest thy self of the Image of God, which is *thine Honour*, and clothest thy self with a Particular Image, which, if it be without Life, is a Stock, or a Stone, if it have Life is a Beast. So, whil'st thou livest in it, thou art but the *Ape* of a Man, and a true Beast; putting on contempt, scorn, and Death; instead of Honour, and Immortality.

2. *A Sinner is a Monster.* When thou sinnest, thou confoundest the *Excellent Image* in thee with a *base Image*, so thou makest thy self a *Monster*.

Gen. 6. 2. *The Sons of God saw the Daughters of men, and took Wives of them.* Then at the fourth v. we read; that *there were Gyants upon the Earth in those days.* Give me leave to make an *Allegory*, or an *Allusion* of this Story, which you please.

The Divine Image is the Man, the *Son of God*: All the Inferiour Images of the Creatures descend from this, depend on this, are the *Secondary*, and *weaker Births* of it. So they are the *Daughters of Men*.

While the Image of God in Man holds the lower Images of things in a *Subjection*, and *subordination* to itself, as *Daughters* to their *Father*: all things then are in their Order, and Beauty.

But when the *Son of God*, the Supream Image, which is Man, looks down, and dotes upon the Inferiour Images the *Daughters of Men*; when it marries, and mingles itself with them, then confusion comes in: then this Beautiful Image, *Man*, becomes a *Monster*, and brings forth Monsters.

Now *Gyants are born:* Man comes forth in a greatness, and force resembling the Image of God in Man, but is in the true Form, and Principle of a Beast. The Divine Image is fallen, imprisoned, dead in the midst of all this Greatness.

Thus of a truth *Sin* is the highest Incest, the most unnatural confusion, the true Engendring of Monsters.

3. *A Sinner makes himself a Devil.* A man by Sin withdraws the Creature from the Image of God: sets it up in its own Principle, and Image: so maintains it in the place of, and against the Image of God.

Rom. 1. 25. St. Paul sets forth the Nature of Sin after this manner. *who changed the Truth of God into a Lie, serving the Creature more than the Creator, who is blessed for ever.* See here the nature of the *Devil* discovered in a *Sinner*.

When

When thou fatherest any Sin, thou by that Act makest thy self the Father of *Idolatry*, *Lies*, and *Murther*.

1. *Thou* makest thy self by Sin the *Father of Idolatries*: Thou settest up the Creature above the Creator, and servest that, more than thou dost him; Sacrificing thy Heart, thy Love, and thy Life to it.

2. *Thou* makest thy self by Sin the *Father of Lies*: thou settest up the Creature; as if it were something *of*, and *in* it self; when as it is meerly nothing, save as it is *in* the Image of God.

3. *Thou* makest thy self by Sin the *Father of Murthers*: Thou killest, and destroyest the Image of God; which is the First Murther, and the Fountain of all Murthers. Thou *changest the Truth of God into a Lie*. Thou makest away that Image of God, which is the *Truth*, and *Life* of all the Creatures; by setting up instead of it those things, which as they are in themselves, without that Image, are not only *Vanity*, but a *Lie* too.

He knows very little of the Nature of *Man*, of the *Creature*, of *God*; who knows not *Sin* to be the most ridiculous *Apishness*, that he may *despise* it: the most horrid *Monstrousness*, that he may *hate* it: the highest *Devilishness*, that he may *tremble* at it, and fly from it.

So much for the Second Instruction, which shews us, *what a Sinner is*.

3. *Instr. What a Saint is.* Then a Man begins to be a Saint, when the *Natural Image* of God begins to be restored in him with advantage; with the advantage of the *Super-natural Image* bringing it forth again *from* itself, and itself *in* it, together *with* it.

The *Kingdom of God* brings forth itself, and the *Kingdom of Nature* a Second time in itself. *Behold, I make all things new*, Saith *Jesus Christ*, when he appears in the Soul.

The *Second Adam* revives, and restores the *First Adam*, in us; but as in its own Spirit, and Bosom; that so the *Earthly* Man may become *Heavenly*, and Immortal.

I will conclude this use with *Consolation* to *Two Sorts* of Mourners, *Gods Mourners*.

1. *Consolation.* You who have lost the Innocency of your Natures in Sin, and Guilt; be you comforted in the knowledge of this: The Righteousness of God, the Eternal Image of Glory shall break forth in your Souls, and bring forth the First Image of Beauty, your Natural Innocency again upon you; with an Increase of Glory.

It is the Lord that justifies, who shall condemn: Saith St. *Paul*, *Rom.* 8. 34. Who, or what Guilt shall condemn thee, or be able to sink for ever the Innocency, and Beauty of thy Nature; though it now have lain long buried under thy Lusts? The Lord, the Lord himself shall come, and this Beauty of thine shall come with him, and thou shall see it again with Joy.

2. *Consolation.* You, who have lost the Chearfulness of your Spirits, and the

the ſweet Pleaſantneſs of your Natural tempers in Melancholy, and Terrours, comfort your ſelves in the knowledge of this. The Spring of Joys, the Eternal Spirit, the Spirit of our Lord Jeſus ſhall open itſelf within you; and ſhall ſend forth from itſelf the ancient ſtreams of your firſt Peace, and joys; of your natural chearfulneſs. Your natural Spirits ſhall once more dance, and ſing together in this Spirit.

All your Springs are in this Heavenly Image: the Springs of your firſt Innocency, Beauty, Peace, Pleaſantneſs. All ſhall open themſelves again upon you from the Boſom of this Image, at the Appearance of it, never to be ſhut more. And this Heavenly Image ſhall certainly appear in you. Only do you wait with Hope, and Patience for the appointed Seaſon.

Do not mourn at the Death of any natural Beauty, or Content, as without Hope ever to ſee it again; the Hour comes apace, and perhaps now is, in which thy dead Innocency, and Joys ſhall hear the Voice of the Son of Man, Jeſus Chriſt in thee, and live again by him.

Do not doubt, but believe. The Earth ſhall hear the Heaven. The Earthly Image of Life, Paradiſe, and Heaven in thee ſhall be awakened again in thy Spirit by the manifeſtation of thy Saviour in thee. Thine Eyes ſhall ſee thy Redeemer; and he ſhall ſtand the laſt upon the Earth. Thine Eyes ſhall certainly ſee Jeſus Chriſt, when he ſhall redeem the Earthly Man in thee with all its Excellency, and Sweetneſs from theſe Powers of Sin, Fear, Death, and Hell, which have carried it captive. And thou ſhalt ſee this Jeſus the Heaven of God, the Heavenly Image, laſt of all ſtanding, and appearing in thy Earth, thy Earthly Man, thy firſt Image.

Be of good chear, faint not. Death ſhall not prevent this Bleſſedneſs. Thou ſhalt live, when God ſhall do all this; thine Eyes ſhall behold it, and thou ſhalt taſte of it, and feed upon it. For God hath undertaken it, and he will bring it to paſs. *Behold I make all things new*; ſaith *He*, who is the *firſt, and the laſt.* Believe, and wait: for *theſe words are True, and Holy*. Revel. 21. 5, 6. *And he that ſate upon the Throne ſaid: Behold I will make all things new. And he ſaid, Write*, (write upon your Hearts this Sentence, behold, I the Lord make all things new.) *For theſe words are True, and Holy. And he ſaid unto me; It is done:* (This is the Finiſhing of all things, the ending of the Myſtery) *I am Alpha, and Omega, the Beginning, and the End: I will give unto him, that is a thirſt, of the Fountain of the Water of Life Freely*, that is, without any thing of *Suitableneſs* to it, or *Satisfaction* for it, without any *Condition*, or *Confinement*.

3. *Part: The Activity of the Soul in God.* This is the *Third*, and *laſt Part* of *Divine Joy*.

The *Pſalmiſt* expreſſeth *Joy* by *Shouting*, and *Singing*: Pſal 65. 13. *The Paſtures are clothed with Flocks*; (the Appearances of God are Green, and Flouriſhing, they bring forth, maintain, and put forth themſelves into nume-

rous

rous Flocks of Saints:) *the Valleys also are covered with Corn*; (The lowest State of things in the Flesh, and the Natural Man are cloathed with Jesus Christ, and grow up into him, who is the Bread, and Beauty of Eternal life.) *they Shout for Joy, they also Sing*. This is *Spiritual Musick*, the working of *Spiritual Joy*, to *Shout*, and to *Sing*.

We read of a *Two-fold Song*, which Spiritual Persons sing, *Revel.* 15. 3. *They Sing the Song of Moses, and of the Lamb*. The *Song of Moses* is *the Law*; *the Song of the Lamb*, *the Gospel*. When the Children of *Israel* had passed thorow the Red Sea, and saw their Enemies lie dead on the Shore: then they Sung the Song of *Moses*, who drew them out of those *Waters*, according to the *Signification* of his *Name*.

When the Soul hath escaped out of the Sea of *Blood* mingled with *Fire*, which is the Dissolution of her *Natural Principles* in Troubles, and Terrours by the *Baptism of the Spirit*; when shee sees her Spiritual Enemies slain on the *Dry Land* of Christs Spiritual Appearance: then she Sings the *Song of the Lamb, who was dead, but is alive, and lives for ever*; the Song of Peace.

Singing *naturally*, with the outward voice, is the highest, and fullest *Activity* of the *Natural Spirits*. So Singing *Spiritually*, and with the Inward Man is the highest *Activity* of the *Spirit* in our *Spiritual Part*.

This *Spiritual Musick*, or *Singing*, which is the working of the Wine of *Spiritual Joy* in the Soul, consists of *Three Things*.

1. *The Heightning of the Soul towards God.*
2. *The Tuning of the Soul to God.*
3. *The Exercise, or Entertainment of the Soul upon God, and with God.*

1. *The Heightning of the Soul towards God.* This is *one Piece* of that *Activity* of *Spiritual Joy*, which is the *true Musick* of the Soul.

In that place cited before, *Psal.* 65. 13. *Singing*, and *Shouting* are put together, 1 *Thessal.* 4. 16. *The Lord Jesus* is said *to descend from Heaven with a Shout*. This *Shout* is the *Awakening*, and the *Elevation* of the Soul, or Body towards the highest State of things, by the *Powerful breakings forth* of the Glory of God upon them.

Psal. 57. 7. *David* had said: *I will Sing, and give Praise*. Then he calls upon himself, v. 8. *Awake up my Glory, awake my Psaltery, and Harp*: *I my self will awake right early*.

Some say, *Davids Glory* was his *Tongue*: but then sure it was such a *Tongue of Fire*, as sat upon the Heads of the Apostles, a *Tongue* of *Spiritual Manifestations*, and Heavenly Glory, like a *Flame*, *enlightning*, and *heating* both at once.

Man is the Glory of God; saith St. Paul, 1. *Corin.* 11. 7. The *Spiritual Man* is the *true*, and *Spiritual* Glory of God. The *Natural Man* is but a *Shadowy Glory*.

David calls upon his *Glory* to *awake*; as distinct from *himself*; and then he saith: *I shall awake*; like that of St. *Paul*, Galat. 2. 20. *I live not, but Christ in me*: there is the *Glory* awakening itself: *and the Life, that I live, is by the Faith of the Son of God*: there is *himself* awakened in that Glory.

Then the *Soul sings*, when the Life of Jesus Christ, which is her *Glory, awakens* itself in her, and awakens her together with itself, into the *Light of God*, to a *Contemplation of*, and *fixing upon* his Beauties. Now the *Soul* is above her ordinary Pitch, as *Waking* is above *Sleeping*. Now she sits above herself, upon the top of her *Spiritual* Principles, as a *Bird* upon the *Top-branch* of a Tree, Singing in the *Sun-shine*, the highest Light of *Divine Discoveries*.

This is the *First thing* in this *Activity*, or *Spiritual Musick*.

2. *The Tuning of the Soul to God*. In that fore-mentioned *Psalm*, *Psal*. 57. 7. *David* speaks of *awakening* three distinct *Lives*: *His Glory*: *His Psaltery, and Harp*: *Himself*. The *Glory* is *Jesus Christ* in the *Soul*. *Self* is the *Soul*. The *Psaltery* and *Harp* those *Heavenly* Principles, and *Powers*, which as *Ministring Spirits*, go forth from Jesus Christ into the Soul, *suiting*, *fitting*, and *tuning* the Soul to her Saviour.

Revel. 15. 2. St. *John saw the Saints, that had gotten the victory over the Beast, stand upon a Sea of Glass mingled with Fire, and the Harps of God in their hands*. Then in the next verse they *Sing*.

The *Sea* is *this Creation*, especially the *Invisible*, the *Angelical* Part of it. In this State it is a *dark, troubled, foaming Sea*. But in the Kingdom of Christ it shall be a *Sea of Glass*, a *Chrystalline Sea*, clear, calm, fresh taking in, and holding forth the Lord Jesus, the *Image*, and *Face* of God, as a *Glass*, as a pleasant Stream. The *Fire*, with which it shall be mingled, shall be the *Spirit of God, and of Glory* resting upon the Creature.

The Saints standing upon this *Sea*, shall have the *Harps of God* in their hands. *Angels* are the *Trumpets of God*. This State of the Saints, which is here described, is their *Angelical State*, when they shall be *like the Angels*. These Harps of God then are *Angelical Tempers*, and *Principles*, which Jesus Christ brings forth, and puts into the Soul, *as Harps* into their *Hands*, by which they are tuned, and fitted, made ready *for Him*, to sing *to Him*.

Thus the Soul is *tuned* to God, being put into a Spiritual, and Heavenly Temper, like an *Angel* beholding the Face of God, and in a readiness to Sing forth, to Sing aloud his Glory.

Coloss. 3. 16. St. *Paul* speaks of *Spiritual Songs*, which they were to Sing *with Grace in their Hearts*. This is that, which *David* calls *his Harp*. This is the *Harp of God in the hands* of the Saints, the *Grace of God in their Hearts*.

This is the *Tuning* of the Soul to Christ, the Receiving of *Grace for Grace* from Christ, the winding up of Grace in the Heart to a pitch of Conformity, and Communion with Jesus Christ, like the *Tuning* of two voices, or Instruments one to another; that so Christ and the Soul may make Musick each to other, and have their *Joy fulfilled* in one another.

So much for the *Second Thing*.

3. *The*

3. *The Exercise, and Entertainment of the Soul upon God, and with God.* This is the *Third thing* in the Souls *Singing* for *Joy.*

David saith in one place: *I will Sing of thy Righteousness*: and in another: *I will Sing of thy Power.*

The *Spiritual Joy*, and *Musick* of a Saint is to fly abroad among the Excellencies of the Divine Nature: to enlarge, and act his Spirit to the Height upon the Beauties, and Brightnesses in the Face of God; the Uprightness, Truth, Perfection in the Heart of God; the Freedom, Fulness, Fruitfulness, Infiniteness, in the Spirit, and Life of God.

David hath often expressions to this purpose: *I will Sing to thee*: *I will Sing to the Lord.* So St. *Paul* speaks: *Making melody to God.* The Holy Soul Sings *of God, to God.*

Spiritual Joy is the *Free letting forth* of the Spirit *with* God, *concerning* God. It is often the Work, and Delight of a Holy Soul to open her mouth wide, to take in to the utmost, the contemplation of God, the communications of his Greatness, Fulness, Sweetness, Glory: and then, when she is fullest, to pour forth herself again into the Ear, and Bosom of her God.

You may see this in the *Psalmist*, *Psalm* 45. 1. *My Heart is enditing a good matter. I speak of the things touching the King. My Tongue is as the pen of a ready writer.*

The Heart was here full. A Spring of Heavenly Sweetness had opened itself in it. It bubled, and boyled up apace. It enlarged itself into a Flood of matter. But all was *touching the King*, the Beauty, the Glory, the Graciousness, the Pleasantness, the Love, the Power of Jesus Christ. And the Heart *full* of this Blessed matter, empties itself again as *fully* upon Jesus Christ. *My Tongue is as the Pen of a ready Writer.*

I have now shewn you the *Third Part* of *Spiritual Joy*, which is the *Activity of the Soul in God.*

Use. 1. *For Instruction. Spiritual Joy* is no *Secure, Slothful, Carnal* thing.

1. *Spiritual Joy is no Secure thing.* It hath the *least*, and the *greatest* Security in it. It suffers a man to be least of all secure in himself, or in any Creature; that he may be most secure in God.

True *Joy* consists in the *Heightning of the Soul towards God.* The Soul, that is acquainted with this Joy, hath a Fear, and Trembling upon her, while she is among the Creatures, though she be in the Fulness of them. She can rest no where, till she get up above them all, and come to God.

God makes a Gracious Promise to a good Man, *Psal.* 91. 14. *I will set him on high, because he hath known my name.* The word signifies the setting of a man in a *Strong Castle* situate on a *High Rock.* The God-Head is the *Rock*, the *Messiah*, or the Humanity of Jesus Christ, is the *Castle* upon this Rock.

A Holy Soul is in *Safety*, and may be in very great Security; but not in her self, nor in the World. Her Safety, and Security lies in being carried upward, and set on high, in being encompassed with Jesus Christ, and God, as with a Tower of Defence.

The Soul hath her *high Rock*, and her Strong Castle of Spiritual Joy, and Triumph; not in the knowledge of any thing here below, not in any Earthly acquaintance; but in the knowledge of God. *I will set him on High, because he hath known me.*

If we be in the Light, as God is Light; then is our Joy full; and the consolations of the Lord Jesus cleanse our Hearts from all Clouds of Griefs, and Fears.

This is the *First Instruction.*

2. *Spiritual Joy is no Sluggish Thing.* It is the *Enlargement*, and *Activity* of the Soul.

I went by the Field of the Sluggard, saith *Solomon*, *and I saw it over-grown with Thorns.* Thy *Spirit* is thy *Field.* If thou be not *plowing* it up with the Cross of Christ; and *sowing* it with the Seeds of Grace, Glory, and Immortality by the Life of Christ; and waiting for, and gathering, and feeding upon the Appearances of these in thee; thou art this Sluggard, and canst expect nothing but Thorns.

That Soul which is not Spiritually *active* in Christ, will be miserably *passive* in Cares, and Confusions,

Divine Joy is the Highest, and most Harmonious Activity of the Soul upon the highest Excellencies of the Best, and most Blessed Object, which is Jesus Christ.

While the Husband-man sleepeth, Tares are Sown. If Jesus Christ be asleep in the Ship, the Winds toss it, and the Waves fill it. A sleepy, or sluggish temper of Spirit breeds Fears, Cares, and all Sorts of Troubles.

Awaken the Lord Jesus in thy Spirit, and be thy self awake in his Spirit, if thou wouldst have Peace, and Joy.

3. *Spiritual Joy is no Carnal, or Fleshly Thing.* This is the *Third Instruction.* The Joy of the Spirit is the *Exercise, and Entertainment of the Soul on* God.

Mark the Temper, and Spirit of *St. John*, 1 John 1. 3. *That, which we have seen, and heard, declare we unto you, that ye also may have Fellowship with us; and truly our Fellowship is with the Father, and with the Son Jesus Christ.* v. 4. *And these things write we unto you, that your Joy may be full.* v. 5. *This then is the Message, which we have heard of him, and declare unto you, that* God *is Light, and in him there is no Darkness at all.*

Spiritual *Joy* springs from *seeing* Spiritual Objects, and *hearing* Spiritual Mysteries. *The Eye is not satisfied with seeing, nor the Ear with hearing*: Saith *Solomon, Eccl.* 1. 8. The Natural Eye, and Ear can convey no Satisfaction to us. For they are but a *Dream.* The Sight, and hearing of the Things of *this Life* can give no Satisfaction; for they are but a *Shadow.*

A *Full Joy*, *Joy*, and fulness both together come by a Spiritual way of seeing, and hearing the Things of *Eternal Life.*

You

You may have a *slight, empty, vanishing* Joy *by Fellowship* with the Pleasures, and Glories of the Flesh.

But if you will have a *full*, and *solid* Joy, which may endure for ever, your *Fellowship must be with the Father, and the Son Jesus Christ.*

Bring before your Spirits the Excellencies, and Delights of the whole World. Let all the Creatures send into your Souls from the *best Hand, Messages* of their Loveliness and Loves. You for all this can have no true Joy, no compleat Joy in any of these things. For all the Creatures have in their highest Sweetnesses, and Glories a Darkness, which will beget Doubts, Fears, and Distractions in you.

Would you have Joy? Seek it in the *Declaration* and Discovery of God, *who is Light, and hath no Darkness in him.* Seek it in the Contemplations of God *by his own Light.*

So long thou shalt have Peace, and Joy, as thou turnest away thy Spirit from the Lying Vanities of the Creature; and takest in, and livest upon *Messages of God*, which are brought in upon thee *by God* himself.

Behold the *Face* of God, and thy Heart shall live in Pleasures. For in his Face is the Fulness of Joy, with all manner of Pleasantnesses, without any uncomfortable Dash, or Mixture of Darkness. But, while thine Eye looks upon the Sparklings, or Appearances of any Creature, thine Heart shall never be without the *biting of the Serpent.*

So much for the *First Use.*

Use 2. *Exhortation.* Press forward toward the High Calling of this *Royal*, and *Joyful State* in Religion.

Your Fears, Doubts, and Servile Tempers in your Religion arise from a want of Growth. Forget that, which you have already attained, and follow hard after Jesus Christ. There is before you a State of Peace, Pleasure, and Perfection in a kind.

Travel on thorow this vale of Tears, in which you now are, from Strength to Strength; till you come to see the God of Gods, on Mount *Sion,* in this State of Royalty, and Joy.

But you may now ask me *Two Questions.*

Quest. 1. Whether is this *Royal* and *Joyful State* of Holiness attainable in this Life? May we enter into the *Kingdom of Heaven,* before we go out of *this Body?* Doth not *St. Paul* say; that *Flesh, and Blood cannot inherit the Kingdom of Heaven?* 1 *Corin.* 15. 50.

My *Answer* to this *Question* is *Four-fold.*

1. *Answ.* So far, as we are *risen* with Christ, while we are on *Earth*; So far we are entred into the *Kingdom of Heaven*, before we are out of the *Body.*

St. Paul speaks to the *Colossians,* as being *Risen* with Jesus Christ, *Col.* 3. 1. *If ye then be Risen with Christ, seek those things, which are above, where Christ sitteth on the Right Hand of God.*

2. *Answ.* We may in this Life attain to a State of *Royalty*, and Joy *Com-*

paratively. We may come to that Degree of Liberty, Power, Peace, and Pleasure in Holiness; which may be a *Resurrection* into the *Kingdom* of God, and Heaven, compared with lower Degrees of Grace, thorow which we pass.

St. *Paul* speaks to the *Galatians*: *But now after that ye have known God, or rather are known of God, how turn ye again to the weak, and beggerly Elements, whereunto ye desire again to be in Bondage? Galat.* 4. 9. Here you have described a *Two-fold State* of *Grace* on Earth. The *First* is in these words: *After that ye have known God, or rather are known of God.* This knowledge of God is *in the Spirit*, and *Truth*. There the Apostle expresseth it *rather*, by a *being known of God*; or, as some interpret it, a *being made to know by God.* The sense is the same, which is this: The coming in of God after a *Spiritual manner*, and making himself *in the Spirit One* with our Spirits; so that God in the *Power* of his Spirit is the *Principle by which* we know: and God in the *Appearance* of his Spirit is the *Object which* we know.

Now *we know God*, not an *Earthly Figure* only of God. Now we are *known of God.* For we are taken up into the *Light*, and *Spirit* of God. Now we are *made to know by God.* For it is God, who both *knows*, and *is known* in us. It is the *Light*, and *Spirit* of God, *in*, and *by* which we know.

The *Second State* described is in these words: *How turn ye again to weak, and beggerly Elements?* The *Principles* of this Creation are these *Elements*, which are *weak*, because they cannot hold forth God to us, but in a very *uncertain* way, full of *Fear*, and *Doubt*. They are *Beggerly*, because they can convey to us very little of the *Riches*, *Fulness*, *Greatness*, *Grace*, *Glory* of God.

When we *first* come to the knowledge of God, for the most part we know him after this manner, by the *Rudiments* of the *Flesh*, the *Elements* of *this World.* And so long we are in *Bondage*, carried on by *Fear*, and *Hope*, in a Servile way: seeing very little Glory, enjoying very little *Freedom* in our Religion.

You that are in this Condition, whose *Fears* are your *Food*, whose *Tears* are your *Drink*, by Day and Night: Up, and be travelling forward thorow this Shadowy Vale, you may come to such a State of Holiness even here in this Life, as will be a Heaven compared with this Wilderness, in which now you wander. When you shall attain to a *Spiritual understanding* of Things, you will think your selves come forth from a *Prison-house*, in which before, like *Samson*, you were made to Grind, with your *Eyes out*; into a *Palace*, where you sit, and reign like Kings, in a Divine *Light*, *Liberty*, and *Joy*.

Thus we may, while we live here, attain to a *State* of *Royalty Comparatively*, in respect to the *former State* of our Spirits, in an *Inferiour Degree* of Holiness.

3. *Answ.* We may enjoy the *Kingdom of Heaven* on *Earth* in the *First-fruits* of it.

Rom. 8. 23. St. *Paul* saith in the name of those Saints, that were as he was: *Not only they,* (that is, the Creature) *but we also, who have the First-fruits*

fruits of the Spirit, even we our selves, groan in our selves, waiting for the Adoption, that is, the Redemption of our Bodies.

The *First-fruits of the Spirit* is the *Kingdom of God* in the *First-fruits.* For the *Kingdom of God is in the Holy Ghost.* And *where the Spirit of the Lord is, there is Liberty.*

These *First-fruits* are not from that Life, which the Soul hath in the *Body.* For in that Life she *groans* for the *Adoption.* But they are from that Life, which she hath above the *Body* in her *Spirit,* of which she hath some *Glympses, Reflections,* and *Fore-tasts,* as she is in the *Body.* And these are her *First-fruits.*

The *Body* is, as yet, *Un-redeemed* from a *Double Darkness,* that of the *Flesh,* and that of the *Devil.* The Soul, as she lives in the Body, hath her *Communion* with *God* in the *Elements of One,* in the *Enmity* of the *Other*; as kept under by a *hard Master,* and opposed by a *cruel Enemy* both at once.

4. *Answ.* We may on *Earth* enter into the *Kingdom of Heaven,* and the *Joy of our Lord,* by *Faith.*

2. *Corin.* 5. 6, 7. *We are alwaies Confident, knowing, that, while we are at home in the Body, we are absent from the Lord. For we walk not by Sight, but by Faith.*

St. Paul plainly signifies; that *our Presence* in the *Body* necessarily imports, and carries along with it an *Absence* from the *Lord Jesus.* But this is in respect to the *Presence* of *Vision,* and *Sight*; not of *Faith.*

While we are in the Body, we may have that *Presence* of the *Lord* by *Faith,* which we shall have by *Sight,* when we are out of the *Body.*

This *Body* is an *Image,* which bears a *Representation* of the Divine Body, or Image of Things in the Spirit; but together with a *Darkness hiding* that Divine Image, which is Christ, and a *Contrariety opposing* it.

The Lord *Jesus* by his Spirit shews forth himself in this Bodily Life to us, so that we see him in the *Fleshly Image,* as in a *Glass*; under a *Fleshly Vail,* as in the *Dark*; thorow the *Contrariety* of the *Fleshly Appearance,* as in a *Riddle.* Yet we see *Him,* we enjoy his true Appearance in the midst of all these *Difficulties.* And while we see him, we see all these *Difficulties* reconciled, and subdued in *Him*; we our selves live in *Him.* Thus we enter into the *Kingdom,* and *Joy* of *Heaven* by *Faith,* even while we are in the *Fleshly Body* to *Sight.*

When we dye, then the Fleshly Body, and Image is swallowed up in Eternal Darkness. Our Souls then come *Home* to Jesus Christ; they enjoy the *Heavenly Appearance* of Things in its own Likeness, *Face to Face,* by *Sight*; no more by *Faith*: no more in a *Glass,* or in a *Riddle*; because the *Fleshly Body* is taken away: but yet in the *Dark* still; not with a Perfect *Clearness,* or *Fulness*; though with a *Nearness,* and *Likeness*; until the *Body* be re-assumed out of that *Darkness,* as a *Divine Body.* Then, as in Christ, so in us, the *Fulness* of the God-Head shall dwell *Bodily,* in its own Body, which is our Body risen again out of *Flesh,* and *Nature* into the *Spirit.*

Till

Till then we have the *Fulness* of the God-Head dwelling in us in a *Contrary Body, before* Death: We have have it dwelling in us *without a Body*, like an *Appearance*, or *Apparition*, like a *Soul without a Body*, *in* Death.

I will attempt to make the *Answer* to this *Question* more plain, and perfect by a Two-fold *Distinction*.

1. *Distinct.* The *Spiritual Man* hath a *Three-fold State.*

1. The *Spiritual Man* at *first* lies hid under the *Natural Man*, as *Seed* under the Ground. So *St. Paul* speaks of it, *Gal.* 3. 19. *Wherefore then served the Law, it was added because of Transgressions, till the Seed should come, to whom the Promise was made: and it was ordained by Angels in the hand of a Mediator.*

While a Man lives under the *Law*, the *Seed* of Promise is not yet come, that is, the *Spiritual Man*, which is One with Christ, and so the *Promised Seed* is not come up, or put forth in the Soul. But it lies hid under the *Ministry* of *Angels*, which restrain Sin by inward *Impressions*, and outward *Dispensations* of the Good, or Evil Things of this World: and it lies hid under a *Mediator*, which is the *Earthly Image* of God, according to this Creation, in which God stands as a *Mediator*, between Man, and Himself in the *Spiritual Image*, which is the Heavenly Person of Jesus Christ. God in this Earthly Image *Heightens*, and *Suppresseth* Sin, by his *Divided Appearances* of Mercy, and Wrath; by his *Divided Administrations* of Allurement, and Terror; Reward and Punishment.

Thus God as a *Mediator* stands between Man, and the Person of Christ; hiding that Person, together with the Spiritual Man, which is in Christ from Man. And so God converseth with Man, at this Distance, after this manner, till the *Seed come*, in which *God* and *Man* are no more *Two*, but *One Spirit* in Jesus Christ.

This is the *First State* of the *Spiritual Man.*

2. *Secondly*, the *Spiritual Man* breaks forth thorow the *Natural Man*, appears *in* it, and together *with* it, *Gal.* 2. 20. *I live, yet not I, but Christ liveth in me; and the life, which I live, is by the Faith of the Son of God*, &c.

Christ, and the *Spiritual Man* are joyned together by an inseparable Union. When these break forth in a Man yet clothed with *Flesh*; they draw the *Person* of a Man, to have his Life *in themselves*, as in his *proper Principle.* They shew forth themselves to him, as that *Appearance*, and *Image* of Things, in which he is to dwell. The *Principles* of *Nature* are now as a Death to a Man, so far, as he abides in them. The *Fleshly Image* of Things, is a *Prison*, or an *Inchantment*, or a *Whorish Woman* to him. He loaths the Embraces of it, though he cannot quite shake it off. A Saint now labours to crucify, and cast off both these. Yet while he is shut up in them, he comforts himself *in*, he casts himself *upon* the Spiritual Man; and the Life of Christ, which dwell *in These* together with him, and look forth *thorow these*, as thorow the *Lattices* upon him,

3. The *Third State* of the *Spiritual Man*, is that, in which he is *Absolute*, free

ſree from the Bonds of the *Fleſh*, no more *Comprehended by*, but *Comprehending* the *Natural Man in* himſelf.

St. Paul ſpeaks of this *State*, 2 Corin. 5. 2. *In this we groan earneſtly, deſiring to be cloathed upon with our Houſe, which is from Heaven.*

As *Jeſus Chriſt* is at the ſame time, Bleſſed, and Glorious in Heaven; yet withal living in thy Fleſh, who art a Member of Him, and ſuffering with thee: So thy Spiritual Man, even while it is *ſtreightned* here below in thy *Natural Life*, is *at Liberty* above in Heaven in Jeſus Chriſt.

This Man at once comes down from *Above* in its full Glory upon thee; and breaks forth from *Below*, from out of thy Fleſhly Life to a full Liberty. And this is the *Houſe*, which comes down from Heaven, to cloath thee, that thou mayſt not be *naked*.

But this *Houſe* from Heaven doth not cloath thee, till thy *Earthly Tabernacle* be diſſolved in Death; as appears by the *firſt verſe* of that *Chapter* cited next before, 2 *Corin.* 5. 1. *When our Earthly Tabernacle is diſſolved, we have a Houſe not made with Hands, Eternal in the Heavens.*

Theſe are the *Three States* of the *Spiritual Man*. The *Firſt* of theſe is the *Legal State* of a Chriſtian. The *Second*, is the *Evangelical State* before Death. The *Third* is the *Angelical State*, that State to which we cannot come, but by *Death*, or a *Change* inſtead of Death, when, as Jeſus Chriſt ſpeaketh, *We ſhall be as the Angels in Heaven.*

Thus much we have ſpoken of the *Firſt Diſtinction.*

2. *Diſtinct.* The *Second Diſtinction* is upon the *Spiritual Man* in the *Evangelical State*; or upon an *Evangelical Chriſtian* in this Life. He alſo hath *Three Diſtinct Growths.*

St. John ſpeaks of all *Three* in *One Place*, 1 John 2. 12. *I write to you Little Children, becauſe your Sins are forgiven for his Names ſake.* v. 13. *I write unto you Fathers, becauſe you have known Him, who is from the Beginning. I write unto you Young Men, becauſe ye have overcome the Wicked One. I write unto you little Children, becauſe ye have known the Father.* v. 14. *I have written unto you Fathers, becauſe ye have known Him, that is from the Beginning. I have written unto you Young Men, becauſe ye are ſtrong, and the Word of God abideth in you, and ye have overcome the Wicked One.*

The *Apoſtle* doubles his mention of all *Three Growths*, for *Certainty*, and *Efficacy*; that we may take the more *Clear*, and *Diſtinct* notice of it, He placeth the *Two Extreams*, the *Children*, and *Fathers*, *Firſt*. Then he puts the *Middle-State* in the *Laſt* Place; becauſe that is the more *Remarkable*, and *Active* in the World. The *Children* are not yet grown up to the *Conflict*. The *Fathers* are paſt the *Brunt*, and violence of it. For the ſame Reaſon in his *Repetition* he adds ſomething, when he ſpeaks of the *Young Men* to encourage them.

Now let us ſpeak a word or two particularly of *Each* of theſe *Growths.*

1. The *Firſt Growth* of an *Evangelical Chriſtian* is his *Child-hood.* The

Spiritual Man, when it first begins to put forth itself in us, suits itself much to our *Natural Capacities*, puts itself into *Fleshly Forms*, and Appearances, as into *Swathing Bands*. Yet it submits and subordinates all these Appearances, to the Spiritual Appearance itself in the highest, and most grown State. It Owns That; It *Depends* upon That: It Directs its Growth to That. Thus it is a *Little Child*, and *Knows the Father*.

2. *Secondly* an *Evangelical Christian* comes to be a *Young Man*. This is then, when thou comest to distinguish between the *Fleshly*, and the *Spiritual* Appearances of the Spiritual Man, or of Jesus Christ in thee.

When a Saint grows strong in Spiritual Appearances, when he begins to *abide firm* in them; then he sets himself against the Fleshly Appearances; because the Devil hath his *Chiefest Strength*, and *Seat* in them.

And now thou hast *overcome the Wicked One*, when once thou hast discovered, and discerned the *Fleshly Appearances* from the *Spiritual Life* itself. When thou labourest to crucify the *One*, as fast, as it Grows up; that thou mayst live more abundantly in the *Other*: thou hast now taken from the Devil his most *Principal Power, and Engine*. He is now falling apace, like *Lightning from Heaven*, in thy Soul.

This is thy *Growth*, when thou art come to be a *Young Man* in Christ.

3. *Thou art a Father* in the Gospel. when *thou knowest Him, who was from the Beginning*. This is the *End*, and *Perfection* of the *Gospel* in thy Heart, to bring forth that *Mystery of God*, which was *hid* from the *Foundation* of the *World*: to *Discover* God in thee, as he is the *First*, and the *Last*; the *Beginning* and the *End*; the *Almighty*; the *All-comprehending*; *the same Yesterday, to Day, and for ever*.

When thou knowest God, as *He was from the Beginning*; thou knowest him, as the *Fulness*, Gathering up all things into *One Glory* in Himself; thou knowest him, as the *Fountain*, sending forth all things from himself; thou knowest him, as a *Father*, living in all things, as his own *Out-goings*, and loving all things for his own sake.

When thou knowest *God* after this manner, thou knowest *thy self*, as thou wert *in God from the Beginning*. This *Appearance* of *God*, and of *thy self*, which was *from the Beginning*, being brought forth in thee, changes thee into their own *Likeness*. So thou becomest *like* God, a *Father*, *Possessing* the *Fulness* of all, *Flowing* forth into all, *Enjoying* thy self sweetly *in*, and *thorow* all.

But this is to be remembred all along, that thou hast this *Discovery* of God, and *Conformity* to God in this *High State*, not *Absolutely*, or *Nakedly*: but thou hast it *vailed* under the *Darkness* of the Flesh, and *mingled* with the *Frailties* of it.

This is the *Highest Degree* of the *Evangelical State* on *Earth*. But it falls short of the *Angelical State* after *Death*. It is *next* to it, the *Image*, and the *First-fruits* of it.

This

This is the *Answer* to the *First Question:How far one may enter into the Kingdom of God on Earth?*

Quest. 2. How may we attain to this *State* of *Spiritual Joy*, which is the *Kingdom of* God?

Ans. My *way* of answering to this *Question* shall be by *Shewing* you those *Mistakes*, which keep very many Saints very long from this Joy; and then by endeavouring to *remove* those *Mistakes*.

These *Mistakes* are Principally *Three*:

1. *Mistake*: *That Spiritual Joy is indeed the Delight, but not the Duty of a Saint.*

2. *Mistake*: *That we are to take the Rise of our Joy from a Reflection upon something in our selves.*

3. *Mistake*: *That Spiritual Darkness, Desertions and Griefs cannot stand together with Spiritual Joys.*

I will begin with the *First* of these *Mistakes*.

1. *Mistake*: *That Spiritual Joy may be the Delight, but is not the Duty of a Christian.* This is a *Secret Principle*, which works very often in the most Upright Hearts: That *This Joy* is rather the *Prerogative* of a grown Saint; than a *Precept* from God to every Child of his: that it is, a *Reward* for great Services, and Progresses in the Way of Christ; but not a *Work* Enjoyned, and Expected by Christ.

I will propound to you *Five Rules* for the taking away of *this mistake*.

1. *Rule*: *The Command in Scripture.*
2. *Rule*: *The Inseparableness of Knowledge, and Joy in Spiritual Things.*
3. *Rule*: *The Inseparableness of Faith, and Joy.*
4. *Rule*: *The Inseparableness of Love, and Joy.*
5. *Rule*: *The Inseparableness of Purity, or Holiness, and Joy.*

1. *Rule*: *The Command in Scripture.* I could give very many *Instances* in the plain *Letter* of the *Scriptures*, where *All* without any *Note* of *Distinction* are commanded to *Rejoyce*.

I will satisfy my self with the mention of that *One Place*: Philip. 4. 4. *Rejoyce in the Lord alway*: *I say again, Rejoyce.*

See how the Apostle *Doubles* the Command, and speaks it with a *vehemency*, and tells you *plainly*, that it is his *Command*, and *Charge* to you from the Lord. *I say again, Rejoyce.* He speaks, as if he knew, how apt we were to *Mistake* in this *Point*, and think *Spiritual Joy* were no *Precept* from God, or *Duty* in us.

The Apostle *extends* the Command to *all Persons*, and *all Times*: *Rejoyce alwaies.* No *Person* is excused, no *Condition* is exempted from this *Delightful Duty* of *Rejoycing*.

St. *Paul* clearly implies the *Reason*, *why* the *Command* is so *unlimited*, in that word: *In the Lord.* Can any Condition be so *Sad*, as to take away thy *Joy* in Jesus Christ? Is there any *Affliction* in which thou hast a *Greater Cause* of *Sorrow*, than thou hast of *Mirth* in thy *Saviour*?

Hath not *He Comforts* for every *Season*? *Cures* for every *Sore*? Cannot *He* make thy *Affliction* itself *matter* of *Glorious Joy*; and turn thy *Covering* of *Sack-cloth* into a *Garment* of *Praise*?

There is no *Person*, which is not a *Proper Subject* for *Joy*, as he *is in Jesus Christ*. There is no *Condition*, which is not a *Proper Object* of *Joy*, if it be *seen in Christ*.

This is the *First Rule*.

2. *Rule*: *The Inseparableness of Knowledge, and Joy in Spiritual Things*. Thou *knowest* no more *Spiritually*, than thou *Rejoycest*. *Spiritual Knowledge*, and *Spiritual Joy* are *born* together, *grow* together, *sleep* together, *wake* together in the Soul of Man.

Thou art no longer in the *Light* of the Lord, than thou art in the *Joy* of the Lord.

Prov. 3. 17. *Her ways are ways of Pleasantness*; *all her Paths are Peace*. *Solomon* speaks of *Wisdom*, and *understanding*. This *Place* hath a *Two-fold Sense*: *First*, all the *Ways* of God, as *He* goes forth in them *by Jesus Christ*, who is the *Wisdom* of God, are *Peace*, that is, a *Sweet*, *Agreeable Harmony* in themselves, and with the Soul of Man. They are *Pleasantness*, that is, a *Sparkling forth* with *Good*, and *Satisfaction* to every Faculty, or Desire.

Secondly: The *Ways*, and out-goings of *Wisdom* in thy Soul carry *Peace*, and *Pleasure* along with them. If the *Light* of God *shine* upon any *Thing* in thy Spirit, it will put a *Joy* upon that *Thing*. So far as thou seest Things in the *Light*, and *Method* of God, as he goes forth in them; thou canst not but have *Peace*, and *Pleasure*.

All *Want* of *Joy* proceeds from *Ignorance*, or a *Fleshly understanding*, which is *Darkness*, and not *Light*; or a *Perverted Knowledge*.

So far as thou hast a *Right understanding*, a *Spiritual Knowledge* of *God*, *thy self*, or *this Creation*, thou canst not but have *Joy*.

1. *First*, if thou hast a *Spiritual Knowledge of God*, thou wilt be fill'd with *Joy*. If thou knowest *God* in the *Spirit*, thou knowest Him in *Glory*. For the *Spirit of God*, *and of Glory* are both *One*, 1 *Pet.* 4. 14.

When thou knowest *God Spiritually*, thou knowest *Him*, as *He* knoweth *Himself*. *For God is a Spirit*, *John* 4. So thou hast the same *Object of Joy*, thou hast before thee the same Image to *Rejoyce in*, as *God himself* hath.

When thou comest to a *Spiritual knowledge of God*, thou standest in a *Light*, in which thou seest all Things, as *Horses of Fire*, and *Chariots of Fire*, of *this Fire*, which is *God in Glory*.

If thou knowest any thing of God *Spiritually*, thou knowest *God*, to *Bring forth All*, to *Fill All*, to *Be All*: Thou seest all Things, as *Light* in *His Light*, *Living* in *His Life*, *Spirits* in *This Spirit*.

Canst thou *want Joy*, when thou meetest with every thing *in God*, the *Fruit of God*, *Full of God*, *One Spirit with God* to thee?

2. *Se-*

2. *Secondly*, if thou know *thy self Spiritually*, thou canst not *want Joy*.

A Spiritual Knowledge of thy self holds thee forth to thy self, as *One Spirit with Jesus Christ*. Thou seest *thy self there*, *where* thou seest *Christ*. Thou seest *Jesus Christ there*, *where* thou seest *thy self*. *He that is joyned to the Lord, is one Spirit with Him*, 1 *Corin.* 6. 17.

Dost thou in any *Sufferings* know, that *Jesus Christ* and *Thou* make but *One Spirit* in those Sufferings ; and canst thou forbear to *Rejoyce* in them ?

Canst thou *think* of no Glory or Blessedness in Heaven itself, but thou knowest, that *Jesus Christ*, and *Thou* make but *One Spirit* in that Glory ; and canst thou chuse, but Joy in it ?

Hast thou this Knowledge, that thy *Saviour* and thy *self* run along thorow all Things. Twisted into *One Spirit*, undivided in Light, and Darkness, from the Beginning to the End of Things? and hast thou not *Joy* in all Things ?

A *Spiritual Knowledge* of thy self teacheth thee to look upon *thy self*, as made in the *Image*, and *Likeness* of *Christ*.

Jesus Christ saith of Himself, *John* 3. 13. *No man hath ascended up into Heaven, but He, that came down from Heaven, even the Son of Man, that is in Heaven.*

Jesus Christ had *One Part* of Himself *above* in Heaven, at the same time, that the *Other Part* of Him was *below* on Earth.

As Jesus Christ *unites* God, and the Creature in his own Person ; his *Face* being as the *Sun* shining in the Highest Glory, when his *Feet* are in the *Furnace*, the Fire and Fading State of the lowest Things : So the *Soul* of Man in her *Natural State unites* the *Heaven*, and the *Earth*, the *Invisible*, and the *Visible Part* of this Creation.

Thy *Soul* in her *Top*, and *Supream Part*, which is her *Truest* self, and *substance*, lives ever Invisibly, and Immortally among the *Angels*. *She* in the mean time subsists here below among these Fleeting Shadows, only in her Lower Part, in which she is, but as a *Shadow* of herself.

He that knows this, hath *this Joy* alwaies, that the Inconstancies, and Tumults of this Life wet but his *Feet*, trouble his *Dreams* only : His *Better Part*, his *Waking Part*, His *Life* is Constant above these *Floods* in the Company of *Spirits*. *Death* catcheth thy *Shadow*, and no more of thee. Thy true self is above the *Region*, and *Reach* of Death, *Immortal*, as the *Angels*.

But behold ! A *Greater Cause* of Joy ! Thy *Soul* in her *Spiritual State* hath a *fuller Resemblance* of her Saviour. That *Life*, which thy Soul hath at the *Top* of this Creation, is yet but a *Dream*, a *Show*, the Feet only.

Psal. 17. 15. *I shall be satisfied, when I awake with thy Likeness* : Saith *David*. The *Soul* in this Creation is fallen into a *Sleep*, she hath her *Sleeping Part* only here ; and her Life at Highest even in the *Angelical State* of it, is but a *Dream*.

The *Life*, the *Truth*, the *Waking*, and *Chief Part*, the *Head* of thy Soul is above *Angels* with *Christ* in *God*.

John 13. 9, 10. *Peter said to Christ: Not my Feet only, but my Hands, and my Head. Jesus saith unto him, He that is washed, needeth not save to wash his Feet, but is clean every whit.*

All of thee, that comes within the Compass of this Creation, thy *Immortal*, as well, as thy *Mortal* Part, all is but thy *Feet*. For *all that* needs *Washing*. Thy *Head*, and thy *Hands* are above *Nature*, in a *Spiritual*, and *Supernatural Glory*, ever *un-troubled*, *un-spotted*, the *same Yesterday, to Day, and for ever*, like *Christ*.

Dost thou thus *Spiritually discern* thy *self*? Thou canst not then but rejoice in the midst of all *Changes*, and *Confusions*. For thou seest thy *Life*, thy *True Being*; thou seest thy self *awake*; in an *Unchangeable State*, with all *Contents* round about thee, as *Christ* in *God*.

3. *Thirdly*: If thou know *this World Spiritually*, thou canst not *want Joy*.

When we look upon *this World* after a Spiritual manner we see it, as a *Show*. *Man walks in a vain Show*, *Psal.* 39. 6. What *Pain* have all the Miseries of this World to Him, that looks on them, as an *Empty Show*, without any *Substance* of Evil? Nay, what *Peace*, or what *Pleasure* do they afford thee, when they are, as a *Tempest* in a *Picture*, or a *Battel* in a *Story*?

A Spiritual Eye perceives this World in all the *Pieces*, and *Particularities* of it, to be an *Image* of Heavenly Glories, *Rom.* 1. 20. *The Invisible things of Him are clearly seen by the Things, that are made: Even His Eternal Power, and God-Head.*

The *Mind* of Man naturally rejoyceth to see a *Resemblance* of any thing, especially of *Excellent* Things, especially of Things *Beloved*. Thou canst not carry a *Spiritual understanding* with thee thorow the World; but thou wilt *rejoyce* over all the Works of God in the World, when thou seest thy God, with his *Beauties*, and *Blessednesses Imaged* forth, and brought to thy mind by them all.

If there be any Thing, which is most Dark to thee; thou wilt say of that: *Yet here is something of my God pictured out, though I know not, what of Him it is.*

This World is a *Principal Part* of the *Mystery of God. When the Seventh Trumpet shall sound, then shall the Mystery of God be finished, Revel.* 10. 7.

This World is indeed a *Deep* of Darkness, yet it hath the *Wonders* of God in it. *They that go down into the Deep, see the Wonders of the Lord, Psal.* 107. 24.

The Soul *sports* itself, and *plays* with the Miserablest Things of the World, when she perceives herself to be in them, as in the midst of the *Mystery* of *God*, and among his *Wonders*.

I have done with the *Second Rule*, by which you see, that your Spiritual *Knowledge*, and *Joy* go Hand in Hand.

3. *Rule*: *Faith*, and *Joy* are ever in an *Equal Degree*, and *Activity*. St. *Paul* prays for the *Romans*, Rom. 15. 13. *Now the God of Hope fill you with all Peace, and Joy in Believing.*

Faith, *Peace*, and *Joy* are Companions of equal *Stature*, and *Favour* in the Heavenly

Heavenly Life. *Faith* and *Joy* are like the *Sun*, and *Light*. *Joy* is the *Daughter* of *Faith*, but ever as old, and strong, as the *Mother*.

There are *Three Joyful Things* in *Believing*.

1. A *Joyful Prospect*. 2. A *Joyful Possession*. 3. A *Joyful Purchase*.

1. A *Joyful Prospect. Faith is the Evidence of Things not seen*: Heb. 11. 1. *Faith* sets Heaven, with all its Angels, Spirits, Joys, Glory, Christ, and God, whatsoever is Excellent, and Invisible, *in thine Eye*. *Faith* discovers all these Things to thee, with a *Conviction*, and *Demonstration* of their *Reality*.

He that believes, hath presented to the *Sight* of his Mind, that *Frame* of Things, in which *God* lives; and that not as a *Show*, or *Apparition*, but in a *Substantial* manner.

The Angel of the Lord pitcheth his Camp round about those that fear him: *Psal.* 34. 7. This *Camp* hath in it all the *Powers* of the *Angelical*, and *Divine Nature*. These continually encamp about a Saint, and encompass him in the midst of themselves. But they are *Invisible*, and Faith is their *Evidence*, the *Discovery* of them to thee, in their *Truth*.

When Jesus Christ had his *Sufferings* upon him, he had a *Joy before Him*, *Heb.* 12. 2. So much of *Faith*, as thou hast *in* thee, so much of *Joy* thou hast continually before thee.

Faith, when thou art in a *Dungeon* gives thee such a *Prospect* into Heaven, and the God-Head; as *reflects* a *Joy*, and a *Divinity* upon the *Dungeon* itself.

2. *Secondly Faith* gives thee a *Joyful Possession*. A Wise man among the *Heathen* tells us, that there are *Three ways* of being united to God; *by Knowledge*; *by Love*; *by Faith*. But, saith he, this *Faith* is no *Empty Image*, or *Thin Persuasion*; but a *Substantial Incorporation* of the *Things* themselves with the *Soul*.

So saith the *Holy Ghost*, Heb. 11. 1. *Faith* is the *Presence* ὑπόστασις the *Subsistence of Things Hoped for*.

Can you *have*, what you *Hope* for, and not have Joy? Do you *Hope* for Heaven, for Jesus Christ, for Freedom from Sin, and Troubles? Do you *Hope* for *Joy*? So much Faith, as you have, so much *Joy* you *have*, so much you have already of all that, which you *Hope* for.

Dost thou say; thou hast *Faith*, and by *Faith* the *Presence* of thy Saviour, the *Possession* of Glory, and yet hast thou no *Joy*? Say not, thou Believest; but shew me thy *Faith* by thy *Joy*.

He, that *believes*, cannot but have *Joy in Believing*; no more, than he that walks in the *Light* of the Sun, can be without its *Heat*.

3. *Thirdly*, there is in *Faith* a *Joyful Purchase*. The *Life, that I live*, saith *St. Paul, is by the Faith of the Son of God, who loved me, and gave himself for me*, *Galat.* 2. 20.

Faith makes an *Exchange* between Christ, and a Saint. If thou believest, the Lord Jesus hath given *Himself for thee*. *Christ* stands in *thy Stead*. And thou standest in the *Stead* of *Christ*.

Christ fills *thy Room*, in the Flesh, the world, and all Sufferings. He bears the *Place* of *thy Person* in them.

Thou fillest the *Room* of *Christ*, and bearest the *Person* of Christ in all these.

Can such an *Exchange*, as this be without its *Joy*, when Christ *stands for* thee in Sorrows, under the *Guilt*, and *Infirmity* of them: when thou *standest for* Christ in the *Mystery* of Them?

This *Purchase*, or *Exchange* is made in *Glory* too. The Lord Jesus is set in *thy place* in Heaven, as *Thou* being the *Principle*, and he the *Deputy*. *I go to prepare a Place for you*, saith the Lord to his Disciples, *John* 14. 3.

Thou shalt be taken up into *Christs Place* there; *Where I am, there ye shall be also*, *John* 14. 3.

My Beloved is Mine, and I am His: saith the *Spouse* in the *Canticles*. Is not this abundant matter of Joy at all Times to thee? *That Glory*, which Jesus Christ hath now in Heaven, is *Thine*, as it is *His*. *That Glory*, which thou shalt have hereafter shall be *Christ's* together with Thine.

Thou hast no *Misery*; *Jesus Christ* hath no *Glory alone*.

This is the *Purchase*, or *Exchange* of *Faith*.

4. *Rule*: So much *Spiritual Love*, as there is in any Soul: so much *Spiritual Joy* is there also, 1 *Pet.* 1. 8. *Whom having not seen, ye Love*: then it follows a little after: *Ye Rejoyce with Joy unspeakable*.

There is a *Two-fold Love*;

1. *A Love of Benevolence.* 2. *A Love of Complacency.*

1. *A Love of Benevolence.* If thou hast this *Love* to Jesus Christ, thou wilt *Rejoyce* to accomplish *His Will*, to *Glorify* Him in thy Self, to make thy Self a *Sacrifice* in any Kind to his Good Pleasure: even, as He offered Himself up in the Flesh to the Father.

2. *A Love of Complacency.* Is thy *Saviour* thy *Delight*? Is He to *Thee*, as He is to the *Father*? Is He thy *Beloved, in whom thy Soul rests*? Then is thy *Joy* the *same*, in the midst of all *Changes*, while thy *Jesus* remains *Unchangeable*.

If Jesus Christ be *Altogether all Pleasantnesses*, all Lovelinesses to *Thee*, as the *Spouse* expresseth *Him* to her self in the *Song of Songs*: then, thou canst want no *Joy*, though thou be in want of all things; while thou hast *Jesus Christ*.

This is the *Fourth Rule*.

5. *Rule*: *Joy, and Purity* are ever in the Soul in a *like Degree*. *Holiness*, and *Happiness* are both *One Thing* in *God*, and the *Soul*. *Each* is an *Elevation* above all *Inferiour*, and *Corrupting*, or *Corruptible* Things: and an *Habitation* in the *Supream Good*.

It is said of God in the Prophet *Esay*, that *He inhabiteth Eternity*; that is, *Himself*, *Isa.* 57. 15.

It is said by the *Saints* to *God* in the *Psal.* 90. 1. *Thou hast been our Dwelling place from One Generation to another*.

Pure Religion, and Undefiled before God, and the Father is; to keep Himself Unspot-

Unspotted from the World, James 1. 27. The World is *Pitch*. For it lies in a *Principle* of *Darkness*, and *Blackness*. Where it *Touches*, it *Spots*.

He only keeps himself *Pure*, who keeps himself *Untoucht* by the World; *Un-affected* with it.

So long, as your *Purity* is *Un-stain'd*: Your *Pleasure* will be *Un-troubled*. For Troubles are *below*, in the *Changeable* State of Things. But a Holy Soul dwells on *High*, in *Him*, who hath no *Shadow* of *Change*.

Trouble is in the *World*, and *in Christ all* is Peace, *John* 16. 33. *Hold up* thy Heart, that it sink not into the *World*: *Hold off* thy Heart, that it settle not on the World; and thou at once shalt preserve thy self from *Sin* and *Sorrow*.

Abide in Jesus Christ, *Act* thy self perpetually *from*, and *upon* Jesus Christ; so shall thy *Purity*, and thy Pleasures flow continually like a *Mighty River*, which is both *Clear, and Calm*.

I have now finish't that, which I had to say in the *Removal* of the *First Mistake*, which hinders the Soul from attaining to a *State* of *Spiritual Joy*.

2. *Mistake: That we are to take a Rise of our Joy from a Reflection upon something in our selves.* We are generally apt to think, that we are to look *into our selves* for the *Ground* of our *Joy*; and that we are to *measure* our *Joy* by that, which we find *in our selves*.

Go to most Christians, when you perceive them full of *Joy*, and ask of them a *Reason* of their Joy: you shall hear them telling you, that they have Examined their Hearts, and find a *Love* to *God*, to the *Children* of God, a *Trust* in God, an unfeigned *Desire* to Please God, an *Universal Indeavour* to keep all the Commandments of God, an *Uprightness* before God, a true *Sorrow* for *Sin*, a *Detestation* of it, a full *Purpose* to forsake *all* Sin, with many other *Goodly Things* in Themselves.

Go to other Christians, who put out the *Flame* of Life in their Hearts by their *Sighs*, and *dim* their Eyes with their Tears: Ask them, why they have no more Joy in their Lives; you shall have some such Answer, as this from them: Alass! What Joy can there be in my Life? God with-holds His *Grace* from me, and I can find no *Abatement* of Corruption, no *Life* of Holiness in my Soul. I have strong *Temptations*, mighty *Lusts*, and no *Power* to withstand them. I cannot *Trust* in God, or *Believe* in Jesus Christ, I find no *Profit* in the *Ordinances*, I take no *Pleasure* at all in *Spiritual* Things.

Obj. But you will say; may I not *rejoyce*, when I discover the *Workings* of *Grace* in my Heart? Is it not a *just Cause* of *Grief*, when I feel my Heart *hardned* from the *Love*, and *Fear* of God?

Ans. There is a *Right*, and a *Wrong* Way of *Rejoycing* and *Grieving* in these Things. The *Mistake* lies here in not *Distinguishing* between these *Ways*.

Psal. 3. 7. *David* rejoyc'd that the *Lord by his Favour had made his Mountain so strong*. But this *Mirth* was quickly turn'd into *Mourning*. It would not have been *so*, if *David* instead of *Rejoycing* in the *Mountain* made *strong* by

the

the Favour of the Lord, had *Rejoyc'd* in the *Lord*, and *his Favour*, which made that Mountain strong.

Or rather, if instead of *that Favour* of the Lord he had made the *Lord* of that Favour his *Joy*.

Psal. 77. *Asaph* abandoned all *Joy*, and gave himself over to *Grief*, for Gods With-drawings from him in the *Sensible Conveyances* of *His Grace* to his Soul. *v.* 2. 3. *&c.*

But he repents himself of *Measuring* his *Joy*, or *Grief*, by this *Standard*; and finds a *Cause* of Joy above these Troubles. *v.* 10. *I said*; *This is mine Infirmity, but I will remember the Years of the Right Hand of the most High.*

I shall speak of *Spiritual Mourning*, when I come to the next *Mistake*.

In the mean time I will give you *Two Rules* for the *Removing* of the *Mistake* in this *Point* of *Grounding* our Joys.

The *Two Rules* are *These*.

1. *Rule : Make God, as He is in Himself, the Object of your Joy, without any Consideration of your selves at all.*

2. *Rule : Take the Rise of your Joy from Jesus Christ, not, as He Communicates Himself to you: but, as He Comprehends you in Himself.*

I will begin with the *First Rule*.

1. *Rule: Make God, as He is in Himself, the Object of your Joy; without any Consideration of your selves at all.*

When St. *Paul commands* Joy, he *confines* us to the *Person* of God, for the *Matter* of our Joy. *Philip.* 3. 1. *Finally, Brethren, Rejoyce in the Lord.*

The *Person* of the *Lord* hath *Space*, and *Room*, and *Entertainment* enough for thy Joys in their largest Extent. Thou needst not wander besides the *Tents* of any Creature, *within* thee, or *without* thee.

Do but still *Pitch* thy Thoughts upon this *Mark*, and thou shalt have *Plenty* of Joy. He that makes *God*, as *He* is *Alone*, the *Matter* of his Rejoycing; will find *Abundant matter* of Joy in *every Season*.

You have *David's* Example in this kind, *Psal.* 118. 14. *The Lord is my Strength ; and Song ; He is become my Salvation.* The Lord is then *Strong in* you, and *for* you, when you receive Him in the *Simplicity* of His Nature, *unmixt* with anything of the Creature.

God is *weakned, and straitned*, when He is *Compounded* with any other thing. You bring Him *out* of Himself, and *below* Himself, when you joyn Him with any thing *besides* Himself.

It is said of *Jesus Christ* in the Gospel; that *in One Place* He could do no *Great Work*, because of *Their Unbelief*.

Faith is the *Emptying*, and *Filling* Grace. It *Empties* the Soul of *itself*, and the *Creature*. It *Fills* the Soul with *God*.

While we abide in *Unbelief*, that is, in any Thing of our *Own*, or the *Creatures*; we *weaken* God in us, we *bind* Him, and make Him *un-able* : *He can do no Great Work* in us.

We

We have God in *Power*, when we have Him in *Purity*; we have Him in *Purity*, when we have Him in the *Simplicity*, and *Nakedness* of his own *Person*.

Thus the Lord is *thy Strength*. And thus must He be thy *Song*, the *Subject* of thy *Joy*. When thou *singest* of God *alone*, then art thou *strong*, and hast *strong Joys*.

The Lord is thy *Salvation*. So far, as thou goest out of thy *self*, and the *World*; so far, as thou entrest into *God*, thou entrest into *Salvation*, *Joy*, and *Heaven* itself.

I will back this *Rule* with some Particular *Motives*.

1. *Motive: Look to God in the Nakedness of His own Person, and you shall see Light, without any Darkness.*

John 8. 12. *Jesus Christ* saith of Himself: *I am the Light of the World, He that followeth me, shall not walk in Darkness, but shall have the Light of Life.* Our *Saviour* is the *Light*, that *points*, and *chalks* out our way to us, He is the *Star* that goes before us, and stands over the *God-Head*, as the *House*, in which He, and We must find our *Rest*, and dwell for Ever.

Follow Christ. Which *way* goes Christ? He goes by the *Cross*, and thorow *Death*. He descends to the *Lowermost Darkness*, Then He ascends *thorow* all things, till He comes *above* All. He goes up above the Highest Heavens, *into God*.

Go you after the Lord Jesus. Tread in the Steps of this Shepherd of the Flock. Go by the *Cross*, the *Death*, and the lowest *Darkness*. Carry every thing of the *Creature* with thee, this *Way* into *These*. Then rise up *out* of *All*, pass *thorow All*, till thou come *beyond All* unto the High, and Holy *Habitation* of the *God-Head*,

If thy *Heart* be *in* this *Treasure* of the Divine Nature, if thine *Eye* be *upon* it, and thy *Way* be *towards* it: thy *Way* itself shall be a *Light* of Truth, and Joy without any *Darkness*.

Psal. 104. 2. *Who coverest thy self with Light, as with a Garment, and stretchest out the Heavens like a Curtain.*

Every Thing of the *Creature* is a *Covering* upon God, even the Brightest, the most Beautiful Piece of the Creature; the *Light* itself.

The Highest, and most Glorious Things, the *Heavens* themselves, are *Curtains* drawn before the Lord, *Hiding*, and *Darkning* Him to us.

You must break thorow the *Light* of *Angels*, the Highest *Heavens*, the Divinest Excellencies of *this Creation*, into the *Open Face* of the God-Head; if you will have the true *Light* of *Peace*, and *Joy* in your Spirits.

While you sit under any Thing *Created*, you sit under a *Cloud*, in the *Dark*: you can never be free from Fears, Doubts, Uncertainties, and Unsatisfactions.

This is the *First Motive*.

2. *Motive. Set your Heart, and Thoughts on God in the Simplicity of His own Nature; and you shall sit down under Love, without any Mixture of Wrath.*

Esa. 27. 4. The Lord saith of Himself: *Fury is not in me; who would ſet the Bryars, and Thorns againſt me in Battel? I would go through them, I would burn them together.* God, as He is in the *Singleneſs* of His own *Perſon*, and *Nature*, hath nothing of *Wrath* in Him, but all Sweetneſs, Love, and Bleſſedneſs.

God in Himſelf is *Light*, and *Love*. He is a Fire, a *Principle* of Wrath, only as He is in the *Fleſhly Creature*, Straitned, Impriſoned, and Reſiſted by the *Darkneſs* of the Fleſh.

If you hold up any Created Strength or Excellency before God; you ſet *Bryars*, and *Thorns* againſt Him, upon which God *Kindles* in his Wrath, as a *Conſuming Fire*.

1 *Corin.* 3. 11. St. *Paul* tells us, that *Jeſus Chriſt is the Foundation*, and v. 12. *If any Man build upon this Foundation, Gold, Silver, Precious Stones, Hay, Stubble*; then ſaith He. v. 13. *Every Mans work ſhall be made manifeſt; it ſhall be revealed by Fire.*

Let thy *God* be laid in thy Heart, as the *Foundation* of thy Joy. He is a *Living Rock*, a *Living Corner-Stone*. If thou *reſign* thy ſelf to Him, and *reſt* on Him: He will grow up unto a *Building* of Pleaſure, and Glory in thee. Living Precious Stones of all Joys, and Beauties, will ſpring up out of Him.

But take thou heed of *laying on* any Thing, thy ſelf, upon this *Rock*. For whatever it be, though it be not *Hay*, and *Stubble* only, but *Gold*, and *Precious Stones*; though it ſhould be the Immortal Excellencies of *Angels*, the Glory of the *Firſt Image* in Nature, the Beauties of the Earthly *Paradiſe*: This *Rock* of the God-Head will be, as an Irreſiſtible *Fire* at the Bottom of them, breaking forth upon them, and Devouring them.

Then thine own *Perſon* may be ſaved, becauſe it is *Rooted* in the *Rock*, and hath the *Foundation* of the Lord in it, which abides *Sure*. But this will be, as *by Fire*. Thou muſt paſs thorow the *Fire*, in which thou ſhalt leave all thy *Joys* behind thee, which have been *thy Super-ſtructures*, and *Additionals* upon the *Foundation*. Thy *Perſon* alone ſhall eſcape *naked* out of the *Fire*, having nothing left, but the naked *Foundation*, or the *Rock*, for a Clothing to it.

St. *John* ſaith: *He, that dwells in love, dwells in God.* So far, as you dwell in any thing of the *Creature*, you dwell under the *Vail*, in the *Fire*, under the *Law*, under an *Adminiſtration* of *Wrath*, and *Death*: you cannot be free from *Trouble*, and *Torment*; *Death* will feed upon you.

Dwell *Nakedly* in *God*, and you dwell *Entirely* in *Love*. Let a *Naked God* dwell in you, and as you take in a *Naked God*, you take in *Naked Love* into your Souls.

Thus much for the *Second Motive*.

3. *Motive: Cloſe with God in the Abſtractedneſs of his own Being, as he is unclothed of all the Creatures; and you cloſe with Eternal Life itſelf, where there is no more any Death.*

See how *David* Rejoyceth: *Pſal.* 18. 46. *The Lord lives, and Bleſſed be my Rock.* David look'd off from all other Things, and turned his Eyes upon the Lord

Lord alone.In the Lord he sees *Life*,and this is *his Life*. He considers nothing Transitory,or Moveable. His *Rock* is alone in all his Thoughts.He *Blesseth* his *Rock*. He triumpheth in the *Blessedness* of his *Rock*. And this is *his Blessedness*.

Follow *Davids* Example, and *thy Heart shall live*, while there is *Life* in God, Say ; my *Friends*, and my *Body* may die ; my *Graces*, and my *Comforts* may wither, but the *Lord lives*. *I* may be miserable, the whole *World* may be miserable round about me ; but Blessed be my Rock: There I see, and find a *Life* in the midst of *Death*, and *Blessedness* in a Heap of *Miseries*.

The Lord *lives Truly* : all other Things below Him, are *Dead*, and have only a *Shadow* of life. The Lord *lives Eternally*: He hath no *End* of Days, no *Change* of Life, or *Shadow* of Change. The Lord *lives Universally* : He *lives* in all Things, He *comprehends* all Lives in Himself, He *gives* a Life to all Things in Himself: *All Things live to God*, *Luk.* 20. 38.

If thou look *to*, or *for* an thing *below*, or *besides* God, thou shalt certainly find it in the Region of the Shadow of *Death*; and *Death* feeding upon it with his *Iron Teeth* of Divisions, Distractions, Cares, Changes, and Griefs.

Look into the *Book* of this *World*, and thou shalt find it a *Book* of *Death*, where thou shalt see every thing *Dead*, or *Dying*, *Betraying* thee to *Death*, and *Amazing* thee with the *Fear* of Death.

Look into thine own *Heart*, and thou shalt find that, a *Book* of *Death*, and *Hell*, fill'd with Darkness, Guilt, Fear, Torment. The best things there, thy *Graces* are written with *Black*, and *Bloody* Letters, in much *Obscurity*, hard to be discerned ; in much *Impurity*, having little Life of *Comfort* in them.

But if thou wilt look into the *Person*, and *Nature* of God, thou shalt see the *Book* of *Life* opened to thee. *God* is that *Book* of *Life*, in which thou shalt see thy Self and all Things *Written* with the *Beams* of the *Light of Life*. Here thou shalt neither read, nor hear no more sad Stories of *Death*. Thou shalt see *Death* itself *Shining* in the Light of Life.

God is a *Bright*, and the *Last* Darkness. The Darkness of Death itself is swallowed up into *Life*, and *Immortality* in Him. O *Death I will be thy Death*.

Live only *to* God, and *upon* God ; Consider nothing but *Him only*. So shall thy *Joy* alwaies be as *Life from the Dead*, as the *Joy of Harvest*, I mean that Heavenly Harvest, the *Resurrection*.

4. *Motive* : *Pitch thy Spirit upon the Single Person of God* ; *so thou shalt fall into an Infiniteness of Satisfaction.*

This is the Advice of *David*, Psalm 37. 4. *Delight thy self in the Lord, and he shall give thee thy Hearts Desire.* The *Desires* of man are *Infiniteness* budding forth from its *Seed* in the Soul. These *Desires* are ever in Motion,and Restless, till they put forth into *Infiniteness* itself. All the Creatures are too Strait, and Narrow for them. They are Unquiet, while they are contained within the Compass of any Creature ; because every Creature is *Finite*.

They beat against the sides of it,till they break thorow it into the *Innfiniteness* of God.

Make God thy Delight; and there is nothing which thou canst *think* of, or *wish* for, but thou shalt have it in him. In God thou shalt meet with thy Self, in any State, or Form, in all States or Forms, which thou canst desire, *at once*. In God thou shalt meet with whatever thou *hast* Enjoyed, and wouldst fain Enjoy *again*, with whatever Enjoyment thou hast *fallen short* of, and *longest* for.

If there be Loss, Shame, Grief, or Evil, which thou wouldst fain have *abolished*, and to be as if it *never* had been. If thou wouldst have any Time past brought back again; any Good, or Content, which hath been defac'd, or stained, renew'd; thou shalt have this *Abolishment* of what thou wilt, this *Restitution* of what thou wilt, in God. For *He will give thee thy Hearts Desires.*

God is *All*, if he be *Alone*. As He is in *Himself*, He is *Infinite*. If you add any Thing to Him, or take Him cloath'd with any thing of the Creature; you make Him *Finite*, and so loose *Him quite*.

It is a Joy from the *Creature*, which is a *Confined* Joy. If thy Joy be *purely* from God; if it be from an *Un-compounded Cause*, it will be an *Un-confined* Joy.

Search then, if thy Griefs encrease, as thou appliest Spiritual Comforts to them; thou then dost but take *something* of God, as a *New piece of Cloth*; and sowest that to the *Old Garment* of the Flesh, and Creature in thee; so the *Rent* becomes worse. For if thou think to *patch* up that which is *Thine*, or the *Creatures*, with that, which is *Gods*; He will tear more of it away and leave thee still more Broken, and Naked.

Let thy Heart go out of all Things into God, make Him thy Delight *Alone*, and He will give thee *All* thy Desires.

These are are the *Motives* to perswade you to the *First Rule*, to make God in the *Singleness* of his own *Person*, your *Joy*.

Obj. But now some one may say: Shall we so give our selves to look up to God in *Contemplation*, as never to look down upon our own *Conversation*? Shall we *consider* God only, and take no *Care* of our Selves? Shall we satisfy our Selves to think, that *God* is most Holy, and most Excellent, though *we* in the mean time be never so Sinful, and Vile? Is not this like Him, who gazed upon the Stars, and fell into the Ditch?

Ans. While we thus *Object*, we err, not knowing the *Power of God*, nor the *Way of the Spirit of Man*. And this is my *Two-fold Answer*: the *First*, from the *Power of God*; the *Second*, from the *Spirit of Man*.

1. *Ans.* From the *Power of God*. The *Light* of God is the *Light of Life*; as *Jesus Christ* calls it. It is no *Dead Light*, it works, *Transplanting* the Soul into the same *Principle*, *Transforming* the Soul into the same *Image* with itself.

As the *Beams* of the Sun have a *Heat*, and *Influence* going along with their *Light*: so have the *Appearances* of God to the Soul, a *Fire* in them, which *baptizeth* it.

The *Discoveries* of God carry the *Spirit* of God along with them, by which those Excellencies of God *are*, and *Act*, wheresoever they *Appear*, according

to

to the *Manner*, and *Measure* of their Appearance, 2 *Cor.* 3. 18. *Beholding the Glory of the Lord, we are changed into the Likeness of the same Image, even as by the Working of the same Spirit.*

To know thee, is Eternal Life; saith *Jesus Christ* to his *Father*, John 17. 3. *Spiritual Changes* are made in *Spiritual Contemplations*. The *Knowledge* of God is the *Life* of God in the Soul, which first brings forth itself in the *Flower*, and then in the *Fruit*.

It was said under the *Law*; *No man can see God, and live*: that is *in*, or *to* himself. But the *Gospel* saith: *No man can see me, and lie dead in Sin, or Flesh*, 1 John 2. 4. *He that saith, I know Him, and keepeth not his Commandments, is a Liar.*

Look unto me, and be ye saved; saith God in the Prophet, *Isa.* 45. 22. *Sanctification*, and *Salvation*, *Holiness*, and *Joy* come *down* upon us when we *look up* to God

2. *Ans.* From the *Spirit of Man*. What is it *Draws* Man on to any Course? Is it not some *Image* set up before the Eyes of His mind? What is it, which *Drives* the Soul swiftly forward in any way? Is it not the *Delight*, which it feels and enjoys?

1. Our *Saviour* tells thee, *Mat.* 6. 22. *The Light of the Body is the Eye: if thine Eye be Single, thy whole Body shall be full of Light.* Such as the *Image* is, Which is in the *Eye*, such is the whole Man. If the Eye takes in One, Pure, Simple *Image* of Him, who is *One*, who alone is *Good*; then is the Eye *Single*: for it becomes *One* with this *Image*: Then is the *whole Body Light*. For every *Member* is formed, and moved according to that *Image*.

But if the *Eye* be Evil, taking in the *Double*, the *Divided Image* of any Creature; then the whole Body is *Dark*; it is *Uncertain*, *Confused*, *Distracted* in all its *Members*, and *Motions*.

This is the *Misery* of Men, that *their Light is Darkness*. They have no other *Images* of Things before their Eyes, no Appearances of God in their *Understandings*, beside those of this World, and the Creature. This fills their *Life* with all manner of Disorder.

It were Happy for us, that we were always in the *Contemplations* of God, that we had *Him alone* in all our Thoughts: so should the *Eye* of our Soul be *Single*, and we should be ever carryed on towards that *Single*, *Supream* Good, according to *Him*, as *Children* of *Light*.

The *Eye*, wherever it is; is the Highest *Image*, and *Representative*; the Immediate *Production*, *Habitation*, and *Inlet* of the Superiour *Principle*, or *Power*:

As the *Appearance* is in the *Eye*; so are the *Actings* and *Out-goings* thorow the whole *Body*.

The same Word in Hebrew signifies the *Eye*, and a *Fountain*.

The *Eye*, and the *Heart* are the same Thing in Spirituals; having only this different *Notion*; the *Heart* is as the *Principle* in the *Image*; the *Eye* as the *Image* in the *Principle*: the *Heart* as the *Unity* in the *Variety*; the *Eye*, as the *Variety* in the

the *Unity*: the *Heart*, as the *Father* in the *Son*; the *Eye*, as the *Son*, which hath the *Father* in the *Trinity*.

But to return, thus you see, that it is the *Image*, which we have in our Minds, which *draws* us to Good, or Evil.

2. It is *Delight*, which *drives* us. This is the *Oyl* to the *Wheels* of our Soul. *The Joy of the Lord is your Strength.*

Where your Treasure, there will your Hearts be: saith our Blessed Lord, *Mat.* 6. 21. That is a Mans *Treasure*, in which he hath *Joy*. O that we had less *Joy* in the *Creatures*, and more in the *Creator*: then would our *Treasure*, and *Hearts* be in *Heaven*!

Cant. 1. 3. The *Spouse* saith to Jesus Christ: *Thy Name is as an Ointment poured forth: therefore do the Virgins love thee.* See the *Kindly*, the Spiritual *Way* of the Lord, with that Soul which he espouseth to Himself.

1. *He poureth* forth his *Name*, the Discovery of his Person, and Excellencies in the Soul. He filleth the *Eye* of the Soul, the understanding of Man with the Contemplation of His Riches, and Glories.

2. *This Name* thus *poured out* becomes as an *Ointment* in the Soul. It *perfumes* the Spirit. It spreads a Strong, Delicate *Sweetness*, and *Delight* thorow the *Heart*, and *Affections*.

3. *This Perfume* of Delight makes the Soul in *Love* with Jesus Christ, makes her full of *Longings* after him, of *Breathings*, and *Cries* to be taken up into *Communion* with Him, and made more *Conformable* to Him.

Thus, as the *Contemplations* of God *draw* the Soul, so a *Complacency*, and Joy in God *drive* her on to *Believe*, *Love*, *Obey*.

And this is according to the *Natural Way* of the *Spirit* of Man. The *Object informs* the *Understanding*, the *Understanding moves* the *Will*, and *Affections*, these put the *Whole Man* into *Action*.

O then fear not any *Danger* in *Delighting* your selves in the Excellencies of God, as he is *Naked* in himself. If you be not *Good*, this *Joy* will make you *Such*. If you be *Good*, this *Joy* will make you *Better*.

So much for this *Objection*; and the *First Rule* for the *Removal* of the *Second Mistake*, by which we are apt to look into our *Selves* for the *Ground* of our *Joy*.

2. *Rule: Take the Rise of your Joy from Jesus Christ; not, as he Communicates Himself to you; but, as he Comprehends you in Himself.*

St. *Paul* expresseth this *Distinction*, and *Rule* in the *Life*, in his own *Example*, 2 *Corin.* 12. 2. He tells us of a *Man in Christ*, *caught up to the Third Heaven.* v. 3. *Such a Man Paul knew.* v. 4. This Man *heard Un-utterable Words in Paradise.* v. 5, *Of such a One*, saith St. *Paul*, *I will glory.*

Three *Distinct Persons* are mentioned in this Discourse. Yet all these *Three* prove *One*.

1. *First*, here is the *Person* of *Christ*, as it is in the *Third Heaven*. The *First Heaven* is the *Starry Heaven*: For so we read: *He called the Firmament Hea-*

ven

ven, Gen. 1. 8. The nature of *Angels* makes the *Second Heaven*. So we read, *Gen.* 21. 17. *The Angel of God called to* Hagar *out of Heaven*, and they are called *The Angels of Heaven*. The *Third Heaven* seems to be the *Natural Image*, and *Presence* of God, as he is the head of Angels. This is called *The face of* God, Psal. 42. 2. Mat. 18. 10.

In this Heavenly appearance was *Paradise*, the flourishing State of all the Creatures in the *Divine Image*. This *Image* was withdrawn at the fall, and not brought forth again in its own *naked* Appearance till Jesus Christ brought it forth to Light, after a *Spiritual* manner, in His own *Person*, by His *Resurrection* from the Dead.

2. *Secondly*, here is the *Person* of St. *Paul*, as it is *wholly Spiritual*, in *Union* with the *Person* of *Christ*; *Comprehended* in *One* Spirit; Ascending, and *Caught* up into *One* Glory, with him.

3. *Thirdly*, Here is the *Person* of St. *Paul*, as it is a *Mixt Person*, partly *Spiritual*, partly *Natural*. This *Man*, as he was *spiritual*, had a fellowship with the *Man* in Glory, knew him, did bear that *Image*, and *Impression* of those *Words* which were spoken, and those *Glories*, which were seen in *Paradise*. But as he was *Natural*, so he could not *Utter* those *Heavenly Words*, nor *Understand* that *State*, whether it were the Last Resurrection to the *Glory* of the *Body*; or the first Entrance, and Abode of the *Soul naked* in Glory, at Death.

Of such an one I will Glory, saith St. *Paul*: *v.* 5. that is of the *Heavenly Man*, the *Man of* Paradise, that is, of the *Natural* Man, as it is *caught* up into the *Spiritual* Man; of the *Spiritual* Man, as it is *Comprehended* in Christ, and together with *Him caught* up into *Paradise*.

Thou mayest Joy, and Glory in that *Man*, that *Self* only, which is above a *Man*, above thy self. which is compleat in Christ, as Christ is compleat in the Glory of God.

Of *Such a One* I will Glory, saith St. *Paul*: that is, of *that Man*, whose *Resemblance*, and Likeness I saw, and was taken up, and transfigured into it, when I had that *Revelation* fourteen years ago.

But of my self, saith he, *I will not boast*. He calls *himself*, the Man in that *Mixt State*, in which he now was on Earth, having the *Power of Christ made manifest in his Weakness*.

This *Rule* hath *two* Parts in it. One is *Negative*, the Other is *Affirmative*.

1. Part, The *First* is the *Negative* Part of this *Rule*, which is This: *Take not the Rise of your Joy from Jesus Christ, as he communicates Himself to you on Earth.*

The *Communications* of Christ to us in the *Natural Man*, are,

1. *Uncertain.*
2. *Imperfect.*
3. *Unsatisfactory.*
4. *Un-safe* for an Object of Joy.

1. *First*,

1. *First*, The *Communications* of Christ in our *Natural Man* are *Uncertain.* They are like the Shining of the Sun upon the Earth, which is ever and anon cut off by a Cloud comi g between the Earth, and the Sun. So *Sins*, *Temptations*, *Desertions* make the *Breakings forth* of Christ upon *Us Fleeting*, and *Changeable*.

Jesus Christ complains of his *Fathers forsaking Him*. Neither is there any Member of *Christ* that lives in the Body, which doth not often find cause to grieve for the *Withdrawings* of Jesus Christ.

The *Psalms* are the *Discovery*, and *History* of a Holy Soul in her whole *Course*, and in all her *Tempers*. How often have ye there Sad mention made of *Gods hiding his Face*.

If thou take thy *Joy* no higher, than from the *Puttings forth* of Christ in thee, thou wilt be very *Wavering*, and *Unconstant* in all thy Comforts. Thou canst have no *Sure*, or *Setled Joy* this way. Thou wilt be able to bear no *Tryal*, when thou shalt be carried thorow the *Waters* of Darkness, and Desolation, thorow the *Fires* of Terrour, and burning Tribulation. The Strength of thy Joy will be *Small*, and thou wilt *faint in the Day* of Adversity.

2. Secondly, The *Communications* of Christ in our *Flesh* are *Imperfect*. They are Imperfect *Two ways*.

1. *In Degree*. 2. *By Mixture*.

1. *In Degree*. All our *Graces* are thus *Imperfect*, while we are in *This World*. *I count not my Self to have apprehended*; saith *St. Paul Phil* 3.13. *I press towards the Mark*. v. 14.

While you look upon your *Graces* for *Comfort*, you can never have a *Full Joy*, because you have no *Grace*, which doth not in *Many Degrees* fall short of the *Mark* in Jesus Christ, the *Glory* of God, to which ye are called.

He that takes his *Joy* from the *Manifestations* of Christ in his *Flesh*, is like him, that feeds upon *Unripe Fruit*, which hath a *Sowrness* in the Taste, and a *Waterishness* in the Nourishment. So will this Man have a *Bitterness*, and *Weakness* in his Dearest Comforts.

2. *By Mixture*. This is a *Second Way* in which the *Graces* of Christ are *Imperfect* in us.

Rom. 7. 21. St. *Paul* complains : *I find a Law, that when I would do Good, Evil is present with me*. How many sad *Throws* have we, how near are we brought to *Despair* full many a Time, when we go to *derive* our Joys, from what we can *discover* of Jesus Christ *in us*? If we pitch our Thoughts upon *Faith*, *Love*, *Obedience*, *Humility*, *Heavenly-Mindedness*; we find these only, as *Weak Inclinations* in us : *We would do good*; But then *Evil is present with us*. At the same time like *Satan* in the midst of the Sons of God, *Unbelief*, *Lust*, *Hatred*, *Pride*, *Worldliness* appear together with our *Graces*, and so *mingled* with them, that it becomes very difficult to determine, which is the *Son*, that is to abide in the heart; and which the *Servant*, that is to be cast out; which is the

True

True, *Predominant* Principle in the Soul, and which is a *Temporary Appearance* only. Who can tell, which are from the proper *Will* of the Soul, as the Children of the *Husband*; which are from *Violence*, as begotten by a Ravisher?

This *Mixture* in thee will make that *Joy*, which depends upon any Thing in thy self, a *Mixt Thing* of *Hope*, and *Fear*; of Pain, and *Pleasure*.

Thy *Life* will be like an *April day*; which hath far more *Showers* than *Sunshines* in it. Thou wilt far oftner with *Paul* cry; *O wretched Man!* than say with him; *I bless God*: Rom. 7. 24.

As the *Hand*, that gathers a *Rose* in the midst of *Thorns*: so will thy *Heart* be, while it gathers its Joys from the *Beauty* of Christ growing up in *itself*. If it do reach any *Sweetness*, it will have with it many a sharp, and Bloody *Scratch* from its *Corruptions*, as from *Thorns*.

3. *Thirdly*, The *Puttings forth* of Christ in us are *Unsatisfactory*. *This One thing I do*, saith the *Apostle*, *forgetting those things which are behind*; *I reach forward towards that which is before*. What is that? Observe, the next verse will tell us: *The Mark of the price of the High Calling of God in Jesus Christ*.

That which is *come forth* of Christ into thy *Natural Man*; that is now *Behind* thee. That which is *Before* thee is, the *Person*, *Possession*, and *Life* of Jesus Christ in the Spirit, and Glory of God. The *Unity* of this *Spirit*, the *Fellowship* of this *Glory*, as it is *in the Person* of Christ: this is *That Mark* which is *Before* us.

All that, which is in our *Persons*, while we are in *Flesh*, is *Behind* us, and to be forgotten by us. It hath a *Darkness*, a *Shadowyness*, an *Emptiness*, a *Transitoriness* from the *Flesh*, in which it is inclosed. So it cannot *stay* with us, or *satisfie* us. It cannot *hold* us. It vanisheth, it passeth *behind* us, and is to be *forgotten* by us.

Our best Things, while we are in this vile Body, are a *Heavenly Treasure in an Earthen Vessel*, as St. *Paul* speaks. They are *Pure*, and *Sweet*, as they flow from the Spirit of Christ, but as they are in our Spirits, they tast of the *Vessel*, they receive an *Unsavouriness*, or *Unsatisfactoriness* from their Communion with our *Earth*, and *Flesh*.

The *Grace* of *Christ* in thee, is like a *Beam*, which is at once in the *Bosom* of the *Sun*, and in the *Bosom* of the *Earth*. That End of the Beam which is to the *Sun*, is *pure*, and *perfect* Light: But that which is towards the Earth, is *Dim*, full of *Motes*, and *Dust*. The *Shinings forth* of Christ in thee, have such a double *Relation*, *to Christ*, and *to thee*. As they are *Christ's*, and in Union with him, they are *Light*, and *Life* in Christ, without any *Emptiness* or *Mixture*. But as they are *Thine*, and have their Being in thy Heart, they are like *Gold* in the *Mine*, partaking very much of the *Earth*, in the midst of which they lie.

The Power of Christ magnifies it self in thy Weakness: as the *Apostle* speaketh of Himself. The Life of Christ in *thy Spirit*, is *Wine* mingled with *Water*. If thou take it *in itself*, and *in Christ*, it is the *Power of Christ*. But if you look

U upon

upon it, as it is in *your Spirit*, it is *Wine* and *Water*, *Power* in *Weakneß*. On Christ's *part* it is *Magnified*, but on thy *part* it is *Weak*, and can afford thee but a *Weak, Unsatisfying* Joy.

4. *Fourthly*, and *Lastly*, The *Communications* of Christ in us become *Unsafe*, when we build our Joys upon Them. St. *Paul* is ever very careful in this One Main Point; when he rejoyceth at any time in the *Grace* of God, to set aside *his own Person*, and to set up that *Grace* in *the Person* of *Christ*. *I thank God thorow Jesus Christ my Lord:* Rom. 7. 1. What ever *matter* of Rejoycing, or Thankfulneß a holy Soul finds, it still finds, and acknowledges *it* to have all *its Vertue*, Sufficiency, and Safety *from*, and *in* the *Person* of Jesus Christ. Therefore doth it draw all *through that Person* out of its *own Person*, lest it should think of *it self* above what is meet.

Look to Jesus Christ the *Beginner*, and *Finisher* of thy Faith, and Joy. For God hath appointed Him, as the *Mediator*, in whose *Person* alone every Thing is made truly *Acceptable* unto *God*, and *Man*: He alone must be thy *Beloved*, *in whom* thou must be *well-pleased*. Thou must be *well-pleased* and Joy'd with every *Grace*, onely *in Him*, as *Thou*, and *It* meet *in him*. Otherwise thou art in danger of Spiritual *Adultery*, and *Idolatry*, by which thou wilt grieve thy *Husband* the Lord Jesus, and rob thy self of his blessed Presence.

This is a *Way* by which thy Soul often falls on a sudden from *High Enjoyments* into a *Dark*, and *Desolate* Condition.

When the Lord Jesus fills thee with the *Warmth*, and *fruitfulneß* of his Embraces, *first* thou lookest upon the *Fruits* of Christ in thy Soul, and art exceedingly taken with the *Beauty*, and *Sweetneß* of these. Now thy *Heart*, and thine *Eye* begin to go a *whoring* from thy Heavenly Spouse, when they begin to look *off* from his *Person*, though it be *upon* something sent forth *from Him*. *Secondly*, thou then reflectest upon thy self with Delight, to see thy *self* so *adorned*, so *strengthened*. Thou thinkest thy self *Rich*, and *Safe*. So ere thou art aware, thy *Soul* makes her self like that *Whore*, which said, *I sit like a Queen*, *and shall see no sorrow*. *Thirdly*, Thy *Saviour* now grows *Jealous*, He turns away his *Face*, He withdraws his *Graces*, the Testimonies of his Presence from thee, He leaves thee to the Power of Temptations, and Lusts. This he doth, that thou mayst learn not to *Exalt thy self by his Gifts*, nor *His Gifts in thy Self*; but *Both in him*, whose *Person* is the *Life* of *Both*, and ought to be the *Only Object* of all thy *Love*, and *Joy*.

Thus the Apostle had the *Buffetings* of Satan, and a *Sting* in his Heart, that *he* might not be exalted by his *Revelations*, but *his Saviour*, and *he* only *in his Saviour*.

Take heed then of looking upon the most *Glorious Graces* of *Christ* in your *own Person*. But keep your Eye unmoved on the *Person* of your *Saviour*, and look upon *Both*, *your Self*, and *your Graces* in that *true Glaß*, and *perfect Image*.

So I paß from the *Negative* to the *Affirmative Part* of this *Rule*.

2. *Part.*

2. Part, *Take the Rise of your Joy from Jesus Christ, as He comprehends you in Himself.*

It is necessary for me here to make plain this *Rule,* by Propounding, and Answering *Three Questions,* which perhaps most of your Spirits will be ready to *ask* in themselves.

1. *Question. First* you may *ask* me, *What I mean by Jesus Christ.*

Answer. I shall answer so far only, as I apprehend most pertinent to the *Point* in hand.

My *Answer* to this Question shall be Six-fold.

1. *Answer.* Our *Lord Jesus* is a *Spirit,* 2 Corin. 4. *The Lord is that Spirit.* A *Spirit* hath a *Three-fold* Power.

1. A *Penetrating.* 2. A *Receiving.* 3. A *Uniting* Power.

1. *Power, Penetrating.* When *Jesus Christ* was made *Spiritual* by his Resurrection, He could pass thorow the *Door,* when it was *shut,* and present himself in the midst of the Room, and the Disciples on a sudden.

All *Bodily* Substances are forc'd to remain one *without* another. They *touch* and joyn only by their *Out-sides.* They cannot mingle, but by *Breaking* themselves into little pieces. So the *Golden Calf* was stampt to Powder, that it might *mix* itself with the *Waters.*

But this is the Excellent Nature of *Spirits,* that they can be a *whole Army* of them in *One Spirit,* or in the *Body* of any Creature, passing into the very *Essence,* or *Being* of it, most *Inwardly,* most *Universally;* and yet neither *Divide,* nor *Stretch* it.

The Lord was in this manner present with His Ten Thousand Thousands of His Angels on Mount *Sinai,* which was a *Bodily* Substance, that might be touched.

So the Lord, and all the Angels, and all the Spirits of Just men; the General Assembly of all Glorious Spirits meet on Mount *Sion,* which is a *Spirit,* that cannot be toucht with hands.

The *Person* of thy Saviour is such a *Spiritual Substance.* He can come into thy *Closet,* thy *Bosom,* thy *Heart.* He can dwell in the *same Body,* in the *same Soul* with thee, in the most *Inward Parts,* in *every Part* of *Both;* and yet take up no more *Room.*

The *Word,* which is *Christ,* is within thee, even in thy *Heart,* and in thy *Mouth;* in the most *Inward,* and most *Outward* Part. *All* of Man, and every Creature is either *Heart,* or *Mouth;* an *Indrawing,* or an *Out-driving Power;* the *Inward Principle,* or the *Out-ward Appearance.*

Our Saviour divides the whole Man into *Heart* and *Mouth,* when He tells us; that *Nothing, which enters into the Mouth, defiles a Man; but that which comes forth from the Heart.*

Jesus Christ is a *Spirit* in thy *Heart,* and in thy *Mouth.* He pierceth to the *Bottom* of the most *Secret Principle* of Life, and Being in thee. He is as *In-*

ward with *That*, and *Thee*, as *That* is with *Thee*. He *passeth* quite *through*, all *over* the Bredth, and Length of that *Body*, that *Appearance*, in which thou walkest. He makes it *His Clothing*, as it is *Thine*.

This is the *First Power* of a *Spirit*.

2. *Power, Receiving*. A *Spirit receives* other Things into self, *as Inwardly*, *as Entirely*, *as* It *conveys* itself into Them.

We read of the *Depths of Satan*, Rev. 2. 24. of the *Deep Things* of *God*, 1 Cor. 2. 10.

We read of a *Pit* for the *Devil*, which can be no other than a *Spirit* of *Darkness*, and *Wrath* in *himself* or in *God*: Rev. 20. 3.

We read of *Chambers* for the *Saints*: Ef. 26. of a *House*, and *Mansions* for them above; which can be no other than *Spirits* of *Grace*, and *Glory* in God.

A *Spirit* hath an *Opening*, and a *Depth* in itself, into which it can receive all things without any Breach in it self.

An *Evil Spirit* hath its *Pit*, into which it taketh in, and swalloweth up, whatever it taketh hold of.

A Good Spirit hath its *Chambers*, and *Mansions*, its *Retreats*, and *Abodes* in it self, for what Guests it pleaseth to admit, or draw in.

Abide in me, saith *Jesus Christ* to his Disciples, *Joh*. 15. 4. As every Thing may be a *Temple* to a *Spirit*. *Your Bodies are the Temples of the Holy Ghost*: 1 *Cor*. 6. 19. As a Saint is the *Temple* of Christ; So a *Spirit* may be a *Temple* to any Thing: So the *Lord Jesus* is a *Temple*, into which the *Saints* may at all times enter, and have Communion with God. *Destroy this Temple, and in three days I will build it again. This he spoke of his Body*, John 2. 21.

The *Body* of Christ was a Temple shut up with a *Vail* before it, while it was *Natural*. But when it was made *Spiritual* by the Resurrection; it was the *most Holy place* set open for thee to come into it, and never to go out more: *Heb*. 9. 1, 3, 8.

Flesh is a mere *Shadow*, which can only *touch* upon Things, but can *take in* Nothing. A *Spirit* is the *Life*, and hath a Depth in it, for which it is compared to *Water*.

This is the *Second Power* of a *Spirit*.

3. *Power, Uniting*. The Spirit is the Band of Unity. 'Tis true of every Spirit, so far as it hath the Nature of a Spirit in it. *Bodies* in *Flesh*, are *Divided*, and *Broken* things, being held together only so far, as they are *Bound* up in *One Spirit*. *Bodies* in *Flesh* converse with all things at a *Distance*, in a *Divided* Manner. Our Saviour is said to take away the *Wall of Partition* in his own Flesh, when he crucified the *Flesh* in himself, for *Himself*, and the *whole World*, Eph. 2. 14.

A *Spirit* is Uncapable of *Division*, being *One* in it self, and making all things *One* with it, which it takes in, or converses with.

Spirits

Spirits are compared to *Flames:* Heb. 1. As *Flames* they *lick* up into themselves, and *Incorporate* (as it were) with themselves, whatever they light upon, or work upon.

So the *Power* which caught up *Eliah* was represented by *a Chariot* of *Fire*. It was, as a *Chariot*, because it took him *into* it self. It was a *Fire*, because it took him up into the Fellowship of *One* Life, Glory, and Spirit with it self.

This is the *First Answer* to that *Question*, which asketh, *What we understand by the Person of Christ*, when we speak of his *comprehending* us.

2. *Answer: Christ* is the *Highest Spirit. He is Lord of all.* We read 2 *Cor*. 4. the last words thus; *the Spirit of the Lord.* It is in *Greek*, *the Spirit the Lord. Jesus Christ* is the supreme Spirit, that Spirit, which is Lord of All.

The *Majesty* of our Saviour's Person consists in this, that he is that *Spirit* which hath the most *Absolute Power* over all Spirits, Persons, and Things; together with the most comprehensive Greatness.

A *Spirit* is like a *Prospect*, the *Higher* it is, the more *Commanding*, and *Comprehensive* it is.

3. *Answer. Christ* is the *Brightest Spirit*. He is the *Brightness* of the Father's *Glory*: Heb. 1. 3. Ἀπαύγασμα, the *Out-shining*.

All the *Effusion of Beams* from the Godhead, is *through* the Person of Christ. All the *Beams* meet within the Compass of that Person.

We before cited a Place of Scripture, which calls the *Spirit*, *A Band of Unity*. The Lord *Jesus* is that *Spirit*, in which all the *Goings forth* of the Godhead are united, as a *Knot of Beams*, a *Band*, a *Bundle* of *Divine Irradiations*, or *Manifestations*.

This Blessed *Person*, and *Spirit* is the Highest, the clearest Light, which as a *Garden-bed*, discloseth, and exposeth all things to view, in the most natural, naked, and distinct manner. This is the *Word*, which being *spoken*, all things are *exprest*. Heb. 4. 12, 13. *The Word of God is lively*: *All things are naked and bare before him, with whom we have to do.*

4. *Answer*. The *Person* of *Christ* is the *First*, and *Fountain-Spirit*. *The Second Adam* is a *Quickning Spirit*, a *Life-giving*, or *Life-making* Spirit.

All *Spirits*, *Persons*, and *Things*, that *have* Life, or *are from* Life: they are in this *Spirit*, as *Waters* in their *Fountain*. They are in Him *Primarily*, and *Eminently*. They are in Him, *more truly*, than they are in themselves. For they *derive* that, which they are *in themselves*, *from Him*.

5. *Answer. Christ is the Image of God:* Col. 1. 15. *He is the Image of the Invisible God.*

But you may say, that every thing is an *Image* of God one way or another. It is true; for St. *Paul* saith, that the *Invisible things of God, are made manifest by the things that are made.* Rom. 1. 20.

Therefore the meaning of St. *Paul* in that other place is, that He is *the Image*, the *Full Image*, the *Proper*, the *Perfect Image of God.*

All

All the *Workings*, and *Manifestations* of God are in this *Blessed Spirit*; and that according to their *several States*, with their *Proper Distinctions*: Otherwise the *Image* were *Imperfect*.

All the *Discoveries* of God are in this *Person*, as *One* with it. For all make *One Image*, and that a *Spiritual Image*.

Thus this *Image* is, as it were a *Body* to the God-Head. All the *Vertues*, *Operations*, and *Appearances* of God are contained in *Jesus Christ*, as *One Body*. Yet every One hath his own Distinct *Place*, *Power*, *Form*, *Activity*, *Enjoyment*; as *Diverse Members*. *The Fulness of the God-Head dwelleth in Him Bodily*, *Colos.* 2. 9.

6. *Answer*. *Jesus Christ is the Head-Spirit. God hath made Him the Head of All*, *Ephes.* 1. 22.

Our *Saviour* is the *Universal Spirit*, that takes in all, and unites all in Himself. *It pleaseth the Father, that all Fulness should dwell in Him*, *Colos.* 1. 19.

He is a *Particular Spirit*, distinct from all. *For God hath given Him a Name above every Name which is named in this world, and that which is to come*, *Ephes.* 1. 21. Thus He is the *Head*.

Thus our *Saviour* becomes a Person, that both *Represents*, and *Presents* all in Himself: that both *Perfects* all in Himself, and Himself *bears* the *Imperfections*, Sufferings *in*, and *for* all.

I have now answered the *First Question*, *what I understand by Jesus Christ*: not according to the Exactness, or Latitude of the Question, but so far, as tends to my present purpose, and the making plain of the *Second Question*, which follows.

2. *Question*: *How we are said to be Comprehended in Jesus Christ.*

I shall indeavour to open the Nature of this, which is one of the most Principal, Spiritual, Profitable, Comfortable, and yet Difficult Points in all our Divinity. I shall proceed in the opening of it by a *Three-fold Step*, which shall be a *Three-fold Answer* to the *Question*.

The Lord *Jesus* comprehends us *Spiritually*, *Mystically*, *Eternally*.

1. *Answer*. The Lord *Jesus* comprehends us *Spiritually*.

Our Blessed Saviour, *as a Spirit*, comprehends us in Himself, 1 *Cor.* 15. 45. *The last Adam was made a Quickning Spirit*. *Jesus Christ* is the *Second Adam*, a *Universal Person*, *comprehending* the Second Creation, in His *Spiritual* Person, in the *Spirituality* of His Nature. He is the *Heavenly Adam*, a *Collection* of all the Saints, as He is a *Spirit*.

Jesus Christ comprehends us *by the Spirit*, 1 Cor. 12. 13. *By one Spirit we are all Baptized into one Body*. Christ, and we live both in One Spirit, so we are *Both* bound up in *One*. It is the *Unity of the Spirit*, *Ephes.* 4. 4. The *Spirit* is *Christs Radically*, and Primitively, by drawing us down, and *Baptizing* us into this Spirit, *Jesus Christ* comprehends us.

The Lord Jesus comprehends thee, *as thou art a Spirit*. *He that is joyned to the Lord is One Spirit*, 1 *Corin.* 6. 17.

Our Saviour, and Husband comprehends us *Inwardly, Powerfully, Fully*: not as *Bodies, Waters, Flames*, but as *Spirits* comprehend one another, nay as One Spirit, as the Highest Spirit comprehends itself.

Christ comprehends thee, as Spirit *of His* Spirit, as a Spirit *in His* Spirit, as *One Spirit*, as the *Self-Image* of Himself.

2. *Answer*: The *Lord Jesus* comprehends us *Mystically*. The *Mysticalness* lies in Three Things, in the *Glory*, or *Diviness* of the Union; in the *Nearness* of it; in the *Distinctness* preserved together with the *Oneness*.

We are comprehended in Christ *Mystically*, because *Incomprehensibly*. The *Love* of Christ *passeth Knowledge, Ephes.* 3. 19. That *Love*, which is an *Affection* only, and *loves* by *Impression*, and *unites* by *Imagination*; such a *Love* may be taken in by *Knowledge* only, which is a Notion, the taking of a *Picture* the Catching of a *Shadow*. Such a *Love* may be known by the *Understanding*, which is a *Faculty*, an *Accident*.

But the *Love* of *Christ* is above *Affections*, and *Impressions*. It is a Naked Comprehension of *Substances*, and *Spirits*, in a *Unity* of *Substande* and *Spirit*. So it *passeth knowledge*, not being to be *represented* by any *Image*, or *Notion*; nor to be *conceived* by any *Faculty*; but to be *Felt*, and *Enjoyed* only, after an Immediate, and unconceivable manner.

We are comprehended in Christ *Mystically*, because with an Appearance of *Contrariety*.

We are *One Spirit*, and *One Body* in Christ. The *Body* of Christ in the Unity of it is a Spirit. The *Spirit* of Christ in the *Variety* of it, is a *Body*.

We are comprehended in *Christ*, as *Members* in the Body. Each Saint hath his *Distinct Person*, Place, *Power*, *Appearance*: I say *Distinct* both from the *Person* of Christ, as the *Head*, and from all the other Saints, as *Particular Members*.

Yet again each *Member* is *One Man* with *Christ*, possessing the *Fulness* of God, and of the whole Body, being in itself *conformed* to the Image of *Christ*.

3. *Answer*: The Third and Last Answer to this *Question* is, that we are Comprehended in Christ *Eternally*, 2 Tim. 1. 9. *Who hath saved us, and called us*, &c. *according to his own Purpose, and Grace, which was given us in Christ, before the World began.* v. 10. *But is now made manifest by the Appearance of Jesus Christ.*

Three Things lie clear in these words.

1. *First*, Thy Person was in Christ from Eternity. Thou hadst a *Capacity*, and a *Subsistence* in thy Saviour, *before the World began.* For thou wert then in Him, as a *Subject*, on which the Father setled his *Purpose*, and confer'd his *Grace*: The words of the Apostle are: *Grace given us.*

2. *Secondly*, Thy Person with all manner of *Grace* and *Glory*, was in Christ before all Times, as it is or shall be in any Time. For One is the *Measure* of the Other. That *Eternal State* in Christ is the *Pattern* of the *State* of *Grace* after-

afterwards, *according* to *That*, is *This* exactly fashioned, *who hath called and saved us according to*, &c.

3. *Thirdly*, That State of our Persons comprehended in Christ is *Unchangeable*.

When Jesus Christ appears *to* us, or *in* us as we are in *Flesh*; then is *that Grace* put upon our Persons in Christ made Manifest. The *Discovery* is *now* of that, which *in Truth* was before. The *Manifestation* is here *below*, but the *Substance* abides still *above*.

The *Manifestation* in thy Flesh is as the *Appearance* of Christ upon thy Flesh, subject to *Change*. But as is the Person of Christ in the Glory of God, so is thy Person of Christ comprehended in Christ, *Unchangeable*.

Let us now pass from the *Second Question* to the *Third*.

We have seen in some measure, what it is to be Comprehended in Christ. Let us now proceed to enquire; how we shall know our selves to be Comprehended in Him. There is indeed *Unspeakable*, and *Unchangeable* matter of Joy for those that are so *Comprehended*; but how shall any Particular Soul be assured of this concerning herself?

3. *Question*: How shall I know *my self* to be comprehended in Christ?

Answer. Art thou comprehended in the *Wisdom*, or *Image* of God? Then thou art comprehended in *Christ*. For he is the *Wisdom* of God in its *Latitude*, and the *Image* of God *in Large*.

Hast thou any place in the *Fulness* of God, or any part in the *Fulness* of the *Creature*? Then hast thou a *Mansion*, and *Habitation* in the Lord Jesus. *For it hath pleased the Father, that all Fulness*, (both of God, and the Creature,) *should dwell in Him*, *Coloss*. 1. 19.

Obj. But you may *object*, and say; It is true, all things, that have a *Being*, or *Subsistency*, have it in *Christ*: *For all things subsist* ἐν αὐτῷ *in Him*, *Coloss*. 1. 17.

But there are *Two ways* of being *in Christ*: *One*, as He is *Head* of the *First Creation*. So Plants, and Brute Creatures have their Being, Motion, and Life in Him, as well as Men, or Angels. What Happiness, or Joy can I have in this?

Another Way of being *in Christ* is, as He is *Head* of the *Second Creation*; the *First-born from the Dead*.

The Lord Jesus in this State comprehends the Spirits of men in Himself with a very great Contrariety; some in *Love*; others in *Wrath*. So we read that there were *Sheep* set on his *Right Hand*; and *Goats* on His *Left*, *Mat*. 25. 33.

What comfort can I have in the Lord Jesus, till I know on which *Hand* I stand? What shall discover to me, whether I be comprehended in his *Love*, or his *Wrath*?

Ans. I entreat thee to understand, and lay up this, which I shall now say, carefully in thine Heart. It is a *Preparation* to the Answer to this *Objection* which thou hast made, and the only way of *Satisfaction*. It

It is this: The *Left Hand* of Jesus Christ is his *Weakness*; his State, and Appearance under a vail of *Flesh*, as he bears the Image of the *Creature* upon Himself.

For this Reason, the Works of *Wrath* are the *Strange* Works of Christ, and God, *Es.* 28. 21. This Expression, *His Strange Work*, signifies; a work with which he is not acquainted *in His own Person*, and *Nature*; a Work, which is *uncouth* to Him, in which the *Height* of his Skill, and Power delight not to put forth themselves; a work in which he is *descended* out of his own Form into some inferiour Form of the Creature, and so become a *Stranger* to Himself.

The *Right Hand* of Christ is the Person, or Spirit of Christ in its full Power, and Glory: as Christ is at the Right Hand of God, that is, in Immediate, and Personal union with the Father.

When the *Love* of Christ is signified by his *Right Hand*, the meaning is that *Love* belongs to Christ in the *Propriety* of His Person. Therefore St. *John* saith: *God is Love*, 1 *John* 4. 16.

Now the *Answer* to the *Objection* follows clearly from these *Premises*, if they be clearly understood.

You shall know, that you are *comprehended* in the *Love* of the Lord Jesus, if you look within the *Vail*, beyond the *Creature*; to the *End*, to Jesus Christ in the *Simplicity* of his own Person, as he is the *Beginning*, and the *End* of all the Works of God, 2 *Corin.* 3. 13.

It is only the Discovery of the naked Person of Christ in you, which can discover your Persons naked in the Love of Christ.

2 *Corin.* 4. 6. *God hath shined into our Hearts, the Light of the Knowledge of the Glory of God in the face of Jesus Christ.* You cannot see the Glory of God in his Eternal Love to your Persons, but by the Shining out of God from the Naked Face, or Person of Jesus Christ within your Hearts.

1 *John* 5. 10. *He that believeth on the Son of God, hath the Witness in Himself*; because He hath the Son of God in Himself, who is the only True, and Faithful Witness.

While you look at any thing below Christ, whether without or within your selves; while you look at any thing *of* or *in* Christ, besides *himself*; while you look upon Christ in any Relation, Capacity, or Consideration; and not in the *Singleness* of his own heavenly and Divine Person: you will sit under a Cloud, though light may be sown for you.

He that followeth me, shall not walk in Darkness, but shall have the Light of Life, *John* 8. 12. You can have Light in your Eye, no longer, than your Eye is upon the Person of Christ. Every other way is Darkness

Then do this: Take off the Eye of your Souls from all Outward Things. Turn it Inward into the Secret of your own Spirits. There lay aside all Appearances of your Self, or any Creature, which would draw your Eye to it;

is a *Glittering Cloud* at best, or a *Shining Vail.* So wait, till Jesus Christ sets his own Person before your Spirits in the Light of God. When you see him, you shall in the same Light see your Selves in Him, and together with Him, *in Love.*

Now for ever after make your self, your Graces, but *Glasses* to see the Face of Christ in; and Christ will be a *Glass* in which you shall see your own Face in the Love, and Glory of God.

Obj. Still you may urge, and say: But *how*, and *when* shall I have this Appearance of Jesus Christ to me?

Ans. 1. St. *Paul* tells thee *how* Jesus Christ shall appear to thee: 2 *Corin.* 4. 6. *God, who hath made Light to shine out of Darkness, hath shined into our Hearts.*

As Light shined out of Darkness, so shall Jesus Christ appear in thine heart out of the midst of Ignorance, Unbelief, Lusts, and all manner of *Contrariety.* Thy Evil shall no more hinder his Discoveries, than Darkness can the shining of the Light. His breakings forth no more depend upon, or are assisted by thy Spirit, than the spreading of the Light through the Air depends upon the *Air.*

As Light was brought forth upon the Waters, when there was no Light, by the Moving or Hatching of the Spirit of God, and by the Word of God: So shall God upon thy Spirit, as easily, as soon, as a Word is spoken; bring forth in thy Spirit the Sight of Christ, where there was no Sight at all of him.

Thus you see *How* the Lord Jesus shall be discovered in thee. But still thou cryest, *How long Lord? When* shall this be?

I *answer* thee to that also; that it shall be in the *Fulness* of *thy Time.* As the World hath its fulness of Time, so hath a particular Soul for the bringing forth of Christ in it.

God hath several works upon thy Soul, various Forms to bring thee thorow, and to bring forth himself in before thee. When these are full, then will he last of all come forth to thee in his Last and full Appearance, which is the Manifestation of the Lord Jesus.

God hath his *Ordinance* with the Sun and Moon, which run their Race from one end of the Sky unto the other. These at length enlighten every part of the Earth in its Season, as they come to it in their Course.

The Ordinance and Covenant of God is, as sure with Jesus Christ, who is the Day-star and Day-light of thy Spirit. He hath his *Goings forth* decree'd and set Him from Eternity. Wait thou for him, as the Watch-men watch for the Morning. For thou shalt so certainly see his Appearance in thy Soul.

The Vision of Christ is for an appointed Time. It is like the Birth of *Isaac*, who was the Type. It hath its *Set time.* In its Set time it shall not fail.

Go thy ways then, be at Rest, have this assurance in thy self, that thou shalt stand up in the Light of Christ, *in thy Lot.* *Cantic.*

Cantic. 6: 13. You have a Song in Parts; Christ and his Angels answering one another, or the Spirit of Man answering it self. *Return O Shulamite, that we may see thee. What will ye see in the Shulamite? As it were the Company of two Armies*; Invisible Things, and Visible; Divine, and Humane; God and the Creature united in a Holy Soul.

Hitherto I have persuaded you to see nothing besides the *Single Person* of *God*, and *Christ*, if you would have true *Joy*. Now you may say to me, *what shall we see* in the Single Person of God and Christ to give us true Joy?

I think it therefore necessary for me to point out to you the *Several Springs* of Joy for all *Seasons* in the Person of God, and Christ, before I leave this *Subject*, that so my discourse upon it may be more full, and Satisfactory to the Soul.

There are various *Springs* in the Person of God, which but look't upon by any Spirit in any Condition, would certainly bubble up a Sweet Delight into that Spirit.

I will indeavour to lead you to these *Springs*.

There are *Five* distinct *Springs* of *Joy* in the *Person* of Christ, or God.

1. *Love.* 2. *Beauty.* 3. *Power.* 4. *Wisdom.* 5. *Glory.*

1. *Spring*, *Love*, Psal. 63. 3. *David* confesseth to God: *Thy Loving Kindness is better than Life.*

Solomon saith: *A living Dog is better than a dead Lyon. Life* is the best of all Created Things. Yet the *Love* of God is better than Life.

Instead of *Better*, you may read *Sweeter.* Did you ever tast a Sweetness in *Life*? In your own Life? Or in the Life of any Thing, that was dearest to you? The *Love* of God can make this Sweetness none at all, overcoming it with a greater Sweetness in it self.

The *Love* of God can Sweeten the Loss of your own Life, or the Life of those in whom you have most Delight; because it is it self far Sweeter.

Waters are Sweetest in their *Fountain.* The *Love* of God is the *Fountain* of Life. All *Lives* derive themselves, as *Streams* from this Head.

Hath *Life* ever been Sweet to you? Come to the *Love* of God, and you shall tast the Sweetness in a Sweeter manner, in its Fountain.

The *Love* of God hath a *Six-fold Sweetness* in it.

1. A *Pardoning.* 4. A *Chearing.*
2. A *Healing.* 5. A *Crowning.*
3. A *Clearing.* 6. A *Conquering Sweetness.*

1. There is in the *Love* of God a *Pardoning Sweetness. David* melts out this, *Psal.* 103. 3. *Who pardoneth all thine Iniquities.*

O hear this, you, who with *Mary Magdalen*, have a full number of *Sins* in you, and those ripened into so many *Devils*: Though your Iniquities be, as a Mountain reaching up to Heaven; the Love of God hath a Sea of Sweetness in it, which can swallow up this Mountain, that nothing of it shall ever appear any more.

2. There is a *Healing* Sweetness in the *Love* of God. *David* adds this in the former place, *Psal.* 103. 3. *Who healeth all thy Diseases.*

The *Woman*, who had many years been afflicted with a Bloody Issue, and had spent all on Physitians, was cured by one Touch of the Hem of Christs Garment. Here is Comfort for you, who have old Sins, or Sorrows, like *Sores* running continually upon you, and can find no help or ease. The *Love* of Christ can cure you in a Moment with *one Touch* onely of its Sweetness upon your Spirits.

3. The *Love* of Christ hath a *Clearing* Sweetness, 1 *John* 5. 20. *The Son of God is come, and hath given us an understanding, by which we may know Him, who is true.*

What *Job* said of himself, is true of the *Love* of Christ: It is *Eyes to the Blind.*

The *Psalmist* makes a Sweet Conjunction of *Tasting*, and *Seeing*, *Psal.* 34 8. *O tast and see, that the Lord is gracious.*

1 *Sam.* 14. 2. *Jonathan* said, *See, I pray how mine Eyes have been Enlightned, because I tasted a little of this honey.* Do but tast this honey, the Sweetness of the *Love* of Christ, and see how the Eyes of your minds will be Enlightned, to a Discovery of Spiritual and Heavenly Things.

4. The *Love* of God hath a *Chearing* Sweetness, the Heavenly Spouse saith to her Saviour, *Thy Love is better than Wine*, Cant. 1. 2.

It is the Advice of *Solomon's* Mother, *Prov.* 31 6, 7. *Give strong drink to him that is ready to perish; and wine to those that be of a heavy heart. Let him drink, and forget his Poverty, and remember his Misery no more.*

The *Sweetness* of our Saviour's Love, is the *True Wine*, the *New Wine*, as He is the *True Vine.* This is strong drink, of a strength to ravish and transport the Soul *out* of, and *above* her self.

Give this drink to that Spirit which is dropping into Hell or Despair. Give this spiritual wine to him that hath a heart heavy with guilt, wrath and terrours. Let him drink freely. One draught of this *Sweetness* shall make him forget his guilt, and remember his fears no more.

The *fifth* Sweetness in the *Love* of Christ, is a *Crowning* Sweetness, *Psa.* 103. *v.* 4. *God*, saith *David* to his soul, *crowneth thee with loving kindnesses and tender mercies.*

The *Love* of God casts its Sweetness all round about thee, that thou canst turn thy self no way, but thou meetest with this *Sweetness.*

Jesus Christ encompasseth thee with a *Ring* of Sweetness, as a Garland of Roses encompasseth the Head. Nothing can come at thy Person, but it must come *thorow* this Sweetness, and so be *Sweetned* by it

St. *John* calls Jesus Christ, *Revel.* 1. 5, 6. *Him that loved us*, &c. *and made us Kings, and Priests to God his Father.*

The *Love* of Christ Crowns us *Kings*: *Kings to God*, not *Imaginary*, but

True

True Kings; not *Puppet-Kings* in the Play of this Life, but *Real* Kings; not Kings *to shadows*, for the Dream of Time, but Kings *for Eternity, to God*; Kings, *as God* and Christ, whose Kingdom is not in this world, but in heavenly places, and in the Power of an Endless Life.

6. A *Conquering* Sweetness. This is the *last*. Of this St. *John* testifies concerning Christ; *Joh.* 13.1. *Having loved his own, he loved them to the end.* The Love of Christ hath a conquering and triumphant Sweetness indeed; for it bring all things, Sin, Misery, Flesh, Time, the World, Death, to an end, but hath itself no end.

Fear not lest thy corruptions or evil should outwear thy Saviour's Love. No; It is made of a durable and everlasting *Sweetness*, which will outlast all things besides it self, or subdue them to itself.

Here you may change the Riddle, and sing; Out of sweetness comes strength, and out of the heavenly meat of our Spirits comes forth the Eater, that devours all other things, and makes them its meat.

Eph. 3.19. St. *Paul* saith of the *Love* of Christ, that *it passeth knowledge*. This is a *Conquering* Sweetness, which conquers all our faculties, our largest, even our Understanding itself.

The *Understanding* is the *Gate* of the Soul; according to the *capacity* of this, so is the capacity of the *Will* and *Affections* of the whole Soul of Man.

The *Love* of Christ is too strong, too great for them all.

All the Powers of Man are here overcome: They cannot take it in. Let them then cast themselves into this depth of Sweetness, and say, *Because we cannot take thee into us, do thou take us into thee.*

2. *Spring*; *Beauty*. This is the *second* ground of *Joy* in the *Person* of God, His Beauty.

David speaks of this, *Psa.* 27.4. *One thing have I desired of the Lord, that will I seek after, that I may dwell in the House of the Lord all the daies of my life, to behold the Beauty of the Lord, and to enquire in his Temple.*

Three things are remarkable in these words concerning the *Beauty* of the Divine Nature.

1. *David* was a *King*, a King in the *East*, where the Pomp and Glory of Courts excelled that of these *Western* parts of the world, as much as Courts here outshine the Countrey. Yet *David* could have for ever left his Court for the Temple, and the Glories of that, for a sight of those Beauties which are in the face of God.

2. *David* was a *Husband*, and a *Father*; he was sweet enough in both Relations, an *Affectionate* Husband, a *Tender* Father: Yet *David* could have been content never to have seen Wife or Children more, so he might have seen continually the Beauty of God.

3. The Soul of man hath a *Seminal Infiniteness*, by which her desires grow endlessly. She therefore is delighted most with those things, which least *bound* her, which still draw forth fresh desires by opening fresh delights. The

The Spirit of Man loves that best, which makes the utmost Satisfaction an Engagement upon a farther pursuit.

Such is the *Beauty* of God. *David* prays, that he may be in the Temple to *behold* it, and to be *searching still*. The *Loveliness* of the God-Head actuates that *Seminal Infiniteness* in the Soul, giving her the sweetest rest by suffering her never to rest from *fresh Enquiries* in her *fullest Discoveries*.

There are *Two things* in the *Beauty* of God, which will make thee glad at all times, if thou turn thine Eye towards them.

1. *The Beauty* of God *drowns* all other Beauties, *Luk.* 5. 39. Our *Saviour* tells us: *No man having drunk old Wine straightway desireth new, for he saith the old is better.* If thou once drink the old Wine of Eternal Beauties in the face of Jesus Christ, thou canst not miss or desire the new Wine of any Creature-Loveliness, while the relish of that Beauty is upon thy Spirit: For thou wilt say; The Loveliness of my Saviour is far lovelier, and all other Loveliness is not lovely, compared with this, which so much excels it.

2. The *Beauty* of God *draws* all other Beauties into itself.

Elihu saith, *Job* 34. 14, 15. *If he set his heart upon man, if he gather unto himself his Spirit, and his Breath: All Flesh shall perish together, and man shall turn again to dust.*

All Creatures are moulded out of Darkness as out of Dust. The Beauty of each Creature is a *Spirit* or *Blast* from God shining upon this darkness, which makes thee different Flesh of all kinds.

As the Sun-beams put out the fire, by *drawing* up the finer fiery parts into themselves; So God sets his face on man, draws in the Spirit of Loveliness to that face of Loveliness in himself. Then the fleshly form fades, and the Dust remains alone.

Keep thine Eye upon this Loveliness in the Person of thy Saviour. So thou shalt never mourn for the loss of any lovely thing, which was, as the Light of thine Eyes to thee: For thou shalt meet with every lovely thing, with every relish of Beauty in this Beauty, as a man meets with the taste of the *Sugar* in the *Wine* into which it was melted, and dissolv'd.

3. *Spring: Power.* No man can ever want Matter of Rejoycing in any Case, that understands and considers the *Power* of God.

Our *Saviour* said to the *Sadduces*, that denied the Resurrection: *Ye err not knowing the Scriptures and the Power of God.* If you err and exceed in Grief at any time, it is, because ye know not the *Power* of God: For if ye did ye would see there the *Resurrection*, and *Immortality* of all your Desires, Hopes, and Joys.

When our Saviour was entring into the blackest Cloud of sufferings, that ever came upon any Creature; He comforted himself in the *Power* of God. *Mark* 14. 36. *Abba Father, all things are possible to thee.*

With this he comforts his *Disciples* in that great matter of their Salvation:

Mat.

Matth. 19. 26. *With men this is Impossible, but with God all things are Possible.*

The *Power* of God can do *Three Things*.

1. *It can change One contrary into Another, and make them to Embrace each other.*

2. *It can call back time that is past.*

3. *It can give a Being to Things, that have been, and have ceased to be any more.*

1. *The Power of God can change One contrary into Another, and make them both to Embrace each other.* Psal. 139. 11, 12. *If I say, the Darkness shall cover me, even the Night shall be light about me.* When thy Soul saith, the Darkness of this Affliction will over-whelm me, and quite swallow me up: then can the *Power* of God make that *Night* of Affliction to be a *Light* of Comfort, and Joy round about thee.

Yea, the *Darkness hideth not from thee,* saith *David* to God, *but the Night shineth as the Day.* No Darkness, no Mid-night of Sorrow can hide, or lock up itself, or a Soul from the Power and Glory of God. These will dwell together with the deepest darkness, and the blackest night. These can make themselves One with them, and so make them to *shine* equal with the cheerfullest day of Prosperity.

The *Power* of God can pierce into the thickest Cloud of Grief. It can bring in thither all the Love, Excellency, Delight of the God-Head. It can make the Darkness of Grief a bright Light to discover all these, and lay them open to the view of your Spirits.

David goeth on: *The Darkness and the Light are both alike to thee.* O Wonderful Union of *Contraries!* O Unsearchable *Power!* O *Powerful Matter* of universal Joy!

God is the onely Truth, and the Measure of Truth, *Darkness*, and *Light* are both *alike* to him, who is the *first*, and *last*.

As *Light* holds forth Darkness, and makes Manifest all Excellencies in itself: So Darkness holds forth Light, and is a manifestation of all Glories, an Image of all Images of Beauty and Pleasure before God.

Light hath its own proper Appearance, and is seen by God in its own distinct Shape, as it is in itself. Yet in the seeing of it all Things are seen. So doth *Darkness* appear before God in its darkest and rightest Form; and all Lights of Comforts, Holiness, Truth appear together with it in the same Appearance.

Blessed are they that abide in God, or are like to God: For no *Darkness* hideth any *Joy* from them, not the Darkness of *Death* itself. The *Grave* shines to them, as Heaven, and shews the same Spirit, Life, and Glory to their eyes.

This is the work of the *Power* of God, which makes Light from above, and darkness from below to meet, and kiss; and like the Man, and the Woman to bear One Image, to become One Light.

Jesus

Jesus Christ Mark 14.35. prayed to his *Father*, *That if it were possible that hour might pass from him.* At the 36th *verse* he tells his Father, that *All things were possible to him.* Then it was *possible* to the Father, that That hour should pass away from him. And so his *Prayer* was absolutely for it.

Other *Scriptures* tell us, that God alwaies heard his Son, and denyed him nothing; and that he was *heard in that which he feared.*

Then it follows, that That Dreadful *Hour did pass* away from Jesus Christ, though it *did not pass* away. This was the Comfort of Christ, that *Power* of God, which could *reconcile* two, which were *contradictions*; that *the sad Hour should pass away, in not passing away.*

2. *Secondly, The Power of God can call back Time that is past, and make it to be present again.* Heb. 13.8. You read of *Jesus, the same yesterday, to day and for ever.* The Lord *Jesus* is the Fulness, the Image, and the shining out of the God-Head.

They are the *Puttings forth*, and Discoveries of Jesus Christ, which make all *Times, Ages* and *States.* Jesus Christ hath *to day* the same Powers and Appearances in himself, which being sent forth made *yesterday.* They are only *drawn in.* If then he please *to day*, to put forth the *same Appearances* to thee, or pull thee into them; he can make *yesterday* present *to day.*

When he shall open himself fully to thee from the Beginning to the End; then he will make the Sun to stand still over thy head; he will make all Times past to *stand forth*, as at the first, and to *stand still* before thee eternally. For he is *the same yesterday, to day, and for ever.*

Rev. 20. 12. We read, that at the Resurrection, the *Books* were opened. *Time* is as a *Book*, which Life opens, and Death shuts. Daies and years passing, are as the turning over of the *Leaves* of this Book. *Whatever God doth, he doth it for ever*, saith *Solomon* in *Ecclesiastes.* Whatever is written in this Book, is never to be blotted out, but remains there to be read to eternity. If any Leaf, or Line were pleasant to thee, and thou mournest, because it is turn'd over, and past; God can at his pleasure turn that leaf or line back to thee again.

3. *The Power of God can make things which have been, and which have ceased to be, to be again.* It is a sweet, spiritual, and deep discourse that, which is between the *Lord* and *Martha*, concerning *Lazarus*; *Joh.* 11.23. Jesus saith unto her, *Thy Brother shall rise again. V.* 24. *Martha* saith unto him; *I know that he shall rise again in the Resurrection at the last day. V.* 25. *Jesus* said unto her, *I am the Resurrection, and the Life.*

Jesus Christ is the *Power*, the *Treasury* of God, *from* which all things are brought forth, *in* which they are laid up again, and ever to be found.

The *Person* of Christ is the *Life*, and the *Resurrection*; while things are, they are *in him*, as in their *Root.* When they are no more *in themselves*, they are still *in him*, as in a *Repository.* They return *into him*, as the beauty of dying Flowers into their *Root*, to come forth again at *Spring*, in a better manner.

The

The *Person* of the Lord Jesus is the *Life*. This world is but as the shadowy Image in the Glass, or Water. All things have their truest, and standing Life in him.

The Lord Jesus is the *Resurrection*. For when he discovers himself to us, then we see all things again in a full, high, immortal manner.

Hast thou lost any comfort by Death, or any other change in this world; do but look with a *Spiritual Eye* upon the *Spiritual Person* of thy Dear Saviour, there thou shalt see thy comforts still *living*. For he is the *Life*. Nay, thou shalt see them *living immortally*, never to dye more. For he is the *Resurrection*.

Thou shalt see them, and enjoy them *substantially*, satisfactorily, without fear of losing them. For that which thou seest in him is not a *Shadowy Image*, but the *Life* it self.

4. *Spring*; *Wisdom*. The *Wisdom* of God rightly understood is a Fountain of Peace and Pleasures, which will flow perpetually into the heart of man.

Two Scriptures testifie of this *Wisdom*.

1 *Scripture*, Eph. 1. 11. This *Scripture* speaketh of God, *who worketh all things after the counsel of his own will.*

These *words* hold forth *four things*:

1. *A Workman*. 2. *The Latitude of his Workings*. 3. *The Pattern*. 4. *The Original of that Pattern.*

1. *The Workman*. This is God, who worketh. The chief Agent, the *Master-wheel* in all Motions is the God-Head. Learned Men say, that if the Heavens should stand still, all Things here below would be immediately at a stand, as in the *Ægyptian* Darkness. It is most true of the *Trinity*, which moves, and makes, and works all things by the *Movings* of that Life, which it hath in itself.

If the *Trinity* should stop in the course of its mutual Communion, and Enjoyments: This stop would be a *Spoke* set in the *Wheel* of the Creation; nothing could stir any more.

2. The *Latitude* of his Workings. God worketh *all Things*.

God worketh all Things *Collectively* in the General and whole Sum.

God worketh all things *Distributively*, in Particulars. *The Earth is the Lords* Work, *and the Fulness thereof*, *Psal.* 24. 1. There is no time, nor any minute, or moment of Time, which is not fashioned, and carried on by God. *My times are in thine Hand*: Saith the *Psalmist*, *Psal.* 31. 15. There is no Affair nor the the least Circumstance of any Affair, be it good, or evil, which is not the Work, and the gift of God. *Shall we receive Good, and not Evil from the Hand of God*; saith *Job*, *Job* 2. 10.

God *rides upon the Circuit of the Heavens*, *Psal.* 68. 4. So he is the *Universal Cause* of Things.

God also *fills All in All*, *Ephes.* 1. 23. So He descends into the *Lowest Relations*, the narrowest Compass, and becomes every where the most *Particular Cause* of every Thing.

God saith of the *Tree* in the *Prophet* for the *Clusters* sake: *Spare it, there is a Blessing in it.* So mayst thou say of any Thing, whatever it be, great or small, for which thou mournest, or frettest: *Spare thy self: There is a Blessing, for there is a God in this Thing.*

God is not only a *Concurrent* cause, working his Part, and leaving to other Causes their Parts apart. But he is a *Comprehensive Cause*, uniting all in himself and spreading himself thorow all, 1 *Corin.* 8. 6. *There is One God who worketh all in all.*

Wherever there is any *Agent* that works: God works all in that *Agent.*

Wherever there is any *Form* of working: God works all in that *Form.*

Wherever there is any *Subject* to be wrought upon, or to receive the work: God works all in that *Subject.*

Wherever there is any *Effect* to be wrought: God works all in that *Effect.*

Not an Angel, or Bird flies, or falls: not a Thought, a Hair, a Dust moves; but as he moves in it, and moves it.

3. The *Pattern* of these Workings. God worketh all Things *according to Counsel. Counsel,* and *Wisdom* are both the same Thing.

This is the Glory of God, and the Happiness of the Creature, that nothing comes to pass, which is not the *Work* of God; and nothing is wrought by God, which is not a Work of *Wisdom. Philosophers,* and the *Scriptures* agree in setting forth the excellent Nature of *Wisdom* by a *Two-fold Description* of it.

1. *Description. Wisdom* is *Knowledge with a Head.* Knowledge is the Image of Things. The Golden Head of this Image is the Heavenly Image of God in the Person of our Lord Jesus.

Colos. 2. 18. 19. St. *Paul* calls the Study of the Nature of Angels, not *Wisdom,* but *Folly,* and Vanity; a vain Puffing up of the Fleshly Mind, why? Is not this a High, and Excellent Knowledge? Yes. But now it was vanity, not Wisdom; a *vain Swelling,* not a *Substantial Fulness,* and Greatness of Spirit in those, of whom the Apostle speaks, *Because they held not the Head.*

God then, who works all things in Counsel, and true Wisdom, holds the *Head* in all His Workings: that is, whatever he brings forth, He brings it forth in the Divine Appearance of his Son; he brings forth the Divine Appearance of his Son upon it, as the *Head.*

Wisdom saith of God, and herself, *Prov.* 1. 27, 29, 30. *When he prepared the Heavens, I was there, when He appointed the Foundations of the Earth: Then I was by Him, as his Delight.*

This may be as truly spoken of every Passage of thy Life, of the least Accident, that concerns thy Person. For the same *God* in the same *Wisdom* hath wrought these; that prepared the Heavens, and laid the Foundation of the Earth.

Thou mayst with as great Assurance hear (in every Thing of Grief or Joy, which thou meetest with in Flesh, or Spirit) the Glorious Person of thy Beloved Saviour speaking to thee after this manner: *God hath prepared this for thee, and*

I am

I am here. This hath the Father appointed for thee; and now am I with thee, to be thy Delight, brought up, and growing up before thee, together with this, and every other Appearance.

You look upon things *vainly*, with a *Fleshly* mind, after a *heedless* manner, if you see not the Brightness, and Delight of the God-Head in the Person of Christ, as a Crown of Rejoycing upon every Providence. You deface the work of God, you look not upon it, as he hath wrought it, *Holding the Head* if you see not the Face of Christ in every Act, or Accident, as in a *Glass*.

God in this Sense hath made Christ his *Only Begotten* Son; in that he brings forth nothing but *Discoveries* of Jesus Christ. For he is the *Head* of all Things; and this is the *Wisdom* of God, the *Holding of this Head* in all.

This is the *First Description* of *Wisdom*.

2. *Description: Wisdom* is the *Fulness* of Things, Jesus Christ is the *Wisdom of God*, and the *Fulness* of *all Things, Colos.* 1. 19.

Wisdom is that Contrivance, that Harmony of Things, that casts the whole Fulness of Things into each Thing. As Members in the Body, amongst whom the Joy of all pertains to every one; and the Grief of each One to all: So are all the Parts of that work, which is wrought in *Wisdom*. *Wisdom* is a Spirit, that conveys the Life, Power, and Sense of all into each Particular; that all may rejoyce, and mourn together every where.

As in a good *Picture*, all the *Proportions* of the whole Face meet, and concenter as it were, in each Line, Point, or Touch; giving you from thence a Cast of the Beauty of the whole: So hath God prepared, and appointed all his Works *in Wisdom*, like an Excellent Picture; that the *Fulness* of the *Whole*, and the Beauty of *all Parts* may shew forth themselves from *every Part*.

Is there any thing so dark, so low, as that the *Wisdom* of God reacheth not to it, and shines not in it? If the Wisdom of God be there, then is there the *Center*, the *Concurrency*, the *Union* of all Things, of all Glory.

If the Wisdom of God shine there, then is there a *Spiritual Light* opening all Divine Beauties, making that Thing, the *Gate* of the *Creation*, of Paradise, Heaven, and the Divine Nature. This is that Traffique of *Wisdom*; which makes the *Merchandise* of it, better than that of *Silver*, *Gold*, or *Pearl*.

4. *The Original of that Pattern.* God works all things according to the *Counsel of his will*. The *Will* of God is the *Principle*, and *Original* of his *Wisdom*.

The *Will* of God is the highest *Rule*, *Rest*, and *Rejoycing* of all manner of Goodness.

The *Phœnix* is said to spring out of a Nest of all manner of Spices laid together, and fired by the Sun, the Will of God is such a *Flaming Nest* of all Beauties, and Sweetnesses at their Height. Out of this *will* the *Wisdom* of God springs forth into every Act of Providence, being Beautiful, and Precious in it.

The *Will* of God is the highest *Reason* of all things. *What if God willing to shew the Riches of his Grace? What if God willing to shew the Power of his Wrath?*

 The

The *Will* in a Spirit is as the *Sea* to a River. All its workings flow *out* of it, and *into* it. It is its *Spring*, and *Fulness*.

Shall not *thy Will* rest, and rejoyce in that, which is the *Will of God*; that is the *Highest Reason*; the fullest Rest, and Blessedness of the Divine Nature?

The *Will* of God, out of which God himself drinks all his Delights, in which he bathes himself: this *Will* is the Eternal *Fountain*.

The *Wisdom* of God is a Large, and Broad *River* poured forth from this Fountain. Every *Creature*, each *Passage* of things in the Creature, is the *Water* of this River. Shall it not be *Sweet* to thee? Canst thou not drink of this Water of the River of God, sent forth from his own Fountain with Delight?

2. *Scripture*; *Deut.* 32. 4. *Moses* sings of God: *He is the Rock: His work is perfect: All his ways are Judgment.*

The *Work* of God is *Perfect* in the *whole*. For all the ways of God in his work in *Particular*, are in Judgment, that is, in *exact Wisdom*.

This place affords us *Three* comfortable *Observations* concerning the ways, and works of God.

1. *Observation*: *Nothing comes to pass, but that which is best.*

2. *Observation*: *Nothing falls out but in the best Time.*

3. *Nothing is brought about, but in the best manner.*

The former place of *Scripture* taught us, that *all* things are the *Work* of God. This teacheth us, that *his work* is *Perfect*, and all the ways of it *Exact*, according to the best *Judgment* of things, and the rightest rules of Wisdom, which are the *Weights* in the *Ballance* of our Judgment.

1. *Observation*: *Nothing comes to pass, but that, which is best. David* saith: *It was good for me, that I was afflicted*: *Psal.* 119. 71.

Goodness is made up of all *Perfections*. *Evil*, by any one *Defect*. Affliction had not been *good* for *David*, if it had not been *Best*. If it had kept out any thing, that might have been *better* for him, it had been an *Evil* to him.

Rom. 8. *All things work together for the good of those that love God.* Where all things *work together* for good, there all things are like *Stones* in an *Arch*, in which every Stone is absolutely necessary. If you pull any one out of its place, the whole Arch falls. Where many things fall into *Conspiracy*, or *Harmony* for good, there the *Stops*, and *Shakes* make the Musick, as well, as the *Stroaks*, and *Sounds*; there every thing is *Best*. For the Alteration of any thing alters the *Harmony*. If all things *work together* for good, than each *Particular* thing with all the *Circumstances*, and *Defects* of it.

2. *Observation*: *Nothing falls out, but in the best time. Eccles.* 3. 11. We learn, that God hath made every thing *Beautiful in its Season*. Every thing is brought forth by God in the *Season* of its beauty, so that you may say; *This Time, and this Thing were fitted one for another from Eternity.*

The Jews say; that Souls were match't, and pair'd in Heaven: and that Marriages prove happy on Earth, when they were first made in Heaven; when a Soul a Soul meets with its first Mate. God hath from Eternity match't every *Thing* to its *Time*. And every *Thing* meets fully with the same *Time* on Earth. So it proves a Lovely, and Glorious Marriage.

Psal. 1. 3. A good man is compared to a *Tree*, that brings forth his *Fruit in its Season*. The good God doth so, much more. He brings forth all the Fruits of his Providence, whether they be Bitter, or Sweet, in their proper Season; in that Season, in which they have a true, and full Beauty.

Good and *Evil* never befal us, but in their own *Season*, when they are Natural, kindly, and Beautiful. If a good should happen to thee in the Time of an Evil, or an Evil in the Time of a Good, it were like the Stars seen at Noon and the Sun at midnight; which would be a matter of Terrour, and astonishment to Mankind; arguing Disorder in Nature, and presaging Confusions to the world.

3. *Observation*: *Nothing is brought about, but in the best manner.* The Jews witnessed of Christ, that he had done all things *well*; not only *good* for the *Matter*, but also *well* for the *Manner*.

There are Three Things, which commend a *Diamond*. 1. *The* Goodness of the Stone. 2. *The* well-setting. 3. *The* well-cutting of it. Every *Providence* of God towards thee is such a *Diamond*. It is *Best* in itself. It is *well-set*, in the best *Season*, and State of Things. It is *well-cut*, all the *Circumstances* are ordered, and polish't with the best skill, like Points of the Diamond, to sparkle forth most Sweetness, and Beauty.

All His ways are Judgment. Every way of God, in each Circumstance of every work is scan'd, and judg'd, and so disposed in the most *Judicious* manner. Not a Mote, or a Hair in any business falls *casually*, or lies neglected, but is weighed in Judgment, and ordered with the highest skill, and care. Never then repine more or say; if it had not been *This*, or *Then*, or *Thus*, I could have born it. For now thou sinnest against the *Wisdom* of God, which hath ordered, and appointed all these Three; *This*, *Then*, and *Thus*: So that *This* was *Best*; *Then* it was most *Beautiful*; and *Thus* it was the greatest *Blessing*.

I will conclude this *Particular*, with that of *Solomon* in the *Proverbs*, Prov. 3. 17. *All the ways of wisdom are Peace, and all her Paths are Pleasantness* This is true *Two ways*.

First, all the goings forth of Wisdom in thy Spirit are Peaceful, and Pleasant. If Wisdom enlighten thy way, and lead thee forth into all things by the Beams of her Discoveries, as the Path of thy Spirit: then all the Out-goings of thy soul into Things, and all the Appearances of Things to thy Soul, will be like a Sweet Tune, or Pleasant Dance.

Secondly, all the goings forth of God in his Wisdom are Paths of Peace, and Pleasantness. No providences would be a Labyrinth or Wilderness to a man, to bring him to a loss; if he travelled thorow them with that *Thread* of Light, with which God went forth into them. Do but go by the *Foot-steps* of God, and

and track his *Wisdom* in the world; and you shall walk continually in a Smooth and quiet Path, in a Path of Rest, and Joy even thorow the Darkest Thickets.

I have spoken of the *Fourth Spring* of *Joy* in God, *His Wisdom.* Now let us pass to the next.

5. *Spring*: *The Glory of God*, *Psal.* 8. 1. David breaks forth into Admiration, *O Lord, our Lord, how excellent is thy Name in all the Earth! Who hast set thy Glory above the Heavens.*

Divines distinguish the *Glory* of God into *Essential*, and *Manifestative*. The *Essential Glory* of God is that which shines Eternally in the Person, and Nature of God. This *Beauty* is the *God-Head's* Self in the *Image*, which is *Jesus Christ*. But I am not now to speak of this. For I spake of this *Glory* before in the *Second Spring*, the *Beauty* of God.

The *Manifestative Glory* of God is that, which he holds forth to us in the *Creature*. *David* speaks of the *Essential Glory* of God, when he saith, that God hath set his *Glory above the Heavens.* No creature can bring forth, or bear the Essential Glory of God. It is above the highest, the most heavenly creature, in respect to its *Excellency*, or *Capacity*. *David* speaks of the *Manifestative Glory* of God in those words: How excellent is *thy Name in all the Earth*! The *Name* is the *Image* of God, the Appearance or Manifestation of his Glory. This *Name* of God is in All the Earth, in the lowest part, or state of the creature, and every thing of it. The *Name* of God is *Excellent*, to *Admiration*, in all the Earth. What a Foundation is this to build Joy upon in every condition? Thou canst not be so low in the Earth, but thou mayest read the Name of God, and see his Glory in thy lowest state.

Look then upon thy greatest Loss, or Cross, and say, *My God, how excellent is thy Name in This also? The Death of my friend, mine own grief shall be precious in mine eyes, because they are the manifestations of thy Glory. I will call nothing dark, bitter, or base, in which thou writest thy Name, and hast thy Beauty shining forth with an excellency.*

I have now finished my Answer to the second *Mistake*, which contains *Directions*, how to look upon the single Person of God, and Christ; what to look upon in That Person, which will fill us with Joy in every condition. Now I am arrived at the *Third Mistake*, which hinders the Soul from attaining to a state of Spiritual Joy.

3 *Mistake*: That *Spiritual Grief* and *Joy* are inconsistent, and cannot stand together. You shall perceive this, as a *Principle* laid down in the hearts of many Christians by the *Reply* which they will make, when they are pressed to *Joy* as a *Grace*, and to continual *Delight*, as a *Duty*. Woe is me, saith one, how can I have any Joy, who have so many corruptions, and sins to mourn for continually? Alas! saith another, should I rejoyce, or take any delight, who am still called to mourning and heaviness by private Afflictions, or publick Calamities? I answer all these, that they err, not understanding aright the

Scriptures,

Scriptures, and the Power of the Spirit of God in the Soul. They erre in supposing that *Joy* and *Grief* in the Spirit do *binder*, and not *help* forward one another. I will endeavour the *Removal* of this *Mistake* by *Two General Rules*, and then by *Particular Application* of these Rules.

The *Two General Rules* are these:

1 *Rule: Take heed of separating those things which God hath joyned.*

2 *Rule: Take not any mourning to be holy, which hath not a holy mirth mingled with it.*

1 *Rule: Take heed of separating those things which God hath joyned. Solomon* saith, *That God hath set One thing over against another*. We may read it; God hath set One thing *By* another, or *For* another. God often sets several things *One By another*, to *compleat* each other; and we set them *One Against another*, to *fight*, and destroy.

God is One, Gal. 3.20. But the name of the Devil is *Legion*: For he is many.

God by *Beholding* all things in One *Light*: by *Possessing* all things in One *Life*; by *Enjoying* all things in One *Love*, is *One*, and Blessed for ever.

The *Devil* by *Dividing* becomes a *Destroyer*, the Principle, and Seat of Destruction.

Jesus Christ is the *Mediator*: He makes things distant to *meet* in him: He *gathers* up all things into One, *Ephes.* 1. 10.

Jesus Christ by *Reconciling* divers *Appearances* of God, divers *Administrations* in Man, makes his *Church* to be of many Members *One Body*; and of *all things* makes *One Beauty*.

We by setting One *Appearance*, or State of the same thing, One *Administration* or Gift to fight with another, make the *Church* a *Babel*, and the Commonwealth a Field of Blood.

The *Spirit* is a *Band of Unity*, Eph. 4. 3. *Unity* is in the *Spirit*; *Division* is in the *Flesh*. The *Spirit* by binding up various *Operations* of the same Grace, various *Illuminations* of the same Truth, in One Band of Unity, makes us *Spiritual* in *Judging*, and *Living*. We first *breaking* off the *Parcels* of Truth, and *Properties* of Grace, then *oppose* them. So we become *carnal*, apt to *miscarriages* in our selves, and *contentions* with others. Take heed then of separating those things which God hath joyned. He is a growing Saint, a God-like man among men, who hath a Spirit Reconciling and Uniting Persons, Things, Duties, Graces, Factions, Affections, Parties, Properties.

This is the *First Rule*.

2 *Rule: Take not any mourning to be holy or spiritual, which hath not a holy mirth mingled with it.*

Be angry, and sin not, saith the *Apostle. Let not the Sun go down upon your wrath*, Eph. 4. 26.

So saith the spiritual man; *I will mourn, and not sin. The Sun shall not go down upon my Griefs.* The Sun of a Saint, the Sun of the Soul is *Jesus Christ*, who

who hath the Light of Life. The ſhining of his Face upon the Soul, makes it cheerful; fills it with beams of Joy; glads it more than ſtore of Corn and Wine can glad any carnal heart. Spiritual *Joy* is the *Sun-ſhine* of Chriſt's face in the ſoul. *The Bridegroom ſhall be taken from them, and then they ſhall faſt, and mourn in thoſe daies*: ſaith *Chriſt* of his Diſciples, *Luk.* 5. 35.

Jeſus Chriſt is the *Bridegroom* of the Soul, as the *Sun* is of the *Earth.* His Preſence and Appearance in the Soul is the Joy of it. Every thing is ſinful in us, which caſts down the Light of our Saviour's countenance in our Spirits. 'Tis Sin to grieve the Spirit of Chriſt, that is, to ſtraiten it and hinder it from rejoycing, and putting forth its Joys in us.

If the Paſſion of Grief or Anger gather to a Thick Cloud, ſo as to Darken the bright Face of the Lord Jeſus in us, it becomes a Corruption, and Tranſgreſſion. We are commanded to *Rejoyce evermore,* 1 Theſ. 5. 16. *Rejoyce in the Lord always, Phil.* 4. 4. Our Spirits are to be playing, and ſporting themſelves unceſſantly in the Light of our Saviours Preſence. It is from the Devil, and the Fleſh, whatever interrupts this Joy, theſe *Sportings.*

The *Rain-bow* was the Covenant of God in the Cloud, that the *Waters ſhould no more cover the Earth* : *Geneſ.* 9. 6, 15.

The *Rain-bow* is ever ſet in a Black, Watery Cloud. But it is begotten by the Reflection of the Sun-beams upon that Cloud, mixing their chearful Beauties, with its Melancholy Blackneſs.

Grief is then alone a *Grace* in thy ſoul, when the Sun ſhines upon the watery Cloud. When the Glory of Chriſt mingles its ſweet Beams with thy Grief, and makes a *Spiritual Rain-bow* in thy Soul. Then is there the *Covenant* of God in the *Cloud* of thy Grief.

This Over-ſpreading of a Spiritual chearfulneſs upon thy Sorrows is a Sign from Heaven, that the waters of Sin, Deſpair, and Wrath ſhall never quite cover the Image of God in thee.

I now come to the *Particular Applications* of theſe *General Rules.*

I will do this under *Two Heads* :

1. *Spiritual Mourning.* 2. *The mixture of Mirth with it.*

1. *Head* : *Spiritual Mourning.* I will here ſet before you the Nature of a *Holy Grief* in theſe *Four Particulars.*

1. The *Matter.* 3. The *Meaſure.*
2. The *Manner.* 4. The *Myſtery.*

1. The *Matter* of *Spiritual Mourning* is *Evil* in all the *Kinds* and *Degrees* of it.

Ecclеſ. 3. 3, 4. *Solomon* couples *Two Verſes* fitly together : *A Time to Kill and a Time to Heal* : *a Time to break down, and a Time to build up. A Time to Weep, and a Time to Laugh, a Time to Mourn, and a Time to Dance.*

Theſe *Times* anſwer one another. The *Killing* Time is the *Weeping* Time: the *Healing* Time is the *Laughing* Time. The Time of *Breaking* is the Time

for

for *Mourning*, and the time of *Building* is the time for *Dancing*. Man is Gods *Cymbal*, or *Harp*. Our Affections, and Passions are the *Strings* upon it. It makes good Musick, when it keeps *Time* with the Administration of God. When the Lord brings forth *Good* Things for us, then he toucheth our *Sweet* Affections, and awakens them. When he brings any *Evil* upon us, then he strikes upon our *sharp*, and sad Passions, to make them sound.

There are *Two Sorts* of *Evil*: The *Evil* of *Sin*, and of *Misery*. *Moses* expresseth both these *Evils* by a *Contrariety*, Levit. 26. 23. 24. *If ye will walk contrary unto me: I also will walk contrary unto you.* The *Evil* of *Sin* is the *Contrariety* of Man to God: The *Evil* of *Misery* is the *Contrariety* of God to Man. *Sin* is the *Running out* of Things from the Glory of God: the breaking of the *Harmony* of Divine Love, Beauty, and Wisdom by a *Discord*. *Sorrow* is the *Return* of Things into this Glory: the bringing of the *Discord* into a *Harmony* again. Both these *Evils* are the *Matter* of Spiritual Mourning.

1. *The Evil of Sin.* We are to grieve for the *Evil* of Sin *in our selves*, and *in others*.

1. We are to grieve for *Sin in our selves*, Psa. 51. 3. *David* cryes to God, *I acknowledge my transgression; my sin is before me.* When *Sin* appears in its right shape to us, it brings forth *sorrow*, as its *Image* in our souls, as naturally, as the face of God begets a face of Joy in our hearts. Mourning is as the *Mouth* by which we confess our corruptions. It is the *Image* and *Form*, in which the sense of guilt holds forth it self in the Spirit. He that grieves, and glories not in the Glory of God, calls *Good Evil*, and *Light Darkness*. He that is merry, and mourns not under guilt, he calls *Evil Good*, and *Darkness Light*. Both lye under a *Curse*; one for turning the *Glory* of God into a *Lye*; the other for Boasting himself in a *Lie* against the *Truth*. Not to feel a *Sorrow* for *Sin*, is to deny the Nature of it, to destroy the Person of Christ, to make void his Cross, to confound, and dissolve the Mystery of God.

2. *We are to grieve for Sin in others*, Psal. 119. 53. *David* complains, *Horrour hath taken hold of me, because of the Wicked, that forsake thy Law.* When the Sun, the Light of the World, laboureth under an Eclipse by the Moon, the Sight of it naturally strikes a kind of Horrour upon the Spirits of Men. For it portends Blood, and Ruine in one Kind or another. In each Sin there is a more Dreadful *Eclipse*. The *Image* of God, which is the True Life, and Light of all Creatures, laboureth, and groaneth being opprest under, and darkned by the Image and will of Man. He that understands this Sight, sees in it a certain Presage of Wrath, and Desolation, which fills him with Astonishment.

Ephes. 4. 30. *Grieve not*, saith St. *Paul*, *the Holy Spirit of Christ*. Sin grieves the Spirit of Christ. As Jesus Christ Sympathizeth, and Suffereth with us, having a fellow-feeling of our Infirmities by a Union of Spirits. So a good man hath a Sympathy, and fellow-feeling with his Saviour, when he sees his Spirit grieved by the Sins of other men. Thus we are to *Mourn* for the *First Evil*, the Evil of *Sin*.

2. *The Evil of Suffering.* We are to mourn for our *own Sufferings*, and the *Sufferings of others.*

1. *We are to mourn for our own Sufferings*, Ef. 22. 12. *In that day did the Lord God of Hosts call to weeping, and to mourning.* What *Day* was this? It was a *Day* of *Calamity*, when Death was before their Eyes. So you may see at the 13th *verse*: They said: *Let us eat, and drink, for to morrow we shall die.* The Providences, and Appearances of God are his *Language*, in which he speaks to us. God requires of us, that we should have an *Ear* to hear, and a *Tongue* to answer him in his own Language. It is said in one place, that the *Heaven should hear the Earth.* Is it not much more fit then, that the Earth should hear the Heavens? The *Heavens* are the Image of God, the Heart of Man is the *Earth.* Shall God speak to us in Wrath, and Ruine; and shall not we hear, and answer him with Fear and Trembling? Shall God speak to us in Thunder, Storms and Blood; And shall not we hear, and answer him with Tears, and Broken Hearts?

2. *We are to mourn for the Sufferings of Others*, 2 Corin. 11. 2, 9. *Who*, saith St. *Paul, is sick, and I am not afflicted? who is offended, and I burn not?* Every good Man is like his God, and Father. All Things are *his*, because he is the *Spouse* of *Christ*, the *Child* and Heir of *God*, one Spirit with Christ, and God. So he suffers in all. As St. *Paul* said; *I make up the Sufferings of Christ in my Flesh*: So saith he; *All Things that Suffer, add to my Sorrows, and make up my Sufferings in their Flesh.*

A good Man is One Spirit with Christ. Thus he is like Christ, a Spirit of Universal Sweetness, which longs, and labours to bring forth itself in Peace, and Pleasures every where. When it meets with a Soul shut up in Griefs, it is straitned and afflicted there, and burns like a Fire, to be at liberty in that Heart. This Spirit suffers with each Heart, till it can make every Heart to rejoyce with itself. It is never entirely Risen from the Dead, while there is any one in the Grave of Sorrows. That One is a Member of its Body; and it is ever present with the whole Body, being all of itself in every Part of that; all in the Sorrows of the Militant and Suffering Part, as truly as it is all in the Joys of the Triumphant, and Rejoycing Part. This is the *Matter* of our *Mourning, Evil* in both kinds, of *Sin*, and *Suffering.*

2. *The manner of our Mourning.* This is the *Second Particular.* My way in this shall be to give you some *Distinctions*, and then some *Rules* drawn from those Distinctions.

The *Distinctions* are *Three.*

First, of the *Appearances of God. Secondly*, of the *State of Things. Thirdly*, of the *Life of Man.*

1. *Distinction*, of the *Appearances of God*: These are *Two-fold.*

1. *The Supream.* 2. *Subordinate Appearance.*

1. The *Supream Appearance* of God is *One*, Blessed for ever, perfect in Glory,

Glory, Unchangeable. This is *Jesus Christ*, the *same Yesterday, to Day, and for Ever: Heb.* 13. 8. This is that Heavenly Image of the God-Head, which gathers up into one, in itself, all Images of things, in all Times. *David* speaks of this, *Psal.* 16. 11. *In thy Presence* (or Face) *is fulness of Joy: at thy Right Hand are pleasures for evermore.* In these words are *Four Things.*

1. *The Presence*, or Face, and the *Right Hand* of God. Both these expressions signify God in his Naked, Highest, and Rightest Appearance. 2. *Pleasures* are here doubly exprest by *Joy*, and *Pleasures.* 3. *There* is *Perfection* in those Pleasures, a *Fulness of Joy.* This fulness intimates a *Solidity*, or Substantiality of Joy for the *kind*; an *Abundance*, and Satisfactoriness for *Degree.* 4. A *Perpetuity* is added to all this. The Pleasures are *for evermore.* This is the Description of God in his *Supream Appearance*, in which there is all *Variety*; but no *Mixture*: all *Communion*, and Communication; but no *Chance.* This Appearance is Light without any Darkness.

2. *The Subordinate Appearance* of God is *Manifold.* God in this respect is called, *the Lord of Hosts*, because he comes forth in an Army of Appearances, which are his Ten Thousand Chariots, his Millions of Angels. God in his Supream Appearance, is *Light*: in his Subordinate Appearance, a *Fire.* He is in this Appearance a Mixture of Light, and Darkness. He hath various effects, Cherishing, and Consuming: Drawing forth all Things, and devouring them again. Here God is various; sometimes blazing forth brightly; sometimes wrapping up himself in a thick Smoak: sometimes Burning Dreadfully; sometimes shining out Sweetly. This is the Appearance of God, as he comes forth in a Created Image to the Creature of the First Creation. This is called by *Moses* the *Back-parts* of God, in which he hath many Names proclaimed before him, which have Change, and Contrariety in them: *Exod.* 34. 6, 7. *Gracious*, and *Jealous*; *Long-suffering*, and *visiting*, &c.

This is the *First Distinction.*

2. *Distinction*, of the *State of Things.* This is *Two-fold*:

1. The *State of Things in the Spirit*, or God.

2. The *State of Things in the Flesh, or the* Creature.

You have this *Distinction* taught you, *Heb.* 2. 14. *For as much, as the Children are made Partakers of Flesh and Blood.* Here you have the *Children before* their Clothing of Flesh and Blood; again you have the *Children in* that Clothing. There is such another *place* as this, which expounds it, and is expounded by it, *Rom.* 8. 20, 21. *The Creature was made subject to Vanity, not willingly, but in Hope*, &c. *It shall be delivered into the glorious Liberty of the Sons of God.* Here is the Creature *before, above, after* the Vanity of this Creation, in the Liberty of the Sons of God. Here is the Creature *under* vanity, and in the Corruptible Creation.

1. *State: The State of Things in the Spirit, or* in God. This is a State of Immortal Beauty, and Joys. *All things live to God, Luk.* 20. 38. *To* God,

 that

that, is, *in* God. *All Things live to God*, that is, as they are seen *by* God for all things are seen by God, *in* God. God never looks *off*, or looks *out* from Himself.

Rom. 8.6. *To be spiritually-minded is life and peace.* All things live and flourish to the spiritual mind, which is born of God, which is both the *Eye* and *Image* of God in the Soul, as they do *to God*. He that hath the Eternal Spirit for the *Eye* of his Mind, hath it also for the *Object* of his Mind. He that seeth things *by* the Spirit, seeth them *in* the Spirit. All things *in* the Spirit are *One* Spirit with that Spirit, Spiritual Appearances of the Spirit. So they are living and pleasant Images of that Life and Peace which is the Activity and Harmony of the Divine Nature.

Rom. 11. 36, St. *Paul* saith of God; *Of him, and through him, and to him, are all things; to whom be glory for ever, Amen.* God is blessed for ever; the Spring and Seat of Blessedness. All things cannot but be Branches of Blessedness, as they have their beginning, their way, their ends in him, who is the Eternal Spirit of Blessedness and Glory.

2 *State. The State of things in the flesh*, or in the creature, or in themselves. This is a *Flourishing*, *Fading*, and *Flaming* State of Things.

We have it described by St. *Peter*, 1 Pet. 1. 24. *All Flesh is as Grass, and all the Glory of the Flesh, as the Flower of the Field: the Grass withereth, and the Flower thereof falleth away.*

All Things in the *Flesh* are, at best, Vanity, and change in their *Principles.* Their *Path* is Corruption, their *Conclusion* is Consumption, as by Fire.

This is the *Second Distinction.*

3. *Distinction: of the Life of Man.* Man hath a *Two-fold Principle*.

1. *A Heavenly.* 2. *An Earthly Principle.*

This *Distinction* is laid down, 1 *Cor.* 15. 45. *The First Man Adam was made a living Soul: the New Adam is a quickning Spirit. Adam* is a *Universal* Name, which includes all Mankind, as in its Root, or Principle. The *Two Adams* are the *Two Principles*, or distinct Roots of Man. One is a *Living Soul*, the Soul of all Mankind in its Natural State. The other is a *Quickning Spirit*, the Spirit, or Principle of men, as they are converted from Nature to Grace, or Glory. These *Principles* are called by the Apostle in this place, one *Heavenly*; the other *Earthly*. v. 47. *The First Man is from the Earth; the Second Man is the Lord from Heaven.* v. 48. *As is the Earthy, such are they that are Earthy; as is the Heavenly, such are they that are Heavenly.* These *Two Principles* are likewise called *Two Images*, the Image of the Heavenly, and of the Earthly Man. *v.* 49. *As we have born the Image of the Earthly, we shall also bear the Image of the Heavenly Man.*

They are likewise stiled in *Scripture* the *Inward*, and the *Outward Man*, Corin. 2. 4, 14. *Though our Outward Man perish, our Inward is renewed day by day.* The Heavenly Principle is as the *Center*; the Earthly, as a *Point* in the *Circumference* shooting forth its Beams from thence only.

The

The Heavenly, and Earthly Principle lie mutually infolded in one another. The Earthly Principle is in the Heavenly, as the *Seed* in the full-blown Flower. The Heavenly Principle is in the Earthly, as the *Flower* lies hid in the Seed. The Earthly is in the Heavenly, as the Flowers of all *Colours* are in the Light. The Heavenly is in the Earthly, as *Light* is in every Colour. These Two are also expressed by the *Spiritual*, and *Natural Man*, 1 Cor. 2. 14, 15. So also by the *New*, and *Old Man*, *Coloss*. 3. 9, 10. Man according to the Diversity of these *Two Principles* is capable of a *Five-fold life* at once.

1. *The Life of the Heavenly Principle in itself.*
2. *The Life of the Earthly Principle, as it is Comprehended in the Heavenly.*
3. *The Life of the Heavenly, as it is in the Earthly.*
4. *The Life of the Earthly, as it is Subordinate to the Heavenly.*
5. *The Life of the Earthly Principle in itself.*

1. *Life* : *The Life of the Heavenly Principle in itself.* Man, as he lives this Life, is uncapable of any blot of Sin, or spot of Sorrow. The *Apostle* speaks with reference to this Life, *Ephes*. 5. 8. *Now are ye Light in the Lord: Walk, as Children of the Light.*

As we live in the *Heavenly Principle*, and that lives in *itself*, we are Children of Light; clear Beams of the God-Head, like Christ, Brightnesses of the Fathers Glory, which can neither be Defiled, nor Darkned. *That which is born of God, sins not, nor cannot sin.* I may add, it grieves not, nor cannot grieve, according to its Heavenly Birth. In this Principle we are *Light in the Lord.* Our *Saviour* tells us, that we shall be in the Resurrection, *as the Angels.* He tells us again; that *the Angels of Little Children behold the Face of God in Heaven:* This Life in the Heavenly Principle is the *Resurrection.* In this we are alwaies, *as Angels.* While we are like little Ones on Earth ; we are as the most Glorious Angels, beholding the Face of our Father in Heaven : while we are inclosed in the Darkness of Flesh, we are at the same time Light in the Lord. It is the Opinion of some very learned men , that the Supream part of the Soul which is above sensible Things, ever living in the midst of Invisible Things, the Head, and Spirit of the Soul; that this is each Mans Angel.

But man hath a *Head* above this Head. *The Head of Man is Christ, as the Head of Christ is God*, 1 *Cor*. 11. 3. Man hath a *Spirit* above this Spirit: *Whom I with my Spirit serve in the Gospel of his Son :* Saith *St. Paul, Rom.* 1. 9. The Heavenly Principle is this *Head*, and *Spirit*. Thou hast an Eternal Life in this Head, and Spirit of thine. In this Life thou art more than an Angel in the midst of the Throne : thou art Light in the Lord : thou art in the Light of the Lord, as He Himself is in that Light.

This is the *First Life.*

2. *Life*: *The Life of the Earthly Principle, as it is Comprehended in the Heavenly.* The Earthly Principle in the Heavenly, is as the Heavenly. *Behold*, saith *Jesus Christ, I make all Things new*, 2 *Corin*. 5. 17. As the Sun riseth upon the

the Earth; so doth the New Man upon the Old, making that also to have a New Face of Immortality, as it is comprehended in the Beams of the New Man. The Glory of God taking up *Elijah*, was as a Chariot of Fire, because as it catcheth up, it changeth, and conforms to itself that which it catcheth up into itself. Such is the Heavenly Principle taking up the Earthly into it.

When St. *Paul* was caught up into the Third Heaven, and Paradise: then he was *another man. I knew a Man*, saith he. *Then* he was that *Man of Paradise.* If he was caught up in the Body: then was his Earthly Body a Paradisical Body, comprehended in the Body of Paradise. When he was let down again, he was an Earthly Man in an Earthly Body, 2 *Cor.* 12. The *Graecian* Poet tells us of an Herb, which had one Name among the Gods, and another Name among Men. All the Things of this world, have one sort of Names and Natures, as they are in their own Principle. But as they are Comprehended, and Converst with by a Heavenly Principle, they have quite other Names, and Natures, which are Heavenly. As *Adam*, so each Principle gives Names to all Things according to itself, and by those Names they are called in that Principle. The Sickness, and Death of the Earthly Principle have other Names, Names of Life in the Heavenly Principle.

This is the *Second Life.*

3. *Life: The Life of the Heavenly Principle in the Earthly* This is, as the Life of Christ in the *Flesh.* It is the Life of the Son of God in Flesh.

This is the *Firmament*, which divides between the Waters of Life above, and the Waters of Grief, and Death below. It reacheth to both, and drinks of both. It hath in its own Principle all the Springs of Peace, and Joy. But as it is in one Person, and Principle with the Fleshly Man, it takes the Infirmities of that upon itself, and bears all its Diseases. And besides all, it hath one Disease of its own, which the Earthly Man bears no part in, and that is, the *Imprisonment*, Restraint, and Contradiction of Sins, and Sinners, which it suffers in the Earthly Principle. The Heavenly Principle in the Earthly is both the *Primary Inflicter* of all Sufferings, and the *Principle afflicted* by those Sufferings.

4. *Life: The Life of the Earthly Principle, as it is Subordinate to the Heavenly.* This is that *Flesh* of Christ, of which St. *Paul* speaks in the Mystery, as of the Spouse of Christ, *Ephes.* 5. 31, 32. This is that *Spouse*, which though it have still a Head, a Principle of its own, yet it *vails* this Head, and subordinates this Principle to the Heavenly Principle, as to its Husband, till it be taken up into it, that so there may be no more *Male* and *Female*; but *one Man* in Christ: no more *Flesh* and *Spirit*; but all according to the New *Adam*, a *Quickning Spirit.* This *Flesh* is indeed washt with pure water, that it cannot sin. But it is Baptized unto *Christ*, as the Jews were unto *Moses*, 1 *Cor.* 10, 2. in the *Cloud*, and in the *Sea.* It is the *Immediate*, and *Proper Subject* of all Sufferings. This is the *Man*, that saith, *Lamen.* 3. 1. *I am the Man that hath seen affliction by the Rod of his Wrath.*

This

This is a *Beast* for *Slaughter*. But it is the *Lamb* among the Beasts. It is a Lamb without Spot, which is slain all the day long. But it is slain, as a *Sacrifice*, not as an *Abomination*.

5. *Life*: *The Life of the Earthly* Principle *in itself*. This is the *Wild Ass* that runs, and snuffs up the Wind. This is the Seat of *Sorrows*, and the Pit of *Pollutions*. St. *Paul*, *Colos.* 2. 11. calls this the *Body of the Sins of the Flesh*. The *Flesh*, as it is in its own Principle is the Womb, and Mother of all Evil. The Devil sows all his several Seeds in this Womb. So the *Body* that springs forth from the Flesh, is the *Devils Body*, in which all the Members are the several puttings forth of those various Seeds, and Divers Principles of Evil cast by the Devil into the Flesh. These Principles are in truth so many particular Devils in him, who is their Prince, and Head. The *Body of the Sins of the Flesh* is then a *Cluster* of *Devils Incarnated*, in which each Member in particular is a particular Devil in Flesh,

Rom. 6. 19. *As ye have yielded your Members Servants* (in a verse before *St. Paul* called them *Instruments*) *unto Uncleanness, and Iniquity*, (that is, to the Principle of Uncleanness, and Iniquity, which is the Devil) *to Iniquity*, (that is, to make themselves one with that Principle, and the various Images, or manifestations of the various Powers in that Principle:) *so yield your Members Servants* to *Righteousness*, (that is, Jesus Christ the Righteousness of God) *unto Holiness*. (to the pure, unmixt, unclouded holding forth of the several vertues of Christ, thorow your several Members.) You see the Life of the Earthly Principle in itself; that it is the *Center*, or *Spring* thorow which the Prince of Darkness, and Devils thrusts forth all his Evil Powers, and Spirits into a Body.

By this means it is made the *Beast*, that bears the *Whore*; it is made an *Ass*, which bows down its back to all the Burthens of every Devil, and Evil. Thus much for the *Distinctions*, which concern the *manner* of our grieving. Now follow the *Rules* which are drawn from these Distinctions to direct us in the Spiritual manner of Mourning.

1. *Rule*: Know the *Ground* of your Mourning to be the *Subordinate* only, and not the *Supream Appearance* of God, *Psal.* 30. 5. *His anger endureth but a moment*; *in his favour is Life*: *Weeping may endure for a Night*, *but Joy comes in the Morning*. When thou grievest, and lamentest most bitterly, then remember; that this Discovery of God, which covers thee with so much Horrour, is but a momentary, and dark one; it is the Night, the Back-part of God. The Morning-appearance, the Face of thy God is Bright, and Shining with Joy. The Living, True, Eternal Discovery, which is above all other Discoveries, is favourable, and kind. When thou lookest upon God, and takest the Rise of thy Mourning at the highest: then say; *my Soul, there is yet a Sight of God higher than this, into which if thou couldst raise thy self, thou shouldst find all their Love and Delight*. It is a Rule among Divines, that there is no *Supream*

pream Evil. Evil hath its Root in the Subordinate Manifestations of God, in his Clothings, and Disguises. Travel on to the Naked Person, to the open Face of God, and thou Travellest beyond all the Fountains, and Heads of Grief, or Evil.

2. *Rule*: Understand well, that the *Object* of all Sorrow is the *State of Things in flesh*, not *in the Spirit*. The *Law* is the *Ministry of Death, and Condemnation*, 2 *Cor.* 3. 7. *Sin* comes in by *Occasion of the Law*, *Rom.* 7. 8. The *Law* is the Occasion of Sin, and the ministry of Death by reason of the *Flesh*, *Rom.* 8. 3. *What the Law could not do* (that is, to make us Holy, or Happy,) *thorow the weakness of the Flesh.* The weakness of the *Flesh* is the Ground, on which all wickedness, and woe is wrought.

The *Flesh* is the Shadow, the Vail, *Hebr.* 10. 20. Whatever evil is the *Object* of thy Grief, so grieve, as knowing it to be in the *Shadowy* part, in the *Out-side* of Things only. 'Tis but a *Leprosie in the Skin. Job* calls the Fleshly State of Things in themselves, and not in the Spirit, but *Skin*, *Job* 19. 26. So doth the Devil in the *Proverb* : *Skin for Skin.* The Inside, the Substance, the Spiritual; and Life-part of those Things, over which thou so sadly breakest thy heart, is Peace. The Altar for Sacrifices was without the vail, all thy Evils are without the vail, let thy griefs then abid without the vail, like the Servants of *Abraham* at the Foot of the Mount. But let thy Spirit enter within the *vail*, and let *Isaac* only go thither with thee, the Child of Mirth, and Laughter. The Sea, and Storms are without the Vail, only in the *Shadow*. The *Anchor*, and the *Rock*; *Rest* is within the Vail, in the Spirit, and Truth of Things.

3. *Rule* : *Grieve so, as having thy Head still above the Clouds of Grief in a clear Light of* Peace and *Joy.* Thy Head is Christ; thy Head is thy Heavenly Principle, thy Life hid with Christ in God, *Colos.* 3. 3. This is your Head, hiding itself in a Divine Light, and Glory, above all Storms and Changes.

Divide your self then in your Sorrows. Let your grief be upon your *Inferiour* parts : but let your *Head* be in Joys. And as your Inferiour Parts are subordinate to your Head: So let the Joys of that be, as the head of your Griefs. They that are washt, need to have their Feet only washt ; said our *Saviour*. Let your *Feet* only be washt with Tears. And then remember, that the *Anointing* of Glory, and the *Oyl* of gladness is upon your *Heads*. So mourn, as that you may be like the Description of *Christ*, *Revel.* 1. 14. 15. that your *Face* may *shine* like the Sun in its Strength, while your *Feet* are in the *Furnace*. Feel your God stroaking your Head with his right hand, while his left hand is striking your Feet with an Iron Rod of Affliction. See how *Job* in a Tempest of Miseries yet Glories in his Head lift up above the Storm, *Job* 16. 18, 19. O *Earth cover not thou my Blood, and let my Cry have no place. Also now behold! My Witness is in Heaven, and my Record is on High.*

When thy Tears and Blood run down upon the ground, when thy Cries fill the Earth; then raise thy self like *Job*, and say : even now, behold! My Head

is

is in Heaven, now I have a Life in my Heavenly Principle, which is an Eternal Record of my Glory, and Blessedness. This testifies of a Beauty, and Joy to me in these very Sorrows.

4. *Rule: Let the Heavenly Principle, as it lives in the Earthly, be the Spring of your Sorrows.* Let not thy Griefs be an *Oppression* to the Spiritual Man in thee, but an *Oblation* from it. Thy Griefs will be an oppression to it, if they proceed not from itself Originally. For then its Joys in the Flesh are taken away from it by another, by the Fleshly Principle. Thy Griefs are an Oblation by the Spirit, when they flow *Primarily* from the Spirit. For then itself layeth down its Joys, as Christ speaketh of his Life. The Blood, which our Saviour shed, is called in Scripture *the Blood of God.* Though the Blood ran thorow the Humane *Nature.* Yet the *Person,* or *Principle,* that bled in that Nature, was God.

Our Divinity ordinarily teacheth us this: that Christ was *Man,* that he might *Suffer*; *God,* that he might *Merit.* His Blood had been of no value with God, if it had not been the *Blood of God.* In like manner your Tears cannot be Heavenly and Divine; if they be not the Tears of the Heavenly, and Divine Principle in you. Though the Earthly Principle be as the *Earth,* in which these bitter Waters bubble up, and run along: yet the Heavenly Principle must be the *Spring* in this Earth, out of which they arise: Otherwise they will be of no *use* to you, nor *value* with God.

5. *Rule: Let the Mourning of your Earthly Principle be a Subordination, and Submission to your Heavenly Principle.* This makes your Sorrow a *Sacrifice,* when without this your Mourning is but *Murmuring.*

Heb. 10. 5, 6, 7. Jesus Christ is brought in speaking to God his Father: *Sacrifice, and Burnt-Offering thou wouldst not, but a Body hast thou prepared me. Then said I, lo I come, to do thy Will O God.*

Thus the Heavenly Principle speaks the same Language in every St. *Thou wilt have no more Sacrifices of Beasts. The Time is past, in which thou hast taken pleasure to have the Inferiour Earthly Principle to be Sacrificed to,* and *by* the Superiour Heavenly Principle, while *thine Image* was present only in the Type, and Shadow. But now thou hast prepared a Body for *me,* thou hast brought me into the Earthly Principle, that I should make a *Burnt-Offering* of my self to thee, as of my *own Body.* They were to bring no *Strange Fire* to the Sacrifice, but to wait till Fire from Heaven fall down upon it and consume it. In like manner is the Earthly man to lay itself on the Altar by the Power of the Heavenly Man, and to wait, till that bring forth a Flame of Sorrow upon it. The Earthly man should say alwaies to the Heavenly, *I mourn, that I may do thy Will, and not mine own.*

Est quædam flere Libido. There may be a *Lust* in weeping, and so there is, when the Outward Man fulfils his own will in weeping, and not the Will of the Inward Man, which is one with the Will of Christ and God.

6. *Rule : Let the Earthly Principle, as it is in itself, be only a Slave to yo in your Griefs.* If the *Flesh* have a Power of its own to make you *Grieve*, to qualifie, or measure your Griefs, it will bring the Curse of the *Serpent* upon you: it will make you to go upon your Belly, to sink altogether into your sensual and Corruptible Part. It will make you feed upon Dust, seek a merit in, and a Nourishment from your Sorrows. When the Flesh hath Liberty to interpose it self in our mourning, it makes our mourning *B rutish*, or *Devilish*. It makes our mourning *Brutish* by deriving it from outward, and Temporal Things; by terminating it on these. So our Lamentations are as the howl of Dogs, and cry of Bears. It makes our mourning *Devilish* by mingling it with discontent, and despair. So the Roarings of our Spirits are like the yellings of Devils to Christ: *Art thou come to Torment us?* The Flesh is to be kept as a *Hewer of Wood*, & *Drawer of Water*. We are to make use of the ways and weaknesses of it, to help to break our Hearts, and bring forth Tears at the direction of the Spirit in us.

The work of our Grief upon our Natural Part, as it is in itself, must be to keep it under; to beat it as a *Slave*, to destroy it as an *Enemy*.

This is the *Ass*, which is not for *Sacrifice*, but to have its neck broke, except it be redeemed by its Subordination to the Spiritual Part.

I have done speaking of the *manner* of *Spiritual Mourning*.

I come now to the *Third Particular* in the opening of the Nature of this *Grief*, which is the *Measure*.

The *Measure* of Spiritual Grief hath *Three Limits*.

1. *Limit : The casting out of* Filth.

2. *Limit : The casting down of* Flesh.

3. *Limit : The clearing up of the* Face *of* God *towards us.*

1. *Limit : The casting out of Filth.* St. *Paul* 1 *Corin.* 5. 3. in the case of the incestuous Person blames the Church, that *they had not mourned, that he, who had done this Thing might be cast out from among them.*

The Case is the same in our own Persons. We are to mourn, that every Evil Thing may be cast out of us. We are to keep our Hearts in a melting temper, till our Lusts be quite melted down, till the Gold, and the Dross be separated one from another. We are to weep, till we have washed our selves clean in our Tears.

Obj. But you may here ask : What Power is there in our Tears, or Sorrows to cleanse us from our Filth, shall we say with the *Papist*, that our mourning merits Grace, if not of *Desert*, yet for desire, out of *Congruity*? Or shall we say with the *Arminian*, that our griefs are a *moral* way of working upon our will, to mortifie that, and make it weary of the Pleasures of Sin, for the Pennance of Sorrow?

Ans. I answer to this, that there is neither any *merit* in the Tears of any Creature to move God ; For if thou be Righteous, it is to thy self. And the Heavens with all their Hosts are Folly, and Filth before Him :

Neithe r

Neither is there any *Efficacy* in the woes of man to purge the will of man. For *who can bring a clean Thing out of an unclean?* Can any one redeem his Brother from Death? Can one Passion or affection in Man by a Death in Sorrow redeem his Brother, another Passion, or affection from the Death of Sin? *They must let this alone for ever.*

But the Spiritual Griefs of a Saint are the Buddings of *Aaron*'s Rod, of the the Cross of the Lord Jesus in him. And from hence they have their *value* with God, and their *Vertue* on us.

1. *First, my Sorrows have a value with God*, as they are the Sufferings of my Saviour in me. St. *Paul* saith of himself, 1 *Colos.* 24. *I rejoyce in my Sufferings, while I fill up that which is behind of the Afflictions of Christ in my Flesh for his Bodies sake.* All the Sufferings of Believers are the Sufferings of Christ propagating themselves thorow his mystical Members. We are one Spirit with our Lord Jesus in our Tribulations as well as in our Consolations. Our Groans, as much as ourOoryings, are the Breathings of that Spirit. As the Soul is all in all the Parts of the Body, making every Member a part of the Humane Nature, putting upon it the Beauty of that Nature: So is Jesus Christ in every Thing of the actings, or Sufferings of Christ any where, giving a Divine Beauty, and worth to it, by vertue of the Union.

2 *Corin.* 4. 10. *Always bearing about in my Body the Dying of the Lord Jesus, that the Life of the Lord Jesus may be made manifest in my Body*: This St. *Paul* saith of himself. The Tears from our eyes are the Blood from the Heart of the Lord Jesus. Though not as *our Tears*, yet as *his Blood*, they have Power with God to bring forth his life in us. Jesus Christ dies over again in thy griefs; that so he may act his Resurrection over again in thy Graces. The Father makes a Promise to the Lord Jesus, *Es.* 53. 10. *When he shall make his Soul an offering for Sin, he shall he see his Seed.* This is an Everlasting Covenant between the Father, and the Son, that when he hath descended to the lowermost parts of the Earth, he should then begin to ascend.

When the Image of the Invisible God hath put itself off into the Strange Forms of Darkness, and Death; then is it to spring up again out of these, and again to behold itself in its own proper shape and power, which is its Seed. Thy Saviour, and Husband makes his Soul an Offering for Sin in all the Sufferings of thy Soul. Therefore mayest thou now challenge it of the Father in the name of Jesus Christ, that he may see in thee his Seed, which is the Power of an endless Life. Thou mayest say; behold, O my God! by him, whoso the Signet, and the Staff is; the Glory and Power of thy God-Head; by him am I in these Pangs and Sorrows. Let then a Man-child be born in my Heart, which may be called after his name, that I may rejoyce in it, and remember my Sorrow no more. Thy *Benjamin* is come before thee into the Land of *Ægypt*, as thy servant in my servitude. Thy *Darling* hath brought himself into my guilt, and griefs; he stands before thee in them. The *Lamb* of God is slain in my sufferings. O then let it be a *Passover*, that the evil Angel of Lust and Misery may pass from the house of my Spirit, when he sees the blood of this Lamb in my Tears sprinkled upon the Posts of the Door.

2. *Secondly, Our Sorrows have a vertue on us, as they are the Sufferings of Jesus Christ in us.* Galat. 6. 14. *God forbid*, saith *Paul*, *that I should glory in any thing, save in the Cross of our Lord Jesus, by which the world is crucified to me, and I to the World.*

As the Person of Christ is the Seed of God, which springs up into many Sons to God: so is the Cross of the Lord Jesus a Seed that remains not alone, but brings forth much Fruit. It grows up into a multitude of Crosses, a Cross in each good Heart, a Cross in every Creature of this world. This Cross of Christ is the wisdom and Power of God making themselves first the *Tree of the Curse*, on which all the Principles, and Spirits of this world must hang: Then the *Tree of Life* bringing forth the Fruits of *Paradise*, and the *Third Heaven*. Every care or cross in a Saint is this Cross of his Saviour sprouting in his Person. The *Lord Jesus* lies hid in each Tear, in each sigh of a Holy Spirit. He is there, as the Seed falling into the Earth, and Dying. By this Death he delivers himself from Death in thy Heart, and breaks out on every side into Discoveries of his Grace and Glory.

Say of thy Trouble; *why art thou cast down O my Soul?* This is that Death of my Saviour in me, by which he destroys the power of Death in my Spirit, Sin and the Devil. This is the way in which thou shalt praise him, and see him swallowing up the Principle of Darkness, in Darkness, that he may bring forth himself in the Light of his Countenance, to be the Light of thy Countenance. I have been the larger in this Objection, that so I may be the more clearly understood both in this, and in the following Particulars. Whatever mention is made of any Beauty, or Grace in a Saint, is not to be imputed to the Saint, but to the Grace, and Face of *Jesus Christ* in him: so is the Excellency or Efficacy of our mourning, the Discovery of our dying Saviour in it. No Persons, no Sorrows are Spiritual, if they be not one Spirit with Jesus Christ. But thus much for the First limit in the measure of our Sorrows, the casting out of Filth.

2. *Limit: The casting down of the Flesh,* 1 Cor. 9. 27. *I*, saith the Apostle, *keep under my body, and bring it into Subjection.* The words are ὑπωπιάζω, *I beat it black and blew*, and δουλαγωγῶ, *I make it to serve.* The end, and so the bound of Humiliation is *First* to bring down the Principle of the Natural Man into a Principle of Darkness, that it may no more put forth itself in its own Light and Life. *Secondly*, it is to subdue that Principle to the Heavenly Principle, that it may be quite slain in itself, and revived in the Spiritual Man a Spiritual Principle.

Rom. 7. 24. St. *Paul* calls the Natural Man, *this body of Death*, or *the body of this Death.* It is a body of Death in a Two-fold sense.

First,

First, Thy Outward Man is the shadow of Death cast upon thy Spirit. It is the Valley of the Shadow of Death thorow which thou walkest here below. Thou art in the Body sunk down to the borders of Death, being already come within the shadow of it. The whole face of things upon thy Person, and round about thee, is a dead Image, and the Image of Death: For he, who hath the Power of Death, hath entred into it with his Principality, and taken away the true Life of it, setting it up now, as an Appearance in, and of *himself*.

Secondly, Thy Outward Man is a Body of Death, because it is appointed to Death. The Body by one Death hath brought it self out of the Divine Life into the Power of Darkness, into a Hellish Root. Now by another Death it must be broken off from this Root, and brought back again into an Eternal Stock. Our mourning then must last, while we are in the Body of this Death, till this be no more *this Body*, but perish in Death. The Devil cast us out of our Innocency, and from the face of God; he set up himself, by setting up the Natural Man in it self. We were turn'd out of *Paradise*, when we came into *this Body*, which is now the *Beast's skin*. *Again*, By the Ruine of the Natural Man, we must raise the Building of God, and cast down the Devil. By putting off the Beast's skin, by the dissolution of the Tabernacle of Beasts skins in Death, we return into *Paradise*. We are therefore to go mourning to our Graves.

3. *Limit: The clearing of the face of God towards us*, *Matth.* 9. 15. Our Saviour tells the Jews, *That his Disciples could not fast while the Bridegroom was with them. But the Bridegroom should be taken away. And then they should fast in those days. The Face of God* in Jesus Christ, is the Soul's *Bridegroom*. Who, that is the Bride of this Bridegroom, can take joy in any thing, when this Face is withdrawn and hid from him? Shall not our Souls fast from the Freedom and Fulness of Natural Delights, when our Spirits are made to fast from the Beauties and Delicacies of *Jesus Christ*? This is the season of Mourning. It is now beautiful to see a holy Soul Widow-like, with a Vail upon the face of all her Glory and Content; when her God is gone a great Journey from her. What can she do but mourn, when he is absent, who was the *Light* of her Eyes, the *Anointing* of her Face and Head? What can set an end to her mournings, till *he return*, and wipe away all Tears from her Eyes, by *setting* himself in the Eye of her Spirit?

Psal. 30. 7. *Thou didst hide thy face, and I was troubled*, saith *David*. Will it not be Winter when your Sun is gone? Can you expect a Spring, till he turns toward your Earth again? Is it not the Presence of the *Lord Jesus*, that makes all things fresh, and full of Beauty round about thee? When he is *withdrawn*, who was the *Image* of God in them, do not all things *droop* and *languish* in thine Eyes? Canst thou then chuse but languish with them? If the *Lord Jesus* be the *Root* of thy Spirit, and his Spirit the *Sap* of thy Comforts, thou

thou wilt grieve in his *absence* without arguments to persuade thee to it; as naturally, as *Flowers* nipt with Frosts *hang* the head. Nay no arguments will be able to raise thee to any degree of chearfulness, except *he come*, and make himself the *argument*. When thy Corruptions, like Fogs from the Earth, have gathered into Clouds, which hide the Heaven of thy Lords Face from thee: weep then, till these Clouds be again dissolv'd by the Showers of thy Tears, and so thy *Jesus* again discover himself over thee as a clear sky.

I have done with the *Third* particular in the Nature of Spiritual mourning, which was the measure of it.

4. *The Mystery*. The Mystery of every thing is in God, *Ephes.* 3. 9. *The Mystery hid in God, who created all Things by Jesus Christ.* This is the Mystery of Things, their ground, their beginning, and end in the Person of God and Christ. Neither can we be Spiritual in any thing any further than we see the Mystery of it, and stand in the Mystery.

The *Mystery* of a holy Grief is Threefold.

1. *Mystery: Conformity to Jesus Christ.*
2. *Mystery: Complyance with the Will of God.*
3. *Mystery: The Compleating of our Persons.*

1. *Mystery: Conformity to Jesus Christ.* We read, *Ephes.* 1. 4, 5. that *we were chosen in Christ before the Foundation of the world: We were predestinated to the Adoption of Children by Jesus Christ.* We sprung up in Eternity, in the Heart of God, out of the Person of the Lord Jesus there, as *Images* of him, who as he rose up in the Divine Nature, the essential Image of it, was Fruitful from the Root of that Nature according to the Power of Life, and Store of Spirit in it. So he multiplied himself by the strength of the Father into many such Images in the heart, and thoughts of God. *Thus we were chosen in, and by him.* Thus also we were *chosen to be Conformed to the Image of this Son,* as you shall read, *Rom.* 8. 29. *Whom he did foreknow, he did also predestinate to be conform'd to the Image of his Son.* The Fathers fore-knowledge of us in his Son, was the ground of our predestination by him, and conformity to him. A chief part in Christ is the dark part, his Sufferings, a chief part of our Conformity to him lies in our Sufferings and Sorrows.

Rom. 8. 17. *Joynt-heirs with Christ, if so be we suffer with him, that we may be also glorified together.* Our whole inheritance is our conformity to the Lord Jesus. This Inheritance lies as well in Suffering, as in being glorified. We have a *double interest in Christ: One in the Unity of his Spirit: Another in the variety of his Body.* According to our *First* interest we are one with Christ, that is, by the Unity of the Spirit, 1 *Cor.* 6. 17. So we are to have the fulness of Christs Sufferings form'd over again upon our Persons in the Spirit, 2 *Cor.* 4. 10. According to our *Second* interest in the Body of Christ we are only particular members, 1 *Cor.* 6. 15. In this particular membership a particular share of Sufferings pertains to us, according to our

place

place in the Body. The portion of ſorrow allotted to every Saint in this capacity, is as much inferiour to the miſeries of our Bleſſed Saviour, as that Member is inferiour to the Head. But for this reaſon the Providence of God leads us to occaſions of ſorrow, and then opens in us a ſpring of Sorrow, that we may *fulfil our meaſure in the ſufferings of Chriſt*, Col. 1. 21. This is the *firſt Myſtery* of our Griefs, our Conformity to Chriſt; that we may be Brethren, Spouſes and Members of Chriſt.

2 *Myſtery. Our Complyance with the Will of God.* We mourn, that we may be like Chriſt; *Brethren* grown up from one Root with him; *Spouſes* drawn forth from his ſide, *Bone* of his Bone, *Fleſh* of his Fleſh; *Principle* of his Principle, *Image* of his Image; *Strength* of his Strength; *Weakneſs* of his Weakneſs. But now you may ask, what the myſtery of all ſufferings and griefs are, as they are Chriſt's firſt, and ſo ours?

Anſw.I anſwer to that by a place of Scripture, *Heb.* 5. 8. *Though he were a Son, yet learned he Obedience by the things which he ſuffered.* There are Two Waies of Learning; one *Speculative*, in the Contemplations of the Spirit; the other *Practical* in the Conformity of the Perſon. There are Two Waies of Obedience; one in the *Will*, being prepared,and ready to all things; the other in the *Work* of Doing or Suffering, being actually undertaken, and thorowly undergone. Our *Lord Jeſus* was ever in all things obedient to his Father, ſo far as that State in which he was, would permit. While he liv'd in Heaven, he was obedient to the Death,in the Contemplations of his Mind,and the Conformity of his Will, ſo far as theſe two Wings could carry him.

But all this while, the Devil might ſay of *Jeſus*, as he did of *Job*; He dyes for his Father in his Speculations, and Purpoſes at a diſtance; while his Father maintains a hedge of Life, and Joys round about him; while he ſees not Death, but as Death it ſelf is a living and beautiful Image in a Proſpect of Glory. Therefore *Jeſus Chriſt* is brought down into Fleſh, that he may try, and ſo experimentally learn another way of ſuffering, by an Actual Deſcent into the Power of Darkneſs, and Miſery, as it is in its own Principle. Our *Father* could have prevented the Riſing up of the Spring, or Principle of Sin in the Heart of the creature: So he could have cut off all occaſions of ſorrow or ſuffering: He could have taken away Sin by a change, and not by a Death; *Transfiguring* inſtead of *Crucifying* us; and this too, by the heavenly Perſon reſting upon us in a White Cloud, and taking us up in it ſelf, without its Deſcent into the Dark Cloud of this earthly Body. Thy Father could reſtrain the Iſſues of Luſt in thee, which ſend forth ſo much Filth, upon which we pour forth ſo many Tears. So our Tears might have been ſpared. But if all this had been, where had been the Teſtimony of our Obedience to the Father? There are *Two* Waies of Obeying God: *One in the concurrency of his Will, and ours; the other, in a contradiction between his Will and ours.* A holy Spirit obeys God the *firſt* way in Heaven and Joys. For there it takes up its Joys, and taſts a Sweetneſs in them, much more out of *Obedience*,

than

than *Appetite*; because they are the *Will* of God, rather than because they *agree* with its own will.

But we obey God the *Second* way on Earth in Afflictions. In Heaven we give up our will to be swallowed up in the Will of God, as a River in the Sea. In our Sorrows we Sacrifice our wills to the Will of God, as the Beasts were Sacrificed by their Death, and by Fire. So *Jesus Christ*, when his will was at the height of contrariety to the Will of God according to its own proper inclination; *If it be possible, let this Cup pass from me.* Yet then he cut the Throat of his will, and laid it panting upon the Altar, to be wholly consumed in the dreadfullest way, in the Fire of divine wrath and vengeance. Thou in all thy Griefs accomplishest the same Mystery after the same manner. Thou *Feastest* the will of the Father by the *Fast* of thine own will. Thou *obeyest* thy God, and servest his *Pleasure* by the *binding*, and *Offering* up of thy *Isaac*, all thy Pleasures.

3. *Mystery: The Compleating of our Persons.* This is yet a Further, and the utmost depth in the Mystery of our Sorrows. The Scripture holds it forth in the *Person* of *Christ* as the *Pattern*; in our Persons, as the *Copies* of that Pattern. We read of *Jesus Christ*, *Heb* 2. 10. that, *he was made Perfect through Sufferings.* That is Perfect, which hath all parts belonging to it. It belonged to the Person of Jesus Christ to act all parts, to appear in all shapes. For he was to be the *dwelling place of all Fulness*, 1 *Colos.* 19. He was to *unfold the manifold wisdom of God in his own Person*, *Ephes.* 3. 10. He came forth as *the Word*, to make a full and distinct expression of God. The Nature of God is the *Glass*, in which all Natures are first formed, and seen. The Natures of Light and Darkness, Shame and Glory, Joy and Misery; to say all, the Natures of Love and Wrath, the two Contrary heads of all distinct Natures are Originally in God according to their Eternal *Ideas*, or *First Forms.* If *Jesus Christ* had not come forth into all these Forms, and taken upon himself these several Natures in their utmost varieties, and contrarieties: he had wanted some parts belonging to his Person, and been imperfect in his *Relation*, as a Son, a Saviour; in his *Office* as a Representer, a Reconciler. Therefore, as St. *Paul* witnesseth, *He descended first to the lowermost Parts of the Earth*, then *He ascended above all Heavens*, and that for this reason; *that He might fill All*: *Ephes.* 4. 10. Thus he was made *perfect by Sufferings. The descent of Christ* was the *drawing* of the Picture of the God-Head upon him in its lowest and outermost Mysteries, or wonders of Glory; in its *Back-parts* or *Feet. The ascent*, was the *Uniting* of the lowest to the highest: the *bringing* of the outermost into the bosom of the Innermost: the *drawing* up of the Feet into the Bed, into the rest, and Glory of the head. The *Scripture* holds forth the accomplishment of the same *Mystery* in our Persons after the same manner. *Jesus Christ* went thorow these Sufferings, as our *Captain*, that he might lead us the *same way* to the *same end*; that he might bring us, as Sons to inherit the same

Glory;

Glory; to fulfil all Righteousness, all the goings forth of the God-Head in our selves thorow Christ, *Heb.* 2. 10.

St. *James c.* 1. *v.* 2, 4. exhorts the Saints to *account it all Joy, when they fall into all manner of Temptations*: and to *let Patience have her perfect work*, which would make *them Perfect, entire, wanting nothing*. We were brought forth upon the uppermost parts, the Face of the Earth in *Paradise*. Let us now with *Jesus Christ* go down into the *Deep*, to the lowermost parts of the Earth, by Sufferings and Sorrows. Let us patiently endure till we are carried thorow all the Chambers of Death, and the innermost corners of that Cave of Darkness; till we be carried out of all, up into Heaven: So we shall be clothed with all the *Wonders* of God, and have his manifold *Wisdom*, his *Fulness* displaid in our Persons as his Sons also, together with our Saviour. Willingly then Travel thorow the valley of *Baca*, of Mourning, and Lamentation; as the way of *Perfection*, the *Accomplishment* of the *Mystery* of God in you. Now I have performed the *first* part of my promise, which was to speak of *the Nature of Spiritual Mourning*. There remains behind, the *Second* part of my promise, which is to speak of *the Mixture of Spiritual Mirth, and Spiritual Mourning*.

I will direct you to this Mixture by *Five Rules*:

1. *Rule: So grieve, as giving Glory to God in your Griefs.* 1 Cor. 10. 31. *Whether ye eat or drink, or whatsoever ye do, do all to the Glory of God.* whether ye *Mourn* or be *merry*, let *both* be to the Glory of God. *Mourn* not, as questioning the *Sweetness* in the *Will* of God, the *Wisdom* in the *Counsels* of God, the *Strength* in the *Power* of God, the *Beauty* in the *Face* of God, the *Pleasures* in the *Person* of God, the *Infiniteness* in *all*. Grieve not to the *Clouding*, but the *clearing* of the Appearances of God in your Spirit. Let not your Sorrows be as *a troubled Sea*, but as a *Sea of Christal*, thorow which you may see the glorious face of God. As the Beams of the Sun shining thorow red Glass, so will the glory of God be appearing thorow your Sorrows. It will beget a *Pleasantness* in your *bloodiest* Pangs.

2. *Rule: Let your Mourning raise, not ruine the Life of the Spiritual Man in you. Though the Outward Man perishes, the Inward Man is renewed day by day*, 2 *Cor.* 4. 16. Let your Sorrows weigh down the Natural Man only, as *one* of the Buckets, that the Spiritual Man as the *other* of the Buckets, may be lifted up. If that Life which is Light in the Lord, be lifted up by your Griefs, It will draw up your Person, and your Griefs themselves into the Pleasantness of its own Light.

3. *Rule: Mourn in the Name of Christ, Colos.* 3. 17. *Whatsoever ye do in Word, or Deed, do all in the Name of the Lord Jesus. The Name of the Lord Jesus* wraps up *Four Things* in it, which I shall express by *Four Rules* in this present case.

1. *Mourn in the Power of Christ*, The Power of Christ is the Power of

Eternal,

Eternal Life, which carries an unexpressible sweetness along with it, even then, when it goes forth into the saddest operations. Thy Tears will be a Spiritual Wine, if they be the Fruit of this Vine.

2. *Mourn in the Image of Christ.* Every thing is delightful to us, which brings our well-beloved into our Thoughts, though it be, but as a Picture, or Shadow of him. Love delights in likeness, especially to be itself made like that which it loves. This will make thy Sorrows *Comfortable* to thy Heart, and *Glorious* in thine Eye, if thou *Transferrest* them upon thy self, as in a *Figure of Jesus Christ.*

3. *Mourn for Christ.* Make him the end of thy Sorrows. *Christ is the end of the Law for Righteousness sake, Rom.* 10. 4. Let *Jesus Christ* be the end of thy Griefs for thy Joys sake. *The End puts a Loveliness, and Pleasantness upon the means, and way to it.* If thy Sorrows be for Self, and from Self-love: they will be like *Brine*, they will have a *Gnawing, Burning* Saltness in them. But if they be for thy Saviour, and from his Love, they will be *Fresh*, and *Sweet* on thy Spirit, as the *Dew* of Heaven on the tender Grass.

4. *Mourn, as in Union with the Person of Christ.* A *Saint* is a Name of *Anointing*, which signifies *Two in one*; the *Ointment*, or Oyl, and the *Anointed*: *the Sanctifier, and the Sanctified. He that Sanctifies, and they that are Sanctified are of one, Heb.* 2. 11. They must also be in One. Our Griefs are never *Saintlike*, or Holy; if they be not in *Consort*, and *Fellowship* with *Jesus Christ*. *Rom.* 8. 17. *Joint-heirs with Christ, if so be we suffer with him.* Our Sufferings are a *Murther*, not a *Sacrifice*; they are to *Death*, not to *Life*; if they be not in Union with *Jesus Christ*. If they be in Union with Christ, that Union unites a *Sweetness*, and *Joy* to them.

These are the Branches of the Third Rule.

4. *Rule*: *Let your Grief be a Grace.* If your Grief be from Nature only, it is carnal, not spiritual; it is such a *Death*, as is a *Sowing to the Flesh*, which will bring forth Corruption, and Death. *Whatever is not of Faith is Sin, Rom.* 14. 23. If your *Mourning* be not a *Grace* in you, one of the *Daughters* of Faith, which is the mother of all Grace: it is Sin, and to be resisted by you, as the *Devil.* But if your *Mourning* be *Gracious*, then it is a *Sowing* to the Spirit, of which you shall *reap Immortality.* Such *Tears* are *Precious Seed*, Spiritual Seed, which have the Sweet Rellish, and Power of Immortal Life in them.

5. *Rule : Let your Mourning be in God. In him*, saith St. *Paul of God, we live, and move, and have our Being, Acts* 17. 28. It is true Naturally of all men. It is much more true of Saints in a Spiritual sense. We live the life of Grace, we Mourn, we have our Spiritual Being and Motions in God. A *Natural*, and *Spiritual* Man have their *Being* in *God* after a *different* manner. *A Natural Man* hath his Being in God, as he is the *Principle* of the First Creation, in which he is as in Thick Darkness. *A Spiritual Man* hath his Being in God, as God is *in Christ, who is the Brightness* of the Glory of God. *Abide in me,*

saith

ſaith *Chriſt*, that is in the Brightneſs of the Glory of God, and *ye ſhall bring forth much Fruit*, *John* 15. 4. 5.

If you will bring forth your *Tears*, as *Fruit* to God, you muſt weep in the midſt of the Glory, and Joys of the Divine Nature. *God* in his Naked Beauties muſt be the Stage, on which you muſt act the ſaddeſt part of your Sorrows. What Part will not ſuch a Stage, and Scene of Delights make Pleaſant?

If thou *mourneſt right*, thou art *in God*, while thou mourneſt, thou *ſeeſt* nothing below, above, on every ſide of thee, but the *Gold*, and *Curious Work* of his Glory. Will not this *Guild* thy Grief, and put a chearfulneſs upon it?

PSAL. XLV. VER. 1.

My Heart is enditing a good matter; I speak of the things, which I have made touching the King; my Tongue is the Pen of a ready Writer.

THis Psalm is believed to be composed upon the same occasion with the *Canticles*; The Marriage between *Solomon*, and the Daughter of *Pharaoh*, which is made by the Holy Ghost, a Type of the Mystical Espousals between the Lord Jesus, and a Holy Soul. The Eternal Spirit delights to play with itself, casting from its Heavenly person the shaded Light of this Creation, then filling every part of it, even the darkest, with figures of its own Sweetnesses, and Beauties. Strange Wives were charged upon *Solomon*, as a Mother-Sin big with many hateful Births. Yet this cloudy piece of Providence is a Vail curiously wrought with the Divine Images of Christ on the Throne, his Queen all in beaten Gold at his Right Hand with their pure, immortal Lovelinesses, Loves, and mutual Joyes; under which Vail lies hid the Living Face itself of all these Glories.

Prov. 25. 2. *It is the Glory of God to conceal a thing: but the Glory of Kings to search out a matter.* It runs thus in the Original: It is the Glory of God to conceal the *Word*: but the Glory of Kings to search out the *Word*. It is a height of Glory beyond the Compass of every created Understanding, the hiding of the eternal Word, which is brighter infinitely than ten thousand Suns all joined into One, under a vail slighter, and thinner, than the most empty shadow, to form the Picture of this Glorious Word upon every part of the shadow, and then again to vail that also with the Darkness of the Shade.

But this is the Glory of Jesus Christ, to bring down these Mysterious heights, and make them familiar to the Eye of the Creature. It is an Eye of Glory in the Saints, those Fellow-Kings to Jesus Christ, by which they discover the Picture in the shade, the ravishing depths of the Life itself in the Picture, and make it their Royal Entertainment to converse continually with the Beauties, and Sweetnesses of the Divine nature in them both invisible to common senses.

This Psalm is entituled, *A Song of Loves.* The sweetest *Matter* exprest in the sweetest *Manner*. Both are a Divine Harmony. The Loves here are a Harmony of the most Heavenly, and most Spiritual *Hearts*. The Song the Harmony of the most Heavenly, and most Spiritual *Voices*. The Loves figure out the Father, the pure, unfathomed, unconfined Spring of Unity, and Sweetness, where all things lie embracing each other in their first, and softest Bed: The Song represents the shining Word, the harmonious Wisdom, the Essential Musick, Beauty and Image of the Godhead, the Son, in whom all the Riches of Love are with an equal Richness, and Loveliness displaid. The Song of Loves, these Loves thus sung, this Marriage of Love, and Loveliness paint out to us the Joyes and Glories of the Third Person the Holy Ghost. But by whom was this Song sung? Some read; *The Song of the beloved Virgins.* These are the friends of the Bridegroom, and the Bride, which sing the *Epithalamium*, or Marriage-Song. In the *Canticles* they are called, *The Daughters of Jerusalem*, which some Interpreters understand to be the *Holy Angels*. Angelical Spirits are expressed by the name of Virgins very fitly: 1. For the preservation of their native sweetness, their primitive beauty, the flower of the Divine Image in them uncorrupt, untainted. 2. For their single Estate, being separate from mixture, and union with any sorts of Earthly Bodies below them, and not yet raised to a marriage with the Divine Body, the Substance, and Fulness of the God-Head in Jesus Christ; because they are the fairest, softest, and sweetest Images of all created Things. It is the manner of the Hebrew Tongue to express the Beauty, and Loveliness of things by the feminine Sex. The Woman is the Glory of the Man. Christ the Brightness of the Fathers Glory is represented in this Form by the *Jerusalem* above, the Mother of us all. In the Proverbs he is figured by a Virgin-Queen in her Pallace, his Angels as Maidens attending on this Virgin-Queen, and sent forth by her to invite her guests. Thus separate and Angelical Spirits, those invisible Beauties, which are the immediate Copies and Springs of all visible things, as also the Mark, and White to which the activity and operations, of all natural Principles, as Arrows are directed, be known by the names of Nymphs, and Virgins.

John the Baptist was the Restorer of the Law, the proper Ministry of Angels, which was ministred by Angels, and by which only the Angelical Life and Glories, as figures of the Divine, were ministred to us. He therefore is called by the Holy Ghost, *An Angel going before the Lord to prepare his way.* He speaks of himself, as a Friend of the Bridegroom, rejoicing to hear his voice, and making one in the Quire of Angels, which sing to the Bridegroom, and the Bride, while they lie on Beds of Glory in the embraces of each others Love.

These *Angels* are those *Friends*, which Jesus Christ calleth upon, in his Song of Songs, when he comes into his Spouse's Garden, *Cant.* 5. 1. *I have drunk my Wine with my Milk, Eat O Friends, Drink, be enebriated with Loves.* St. *Paul* expounds this Scripture, *Eph.* 3. 10. *That unto the Principalities, and Powers in Heavenly places might be known by the Church the manifold Wisdom of God.* The Hearts, and the Lips of the Spouse of Christ; the Marriage-Union between Christ and a saint, in the spiritual and Heavenly Image, is the Golden Cup, out of which the Angels drink in rich Discoveries of God, the Glories and sweetnesses of the Divine Nature, which are there poured forth immedi-

ately

ately from their Fountain, which are that Wine of Love, with which Christ, and his Spouse entertain each other. O the Dignity! O the Delights of a Holy Soul! Angels sing to it; Angels pry into its Beauties, and Joys; Angels draw the Waters of their blissful Light, and Life from this Well. The Sounds, Operations, Lives, Essences of Angels are only a Musick, Songs of Love, and Joy to the beloved Soul, and her Bride-groom in their Union. In this sense Christ, and a Saint in their Spiritual Glory, ride together upon the Cherubims. The Angels are made as perfumed gales of Wind, on which they Flie; Flames of a Divine Fire of Love, Joy, and Glory, which continually spring up, shine before them, and round about them; penetrate thorow all things, converting all things into the same Ministerial Brightnesses, and Harmonies of an Immortal Life, and Love under their Feet.

But there is another passage worth our observation, before we leave the Title to this Psalm: *To the chief Musician upon Shoshannim. Shoshannim* was an Instrument of six strings, upon which the Tune to this Song was plaid. If there be, as Divines say, *Tot Mysteria quot Apices*, so many Mysteries, as points of words, letters, or Marks in the Holy Scripture, we may well believe this six-stringed Instrument to allude to the Creation made up of the several Works of six several Days. He that hath Eyes to see what the Spirit doth, and Ears to hear the Sound of the Spirit, understands this great frame to be a well-tuned Instrument of so many strings, as there are Creatures in it; the whole Composure of Providence from the beginning of the world to the end of it, this Song of Loves plaid upon it by Jesus Christ to his Heavenly Bride, whose Spiritual senses see the Harmonious, and Delicate Motions of his Hand upon every string, and take in with unexpressible delight the ravishing Melody.

Shoshannim signifies also the six-leaved Lilly. *Can.* 2. 1. It is doubtful whether the Holy Spirit speak in the Person of Christ, or the Church, when he saith in his Song, *I am the Rose of Sharon, and the Lilly of the Valleys.* It is generally understood of Christ. In that Mysterious History of *Esther*, as *Esther, Mordecai*, the Jews, so the City *Shushan*, the City of the Lilly represent the Church of Christ in general, or each holy Soul in particular. Interpreters here apply the Lilly to the Bride, It is in the plural number Lillies, and the clause may be rendred, concerning the Lillies. So the Subject of this Song of Loves is signified to us, Jesus Christ, and his beloved Bride, two Lillies upon the same Root, Flourishing with the same Beauties, smiling Reflections each of other. Either of them with his six leaves comprehends in itself the perfections of the whole Creation in their Original Purities, and Sweetnesses. Both alike, in that Spiritual Image in which they are united, are to the variety of Creatures, as the Seventh Day to the other six, a Bed of Rest, and Delights with a Canopy of Glory; their Rest, Sanctification, and Blessedness.

But it is time to pass from the *Title* to the *Psalm* itself. The first verse is a Preparation to the matter contained in the Song. It consists of Three Parts.

1. The

1. The Flame, and fulness of the Author; *My heart enditeth a good matter.* The word, *Enditeth*, is used only this once. Some expound it, boileth with a good matter, and make it an allusion to Meat-offering in the Sanctuary prepared by fire in a Frying-pan. So the eternal Spirit, which is Love, hath the place of the Holy Fire. The Heart is the Frying-pan. The Excellencies of Jesus Christ in his own Person, and his Brides, with their mutual Affections, and Joyes are the Meat-offering.

Some interpret this Boiling by the bublings and wellings forth of a Fountain. Thus the Chrystalline Waters of the Light, Life, and Beauties of Christ, mingled with the Heavenly Fire of his Love, are the Sea. The Heart is the Spring into which this Sea by Invisible Tracts, and hidden Passages conveyeth its flowing Treasures, which from thence pour themselves forth into rich, pleasant, and plentiful Streams.

2. The Excellency of the Subject, *I speak of the things, which I have made touching the King.* This King is called God, and seated upon the Throne of Eternity, *v.* 6. which verse is cited, and applied to Jesus Christ, as he comes the second time into the World, attended by all his holy Angels after his Resurrection; and Ascent to the Throne of his Father. This is the King, this is the Bridegroom, and the Beloved of the Soul; Jesus cloathed with the Royal garment of his Divine Nature, crowned with the Glory of the Father, perfumed with all the good ointments of the Holy Ghost.

3. The Power, by which the Author is inspired in the composing of this Song *My Pen is the Tongue of a ready Writer.* Holy men of God spake, as they were moved by the Holy Ghost. 2. *Pet.* 1. 21. As the Son is the Wisdom, Power, and Glory of the Father: So the Holy Ghost is the Love of the Father, and Son, he is called by the name of Charity, or Love, 1 *Cor.* 13. *v.* 1. 8. He is that Love, by which God and a Saint dwell one in another, as Love is described to be the Union between the Lover, and the beloved Object. So he is spoken of. 1 *John* 4 16. God is Love; He that dwells in Love, dwells in God, and God dwells in him. It is the Inspiration of this Holy Spirit of Love, by which this Song of Loves was penned.

My Heart is enditing a good matter. My heart is full, boileth up, and floweth forth with a good matter, sweet, beautiful and profitable, This Heart represents every Member of Christ, which all have one, and the same Spirit. These words thus opened, afford us this Doctrine.

1. *Doct.* A good Heart is a Treasury of good things. *Matth.* 12. 35. *A good man out of the good Treasure of his heart bringeth forth good Things.* A Treasure, or Treasury implyeth two things:

1st. *A Place.* A good Heart is a Treasury like Heaven in three respects; 1. It is great, and spatious. It comprehends all things within itself. It hath nothing above it, or without it, to shut it up, and confine it. 2. It is of a shining, and glorious Substance, made of Light. 3. It is incorruptible, immo[illegible]

impreg[illegible]

impregnable. No Thief can there break in to steal. No moth, or rust consumes: There is no Principle of corruption, or decay within: No power from without can prevail there.

2. Precious things laid up in this Heavenly Heart make it a good Treasury. All the precious things of the Sun, and Moon, of the Heavens above, and the deep below, are here. Here are *Eden* and *Paradise*. Gen. 2. 10. A River went out of *Eden* to water the Garden. The Jews observe from this place, that there are two *Paradises*, a Superiour, and Inferiour; One above, Another below. In that above is the Fountain of Pleasure, from thence the stream descends, which makes that below ever-green, and flourishing with delights. *Eden* signifies Pleasure or Delight, which name in another word is given to Christ, as he was eternally in the bosom of the Father; *Prov.* 8. 30. I was by him, one brought up with him, Delights from day to day. Jesus Christ in his Heavenly Image, in the Substance and Essence of the eternal Light, is *Eden*, the Paradise above. In his earthly Image, the sweet Shade where all his Beauties seem at once to sleep and spring, he is the Paradise below. There is he the *Eden*, and the Fountain in the midst of *Eden*. Here the Garden watered by the River going forth from *Eden*. A good Heart hath in itself both these Paradises; the Fountain, and the Stream; *Eden*, and the Garden. *Cant*. 4. 15. The Lord Jesus calls his Spouse, A Fountain of Gardens, a Well of living Waters flowing from *Libanon*. The holy Heart is both the Fountain which makes all things Gardens, Paradises, which way soever it flows, and those Gardens too. It is both *Libanon* with the Fountain in it; and the Gardens below in the vallies, in the midst of which the Living Waters from this Fountain run along.

Reason. The Heart is that Spirit, which is the first Spring, and Principle of Life in man. *Prov*. 4. 23. Keep thine heart with all Diligence: For out of it are the Issues of Life. All the treasures of this World, its Light, Forms, Vertues, operations are first in the Sun. From thence they flow forth in various Streams all round about him, while yet they are still comprehended in him, as being not only their inmost Center, but also their outmost Circle of Light, and Life. So is the Heart, or Spirit of Man, an Invisible Sun in the midst of him, far more great or glorious than this which we see; in which all forms, and acts of Life, like Beams, rise up first, and fullest; from whence they are dispensed, and dispersed.

The Hebrew word, to keep, imports a double sense. 1st. Diligently observe thine Heart, what Spirit, or Principle it is, by which thou art acted. Such as this is, such is thy whole Life. If thy Heart be a Substantial, true, pure Spirit, thy whole way, and work, all thy Joyes are Substance, Truth, Light, Immortality, as the Visions of God. If the Heart which is in thee, be shadowy, thy Life is vain and empty, the dream of a shadow. Is thy heart corrupt, and polluted? then are all thy Streams poisoned, death lurks and sports

itself

itself in them with an innumerable company of Devils. 2. Keep, that is, preserve thine own, thy true Heart with all diligence. Abide in Christ, and his Love, as the only root of Life, from whence alone spring the sap, greennesses, flowers, fruits of true Sweetnesses, Beauty, and Blessedness. Watch day and night, that no other Spirit put forth itself in thee; for every other Principle besides Christ, and his Love, will certainly prove a Counterfeit, and instead of a Heart, out of which the Issues of Life ought to be, a root of bitterness.

There is a Twofold Heart: 1. Natural. 2. Spiritual.

1. There is a Natural Heart. This is the supream part of the natural Soul, the Angelical Spirit in Man. 1 *Thes.* 5. 23. St. *Paul* prayes: *The very God of Peace sanctifie you wholly: and I pray God your whole Spirit, and Soul, and Body be preserved blameless unto the coming of our Lord Jesus Christ.* Here we have the natural Man divided into three parts, which are equally capable of being sanctified, or by defilement made subject to blame. 1. Spirit. 2. Soul. 3. Body. The Spirit is as the Fountain; the Soul the Stream of Life: The Body the Channel in which this Stream runs along. The whole Man is one Beam sprung immediately from the Divine Glory. The upper end of the Beam, where it is fullest and brightest, immediately united to, and rooted in the supream Light, makes the Spirit. The lowest point, least and darkest, almost vanishing into the Shade, with which it mingles its light, where it toucheth the Earth, is the Body. The Soul is the middle of that Beam, partaking of both these, dividing and uniting them, like the Firmament between the Waters above and the Waters below; the Angels being the Waters above the Firmament; and Corporeal Lives those below.

The Spirit is the Angel in Man, or Man in the Similitude and Society of Angels; the invisible Image, the first Treasury of all his Natural Beings, Beauties, and Life, which afterward descends, and distinguisheth itself into the varieties of Inferiour Acts, and Appearances. St. *Paul* therefore in the forementioned place calls it their whole Spirit.

The Body is the Outward and Visible Image, the Shadow below of this above.

The Soul is the Life, by which the Spirit descends into the Body, maintains communion with it, and gathers it up again into itself.

According to these Distinctions and Descriptions *Solomon* discourseth, *Eccles.* 12. 7. *Then shall the Dust return to the Earth as it was: and the Spirit shall return to God, who gave it.* The name of God there signifies Gods or Angels, for whom it is frequently, and expresly used in the Holy Scripture. The Jews say it properly imports the Divine Nature, as it is cloathed with the Angelical; God in the midst of all his Holy Angels, coming forth into the Creation, descending to be the Head of it.

It is an *English* Proverb: If men could live without the company of Women, they should converse with Angels. This is true; when the Spirit, which is the Head, and the Man in us, withdraws itself from its Shadowy Image, the Body, which is as the Woman, it finds itself in the Form of an Angel, and in the Society of Angels. From the Angelical State and Company it descends into the Body. Thither it returns again, when it leaves the Body.

This is the Natural Heart, the Angelical Spirit in Man, made in the Similitude of God, as he cloaths himself with the Angelical Image, as with a Garment of Light, and so vailing his naked, unaccessible Glories comes forth to be the Head of Angels. This Spirit is the Immediate Seat of the Divine Presence, the Glory the Angelical Throne. Here the precious things of the Sun, and the Moon, of the Invisible, and Visible Image of the Divine Nature; here the Riches of the whole Creation appear together in their fullest Lustre, and most beautiful Order. The Letters of the Latine Name for Heart, *Cor*, make the first Letters of those word, *Camera Omnipotentis Regis*, which being interpreted are, the Chamber of the Almighty King. It is a common observation, that the Heart of Man is Triangular, which therefore cannot be filled with the round World, but only with the Trinity. This Heart, of which we speak, is properly Triangular, consisting like the Angels, of these Three, Essence, Understanding, and Will, the proper, and Immediate Type of the Trinity, which as it can be fitted, and filled up only with the Truth of that Type, those Three ever-blessed Persons, as their Seal in the noblest mettal, next themselves, it contains more expresly, more at large, and more gloriously all those Figures, and Draughts of Divinity, which are imprinted upon the Face of any Creature. O the inestimable Treasures of Mans Natural Heart, if Sin change it not from a Palace of Angels to a Prison of Devils, or a Grave!

2. There is a Spiritual Heart, 1 *Corin*. 6. 16. He that is joyned to the Lord, is one Spirit. Mark the Absoluteness, and Universality of the expression: one Spirit. He who is joyned to the Lord Jesus by believing, is one Spirit with Christ, one Spirit in Christ, one Spirit, as Christ is one.

Galat, 3. 19, 20. St. *Paul* thus distinguisheth between the Law, and the Gospel: The Law was ordained by Angels in the hand of a Mediator. Now a Mediator is not a Mediator of one; but God is one. There is a Two-fold Mediator; one, who hath his Ground in the Distance, and his End to maintain the Distance between Two Parties. The other is founded in an Unity, and his work is to manifest, and make perfect this Unity. The Character of the Law is Duality, and Division. God, and the Creature are presented each to other, as two upon different Principles, treating on a Covenant of works, containing different Terms to be performed by each apart. In the Gospel God reveals himself, as he is One, as he is the Ground, the Object, the End of all his affections, and operations; as he comprehends himself, and the Creature in one Person, and in one Spirit in our Lord Jesus; as he loves the Creature with the same love, with which he loves himself, and beholds it in the same Glory, with

which

which he beholds himself in Christ. This is the Covenant of Grace, in which the Lover, and the Beloved are both One.

You may now ask me two Questions:

Q. 1. How God is One?

Q. 2. How a Believer is one Spirit?

Q. 1. How is God One?

An. God is one four wayes. 1. He is perfect. He comprehends all parts of Excellency in every kind and degree, Essentially in one supream, and undivided Point of Being within himself. He is to himself the Eye, the Light, and the Object; the Love, the Lovelinefs, the Joy and Fruit of both; all in One. The most curious Composition of all Sweets in one Ointment, or Perfume; The most natural extraction of the vertues of all herbs and flowers into one Sweetness in Hony falls infinitely short of the Unity of all Perfections here, and the Perfection of this Unity.

2. God is Pure. There is no mixture in him. As they say of Gold the purest Mettal; It is *plenum sui*, full of itself: so is God in the highest sense. Every grain of pure Gold, is Gold. Every thing in God is God. There is no mixture, Division, Allay, or Bound. The Divine Nature is endlessly compleat, and entire within itself, like a Sea of unshaded Light, which hath no shore, or Bottom. God is Light, and in him is no darkness. 2 *John* 1. 5.

3. God is unchangeable. He is the Rock unmoveable; He is the Rock of ages. All successions of Time, like Waters of a River pass by him, and behold him through all revolutions fixt in the same place, and State. He is the Rock of Eternity. As Wheels turning round in a Cave within a great Rock: So all the Times and Changes of this World are comprehended within the Unchangeableness, and Eternity of his Essence.

4. God is the Fountain. He is not a Broken, Barren, but a perfect, and pregnant Unity. *Rom.* 9. 36. Of him, and Through him, and To Him are all things, to whom be Glory for ever. As all numbers are a Unity multiplied, so are all things various Sparklings of this Divine Unity; Emanations, and Manifestations of the same God presenting himself to us at sundry times, and in divers manners. Love is defined to be *Partus in pulchro*, a Birth in a Beauty. This is the true nature of things, that Divine Love, which is the Birth of all Varieties of, and in this Beautiful, this Blessed Unity.

2. *Q.* How is a Believer one Spirit?

1. That One, Eternal Spirit brings forth the Spirit of a Saint, as his own immediate, proper and Peculiar Birth; as the dear Reflection of himself. A Saint is the Workmanship of Jesus Christ, not as a Picture is of a Painter, but as a Child is of the Father, one Spirit, one Life, one Divine Nature is in Both.

2. This one Spirit begets, and brings forth the Spirit of a Saint in his own likeness. *Rom.* 8. 29. *God hath predestinated us to be conformed to the Image of*

his Son; that is to his heavenly Image, as he is the quickning Spirit: 1 *Cor.* 15. 45, 49. The Lord Jesus is our Father, the Father of the new World, the New Birth in us, as he is the Heavenly one, that Spirit, which is the supream Unity, the Lord and Fountain of Life, and Spirits. So he brings us forth in the Image of the same Heavenly Form, and of the same Divine Unity. Thus he prays to his Father; *John* 17. 22. *The Glory which thou gavest to me, I have given to them, that they may be One, as we are One.* Behold the Divine Birth of a Saint, the Divine Likeness into which he is born, and the Divine Unity, the Ground, and Form of the Divine Birth, and Likeness.

3. The Eternal Spirit unites itself to the Spirit of a Believer thus regenerated in the most Intimate, Entire, and Inseparable manner. They mutually inhabit, fully possess, perfectly enjoy each other. In life, and death, time, and eternity they are undivided. Thus this Heavenly *Adam*, the Unity, and Fountain of Spirits casts himself into the sleep of Humane Life, and of Death, that he may bring forth from his Side, and his Bosom this Sister-Spirit, this true *Eve*, the Mother of all Living, of all Heavenly, and Spiritual Lives, as he is the Father. Then, when he awakens in the Resurrection from the Dead, he takes her to be his Spouse, as she is his Sister in the Fellowship of the Divine Unity, which is the glorious Ring, and Circle of all Relations. So she, who is Spirit of his Spirit, in the likeness of the same Spirit, is made one Spirit with him.

Thus you have an Answer to these two Questions. You see, how God is One; How he, that is joyned to the Lord, is one Spirit. O that men knew God unvailed, revealed in the Light, and Grace of the Gospel, as he is One! O that they they did rellish the Sweetness of this Unity of the Spirit, which is the height of all Relations, by which God is one to a Believer in all times, and things, one in him, one with him; by which he also is one to, in, and with God! This sight and sense would make us to be continually in Pangs of longings to be regenerated, and brought forth into this Spirit, and Unity; as Jesus Christ is always in pangs of Love to bring it forth, and form it in us.

But to conclude this Reason;. This Holy Spirit, this Spirit of Unity, and Unity of the Spirit is the Spiritual heart, of which we speak. St. *Paul Ephes.* 3. expresseth it by being rooted in Love. This is that Root, which we have in the eternal Love of God, in that Love, which is God, in God, as he is Love. This is the new Heart, which is bred and cherished in the bosom of the Father. These Heavens above us comprehend in their Circuits all things here below, which, as learned men teach us, are figures, & images of their vertues sent forth from them. But they have fixed in themselves innumerable Bodies of Light, and Glory far exceeding all things here. They say, that these Heavens are Circular, because that round Figure is most capacious, and beautiful, as being an Image of the Unity of Angelical Spi[illegible] How great and glorious a

Circle

Circle then vastly transcending the Heaven of Heavens is this Divine Unity; this Spirit which is the new heart of a Saint? All the Heavens, and this earth lie within the compass of it, as Light shadows which it casteth from it self. But as for those Treasures which are proper to it, which are fixt in it, how infinitely more innumerable, how infinitely richer are they? The mind of Christ with all the Beauties, and Brightnesses there; the deep things of God, with all those Lights and Joys unfathomable to every natural Eye, and Heart, lie within the Circuit of this Spiritual Principle. A great Philosopher call'd the Angelical Spirit in man, which is his Natural Heart, the Flower of the Soul. It is so indeed, as the Blossoms upon Fruit-Trees; but the Divine Spirit, the Spiritual heart is the Fruit,

1. *Use.* Seek this good heart, which hath so good a Treasure in it. That you may seek it with all affection, and diligence, take these Three directions: Believe the Truth of this Principle: Consider the Preciousness of it: Understand your Propriety in it.

1. Believe the Truth of this Principle. When the Apostles asked the Christians in *Samaria*, whether they had received the Holy Ghost, they answered, that they had not so much, as heard whether there were a Holy Ghost or no. Is not this the temper of many amongst us, of most, of the sensitive, and natural Spirit in us all? We do not so much as believe, that there is a Holy Ghost; much less, that this Holy Ghost is poured out upon any Soul, as a Heavenly Anointing from above; or dwells in any heart, as the Principle of a supernatural, and eternal Life. He that comes to God, must believe, that God is, and that he is a Rewarder of those that diligently seek him: *Heb.* 11. 6. Fix in thine heart with an unshaken faith, these two Radical Truths, from which all the fatness, and sweetness of the Tree of Life is derived into our Spirits; 1. That God is. 2. That there is a Union between God and Man in One Spirit. Say frequently to thy self: It is true, It is the first Truth, upon which all other Truths are built; that there is a supream, incomprehensible Being, which shines through all, and fills all, the Fountain, and Measure; the End, Perfection, and Blessedness of all Beings. It is as true, that this ever-glorious God descends in Jesus Christ to sow himself by his own good Spirit as a Divine Seed in the heart of man below; that by the unvailing of his original Excellencies he shines, as a spiritual Sun from above into the Soul, to quicken, awake, and call forth this Seed, in the vertue of which the Soul springs into a new, and heavenly Being, comes to God by the fresh Participations of his life, grows up into his Likeness, pleaseth him, is possess'd, and enjoy'd by him, possesseth, and enjoyeth him with an unexpressible fulness of all mutual, and Divine Pleasures. When the Merchant in the Gospel found a Pearl in the Field, he went, and sold all to purchase this Field. If you have discovered this rich Pearl of the Divine Nature, as a Root at the bottom of your Spirits: go, exchange every Principle, Power, and excellency to give y

self up to the conduct, activity, fruitfulness, enjoyment of this alone.

2. Consider the preciousness of this Heavenly Principle, *Es.* 6. 13. God compares his people in the greatest desolations to an Oak, whose Substance is in it, when it hath cast its leaves: so saith he, the Holy Seed shall be the Substance thereof. Consider here three Precious Things in this good Heart, which is the Seed, and Principle of Grace in us.

1. This Spiritual Principle is a Substance. *Solomon* complains of all things under the Sun; the Eye is not satisfied with seeing, nor the Ear filled with hearing. He brings this as an Argument, and effect of their vanity. All things here are Shadows only, and so empty, unsatisfactory, endlesly raising expectations, and desire, but never answering them. When this Spirit, which is far above the Sun is received by thee, when this becomes the Principle of all thy faculties, which sees in thine Eye, hears in thine Ear, understands, and wills in thine heart; when this is the Treasury, from which all Objects come forth to act those faculties: then thine Eye will be satisfied with seeing substantial Beauties, thine Ear will be filled with substantial Melodies, thine Understanding will sit down to a Heavenly Feast of substantial Lights, and Truths, thy Will shall lie down to a Sweet and Eternal rest in a bed of substantial Embraces, and Joys, in the midst of the Substance, and Essence of Goodness itself.

2. This is the Holy Seed. The Heavens over our Heads are pure. They are free from that gross, and dark Matter, with which all Forms of things are mixt here on Earth. This Purity of theirs, is their Transparency, Light, Lustre, Harmony, Vertue, Incorruptibility. Yet they are Corporeal, and Bodily; their bright Beauties shall be turned into Darkness, and Blood. The Angels are purer far, than these Heavens. They have no Cloud, Clog, or Dross of Bodies. Yet are they mixtures of Light and Shade. Their Glories are vails upon the true Glory. They wax old, as a Garment, and are changed. Their Nature is subject to stains, and falls. But this Principle, which is the Seed, and Heart of a Believer is purer than the Heavens, or the Angels. It is the Spirit of God, the true Light, in which there is no Darkness; Simple, incorruptible, Unchangeable.

3. This Principle is durable. It is a Fountain springing up in the Soul to Eternal Life, *John* 4. O precious Treasure! Eternity is defined to be the full, and unbounded Possession of all Good at once, in One. Pearls have their price, because they have their lustre in a lasting Substance. This Holy Seed is the onely Pearl of price, both for its Lustre, and for its lastingness.

The Will of Man naturally moves to good. The greater the good is, and the more clearly it appears to us; so much the more natural, and powerful are the motions of our Will to it. Did we understand the goodness of this Spiritual Principle for the Reality, the Excellency, the Eternity of it; the Waters are not carried so naturally, so constantly to the Sea, nor Fire upwards to the Bosom of Heaven; as our Souls would to this Sea of Life, and Bosom of Love,

Union

Union with God in the Unity of his own Spirit. Thus we have done with the 2d Direction to quicken us in our pursuit of a new Heart, a Spiritual Principle, which is to consider the preciousness of it.

3. Understand your Propriety in this Divine Principle. 1. You were made in the Similitude, and Image of God. He is your Original; the Substance and Truth of your Being; more truly your selves, than you are your selves. 2. God is your Father, *There is one God the Father, of whom are all Things*, saith St. *Paul*, 1 *Cor.* The Cheeks of Christ are said to be Beds of Spices: *Cant.* 5. *v.* 13. Our Immortal Souls, our whole Persons are sprung up out of the Glories of the eternal Spirit, as Spices, and Flowers out of their Beds in the Gardens. When we are united to this Spirit, we return to our own Original, like those flowers; we sink down into our proper Beds and Roots, to receive a fresh Life and Beauty. 3. We are made by, and in Christ, *Col.* 1. By Christ, as our immediate Principle, and Pattern; In Christ, as our proper Habitation. The Original Sin of Devils, which infected Mankind, is plainly set down to be this: *Jude* 6. They kept not their first State, in *Greek*, Principle: but left their own Habitation. Propriety begets Love; for both Love and Propriety have their life and root in Unity. There is nothing which is so much thine own, as God, as Christ, as the Spirit. These are thine own Father; thine own Habitation, where thou art at home; thine own Principle; thine own Original; thine own truest and best Self. Let this Propriety then by Love ascending from thee, by the sense, and influence of a greater Love far descending upon thee, encourage, allure, and attract thee to this Divine Principle, this Spirit of Union, by which thou becomest one Spirit with Christ, and the Father. Thus return, O man, whosoever, whatsoever thou art, to thine own Home, to thy proper Unity, as the wandring Bird to her nest; and the Wife of Adulteries to the bosom of the Husband of her Youths, where she finds a Fountain of Heavenly Loves still flowing fresh for her, as at the first; into which she casts her self, and finds all the Beauties of her Youth, and Purity restored unto her, as in the beginning; her sins and sorrows flying away, and vanishing into the Air of this eternal Spirit, as Shadows of the Night, and Dreams of a man asleep, when he waketh.

Use 2. This good Treasure of a good Heart is a Cordial, and Comfort against Losses, or Sufferings. *Heb.* 10. 34. The holy Penman tells the Disciples, to whom he writes, they took joyfully the spoiling of their Goods, knowing in your selves, that ye have in Heaven a better and an enduring Substance. Some read it knowing that you have in your selves in Heaven a better, and an enduring Substance. This Scripture upon the riches of the Spiritual Principle in a Believer groundeth five sweet and full Consolations.

1. Thou hast the Substance. A Lacedæmonian invited to hear one sing like the Nightingale answered, To what purpose, when I can hear the Nightingale itself. When thy sense mourns to thy Soul, and saith: They

have

have taken away our Estates, our Friends, all the joys of Life. They will take away our Lives also: let thy soul reply; why should we mourn for the Shadows, when still we have the Substance?

2. Thou hast all things better. Philosophy saith, that every plant below, hath its Star in Heaven; each Star its Angel above; the Angels their Idea's, or Original Essences, and Truths, in God, to which they are as Types only. Is thy Flower withered? Thou hast it in a Star. Is thy Star darkned? For thy Star thou hast an Angel. Are the good Angels, which ministred to thee, withdrawn from thee? They are present, and appear to thee in a better manner, in the Form of God. Canst thou grieve for the loss of a Figure in Wax, when thou hast the same Figure in a Gold-Seal, from which the Impression of that Form was made upon the Wax?

3. Thou hast all to endure for ever. The Scripture compares Spiritual, and Heavenly Things to Spices, for their Sweetness, and Incorruptibleness, because they partake much of the Sun. Spices are prefer'd before Flowers, because they have a more lasting Sweetness; and not only so, but they preserve us both living, and dead from corruption. Therefore they are used for preservatives from Infection, and for Embalmings. Thou seest thy Flesh, and all the Glory of the Flesh round about thee wither, and fade away. Trouble not thy self. In stead of these Flowers thou hast Spices. Thou hast all thy pleasant things in an incorruptible Spirit, where they not only preserve their sweetnesses ever fresh for thee, but thee also ever flourishing in the enjoyment of them.

4. Thou hast all in Heaven. A Believer is ever in Heaven, and hath Heaven in himself. For that Spirit, which is his Principle is the highest Heaven. The Joys of the Gospel are compared often to a Feast, to a Wedding-Dinner at the Marriage of a Kings Son. Now there go to make up a Feast, not only costly, and curious fare, but all things suitable, Stately, and rich Rooms, Musick, Perfumes, excellent company, all the Furniture, and Entertainment great, beautiful, and delighting. Thus thy Sufferings only change the Scene. What thou hadst before on Earth; now thou hast in Heaven, in the glorious Fellowship of all Angels, and Triumphant Spirits, with the Ointments of the Holy Ghost, the Melodies, and Harmonies of Divine Love sounding thorow all the Beauties of the Divine Nature, in the purest Light guilding all; Joys, and Immortal Pleasures like Doves with Silver Wings, and Golden Feather flying about every where, being nothing but the Spirit of all Grace, Joy, and Glory in various forms.

5. Thou hast all this Substance, this Heaven in thy self. A Believer hath these Heavenly Things in himself by a threefold Union.

1. By a Union of Love. As these Heavenly things are thy Beloved; so thou art their Love. As thou beholdest all pleasantnesses in their faces: so thou art their Garden of Pleasures, where all precious things, new and old, are

trea-

treasured up for thy Beloved. They are thy rest, and delight: their Desire is towards thee. You are in the Unity of the Spirit, as One made Two, and Two made One again.

2. By a Union of Likeness. Those Heavenly things, and thy Spirit are as Brother and Sister that suckt the breasts of the same Mother; as Twin-Lilies, or Roses springing from the same Root of Love. They are to you, and you to them, as clear and shining Glasses, in which you mutually see the Faces each of other, and your selves as reflections of each others Beauties. Jesus Christ in the *Canticles* often calls the Holy Soul his Sister-Spouse. He calls her, *Can.* 1. 9. My Love. The word in Hebrew according to its Root is the same with that, which signifies a Friend, who is described to be *Alter Idem*, the same in another Person. It properly imports One made into Two by a Division, as *Adam*, and *Eve*; the other half on Ones self.

3. By a Union of Substances. Bodies can never meet in One. No one Body can ever be in two places at once; nor two bodies ever in one place. They unite only by Touches, by their outsides, by Accidents, and Shadows. A Holy Heart, and Heavenly Things unite, as Spirits, as the purest Spirits, where the Unity is most perfect. These intimately, totally, essentially, formally penetrate, possess, fill, and actuate each other. You have a shadow of it in the mixture of Lights; or in two clear, and bright Eyes, when they look full, and stedfastly one upon another. So Christ prays, *John* 17. 21. That they all may be one, as thou Father art in me, and I in thee, that they may be one in us. Again, *v.* 23, I in them, and thou in me, that they may be made perfect in One. The Radical, and Original Unity is that of the Blessed Persons in the Trinity; the most immediate Branches, and liveliest Copies of it are those Two, of the Divine, and Humane Nature in Christ's Person; of the Head and Members in his Mystical Body. But this shall suffice for our present Doctrine, that a good Heart is a Treasury of good things.

PSAL. XLV. VER. II.

Thou art fairer than the Children of Men: Grace is poured into thy lips: therefore God hath blessed thee for ever.

THis *Psalm* is a *Song of Loves*. It containeth the whole mystery of the Gospel, and of the life of a Saint with his Saviour, both in the Figure and Substance, which is all an Heavenly *Song* of Spiritual, and eternal *Loves*.

An Holy Soul in love with *Jesus Christ* is altogether taken up with this *Threefold* exercise. 1. The Description, and Contemplation of the Person of her Beloved. 2. The Desire, and continual longings by day, and by night to be possess'd of, to enjoy this Person. 3. The care, and labour to be like him, to partake of his Beauties and Graces, to derive them by the channels, and streamings of the Spirit into itself, to transform itself into his Likeness.

St. Paul spends the first part of his discourses in drawing aside the Curtain, and setting the Person of Christ in its entire form, naked glories, and native sweetnesses in the Eyes of Believers. Then he leadeth, and presseth them to the enjoyment first, next to the Imitation of this *Jesus* upon the ground of his own Loveliness, Love, and Life.

The *first* part of this *Psalm* is spent in like manner upon the Person, and Praises of the Lord *Jesus*. This *Verse* hath *Three Parts*. 1. The Beauty of Christ; *Thou art fairer, than the Children of Men*, 2. The Love, and Sweetness of Christ; *Grace is poured into thy lips*. 3. The Seal of the God-Head, of the Father, of his Blessedness, and Eternity upon the Person of *Christ*; *therefore God hath blessed thee for ever*.

1. The *first part* in the *Text* is the *Beauty of Christ*; *Thou art fairer than the Children of Men*. *Jesus Christ* is the fairest of all men. He is fairer than the whole generation of Mankind. He is fairer than any person born of Man.

The Lord *Jesus* excells all Mankind in Beauty, in *Three respects*.

1. The *Humane Nature* of *Christ* taken by itself, was born of a Virgin-Mother, and God immediately supplying the place of a Father. So it was, as a Morning-beam begotten between a pure Sun, and a clear sweet Air. Then it was born without Sin, the proper, and only deformity of Spirits. Thus his Soul and Body were like a Silver stream, flowing quietly in a clean channel, where the Image of the Skie, and all the Heavenly Bodies figures itself constantly, and clearly. So did the Mind, Will, and Workings of the God-Head figure themselves, and shine in the Manhood of *Christ*. Lastly it is the common sense of Divines, that the Complexion of *Christ* was very delicate, and pure,

pure, arising from the most accurate proportion of the Elements, the most exact Harmony, and purity of the Humours, and Spirits in his Body. We never read, that he was at all Sick. As this made all his Sufferings the greater thorough the quickness of his sence; so it made him in his outward Form extreamly sweet, and lovely above the rest of men.

But besides all this, the *Holy Ghost* seems to fix its eye upon the Humane Nature of *Christ* in two other States different from that of his *Incarnation* by the Virgin *Mary*; as he is the *First-born* of the whole Creation, or of every Creature; and as he is the *First-born* of those that rise from the Dead; *Coloss.* 1. 15, 18.

The *Jews* say, that the *Messias* was the *first Creature*; that all the rest were made *by Him*, *in Him*, and *for Him*, as Pictures to the Life, and Copies to the Original. A German Divine teacheth, that he who receives the Body of Christ, receives at once all, that is good, or fair in the whole world from the Beginning to the End of it.

But the Humanity of the Lord *Jesus*, as he is the *First-born* of those that are risen from the Dead, excels *Adam* in all his Innocency, and primitive Perfections, yea, and *Himself* also, as he was the *First-born* of every Creature, the Natural Head of Angels, as much as Heaven exceeds the Earth, or a Paradise in the third Heavens an Earthly One, 1 *Corin.* 15. 49. The *former* was an *Earthly* Beauty, fading, designed for a Sacrifice, to be exposed to all sorts of shame, and Sufferings, to be made a Prey to the devouring jaws of Death. This *latter* Beauty is *Heavenly*, Incorruptible, seated upon a throne, which indureth for ever, and ever.

2. The *Second Respect*, in which *Christ* is fairer than the Children of men is, the *Union* between the *Divine*, and *Humane* Nature. All the Beauties of our Saviours Manhood are heightned by this Union to that Lustre, and Loveliness, which cannot be express'd in any meer Creature; as a fine Cloud, a Garden of Flowers, a Statue of Gold are quite other things, when the naked Sun sheds his Beams immediately upon them, than when they are seen in a common, or reflected Light.

By vertue of this *Union* the Humane Nature of *Christ* is *One Person* with the Divine. As precious stones are a common water congealed, but inclosing particles of the Heavenly, Ætherial Light, and Spirit: So the Manhood of the Lord *Jesus* in its lowest state of Flesh, in its Blood, in the Grave, excel'd in vertue, outshined in Lustre, Rubies, Diamonds, all the precious things of the Creature in Heaven, and Earth, by vertue of this *Union*. For in all these States God was the *Person* there; all subsisted in him, as Branches in the Tree of Eternity. As *Thomas* did to the Wounds of *Christ*: So may we to our Beloved in every form, in the Ghastliness of Death fall down ravished with the greatness of his Glory, and cry out; *My Lord, and my God*. Every thing of our *Jesus* seen into the depth, and inside of it, or in a right Light is an Heaven

 of

of Heavens, *John* 1. 14. *The word was made Flesh, and dwelt among us, and we saw his glory, the glory, as of the Onely-begotten Son of God.*

3. *The last, and highest consideration of* our Saviours Beauty is, as he is *God*, One with the Father, the Onely true God. This is the Head of fine Gold, of solid Gold, to which all his other Beauties are, as the Locks, and Curles of his Hair, black as a Raven, Shadows, and Foils. *Can.* 5. 11. This is your Beloved, and this is your Friend, O believing Souls.

I shall now give you a *Proof* from *Scripture*, and *Reasons* concerning the whole Person of *Christ* after this explication of his Beauties in particular Forms, and States.

Man was made in the Image, and Similitude of God, of the whole Trinity. For so Divines expound that, *Gen.* 1. *Let us make man in our own Likeness*, of the *Three* ever-blessed *Persons* in the God-Head. Some make it a consultation of the Deity in the Assembly of all the Holy Angels to make man an Image, where all their various Excellencies should meet in the Unity of his Person, to make Man a Musical Harmony, of which every Angel makes a part only. Upon either of these Interpretations Man is the most beautiful of all Creatures, having the perfections of all Summed, and Sealed up in himself, to make a compleat similitude of the Divine Nature; like mystical Letters in the *Living Word*, of which the *First Adam* is a Figure. In the 1. *of Ezek.* The living Creatures full of Wings, and Eyes, by which the Angelical Nature is represented among their other manifold Forms, which appear in every particular Angel, is the Form of a Man. This Humane Form is the Image of God, the Beauty of the Angelical Essences, and the proper Essence of man.

Let us then enlarge our Doctrine, and confirm it in its Latitude.

If *Jesus Christ* be fairer than the Sons of Men, *He is the fairest of all Things.*

Proof. Can. 5. 9, 10. The Spiritual Bride, which is the Church in general, and each believing Soul in particular testifieth of *Christ* by the Spirit of Truth, that *He is white and ruddy, the chiefest of Ten Thousand.*

We have here the Beauty of *Christ* set forth, *first, Absolutely*; *then Comparatively.*

First, Absolutely; *He is white and ruddy.* The *Hebrew* word for *white* signifieth smooth, clear, shining brightness, like that of the Body of Heaven in the fairest, and calmest day. That for *ruddy* imports the purest, and most sparkling red, like that of a Ruby. The same Word for the substance is set for the richest Ruby, *Lament*, for the Ground out of which the First Man was made, *Gen.* 2. which, say the *Jews*, was the fairest Composition of all the finest parts of the Earth, with its most precious vertues far beyond the finest Gold. The same word also is used for the First Man in his First Make, when he was the fairest Flower in Paradise.

The most perfect *white* is the purest Light, which hath no Darkness in it. The purest red, is the most exact mixture of Light, and Shadow.

In

In General these words import a compleat beauty in the Person of *Christ*-a beauty suitable to us, fitted to the Eye of our Faculties, our Sense, and Understanding. It is the manner of Men to express the most perfect beauty of a Face by pure White, and Red. We have also a signification, that the choicest beauties here are Shadows only of *Jesus Christ*. White, and Red in the loveliest Face below is the *Type*, and *Figure*; in that glorious Person it is the *Truth*, the *Original*. Divines call the Creatures with all their Excellencies *Vestigia Dei*, the *Foot-steps* of God. If the Print of *Christs* Feet in the Dust make such Beauties in Flesh and Blood, in these Heavens, in the Angels; what are the Beauties of his own Divine Person?

1. *In Particular*, 1. *White* is the Unity of Light in its simplicity. This is the Person of *Christ*. *Red* expresseth the variety of Light and Darkness with all their Degrees, and Mixtures, as they lie in the Unity of a pure, and simple Light. This is Light in its several Forms, and Dresses. This is the high, and Universal Harmony, which maketh all sorts of Musick, and Beauty thorow all things in Heaven, and Earth, as it sendeth forth Sounds, and Glympses of itself any where. This hath all things in itself in their several perfections. This maketh every thing in itself a Divine Musick, and Beauty to the Spiritual Eye, and Spiritual Ear.

2. *White* is the *God-Head* in *Christ*, making a Day of Beauty, which hath no night going before it, or coming after it. *Red* is the Lord *Jesus*, as he is *God-man*, where the Day, and the Night make one entire Day of perfect Beauty, the Night sweetly shadowing the Day, the Day shining beautifully thorow the Night. Here Beauty hath all its Charms and Sweetnesses of its Mornings and its Evenings.

3. *White* is *Christ in Glory*. *Red* is *this Christ*, *this Glory* descending to the Depth of all Sufferings. *Red* is the Colour of Blood. Nothing is more apt among Natural things to delight, and ravish our Souls, than the Musick of an excellent hand carried down in just degrees by soft, and melting strains to the lowest, and there, as it were, quite silenced; then on a sudden carried up again to a Sprightly, and Triumphant height. How agreeable, how delightful a Spectacle is this to the Eye of the Spirit, to see the Lord *Jesus*, who is Glory itself descending with beautiful Conformities to the Wisdom of the Father, with sweet meltings of himself into the Will of the Father, thorow all degrees of Sufferings into the Silence, and Darkness of Death itself; then in a moment to spring up into Glory, and Immortality by the Resurrection from the Dead? What believing, and loving Soul, when she seeth these beautiful goings of her *Jesus* on the Earth, on Mount *Golgotha*, in the Grave, would not gladly go down with him in the Fellowship of his Sufferings into the same Grave, as into a Spiritual Marriage-bed, to come forth immediately in the glorious Morning of the Resurrection, as a Bridegroom out of his Chamber?

I have hitherto spoken of the *Absolute* Praise of Christs Beauty in this Scri-

pture;

pture; *He is White, and Ruddy.* I am now to ſpeak of the *Comparative* Praiſe; *He is the chiefeſt of ten thouſand: Ten thouſand* is a particular number ſet for All. The *Hebrew* word ſignifieth the greateſt number; it is applied to Angels, *Pſal.* 68.18, *The Chariot of the Lord is ten thouſand*; Angels are underſtood. The Angels are the faireſt of all creatures. Our Saviour is the faireſt of all the Angels. The word *Chiefeſt* is in Hebrew a *Standard-bearer.* The *Standard-bearer* carries the *Banner.* The Banner is the Mark and Prize under which all the Troop march, for which they fight, to which, and under which the whole Troop is gathered together. The Beauty and Lovelineſs of *Chriſt's Perſon*, is the *Banner* ſpread over all things, under which, in the force of which, for which all things move in their ſeveral courſes, to which the gathering together of All ſhall be. The *Inſtinct* of this is *All Love.* The *Poſſeſſion* and *Springing* forth of this *All Joy.* We read in the *Acts* of an Altar with an Inſcription, *To the unknown God.* St. *Paul* preaching upon this *Text*, telleth the *Athenians*; *Him, whom ye ignorantly worſhip, preach I unto you*; meaning *Chriſt.* In the whole frame of Nature every Heart, every Creature, every Affection, every Action is an Altar with the ſame kind of Inſcription; *To the Unknown Beauty*; *To the Unknown Jeſus.* This is the Mark, the White, which every Being in nature ignorantly moveth to, which every motion ignorantly aimeth at; this is that which all Underſtandings, all Loves ignorantly worſhip, eſteem and adore; this Beauty of *Jeſus Chriſt*, concerning which we now ſpeak. Bleſſed are your hearts, O Believers, which are Spiritual Altars with the Perſon of *Chriſt*, engraven upon them by the finger of God, flaming with the fire of an heavenly Love, and bearing this Inſcription; To the known Beauty of that Jeſus, whom we know, whoſe Perſon our Eyes have ſeen, our Ears have heard, our Hands have handled, the Arms of our Spirits have embraced.

I come now from the *Proof*, to the *Reaſons* of the Doctrine, which are *four.*

1. *Jeſus Chriſt is Beauty in its Original.*
2. *He is the Perfection of Beauty.*
3. *He hath all the Parts of Beauty moſt compleat in his Perſon.*
4. *All Beauty is derived from him.*

Reaſ. 1. *The Perſon of Chriſt is Beautiful in its Original.* He is the *Firſt*, ſo the *Higheſt*, and *Beſt Beauty*, *Heb.* 1. 3. *Chriſt* is ſaid to be *The Brightneſs of the Glory of God. Four* things go to make up the Glory of God: 1. *Excellency*; 2. *Excellency at the height*; 3. An *Union* of *all Excellencies* reflecting upon, imparting themſelves to each other. All center themſelves in the boſom of every one. All ſee themſelves living and ſhining in the face each of other, as in a living Looking-glaſs. Our Beloved is that *Image*, into which this *Glory* ſo brings forth it ſelf, that it is *One* with it ſelf.

Brightneſs implies three things; 1. *Glory* at the *Height*, as Light in the Sunſhine; 2. *Glory appearing*, Glory in an Image; 3. *Glory* in its *Purity.* The *Perſon* of our *Jeſus* is ſuch an *Image*, as is the *Glory* itſelf, a *Deep* of *Glo-*

ry,

ry, a pure, unmixt, unconfined, infinite *Glory*. He is an Image of so clear Glory, so One with the Glory, that All the God-Head appears in Him, and nothing of it can hide itself from being seen there.

The *Person* of *Christ* is the *Essential* and *Eternal Glory* of the God-Head in its own proper Form, in which it may be seen by Spiritual Eyes, in which it may be a heavenly Bridegroom capable of being possessed, embraced, and enjoyed by the Spiritual Bride, the Wife of this Lamb, without spot or blemish.

Can any soul that hath had the least glympse of this *Mine*, this *Mass* of Glory, the Blessed *Person* of *Christ*, be so treacherous, like *Judas*, as to value him at, and sell him for thirty pieces of silver, the Riches of this world? Can any Spirit, upon whose inward Eye the least Beam of his Beauty hath faln, be so prophane, as *Esau* was, to sell his Birthright, his Inheritance in this Kingdom of Beauty, the Glorious Person of his God and Saviour, for a Mess of Pottage, for sensual satisfactions, for a lust, for a shadowy life on Earth?

It is added, *Heb.* 1. 3. That He is *the express Image of His*, (namely, God the Father's) *Substance*, or *Person*. *True Beauty* is defined to be the proper and native Image of some *True Good*. The *True Beauty* calls, and allures all hearts to it. The *True Good* gives them rest in the bosom of that Beauty. *Beauty is Goodness visible*: *Good* is the *Invisible Spring* and *Center* in that *Beauty*. *God* is the *First and Supreme Good*; *Jesus Christ* then, who is the *Express Image of His Substance* and *Person*, in whom He is figured after the most exact and lively manner, is the *First and Supreme Beauty*.

God the Father is the *First* and *Supreme Good*, as the *God-Head* in the *Root*. *Jesus Christ* is the *First* and *Supreme Beauty*, as the *God-Head* in the *Flower*, springing out of, and standing in the Bosom of its *Root*, having all the virtues of the *Root* in clear and full figures forming themselves most gloriously, and most amiably upon it. The *Holy Spirit* is the *First*, the *Supreme Love* and *Joy*, as the *God-Head in the Fruit*, in which all the precious virtues of the *Root*, all the lively and lovely *Beauties* of the *Flower* are tasted, feasted upon, and enjoyed. To make our Esteem, Admiration, Adoration and Love yet greater, we must also observe that these *Three* in the *Divine Nature*, in the *Person of Christ*, the *Root*, the *Flower*, and the *Fruit*, are inseparable; they all mutually comprehend each other, that every One may be perfect, having the Other Two entire in it self.

Ho! every one that sitteth under the shadow of any melancholy, any grief, or fear; that saith, who will shew us the True Good? Who will shew us Beauty indeed, or where the place of Love is? Who will make us to drink of the Fountain of Joy? Come hither to the *Person of Christ*. But come boldly, stand not without the Vail, press into the *Holy of Holies*, come near to the *Person* of *Christ* himself. Come past all shadows of Glory; come to the brightness of Glory, the naked Person of your *Jesus*. Here shall your Eyes be satisfied with Beauty; your Souls shall rest in Goodness; you shall take your fill of Love, and Joy.

Reas. 2.

Reaſ. 2. *The Perſon of Chriſt is the perfection of Beauty*, Pſal. 50. 2. *From* Sion *the Perfection of Beauty God ſhall ſhine.* There are *three Things*, which I would make clear to you in this Scripture. 1. That *Sion* is the *Third Perſon* in the Trinity, the *Holy Spirit*, 2. That the *Perfection of Beauty* is a deſcription of the *Second Perſon* the Lord *Jeſus*. 3. Why theſe *two* are ſo joyned, as if one only were meant. This *verſe* hath a deep Myſtery of Divinity in it. Glorious Perſons are contained here. But there is a Vail of borrowed Names from inanimate things upon them. It will be worth your time, and patience to ſtay a while at this place, to ſearch into the Myſtery, to take off the Vail, and diſcover the Beauty.

1. I think it will be plain to every underſtanding, that the bleſſed *Spirit* is figured by Mount *Sion*, if you compare *three Scriptures*, Gal. 4. 26. *Jeruſalem above is free, which is the Mother of us all*, Gal. 4. 28, 29. *We Brethren are the Children of the promiſe, as* Iſaac. *As therefore it was then, ſo it is now, he that is born after the Fleſh, perſecuteth him that is born after the Spirit.* In the *firſt* of theſe *verſes*, *Jeruſalem above* is ſaid to be the *Mother of us all.* In the *Second* theſe, *All us*, are expounded to be the *Children of Promiſe.* In the *Third verſe* the ſame perſons are deſcribed by being *born after the Spirit.* This Phraſe of being *born after the Spirit* is fully explained by that of *Jeſus Chriſt*, from whence it ſeemeth to be taken, *John* 3. *That which is born of the Fleſh, is Fleſh: That which is born of the Spirit, is Spirit.* To be born *after the Spirit*, and *of the Spirit* ſignifie both the ſame thing. Is it not then evident, that the *Jeruſalem above, which is free, which is the mother of all the Spiritual Seed*, is the Eternal *Spirit*, after which a Saint is born, that is, *of this Spirit*, and in the Image of this Spirit, where there is Liberty, 2 *Corin.* 4.

Now lay the *Third* Scripture by theſe *two*, *Heb.* 12. 22. *We are come to Mount Sion, the Heavenly Hieruſalem, the City of the living God, to the Millions of Angels, the general Aſſembly, to the Church of the Firſt-born written in Heaven, to the Spirits of juſt men made perfect, to God, to Jeſus Chriſt.* Before, we ſaw *Hieruſalem above, and the Spirit*, now we ſee *Mount Sion, and the Heavenly Hieruſalem* to be the ſame. Is it not then an infallible demonſtration, that *Sion* and the *Holy Spirit* are One, as the *Type*, and the *Truth*? Can any other be the living City of the living God, where all the Holy Angels the Firſt-born of the Father, the Spirits of all Saints, as well on Earth, as in Heaven, *Jeſus Chriſt* in his Mediatory Kingdom, the Father upon the Throne of Judicature meet, and appear together in the full liberty of Eternal Light, Love, and Joy; beſides the Unity of the Spirit, which is the Sweet and Sacred band between the two Glorious Perſons in the Trinity, between all pure, Spiritual, Divine Beings above and below? This is the *Spring*, and Immortal *Seat* of them all.

2. We have in this place another *Perſon* ſet forth by this bright, and lovely Character, *the Perfection of Beauty.* We may diſcover our own Beloved, and Bridegroom the Lord Jeſus under this Title, if we bring to it the Lights of

two other *Scriptures* shining like this by his Appearance in them. In *Heb.* 1. 3. He is stiled *the Brightness of Glory.* Is not this the same, as to say; *The Perfection of Beauty*? 2 Corin. 4. 6. *God hath shined in our hearts unto the Light of the Knowledge of the Glory of God in the Face, or Person of Jesus Christ.* Can Face answer Face in a Glass more exactly than these *Two Scriptures* answer one another? In both you have *God, God shining*: in one you have *God shining from the Perfection of Beauty*: in the other *God shining with a Light of Glory in the Face, or Person of Christ.* God in all the Creatures, whether they be Visible, or Invisible casts forth *Shadows* only of Himself. Then he appeareth in the *Perfection of Beauty*; when he appeareth in the Person of *Christ*, as Light in the Body of the *Sun.*

3. But why are these *two* so joyned, as if they were the same Thing, *from Sion the perfection of Beauty*? I will not examine, whether we may not disjoyn them in reading, by putting in between them, *and*, or *in*, Particles frequently understood; from *Sion, and*, or *in* the Perfection of Beauty God shineth. This needeth not. There is plainly a difference between the *English*, and the *Hebrew*. The *Hebrew* runneth word for word thus: *From Sion, from the Perfection of Beauty God hath shined.* So you have the *Three Persons* of the ever-blessed *Trinity* clearly distinguished, and united in this shining of the God-Head. The *Father* shineth, from the *Spirit* his holy hill of *Sion*, from the *Person of Christ* the Perfection of Beauty. These *Two Persons* are placed here, as One in Another, a Globe of Light in a Globe of Light, and the Father shining from them both to awaken in us this great, and glorious Truth, that the Persons of the Sacred Trinity have their Perfection in each other, and are ever undivided, when they appear nakedly in their proper Forms. The whole Trinity is the Crown of Beauty upon every one of them.

In particular *Jesus Christ* never appears, as the *Perfection of Beauty*, but when he, and the Spirit appear both in One, 2 *Cor.* 3. from the 14th to the end you read of a vail upon the Face of *Moses*, the Person of Christ in the Type; then of a vail upon the Hearts of the Jews. These are both the same vail. For the vail is never upon the Person of Christ properly, and simply, but upon the Eye of our Spirits; as the Cloud is never upon the Body of the Sun, but upon our Corporeal Eyes. For, as that doth in the midst of its world; so doth the Person of *Christ* in the midst of all things ever comprehend, and contemplate himself, and all things, in the simple and pure Light of his own naked Beauties. But then in the same place we read, that the *Vail is taken away in Christ*; and *where the Spirit of the Lord is there is Liberty*; that is, freedom from the Vail; Christ is seen unvailed in his naked Glories. It is added; *Now the Lord is that Spirit.* Then mention is made in the last verse; of *beholding the Glory of the Lord with open Face*; that is, Eye to Eye, the naked Eye of our Souls to the naked Eye of his Beauties; every Spirit being all Eye. The *verse* is closed thus; *as by the Spirit of the Lord*; or more agreeably to the *Greek*, *as of the Lord the Spirit.*

I have

I have alledged all this to make it plain to you, and to seal it upon your understandings, and memories, that *Jesus Christ* is then only seen in his *true Person* and shape, without a vail, when he is seen in the *Spirit*, when Christ and the Spirit are seen, as *two distinct Persons in One*. *Sion*, the *Type* of the *Spirit* signifieth *Vision*. *Hierusalem* the Figure of the same *Spirit*, the *Heavenly Hierusalem* is by interpretation the *Heavenly Vision of Heavenly Perfection and Peace*. The Lord *Jesus* is the *Perfection of Beauty*, the Heavenly Harmony of all things, the Peace of all Hearts, and Desires. The *Person* of the *Spirit* is the *Heavenly Vision* of this *Heavenly Perfection*.

By the way observe, that the *Holy Ghost* speaks in this 50 *Psal.* of the Day of Judgment the Second, and last Coming, and Appearance of our Lord and Saviour, after which he shall go away, and disappear no more. See here, what manner of Appearance this is; in what State, in what Form the King of Glory comes to the Marriage of his Bride, and to reign upon the Earth. He comes in a Spiritual, and Divine Form, in the *Person* of the *Spirit*. The *Eternal Spirit* is an anointing of Beauty upon the whole Person of our Beloved. He again is a Sun of Beauty looking forth in the Person of *Spirit*. Nay, the Lord *Jesus* cometh in the Glory of all the *Three Persons*; the *Father* shineth in the Person of the *Son*; the *Son* shineth in the Person of the *Spirit*; all *Three* in *One* shine together in the glorified *Humanity* of the Lord *Jesus*, all three glorifie that with themselves; Inhabiting, and shining forth round about with a full Light of glory in it, Figuring themselves in their Divinest Forms upon it; overshadowing it, and cloathing it with the Brightnesses of their own most entire, and most naked Appearances.

Thus is *Jesus* the *Perfection of Beauty*. The Glory of the God-Head is now consummate in Him, when all the *Three Persons* appear quite unvailed in his *Person*. You who love and wait for this Appearance of your Heavenly Bridegroom; who see this day, which his Spiritual Beauties make, and rejoyce to see it with a Joy unspeakable, and glorious; you, who live in the sweet dawnings of this day upon you; you, who have any thing of the Spirit of the Bride in you; cry continually; *Even so, so come quickly Lord Jesus in this Thrice-Beautiful, and Thrice-Blessed Appearance.*

Thus the *Person of Christ is the Perfection of Beauty.*

Perfection implyeth 3 *Things*. 1. *Clearness*. 2. *Compleatness* 3. *Comprehensiveness*.

1. *Clearness*. That which is perfect, is pure, hath no spot, or mixture of any thing Forreign. As every drop of Milk is Milk: so every thing, the smallest Point in the Person of *Christ* is Beauty. He is Beauty itself in the *abstract*, in its simple Essence. This Finite world cannot satisfie our desires, because they are infinite. Behold here the Person of *Christ*, a world of Beauty, and infinite to terminate, and satiate your infinite desires. For every thing is bounded by another, or by its Contrary; nothing by itself; as Light by Darkness, Life

by

by Death. Our Lord *Jesus* is a Light of Beauty, where there is no Darkness, and so no bound to set a stop to it from multiplying itself endlesly within itself; meeting no where in its utmost Circles of glory with any thing besides itself. It is this Beauty, which is sown in every Spirit, shooting up, and budding in desires, flowring in delights. Love is this Beauty in the Seed, desires the sproutings of this Love. Therefore are our Loves, and Desires infinite, because this *Jesus*, the *Beauty*, which is their *Root*, and their *Fruit*, is so.

2. *Compleatness*. The Beauty of *Christ* is perfect; nothing can be added to it, *Solomon* saith, *Eccles.* 1. 7. *All rivers run into the Sea, and the Sea is not at all the fuller.* It is the Person of *Christ*, which is this Mystical Sea of all Beauty, and Sweetness, all the rivers of created Beauty, and Sweetness go forth from him, and take away nothing. They all return into him again, and add nothing. When *Lot* had been made to drink Wine freely by his Daughters, he perceived not when they lay down, nor when they rose up. Believing beloved Souls, drink in the Lovelinesses of your own Heavenly Husband, drink abundantly of them; so will ye have little, or no sense of the presence of the Sweetness of any Object, or Relation among the Creatures, when ye lye down in its embraces; or of its absence, when ye rise up from it never to return to the enjoyment, or sight of it any more. Your *Jesus* in his single Person is all Loveliness compleat in itself. He is the same; that which all Creature are; that which they are not; with them, and without them. Their presence, and their absence are the same, equally full of the same Beauty, and Sweetness in him.

3. *Comprehensiveness*. The Perfection of Beauty comprehendeth all Beauties, and Beautiful Things in itself. It is the *First*, and *Essential Beauty*, which by its presence beautifies every thing. The Beauties of Angels, Stars, and Flowers; of Bodies, and Spirits, all flourish together eminently, and unfadingly in the Person of *Christ*, which is the Paradise of God, and the Bed of Flowers there.

Thou, who mournest, and loathest thy self for some Deformity, or Defilement of Spirit; who bemoanest thy self for some defect, comfort thy self concerning this in the Person of *Christ*. God is said in one place; to call all the Stars by name, and no one of them is wanting. The Person of thy Saviour hath all Spiritual, and Natural Beauties in itself. Here thou mayst call by Name the proper Beauties of thy Person, to cloath all thy shame with Glory, to supply all thy wants with suitable Grace. Thou shalt find no one wanting. Every one will answer readily; here am I; behold I bear thine Image, and the Inscription of thy Name upon me. I have been laid up from Eternity in the Perfection of Beauty, and kept for thee, unto this Season.

You that complain for the want of any Loveliness, come to *Jesus Christ*; that you may have it, and have it in abundance, richly to enjoy. He is that well of Beauty springing up to eternal Life, that is, with All, with Infinite, with Endless Beauties.

You, who find your hearts captivated by any thing lovely on Earth, come hither. Where the Person of *Christ* is seen, as he appears in the Spirit, unvailed; there is Liberty; the fulness of a Divine Beauty, the freedom of a Divine Love taking off from our hearts the Chains of every ensnaring, and enslaving passion. Behold that which thou lovest, in *Christ* the perfection of Loveliness, where it is truest, and sweetest; so love it in him. Behold *Christ* beautifying by his presence every beautiful Object, like the Sun-shine on Flowers; so love him in it.

One said; if a man know not the way to the Sea, let him follow the course of a River. Every stream of Sweetness flows from our Saviour, and runs into him, Let thy heart accompany it in this course, so shall it be led by a pleasant Guide to *Jesus Christ*. The nearer thou followest it to *Christs Person*, the larger and fuller will the Sweetness be, as a River near the Ocean; till it be perfected in him.

When thy heart breaketh over any departing Beauty, or dying Sweetness in a Friend, Child, Wife or Life, then think upon the *Comprehensiveness* of *Christs* Beauty, which holds all other Beauties in it, as Heaven doth the Angels. *Solomon* saith in *Ecclesiastes, When man dieth, the body goeth to the Dust, from whence it came; the Spirit to God, who gave it.* Each thing returns to its Original, to the Element from whence it is taken, and of which it is ever a part. Darkness sinks down into the Pit of Darkness: the Spirit, which is the Light, Life, Sweetness every where, every Spark, and Image of Divinity re-ascends, and retreats into the Bosom of the first Image of God, which is *Christ*. Each pleasantness, each beam of loveliness, is a glance, and sparkle of this Eternal Image of Essential Beauty, which enfoldeth all things, and mingleth itself with all things. That which thou callest the fading of any Sweetness dear unto thee, is only the hasting of the loving stream to its beloved Sea; the disappearing of the bright flame of Life into the glorious Brightness of its unseen Element. Thou sayst; it is now dying, now dead, when it is emptying itself into the Ocean of Beauties; retreating into the pure, and incorruptible Element of Beauty, the Blessed Person of *Christ*. Cleave to it in this view of it, cast thy self with it into these secret, and sacred depths of Life, and Loveliness; so shalt thou never lose it, or thy self, save by being both together swallowed up into the perfection of Beauty, the Eternal Treasury of all Beauties, *Jesus Christ*.

I have now finished the *Two first Reasons* of the *Fairness* of *Christ* above all things; the *Original*, the *Perfection* of Beauty in his Person. Before I pass to the other *Two Reasons*, let us look down a little upon our selves, and make some application of these Beauties, which we have seen in the *Person* of our Lord, to our own *Persons*, to enlighten the Darknesses, and redress the deformities there.

Use. 1. *A Caution.* Let us take heed, that we make no inference, take no encouragement from the Loveliness of *Christ* to make our selves unlovely in

his

his Eye, to defile his Spouse in our selves, to stain his Glory by Sensuality, Lust, or any presumptuous Sin. Our Saviour now dying saith to his Father of his Disciples: *I sanctify my self, that they also may be sanctified*, John 17. *Jesus Christ* put off in Death every thing of Earth, and Flesh. He lifteth himself up by his Cross into Glory; that he may present himself again to the Eye of our Spirits in the Spiritual, and Heavenly Brightness of the Divine Form, and Glory; that he may baptize us into the same Sea of his Blood, and into the same white Cloud of his own Spiritual Beauties; that we also by him may die to the Flesh, and live with him in the Spirit. Hath Jesus Christ to this end made himself *higher than the Heavens, Heb.* that our Hearts, and Lives should be low and vile, as the Earth? Is he ascended above all the Angels, all the Principalities, and Powers of Light, that we should become like Beasts, and yield up our Bodies, and Spirits Instruments to the Principalities and Powers of the Darkness of this World, and of Hell?

Is there any hope of renewing such a Person by words, who thus turneth the rightest, and pleasantest words of the Lord Jesus, and his Beauties unto nourishment to vain, and filthy Lusts, to Corruption? Is any more to be done, but to leave him to that Dreadful, and Delightful *Maran Atha*; which is by interpretation, *The Lord cometh*; to the Person of Christ himself in his own immediate Appearances, when those glorious and unexpressible Beauties of the Spirit, and God-Head, in which he shall appear, shall be Flames of Fire burning upon, and consuming every Earthly, Fleshly Principle, or Spirit in every Form.

Use. 2. *A Conviction* of the Evil of Sin, which blindeth us to the sight of this Beautiful, and Blessed Person of our Lord *Jesus*. How should we all curse to the Pit of Hell, from whence it arose, that Charm, or Enchantment, if any had such force to change the Sun into Sack-cloath, or hinder it from shining any more upon the Earth? How much worse than a Grave would it make the whole world, when we should have eyes open, and no Light? Far greater is that mischief, which the Devil worketh by Sin. By the charm of this world, which he raiseth, as an Apparition, and Lying Image from Hell, together with the Lusts, which he awakeneth by it, he taketh away from us the glorious Light of *Christs Person* ten thousand times brighter, sweeter, and of more consequence to us, than the Sun in Heaven, 2 *Corin.* 4. 4. By this means all our faculties are, as so many Eyes continually awakened, continually benighted with the blackness of Darkness, deluded with empty Shadows, and disappointed of the beloved Substance. So are our Spirits wandring in an everlasting Darkness, tormented night and day with the fire of their own restless, eager, and unsatisfied desires; while *Jesus Christ* their only Light, and Food is hid from them under the Cloud of their Corruptions.

Take heed especially of *three Sins*; of *Covetousness*; *Uncleanness*; *Enmity*.

1. Take heed of *Covetousness*, *Mat.* 6. 22. Our Saviour warneth his Disciples to take heed, what they made their *Treasure*, because where the Trea-

sure is, there the Heart will be. *v.* 21. The beloved Object irresistibly draweth the Heart to itself, and transformeth it into itself, as Seed doth the ground in which it is sown. *The Eye,* saith *Christ, is the Light of the Body. If thine Eye be single, thy whole Body shall be full of Light, But if thine Eye be evil, thy whole Body shall be full of Darkness; and if the Light, which is in thee be darkness, how great is that Darkness?* The whole Soul, and every Spirit is an Eye. The understanding is an Eye of Light; the Will is an Eye of Love. The same word for the substance of it in the Hebrew signifies an *Eye*, and a *Fountain.* The *Object* is the Light of this Eye, which sheds abroad in it the Beams of its Light, Sweetness, and Influence. These are the waters springing up in this Fountain.

The *single Eye* in the Language of the Scripture is the *good, the liberal, large, open Eye.* The Eye is single from its Object, when it hath fixed unchangeably in it that single Object, which is truly and eternally One; when it looketh upon all things only as they are comprehended in this Unity. This is such a singleness, such a simplicity, that the Eye, and the Object are both One; the Supream, and Eternal Unity is both the Eye and the Object in this Spirit; and so the Fountain, which goeth forth from its own *Eden*, maketh the Soul a Paradise, and watereth the whole Body.

The *Evil Eye* is a *contracted, divided, narrow, covetous, envious, malicious Eye.* Beware O man, that the things of this world, that this world be not in thine Eye. As *Jesus Christ* is the Image of the Invisible God: so is *this World* the Image of its God, the Devil, the Prince of Darkness, by which he becomes visible to thee, enamoureth thy Soul, setteth himself in thine Eye, and thine Heart, with all his Hells, and Fires hid within this Cloud, And now a blackness of Darkness big with a dreadful Tempest of Wrath dwelleth within thee, and covereth all things round about thee.

But if *Jesus Christ* be the Object of thy Love, he will be as a Divine Sun in the Center, and midst of thy Spirit, powring forth a great plenty of rich, and glorious Beams thorow all parts, every point of thy Soul, thy Body, every thing round about thee. Now all things shall be to thee one entire, and beautiful Body of Divine Light.

Indeed the world compared with the great, and glorious world of Light, and Beauty in the Person of *Christ*, is as a Mote in the Sun. But if this Mote be in thine Eye, it will deprive thee of the sight of this Sun.

2. Take heed of *Uncleanness.* St. *Jude, v.* 23. teacheth us to *hate the Garment spotted with the Flesh.* The Holy Spirit seemeth here to represent a Saint after this manner; *Jesus Christ* in the inward, and Spiritual Man, as a Sun shining in Heaven; The outward and natural Man, as a Garment of Light sent forth from this Sun, thorow which the Sun itself is seen in every point of it. As often as any unclean thought, or fleshly Imagination ariseth in us, this becomes a spot upon our Garment. Now the White is turned into Blackness of

Dark-

Darkness, the Beauty into Burning, the Face of Christ, and of Heaven are clouded, and appear no more.

Blessed are the pure in heart, for they shall see God, saith our Saviour, *Matt.* 5. All vision dependeth upon the suitableness between the Eye, and the Object. All sense in every kind of things proceedeth from the suitableness between each Faculty and its proper Object. Suitableness is the visible Image, and effect of an hidden Unity, and awakeneth that, as the Sun doth its own Seminal vertues in the Earth, which spring up into all manner of Plants, Flowers, and Fruits. The pure Beauties of *Christs Person* are seen only by a pure Eye, which Eye is the living Image of the same Person in the Unity of the same Spirit, and awakened in us by the Appearances of that Glory. There is a *Three-fold Purity*; *Moral*; *Legal*; *Evangelical*.

If we would see the Image of God in the visible Frame of Nature, which is the *Person* of *Christ* in its *Shadow*; we must be baptized into the *Blood*, that is, into the *Principle*, and *Spirit* of this Image; we must be washed in this Laver from all the gross disorders, and pollutions of the Flesh unto a *Moral Purity*. If we would see the Divine Image shining in the midst of the Intellectual, Angelical, Invisible things of Nature, which is the *Person of Christ* in its *Picture*; let us baptize our selves into the *Blood*, that is into the *Spirit* and *Principle* of this Image. Let us in this Spring wash off, by the Fire upon the Altar offer up all sensitive Forms, which is the Sacrifice of Beasts, that our Spirits may be like the vail of the Tabernacle having *Cherubims*, the Forms of Invisible, and Heavenly things only formed upon them. This is our *legal Purity*.

But would we see that Image of the invisible God, which is itself invisible to every Natural Eye, of Men, and Angels? Would we see, not the *Shadow*, the *Picture*, but the *Brightness of Glory*; the *Person* of *Christ* in the *Life* unvailed? We must then be baptized into the *Blood*, the *Spirit*, the Principle of this Eternal, Essential Image of God. This alone *can purify the Heavenly Things themselves*, *Heb.* This alone can wash out the impression and similitude of every Creature in its Natural State, that the uncreated Glory, which alone is the *true Heaven*, and lies hid under the other, as a Diamond in a heap of rubbish may shine forth. This is our *Evangelical Purity*, and our *Evangelical Vision* of God in the *Person of Christ*.

When thou art come never so little past the *lusts* of the Flesh; thou shalt meet with him, whom thy Soul loveth, *Jesus Christ* in his *Shadow*. This will be an *Earthly Paradise* to thee springing up thorow thy body, thy senses, all visible things round about thee. When thou art come never so little past the *Flesh* itself, and all Appearances of things in that; thou shalt meet with him, whom thy Soul loveth, in a lively, lovely *Picture*, thy *Jesus* in the Form of an *Angel*. All that was dear to thee, and present with thee in the *dark shadow*, thou shalt now see again with gain, and enjoy in the *bright Picture*. Thy *Earthly Paradise* shall be grown up, transformed, and enlarged with thee into a *Heaven of*

Angels.

Angels. When thou art come never so little past these *Watchmen* themselves, the *Angels*, without the walls of the City of this whole Creation; thou shalt meet with him, whom thy Soul loves, the Lord Jesus in his naked, living, and eternal Beauties. Here thou shalt see the *Light of Life* far above all *Shadows* and *Pictures*, enlarging itself to take in, and comprehend them also. Not only the *Persons*, and *Things* represented in those lower Scenes, and Forms: but the Scenes, and Forms themselves appear again, and appear eternally in this last and highest opening of the Mystery of God. Not only that *Rose*, which was the Treasure hid in the *Seed*, the *Stalk*, the *Leaf*, the *Thorn*, sheweth itself full blown in all its Beauties, and Sweetnesses, but that *Seed*; *Stalk*; each *Leaf*; every thing of the *Rose-Tree*; every *dust* of the Earth round about it, is now a *Distinct Rose*. This is the *Rose of Sharon*, our *Jesus* seen, *as he is*, the vail taken off in the Gospel by the *Holy Spirit*. Follow after Holiness in all degrees of it, that you may see this *Jesus*, as he ascends thorow all Degrees of things. Fly from every degree of uncleanness which will be a spot upon your Garments, that the Beauties of *Christ* cannot shine in them, neither in your outward, and Earthly, or your Inward, Angelical Garment.

3. *Beware of Enmity.* The *Holy Ghost* saith; 1 *John. He that hateth his Brother, walketh in darkness until now.* Every Saint, every Man, every Creature, each Providence is our Brother, as it is the work of God, the Birth of God by *Jesus Christ*, and beareth the Image of him, who is the *Wisdom* of God. All *Hatred* is a Twin-birth with *Darkness*. Both arise immediately out of the departure and separation from the *Unity*, which is the womb, from whence spring together that Blessed Pair, *Light* and *Love*. All Enmity and Hatred besides that, which is the loving, and lovely opposition of *Love* itself to *Hatred*, and Enmity, is the seed of the Serpent, out of which himself ariseth, and by which he propagateth his Serpentine brood. The *Jews* say in their *Proverbs*; *The Spirit of God resteth not upon an Angry, or a sad Man.* While thy Soul is wrapt up in a black Cloud of Malice, or tossed with any Tempest of wrath, the *Sun* of *Love*, the Glorious Person of thy Saviour, which is all an immortal Flame of Love appeareth not to thee, neither can it be seen by thee, all whose Lovelinesses are the Beauties, and Beams of Love.

Rom. 3. 24. *Jesus Christ* is called the *Propitiation.* This was in the Tabernacle and Temple the *Golden Mercy-Seat*, on which God sat between the *Cherubims*, and talked with *Moses*. In allusion to this we read of the *Throne of Grace, Heb.* 4. 16. The *Person of Christ* in his Heavenly Form is *the Propitiation, the Golden Mercy-Seat, the Throne of Grace, the Throne of Love*, of the *freest, sweetest, purest Love*, If you streighten a Flame, and bar it from its *Liberty* of extending, and dilating itself, you extinguish it, and lose at once its *Light*, and *Heat*. If you contract the *Love* of *Christ* in you by Wrath, or Enmity, you make your self uncapable of the sweet *Light* of his Appearances, and of the Heavenly *Heat* of his Graces, and Consolations. While there

is

is among you strife, anger, malice, murmurings, whisperings, hard thoughts, evil speakings, or any such thing; Heaven is not now open upon you, neither do you see *Jesus*, as he comes up out of the Baptism of his Sufferings into a Resurrection of Glory with the Eternal Spirit in the Form of a *Dove*, in a Form of *Love* resting upon him.

The Priests in the Temple were Morning and Evening to trim the Lamps in the Golden Candlestick by pouring in fresh Oil, that the Light might not go out by day, nor by night. Your Persons, O ye Saints, are the Temple, your Spiritual and Divine part the Golden Candlestick, the Heavenly Person of your beloved is the Light in the Lamps of this Candlestick. If you would preserve this Light of Glory continually shining in you, be continually pouring in from that vessel of Love, the Heart of the Father, fresh Love, which is the Golden Oyl of the Spirit, in which the Life, and Light of the Divine Nature burneth, and shineth eternally.

But to conclude my discourse concerning these *Three Sins*.

The *Scripture* saith; *Covetousness is Idolatry*. We make an Idol of every Image besides the Lord *Jesus* alone, which we set up in our Hearts, as real, and excellent to bow down our Souls to it by our esteem, and affection. Every Idol hath its Devil in it. *St. Paul* saith plainly; *What the Gentiles Sacrifice to Idols, they Sacrifice to Devils. You cannot eat of the Table of the Lord*, which is his *Glorified Person*, to feast upon the Delicacies of his Beauties set before your Spirits there, and *eat of the Table of Devils*, which is this world; to feed upon the Dainties of the Flesh here. *You cannot drink of the cup of the Lord*, which is *his Spirit*, to take in the Wine of Spiritual Sweetnesses from this, *and drink of the Cup of Devils*, which is the Spirit of this World, to swallow down the riches, and pleasant things of that.

2 *Pet.* 2. 13, 14. We read of *Spots* at the *Feasts* of the Saints, who are those that have *Eyes full of Adultery*. *St. Jude* expoundeth those *Feasts* to be *Feasts of Charity*, that is, *Love-Feasts*, which were joyned with the Supper of the Lord. The Appearances of *Christs Person* in the *Visible, Angelical, Divine* Images, are our several *Love-Feasts*. An adulterous Eye in the moral sense, which looketh upon any visible Object after an undue manner, is a *Spot* upon the *First Love-Feast*. The adulterous Eye in a legal sense, which looketh upon any Fleshly, or visible Figure of things, is a *Spot* upon the *Second*. The adulterous Eye, which setteth its Love upon Created Forms on Earth, or in Heaven, is a *Spot* upon the *Last*, and *best Love-Feasts*. All these *Spots* are Clouds upon the *Person*, and stains upon the Beauty of *Christ*, which at once dishonour and grieve him, darken and defile us, making us unworthy, and uncapable of his blessed Appearances to us.

As an adulterous Eye of Lust, so the blood-shot Eye of Wrath is unable to look upon this Heavenly Object, or to bear the brightness of his Glory.

I will wind up this *Use* with this solemn adjuration, and charge: If there

 be

be such a Person as our *Jesus*; if this Person have such unsearchable Treasures of Beauty, and Joy in it; if the presence, and appearance of this King in his Beauty, as a Bridegroom, as a Spiritual Sun in the hearts of the Saints be no dream, or fancy, but the very Spirit, and Truth, and Life of the Gospel; I adjure, and charge you, all his Saints, by the *Hinds*, and *Roes of the Field*, by the lovely *Person* of your *Christ*, by the pleasantness of his Appearances in you, that laying aside *Covetousness*; casting away all *Filthiness* both of *Flesh*, and *Spirit*; putting off all Wrath, Malice, Envyings, and evil speakings, you fix your Eye upon, fill your Souls with the Beautiful, and blessed Person of the Lord Jesus. This is your own Fountain. Drink waters from this Fountain alone. Behold your selves, one another, all things in the Light of *this Person*, of these Beauties, as they lie here, as they are comprehended in this fairest, greatest, and most Divine Image of all Loveliness. *Christ* is *the Truth*. The Appearance of things in the sweet Light of his lovely Person is *True*, This is that Truth, which if you walk in it, shall dwell with you for ever, shining with a precious, and living lustre in the darkest places of Sorrow, or Death. In this Truth live at peace, live in love within your selves, with one another, with all things. So the God of Peace, and Love shall be with you. *Amen*.

Reas. 3. I now come to the *Third Reason* of the *Doctrine, our Lord Jesus is the fairest of all things, because he hath all the parts of Beauty compleat, and entire in his Person.* That work with my own Spirit, and with all Spirits, which is my design, and delight, is to woo them for *Christ*, and espouse them, as chast Virgins to *Christ*. *Eccles.* 12. 10. We read, that *the Preacher sought out acceptable words, and the words, which he found out were upright. Solomon* was a figure of *Christ in glory*, King in the *Hierusalem above*. This Glorious Person is the Preacher, the Text, and the Sermon. *Acceptable words* in the Original Language are *words of delight*, as you may see in the Margin. If ever it be fit to seek out pleasant, and delightful words; it is on this Subject, when we treat of the Lord *Jesus*, and *his Beauties*. If ever it be necessary to take care to speak right words; it is now, when we speak of him, whose *Person* is the Center, from which all the lines of the Gospel, of Evangelical Truths, Graces, Comforts, Glories, Spirits are drawn; into which they all run; in which they all meet. My endeavour therefore is, that all my discourses may be steps from one Scripture to another, that by the explications, and applications of these I may enlighten your minds to the sight, and warm your affections to the love of these Blessed and Heavenly Beauties.

There are *four Parts*, of which all Beauty consisteth; 1. *Variety*. 2. *Harmony in the variety*. 3. *Light in the Harmony*. 4. *Life in that Light*. These *four* meet all eminently, and transcendently, in the highest degree in the *Person* of our Saviour.

1. There is *all variety* in the *Person* of *Christ*. Colos. 1. 19. *It pleased*

ed the Father, that in him all fulneſs ſhould dwell. Obſerve how St. Paul cometh to this total Sum at the foot of the Account, to this Concluſion of *all Fulneſs in Chriſt.* From the 15*th v.* to *this* you have the whole Compaſs of Things in *Nature, Grace,* and *Glory.* From the 15*th* to the 18*th* you have the Circuit of *Nature* in the full extent of the Creation with its Creator. *Firſt* there is *God,* as he is the Author of Nature. *Jeſus Chriſt* is *the Image of the Inviſible God*; v. 15. Then you have the whole *Creation. He is the Firſt-born of every Creature*; or *of all the Creation.* The *Firſt-born* is the *Excellency of Dignity,* the *Excellency of Strength.* Every Creature is in *Chriſt,* as in the *Excellency of the Divine Strength,* in its Divine Root, Power, Life, Vertue; as in the *Excellency of the Divine Dignity*; in its Divine Form, Beauty and Fruit. As our Lord *Jeſus* is *the Image of the Inviſible God,* ſo the whole Creation lieth in him, as in a Glorious Fountain-Head, in a Beautiful Womb, In a Beautiful Pattern, in one entire Form of Beauty. As our *Lord Jeſus* is the *Firſt-born of every Creature*; ſo each Creature is ſeen diſtinctly in Him, and he appeareth diſtinctly in each Creature, in its Primitive, Pure, Paradiſical State.

In the *next* place you have this *General* drawn down into *Particulars,* the *Heaven,* and the *Earth*; the *Viſible,* the *Inviſible* things of the Creature; Angels with all their Orders; all comprehended in the Light of *Chriſt's Beauties,* like the living Creatures in the *White Sheet* let down out of Heaven to St. *Peter,* as he prayed on the top of the houſe. All are *For, By, In Him*; v. 17.

Laſtly, For a cloſe you have all the Forms of Nature, like Flowers of Silk in a Garment of Needle-work, ſhining together in the *Perſon of Chriſt*; v. 19. We read in the latter part of that *verſe, All things ſubſiſt by him.* It is in *Greek* word for word, *All things have ſubſiſted together in him.* As Beams of Light ſtand in the Sun, and out of the Sun; ſuch a Sun is Jeſus Chriſt, ſuch a Viſible Image of the Inviſible God at the Head of the Creation, *in* which, and *out* of which all the Creatures ſtand; like a Bright, and myſterious knot of Millions of Diſtinct Beams: As a great and freſh Picture taken from the Life made up of many leſs Pictures, which ſtand in it, of which, ſeveral Copies are taken from itſelf, and Copy from Copy: So is our Beloved *the firſt born of every Creature,* in which all the Creatures ſubſiſt together in their *proper Diſtinctions,* and their *Univerſal Harmony.*

After this *firſt Circuit* of *Nature,* St. *Paul* paſſeth to the *ſecond Circuit* of *Grace, v.* 18. Here alſo all things appear *in Chriſt,* as their *firſt Principle,* and their *proper Habitation,* Jude. The *Garden* of *All,* the diſtinct *Root,* and *Flower* of *each* Spiritual Plant. *He is the Head of the Church*; *the Beginning,* the Principle; the *firſt-born from the Dead.*

Both theſe *Circuits* St. *Paul* bringeth into one *Divine Circle* of *Chriſt's Glorious Perſon,* like two diſtinct and pleaſant Apartments, one excelling the other

in

in Riches, Greatness, and Beauty, within the same Palace, in which all the pleasures of the God-Head, and of the Father, lie. *For it pleased the Father that in him should all fulness dwell.* v. 19.

Thus we see how St. *Paul* bringeth all *fulness* through all *Generals*, and *Particulars* of things every where into *Jesus Christ*, like the Silver and Gold out of all the Mines of Nature, and Grace, refined, and fashioned by the Hand of a curious Workman, the *Divine Spirit* into one Jewel.

Behold! *All Fulness*, the Fulness of all *Kinds* and *Degrees*; *All Fulness*, the Fulness of all *Things*, Invisible, and Visible; Angels, and Men; Heaven, and Earth; Flesh, and Spirit; God, and the Creature; *All Fulness*, the Fulness of all *States*, Light, and Darkness; Honour and Dishonour; Pain, and Pleasure; the Griefs of all Sufferings, the Joy of all Glories; the deepest Guilt of Sin; the brightest Crown of Righteousness; *He was made Sin for us, that we might be made the Righteousness of God in him*; Life, Death, the Resurrection from the Dead, Immortality; The Earth with its nethermost parts, the Heavens with all the Heights above them; in a word, Love and Wrath with all their Changes, and Dresses; *All Fullness* dwelleth together in *Jesus Christ*.

O the Greatness of the Majesty, and Fulness of this Heavenly Person! *Job* saith of *Wisdom*, which is one of the names of *Christ*, Job. 11. v. 6. *The Secrets of Wisdom*; *it is double to that which is.* The *Person* of *Christ* in the Secrets of its Spiritual Treasures, containeth all things, which are, and appear in the Light and Eye of the Creature; and besides these which are *Copies*, their *Originals*. Thus is it *double to that which is*; having in itself the *Shadow*, and the *Substance*; the *Picture*, and the *Life*; whereas all *that is*, is *Shadow*, and *Picture* only. The *Platonists* call Secondary, and created Beings; ὄντα, *Beings*; the Original they call Ἓν, and ὑπερὸν, an *Unity above all Being*. But *Job* going on to speak of Jesus Christ, addeth; *Canst thou find out the Almighty to Perfection?* v. 7. *As high as Heaven, deeper than Hell*; v. 8. *The Measure thereof is longer than the Earth, broader than the Sea.* That is observable; The Divine *Wisdom* called also the *Almighty*, is *as high as Heaven*; but *deeper than Hell.* His *Heights are all Heavens*; and his *Depths* are *Heaven below Hell* itself. What are the Dimensions, what are the Comprehensions of this Spiritual Person? It is the Heaven of Heavens for height of Glory. It stretcheth the Compass of its everlasting Beauties and sweetnesses, beneath Hell itself, comprehending that in its Depths, amidst the precious things of its sacred deep below. Its Measure extendeth beyond both Earth and Sea in all their Literal and Mystical Images. As the Earth hangeth in the midst of the Air; as the Air moveth in the bosom of Heaven: So Earth, Hell, Sea, Air, Heaven, and all live, move, and have their Being in this most high Person, and Spirit. O the Greatness of the Majesty, and Fulness of Christ!

I think

I think not fit to pass over this *Part* of our Saviours Beauty, the variety in him, without *Two Notes*; *one* of the happiness of Believers; the other of the Unhappiness of Sinners.

1. *Note.* How happy are they, who are persuaded in their hearts to trust in *Jesus Christ*, and by faith to abide in him? They dwell together with, and in all Fulness. When they travel through the valley of *Baca*, of *Weeping*; they go *from Strength to Strength*, from *one part* of the *Variety*, from one *Beauty*, in the Person of their *Beloved* to another; So they see, the *God of Gods* in *Sion*; the open face, and full Beauties of their Bridegroom in the Unity of His eternal Person, and Spirit in every form of things. Every *Pit* the deepest, and darkest is filled with Divine Beauties in him, and his Fulness,

Psal. 139. v. 6. *David* cryeth out; *This Knowledge is too wonderful for me.* The *Name*, that is, the *Person* of *Christ* is *Emmanuel*, that is, *God with us.* Mat. 1. v. 23. God inhabiting all Forms of things, that all Fulness may dwell in him, and so he may be with a Believer, a Believer with him every where, at all times. *David* was in this Contemplation of *Christ's Person*, and ravished with it; *Thou compassist my path*; v. 3. *Thou hast beset me behind and before*, v. 6. I am encompassed, and shut in with thy Person behind, and before, from Eternity to Eternity; in every Form of Darkness, or Light; Earthly, or Heavenly. I am still with thee. All these are Varieties only in thee. It is thy self, thy Person, besetteth, compasseth, comprehendeth me, and my way in them all. O Believers, when you see *Jesus Christ* in the least glance of *His Person* with the same Eye of Light, and Love, as *David* saw him with; do not you also meet with wonders of Delight, and Glory, which are too great for your Hearts, Affections, or Understandings to take in? Do not the lowest, and least things seen in him, appear to you as Divine Wonders, with such a height of Light in them, as no created Eye can reach.

But *David* caught up into the view, and Embraces of *Jesus* in his Heavenly Form proceedeth in his Rapture; *Whither shall I go from thy Spirit, or whither shall I flee from thy Presence, Face, or Person?* v. 7. The *Spirit*, and the *Presence*, or *Person* of *Christ* are here both one, to teach us, that this *Person*, and Presence of our Saviour, in which he is the *same, yesterday, to day, and for ever*, in His Appearances to the Saints under the *Law*, under *Grace*, in *Glory* is entirely *Spiritual*, a *pure Spirit*. *If I ascend up into Heaven, thou art there*; *if I make my Bed in Hell, behold thou art there*; v. 8. *Hell* in *Hebrew*, and *Greek* signifies no more th[...]n the *Grave*, or the *State* of the Dead. It is added in *Hebrew*, Behold! Thou! These words, *art there*, are put in by the *Translatours*, as you may see by the Change of the Letter. *If I take the wings of the Morning, and dwell in the uttermost parts of the Sea*, v. 9. *even there shall thy hand lead me, and thy right Hand shall hold me*, v. 10. *If I say the Darkness shall cover me, even the Night shall be light round about me*; v. 11.

Yea

Yea the Darkneſs hideth not from thee; but the Night ſhineth as the Day; the Darkneſs and Light are both alike to thee, v. 12. Theſe laſt words too are added; *to thee.*

Go thy wayes, O Believer! O beloved Spouſe of this Heavenly Lover; ſay to him with the ſame tongue, in the ſame language of Light, and Love, as *David* doth: Wherever I fly or fall, I am ever encompaſſed with, ever wrapt up in thy Spiritual, and Glorious Perſon, as my Heaven, as the Air of my Life, O my Beloved! If I fly, it is in the face of theſe Brightneſſes; If I fall, I lie in the Boſom of theſe Beauties. When I aſcend up into *Heaven*, behold thou art there. *Heaven is*, as a great Room of State, and Pleaſure in the Divine Building of thy Perſon. The Light of this is all the Glory; the Love, and Lovelineſs of this are all the Treaſures, and feaſts of Joy there. The ſeveral Appearances of thoſe Diſtinct Varieties in thy Perſon, ſhooting forth themſelves like Beams with a Divine Luſtre, Warmth, and Life, make all the Angels in Heaven. The Aſſembly of Glorified Saints is the *Fruitfulneſs*, and *Fulneſs* of thy *Perſon*; firſt thy *Birth*, and then thy *Bride*; like *Eve* to *Adam* in Paradiſe; the *Heavenly Eve* to the *Laſt Adam* in the Heavenly Paradiſe; thy *ſelf* multiplying it *ſelf*, that it may have a *meet Help* for it *ſelf* to be the *Object* of all its Loves, the *Subject* of all its Joys, the *Mother of all Living. What have I in Heaven beſides thee?* Pſ. 73. 25. Thy Perſon filleth all thoſe ſhining, and ſmiling Forms of things in Heaven. They are all the Beauties in thy Face; the ſmiles in thine Eye.

If I die, *behold thee!* Death itſelf is firſt an *extaſie of Love*, in which thou overſhadoweſt me, in a moment ſnatching me out of the Light of this world into the ſweet, and everlaſting Light of a far greater, and more Bleſſed world, thy Perſon. Then is it an *extaſie of Joy* to find the ſame *Jeſus* cloathed with the ſame white, and ſhining Rayment in the Grave, as I beheld him in Heaven. The Grave becomes a Bed, and that Bed thy Boſom. *Luke* 16. 22. *The Begger died, and was carried by Angels into Abrahams Boſom: the rich man alſo dieth, and is buried.* That which the *Grave* is to the rich man, that to the Begger, to the pooreſt Saint, is the Boſom of *Jeſus*, figured by *Abraham*, in whom he lay hid, as the *Seed* of Eternity. *Ere I was aware, my Soul made me, as the Chariots of Aminadab*; *Cant.* 7. *Aminadab* is *my Princely People*; *a Chariot of Angels of Glorious Spirits.* This is the manner of the Death of *Chriſts* Spouſe: Ere ſhe is aware her Soul ſetteth her upon, or rather itſelf becometh to her a *Chariot of Angels*, where ſhe ſitteth upon a Golden Throne of Love, encompaſſed with Curtains of Light, and ſo is tranſported in the twinkling of an Eye into the Arms of her Beloved; her whole way itſelf lying in the ſame embraces, which are the end of her way; and thoſe Angels being the varieties, and the movings of thoſe Fulneſſes of beauties in the *Bridegrooms Perſon*, which is the ſame *Spring*, and *Reſt* of love in them all.

Go on then, believing Soul, with *David*, and ſay to thy Saviour: but the

time

time may come, when I ſhall neither reſt on thy boſom, as a Throne of Grace in Heaven, nor as a Bed in the Grave, in the Fellowſhip of thy Death. I may be hurried to the uttermoſt parts of the Sea; to that State, where ſtorms of malice, and wrath rage moſt in the midſt of the blackneſs of Darkneſs: But when it is ſo, *even* then thou riſeſt upon me, and ſweetly breakeſt, like a lovely morning, in the Beauties of thy Perſon round about me. Thou takeſt me upon thy Divine Beams, as upon Silver Wings with Feathers of Gold, in which the Glories of the Divine, and Humane Nature are united. As thou in thy courſe circleſt thorow all the infiniteneſs of differing Beauties within thy ſelf, thou carrieſt me upon theſe Wings of thine to the extremities of this Sea of Darkneſs, and Tempeſts. *Even* here alſo, as in Heaven itſelf *thy hand*, which is thy ſelf, thy Spiritual Perſon, thy Divine Life in Act; the Activity, and Appearance of thine inſeparable Glories *lead* me, as my Strength within, my guide and way before me, my light round about me. Yea *even* here *thy right Hand*, which is thy Perſon in the ſweeteſt, fulleſt Act, and appearance of Love, Beauty, Majeſty, and Power, *holdeth* me; at once bearing me up in itſelf, encompaſſing with itſelf. Thus the Sea, and Tempeſts are ſtill *thy Perſon* in the ſame Lovely, and Eternal Form opening new Wonders of Beauty, and diſcovering greater Riches of vaſter varieties within the bright Bound of its own Spiritual Fulneſs.

Yea if I ſink ſo low, that I begin to faint, and ſay; *now the Darkneſs will cover*, and overwhelm me; now the night will ſeal up my Eyes from the ſight of my Beloved, and hide him from me: then the *Night* it ſelf becomes a bright Sun round about me in the Heaven of *thy Perſon*, where every ſpot of Darkneſs, as well as Beam of Light is a ſhining Point, or line of Beauty; and all ſo many ſeveral Suns ſet thick one by another.

Can. 5, 11. *The Head* of Chriſt is ſaid to be *as fine Gold*; *the Buſhes, or Curles of his Locks black as a Raven*, which is the *Bird of Death*. The blackeſt Darkneſſes, with the moſt affrighting Horrours are but thoſe black Locks with their Buſhes, and Curls, which grow, and live upon the Golden Head of my *Jeſus*, and are a principal part of thy Beauties. Thy Golden Head is in the midſt of them, ſhineth thorow them every where; like a mid-day Sun ſhedding his Beams of Gold thorow a pleaſant Grove, making ſo perfect, and delightful a mixture of the Light, and the ſhadow, that both ſeem one. The Shadow heightens, and ſweetens the Light; the Light ſhineth in the Shadow, ſweetneth, and ſoftneth it. Each appeareth, as the ſame Beauty, the ſame *Perſon of Chriſt*, in a different poſture, in a different dreſs. Thus the Light and the Darkneſs are both alike in thee to me. The Light is thine *Eye*. Thy Perſon is all an Eye of Life, Beauty, Love. The Darkneſs is the *Apple* of thine *Eye*. Here all inferiour excellencies are loſt, and covered in a deep ſhade. Here thy Spirit and Perſon is moſt naked; here it uniteth all the Beams, and Forces of its lovelineſs, and love; here I ſee my ſelf, mine own Image, and Perſon ſhining with an Immortal light round about it. The Darkneſs is the variety making the

Beauty,

Beauty, and distinguishing the unity of Light into the Riches of manifold Divine Colours, Shapes, and pleasant Operations of Love-delights, in thy Person. The Darkness is the excess, and depth of thy Light swallowing up every Eye of Nature in me, then giving me a new Eye, and a new Vision of things in itself. *Day unto day uttereth Speech ; Night unto night declareth Knowledge: Psal.* 19. 2. Thou my *Jesus*, the Immortal word, and onely wisdom of thy Father, art this *Speech*, this *Knowledge*. The Day and Night agree in this ; both are Divine Sounds of the *Living Word* ; Divine Representations of the Heavenly Image, Divine expressions of the eternal wisdom ; that is, both are thine Appearances, distinct Appearances of the same Beautiful Person ; several parts of the same fulness lying together, as Lines, and Colours in the delightful Bosom, and Face of one Transcendent, Spiritual Beauty. Thy Person appeareth in them both with equal fulness, and is equally the fulness of both. Thus in this one blessed Person of thine both are made one, and are alike to me. This is the happiness of every Believer. This is my *First Note*.

2. *Note. How unhappy is every Sinner, Prov.* 5. 14. There is one brought in bewailing himself : *How had I almost fallen into all Sin in the midst of the great Congregation?* Thou canst never Sin out of the presence, from under the Eye of this *Jesus*, whose *Person* is the *great Assembly* of all Living, Immortal Beauties, pure Beauties, Spiritual, the Beauties of Holiness. A Poet in a clear night surprized by Thieves, as he Travelled, when they were now about to murther him, pointing to Heaven ; so many Stars, saith he, as are yonder, so many watchful Eyes are there witnesses of this Murther: So many Forms of things, as are round about thee ; so many Eyes of Heavenly Beauties look upon thee, make the darkest night to shine bright, as day round about thee, when thou thinkest to hide in the greatest secrecy the practice, or thought of any Lust. When thine Eyes shall be unsealed, how will thy Spirit within thee be amazed, and confounded, how will thine heart within thee be melted to see, that thou hast covered thy self with the loathsom, abhorred deformities of so many pollutions, so many profannesses in the midst of the great Congregation of all living Lovelinesses, and Loves walking round about thee, and seeing thee, though thou lookedst not to them? But thus much for the *First part* of *Beauty in Christ* ; the *Variety*.

2. The *Second part* is the *Harmony in this Variety.St.Paul* after that he had said ; that *all Fulness dwelt in Christ*, addeth: *and having made peace by his blood* it pleased the Father *by him to reconcile all things to himself, whether they be things in Heaven, or things in Earth, Col.* 1. 20. The Spiritual Form of *Christ* is, as a Musical Instrument. All varieties of things in Heaven and Earth are so many strings upon this Instrument, which are all by the life and vertue of the Instrument itself so tuned one to another, and made to sound in Consort, that they fill the Ears of God himself with a most Divine, and pleasing Melody.

There is another Scripture, which agrees with this, and goeth further expressing

pressing the *Harmony*, and the *Ground* of it, *Ephes.* 1. 10. *That in the dispensation of the fulness of times he might gather together all things in One in Him, both things in Heaven, and things on Earth, in Him.* Here you have the *Variety, all Fulness, the Fulness of Times*; then *the Harmony*; this Fulness *gathered up into One*; & both these in *Christ, in Him.* Then the *Fulness* is explained; *Things in Heaven, and things on Earth.* Then he brings it in a second Time, *in him. Unity* is the ground of all *Harmony.* The *Unity* of *Christs Person,* maketh the *Harmony* in him by a concurrence of *four Particulars.* 1. The Unity of this Spiritual Person, which is most entirely one, springeth up into all variety within itself, 2. This Transcendent Unity boundeth all this infinite variety with itself. 3. This glorious Unity runneth through the whole variety, as a string of Silk through a row of Pearls. 4. The entire unity of this high and Heavenly Person standeth compleat in every branch, and point of all the vast variety at once; as the *Soul* is said to be *all in the whole Body, and all in every part of it*; or as if the Body of the Sun in stead of encompassing the Heavens successively should at once shine with its entire Body of Light in each point of the Firmament, as the same, and yet so many distinct Suns, being an Unity of all Lusters, and yet that Unity set in so many distinct Varieties, which are as highly, and ravishingly various each from other, as the unity is one in itself.

This is that wonderful *Person* of *Christ*; this is that *Word,* that *Image of God,* which is the Supream, and Universal Harmony, the Supream, the Universal Musick, and Beauty. This maketh all the Beauty, and Musick through Heaven. and Earth, as it giveth forth any where any Glance, or sound of it self. This Harmony comprehendeth all particular Musicks, and Beauties of the Creature with their several sorts and degrees in their distinct Perfections within itself. This maketh all things with all their motions, Musick, and Beauty by its Universal Presence with them, and comprehension of them. Blessed is he who hath a *seeing Eye* to discern this Beauty in every Appearance, the most rugged, black; blessed is he who hath a hearing Ear to take in this Musick from every motion, the most sharp, the most confused. Yea blessed is he who lies with his whole Person, and Life wrapt up in this Harmony; who moveth, as always carried on in the Chariot, upon the Wings of this Harmony.

A Caution. Naturalists report a Serpent to be often bred of the Brain, and Marrow of a mans back, when he is dead. So too often that Serpentine Spirit, which feedeth upon the dust of sensuality, and beareth an enmity to the Holy and Heavenly Dove, is engendred from the sweetest, and most substantial Truths, which are as the Marrow and Brain of Divine Wisdom, when they are become corrupted, and dead notions, in dead and corrupt Spirits. How are these two glorious Principles the Golden Pillars on which the whole Gospel is established; *That all Fulness dwelleth in Christ*; *That every thing of Christ, in Christ is altogether lovely*; improved by many unto the grossest Pollutions, and greatest Profanenesses? But these are willingly ignorant, that as *God is*

 the

the God of order, and not of confusion, so all variety lieth in *Jesus Christ* in that perfect Harmony, which is the Beauty of Holiness, and the excellency of the Divine Wisdom.

All natural things stand in *Christ* in a *double Harmony one with another*; and *with the Divine Nature*, as faultless Figures of that purity, and glory in the Eternal Spirit. So *Jesus Christ* is both in one, the *Image of the Invisible God*, and *the First-born of every Creature*, *Colos.* 1. 15.

Then this Beautiful Nature of things in *Christ* is made a Sacrifice upon the Altar of the Cross in Death; that it may put off the Negative Imperfections, the Shadowy Darkness, Slightness, Confinement, Mutability inseparable from a meer Figure. Thus is this State of things subject to a double Law without it, and above it; *one* of *its Pattern* on the top of the mount above Nature; the *other* of *Death*, that it may by putting off itself in the *Shadow* put on its *truer self* in the *Eternal Original*. Thus we read that *Christ*, as he was the *First-born of the whole Creation* became *the First-born from the Dead*: *Colos.* 1. 18.

Thus thorow Death, being purified by the Blood of the Lamb the Creature passeth out of that Shadowy State by rending the Vail of Flesh, where it is in Bondage, into the Liberty of the Sons of God, where it is a Royal Law of Life, of Love, and of Liberty to itself in the Spirit of God and of Glory.

The Heavenly Person of our Lord Jesus is a Circle within a Circle.

1. The *first* and innermost Circle is the First Image of God in Nature. This comprehendeth the whole Creation. This is made up of its Day and Night; Light and Darkness. All things of Light, of Truth and Goodness, are embraced by a Light of Divine Love. All things of Darkness, of the evil of sin, lye in the Darkness of Divine wrath, where the Evil of Sufferings, as a Secret Fire consumeth them.

2. The Circle which immediately infoldeth this, is that of the Death of our Saviour. Here the First Image entreth into a Divine Shade, where by degrees it loseth it self and vanisheth, as to its former appearances in the Figure, sinking into its Eternal Seed. The Spirit of Glory in this Divine Shade is the Blood of Christ purifying the Heavenly Things in the Creature by washing away the Earthly Forms. This State the Jews call the *lower Paradise*, the *Paradise, under the Earth*. For as a Seed hath in it self all the Beautyes, and Sweetnesses of the whole plant under the vail of a naked Grain: so here all things are as Spiritual, and Divine Plants full of all Beauty, and Sweetness under the covert of this Purple, Perfumed Shade of our Saviour's Death, to which the *Holy Ghost* was an anointing of all precious Spices, and a Lamp shining in the midst of it. This Spirit is also, as a Fountain from *Eden* running along in the midst of this Paradise, like a River, and Gardens under ground in the Secret of the Earth.

The *third Circle* is the Kingdom and Glory of *Christ*. In this the two other Circles

Circles are ſeen, the Firſt thorow the Second, as Faces in a Glaſs of Glory. Here the Heaven of the God-Head is open'd, and all things appear as Angels of God aſcending, and deſcending in the *Perſon of Chriſt.* This is the *Spring* of the Spirit, in which all created Forms flouriſh like green Leaves, and flowry Bloſſoms in the Tree of Life, never to fall or fade; the Eye of the God-Head as a riſing Sun ſhedding for ever ſweet Beams of Love, and Life upon them.

4. The *laſt* and *greateſt Circle*, the Crown of Life, and Beauty, is the Glory of the Father. This is the Autumn, and Seaſon for Ripe Fruit. Now is *Jeſus* returned thither, where he was at firſt. Now is he revealed, who was from the Beginning. God is the firſt, and the laſt; all in all. All things ſee, and enjoy themſelves; all things are ſeen, and enjoyed in their unchangeable Originals. This is that Spiritual and Heavenly Form of *Chriſts Perſon,* into which he is aſcended; in which he is, as on the Throne of the Father, which endureth for ever and ever; in which he hath gathered up all things into one. This is that Head of our Lord *Jeſus,* which is of the fineſt, and ſolideſt Gold.

Thus we have ſeen the *Order,* in which all things lie in our Saviours Perſon, according to which he deſcendeth firſt, and then aſcendeth within himſelf: The Unity of this firſt and higheſt Form, which is the Supream and largeſt Circle, the outmoſt, and inmoſt to all the reſt, as their Root, and their Crown, in the boſom of which all the reſt lie as Colours and Figures in the Light. This ſo goeth down into the other, that it maketh all one, and reſteth itſelf entirely upon each point of every one, and enfoldeth the whole in itſelf, ſo that all have the *Truth,* and the *true manifeſtation* of their *Being* and *Beauty* only, as they lie in this pure, and perfect Light.

Every inferiour Circle, or Form of things is comprehended in the Superiour, and hath there a double Appearance. 1. *In plain.* So it is a native Flower in that Myſtical Garden; a fair feature in that Face of Beauty; a Spirit of that Spirit in that Spirit, one Spirit with it. 2. In *Perſpective.* Thus the lower is ſeen in the higher, as at a diſtance, as at the end of a Cave, as it was in itſelf, as paſſed away according to that faſhion of it.

Coloſ. 2. 17. *St. Paul* complaineth of thoſe, who intrude themſelves into Heavenly myſteries, which they have not ſeen, *not holding the head.* Theſe, as *St. Jude* ſpeaketh, are *Senſual,* that is, men acted only by a natural and common Soul, *not having the Spirit.* So in thoſe things of our Lord *Jeſus,* which they know, as brute Beaſts, they corrupt themſelves. They have not anointed Eyes, to ſee the Harmony, and Spiritual Beauty of all things in the *Perſon* of the Lord. They diſcern not how the Original, and firſt Glories by ſit ſteps, ſhoot forth themſelves into Figures, and Shadows; how they lie hid as the immortal Seed and Subſtance in them; how like the Inviſible, and firſt Sun, they ſhine in the midſt of them, ſhine quite thorow them. They behold not the Figures aſcending like a Pillar of Smoak perfumed with all the Spices of the Apothecary

cary from this golden Altar of Christs glorious Form comprehending them, and being ever beneath them; how they lose themselves by degrees in the sweet shade of *Christs Death*; how they spring again new in the brightness of his Resurrection; how they lie continually in the Original Glory, where the whole mystery is entirely comprehended, perfected, and finisht.

These men set not their hearts upon this glory of the Father in *Christ* to make that their Righteousness, their Strength, and their Song in every other Appearance, as in the house of their Pilgrimage. They take no pleasure in the joints of all the members in this Divine Body, which are Jewels wrought by the hand of a skilful workman; this *Unity* being itself the mysterious joynt every where setting all, and binding all together in itself in that *Wisdom* of God, which is *this Beautiful Person* of whom we speak.

But enough of this *Caution*, and of the *Second Part of Beauty* in our beloved, the *Harmony in the variety*.

3. The *Third Part* is the *Light* in the *Harmony*, *John* 8. 12. Our Lord saith of himself; *I am the Light of the World*. As the Sun, the chief and most glorious Body, is the Light of all Corporeal and bodily Beings: so this blessed Person of our Saviour, the first and best Spirit is the Light of all Spirits; the first and most Glorious Form is the Light of all Forms of Things, Bodies, and Spirits. He is the First, the Supream, the universal Light. He is that highest Circle of Light, which rideth forth upon every Circle, or Beam of Light, each point in every Beam, *Psal.* 36. 9. *David* saith to God; *In thy Light shall we see Light.* The Light of the Father is *Jesus Christ*, the express Image and Glory of the Father. These words of the *Psalmist* have *Two senses*. 1. As colours are seen in the light of the Sun; so every colour, Light, and Being, the Light of the Sun itself is seen only in the Light of *Christs Person*, as this pure and eternal Sun shineth *upon* every other Light and Form *in* it, and *thorow* it. 2. Every thing as it is seen in the Light of this Heavenly Form, is a *precious stone* of the *new Hierusalem*. It hath a spark of this everlasting Light, which playeth in it, and is incorruptible.

The Sun is changed into Sack-cloath at the presence of an Angel, whose Light so much excelleth that of the Sun, that it hath no Light, when that other Light shineth forth. The highest Angels vail their Faces with their Wings, lose all their Light and Glory, when *Jesus Christ* appeareth upon the white Throne of his proper Forms, and naked Person. What manner of Light is this then, how pure, how full of Glory, how unexpressible, incomprehensible? This Light, this Lustre of the God-Head is that Scene, that Circle in which all the variety, the ravishing Harmony of Things lieth in *Christ*. This is the Form of his *Person*.

4. The *last Part* of *Beauty in Christ* is the *Life in the Light*. Life is a Spring of Beings, which maketh every thing fresh, and new every moment. Newness is attributed to the *Spirit*. The *oldness* of the *Letter*, and the *Newness* of the

Spirit

Spirit are opposed one to another, because the *Spirit* is *Life*. Life is the Spring of Motion, which is the Chiefest Charm in Beauty, and in which all Pleasures consist.

Jesus Christ, John 8. 12. calleth Himself *the Light of Life*. The *Person* of our King is that Light which is the Flower, and Crown of the Divine Life; and that life which is the lustre, the Sparkling, the Perfume of this Crown, and Flower. He is the Fountain of Life. *Psal.* 36.9. *With thee is the Fountain of Life.* This Lovely Person is the Fountain of Life in the Bosom, and Heart of the Father Himself. He is the Quickning Spirit, 1 *Cor.* 15. 45. *The Lord is that Spirit* which is in its own Essence, and proper Form: *Life itself in the Fountain*, where it is most pure, most plentiful, most powerful, most pleasant. How do all Varieties of things lye in the Youth of all Beauty in this Fountain of Life? How do they renew their Youth, their Beauties every moment, endlesly? Into what mutual traffick of Beauties, and Sweetnesses, into what uncessant, Sprightly, Pleasant motions, what Divine Acts of Love, Joy, Delight do they spring up? How is the Beauty, and Joy of All fulfilled in every one? How are all the Beauties, and Joys of All eternally varied, multiplyed, and increased, when all lye together in this Fountain of Life, and every One hath this Fountain of Life in Himself.

This *Person of Christ* is the Fountain of the Divine Life, that Springing Fulness of the Divine Nature in each Form. Here the *Father*, the *Supreme Love* eternally generateth the Son, the *Original Beauty*. *Both* in the *Spirit* eternally embrace each other, infuse themselves into each other, renew themselves each in other, which is the *First and Universal Joy*, the Fountain of Delights.

Use. *Make the Single Person of Christ the Sole Ground of your Faith; the onely Object of your Love; the Fountain of all your Comfort and Joy.*

1. *Make the Single Person of Christ the Sole Ground of your Faith. Rom.* 10. 17. *Faith cometh by Hearing, and Hearing by the Word of God.* Our *Jesus* in His Spiritual Form of Glory is the *Word of God*, as the Sun itself is *Lux*, the *First Light*. The *Scriptures* are the *Word of God*, as the Sun-shine, *Lumen*, the *Secundary Light*. The *First is a Living Light*, a *Light of Life*. The *Second* in it self is Light alone without Life. Look thorow the outward Word for the *Person of Christ*. When He cometh in to thy Soul by His Spiritual Appearance, He will be a Light of Life in thee, at once revealing His Excellencies in thee; Giving thee an Eye to see these Excellencies; by this Sight Setting them in thine Heart, Setting thine Heart. upon them, as a Root of Faith.

Esa. 45. 22. *Look to me, and be saved all ye ends of the Earth*; saith *Jesus* from His Throne, High, and lifted up, on which *Esay* saw Him sitting, which is His Divine Form. Behold! the Person of thy Saviour setteth it self before thee to attract and allure thine Eye by the Light of His Beauties. When thou lookest to Him. He holdeth thine Heart fast for ever fixt, as a Seal, upon His Heavenly form by the Fulness of all things Good, Great, and Glorious in Himself:

ſelf: He ſoweth the ſeed of his own Form and Fulneſs in thee by the flowing forth of the Life together with the Light of his Beauties.

All Objects for Faith to fix upon; the anſwers of all objections againſt believing; the way to believe; the power of believing; the act of Faith itſelf; with the Sweetneſs, and Fruits of it; all theſe lie folded up in the rich Treaſury of *Chriſts Perſon*; all theſe flow in at once upon the Soul, ſpring up together in it, at the unvailing of the Face of the *Lord Jeſus*; as the whole knot of Beams pour out themſelves in a moment thorow all the Air to enlighten, quicken, beautify and cheer it, when once the Body of the Sun appeareth. Look then to *Jeſus*, O poor burthened Spirit. Look to him that his Light may ſhew him; that his Living Light may be an Eye in thee to ſee him; that thorow this Eye thou mayſt drink in by the ſtreams of this Light of Life, him, and all his Beauties to be a Well ſpringing up to all Grace and Glory, to everlaſting Life in thee.

I ſhall divide this *Exhortation* into *Two Parts*.

1. Let the ſingle *Perſon* of *Chriſt* be the *only ground* of *Faith* in thee unto *juſtification*, Eſ. 60. 1. *Ariſe, and ſhine; for the Glory of the Lord is riſen upon thee*. Thou who lyeſt in the Duſt, bearing thy ſhame, as one free among the Dead, be no longer unbelieving, but believe. *The Perſon of Chriſt* in the Glory of the Father is riſen upon *thee*, filleth all things round about thee; ariſe and ſhine in the brightneſs of his Appearance. Conſider the Fulneſs of Beauties in *Chriſt*, and ſay thus with thy ſelf; *Hath the Sun Beauty enough to gild every Dung-hill, and Dung-heap here below, though that be on Earth, and he in Heaven*? Is not my *Jeſus* then rich enough in Glories to overſpread my ſhame, and nakedneſs, to make my Perſon ſhine in the Beams of his; though he be higher than the Heavens; I fal'n down to the nethermoſt parts of the Earth?

The Perſon of Chriſt is an *overflowing Sea* of Spiritual Beauties. For *all Fulneſs dwelleth in him*. If thou canſt not caſt thy ſelf into him; ſtand ſtill, and ſee how he breaks forth on every ſide, cometh on upon thee with mighty Floods, with a Deluge of Light and Beauty till he cover thee, and ſwallow thee up into his Bottomleſs depths of pure and Divine Glory, as a veſſel in the Ocean, which is fill'd within, and overflown without with the Waters of the great, and wide Sea.

2. Let the ſingle *Perſon* of *Chriſt* be the *ſole Ground* of *Faith* unto *Sanctification*. *All Fulneſs*, the *Fulneſs* of a *Sea*, and of a *Spring*, is in *Jeſus Chriſt*, *Num*. 21. 17, 18. You have an excellent Figure in a Hiſtory. The Children of *Iſrael* wanted water in the Wilderneſs. God gave them a Well. Then they ſung this Song. *They encompaſſed the Well; they ſung to it, Spring O Well; the Princes digged it with their Staves at the direction of the Law-giver*. Doſt thou want ſtreams of Grace? Is thy Soul a dry and barren Wilderneſs? Behold *Jeſus*, whom God hath given thee for a *Well*. At the direction of this Law-giver dig up the ground in thine heart, till this *Well*, this *Jeſus* appear.

Then whatever Grace thou wantest, at all times encompass his Spiritual Person in thy Soul, and sing to him; *Spring O Well.*

Joh. 4. 14. *The Water which I will give him,* saith *Jesus Christ, shall be a Well springing up in Him unto everlasting Life.* Take but in One Drop, the least Drop of the Sweetness of Christ, the least glance of His Beauty into thy Spirit; in this thou takest in the *Person* of *Christ Himself,* the *Fountain,* that shall spring up within thee unto the Life of Holiness which is the same for *Nature* and *Duration* with Eternal Life in Heaven; *Divine,* and *Incorruptible.*

2. *Make the Single Person of Christ the only Object of thy Love.* Let all the Fulness of thy *Love* be poured forth upon *this Person,* which hath *All Fulness* of *Beauty* in Him.

There is a *Twofold Love*; of *Benevolence*; of *Complacency.*

1. *Love thy Lord Jesus with all thy Love of Benevolence.* St. *Paul* complaineth, *Philip.* 2. 21. *Every man seeketh his own things: no man the things of Jesus Christ.* Seek, and pray for the prosperity of *Jesus Christ* all thy daies in *His Truths,* in *His Graces*; in *His Glory* thorow the whole Earth; in *His Church*; in *every Creature,* where he is sown as a Seed. Love him with the Love of Wife, Children, Friend, Country, Parents, Life. *In Isaac shall thy Seed be called,* said God to *Abraham.* In *Jesus* let all Relations, even of *thy self,* to *thy self,* have their Name, Truth and Vertue to thee. Let all those Blessings, with which thou shalt bless any of these, come upon the Head of the Lord *Jesus.* Wish well to, bless all these in the name of the Lord *Jesus.* Say continually, let the *Immortal Word upon its Wheels* run, and be glorified thorow all these, thorow the whole Heavens and Earth. Those that are Florists and love Flowers, procure the choicest slips of Flowers, set them in their Gardens, water them, watch them, cherish them with the greatest tenderness and care. So do thou love *Jesus Christ.* Be continually sowing and setting him, his Beauties in thine own, in every Spirit, in every Appearance. Water them, cherish them by Word, Example, Faith, Prayer. Go out often into the Fields; go down often into the Gardens to see whether these precious Plants bud and Blossom.

2. *Love the Person of thy Beloved with all thy Love of Complacency,* Prov. 18. 1. *A man through desire separating himself, intermedleth with all Wisdom, or with all Substance.* Behold here the Spouse her love of Complacency to her Spiritual Bridegroom in *three Steps*; *Desire*; *Separation*; *Enjoyment.*

1. *Desire.* Thy Saviour is called in the Prophet, *Hag.* 2. 7. *The desire of all Nations.* Thy *Jesus,* who hath all Beauties for all Eyes and Spirits, who hath all desirable things in himself, is the desire of all Nations. Shall not he then be the desire of all Principles, and Powers of Life or Being, in thy whole Spirit, Soul, and Body? shall not he be the Object of all thy desires? *This Person,* who is the Sealed Sum, and perfection of all Beauties, putteth this Song into thy mouth, *Can.* 7. 10. *My Beloved is mine, and I am his, and his desire is towards me.* As the *word* there signifieth; he continually is circling round

about

about me, hovering over me with the Eyes of all his Beauties, and Loves, upon me; as a Kite about his Prey. Do thou add to thy Song this part also; *and my desire is toward him*, Psal. 27. *David* saith; *one thing have I desired of the Lord, that I may be all the days of my life in his Temple, beholding his Beauty, and seeking still.* The Heavenly Form of Christ is the *Temple*, or *Palace*; and the *God*, or *King* in it, the Beauty of all. Say thou to *Jesus Christ*: *I now, for what is my sighing before thee? This is all my desire; that I may be continually in the Heavenly Light, and Divine Form of thy Person; that I may be continually feasting all my Faculties and Senses on thy Beauties, and endlesly* making fresh Discoveries of new Beauties in thee.

2. *Separation, Cant.* 8. 6. The *Church* cryeth to *Christ*; *Set me as a Seal upon thine Heart, as a Seal upon thine Arm. For Jealousy* (*that is, Love in its Strength, at its Height*) *is strong as Death, cruel as the Grave, the flame of it is as the Flame of the Lord. Love* and *Death* both agree in this, that they are a *separation. I protest by my Rejoycing in Jesus Christ, I dye dayly*; saith *St. Paul.*

The *Love* of a Saint to *Jesus Christ* is a *Daily Death*; a *Separation* from all created Objects, a Retirement out of this whole World visible, or invisible, into the World of the Blessed, that World of Eternal Light, and Beauty; to be alone with Him, and in Him; to be inseparably united in One Love, in One Loveliness; in One Spring, and One Stream of Beauties with Him, as *a Seal upon His Heart*, as *a Seal upon His Arm.* Where we read, *Cant.* 8. 6. *Love is strong as Death, cruel as the grave; the coals thereof are coals of Fire, which hath a most vehement flame, which hath*, is put in by the Translatours, *a most vehement Flame*, is in Hebrew, *the Flame of Jah*; of the *Lord*, of *Jesus.*

Learn here the Divine Mystery of *Love in Death.* The Death of a Believer, a Lover of *Christ*, is Love itself, which is the Fire of God burning from the Center of our Spirits, from beneath the Foundations of our Natural Being, till it have consumed the whole frame of this Creation in us, and transformed us into one everlasting Flame with itself; till it have separated us from every Form of things into his own Shining, and Flourishing Form, which is the *Person of our Beloved*; the *Temple, Palace, Paradise* of *Love*, of the *God-Head*, which is that *Primitive, the purest Love.*

3. *Enjoyment.* This is the *Third Step* in the *Love* of *Complacency. The Intermedling with all Wisdom*, or *all Substance.* Our *Jesus* is the only *Wisdom, Substance*, and *Truth.* The Fulness of things in Harmony, as they make all Beauties and Pleasures; in their Substances and Truths, as they have the first, & freshest Glory upon them, and are incorruptible, lie in the Person of *Christ.* The *Hebrew word* to *intermeddle* signifieth to *mingle with*, or roul our selves in the midst of all Wisdom, and Substance, that is, *in the Bosom of Jesus.*

O believing, loving Soul! Thy Beloved, when He cometh into thy Spirit, saith, *Can.* 1. *I am come into my Garden, my Sister, my Spouse, I have gathered my Spice, I have eaten my Hony with my Hony-Comb, I have drunk my Wine,*

and

and my Milk. When thou comest into his Bosom, and Spirit, say thou to him: *Now am I come into my Garden, my Brother! my Bridegroom! I gather all pleasant, precious, and incorruptible Fruits in thy Person, together with their Root, thy Person. So I transplant them into my Spirit and Person. I eat of the excellencies of Wisdom, which are sweeter to my Soul, than Honey is to the Palate, I eat them in, and with thy Person, the essence of Wisdom itself, as live Honey with the Honey-comb. I drink in my Wine and my Milk; the Spirit, and Sweetness of thy Divine and Humane Nature; of the New Heaven, the naked Appearance of the God-Head, and the new Earth, the Divine Appearance of the whole Creation in thy Spiritual Form. Thus I stretch my self at large, I roul my self at liberty in the midst of all Beauties and Delights. Here I rest in Eternal Joy with the perfect Complacency of all my Faculties, of my whole Spirit, Soul and Body, in thine Heavenly Person.*

3. *Make the single Person of Christ the Fountain of all thy Comforts.*

1. *Consider*, that there *is indeed such a Jesus, so Beautiful*, Eccl. 11. 7. *Solomon* telleth us; *the light is sweet, and it is a pleasant thing to behold the Sun.* If the light of this Heaven be sweet, and the sight of this Sun infuse a pleasure into us, when we look upon it: what is the Light that shineth in the *Person of Christ*? What doth once glance of this Sun of the Divine World? How doth it make the heart in our bosom leap to him, and dance about him, as the Needle to the Loadstone?

To go forth in a fair Summers day to look upon the green Fields, and clear Skie, is a refreshing to our Natural Spirits, and begetteth a lightsome Joy in us. come forth ye dark, and melancholy Souls! see *this Jesus* in his unvailed Person, as he rideth forth upon the Circuit of the whole Heaven and Earth in his name *Jah*, in his Divine Form, in which he comprehendeth and filleth all; see that New Heaven, and New Earth, which he maketh in himself. As Snow at the shining forth of the Sun; so will the heaps of Snow, the Mists and Clouds about your Heart dissolve into an unexpressible Sweetness, and Light of a secret Joy and hope at this Sight. By the *Light* of the Beauties of this Person cometh the *Sight* of him: by this *Sight* cometh *Faith*: then cometh all *Peace* and *Joy* in *Believing*.

Could *Davids Harp* chase away *Sauls* evil Spirit, which vexed him? Is there any evil Spirit, which will not be chased away; any vexation, or melancholy, which will not be charmed by this *Harp of God*, by the Harmony of all Heavenly Beauty, and Musick in the *Person of Christ*.

2. *Consider, that this Jesus is Beautiful to make thee Beautiful.* Ephes. 1. 6. God is said, *in his Grace*, that is, in his sweetest, and richest Love, to have *made us acceptable*, that is to have made us lovely in the Eye of his Love, to have set us in the Embraces of his Love, *in the Beloved One*, in the *Person* of *Christ*. When thou liest on the ground covered with Sack-cloath, and ashes, in thine own Spirit, then think thus with thy self: *When the Lord Jesus appear-*

 eth

eth in all his Glories before the Father, then doth he represent me, then doth he present my Face and Person to the Eye, and heart of his Father in the Glass of his own Beauties. Will not this revive thy Soul within thee, to understand, that the Father taketh that Beautiful Image, and sweet Impression of *thee* upon his heart, which he receiveth from the most lovely sight of *Jesus Christ* in his fullest lustre? that all the thoughts, and works of the Father concerning thee pass thorow *this Medium*, the Beautiful, and Blessed *Person of Christ* ?

Thou sittest on the dunghil of this Body of Sin, this Flesh covered from Head to Foot with the Sores of thy Corruptions. Thou liest in the Grave of this Body of Death, where all cares, and fears, like Worms feed upon thee. But see, *Jesus* boweth the Heavens, and cometh down. He descendeth in that Form of Glory, which is the Heaven of Heavens, encompassing thee on every side, transfiguring thee into a shining Glory, as the white Cloud of the most excellent Majesty transfigured him, when it rested upon him.

3. *Consider, that this Jesus is Bautiful for thee, to make thee happy in the enjoyment of Him. David* in a pang of grief comforteth himself after this manner; *Why doest thou cast down thy self; O my Soul! why art thou so troubled within me? Hope in the Lord ; I shall yet praise Him, the Health of my Countenance, (or, the Salvations of my Persons, of my Person in every Form, and Appearance) and my God, Psa.* 42. 11. Thus do thou discourse with thine own Soul, when it is overcast and bowed down with fear, care, or sorrows: *Why droopest thou my Soul! Why doest thou mourn, and groan? Why art thou thus unquiet within me? Look to thy Jesus; I shall yet sing new songs of my Beloved, and praise His Beauties, these are the Spiritual wine, that maketh glad my Heart; the Oyl of Joy, that maketh my face to shine.* He is a Million of Salvations, and Heavens to me in every state. He is my God.

Why art thou cast down, O my Soul! Lift up thine Eyes to the Person of Christ. Is not this Anoynted One, with all the Beauties of the God-Head, ever before thee? Doth not he continually encompass thee, and shine round about thee with all variety of pleasantnesses, and glories, like the Rainbow round about the Throne of God? Rev. 4. *Is not His Desire towards thee, that thou mayest rule over His Beauties, and satisfie thy self at all times with these Breasts of Divine Sweetness? Feed then like a Roe, among these Lillies. The Person of Christ is not His own, but Thine; Thou hast power over it, and all its Heavenly Treasures. Let Him then with all His Excellencies lye like a bundle of Myrrhe between thy breasts all the dark Night, breathing Sweetness into thy Spirit, and as a Cordiall fortifying thy Heart against all assaults, with a glorious Joy. Here make thy self, with all thy flocks of thoughts, and affections to lye down, O my Soul! Here lose thy self, and this dark appearance of Things, in these Lovelinesses of thy Saviour's Person, which cometh forth, like a Brdegroom out of His Chamber of Eternity, of His Father's Bosom, like a Sun fresh in all His Morning-Beauties, to run his race of Glory in thy Person, and to swallow up that into the Circles of His Pure Light.*

Reas.

Reaſ. 4. I come now to the *4th* and *laſt Reaſon,* why *Jeſus Chriſt* is the *Faireſt* of all things. *All Beauty is derived from Him.* Beauty any where in the Creature is an Image of the Divine Nature, by which that maketh itſelf viſible, teſtifieth its Preſence, awakeneth the Soul to a ſenſe of *itſelf*, and to ſeek after it. The Lord *Jeſus* is the Firſt Image of the Inviſible God, the Supream Beauty. So every other Image, is drawn from Him, dependeth upon Him, and is comprehended primitively, purely in Him. Every other Beauty is a *Copy* of Him, taken from Him, who alone is the *Life.*

Col. 1. 18. All things are made *by Chriſt*, inviſible, viſible; in Heaven, on Earth; Angels; all were made *by Him*, and *for Him*; *by Him*, as the *Exemplar Cauſe*; *for him*, as the *End*, that thorow the *Picture* the *Perſon* Himſelf might, as a Sleeping Seed, ſtir up itſelf, and ſpring in the Light of every underſtanding and ſenſe, in the Love of every Heart.

All Things are By *Chriſt* Two ways, 1. *As the Pattern of the Work*: 2. *As the Power Working.*

1. Every thing is *by Chriſt*, as the Pattern of the Work. Our Lord *Jeſus* is the *Wiſdom* of God. Wiſdom is an Inward Image in every Spirit, according to which it ordereth its way, and faſhioneth its work that the Whole may be One Piece, and a Beauty may reſult from the agreement of all Parts in the unity of the whole; as alſo from the Harmony of the outward Form, and the Inward Image, which by their mutual reflections pour forth pleaſures, and joys into the boſom of each other. In Nature the Spirit included in the Seed of a Roſe, hath within it ſelf the Image of a Roſe-tree, with all its proportions; leaves and flowers; beauties and ſweetneſſes, ſeveral growths, the bud, and the full-blown Roſe. According to this Image, the Seed putteth forth it ſelf; the Spirit in the Seed formeth it ſelf upon the outward Matter, and figureth the whole Plant in all the progreſs, and perfections of it. The *Perſon* of our Beloved is the onely Image in that *Eternal Spirit*, which is God bleſſed for ever. In this glorious Image doth He ride forth upon the face of the whole Creation from the beginning to the end. In all His works of Power and Providence, He conſulteth onely with this Beautiful Image in His own Breaſt, in which all the Treaſures of Wiſdom and Knowledge, all the Patterns of Beauty and Excellency are laid up. He figureth this Image upon every Creature, and Work: he fixeth this Image itſelf in every Creature, and Work, which by the luſtre of its preſence, putteth a Life in the Figure, and giveth a gloſs to it, as the Sun-ſhine to a Flower.

Gen. 40. 38, 39. We have the Hiſtory of *Jacob* laying ſtreaked and ſpeckled rods in the Water-troughs before the Cattel. When they came to drink, they ſaw theſe, conceived, and brought forth their young ſtreaked, and ſpeckled like to theſe. Thus God the Father in all the Excellencies of the God-Head generateth *Jeſus Chriſt*, and ſetteth his Perſon before him. When he cometh to drink of theſe waters of Life, to take in, and feaſt himſelf upon the

Joys of his own Essence, and of the Divine Nature, he hath his Beloved Son in his Eye continually. From this Beatifical vision he is filled with the Innumerable Forms of his Son's Beauties. From this Fulness the Father becometh Fruitful, and bringeth forth the Creation with all the Forms, and changes of it in the Figure of these Eternal Glories.

2. *All things are by Christ*, as the *Power working*, Job 38. 14. *It is turned as Clay to the Seal; they stand as a Garment.* How sweet, and clear a Depth is this Text? How doth *Jesus Christ* in it shine from the Face of every Creature, and from the unfathomable Light of his own Person? What is this *it*, *it is turned*? You shall see in the *verse* immediately before, *it* is the *Earth*, which frequently is taken for the whole Creation in the language of the Scripture, as *Heaven* for God. But what is this *Seal*, to which the *Earth* is turned like *Clay*? *Two verses* before will shew you, that this *Seal* is the *Day-light*. *Luk.* 1. 78. *Zacharias* in his Song expresseth *Jesus Christ* by this name, the *Day-spring*: These are his words; *The Day-spring from on high hath visited us.* As the *Day-light*, when it springeth in the morning, overspreadeth the whole visible World, and setteth a new Form upon every thing: so the Lord *Jesus*, as a Seal by the presence of his *Person* with every Creature imprinteth the figure of himself in a beautiful Form upon it.

Thus *it is turned, as a Clay to the Seal. Job* addeth; *they stand, as a Garment.* The Creation is spoken of first *Collectively, It*; then all the Creatures *in particular distributively, They.* There are two rich Glypmses given us of the glorious *Person* of our Lord in the Creation by these words.

1. As the whole Creation in *general*, so each in *particular* is sealed with the *entire Person* of *Christ*.

2. All the Creatures are *Sealed* with the *Person of the Lord Jesus without*, and *filled* with the *same Person within*. Every Creature rightly seen, is as a *Garment of Light* cloathing the Body of the Sun, the *Person of Christ*; and wrought in every part of it with the *Figure* of this *Spiritual Sun.* The *Type* of it was the *Vail* before the *most Holy Place.* Within were the *Cherubims* of Massy Gold. Upon the Vail was wrought the *Similitude* of the same *Cherubims* in all manner of rich Colours.

Thus the Earth is turned to *Christ*, as a *Clay* to the *Seal*; and every thing in it standeth, as a *Garment* upon him.

Perhaps he who peruseth this place in *Job* will find reason to believe, that the *Holy Spirit* pointeth at *Three States.* 1. The *Creation*, as the *Figure*. 2. The *Person of Christ* incarnate, as the *First-fruits.* 3. The *Reformation*, as the *Life* in the *full Harvest.* Neither will it seem unlikely to those who compare the *Scriptures*; that *Zacharias* alludeth to *Job*, and *Job* here to the *first of Genesis.* In *three* things all agree; 1. a *Darkness*. 2. A *Light* rising in this Darkness, and triumphing over it. 3. A *New Form*, given to all things by this Light.

But to return; *Heb.* 1. 3. Our Lord is said to be, *The express Image of his Fa-*

Fathers Substance. The *word* is *Character*, which signifieth *an Ingraving*, as upon a *Seal.* Great Persons first engrave their Arms upon some precious matter, as Gold, or a rich stone. This is their Seal. With this they stamp the same Image upon several pieces of Wax, as they have occasion. So God the Father setteth deeply, and richly, the compleat Form of his *Divine Person*, and *Substance* upon the *Person of his Son.* Then he setteth him, as a Gold-Seal upon the Creation, as Virgin Wax, and so imprinteth all his Beauties upon it. But the *Lord Jesus* stampeth one part of the Creation with the Impressions of his Person thorow another; so that the Figure is more clear and perfect in the invisible part of things upon Angels, and Spirits; more obscure, and imperfect upon the Visible part, the Things of Sense.

Before I leave this we are to take notice that the *matter* of the Creation, which *Job* calleth *Clay*, is expressed by *Water* in the beginning of *Genesis.* If you set a seal upon water, it receiveth the Impression without resistance, but keepeth it only by the continuance of the Seal itself upon it. Thus the Preservation of the Creature to the end, is the same thing with the Creation of it at first,, it is the Impression and Figure of our Saviours Beautiful, and Blessed Person, which is the Essence, and Form of each Created Being. It is this Glorious Person itself, the Fountain of all Forms fixed in the Impression, which alone every moment preserveth each Essence, and all Beings, by renewing them. If the Seal be taken off, immediately the Figure vanisheth, and is no more.

Use. 1. Let all this, that hath been spoken of the *Person of Christ* perswade us to study *this Person*, in which such unsearchable riches are laid up, and to seek the knowledge of him. Beautiful things alone are worthy of knowledge. This *Jesus* then is worthy of our knowledge. For he is fair. He is fairer than all things; and so most worthy to be known; all Beauties are comprehended in, and derived from him. *His Person* then should be the Center, where all the lines of our knowledge meet, and from whence they are drawn.

I shall press upon you the Study of your Beloved in the simplicity and nakedness of his *Heavenly Person* by *Two Arguments.* 1. *The Easiness.* 2. *The Excellency.*

1. *The knowledge of Jesus Christ is Easy.* Heb. 5. 11. The *Holy Spirit* had made mention of *Melchisedech* in the *verse* before. In this he addeth: *Of whom we have many things to say, and hard to be uttered by reason of the dulness of your hearing. Melchisedech* signifieth *the King of Righteousness.* This is *Jesus Christ* in that Spiritual Form of Divine Glory, which is the Throne of Righteousness. In this he was eternally with the Father, in his heart, and Eye. In this he was with the Saints from the beginning of the World, the Immortal Seed in their Hearts, the Joyful, and Glorious Object in the Eye of their Faith. In this he appeared frequently to them thorow outward Figures.

The *Holy Ghost* telleth the *Hebrews*, that He hath *many things* to say to them *of this Person.* He hath many, innumerable Beauties in Him to unvail, and

shew

ſhew to them. He hath many things to ſay, many words, and expreſſions, to declare the riches of each ſingle, Beauty. When *David* ſaw this *Perſon of Chriſt*, as a City compact in it ſelf, where all Spiritual Beauties, and Beautiful Spirits dwelt together in a moſt Beautiful Order in the unity of this Firſt and Great Spirit, in the Eternal Palace of His Spiritual Form, he cryed out: *Glorious things are ſpoken of thee, O thou City of God! Pſal.* 87. 3. So ſaith the *Spirit* here: *of whom I have many things to Say*; Then He addeth; *and hard to be uttered.* This ſeemeth a ſtrange Teſtimony to bring, to prove the Knowledge of *Chriſt* to be eaſy, which ſaith plainly; the things of *Chriſt* are *hard to be uttered.* But you will preſently ſee theſe words to have in them a full, and manifold proof of this, which we intend.

The Beauties of *Chriſt* are hard to be uttered. Whence ariſeth this Difficulty? From the Nature of the Things? *St. Paul* teacheth us, that *Every thing, which maketh manifeſt, is Light*; *Eph.* 5. 13. If that which maketh every thing manifeſt, be Light; then is the Light itſelf moſt manifeſt of all things; then the higher, and greater the Light; the clearer, the fuller is it in the Manifeſtation of Itſelf, and of all other things. The *Perſon of Chriſt* is the moſt pure, moſt perfect, and moſt univerſal Light. Nothing ſhineth ſo openly, ſo clearly in every creature, in every place, in every Spirit; Nothing ſo eaſy to be ſeen, as the *Perſon* of this Lovely One. Whence then is the difficulty of uttering His Glories? The *Spirit* anſwereth the Queſtion. It is from *the Dulneſs of our Hearing.* How evident an Argument is this of the Preſence of our Beloved with us, that He is before our Eyes in every Appearance of Things, that He is in the midſt of us? How plain a Teſtimony is it of the openneſs, and clearneſs of His Beauties, of their nearneſs, and ſuitableneſs to our ſenſes; that it is a *Dulneſs* in us not to ſee this Perſon, theſe Beauties? We never account it to be a *Dulneſs* of Senſe not to diſcern things Diſtant, or Difficult.

Solomon ſaith, Prov. 14. 6. *Knowledge is eaſy to him that underſtandeth.* The *Knowledge*, which this Divine King had his eye upon thorow his whole Book, was that *Wiſdom*, which is the *Brightneſs of the Glory* of God ſhining forth in the Soul. The *Holy Ghoſt* ſeemeth thorow this book of the *Proverbs* to expreſs by *underſtanding* a Divine Light and Senſe, which is the *Spirit* of *Chriſt* in us; by *Wiſdom*, that *Divine Object*, which is the *Perſon* of *Chriſt* riſing in us, like the Sun in his proper Sphere. This Earth which we tread upon, This Heaven, which we ſee ſhining round about us, are not ſo manifeſt to our natural Senſes; as *Jeſus Chriſt*, that *Power* of God, which bringeth forth, beareth up us and all things; that Wiſdom of God, which encompaſſeth us round about with its various brightneſſes and beauties is preſent, open, and evident to the Spiritual Eye.

Doth not this move us; to underſtand, that there is an *Heavenly Perſon* ever with us, in whom are ſet before us all the Delights of our Eyes, all the Deſires of our Hearts; and that the only Bar between us, and theſe Beauties, theſe

Bleſſed-

Blessednesses is either our want of Senses, or the Dulness of our Senses, that we discern them not? *Mar.* 10. 51. *Bartimeus* the blind beggar, hearing that *Jesus* passed by, cryeth out; *Jesus thou Son of David have mercy on me*. He ceased not to cry, till the Lord maketh a stand, and asketh him; what he would have. He answereth; *Lord, that I may receive my sight. Isa.* 50. 4. The Prophet saith of God: *He waketh mine Ear morning by morning: he wakeneth mine Ear to hear, as the Learned.* You that are no Christians indeed, who have no Spiritual Senses, cease not crying, *Jesus, thou Brightness of the Father's Glory, have mercy on me, that I may receive my sight.* You that are in truth Christians, and have Spiritual Senses drowsie, and dull, whose heart is awake in you, while you sleep, cry to the Lord *Jesus* to awaken your Eye, and your Ears morning by morning, moment by moment that you may see his Shape, and hear his voice. This is the *first Argument* to press you to the study of the *Person of Christ*; the *Easiness* of this *knowledge*.

2. The *Second Argument* is *the Excellency*, which consisteth of *two Parts*, the *Comprehensiveness*; the *Efficacy* of this *knowledge*.

1. The *Comprehensiveness* of the knowledge of *Christ* is the *Excellency* of it, *Col.*2.2. *All treasures of Wisdom and Knowledge are hid in him.* Several Propositions of great value and vertue, lie wrapt up in this single Proposition.

1. *All Things, that are to be known, lie together in the Heavenly Form of Jesus Christ.* All things are here in their first, and proper Being, in their Truth and Substance, in their immutable essences, as they are capable of being known. Every thing as it is seen without this Circle of Divine Light the Person of *Christ*, is a Shadow, an Apparition, a Mockshow of itself. It may beget a Fancy, or Opinion in our Souls, but no Knowledge.

2. *That Light, in which alone things are known, is only in Christ.* He is the true, Supream, and universal Light. *All things are naked, and manifest before him: Heb.* 4. 13. This is that Divine Light, in which every thing appeareth in its Divine Form, in its naked Substance, and Essence, uncloathed of every Disguise, and Vail, as it lieth in the Divine Understanding, which is the measure of all Truth. Therefore our Lord *Jesus* in that place, *Heb.* 4. 12. where all things are said to be naked and manifest before him, is in the *verse* before called; the *Word of God*; *the living Word*; the living Word of the Divine understanding, in which it bringeth forth at once, and eternally all knowledge to itself, and beholdeth, as in a Glass, the eternal Truths, and Essences of all things.

3. The *Eye, which taketh in all Knowledge is in Christ*; As the *Spirit* of this world is both the Fountain, and the Eye, which sendeth forth, and taketh in all natural Images; then our Spirits by being comprehended in this Spirit, become Springs in that Spring, Eyes in that Eye, bringing forth from themselves and contemplating in themselves the various Forms of being in this world; so is a Saint *Light in Christ*; a Child of Light in this great *Father of Lights. Jesus*

Christ

Christ in His Divine Form is the *Light of Life*; *that is.* 1. The *First Light*, as the first Picture is called *the Life*. 2. The *True Light*; every other Light is a Picture of Light, and no more. 3. *A living Light*; and so both a *Fountain*, and an *Eye*. In the *Hebrew* the same word for the substance signifieth both. A Saint Springing up in his inward man out of this Spiritual Form of *Christ*, and standing in it, is made itself also, *a Fountain of living waters flowing from Lebanon*; of all living Glories flowing from the high, and flourishing Mountain of the God-Head in the *Person of Christ*: *Can.* 4. 15. He is made also an *Eye set fully*, *Can.* 5. 12. *Aben Ezra* in his notes expounded that to be *an Eye*, in which is set the *full Image* of the whole Nature of things; in which, according to the language of the Gospel is set the Person of its Beloved, that entire Image of the God-Head, and of both worlds, where all Fulness dwelleth together in a Divine Form, and Glory. This is spoken of Christ first, then is true of a Saint, as a Saint is the Image of *Christ*.

4. *All Things, as they are known in Christ, are a Treasure. That which is born of the Spirit, is Spirit*; *John* 3. 6. That which is seen in this Spirit of Immortality and Glory is an Immortal, and Glorious Spirit. This is the true multiplying, magnifying, and glorifying Glass. Each Dust is here known in the bright Form of a Beautiful Star; each Star is discovered here to be an Heaven of Stars, a new world of Glories. Every thing as it appeareth in *Christ*, is something *of Christ*. *Christ altogether is Lovely*; *Can.* 5. 16. It is in the Original; *Every thing of him is desirablenesses*. The least Point, that a Spiritual Eye can touch upon in the *Person of Christ*, is a fresh spring, a full Sea, a great, and bottomless deep of all Beauties, Excellencies, and Joys that may render any thing perfectly, universally desirable.

5. The *Knowledge of things in Christ is a Treasure*. It is *Wisdom*, as well as *Knowledge*. It is a knowledge of things *in their Head*, in their highest Beauty, Life, and Truth. It is a *Fulness of Things*. It is a *Transforming Knowledge*. We are changed into the things themselves, and they into us. By knowing we possess, and enjoy them; we are possessed, and enjoyed by them; we stand both in one Image, and Spirit mutually comprehending, and comprehended; mutually cloathing, and cloathed.

All this Treasure is hid in *Christ*, not as in a *Cloud*, but as in the *Sun*; by no darkness, or obscurity there; but by the Excess, and Transcendency of the Glory; by the Perfection, and Purity of the Light; as *Christ is hid in* God; *Col.* 3. This hiding maketh the Object more a Treasure, and more evident to a suitable Eye, in as much, at it is a Divine Form in a Divine Light; a Form of Light dwelling in the Fountain of Light. How worthy is this Knowledge of that zeal to it, and pursuit of it, which the wise King stirreth us up to, *Prov.* 2. 3, 4, 5. *to cry for it*, to the Fountain of wisdom above, with the voice of our Faith; *to seek it as Silver* in every thing round about us, the pure mettal in the oar of the Creature, by the Flame of our Love; *to dig for*

it

it, *as hidden Treasures* within our selves, below the Foundations of this Creation, by Humility and the Cross?

This is the *Comprehensiveness of the Knowledge of our Saviour.*

2. The *Second Excellency in this Knowledge is the Efficacy.* This divideth itself into *three Branches* : *It worketh Grace.* 1. *Universally.* 2. *Powerfully.* 3. *Kindly.*

1. *The Knowledge of the Lord Jesus worketh Grace Universally.* It worketh all Grace together in a sweet Harmony. *John* 17. 3. In a bosom-discourse between himself, and his Father, where he is most naked, sweet, and free, the Lord *Jesus* saith to his Father ; *This is Eternal Life to know thee the only true God, and Him whom thou hast sent, Jesus Christ,* God is True, the Truth, as he is God. He is the True God, as he is the Onely One. *Jesus Christ* is sent forth from him, as he is the Brightness, the Effulgency, the Outshining of his Glory ; his essential Image. Thus is he also one with him. The Father cannot be perfectly known by him, if he be not *perfectly* one with him. This verse hath in it a figure called Ἓν διὰ δυοῖν: One thing expressed, as two ; like that; a Cup, and Gold, for a Golden Cup. So here ; to know *the only true God,* and *Jesus Christ* sent forth from him, is to know that God, who is the Unity, and Truth in *Jesus* his essential Image, in which he comprehendeth, and cometh forth into all manner of various Images ; the outgoing of his Divine Essence in Eternity and Time.

Eternal Life is the whole Work of God upon the Souls of the Elect from the Beginning to the End ; the Divine Life begun in Grace on Earth, compleated in Glory in Heaven. I have formerly said, that Knowledge maketh the Spirit One with that which is Known. How should this endear the Knowledge of our Blessed Lord, and quicken us to follow hard after it ; The true Knowledge of our Beloved maketh us One Spirit with Him, and transformeth us into His Image, which is the whole Armour of God put on at once ; the compleat frame and fabrick of all Grace rising up at once in the Heart ? All Graces are One in the Person of *Christ.* By taking him in, and being made One with Him, we take in All Grace, and are molded into All Grace in One, according to the measure of the Revelation of our Lord *Jesus* in us. The want of having this Pattern upon the Mount, *Jesus* in His Heavenly Form in the Eye of *our* Spirits, is the great reason why the Tabernacle of God goeth up so imperfectly, and brokenly in us. One Saint is careful of his way, but goeth sadly on; another is chearful, but careless. One is sweet and slight, another serious and soure, censorious. One is zealous and ignorant ; another high in his Light, and loose in his Life. Particular rules and precepts, are like a Watering-pot, which a man carrieth up and down in his hand, watering his flowers and plants singly and slightly. While one is watered the other withereth. The Discovery of our Saviour in His Spiritual Person to the Eye of our Spirits is, as the gentle Rain from Heaven, which at once watereth thy whole Garden, and descendeth to the Root of every Truth, Grace, and comfort in thee. *Grow,* saith *St. Peter, in Grace, and in the Knowledge of Jesus Christ.* 2 *Pet. l. l.* Grace indifferently, universally in the whole Nature, and Kind is inseparable from the Knowledge of *Jesus Christ.* These two mutually breed, and feed each other. All Grace in the entire Frame and Harmony is the similitude, the Image of *Christs Person,* as it is in Glory, formed in us. As *Christ* riseth and shineth forth upon us, this Image springeth up, groweth clearer and fairer. As this Image cometh to perfection; so *Jesus Christ* is seen more perfectly in it, as in a Glass. If you be compleat Christians, grow at once proportionably in all Grace, in Light, in Life, in Love; study the Heavenly Person of your Bridegroom, grow in the Knowledge of him. As the Eye of the Husband should be the Looking-glass of the Wife, by which she adorneth her self: so let this glorious Person of thy Beloved be that Spiritual Glass, in which thou O Queen, O Believing, and loving Soul, dressest thy self.

2. *The Knowledge of our Lord Jesus worketh Grace powerfully.* Psal. 19. 5. *The Sun cometh forth like a Bridegroom out of his Chamber, and a strong man to run a race. His going forth is from the end of Heaven to the end thereof, nothing can hide it from his Heat.* St. *Paul* testifieth to us, *Rom.* 10. 18. that the Lord *Jesus* is the subject of the Spirit in this *Psalm.* When he cometh forth from the Chamber of Invisible, and Spiritual Glories in his Resurrection: He cometh into the Soul at once; as a Sun for Light, and Glory; as a Bridegroom for Love, and Beauty; as a strong man for Life, Power, and Progress. When he riseth, and shineth out in us, he encompasseth our whole Person, and Life from one end to the other; he searcheth out every corner in both. There is nothing so close, so dark, so corrupt, so hard, so unclean, so dead, so comfortless; that can hide itself from the convincing, enlightning, consuming, softning, cleansing, quickning, comforting heat, and power of his Appearance.

Every Beam of the Sun is a Figure of the Sun, sheweth the Sun itself, and carrieth along with it three Things, Light, Heat, and Influence or Vertue. Such is every Spiritual Truth in the Soul. It is a Beam from the *Person of Christ.* It beareth a Figure of his Person, and setteth his Person open, and naked, like a clear Sun before the Soul, drawing the Eye of the Spirit to that, and terminating it alone upon that. Each Spiritual Beam, each Glance, every Discovery of *Christ* bringeth with it into the Soul, a Light of Knowledge; a Heat of Love; a Convincing, Converting, Melting, Transforming, Chearing, Sanctifying, Spiritualizing, Glorifying Influence, and Power. Go then in all thy pantings, in all thy Prayers by night, and by day cry to this Blessed Person; *Arise O Sun; shine O Light that my Soul may become a Spiritual Garden; that my Garden may flourish with all Spiritual Plants of Truth, Grace, and Joy; that all my Spiritual* Plants may give forth their smell, and vertue by thine Appearance.

3. *The Knowledge of Christ worketh all Grace, and maketh it most kindly.*
Psal.

Psal. 110. 3. The *Spirit* saith to *Christ*; *in the day of thy power thy people shall be a willing people, in the beauties of holiness, from the womb of the Morning, the Dew of thy Youth.* The word *Power* signifieth also *Armies. Willing* hath a twofold sense; *a natural, pleasant Freedom*; and *a Princeliness.* The *Morning* is the *Person of Christ* in the Glory of the Spirit, who is called in Scripture the *Day-spring*, the *Light*, the *Sun-rising*. When this lovely morning breaketh upon thy Spirit from the midst of the shades of unbelief, and thy natural State, it maketh a *day of Power, a day of Armies. Jesus Christ* appeareth now in the Glory of his Father, in his own Glory, in the Glory of all his holy Angels. He boweth down all these Heavens, and with them descendeth from above into thy Spirit. With these Armies of Glories he fighteth against all the Powers of Darkness in thee. With the Power of these Glories he subdueth thee to himself, winneth thy Love, transformeth thy Spirit and Person; shineth upon, and draweth forth to maturity every Seed of Glory in thee.

The *Person* of thy *Jesus* shining out in thee is that *Morning*, from which, as from a Beautiful, and Blessed *Womb*, falleth the *Dew of Christs Youth*, which is his Spirituality, his Eternity ever-full, ever-flourishing with all Divine Beauties upon his Person. This *Dew* maketh all Graces to spring in thy Soul; powerfully; plentifully; beautifully; pleasantly; with State and Majesty. As that Vine, which hath most of the Sun, bringeth the most kindly Grapes; the greatest Clusters; the fairest, and best coloured; the sweetest, the largest Grapes; the most abounding with Spirit and Heat yielding the best Wine: so doth that Soul, which liveth most in the Eye of the Lord *Jesus*, under the Beams of his Person unvailed, bring forth the most kindly Fruits of the *Spirit* in all these respects. 1. All Grace aboundeth most; it is as the Dew. 2. It is pleasantest. *Thy people are a willing people.* There is most of Love, of Life, and Delight. 3. It is most Beautiful. There are *the Beauties of* Holiness. 4. Every Grace is greater, spreadeth, and enlargeth itself more; hath more vertue and force in it. The Appearance of *Christ* maketh a *Day of Power*. 5. It is more Princely, hath enstamped upon it more of the *Person* of the Lord *Jesus*, and so more of the Majesty of the Divine Nature. 6. It yieldeth the most excellent wine of Heavenly Joys to make glad the heart both of God, and Man. It is the *Dew of Christs Youth.* It hath in it a Confluence, a Concurrence of all the Lovelinesses, Sweetnesses of the *Person* of our Lord in his Spiritual, his Immortal State, which is his *Youth* flourishing in the height of all Divine Pleasantness, and Glory never to fade, or decline.

O! Let us all be found in the number of the Watchmen, that watch continually for this morning. Let us go forth from under the Vail, from out of the Cave of the Flesh, and of the world, into the Light of this morning; into the sweet breakings of the Eternal Day from the glorious Person of our Saviour. Let us receive the Dew of his Youth falling upon us. Let us see the Dew of his Youth falling upon all things round about us, making the Desert to Blossom as the Rose; our Hearts, all things to us Spring, Blossom, and Flourish with the Spiritual, and Immortal Beauties of our Beloved. This Dew is his Sowing, his watering them every where.

Use 2. *A Direction* to the Knowledge of the Person of our Saviour, and his Beauties. The Lord himself saith, *The words that I speak unto you, they are Spirit, and they are Life*; *John* 6. 63. *Jesus* had been speaking of *Himself*, of *eating his Flesh*, and *drinking his Blood*. He meaneth by *words*, the *Things*, which those words signify. The *Person of Christ*, the excellencies, and vertues of his Person, concerning which he spake to them, are not *Flesh, and Blood*, which are the Shadows only, dying, dead, yea *Death* itself; nor meerly Spiritual; but *Spirit Substantially*, and *Essentially*, which is *Life* not by *Participation*, but *Primitively*, in the Essence, in the Spring.

This is the ground, which I lay for the direction, which I am to give you in your study of the Beautiful Person of *Christ*; *Christ and his Beauties are Spiritual.*

Now not I, but *St. Paul* giveth you *two Rules*, 1 *Corin*. 2. 7, 8. The *Holy Apostle* speaketh of the Knowledge of *the Wisdom of God in a Mystery*. Then he expresseth this *Wisdom of God in a Mystery* to be *Jesus Christ, the Lord of Glory*; the *Lord*, whose Person is all Glory, whose Principality, and Kingdom is Glory in the Abstract, Glory in its utmost extent. He had said, this was unknown to all the *Princes of this world*, the Princes in Wisdom, as well as Power, the highest ranks, and orders of Men or Angels. To confirm this he citeth a *Scripture* in the *next verse*. *v*. 9. *Eye hath not seen, nor Ear heard, neither have entered into the heart of Man, the things which God hath prepared for them that love him*. Observe by laying these *three verses* together, how *St. Paul* meaneth one Thing by these three expressions; *The Wisdom of God in a Mystery*; *the Lord of Glory*; *Things prepared by God for those that love him*. The *Person of Christ* is that Image of Glory, and of the God-Head, in which lieth the entire Mystery, Wisdom, and design of God from the Beginning to the End, with all its way. He is a Collection of all those Beauties, and Blessedness; Loves, and Joys prepared by the Father for his Beloved Ones to feast upon to Eternity. Of these *St. Paul* determineth; that the noblest, highest, largest senses, understandings, hearts of the most excellent Creatures are uncapable of the least Glympse, or tast of them. This he draweth down afterwards to a Rule, which is my *first Rule*.

Rule 1. *Spiritual Things are Spiritually discerned*, 1 *Cor*. 2. 14. This Rule divideth it self into *Three Branches*.

1. *Spiritual things are discerned by a Spiritual Eye*. St. *Paul* saith *The natural man receiveth not the things of the Spirit of* God; *for they are foolishness to him*; *neither can he*; *for they are Spiritually discerned*, 1 *Cor*. 2. 14. Nature hath a *Twofold Eye*, the *Eye of Sense*, the *Eye of Reason*.

The Eye of *Sense* is common to Man with Beasts, and is the *Bestial Eye*. This dis-

discerneth the Beauties of Flesh and Blood. We have histories of Beasts, Birds and Fishes, which have been in love with Beautiful Virgins and Youths. But this Eye is blind to Spiritual Objects. A Material and Corporeal Object, if it excel, and be transcendent in Sweetness, Harmony, or Beauty, destroyeth the Sense, as the Sun dazleth, darkeneth, and putteth out the Eye. How much more unable are our Senses, to take in, or bear Immaterial and Spiritual Glories?

Nature's other Eye is that of *Reason*, of the Mind, the Intellectual Eye, which is common to Man with Angels, This is the Angelical Eye in Man. This can discover, can take some measure of the Invisible things of the Creation, and maintain some Commerce with Angels. But the Darkness of this Eye to the Beauties of *Christ* is painted forth in a lively manner by that sweet and sublime Prophet *Isaiah*, *c.* 6. *v.* 1. *The* Lord *Jesus* appeareth sitting upon the Throne of His Spiritual and Divine Form; His Train of Glories filled the Temple, *v.* 2. The *Seraphims* themselves, which are reputed the Highest Order and Degree of Angels, cover their faces with two of their Wings, as uncapable of the Brightness of this Blessed Appearance.

We generally profess to abhor the Principles of *Sadducees* and *Socinians*. O that we did not most of us fall in too far with them in the real and practical part! The *Sadducees* deny both *Angel and Spirit*. They allow nothing besides that which their Senses can take hold of and assure to them. Let us awaken our own Souls, and examine our selves. Are we not very apt to reject and condemn *Jesus Christ* Himself, if He come in any Appearance of Beauty, and Glory, which beareth not the Figure of, which hath not some proportion to the Forms of Flesh and Sense?

The *Socinians* acknowledge both Angels, Created Spirits, and the Eternal uncreated Spirit above them. But they admit nothing more of these, than their reason can give reception to. They ascend no higher to these, than the Wing of their Natural understanding can carry them. They make reason the only Rule, and Judge of Divine Things. The men of *Sodom* went about groping for the door, at which the Angels went in, and could not find it; because they were blind. Is not this too frequently our case? How many? How often do we all go about in our searches, groping for that Gate of Heaven, by which the Angels, all Divine Appearances go in and out at the Heavenly Person of our Saviour; but find him not; because we seek him with those natural Eyes of our own sense, and understanding, which are perfectly blind to his Beauties?

Divines teach us, that one way of knowing God is by *Negations*; when we run over each particular good in every Creature; when we lay all the good of the whole Creation together in one heap and then say; nothing of this is God; all this is nothing of God, as he is in himself; his Nature, and Person is infinitely beyond, and above all that is here. We were advanced to a good degree in the Knowledge of our Lord *Jesus*, if we were arrived at this *Negative* way of knowing him; if when we were gone as far, risen as high, as our outward sen-

ses,

ses, our inward faculties could enlarge, and lift up themselves; we then said of all; *this is not Jesus Christ*. No, he is made higher than all the Heavens of sense, than all the Heavens of Reason, and of Angels.

When we are thus stopt, and bounded, let us turn to Prayer, and wait for the opening of a *New Eye* in us. *David* cryeth out, *Psal.* 24. 7. *Lift up your heads, O ye gates, and be ye lift up ye everlasting Doors, and the King of Glory shall come in*. So do you cry; *Thou everlasting Door, thou Eye of Eternity, thou Spiritual, and Divine Eye, open thy self in me; that by thee the King of Glory may come in to me, and fill all my Soul, and Senses themselves with His Train. So shall I see my King in His Beauty.*

2. *Spiritual things are discerned in a Spiritual Light*, 1 *Joh.* 1. 7. *If we walk in the Light, as He is in the Light, we have fellowship one with another, and the blood of Jesus Christ His Son cleanseth us from all sin. As He is in the Light*: He is God the Father, as is manifest by that part of the *last clause* in the *verse*, *Jesus Christ His Son*. That term, *As*, is Emphatical, and Distinguishing. There is a *Twofold Light*; *One* in which the Creature is; *Another*, in which God is. *One* God *maketh*; the *Other* God *is*. The Creature is in a Derived, and Changeable Light like the Earth. God is, like the Sun in His own Light, inseparable from Himself. *St Paul* distinguisheth between these two Lights; *God who commanded the Light to shine out of darkeness, hath shined in our hearts the Light of the Knowledge of the glory of God in the face or Person of Jesus Christ*, 2 *Cor.* 4. 6. Behold here *One Light* which is commanded, by the Creating Word of God, out of Darkness, which is called up out of the Possibility, and Principles of the Creature; *Another Light*, which is the immediate *Shine* of the God-Head itself in the Face of *Christ*. As the Sunshine is called the Flower of Light, because it springeth, and flourisheth in the Body and Face of the Sun itself; so is this called here a Light of Glory in the Face of *Christ*.

God Himself is called *the Father of Lights*, *Jam.* 1. 17, that is, the Eternal Sun; the Sun of Spirits; the Supreme Sun of all Beings, Spiritual and Corporeal. He is the Fountain of Light, the first, and purest Light; His Essence is a Light of Glory. This Essential Light of his own unchangeable Glories is the Heaven, in which he is. *St. Paul* saith of him; *he only hath immortality dwelling in the Light, which no man can approach unto, whom no man hath seen, nor can see*, 1 *Tim.* 6. 16. The Light of God is so pure, that it is invisible to every Creature. It shineth with such a Strength, and Fulness of Glory, that no mortal Eye, the natural sight of no Man, or Angel, can approach it, or pierce into it. In this God himself dwelleth, as in a Palace composed of the Beams, and Brightnesses of his own God-Head spread round about him, and encompassing him on every side. In this Palace he resideth in the Center, and midst of every Spirit, every Being, hid from the search of all. In this high, and strong Tower of Divine Light *Jesus Christ* dwelleth together with the *Father*, and is hid there after the same manner; *Colos.* 3. 3. *Our Life is hid*

with

with Christ in God. He is hid in God by the excess of Light, in an Abyss of Glory.

But how then shall we see *Jesus Christ* in his own Light, if that Light of his Person, and Beauties by its unsearchable Riches, and Incomprehensible, unapproachable Glories hide him from us? *St. Peter* answereth this objection; 1 *Pet.* 2. 9. *Ye are a chosen Generation, a Royal Priesthood, a peculiar people, that ye should shew forth the praises of him, who hath called us out of Darkness into his marvellous Light. His Light* in Greek is properly *his own Light.* Every Light in the things of sense is from the Sun. But that is the Suns own Light, which is inherent in the Body of the Sun, which floweth immediately from it, in which the Sun himself is seen. In like manner that is Gods own Light by way of eminency, peculiarity, and distinction from every other Light; which is the very shine, and sparkling of the God-Head in itself, upon itself; in which it seeth, and rejoyceth in it self; in which alone it is seen; which is inseparable from the Divine essence, and Persons, as the Sun-shine is from the glorious body of the Sun.

This is a *Marvellous Light.* This Light itself is a Divine Wonder. It is above the reach of every Humane, or Angelical understanding. It is a Light, which openeth a Divine World of Glorious Wonders; every thing is then only seen right, and in its true state, when it is seen in this Light. Every thing seen in this Light is a Divine Wonder; a Divine, Mystery, Incomprehensible, for the greatness of the Glory, to sense and reason; but familiar, and plain to the Spiritual Eye, as bred up with it, and continually before it, known to it from the Beginning. The Spiritual Bride meeteth her beloved here with all his Beauties in this Light, and kisseth him, as her Brother, as born of the same Mother. There is no strangeness between them.

This Light is indeed the Temple, the Palace of the God-Head, of Eternity. The *Father*, and *Christ* are here upon the Throne of their Kingdom, in the Glory of their Divine Nature. But a Saint is a Royal Priesthood; a King, and a Priest. So he is taken in, called by God into this Sacred Palace, and Temple, to behold the Beauties, to contemplate the vertues of both, the *Father*, and the *Son*, that they may declare them by the Divine Power of their words, and the Beauty of Holiness, which is the Sun-shine of the Divine Nature in their Lives.

We are now by this Circuit of *Scriptures* brought back to that *First*, on which we grounded this *Second Branch* of our *Rule*, and for the explication of which we have taken this compass. *If we walk in the Light, as he is in the Light, we have Fellowship one with another, and the Blood of Jesus Christ his Son cleanseth us from all Sin.* Who are these, that have Fellowship *one with another. St. John* had said before: *These things we write, that you may have Fellowship with us: And truly our Fellowship is with the Father, and the Son, v.* 3. Philosophers tell us, that we must come within all the Beams of the Sun to the

the Body of the Sun itself, if we will see the Sun in his true, and proper Glory. Some speak of a Blessed world in the Sun, the Rarities, and Beauties of which are seen only by the Inhabitants of the Sun. Gods own Light is a Divine World, in which the Father, the Son, all the Saints dwell together eternally, have their proper life of Divine Sweetness, and Blessedness, appear in their proper Forms of Divine Purity, and Beauty. If ye will be admitted into this Society, to a sight of these; you must go beyond, you must come within every Light of the Creature, all Beams into the Bosom of God himself, into the Brightness of the Divine Essence, which is the *Living-looking-Glass of the Holy Trinity.* Here you shall see your *Jesus*, as he is. You shall see him, as you are seen by him.

For now *the Blood of Christ cleanseth you from all Sin.* This Light of the Divine Nature which is the Light of Life, and the Spirit Himself is the *Blood of Jesus* eminently, in the vertue of it, as it is Incorruptible. This is that which poureth forth itself thorow the Humane Nature into the lowest Forms of Dust, Darkness, Wrath, and Death, in the place of Sinners, as a Ransom of Infinite value. This is that Precious Blood of the true Vine, which when Justice and Wrath have drunk of, they are satisfied, sweeetned, and changed into Grace and Glory; an over-spreading Loveliness, and an overflowing Love. This is that Blood, in which the Life is, which, as it is let forth in Death, wrappeth up all things in it self, washeth them from filth, and flesh; then riseth up again as high, as its own Spring in the Heart of the Father, and carrieth up all things with it self into the Newness of the Glory of God.

Nothing is so directly contrary to the Divine Light, as Sin. Therefore it is expressed by Darkness, and the Night. As the Light of the Day cleanseth all Forms of things from the Darkness of the Night which lay upon them; that now they have fellowship one with another, mingle their Beams and Beauties with mutual Joy: so doth this *Blood of the Lamb*, the *Light* shining in the *Person of Christ*, when it breaketh forth from the Shades of Death in the morning of the Resurrection, sanctifie the Heavenly things themselves, bring forth from under every cloud, stain, and dust, the *Heavenly Persons* of a *Saint* of *Jesus Christ*, of *God*, the *Heavenly Truths*, and *Lives* of all Things; that they may in the Unity of this Light maintain a precious commerce. and traffick of all interchangeable Sweetnesses & Excellencies with Immortality unto a full Joy.

Psal. 4. 6. *David* thus openeth the Hearts, of the multitude, and his own Heart; *Many will say, Who will shew us any good? But Lord lift up thou the Light of thy countenance upon us.* When all thy faculties and Affections, all the Powers of thy Soul cry, *Who will shew us Jesus Christ in Glory.* Let thine Heart answer to God, and say, *Lord, lift up thou the Light of thy face upon me. In the Shinings of thy Face is my Jesus hid; and in these Shinings alone will He be seen by me.* Thus the Spiritual Beauties of *Jesus Christ* are to be discerned only in the Spiritual Light of His own Person,

3. *Spiri-*

3. *Spiritual Things are to be seen in Spiritual Forms.* This is the *Third Branch* of the *Rule, Joh.* 20. 30. When the Lord after his Resurrection had appeared to the Apostles in a *Body of Flesh*, as He had been crucified; the *Holy Ghost* addeth, *And many other Signs did Jesus in the presence of His disciples.* Observe this expression well; His Appearance in a Natural Body, the same, in which He had formerly lived with them, was not the *Truth* it Self, but a *Sign* of it.

Luk. 24. 38. *Jesus* shewing Himself after the same manner to His Apostles, raiseth them from their fears, that This was the Apparition of some Spirit, by these, words: *Behold my hands, and my feet, that it is I my self. A Spirit hath not Flesh and Bones, as you see me to have.* The Lord seemeth to speak to them after this manner. "You have not yet received the Spirit; but are hitherto carnal. If I should shew my self to you, as I am now in the Glory of my Resurrection, in which I am altogether Spiritual, and a Spirit; you would not know me; you would not believe, that I were the same Person; you would be afraid of me. I have therefore wrought this Miracle, and given you this Sign in a tenderness towards you, and a Condescention to your present weakness. By that Almighty Power over Heavenly and Earthly Things, which I am now cloathed with; by the virtue of that Spiritual, Divine Form and Substance, into which I am now raised, which comprehendeth within it self all Form, Substances and Virtues; I present my self to you in that *same Body*, composed of the *same Flesh and Bones*, in which I lived with you, and died upon the Cross before your Eyes, with the *same Wounds*, which I then received. And, because this is a Sign, therefore do I accompany it to your Senses, and to your Spirits with a Double Evidence and Seal from my Divinity; One, that this is no Imposture, or Apparition, with which Evil Spirits have power to deceive your Sight, your Hearing, your Touch, all your natural Faculties; but that Individual and Substantial Body of mine, as it was in Flesh: the Other, the awakening of Spiritual Senses in you, the Shining forth of my Glorified Body, and my Divinity by their own Light upon these, thorow this Sign of my Natural Body reassumed for this Service. But now beware that you make not this Sign a Stumbling-block to you, to make you think me now like your selves, and such a one as formerly I was, to have a body of an Earthly Substance, or Figure, consisting of Flesh and Bones. No, the Days of my Flesh are past. I was put to Death in my Flesh, and to the Flesh, I am now quickened by the Spirit to live for ever in the Spirit. A Spirit hath not Flesh nor Bones, as you see me now to have. This seemeth to be something of our Saviours sence in this place.

St. *Paul, Rom.* 8. 6. saith, *To be carnally-minded is Death; but to be spiritually-minded is Life and Peace.* The Greek word comprehendeth an Act of both the Faculties of our Souls; our Understanding, and our Will. To look upon things in their Fleshly Forms, to savour and rellish a Fleshly Sweetness in things, is Death. To see things in their Spiritual Appearances, to savour and rel-

rellish them in a Spiritual Sweetness; This is Life, and Peace, which is the Harmony, the Musick, the Crown of Life. When the Disciples looked down into the Grave, for *Jesus Christ*, the Angels reproved them saying, *Why seek ye the Living among the Dead? He is not here; He is risen; He is gone before you into* Galilee,*as Himself spake unto you.* The Flesh was our Saviour's Grave, and is still the Grave of the Spirit. All Forms and Beauties of the Flesh are Grave-cloaths bound about Him. Let us no more seek the Living and Immortal Person of our Beloved, nor His Living and Immortal Beauties, which are all *Spirit and Life*, among the Dead things of the Flesh. He is not here in Flesh any more. He is risen, and gone before us into the Spirit. Let us follow Him thither. I have done with the *First Rule* to direct us in the Knowledge of the *Person of Christ*; *Spiritual Things are to be discerned Spiritually.*

Rule 2. *Spiritual Things are to be compared with Spiritual*, 1 *Cor*. 2 13. *The Holy Ghost teacheth comparing Spiritual things with Spiritual. This Rule* bringeth me to the Mark and White which I aim at. That I may hit it the more exactly, I must fix a while upon that *Scripture*, 1 *Cor*. 15. 35. and so forward. I lay this Groundwork for the Building, which I intend to raise upon this *Scripture*; The set Design of the *Apostle* here, is to discourse of the Resurrection of the *Body*. He therefore frameth this *Question* to himself, which containeth the Great Subject of his whole Discourse in this place: *How are the dead raised up, and with What Body do they come?* *v*. 35. In *answer* to this question he treateth of the Bodies of the Saints in general, of the Body of *Christ* in particular, as the *Root*, and *Rule* of the Resurrection to all the rest.

Upon this ground I shall raise *three Propositions*, as *three Stories* in my Building, which will take in the greatest part of St. *Pauls* words upon this Subject in this Scripture.

Prop. 1. *The Body of Christ risen from the Dead is not to be compared with the Body of Christ living upon the Earth, or Dying. St. Paul* likeneth by a large similitude the *living Body* to a *Seed*, the *Body raised* to a *perfect Plant* sprung up out of that Seed. *v*. 36. 37, 38. *St. Paul* maketh expresly *three Differences.*

1. The Life of the one is a Death compared to the life of the other; and so the world, in which it is a Grave, to that Image of things in the Resurrection; *v*. 36. *That which thou sowest, is not quickned, except it die.*

2. They differ as two several Bodies for Substance, and Shape. *Thou sowest not that Body, that shall be.* *v*. 37.

3. One is as bare Grain, naked; dark, deformed, little, slight: the other hath a Body, a Substantial, Beautiful, Distinct fulness, It hath a Form of Light and Beauty; proportions of greatness, and magnitude; a fulness of Substance. It hath a Divine Body, a Body drawn forth from the Treasury of the God-Head; *God giveth it a Body.* *v*. 38. It is a Body, a Form, and Fulness sprung forth from the Divine Wisdom, and Will, bearing the Glorious stamp of these,

in

in which themselves rest with a full Complacency. *God giveth it a Body, as himself pleaseth. v.* 38. It is also to the Seed *its own Body, and to every Seed its own Body. v.* 38. As *John the Baptist* saith of *Jesus Christ*; *he is prefer'd before me, because he was before me*; as in the purity, and Paradise of the Creation the perfect Plants were first in the Fulness of their Beauty, and Fruit, bearing their Seed in them: so in the Paradise of Eternity before the World, which is *Christ* the *Word*, the *Wisdom* of God, the Immortal, the Glorious, the Divine Bodies, and Forms of things were first, as the Flourishing Tree, comprehending in themselves the Bodies, and Forms of Flesh, as Shadows, or naked Seeds, hid in the Light, or Bosom of the beautiful Substance, and Fruit. Then came forth the Earthly Forms of things into the State of this Creation. These are *Shadows*, under which the Divine Substances are vailed. These are *Seeds*, in which the Tree itself lieth hid, as a *Divine Mystery*. By the breaking up of these Shadows, and the dying of these Seeds, the Immortal Bodies, and Glorious Substances themselves spring forth thorow them. So every Seed hath its own Body in the Resurrection. 1. It is that Body of Glory, in which it lay, and to which it relateth, as its Divine Original, or first Idea in the mind and will of God. 2. It is that which lay hid virtually in it. 3. It is that, which springeth up out of it, and changeth it into itself; Thus the Body of our Lord risen, is the same Body in relation to the same Idea, or Pattern in God; to the same Soul, to which it is joyned, as its proper Form in the Person of *Christ*; to the same first Matter, out of which it is taken; *God giveth it a Body, as it hath pleased him, and to every Seed its own Body, v.* 38. My Brethren, what joy is it to think, that the Body of our loving, and beloved *Jesus*; that our own Bodies; that the Bodies of our dearest Relations, and delights lose nothing of themselves in Death; yea are much more themselves by Death in the Resurrection; as a man awake is much more himself, than in a Dream; a King upon his Throne, than in the Grave, and Tomb? We shall lose nothing of our selves, nor of our distinction.

But I fear I go to far for common understandings to follow me. I will therefore conclude *this Proposition* with a plain representation of the Truth to you.

As the thing figured, exceedeth the figure: so the difference between the *Body* of our *Lord Jesus* before Death, and after it, is much more large than that, which is between a single grain of Wheat cast into the Earth, and the standing Corn upon the ground full-ripe with many perfect grains of Wheat in the Ear; than that between the single Seed of a Rose, and a Rose-Tree full of fresh, and flourishing Roses; or the Seed of an Apple, and a well-grown Apple-Tree laden with ripe Apples.

What Image could any man frame to himself, or what conjecture would he make of a Rose-bush, or a Rose by the single Seed, if he had never seen the things themselves? No more is it possible for us to take any measure of the *Body of Christ* in Heaven, or at all to guess, what manner of thing it should be, by his Body on Earth.

1. *John.* 2. 3. we read from the mouth of the Beloved Disciple, who lay in the Bosom of *Christ*, knew most of His Divine Secrets, and was best accquainted with His Person in Glory ? that, *now we are the Sons of God, but it doth not appear, what we shall be : but, when he appeareth, we shall be like him; for we shall see him as He is.* Now we have the Seed of God in us : now we have in us the Seed of a Divine and Glorious Soul, of a Divine and Glorious Body. But, what this Seed, which is sown in our Earth, will be, when it is a Tree in the Heavenly Paradise; what this Glorious Soul, and body will be, when they are come forth, grown up, and perfected, we do not at all know. Only this aim we have. We are sure, that we shall be capable of an immediate Sight, and Enjoyment of God, without any Vail, or Garment, without any Representation, or Distance ; *as He is* in His naked and simple Essence, in His own proper and immutable Form. This is an infallible Argument ; that then we shall *be* in the Form of God. For otherwise it would be impossible for us to *see it*, and take it in.

St. *Paul* illustrateth this difference between the Body of a Saint in its Life on Earth, and in the Resurrection, by two Comparisons ; the Varieties of *Flesh* and of *Bodies. All Flesh is not the same Flesh. There is one Flesh of Men, another of beasts, another of fishes, another of birds, v.* 39. *There are Terrestrial Bodies, and Cœlestial ; the Glory of the Terrestrial is One, the Glory of the Cœlestial is another. There is one Glory of the Sun, another of the Moon, another of the Stars ; One Star differeth from another in Glory : so also is the resurrection of the Dead. v.* 40. 41. 42. It is a very great mistake to think, that the *Apostle* intendeth here to set forth the different Glories of Saints in Heaven. He hath a far higher, and nobler design. This is his sence, and the force of his arguing : " You must " not think, because we have Bodies on Earth and Bodies in Heaven, that upon " this Ground these Bodies must be of the same Nature, and Kind, or at all like " one another. How vast a variety of Bodies do we behold with our Eyes on this " Earth, and in this Heaven ? As great as the number of the Stars in the visible " Heaven; so great, and incomprehensible is the Variety, and Several Sorts of " Bodies. For every one of these differeth from the other. Such, yea, far great" er, is the Difference between a Body, when it is sown in Death, and a Body, " when it is raised up. A Body raised, though be it still a Body doth more " vastly differ from it self here, than any two Bodies differ in the frame of " Nature, or within the Compass of the whole Creation.

The properties of a Body in Heaven, by which it is distinguished from a Body on Earth, are four as the *Apostle* reckoneth them up ; *Power* ; *Glory* ; *Incorruptibility* ; *Spirituality* ; *v.* 42. 43. The ground of these differences he layeth in that Primary, and Radical One ; *It is sown a Natural Body* ; *it is raised a Spiritual Body* ; *v.* 44. The Sun doth not so much differ in *matter*, and *make*, from a Clod of Earth ; as a glorified Body doth from itself on Earth. For both those are *Natural* : here one is *Natural*, the other is *Spiritual*. Nay an an Angel doth not so much differ from a Worm in its Essence, and Image. For an Angel is still a piece of Nature, a part of the first Creation, all which the Holy Ghost comprehendeth under the term of *Natural.* But a Body risen from the dead is *Spiritual*, of a new Creation; for *Matter*, and *Form* vastly different from, vastly above every thing within the compass of this whole world in the visible, or invisible part of it.

To conclude this Proposition, observe how St. *Paul* begins this discourse with a quick touch; *Thou Fool!* Thick skales of folly do lie indeed upon the Eyes of our mind, if we perceive not all things in this Flesh to be in a disguise of Sin, Death, Wrath, the Devil, by his Sorceries. That which we call Death, is the casting off the disguise. In the Spirit we see, and are seen with open Face.

Prop. 2. The *Second Proposition*, which is the *Second Story* in my building raised upon this *Scripture*, is this; *we may not compare the Body of Christ in Heaven, with the Body of* Adam *in Paradise.* This Proposition riseth up plainly out of St. *Pauls* words, *v.* 46. *And so it is written; the first man* Adam *was made a living Soul; the last* Adam *was made a quickning Spirit.* Three things lie plain in these words compared with the *Context.*

1. The Apostle speaketh of *Adam*, and *Christ* with a peculiar, and principal respect to the *Bodies* of either. The *Subject*, which he now professedly handleth, is the Resurrection of the *Body.* He bringeth this up to its *Principle*, and *Pattern*, the *Glorified Body of Christ.* In the *verse* before he established this Assertion, as a Pillar, on which the whole Frame and Fabrick of Divine Truths here delivered doth lean; *There is a Natural Body, and there is a Spiritual Body,* He strengtheneth that distinction by this Root, and main reason of it in the *verse* immediately following; *And so it is written; the first man* Adam *was made a living Soul; the last* Adam *was made a quickning Spirit.* You see clearly, that this relateth to the *Natural*, and the *Spiritual Body.*

2. *Adam* is here spoken of in respect to his *Paradisical Body*; *Jesus Christ* to his *Heavenly Body.* The place from which this is cited is the History of *Adams* Creation, as he was brought into Paradise; *Gen.* 2. 7. As his Body was taken new, and pure out of the Virgin-Earth before the fall, and the curse: *The first man was of the Earth Earthy*, *v.* 47. such as the first Earth, of which he was composed, which was then, say some, far finer than Christal, Gold, or Pearl, yea than the Sun is now; *Angelical Earth*, *Jesus Christ* in that Body, which here is meant, is *The Lord from Heaven.*

3. As much, as a *living Soul* differeth from the *quickning Spirit*; that is, as much, as a small Stream of Life from the Ocean, which hath its Fountain in itself, which is therefore unconfined, and infinite; as much, as a little Shadow from the Eternal, Incomprehensible Truth, and Substance: such is the dissimilitude, and disproportion between the beautiful Body of *Adam* in *Paradise*, and the Blessed Body of our dear Lord in *Heaven.* As the Earth in *Es-*

sence,

sence, and *Appearance*; in *Greatness*, and *Glory*; in *vertue*, and *Comprehension* differeth from Heaven, not only this Heaven, which we see, not the Heaven of Angels above our sight; but that Heaven, out of which our *Jesus* cometh, as Lord of all, an Heaven higher, than all created Heavens: such is the difference between the New-created Body of *Adam*, our first Father, which shone about his spotless Soul, as the Light about the Sun; and the glorified Body of *Jesus*, our first, and last Lord, and Love. O all ye, that hear, and believe, admire with me the infiniteness of the wisdom, and love of our God, who hath made the loss of Paradise by Sin so great a gain to us, instead of that, giving us our *Jesus*.

But we shall come yet more clearly to the mark, at which we aim, if we examine these words more exactly. To that end I shall propound *three Questions*.

1. *Question*, What the general Nature of a *Body* is.

Answ. A *Body* is the compleat *Image*, *Instrument*, and *Fulness* of that *Soul*, or *Spirit*, to which it doth belong, *Col.* 2. 17. A *Body*, and a *Shadow* are set opposite one to another. *Which are a Shadow of things to come, but the Body is of Christ, or is Christs, is the Body of Christ.* A *Body*, and a *Shadow* agree in being an *Image*. But the *Shadow* is a *confused*, *useless*, *empty Image*: the *Body express*, *Instrumental*, *Substantial*, and full. In the same Chapter a little before, *v.* 9. we read of the Lord *Jesus*; *in him dwelleth all the Fulness of the God-Head bodily*. God is the *Person* in *Christ*, the *glorified Body* of our blessed Saviour is the *express Image* of the God-Head. God is seen there, as a Man is at home in his house; nakedly, clearly, familiarly, constantly, entirely, in all Forms, and Postures. This glorious *Body* is the Universal, and Immediate *Instrument* of the God-Head, the *Sphear* of its Activity. God judgeth all, acteth all, exerciseth all the operations of the Divine Nature, and life here, as the Sun runneth his race from the beginning to the end of it in his proper Orb, and Heaven. God dwelleth with all his fulness in this Body. He delighteth to pour out into the Body of our Beloved, and his Beloved, all the precious Treasures of his God-Head. Here he delighteth to possess, and enjoy them in a Bodily Form, in the Form of a Spiritual, Heavenly, and Divine Body. As at the *Incarnation* the *word was made Flesh. A Body of Flesh, John* 1. 14. *by emptying* itself to nothing: so now is the *Eternal Word* again in the *Resurrection* made a *Spiritual Body* by returning, and rising up into all its Fulnesses in the same *Body* in which he had emptied himself.

The Lord *Jesus* speaketh of himself in Glory, when he saith; *In my Fathers house are many Mansions*; *John* 14. 2. The Body of our Bridegroom is a Spiritual Palace, in which all the excellencies, and Off-springs, all the operations and works of the Divine Nature have their several distinct Mansions, and apartments. We read of a Tree, in the branches of which all the Birds of Heaven have their Nests. The Spiritual Body of *Christ* is the Tree of Life,

and

and of Love, which hath Branches enough, and large enough for all the Birds of the highest Heaven, the seven Spirits of God with all their Train, all the variety of the God-Head to make their several Nests in them. I may add also; for all the Beasts of the Field, all inferiour Forms of Things to lodge under its Shadow.

You, who love the Lord *Jesus*, and his Appearances, doth not this move you, doth not this make your hearts to spring, and dance in your breasts, to hear, that your Saviour is cloathed with this Heavenly Body, so full of Glory, and of God? Can we forbear now from saying to our own hearts, and one to another these *five short words*.

1. *If we have formerly known any thing besides our Jesus, let us now know it no more.* If we have hitherto known *Christ after the Flesh*, let us know him so no more. This is the only object worth all our knowledge, and study; *Jesus* in his *Spiritual Body*, purer, and brighter than the Body of Heaven in Paradise, far beyond that in the height, variety, and compass of its Glories.

2. *How black doth every Sin appear in this Light of our Lords glorified Body.* When a Soldier was about to kill *Cresus*, his dumb Son cryed out; *thou killest the King.* So cry to every Lust in thine heart: thou crucifiest my Jesus in his Spiritual Body, the Body of all Divine Beauties shining like a Divine Sun upon thee, comprehending thee, as the highest Heaven. In every Creature in which thou seest not the blessed Light of this Body, in which thou doest not kiss it with the pure mouth of the Spirit in thee, thou doest crucify it.

3. *Is not this Bosom, this Heavenly Body of our Beloved, a Field of Lillies indeed, the Field of all Spiritual Beauties, and Divine Graces? Shall we not, like pleasant Roes be ever feeding here?* As *Booz* said to *Ruth*; let us never go into any other Field, to gather, or to feed? Is not this the Paradise it self in the third Heavens, where all the Fulnesses of the God-Head are in a *Body*, a Divine Body.

4. *How pure, and Spiritual are we to be in Body, and Spirit, if we are to be Brides to this Lamb of God, whose Body outshineth all the Angels, and is raised to a degree of Spirituality far above them?*

5. *Is this that Body, of which the poorest believing Soul may say by the Law of its Spiritual Marriage; my Jesus hath not power over his own Body, but I have power over it, to command its presence with me; to delight my self in it, as my Garden of Eden, of pleasure; to bring forth Fruit by it?* Is this that glorious Body of *Christ* to which these vile Bodies, yours and mine, are to be made like by that Power, by which he is able to subdue all things to himself, to the similitude of this Body of Divine Glories? Is this the Body, into which we are taken up, and which we are at home with, when in death we are withdrawn from these Bodies of our Pilgrimage here?

Qu. 2. What the force of this phrase is, *A Living Soul. The first* Adam *was made*

made a Living Soul. Was he not made a *Body* as well, as a *Soul*? The Body seemeth to be so far from being concerned here, that it is excluded.

Ans. This Word *Soul* hath *Three* Acceptions in the New Testament, and so that, which answereth it in the Old.

1. It is taken for the *Person* composed of Soul and Body. So *Gen.* 46. 26. *All the Souls which came with* Jacob *out of* Egypt, *which came out of his loyns*; that is; All the *Persons*. For the Immortal Soul cometh not out of the Parent's loyns.

2. The *Soul* signifieth the *Natural State* by the *first Creation* in distinction from the *Spiritual State* by *Grace*, 1 Cor 2. 14. *The Natural man receiveth not the things of the Spirit.* It is properly; The Man of *Soul*. So in this; 1. *Cor.* 15. 44. *There is a Natural Body; there is a Spiritual Body.* In Greek it is *There is the Body of a Soul; and the Body of a Spirit.* The word is the same there, and in *v.* 45. A Living *Soul.*

3. By *Soul* is meant that *Life*, which the Soul exerciseth in the Body, and which dependeth upon the Body; The Life of *Sense*, and *Reason*, as it is inseparable from *Sense*, Jude 19. *Sensual, not having the Spirit.* The word *Sensual* is the same with Soul; *Men of Soul.*

From these Scriptures laid together you may collect this Explanation of a *Living Soul*: A Natural Person living a Life of Sense and of Reason awakened by Sense, and inseparably tied to Sense in an Earthly Body. The Body is as the tree; the Life as the Sap; the Root as the Person, out of which both spring, and in which both are comprehended. Such as the Tree is such is the Sap, and such the Root, which have their perfection in the Tree. Such as the Earthly Body is, such is the Life, such is the Person of the first *Adam*. For the Body is the Result, and proper Image of the other two.

But the surest, and clearest Light into this Phrase, *a Living Soul*, will be that *Scripture*, where it is first used, and whence it is cited: *Gen.* 2. 7. *And the Lord God formed man of the dust of the ground, and breathed into his Nostrils the breath of Life, and man became a Living Soul.* Three things lie plain in this Text. 1. The denomination of *Man* is put peculiarly, and signally upon the *Body*. *God formed Man of the dust of the Earth.* 2. That part in Man distinct from the Body is expresly here named *a breath of Life*. 3. The *Living Soul* is the Body having received the breath of Life into it. *Man became a Living Soul. Man* relateth evidently to the beginning of the *verse*; *God formed Man, that is, the Body, of the dust of the Earth.* So in this Chapter to the *Corin.* The *Body* is called the *Man. The first Man is of the Earth Earthy. v.* 46. The reason why the *Holy Ghost* peculiarly respected the *Body*, while he speaketh of Man, seemeth to be this; the Body was the united Image, and Fulness of all those Beings, and Beauties, which were divided thorow the whole Creation; a most harmonious Body, and sacred Collection of all those Divine Excellences, Appearances, and Operations of the Eternal Spirit, which

made

made up the several Creatures like single Flowers in a Garden. Thus the Body of *Adam* was a Paradise in Paradise, the Paradise of Paradise. The breath of Life was in this glorious Body, as a Spring in a Garden, to quicken, and to animate it. Without this Body, the breath of Life is naked, and solitary, except *Christ* above the Law of Nature be in the place of a Body to it; which *St. Paul* signifieth; 2 *Corin.* 5. 6, 8. Where he speaketh of *being at home in the Body, and absent from the Lord*; and again of *being absent from the Body, and present with the Lord.*

By this time it appeareth with some clearness, that the *living Soul,* is either the *Body* of the *First Man* having received the *breath of Life* into it; or at least, his *Person* consisting of *Both*, comprehending Both, but with a Principal respect to the *Body*. This only I will add, that nothing is more frequent with most Authors, and Languages, than to express the *Soul* without the *Body* by a Shade, or *Shadow*.

I have now finished the 2d. Question, What we are to understand by a *Living Soul.* Before I pass from it, let us make a stand here while we hearken to a Twofold Voice from Heaven founded in the very Essence of a *Living Soul*: 1st. O Living Soul! cease from thy self, and from every thing round about thee. 2. O Living Soul! cast thy self into the Bosom of thy Saviour, and cleave to Him.

1. O *Living Soul! cease from thy self, and from every thing round about thee* Consider, what thou art, what an Emptyness, what a Vanity what a Nothing. Thy Body is of the Earth Earthly. The Earth is a meer Darkness, without any Form or Vertue, except that which it receiveth by the impression of Heaven, above it, figuring itself upon it, like the Images of the Sky in the Waters. Thy Body is a piece of this Darkness. All that which it hath of Being, Beauty, or Goodness, is the Figure of the Heavenly Body of Christ cast from above upon it. Thus thy Body in Paradise was a Shadow onely, What then is the Breath of Life in this Body, which is suitable to it, and confined to it; which hath this Body for its only Cloathing, for its proper Image, and Fulness, which hath the Compleatness, of its Subsistency, and Operations in it; which hath it for its Glass, in which alone it beholdeth it self, and all Objects, in which alone it converseth with them? This is a Shadow of a Shadow, a Shadow in a Shadow, the Dream of a Shadow: The Body a Shadow, the Life of this Body the Dream of a Shadow. The Person then, which consisteth of this Shadowy Life in a Shadowy Body, can be but a Shadowy Person. This is the Best of Man in his best Estate; the Living Soul in its primitive purity and Glory; *Adam* in Paradise; a Shadow, and no more. So saith the Holy Ghost, *Rom.* 5. *The first man was a Figure*, a rude Type, a confused Shadow *of Him, who was to come.* The Shadow lyeth upon the ground, often moveth, and appeareth before the Body. But the Body is first, is above it, casteth the Shadow from it, and governeth all its Motions. If this were Man, the golden Head,

 and

and Sun in the Paradisical world; if all the Creatures in their Paradisical Births, and Beauties went forth, were renewed every moment from the Divine Presence resting in the Center of his Person, and surrounding him; as Beams go forth from the Sun; what then were all the pieces of Nature in their first Strength, Lustre, and Sweetness, but Shadows of this Shadow? None had the Principle, or Truth of its being in itself, nor the Power of itself for a moment. But now Man, and the whole Creation are fallen by Sin; the Figure in the Shadow is defaced; the Impression, and Image of the Eternal Glory in the Darkness of the Creature, which gave it a Being, a Beauty, a Force, are withdrawn. The Frame of Nature is now a Pit of Darkness full of Confusion, where Death reigneth in the midst of all sorts of deformity and weakness.

That Counsel of the Lord was seasonable in Paradise itself: *Es.* 2. *l. Cease from Man, whose breath is in his Nostrils*, who hath only a Shadowy life in a Shadowy Body; *wherein is he to be accounted of*? Cease from every thing of Nature, and the Creature. It was at best a Shadow. What Excellency then hath it to be esteemed of, and reckoned upon? What stability, or Strength to be trusted to, and relied upon? Can you fill your Embraces with an empty Shadow? Can you hold fast in your Arms a flying Shadow? Will the Eye of your Spirit be satisfied with seeing Light; your heart be filled with Life; shall your Soul feed upon Substance in a Shadow? This is the *first voice* from Heaven founded in the very essence of a *living Soul.*

2. *O living Soul cast thy self into the Bosom of thy Saviour, and cleave to him.* Dost thou not now perceive plainly, that he is thy Root, thy Substance, thy Life, thy Strength, thy Fulness, thy Light, thy Righteousness, thy Perfection, thy Glory; in a word, thy true self; when thou art in thy best state a Shadow only of him according to the first Creation? Is not this the Beauty of Nature in thee, and thy Moral Righteousness to bear the Figure of him, and his Tabernacle in thy Person? Is not this thy Spiritual Glory, thine everlasting Righteousness to be taken up into him, and to be cloathed with him, to have thy Shadow drunk up into his Light? Is not this the Life, Strength, and rest of both states to be united to him, to be acted by him in that Union, to be resigned again to him in, and thorow all Actings, or Sufferings?

Let us consider what wretched things we were in death, if it were not for *Jesus Christ*. How would our poor Souls, when they were thrust forth, and cast out of these Bodies wander eternally naked, empty, in the dark, and desolate, driven up and down with the Storm without, burnt upon within by the unseen Fire of Divine wrath? But now *Jesus Christ* hath been to all his Saints from the Fall, the *Seed of a glorious Body*, into which they retreated passing from hence, and were at rest, as in a Bed of Love, which was green, and springing. Since the Resurrection our breath of Life in Death, and in the Fall of this frail Body drops into the Bosom of that Heavenly Body of our Beloved, as the ground of Divine Life and Glory, from thence to grow up into, and flourish

in

in an Immortal Body of its own, like unto it, and by a Divine Union joyned with it in Eternal Embraces.

Quest. 3. In what sense the Lord *Jesus* is here said to be a *Quickning Spirit.*

Ans. To this I answer *three things.*

1. The *Person* of *Christ*, as it comprehendeth both Natures, Divine and Humane; both parts of the *Humane Nature, Soul* and *Body*, is a *Quickning Spirit.*

2. The *Humane Nature* is expresly spoken of to be a *Quickning Spirit. The last* Adam *was made a Quickning Spirit. Again; the Second Man is the Lord from Heaven. v.* 47.

3. The Body of our Lord is principally intended under this description of a *Quickning Spirit.* This appeareth by the whole Scope of the *Apostle* in this place, which is to shew with what Bodies the dead Saints are raised and come again. *v.* 35. This is manifested by the *Context.* All the foregoing, all the following *verses* treat of this Subject, the *Body* in the Resurrection. Mention is made of a *Natural,* and a *Spiritual Body* in the *verse* immediately before. *v.* 44. The same are again brought in immediately after. *v.* 46.

Then the force of the Comparison, and Opposition maketh this plain. It is a sure Rule; Comparisons, and Oppositions must speak of the same thing, to the same point, and in the same respect. We have endeavoured to prove, that the *living Soul* chiefly, and emphatically marketh out the *Body* of *Adam* in Paradise, when his Body had more of Life, and was more a Soul, more Angelical, than our Souls are now. Therefore the *Quickning Spirit* opposed to the *living Soul* must especially design the *Body* of our *Jesus* in Glory.

Lastly, other Scriptures say the same thing. *John* 3. 6. *That which is born of the Flesh is Flesh. That which is born of the Spirit is Spirit.* That which is born of the *Spirit* is not only *Spiritualized,* heightned, and adorned with Spiritual qualities, like the Picture of a Man with Lines, and Colours; or the Statue of a Man richly gilded; One is a Stone, the other a piece of Canvas still: But it is a Spirit substantially, and essentially. It is a Spirit, not as a Soul, or an Angel is a Spirit; but as that Spirit is, of which it is born, after the same manner, in which; *That which is born of the Flesh, is Flesh substantially,* and Flesh of the same kind with that, which bringeth it forth.

As the Father and the Son have both the same humane Nature in a humane Form: The humane Nature is one in both. But the humane Form is distinct in each, and maketh them *two Persons:* so the Divine Nature of the *Eternal Spirit* springeth up in a Divine Form in that, which is born of it. The Eternal Spirit bringeth its Birth forth in a Divine Form, and at once together with that, itself with its own Divine Nature, and Divine Form dwelling in it; as the Root, the Life; the Form, the Fulness, the Fruit, the Perfection, the Truth, the Glory of it; the Spiritual Temple, the God in the Temple; both Spirits in the same Form; both mutually Temples to each other; both one

Spirit. Thus it is made a *Spirit*; in the same Form with its *Mother-Spirit*, the *Eternal Spirit* itself. It is made a *distinct Spirit*. It is made one Spirit with the *Fountain Spirit*. It is made a *Quickning Spirit*, having the Fountain of Life, and Spirits in itself.

Now the *Body* of our blessed Saviour in the Resurrection is new-born from above, of the Spirit of Life. It is therefore a *Spirit of Life*, a *Fountain-Spirit*, a *Quickning Spirit*. The Resurrection doth not gild, doth not spiritualize the *Personal*, or *Mystical Body* of *Jesus Christ*. It maketh them Gold within, as well, as without. It maketh them all throughout pure, and fine Gold; a Spirit of Glory. In this Creation, and in natural things, all excellencies are Qualities, Accidents; all Beauties are no more, than skin-deep. In the new Creature, in Spiritual Things every excellency is a substance, every Beauty is the Essence, and Person itself; there a Spirit is not excellent, or Beautiful, or Immortal. But each Excellency, each Beauty, Immortality is that Spirit. The Person, the Spirit is the Excellency, the Beauty, Immortality itself. Each distinct excellency is a distinct Spirit; and all Excellencies, all Spirits are one in each one, making that a full Assembly the whole Quire in itself. They all dwell together, and are made *perfect in one*. This is the *New-Creature*, the *Spiritual Birth*, the Resurrection from the Dead. How happy, and blessed are they, who have their part in this Birth, in this Resurrection!

There is another Scripture to this purpose, 1 *Corin*. 6. 17. *He that is joyned to the Lord is one Spirit*. In the verse before he had said; *What, know ye not, that he who is joyned to an Harlot is one Body. For two*, saith he, *shall be one Flesh. v.* 16. Here the discourse is clearly of the *Body*. As the earthly Marriage maketh *two Bodies one Flesh*: the Heavenly Marriage maketh them one Spirit. The union between our glorified Lord, and our Bodies in the Resurrection is as immediate, and entire, as between our Saviour, and our Souls; so that these also are Spirits, and one Spirit with him. Is not his Body then first a Spirit? Doth not the Union between the Divine Nature, and his Blessed Body make that a Spirit, and one Spirit with itself? The glorified Body, and Soul of a Saint are one Spirit. They are one Spirit with the glorified Body, and Soul of their *Jesus*, with the three Persons in the Trinity, with all Beautiful, and blessed Spirits. All are one Spirit. Yet are they all distinct Spirits. If the distinction were taken away, the Harmony, the Beauty, the Musick, the Marriage-joy, and Marriage-love in Heaven were all lost.

Obj. But you will say; how can this be? Are not *Body*, and *Spirit* contrary? How then can a *Body* be a *Spirit*?

Ans. *Flesh*, and *Spirit* are every where in *Scripture* opposed one to the other: but not so a *Body*, and a *Spirit*.

Those very Terms, on which the Contrariety is set so frequently by the *Holy Ghost* between *Flesh* and *Spirit*, shew that the Heavenly Body, the true Body, the Body of Life, and Glory is a Spirit. I shall instance only in a *Two-*

fold

fold Opposition ; one where the *Flesh*, and the *Spirit* are set as *Life*, and *Death* ; the other, where they are set as the *Truth*, or Beauty itself, and the *Vail* upon it.

1. The *First* is *Rom.* 8. 6. *To be carnally minded is Death* ; *but to be Spiritually-minded is Life*, *and Peace*. In each of these Words *Life*, *Peace*, all Joys of Life and Immortality are expressed by the language of the Spirit. Both together are Joys heaped upon Joys ; Blessedness upon Blessedness, to express the Infiniteness in which they rise up ever New, though there can be never any thing more ; Or the Circle of Eternity, where all Fulnesses of Life, and Joy run one into another, multiplying themselves upon themselves endlesly.

Life is the Flourishing State of Things, a Perpetual Spring. The Happiness of Princes, the Blessedness of the Divine Nature is sum'd up in Life. *Live, O King* ! *The Lord liveth.*

Peace is the whole Gift and Legacy of *Christ* to His Saints. *My Peace I leave with you, My Peace I give unto you.* It is All the Good that goeth along with His Presence and Appearance in His Immortal state. Hee stood in the midst of them saying ; *Peace be with you*, when He appeared to them after His Resurrection. *Peace* is the Plenary Rest of all Parts and Faculties of the whole Person in a perfect Union with, and full Fruition of their proper Objects in Perfection.

The *Greek* Word for *Peace* signifieth the *Band* of all Perfections, the Circle of Eternity ; All things within and without, linked together in the Golden Chain of a Blessed and Divine Harmony, making an Ornament of Beauty for the Soul to put on, making a Musick to charm the Soul into the Divine Sleep of the sweetest, and deepest Complacency. The *Hebrew* Tongue expresseth Both *Perfection* and *Peace* by one Word. This is the Name of him, who was the Eminent Figure of *Christ* in Glory ; *Solomon*. This is the Name of *Jesus* Himself, as He sitteth upon the Throne of the Divine Nature in the Kingdom of the Spirit, *Isa.* 9. 6. *The Prince of Peace* ; Some translate it very properly ; *The Prince* ; *The Peace* or *Perfection*, *Shalom*.

But to apply this to our purpose ; The Image of things, as they stand in the Spirit, is in it self ; the Appearance of things in this Image is, to those who see it, *Life, and Peace* ; that is, Eternity of Blessedness, Heaven it self. But the Image, and Appearance of things in *Flesh* is not onely Dying, or Dead ; It is *Death* it-self. The Life of Nature, and of Flesh, is a Shadow onely of Life, and the Death of the True Life, which is in the Spirit. This universal Image of things, which we call *the World*, comprehending the whole Creation, in all its Beauty, is no more than the *Grave* in which the Spiritual Image lyeth sleeping the sleep of death.

2. The *second Opposition* between *Flesh* and *Spirit*, is that of the *Truth*, and the *Vail* upon the Truth, *Joh.* 4. 24. Our Saviour saith ; The Father seeketh such Worshippers, as *worship Him in Spirit, and Truth*. *Spirit*, and *Truth*, are here joyned in the same sense, as *Spirit*, and *Life* go together, *Joh.* 6. *v.* 63.

The

The words, that I speak, they are Spirit, and they are Life. The *Spirit* is the *Truth*, and the *Life*. The *Flesh* is a *Dead Counterfeit*, as a *Picture* is the Counterfeit of a Man, being neither the Life, nor the Truth, 1 *Joh.* 6. 6. *The Spirit beareth witness. For the Spirit is the Truth.* The *Spirit* is the last, and onely Witness. For the *Spirit* is the Truth itself, the Universal and Eternal Truth. There are *two Maxims* in Philosophy, that All *Truths*, and the *Essences* of things are Eternal. The Truth then, and Essence of a Saint's Body, and of Christ's, the true and essential Body, is a Spirit in the Eternal Spirit. It is not Living, but Life it self.

The *Body of Flesh* is a *Vail* upon this *True Body*, which is an Immortal Spirit. So it is expresly named, *Heb.* 10. *v.* 20. where *Christ* is said to have entred, and made a living way for us into the most Holy Place, *by the rending of the Vail that is, His Flesh.* The true Body is a Spirit and Spring, of Immortality in the most Holy Place, the Eternal Spirit. When it cometh forth from thence into the open streets, and fields of this Creation, it casteth over itself the Vail of this Fleshly Body. In Death it rendeth, and casteth off this Vail of Flesh; so it returneth pure, and naked in the Resurrection into the most Holy Place, into the Eternal Spirit again, where it ever stood after an unchangeable manner in its simple, and unvailed Beauties. So is that Mystery of the Gospel accomplished in the blessed Body of our Saviour: *No one goeth up into Heaven, but he, who came down out of Heaven; the Son of Man, who is in Heaven.*

Qu. But you will ask me now; *What becometh of this Body of Flesh in the Resurrection?*

Ans. What becometh of the *Seed* of a Plant in the Spring, and the Summer? The Plant first contracteth its Parts, and Powers; its Beauties and Sweetnesses under a *Vail*, while it maketh itself a *Seed*. Then again it breaketh this *Seed*, casteth off the *Vail*, discovereth by degrees its entire Form with all its Flowers and Fruits, As before the Plant was hid, and imprisoned in every point of the Seed; so is the Seed now Flourishing, and rejoycing with all its several vertues, and pleasant Forms in every part of the Plant. We read, *Joh.* 1. 14 *The Word was made Flesh.* The true, and Spiritual Body, which is an Immortal Plant in the Heavenly Paradise according to the Almighty Power, and Mysterious Will of the Eternal Word, in which it standeth, and Flourisheth, maketh itself into a Body of Flesh. Again by the same Power in the sweet, and glorious Mystery of the same Will, it maketh this *Flesh* a *Spirit*, If you ask now, where it is; it is Singing and Triumphing throughout all the Divine Powers, throughout all the innumerably various Forms of Eternal Life, Beauty, and Joy in the Heavenly Body, for that which was *Flesh*, is now *Spirit*.

As the *Tabernacle* was removed into the *Temple*, when the Temple was built up, and set there, as a part of the Sacred Mysteries in that Holy Place: so the Spiritual Body, when it is raised, taketh up into itself, and comprehendeth

in

in itself the Vailing Form of Flesh, as a Beautiful Form in that Divine Mystery, which it finisheth in itself.

Qu. But you will say now perhaps; *How is this done, by what Power,* and *in what manner* is the *Body* of our Lord in the Resurrection made a *Quickning Spirit*?

Ans. I answer, that it is done by vertue of the *Personal Union* between the *Divine* and *Humane Nature* in *Christ*. The *Person* is the *Word*, the *Eternal Spirit*. This *Word*, the *Soul*, the *Body* of our beloved *Jesus*, are all *one Person*, so all one Eternal Spirit, the Fountain of Life.

As the Soul is said to be all in the whole Body, and All in every part of it: so is the *Person* in *Christ*, the *Immortal Word* All in the whole Humane Nature, and All in every part of it, either *Soul*, or *Body*. The Union between the Divine Nature in our Bridegroom, and his glorified Body is equally immmediate, and entire, as between that, and his Triumphant Soul.

The Humane Nature subsisteth, and standeth in the Divine, as a Tree in its Root. But this Union in the days of his Flesh is as that between the Tree, and its Root in Winter. The Resurrection is our Saviours Spring-time, and Summer. Every living Root in Spring ceaseth not to send forth its Sap into the Tree, until it have brought forth the Tree into that Form, and laden it with those Fruits, which are proper to the Root. In the Resurrection the Divine Nature riseth up with all its Sweetness, and Fatness, all its Vertues and Powers into the Humane Nature, till it have spread, and fashioned it entirely into its own Form; till it have laden it all over with the precious Fruits of its own excellencies, Joys, and Glories. In every power, part, and point of Soul, and Body, though never so mean, so small, the Fountain of the God-Head openeth itself; the Fulness of the God-Head poureth forth itself, that as the Waters cover the Sea, so every distinct Part, or Point appeareth, as a distinct Sea of the Divine Life, Joys, Loves, and Glories without bottom, or bound.

This, O shadowy Man, O faln, lost Man, is *thy Jesus, thy Life, thy Saviour*! Look to this *Jesus* with an Eye of *Faith* with an Eye of Love, live *by Him*, live *in Him*, live *to Him*. Triumph thou because of this *Jesus*.

Look to Him as, 1. Thy *Principle*. 2. Thy *Pattern*. 3. Thy *Price*. 4. Thy *Portion*.

1. Look to this *Jesus*, who is All-Beautiful with the Beauty of the God-Head itself, as thy *Principle*. *I am the vine, ye are the branches. He, that abideth in me, and I in him, bringeth forth much fruit. Without me ye can do nothing*, saith *Jesus Christ, Joh.* 15.5. The Tree first comprehendeth the Branch in itself, then sendeth it forth, supplying it continually with its own Life and Sap. By the vertue of this Life & Sap the Branch taketh hold of the Tree, sucketh in continually fresh and vital nourishment, by which it flourisheth, and bringeth forth much fruit. What shall I say for thee, who yet partakest not of the sweetness, and fatness of this Spiritual Tree of Life, and love? Thou canst bring forth no

Fruit,

Fruit, thou canst do nothing towards thine own fruitfulness. Without this *Jesus* thou canst do nothing.O that thou didst understand thine own Emptiness, and the Fulness of Sap in this Vine:How truly All things Angels, Men All the Creatures can do nothing, are nothing without this *Jesus,that Spirit*,which is the onely Truth,the onely Lfe in,and thorow All! I will pray over thee with inward bleedings of Divine Love from my heart; O that *Jesus* thy Root, who comprehendeth even thee also in the Fulness of His Heavenly sap,and vertue, would bring thee forth by a new birth,as a Heavenly branch in Himself! O that He would continually milk forth from His Breast the streams of His Life into thee! Thus He abideth in thee.Now do thou, now wilt thou by Him abiding in thee abide inHim.Shoot forth thy self into Him,as roots do theirSprigs, and Branches into the Earth beneath, by the actings of thy Faith upon him. Draw his Spirit, and Grace into thy self. Be green, be fair, and flourishing in the Eye of Heaven. Bring forth much Fruit for thy self; thy Saviour, thy Heavenly Father, all Angels,and blessed Spirits to feed upon in Eternity.

2. Look to this *Jesus*, as thy *Pattern*. What thou hast seen done in his Soul, and Body, by the Union between these and the God-Head; the same Glory shall be brought forth in thy Soul, and Body also by the Union between him, and thee; if thou in thy Soul, and Body adhere, and stick to his glorified Soul, and Body, as they are full of the Eternal Word dwelling in them, and resting upon them. The Angels reproved the Disciples, when *Christ* was taken up into Glory, because they looked to a visible Heaven to see their glorified Lord still with Eyes of Flesh: *Why stand you here gazing up into Heaven? This same Jesus, who is taken up from you into Heaven,shall so come in like manner, as ye have seen him go into Heaven.* I say to you in another sense: stand, and look upon your *Jesus*, as he ascends.This is your *Pattern*. As you have seen him in his Humane Nature go up out of all Fleshly, and Visible Images into an *Invisible Glory*; as you have seen him taken out of the sight of every created Eye in the white Cloud of the most excellent Majesty of the *Father*, which is the Heaven of Heavens, so shall the same *Jesus* in like manner come again in your Souls,and Bodies, descending into them uponthose Spiritual Heavens, and changing them by degrees from Glory to Glory, till they also put off every thing of Flesh,and disappearing to every natural Eye, be made perfect in the same Spirit, to be for ever together with him there,where he is,and like him.

3. Look to *Jesus*, as thy *Price*.The Lord taketh notice of the low thoughts, and disesteem, which the *Jews* had of him by that, which they gave for him thirty pieces of Silver: *This*, saith he by the Prophet, *is the Price, at which they valued me*. Thou that seemest to thy self the least, and poorest in all the flock of *Christ*, see the great, the unimaginable thoughts of esteem, and love in the heart of God for thee; O man see the honour, and affection, which thy God hath for thy Soul, how precious it is in his Eye.This is the price, at which

which the Father valueth thee, this *Jesus* his onely Son, full of God, and of Glory, enriched all over in his whole Person, with all the Treasures of the God-Head laid out upon every part of him. Learn O man, to believe; Learn O believer, to value thy self by this *Price*, at which the Father hath valued thee, this *Jesus*. O Sinner, expect as much Love, and Mercy, as much Grace, Comfort, and Glory to raise thee above the lowest depths of Sin in the Guilt, Filth, and Power of it; in the sting, shame, sufferings, and wrath, which go along with it; as this *Price* can purchase, this all-glorious *Jesus* is worthy of, with the Fulness of his God-Head multiplied innumerable times over, in his Divine Nature, in all parts of his humane Soul, and Body. O Saints, let your Faith, and Hope stop no where, until you find that brought forth in you, which may answer so inestimable a *price*, until you find your self raised to that pitch of Beauty, Blessedness, Glory, and Spirituality, which may be worthy of this *Jesus*.

4. Look upon this *Jesus*, as your *Portion*. Thou, who canst say, as *David* doth, *Psal.* 16. 5. *The Lord Jesus is the Portion of my Heritage*; mayst add, as he doth. *v.* 7. *The lines are fallen unto me in a pleasant place*; *I have a goodly heritage*. This is a *Fountain sealed*, and a *Garden inclosed*, a Fountain sealed, a Garden inclosed from every natural Spirit; but inclosed with walls of Fire, the Fire of Eternal Love, and Glory for thee; sealed with thine Image, and the Inscription of thy name upon it, who believest. Walk in this Garden, delight thy self with the pleasant beauties, sweet smells, divine vertues, precious Fruits of the God-Head there. Go down into this Fountain; bath thy self in the depths of it, lie there overflown with its living waters, till thou be changed into the same waters, and become one Fountain, one Spirit with thy *Jesus*, till thy Soul be made like his glorious Soul, thy Body be made like to his glorious Body; till the Fountain of the God-Head be opened, and the Fulness of the God-Head poured forth in every part of These, as of Them by their mutual Union, and Marriage in one Quickning Spirit.

Propos. 3. I drew the Platform of a Building for the countenancing of my *Second Rule* in *Direction* to the knowledge of the *Person*, and *Beauties* of our glorified Saviour. I laid the ground of my Building in the latter part of that, 1 *Cor.* 15. I cast this Building into *three Stories* comprised in *three Propositions*. I have finished *two* of them according to my model.

The *Second Rule* for the sake of which I designed this Frame, and Fabrick was, that *Spiritual Things are to be compared with Spiritual*. The two *Propositions*, which were as the two Stories in the Building were these. 1. *The Body of our Jesus in Heaven is not to be compared with his Body on Earth, either living, or dying.* 2. *There is no Comparison between the glorified Body of our Beloved in Heaven, and the first, the fairest Body of* Adam *in Paradise.*

I am now to add the *Third Story*, so to lay the Top-stone, and to compleat my Building.

Prop. 3. *The Third Proposition* is this: *The Spiritual Body of our Blessed Saviour is to be compared with its own Spiritual Principle, and Pattern*, The Materials, Form, and Furniture for this Piece of the Building are taken out of that *Scripture*, 1. *Cor.* 15. 47. *The first man is of the Earth, Earthy: the second man the Lord from heaven.* See here Two distinct principles, and Patterns of two several Men, differing not onely, as distinct Individuals of the same Kind; but in their whole Essence, and Nature, as Heaven, and Earth; the Shadow, and the Substance; the Life, and the Picture.

The *Principle* of the *First Man* is *Earth*: the *Principle* of the *Second Man* is *Heaven*. From these *two Principles* these two Men take their whole *Nature Name*, and *Image*. They take their *Nature* entirely from their *Principles*. *The first man is of the Earth, Earthy: the second Man is the Lord from Heaven. v.* 47. As the Mettals take their Essence, and Substantial Form from the Mine, in which they are bred, and out of which they are drawn: so the *first Adam*, from the Mine of Earth below is Earth in his Substance, and Essence. The *second Man Jesus* risen from the Dead is pure Heaven quite thorow in the Fundamentals, and Essential Parts of His Immortal Substance, as well, as in the Ornaments, and Beautifyings of it. For He cometh forth from a Mine of finest Gold. Hee is the *Lord*, of a *Nature* in it self above All, and over All, *from Heaven*.

These *two Men* take their *Name* also from their *Principle*. *As is the Earthy, such are they that are Earthy: as is the Heavenly, such are they that are Heavenly*: *v.* 48. Behold the Earthy, and the *Heavenly*.

They take their *Image* too from their *Principle*. *As we have born the Image of the Earthy: we shall also bear the Image of the Heavenly.* The *Heavenly One* beareth the Image of His proper Heaven, out of which He cometh, and so bringeth Heaven down in Himself, The *Earthy One* is cloathed with the Image of the Earth, out of which He is taken. Thus the *Principle* is the *Pattern* also. Each Man is All that, which He is, for Matter, and Form; Substance, and Image; Stuff, and Trimming; Metal, and Fashion from his own *Principle*. The *Principle* is both the Mine, and Mint. Each Man of these Two comprehendeth His Principle in Himself; the One, the Earth; the Other, Heaven in His Heart, and Face; in His Root, Substance, and Sap, as also in His Form, Flower, and Fruit.

I Know no piece of Knowledge in the whole Gospel, of more consequence, upon which more of Divine Light; more of Divine Life, and Strength: more of Divine Sweetness, Comfort, and Joy dependeth, than a right Understanding of the Difference between these *Two*, the *Earthy*, and the *Heavenly* One. This is the Golden Key, which openeth not the little Wicket, but the great Gate into the Kingdom of God; the Several Natures of *Adam*, and *Christ in His Humanity*; the *Son* by *Creation*, and the *Son* by *Adoption*; *Man in Paradise*, *a Saint in the Spirit and in Heaven.*

These

These are to be Known by their *Principles* onely. For their *Principles* are their Patterns.

Their Principles are *Earth* and *Heaven*. These will be best Known by their Answering, and Opposition one to another. All, that is, is divided into Heaven, and Earth.

1. The *Earth*, which is the Principle of the *First man* is to be sought out and discovered, that we may upon that Foot-stool ascend to the Throne; that we may come more distinctly, and clearly by Degrees to a Sight of that Heaven, which is the Principle of the Lord *Jesus* in Glory.

This lyeth clear before us, that the *Heaven* understood in this place cannot be any Visible, or Common Heaven, no, not any of the Created Heavens. This is an Heaven above All. For He, who cometh forth from it, is Lord of All. He is *made Higher than All Heavens*, by ascending into this *Heaven*, which is of another Make different from all things of the First Creation; and hath a New Name above every Name, that is named in this World, or that which is to come; the World of Sense, or the World of Angels: *Heb.* 7. 26. *Eph.* 4. *v.* 10.

The *Earth* then of which we speak cannot be the Common Earth. It must be as large, as that mentioned, *Gen.* 1. *v.* 2. out of which the Heavens themselves were made. The *Earth* intended here by the *Holy Ghost* taketh in all things below the *Heaven* mentioned, and meant by Him. Angels with all the Invisible Glories of the First Creation are Gods arising up out of this *Earth*, and comprehended within the Compass of it.

I will set up *Three Lights* before you, by which I shall endeavour to give you a Prospect of this *Earth*, and of the *First Man* arising out of it, so, as to be a Shadow, and a Figure of the *Heaven* we aim at, with our Bridegroom coming down out of it, coming down in it, as His Mother of Eternal Love; His Garment, and Crown of Divine Beauty; His Chariot of Life, and Light; of Power, and Pleasure.

1. *Light*: God, as He is the Head of the First Creation, cometh not forth Naked, but in a Shadowy Image of Himself, which He casteth, as a Vail, over the true and proper Beauties of His own Person, which the Eye of no Creature ever saw, or can see, *Psal.* 104. The *Psalmist* singeth the praises, and wonders of God in the Creation. After the preface he beginneth thus: *Who coverest thy self with Light, as with a Garment, and stretchest out the Heavens, as a Curtain*; *v.* 2. You have a manifest allusion here to the Works of the First, and Second Day; *Gen.* 1. The *Jews* say from this *Scripture* in the books of their wise, and learned men, that God to make this World, appeared not in His naked Beauties, but *cum Indumentis suis*, with a Garment for a Covering upon Him. The Light, in which God shineth forth at the Beginning to form a Mass of Darknes into a beautiful Creation, was onely a Shadow of the Eternal Light of His own Nature, and Substance, and a Vail upon it. The Glory

itſelf, the Divine Preſence, and Appearance at the Head of this Creation, which was ſpread over the whole Compaſs of it, as an Heaven, was a Curtain drawn before the true Heaven, the true Glory, which ſtood behind this Curtain; like the Oracle, in the moſt Holy place, while the Firſt Tabernacle was not yet removed This is the *Firſt Light*.

2. *Light*: God in this Shadowy Image of himſelf is *that Earth*, the Divine Earth, out of which the firſt Man is made with a Divinity reſting upon him. *Gen.* 1. 26. *God ſaid*; *let us make man in our Image, after our Likeneſs*. The word *Image*, in Hebrew *Tſelem*, ſeemeth to be a contract of two words, *Tſel Maveth*, the *Shadow of Death*. It is uſed, *Pſal.* 39. 6. *Man walketh in a vain ſhow*; *they are diſquieted in vain, or in vanity*.

That other word uſed, *Gen*, 1. 26. *Our Likeneſs*, ſignifieth *ſimilitude*, *ſilence*, an *imagination*, a *cutting off*. Both import thus much, that the Divine Image, the Mother of the *firſt Adam*, in whoſe Womb he was formed, out of whoſe Womb he ſprung forth, upon whoſe breaſts he hung, was a ſhadow, a ſilent vaniſhing Shadow of the Eternal word, in which that ſlept, as in its Night, or Death. As Dreams are Imaginations in the Fancy, which act their parts while the Man ſleepeth: ſuch was this Image, after which Man with the whole World was made. This was the Mother-Earth, which brought him forth, which beareth him, which nurſeth him in her Boſom, and dandleth him on her Knees.

We read; *Gen.* 2. 7. God formed Man of the duſt of the ground. The word *Ground* is the ſame with *Adam*. It ſignifieth in its root a ſparkling Luſtre, and Ruddineſs, like that of the beſt Rubies, to expreſs which it is alſo uſed. A ſweet and glorious Light ſhining thorow a dark ſhade, like a roſie morning; or the Sun ſetting red in a lovely evening, becauſe being low he ſhineth with his bright Beams thorow the riſing miſts, and vapours of the Earth; is properly intended by this word. The Light of the God-Head ſparkling in a Shadow of himſelf, glowing under a Cloud, like a living Ruby from the Rock of Eternity; this was *Adamah*, the *Ground*, the Mother of *Adam*.

God formed *Adam* of the duſt of this ground. The learned Jews paraphraſe after this manner upon the *duſt* here. As the skilful Apothecary beateth his Spices to a ſmall, and fine powder, that by a more curious, and exact mixture of them he may make them into a rich ointment, or cordial: ſo God in the ſmalleſt, and leaſt parts perfectly mingleth, and uniteth all the Principles, Powers, Forms, and Vertues of the ſeveral Creatures, as they lay together in their firſt, and faireſt Image, in their Firſt-born ſtate in himſelf. Of theſe thus tempered he formeth *Man*, the *Second Image* of the whole Creation next to that in his own Perſon. Thus Man is as a living Cryſtal, in which the entire Form of all the world viſible, and inviſible is ſeen tranſparently in the whole Glaſs, and in every point of the Glaſs, by a raviſhing concurrence of all parts in each, the minuteſt part, with a moſt beautiful, and divine Har-

Harmony arising from the accurate Mixture of that Precious Dust. Thus Man is an Universal musick, where the well-measured Motions, and sweet Sounds of all the Strings meet in every skilful Touch of every String; as a New Circle of Heavenly Melody, and Delights spread from a New Center of Life, and Love. Thus I pass from the Second to the *Third Light*.

3. *Light*: The *First Adam* was the Golden Head of the First Creation next to God in *Jesus Christ*. *St. John* in the 1. *chapter* of his Gospel describeth the order, and manner, in which the Unfaln World came forth from God. The *Word*, which was *Jesus Christ*, as He is God, the Essential, and Eternal Image of the God-Head, was made by His own Almighty Power, according to the Unsearchable Counsel of His own All-Gracious, and All-Glorious Will, a Shadowy Image of Himself. As upon the Vail of the most Holy Place were wrought in pleasant Colours the Figures of those *Cherubims*, which stood within the Vail shining in a rich Substance of Massy Gold: So was it in the most Holy *Person* of our Saviour, the true, and living Temple of the Divine Nature, The Glories of the Essential Image figured themselves upon this Mystical Vail of the Shadowy Image. So the Beloved *Apostle* saith to us, while he openeth the Mysteries, and Births of the Divine Love; *v.* 2. *All things were made by Him*; by his Lord, and his Love; our Lord, and our Love, our *Jesus*. As He was the Essential Image, and the Pattern upon the Mount of Eternity, All things were made *by Him*; They were Copies taken of Him, Shadows cast from Him by the Abundance of an Overflowing Life, and vertue in Him. *Without Him was nothing made*, *v.* 2. That expression *Without Him*; properly signfieth, apart in *separation*, or *disunion* from Him; in a Self-Subsistency. All the Creatures in their Flower, in their Virgin-purities, and perfections stood, and flourished together with their united Beauties, and Sweetnesses in the *Person* of our Bridegroom, as He made Himself a Shadowy Image. After this manner, was our *Jesus The Beginning of the Creation of God*; and *the First-born of every Creature*.

St John addeth; *v.* 3. *In Him was Life*. Some Interpreters joyn the latter end of the *second verse* with the beginning of the *third*, and read; *That which was made, was Life in Him*. The sense is the same. All the Creatures in the *Person of Christ* did flourish, and shine together in the unstain'd Lustre, and Harmony of One Divine Beauty. They did rejoyce, and sing together in the Fellowship of One Divine Life, and Love. Here they see the Beauties, they smell the sweetnesses, they tast the pleasant vertues, they feast upon the precious Substances, they drink in the pure Lives, and Spirits of each other continually.

This Life was the Light of Man, *v.* 3. From this Life-Image of the Creation in *Christ* propagating itself Immediately, and entirely, springeth forth the Essence, and Form of Man. Man is now a Light of Glory shining freshly, and fully from the First Created Light, which subsisted in the Person of the Eternal

nal

nal Word. In this Light of Glory stood Paradise with all the Creatures in their Primitive, Pure, and First-born State, next to their First-born State in our Lord *Jesus*. From the Fountain arising here, and going forth from this *Eden* all the Creatures sprung up fresh, and new every moment, in their several Beings, and Beauties, as they grew upon their proper, and distinct roots.

By this you may understand the sense, in which *Adam* is said to be set in the Garden *to dress it, and to keep it*; Gen. 2. *To dress it*, signifieth *to serve it*, or *minister to it*. The Lord *Jesus* by his Resurrection from the dead is set in the Heavenly Paradise to dress, and keep that. So he saith of himself: *I go to prepare a place for you*; *John* 14. The Paradise above is set in the glorified Person of the Lord *Jesus*. From the Father the Fountain of the God-Head opening himself in his Bosom, he riseth up with an Eternal Form of Divine Glory into every particular Saint, as into a Spiritual Plant of the Heavenly Paradise, which comprehendeth all Paradise with its Root, Body, and Branches in itself. *Jesus Christ* is the *Tree of Life* in the midst, the Center of the Eternal Paradise, on which all the Fruits of this Garden grow. Each Fruit, each Plant in like manner is a Tree of Life compleat in itself bearing all the other Love-Plants, as its own proper Branches, and Fruits. Thus this Paradise in the third Heavens standeth *in* the *Person of Christ*, and standeth *out of the Person of Christ*.

After the same similitude the Paradise below standeth first, standeth entire in the Angelical Person of the first *Adam*. The Lord *Jesus* in his Shadowy Image riseth up first here, here first he formeth the fairest, and fullest figure of himself. Every Angel, every Star, every Flower hath here its first, its freshest Life, Beauty, and Sweetness. All fall in, and stand here, as parts of the Musick in the full Harmony. As all the parts of Musick flow forth from the Universal Harmony, and are measured by it: so doth the *first Man* from the Fountain rising up into the universal Form of the whole Creation in himself, go forth every moment freshly, and newly into the temporary Forms of each particular Creature, each Angel, each Star, each Flower, ministring to them the number of their parts, the measure of their proportions, the weight of their vertues. I have been the larger in this place, that we may enjoy the sweetness of the Light of that Scripture more fully by seeing it more clearly, *Rom.* 5. 14. *The first Man was a Figure of him, who is to come.*

This is the *Earth*, of which we speak, God in a *Shadowy Image*; the *Moon* which *Pythagoras* called, an Heavenly Earth; or an Earthly Heaven. Thus is the *first man* of this Earth, Earthy.

I believe you run before me in your thoughts, and by this time have some prospect into that *Heaven*, from which the *second Man*, the Lord of Glory cometh. I am now to proceed to this, which is our Rest, and the end of our [illegible]

[illegible] not be unprofitable, nor unpleasant to stay here a while, and re[illegible] beautiful Earth, this blessed Man rising up out of it.

It

It will afford us *two Lessons* of much use, and comfort.

1. *Lesson.* Fear, tremble, be confounded at the sight of Sin, and fly from it with all your might. O Man! What a glorious Angel wast thou? How wert thou in the similitude of God? the Crown of the whole Creation? Every precious stone was there. How is this goodly Creature faln? Thou art become by Sin a Worm, and no Man; a Serpent creeping upon thy belly, and feeding upon the dust of the Earth. All the Creatures grew, and flourished together, as a Nose-gay in thy Bosom, being in their Paradise there, and living upon their Root. How art thou made a filthy, noisom sink, in which all the Creatures lie covered with dirt, withered, and dead? O the Curse, that goeth along with every Sin!

I have heard of an Holy Divine, strong in Faith, who, haunted by an Apparition of the Devil in the form of an Hog, thus reproached him: *Fie Satan once a beautiful, and blessed Angel, dost thou now appear in the shape of a vile, filthy Hog?* The Devil was so stung with this reproof, that he went presently away out of countenance, and vanished out of that good Mans sight. When we are tempted to any Sin of Lust, Covetousness, or Wrath, let us in like manner say to our selves: *Fie my Soul, once in the Likeness of God, once a Quire of Angels, a Paradise in thine own Person; wilt thou now make thy self a Hog, a Dog, a Toad.*

2. *Lesson.* Set a high value upon *Jesus Christ*; set your hearts upon him; believe in him; love him; run into his arms; cleave to him. That Paradise, that Purity, that Innocency, that light of Life, and Beauty, which you have lost, are found again in his bosom changed from the Shadow to the Substance. He, that was the Figure in the *first Adam*, and vanished out of your sight, leaving you alone, naked, and desolate; the same is come again to you in the *second Adam*, in the Truth, and life, to abide for ever with you. *Augustus Caesar* gloried, that he found the Buildings of *Rome* Bricks, but left them Marble. Our Paradise was at first Earthly, and fading. Our *Jesus* hath prepared for us in himself an Heavenly, unfading, eternal Paradise. When *Caesar* found *Cato* his Enemy slain by his own hand, that he might not come into the power of the Conqueror; *Caesar* spake these words over the dead body: *I envy thee* Cato *the glory of thy Death; seeing thou didst envy me the glory of thy Life.* Poor man! faln from thy first Beauty, and Blessedness; lost in Death, and Wrath; come to *Jesus Christ*; do not thorow unbelief deny to him the glory of restoring thy Beauty, and Blessedness to thee better, than at the first, by restoring thee to the naked Bosom of Eternal Love, and the Substantial Joys of eternal Life.

But now it is time to pass on to our *second Discovery*, unto which all this hath been a preparation only. We have seen the flourishing Earth of the *first Man*, which is only as a sight in a Cross-bow, or Gun to direct our Eye to the mark, which is the *Heaven* answering to this *Earth*. Blessed shall our Eyes be, if they see this Heaven opening itself, and the Lord coming down out of it, with all its glories under his Feet, and round about him.

2. *Hea-*

2. *Heaven*: God in the brightness of his own Substance, uncloathed of every garment, appearing in the naked Beauties, and Loves of his *Divine Nature*, and *Person*; this is the *Heaven* into which the Body of our Saviour ascendeth, out of which it cometh, as a Bride from the bosom of her Bridegroom as the *Heavenly Eve* from the side of her *Heavenly Adam*; Beauty of his Beauty, Love of his Love; joyned to him inseparably in one Spirit, and one eternal Glory.

This is the *Heaven* over the head of the shadowy Image, the essential, and eternal Image of the Father. This is the Resurrection of our *Jesus* from the Dead; this is the sweet, and sacred Mystery of our Saviours death; the opening of the shadow, as a Grave, in which the true Glory slept, that this might come forth, and as it riseth, overspread the shadow; as it overspreadeth it, gather it up into itself, which is the swallowing up of Death into the Victory and Triumph of Eternal Life; the darkness of the shadow into the everblessed light of the beloved substance.

Our Love is never awakened, or stirred up till himself please. When the Beautiful, and Acceptable time is come, the true Glory, which lieth buried in the shadow awakeneth, by a mysterious touch upon the shadow rendeth it, as a *Vail*; then it looketh forth, and springeth like the morning, like the fair Moon, like the pure Sun, the Figure, and the Life, all shining together with one Glory in the calm, and clear day of Eternity.

I shall endeavour to explain, and confirm this to you by *one Scripture*; John 17. 5. *Father glorify me with thy self, with that Glory, which I had with thee before the world was.* Our dying Saviour prayeth for his humane Nature, and for his divine Nature, only as it was united to, and sympathised with his Manhood. The God-Head in its own single state, and simplicity is ever above all passion, and so all prayer. *Jesus Christ* prayeth to be glorified *with the Father* in that Soul, and Body, in which he was presently to be crucified with Thieves; that *in these* he may be there, where the Father is, that is, *in the high, and holy place of Eternity*; to this end that *in these* he may partake of the glory of the Father there, in Eternity. *Eternity* is defined to be: *The possession of all good together, and at once*; without any bound terminating it before, or after, or in any kind. This is the *high place of Eternity*, above all Time, Change, Succession, or Division. For this reason is our Lord said to be *Higher than the Heavens.* All Created Heavens are below Eternity. They have Measures, and Limits set to the Forms of their Beings, and to their Durations, which they cannot pass. They are continually rouling thorow successive Changes. As the Sea lyeth all in Waves: so do the Essences of the most great, and glorious Creatures consist of manifold, and various Changes. *Jesus* alone in His Manhood is ascended to the Height of Eternity above all Changes; and in this Height of Glory He cometh the *second* time into the World, when it is said to him; *Thou changest the Heavens, as a Garment, and they are changed. But thy throne, O God endureth for ever and ever, Heb.* 1. 8.12.

So

So the Lord *Jesus* expoundeth Himself in that prayer of His ; *Father, glorifie me with thy self, with that Glory, which I had with thee before the World was.* The Glory, which *Christ* prayeth for in behalf of His *Humanity*, is a Glory above the Creation. For it was before the Creation. The Glory of Christ's Humane Nature in the Resurrection from the Dead, is a Glory in Fellowship with the Father, with Him, who was from the Beginning, an Eternal Glory, a Glory, which is, when yet the World is not ; a Glory, which is the same, while the World standeth, before which the World is not ; a Glory, which is, when the World is no more. Eternity hath neither Beginning nor End ; neither Succession, nor Change.

We may now understand, how *Jesus Christ* was with the Father, before the World was. 1. His *Divinity* was there. For in that He and the Father are One. 2. His *Humanity* was with the *Father* before the World *Personally*, in its *proper Person*. For the Divinity is the *Person* in the Humanity. 3. The *Soul*, and *Body* of Christ were there in their *Root*, in their Original, in the Will of the Father, which is Eternal Love in its unconfined Absoluteness ; in the Wisdom of the Father, which is Eternal Beauty in its unlimited Greatness, and Universal Comprehension. They were also with the *Father* before the World in their glorified State. For their Glory, which is *Themselves* in Truth, and Perfection, is Eternal, was before the World was.

Thus our Saviour in His Glorified Humanity is that *Melchisedech*, mentioned in the Hebrews, *c.* 7. *v.* 3. *without Beginning of Life, or End of Dayes* ; whose name is always ; *I am*, *Joh.* 8. 58. which met *Abraham* with Bread, and Wine, when he came from the slaughter of the four Kings.

Blessed art thou, when thy *Jesus* thus appeareth to thee in the Form, and Glory of *Melchisedech*, when He is known to thee by this His new and His old Name of *Melchisedech*, the King, and Priest of the most high God, which, *liveth for ever*, liveth in Eternity above all Times past, present, or to come. Thou who thus seest, and embracest Him, to thee He cometh with the Bread not of Angels, but of God ; with the new Marriage-Wine of the Kingdom of God, Upon these the Father, your Beloved, and you sup, and Feast together while every One in Him, is both the Guest, and the Feast.

Blessed is he, who in like manner thorowout the whole Mystical Body of our Saviour seeth that high, and sweet piece of Divinity to be true, which droppeth from the Lips of *Christ* like Myrrhe from Lillies ; *Joh, c.* 3. *v.* 15. *No one ascendeth into Heaven, but He, who cometh down out of Heaven ; the Son of Man, who is in Heaven.* Mark, how the Lord to prevent all Objections fixeth that Title, *the Son of Man*, upon that, which hath its constant abode in Heaven all along the several degrees of its *descent*, and *Ascent*. *Jesus Christ* encompasseth, and circleth in His Human Nature Descending, walking sadly on the Earth, hanging on the Cross, lying in the Grave with the Glory of the same Humane Nature Eternal in the Heavens.

I will now finish my Building, and lay the Top-stone by giving you *three Representations* of the *Person* of your Beloved with its Beauty in the Resurrection; as his Spiritual Soul, and Spiritual Body stand in the same Glory with their Spiritual Principle, and Pattern; as they are two distinct Heavens exactly answering that Heaven, from which they come, it being both their *Mine*, and their *Mint*. So I shall conclude this *use*.

1. *Repres.* All my representations shall be grounded on clear Scriptures. *Can.* 8. 6. The Spouse prayeth to *Christ*: *Set me, as a Seal upon thine Heart, as a Seal upon thine Arm.* The prayers of the Heavenly Bride are made by the Spirit according to the will of God, and so are always answered. The Divine, and Humane Nature are Bridegroom and Bride married together in one Person. As the Impression of a Seal in Wax hath all its Substance, and Subsistence in the Wax, is nothing, but what the Wax is in that Form; so the glorified Soul, and Body of our Blessed Lord stand, as Seals, as Impressions in that glorious depth of Love, of Light, of Life, of all Being, which is the Root, and *Heart* of the God-Head; they stand, as Sealed Impressions on the *Arm* of God; that is, on every Excellency, every Beauty, every form of Glory, in which the God-Head with endless variety, with incomprehensible, Sweetness and Majesty spreadeth forth itself. This is all that, which they are; the unfathomable Love, and Innumerable Beauties of the Divine Nature in the Forms of a Divine Soul, and a Divine Body.

2. *Repres. Job c.* 38. 14. speaking of the *New Heaven, and Earth* telleth us, that they are turned to the Eternal word, *as Clay to the Seal.* The Manhood of *Christ* in Glory hath the first Model of these in itself. As a Golden Seal maketh the Impression of itself on Wax, and then fixeth itself unto a constant abode in the Impression, which it hath made: so the Eternal Word imprinteth by itself immediately upon its own Soul and Body, a clear, deep, and full Image of itself in all the Treasures of its Immortal Life, and Blessedness; uniting itself in its *Divine Substance* to this *Divine Image* most intimately, most intirely, inseparably. After this manner the Glory, with which the Humane Nature of *Christ* is glorified, is the Form, and fulness of the Divine Nature, in its Purity, unmixt with any other Substance, or Image, in its Perfection, possessing, comprehending, enjoying itself in each distinct part here, distinctly, and compleatly.

The God-Head by its unvailed Presence, and full Appearance, at once fashioneth the Manhood of our *Jesus* in every part, and point into its own *Supream Form*; and filleth that *Form* throughout with its own most glorious *Fulness.*

3. *Repres. St. Paul* telleth the Saints, that their *Souls, and Bodies are Temples of the Holy Ghost.* 1 *Corin.* 6. 19. If it be so in the Members, it is so without question in the Head. *Jesus* himself calleth his Body a *Temple*; *Destroy this Temple, and in three days I will build it up again. This he spake of his Body.*

The Divine Nature, the Glorified Soul, the Spiritual Body of our Heaven-

ly

ly Bridegroom are three wonderful Temples. The matter of which these Temples are made is all Spirit of the Eternal Spirit; the Light of Eternal Life in the Spirit. The fashion of these Buildings is the form of God. All the Beauties, and varieties of the Essential Wisdom, all the ravishing delights of the first, the highest, and most universal Harmony in the God-Head, shine in every part of these living structures. Within is seen the high, and Holy Trinity with all its deep, dazling, and delightful Mysteries unvailed; all the Persons appearing in the Lights of their naked, and united Beauties. In the pure, and transparent brightness of this Supream Glory, which is the *first*, and the *last*, are seen all things, that ever passed, or are to pass over the Stage of this Creation from the Beginning to the End with their several Motions, and Changes; yea, Forms far more innumerable, and greater, than ever were, or can be seen in this world; the whole compass of Eternity, and Time, as it cometh down out of Eternity, as it beareth the Figure of it, as it returneth again; as it lieth in the bosom of Eternity, as it is one piece with it, and maketh a Triumphant part of the Divine variety there. All these are seen in the amiable, and admirable Face of the Trinity within these Temples; as they are continually rising up out of their Fountain, the Unity of the first, and most transcendent Love, the Father of all; as they are continually falling down into this Fountain again; as they are ever playing upon the bosom of it. All things are seen here, as rich varieties in the Harmony of an entire, and Immortal Beauty, which comprehendeth all Forms, and hath no bound besides itself, which sitteth entire, and undivided upon every Form, and Part throughout the whole, which is the only Birth and Image of the Father. All things are seen here, as they make up one unexpressible Marriage-Joy between this Love, the Father, the Original, and this Beauty, the Birth, the Son, the Image by which they both breath forth themselves into one Spirit, the Band, and Union, the Inmost Center, and outmost Circle of all Sweetnesses, Graces, Amiablenesses, Pleasantnesses, Pleasures, Rests, Complacencies, Delights and Joys thorow Heaven, Earth, Time, Eternity.

In these three Temples these Things are to be observed, that we may understand their Divine Nature, and wonderful make aright.

1. All three are perfectly distinct in the highest degree of distinction each from other.

2. All three perfectly answer, and are alike to one another.

3. Every one comprehendeth the other Two exactly, and entirely in itself; that all Three stand together in each several Temple.

4. All three Temples joyn perfectly into one Temple.

5. The first Temple is the precious, and living Stone, out of which the other two grow up into living Temples. It is the Root, the Life, the Substance, the Form, the Fulness, the perfection, the glory of the other Two.

I must interpose here *two Cautions* to prevent mistakes.

1. *Caut.* Preserve carefully the *distinction* between Spiritual Things, both in the *Person* of our Saviour, and in *his Mystical Body*. The *Spirit* taketh away all Separations, and Divisions *from* God. All breaches upon the Unity of God are wounds with which Sin pierceth the Prince of Life. The *Spirit* healeth these breaches. But it preserveth entire all distinctions of things *in* God, in the *Divine Unity*. The *God-Head*, the *Manhood*, the *Soul*, the *Body*; the *Persons* of the *Saints*; and of their *Saviour* ever keep their proper parts in the *variety* to make the Musick of Heaven pleasant. As *Spirituality* heightneth the *Unity* beyond every Created comprehension, that the Sweetness, and the Glory may be heightned in like manner: so doth it enlarge the *variety* beyond all finite proportions, that the Marriage-Joy may be more free, more fresh, more full:

2. *Caut.* Preserve carefully the *distinction* between *God*, and the *Creature*, God is that, which he is *in* himself, and *of* himself. The Creature is that, which it is by its Union with God. This is the Incommunicable Name of God; *I am that, which I am.* The name of every Creature on Earth, and in Heaven is: *I am that, which I am in God*; *I am that, which God is in me.*

I have now made an end of my *third Proposition*, which was this, that *the Spiritual Body of Christ is to be compared with its Spiritual Principle, and Pattern.* *Jesus* speaketh to this sense in one place. *If they had known the Father, they would have known me; if they had known me, they would have known you also.* The Person of the Bridegroom is known aright only by its Pattern, and in its Principle, which is the *Father*; as he is the brightness of the Fathers Glory, the express Image of his Substance, and sporteth eternally in his Bosom. The Person of a Saint is then only seen aright, when it is seen by its Pattern, and in its Principle, which is the Heavenly Bridegroom; as it is the brightness. and fulness of him, who shineth thorow, and filleth All in All; the Glory of *Christ*, in *Christ*, like the purest Light rejoycing continually in the Bosom of the Sun.

I am now arrived at the end of my second Rule; to *compare Spiritual Things with Spiritual.* And thus I have concluded my present *use*, which is a *direction* to the knowledge of the Person of *Christ*, and his Beauty.

Use 3. *An exhortation* to Holiness, and Comfort thorow Faith in *Jesus Christ.* This exhortation is raised upon these *three Grounds*,

1. *Ground: The Person of our Lord is unchangeable.* For he is in his true Person, when the Vail is taken off from him, an Eternal Spirit in an Eternal Glory. *John* 8. 58. He saith of himself; *Before Abraham was, I am. I am*, is the name of Eternity, and unchangeableness. See how the Lord *Jesus* comprehendeth all the Successions, and Distances of Time before *Abraham*, from *Abraham* to that moment as one, present, fixt, undivided point in himself. As a Rock standeth firm on the Shore, while Millions of waves rise, and fall at its foot: such a Rock of glory, and Eternity is our Saviour. While all the

Streams

Streams of Time roul along successively, and pass away; while all the waves of change lift up themselves & reak & bury themselves one in another, this Beautiful, and blessed Person standeth unchanged, unmoved, in the midst of them all. How great an Encouragement is this to you, who are tost with the Tempests upon the Sea of this world, and find no rest, to retire, and withdraw your selves into *Jesus Christ* by Faith? His glorious Person is a perpetual Calm with Sun-shine. Here, in him, in the midst of all the Storms of this world is the same sweet untrou-bled Calm, which was in Eternity before the world was.

Mal. 3. 6. Our Saviour is brought in speaking after this manner: *For I am the Lord, I change not: therefore ye Sons of Jacob are not consumed.* The unchangeableness of the Lord *Jesus* is founded upon the unity of his Person, in which he comprehendeth, beholdeth, converseth with himself, and all things. It is said to this *Jesus* by the *Psalmist* cited, *Heb.* 1. 8. *Thy Throne, O God, endureth for ever, and ever.* This Throne in the same Epistle is stiled, *a Throne of Grace*, that is, of *Love*; The *Person* of *Christ* in its *Unity* is the *Throne* of *Love*, and *Eternity.*

Hear this Word, all Sinners, and Saints! Hear this, you who have an ear to hear, what the Spirit saith of the Person of *Christ*. You, that have none, let this word come to you, and make in you a hearing Ear. Hear this, you, who believe not, that you may believe; you, who have Faith, that you may have it in greater abundance. The same Eye, with which *Jesus Christ* looked upon you, the same Beauty, in which he beheld you, the same Love, with which he embraced you in himself in Eternity, before that Sin or the world had any Being; with the same Eye he now looketh upon thee, in the same Beauty he now beholdeth thee, with the same Love he now embraceth thee in the midst of all thy Pilgrimages through so many Darknesses, and Deaths. For he is unchangeable. All the Waters, all the Fires of Temptations, and Troubles, thorow which thou passest, cannot drown, consume, or at all empair thy Beauties, thy Joys. For thou awakest, and findest thy self ever with thy Beloved, thy *Jesus*; thou findest him the same to thee; thou findest thy self the same in him. For he changeth not. So those Waters, and fires vanish, as a Dream.

2. *Ground: The Person of Christ comprehendeth all Changes in it self after an unchangeable manner. Heb.* We are commanded to *look to Jesus, the end of our Conversation; the same yesterday, to day, and for ever.* As all successions of Time lie united in one point, in one present, undivided moment in Eternity; where all things past, and to come are ever present, and every thing of Time appeareth cloathed with the Form of Eternity: so do all changes lie in one unchangeable Glory in the Lord *Jesus*. The *Yesterday* of Infiniteness before the world; this worlds *Day*; *Eternity* after this world are all one Infiniteness, one Eternity of Life and Love in this blessed Person. This world in it self lieth, as a small Island in the midst of the Ocean of Eternity bounding it

on all sides. In the Heavenly Person of *Christ* this Island is sunk, and swallowed up into the Depths of that Ocean. Which way soever you look, there is nothing but Heaven and Eternity. Are you wearied with the Changes of your own Heart, and This World? Retire into the bosom of your Loving God, and Saviour. There every Change lyeth in an Unchangeable Beauty, and Blessedness. Do variety of Objects with their Changes distract, and divide you, making you unsetled, and unsafe? Would you be unchangeable in a Holy, and Heavenly Frame of Heart? Would you be unmoved in the Work, and Joy of the Lord? Fix your Eye on *Jesus Christ*; Abide in *Jesus Christ*. There you shall *see the Same*; there you shall *be the Same, Yesterday, to Day and for Ever*. The Lord was buried in a New Tomb hewed out of a Rock in a Garden. What a Mysterious, what a beautiful, what a blessed Figure is this? Let us fear none of those things, that are to come upon us. A Sick-bed, a Prison, a Grave, every change lieth in the Person of our Beloved as a Mansion cut out of the Rock of Eternity, in the flourishing Garden of Eden, in the Paradise of the Divine Nature.

3. *Ground. The Person of Christ hath passed thorow all Changes after an Unchangeable manner, St Paul* teacheth us that the Lord *Jesus* hath descended to the *Nethermost parts of the Earth, and ascended above all Heavens to this end, that He might fill All*, Eph. c. 4. v. O that I had the tongue of the Learned, the Learned with the Learning of the Holy! that I could speak to you with Words taught by the Holy Ghost! O that you had hearts to take in and understand more, than I can express! *Jesus Christ* our forerunner is gone into every Form of things from the Height of the God-Head above to the lowest Deeps of the Creature to this end, that He might fill every Form of Things with the Unchangeable Fulness of His own Person, in which All Fulness dwelleth together in a Spiritual and Divine Body. He hath by this means filled every point of time with Eternity: every spot of Earth with Heaven; every Change on Earth, in Time, with the Unchangeableness of Heaven, and Eternity. St. *Paul* said to his Friends: *This I know, that Bonds await me in every place. But my life is not dear to me for the Testimony of Jesus.* A Believer in a contrary sense may say, This I know, that my *Jesus* in the fulness of Unchangeable Loves, Beauties, and Joys, waiteth for me in every Change; as a Spiritual Bridegroom in a Spiritual Bed of Loves, which is ever green, which hath a Perpetual Calm upon it, and a Perpetual Spring. Nothing therefore is dreadful, or melancholy to me for the unchanged Pleasantness of my *Jesus*.

In the Eastern countreys they imbalmed the Dead Bodies within, anoynted them without with costly Spices; that they might be preserved from putrefaction: and might have a sweet smell. When the Woman in the Gospel poured forth a Box of pretious Spikenard upon the feet of *Christ*; He said to some, who were offended with the wast: *Trouble her not. She hath done this against my burial* The Lord intimated, that this was a Sacrament dispensed by a Divine Hand representing for His Consolation this high, and holy Mystery; that

Death

Death, and the Dead Body in the Person of *Christ* are so embalmed, anoynted with the pretious Spikenard of the Eternal Spirit; that the Dead Body is Incorruptible, Immortal, and Pleasant; Death itself is a Flourishing Life, a fragrant sweet-smelling Joy, as it lyeth in, and is filled with this Unchangeable Person. O! with what a sweet Indifferency may we now walk thorow all the Changes of Life,and Death, when our Heavenly Spouse hath thus embalmed, anoynted, filled all with the Delights, and Glories of His Unchangeable Person, and Presence!

Use. 3. The Knowledge of the Lord *Jesus* in His Beauties sanctifieth, and sweetneth our Life in this World, our Death, and Departure out of the World. This *Use* hath *Two Parts.*

1. *Part*; The Opening of the Person of Christ upon us in His Spiritual Glories sanctifieth and sweetneth this Life. There are *three Principles* of the Knowledge of *Christ* in His true, and unchangeable State, which will bring home His Heavenly Beauties warm, and shining to your Hearts on this Earth by natural Deductions from each Principle.

1 *Principle.* This World in its pure Naturals is the Shadow,which falleth from the Heavenly Body of Divine Glories in the Person of our Fair One. This hath been proved at large above.Learn then from this Truth 4. *Lessons.*

1. *Lesson.* Live unconcerned in this World. This Divine Lesson is taught us from Heaven by the Holy Ghost upon this Ground; 1.*Cor.*7.29,30,31. *But this I say Brethren, the time is short. It remaineth,that both they that have wives, be, as though they had none; And they,that wept as though they wept not;and they,that rejoyce,as though they rejoyced not;and they,that buy,as though they bought not;& they that use this world,as not abusing it: For the fashion of this world passeth away.* The *Apostle* here divideth all this World into 4. *Heads*; 1. Relations; 2. Passions; 3. Possessions; 4 Employments, and Entertainments. *Solomon* saith in one place; *Why shouldst thou set thine heart upon that,which is not.* There is no real Difference between having a Husband, Wife, or Children, and having none; between being in Grief, or Joy, and being without Grief, or Joy; between having an Estate, and having none; between being in the height of all Employments, or Entertainments, and being out of all. This world hath nothing real. It is all a Shadow. Seeing then the various States of things on Earth have no real Difference; pass thou thorow all estates with a perfect indifference of Spirit, in a constant calm. *Eccles.* 1. This is an Expression of the Vanity, of all things here; *One Generation goeth, another cometh but the Earth standeth for ever.* The Scripture in several places makes this one of the Names of God, *The Earth*; the *Ground*, out of which all Generations of Things arise, and into which they return again. Divines interpret, that *Land of the Living* mentioned, to be the Divine Nature. In this let our Spirits be a Divine Earth standing for ever unmoved upon its own Center of Eternity, while one change after another cometh, and passeth away again. The *Holy Ghost* presseth it upon

us

us by *three Arguments.* 1. This World is a Fashion, a Figure only, a Shadow: The *fashion of this world.* In having this world thou hast a Shadow. The Substance is above. Let the world in having thee have thy shadow only. Let thine heart be in Heaven with *Jesus Christ.* 2. This world vanisheth, as a shadow. *The fashion of this world passith away.* The Colours in a Rain-bow are Appearances of Colours, and no more, made by the reflection of the Sun upon a dark, and watery Cloud. So they suddenly break up, and are seen no more. The Colours of a Flower upon its stalk in the Garden are real, living, and lasting. Such is the difference between Things on Earth, and Things in Heaven. Nothing here hath either Substance, or Root. 3. This world is a flying shadow suddenly gone. *The time is short.* As the shadow upon a Dyal in a short Winter-day moveth swiftly, passeth away presently, the Sun being low, and immediately going in, or going down: so is every condition, every comfort in Flesh. This is the *first Lesson.*

2. *Lesson*: Live without care, and with content. *Let your moderation be known unto all men. The Lord is at hand. Be careful for nothing: but in every thing by Prayer, and supplication with Thansgiving let your requests be made known unto God, Phil.* 4. 5, 6. You have in these words. 1. *A Precept* for moderation. Moderation is that measure of Things, by which they are proportioned, and tuned each to other, so as to fall in, and agree in one. This is that which maketh Beauty in Sights, and Musick in Sounds. A contented frame, composed, and equal motions are the Beauty, and Musick of your Spirits. 2. *The Reason* of this Precept followeth; *The Lord is at hand,* is near: nothing will so quiet the Soul, and bring it to rest in every Appearance of things here so, as a right sence of the near, and immediate presence of the Lord *Jesus* in Glory with all these things, after the same manner, in which the Body, or Substance is present with its proper Shadow. The Body is present with the Shadow *four ways*; as sending it forth immediately from itself, and keeping it hanging upon itself by an immediate touch, and union every moment; as governing all its motions by its own Acts, and Operations in itself; by its own Appearance there in its Figure, and Similitude; by its Approach, and Readiness to break up the Shadow by its breakings forth thorow it. Canst thou think that thy beloved in the sweet shinings of his Beauty, in the wonderful actings of the Divine Life, in the pleasant motions, and mysterious operations of his Love, is thus near to every Creature, every Providence; and not answer this Beauty with the Beautiful smile of a contented mind, this Musick with the melody of a well-pleased, and harmonious temper of Spirit: many that were sick, were healed by the shadow of St. *Peter* overspreading them, as he passed by. When thou art sick with discontent for any passage of things in this world, submit thy self to it, as the shadow of thy dearest Lord, with which he overspreadeth thee from his own Blessed Person, being himself ever at hand there, where his shadow is; figuring himself with his own Divine

motions

Motions, and Operations upon it; being even now ready to diſcloſe himſelf thorow it, as the Roſe breaking out of the Bud. Lie down under every accident, as ſuch a Divine Shadow of this Divine Lover with his Love; and thou wilt find thy ſelf healed of thy ſickneſs of Mind, of every Grief, and Melancholy.

3. *A third Thing* in this Scripture alledged is a *Prohibition* of Care. Be careful in nothing. Care is a Sin univerſally, in the greateſt things, as well as the leaſt; in the higheſt things, as well as in the loweſt.

Qu. But you will ſay, what Care is that, which is Sin ?

Anſ. I anſwer; that Care is a Sin, which breaketh the moderation of your Spirits, which defaceth the Spiritual Beauty, which diſturbeth the Spiritual Muſick of a well-pleaſed, and contented mind in you; which putteth your Spirits out of tune, cloudeth the clearneſs, diſordereth the Harmony of your Spirits, diſtempering them, and making them to jar with diſcontent. Again that care is ſinful, which is contrary to this Three-fold ſenſe of the preſence of the Lord *Jeſus* with every Creature, and Occurrence on the Earth, as with his own Shadow; his Powerful Preſence giving it Being, and Motion from himſelf, faſtning it immediately to himſelf; his Beautiful Preſence imprinting the Likeneſs, and Image of himſelf upon it; his Love-Preſence calling the Soul to himſelf by it, coming down to meet, and embrace the Soul there, ready to ſet himſelf in the place of his Shadow, making that the mark, and forerunner of his Perſon, and Loves in their full Light and Heat.

4. In the *laſt* place the *Holy Spirit*, that skilful Apothecary preſcribeth a *Cordial* to preſerve you from this trembling of the Heart, from carefulneſs. This Cordial is made up of ſix precious Ingredients.

1. *Ingred. Prayer. With Prayer.* The word is προσευχῇ. It importeth thus much: ſtand not at a diſtance; tarry not without. Come boldly up to the Throne of Grace, to God in the pureſt, and moſt raiſed heights of his Glory, and Love; to Love, as it is ſeated upon its higheſt, and moſt glorious Throne, the Heart of God; to love, as it ſhineth with its ſweeteſt ſmiles in the Divine Nature unvailed, and naked. Enter boldly within the Vail, behold God Face to Face, ſo talk familiarly with him, as a Friend doth with his Friend. Like the beloved Diſciple, lay thine head in his Boſom, ſo ſpeak to him, as a Bride to her Bridegroom.

2. *Ingred. Supplication. By Prayer, and Supplication*; *v.* 6. The word rendred *Supplication*, ſignifieth in its root three things, *Want*, a *Band*, *Decency*, or *Harmony*. Have a Divine ſenſe of thine own Shadowineſs, and Vanity upon every want which thou feeleſt. Go by a Divine Power, and in the Divine Myſtery empty thy ſelf into God, bind thy ſelf up together with him in that Golden Band, the unity of his Spirit. So move, be carried along thorow all things in the Order, Decency, and Harmony of the God-Head, of the Divine Wiſdom, and Will. As when Sugar is caſt into Wine, the Wine penetrating into all parts of the Sugar diſſolveth, and melteth it entirely into itſelf:

o in every state, in every streight cast thy self by the Blessed Spirit into that Spirit, which is the Wine of the Kingdom of the Father; let that Spirit wind, and work itself into every part, and power, into every thought, and affection, until it have drawn thee quite down out of thy self into one Stream, one flood of Desires and Delights, of Sweetness, Strength, and Fulness with itself.

Moses ascending upon Mount *Sinai* passed thorow the clouds, and fires; so he came to the top of the Mount, where he saw God face to face. The Eternal Spirit is Mount *Sion*, the Mount of Prayer. Here are white Clouds of Glory, which do much more overshadow the Creature; and Love-fires, which do much more melt down the Soul, and devour it. From the Valley of every low Condition betake thy self to this Mount of Prayer. Wait for this Holy Mountain, the Spirit of Prayer to spring up in every Valley, and take thee up, and carry thee along upon itself. As thou ascendest, pass thorow these Clouds, lose the light of thine own Beauties, and Being, before this excelling brightness. Pass thorow these Fires. Lose thine own Fleshly Substance, and Subsistence in the flame of the Spirit, Lose thine own Life, and Form in the Unity of Divine Love. So shalt thou arrive at the top of this Mount, where thou shalt see God Face to Face, with Life answering Life, Love answering Love, Beauty answering Beauty; being in the full view of his naked Glories transformed into the same Glory by the same Spirit, 2 *Cor*. 3. *l*.

3. *Ingred. Thanksgiving*; *with Thanksgiving*. What a powerful Antidote against Care in every Cross, or Difficulty is this, to give thanks? To see a Divine Glory? To tast Divine Love? To behold God descending in that Darkness, as in a Chariot of Clouds, of Angels; taking us up to ascend with Him thither, into His Palace above, where this Cloud shall become a Throne, this Chariot a Bed of Love, this Angel an Eternal Glory in the Form of God, where our Beloved, and our Souls shall reign together, feast together, ly down together in mutual Joys, and embraces for ever?

O Believing Soul art thou in Darkness? Open the Eye of Faith; see thy Jesus, and thy self from the supream Circle of the God-Head running forth with all Lines of Life, Light, Love into this Darkness, as the Center in the midst of this glorious Circle, where all the Lines from every Point of it meet in One. Again O Believing Soul in this Sight, in this Sense, in the vertue of these Divine Descents, return, and spread thy self by all these Lines of Glory together with thy God into the Circle of *Eternity*. There comprehend All, thy self, and All in the Incomprehensible Mystery of God, There see, hear, tast, enjoy Him, as Beauty itself, Sweetness itself, Musick itself, Joy itself in All. See, Hear, tast, enjoy All, as that Beauty, that Musick, that Sweetness, that Joy in him. Thus call him by every name, that is named in this world, or that which is to come. Call every thing in him, by a new name above every name, which is named in this world, or that which is to come.

When

When *Jacob* saw the Chariots, which his Son *Joseph* sent to bring him down into *Egypt*, his Soul revived, and he said; it is enough that my Son *Joseph* liveth; I will go see him, before I die. When thou seest Clouds of Enemies, or oppositions in thy Affairs, which are apt to perplex thee, and fill thee with care; shut this Eye of Flesh, which representeth all things false; open the Eye of the Spirit. Then look again, and see the Chariots of fire, and Horses of fire, a Spiritual fire shining with Glory, burning with Love, refining, and spiritualizing all things, as they ascend with them. Now let thy Spirit revive within thee from its care to a Heavenly calm, and to praises; Say, it is enough; my Jesus liveth, and loveth me. This is his Chariot. The Flames of it are Flames of Love. He is himself in the midst of it upon a seat of Gold. I see him. He cometh to carry me up above this world into his Heavenly Kingdom. I will ascend with him.

4. *Ingred. The making of our requests known to God.* What Hearts-ease is this to have the priviledge of expressing all our desires to God himself with freedom, and familiarity, at a banquet of Wine, of Spiritual Loves better than Wine? The Husbandman planteth his Vine against a South-wall, and spreadeth all the Branches of it there, where it may receive the Sun fullest, and longest, that by this means all the vertue of the plant may be drawn forth into a great plenty of fairer, and sweeter Grapes. Let thy Spirit be a Heavenly Vine planted by the Eternal Spirit in thee. Let thy will be the Heavenly sap of the Divine Will, and the Divine Love in thee. Instead of cares spread all thy desires, like the Branches of this Vine, fasten them continually before thy Invisible Sun, the Face of God, where the Beams of his Love, and Excellencies fall with greatest heat, and constancy. So shall all the sweet Sap of thy Vine, all the Divine Will in thy Will, that is, all Seeds, all desires of Good, of Love, of Loveliness, of Joy, of Blessedness be made to grow, and be ripened in their proper season unto the most perfect, and most pleasant Fruit.

5. *Ingred. Universality. Be careful in nothing; but in every thing by Prayer, and Supplication with Thanksgiving make your requests known to God.* There is nothing too great for us to be assured of the Ear, and Heart, and Hand of God in it. There is nothing too little for us to trouble him with. Every thing that can befal us is an opportunity, a Scene for all manner of Communion with God, for Faith, and Love to act all their parts upon in all their several Habits, and Dresses. Prayer, Supplication, Thanksgiving, Requests find a place in every Providence. Day unto *Day declareth Knowledge: Night unto Night uttereth Speech, Psal.* 19. 3. Every State, every season of Light, and Darkness in all senses bring down from Heaven to us in one lovely Love-Appearance, or another *Jesus Christ* with the Heart of the Father. Let every day and every night, as it returneth to Heaven again, carry up *Jesus Christ* from our Hearts, and our Hearts in him, in some Spiritual dress to the Bosom of the

Father. In every thing thy God acteth all manner of Loves, expresseth, and conveyeth all his Glories to thee. In every thing do thou meet him, return to him the activity of all thy Loves, and the exercise of all Graces.

6. *Ingred.* The *Ground* of all these Ingredients, and their vertue in this Cordial; *The Lord being at hand. v.* 5. The Philosopher in a Mill seeing his Friends making a doubt of coming in to him there, out of a disesteem of the place, and of him for being found in that place, invited them in with these words; here also are the immortal Gods. When thou feelest thine heart standing at a distance from any condition for the obscurity of it; or disquieted with cares in any condition for the troubles of it, say to thine heart after this manner; here also is my *Jesus* with all his Train of Immortal Glories, Loves, Angels, and Spirits. Here he is in a Figure of himself. Here is he in Person under this Figure. Here he is ready to shine forth, and appear gloriously. This is his Shadow; This Shadow is his Tabernacle, in which he dwelleth with me. Upon this Ground will I tune all my cares, all the unquiet motions of my Spirit to Prayers, and Praises, to the Melody of Faith, Love, and Joy. Thus much for the 2d *Lesson* of living without Care, with content upon this *First Principle* in the knowledge of the Lord, and his Beauties; that he maketh this world a Shadow falling from his Beautiful Person.

3. *Lesson.* Live beautifully, and purely, as Priests to God in this present world. For this world is the Temple of God, in as much, as it is *Jesus Christ* in a Shadow. *For the Invisible things of him from the Creation of the World are clearly seen, being understood by the things that are made, even his Eternal Power, and God-Head, Rom.* 1. 20. Four things make a Temple. 1. *A Divine Authority* for the building of it. This World is the Creation of God. 2. *A Divine Pattern.* The Invisible things of the God-Head, of the Lord *Jesus* the power of the God-Head, of Eternity are figured upon this World. 3. *A Divine End.* The proper end of these Figures is to form notions of the Divine nature upon our minds, to lead us to converse with it, to bring us into the Participations of it, that it may enjoy itself in the reflections of its own excellencies, and Glories from us; *v.* 21. *When they knew God, they glorified him not, as God.* They emproved not these Figures, and Notions to an entrance within the Vail into the Glory itself, which was the Divine end of them. 4. *A Divine Presence. Jesus* is he, *who filleth All in All, Ephes.* 1. *l.*

In what a Calm, in what Serenity, in what Purity, with what Beauty should we appear in this world, as Priests in the Temple, and in the midst of the Mysteries of God?

Psal. 29. 9, In his Temple doth every one speak of his Glory. In the Hebrew you may read *every Thing*, as well as *every One*. So the Margin hath it; *every whit of it*; that is, *of the Temple uttereth Glory.* Such should we ever be, as those who see the essence of Beauty, who hear the Soul, and Spirit of Musick, who tast, take in, and feel the pure, the primitive Life of all Sweetness,

and

and Joy in the Glory, the God-Head itſelf inhabiting every part and point, every paſſage, motion of Things in this whole Creation, as in a Temple. How would our Perſons, and lives ſhine with a ſpiritual Luſtre; how ſweet would the Muſick of our Spirits, and Converſation be, if we did thus take up, and bear this Natural Image, as the Tabernacle, and the Star of our God, our Beloved Jeſus? Figures made by the Eternal Spirit, to worſhip, and enjoy him, as St. *Stephen* ſpeaketh, *Acts* 7. 43.

Eccleſ. 3. We read, that there is *to every thing a Seaſon, and a time to every purpoſe under Heaven.* v. 1. *To be born, and to die; to plant, and to pull up.* v. 2. *To kill, and to heal.* v. 3. *To weep, and to laugh.* v. 4. *To love, and to hate; for war, and for peace.* v. 8. *He hath made every thing beautiful in his Time, or in its Time.* v. 11. *And whatſoever God doth, it ſhall be for ever.* v. 14.

In the Tabernacle, and Temple every part, every pin anſwered to the Pattern on the Mount, which were the Heavenly Things themſelves in the Spirit, in Eternity. All objects, all actions in the Temple, the Beaſts, the cutting their throats, the taking off their skins, the taking out their Entrails, the cutting them in pieces, the boyling, the burning them were ſacred Figures of Divine and Immortal Glories, to which the Muſick of the Levites round about upon the walls with their Inſtruments, and voices kept time.

Thou, O Man, art ſet in this world, as a Prieſt in this Temple. Behold! Both the Intellectual, and the Beſtial part in it; Love, and hatred; War, and Peace; Joy, and Grief; Light, and Darkneſs; Weepings, with Howlings, Laughter with Shouts; Life, and Death with all that is delightful, or diſmal belonging to them; all theſe Heavenly, and Divine Myſteries. Every one anſwereth to a purpoſe in the Heart of God, to a Pattern in the Eternal, and Eſſential Form of God. Every one anſwereth to the Muſick of the Holy Angels, which ſtand in Quires in the uppermoſt parts of this Creation, as the Levites upon the walls of the Temple. The baſeſt, the bloodieſt Perſons, and Offices; thoſe that kill, and thoſe that are killed, bear the Figure of *Jeſus Chriſt*, like the Beaſts for Sacrifice, or the Sacrificing Prieſts in their linnen Garments ſtained with Blood.

Every thing is beautiful in his Time. The Time of every thing is Divinely ſet; by a Divine Pattern, in a Divine Proportion; by a Divine Power. Thus each thing is cloathed with a double Beauty. 1. The Divine Harmony of the Univerſal Image in Nature, reſulting from, and reſting upon each particular fitly ſet with a ſacred proportion, and contrivance in its own Time, and in his Time, that is, by a Divine Hand in a Divine Time. 2. An exact, and raviſhing Harmony with the Eternal Image of the ſupream Glories in God. As line for line, feature for feature, colour for colour, motion for motion from a Face in a Glaſs anſwer to the Beautiful Face, which beholdeth itſelf in the Glaſs; ſo is God, and this world; the Face in the water, and the living Face; Beauty itſelf, by looking upon the water, at once Figuring itſelf upon it, and be-

beholding itself in it; all being reflections of its own Glories.

Obj. But you will say, we see not now this resemblance of the Divine Glory in the face of the Creature.

Ans. What God doth, he doth for ever. v. 14. As *Jesus* said to *Peter* of the washing his Feet: *What I do, thou knowest not now: but thou shalt know hereafter*; that may be applied here. The work of God in this World, and Time, is for Heaven, and Eternity, to be understood, and enjoyed there. When we shall come into the presence of the Life, and the Original, then shall we look again with another manner of Eye upon the Picture, and have an unexpressible pleasure to behold one in the other. As the Tabernacle, when its season was past, was taken into the Temple. So when Time, and this world are past away, Time, and this world from the Beginning to the End shall be taken up into their first Patterns, into Eternity. God shall call every thing to the least dust, or moment by its name, and no one shall be wanting. There shalt thou see the Beauty of the whole, and of every part in the light, and life of its Glorious Original. Then shalt thou know, what God hath done from the Beginning of the world to the End. Thou shalt now possess, and enjoy all with unexpressible pleasures, when thou shalt thus meet them again in a new Light, to be for ever with thee.

In the mean time, as *Christ* said to *Martha*: *Believe, and thou shalt see the Glory of God.* Thy *Jesus* is the Resurrection, and the Life; and that now, and that within thee, in thy Spirit. *John* 1. 14. *The Word was made Flesh, and dwelt (tabernacled) among us; (and we beheld his Glory, the Glory, as of the only begotten of the Father,) full of Grace, and Truth.* O Man, O Christian, open the Eye of thy understanding, open the Eye of thy Faith; see this world the Tabernacle, the Temple of the Eternal Word; behold all things full of the Grace, and Glory of his Person in Shadows, and Images formed by himself; behold himself in the truth of all this Grace, and Glory; in that height of Glory, which is proper to his own Person, as he is the only begotten of the Father, dwelling with thee in this Temple, behind the Vail of every Shadow and Image. Behave thy self, as in the House of God. Walk in the midst of all Creatures, and Occurrences, as in the midst of so many Divine Mysteries; as a Priest in the Temple. In purity, in peace, in wisdom, in love, bear in every state the Figure of thy Jesus, and his Glories; converse with it in every thing; walk in it at all times. See thy Glorified Jesus him self together with his shadow; make him the mark of thine Eye, and thine Heart; terminate all the workings of thy Spirit upon him, as the Truth, and Substance. So wait continually for the breakings forth of the glory, as a Heavenly Flame thorow the Shadow upon thee, to take thee up into itself. And thou, as thou ascendest, carry up the Shadow with thee.

4. *Lesson.* Live abstracted from this world in the world. Distinguish, and separate thy self from the Natural Person, Life, and Image, which are all the

Shadow, and no more; that thou mayst stand in an Immortal Person, a Life of Glory, the Essential Image, which is the Truth. The Lord *Jesus* saith: *I tell you the truth; it is expedient for you, that I go away. For if I go not away, the Comforter will not come unto you: but, if I depart, I will send Him to you, Joh.* 16. 7. *Jesus Christ* in the Shadow, in the Flesh is the Crucifier, and the crucified. Jesus Christ in the Substance, in the Spirit, is the Comforter, and the Comforted. How expedient is it for us in the midst of these Shadows to withdraw our selves into the Life, and Truth; that when all things there are dying upon the Cross, all things here may be Comforters, and Comforts, which continue for ever?

The Lord *Jesus* saith to the Father *Sacrifice*, and Burnt-offering thou wouldest not have; but a Body hast thou prepared me; that is, to be offered up in the place of all Sacrifices, *Heb.* 10. 1. We read *v.* 1. that *the Law hath a Shadow only of good things to come. Jesus*, and all His Members have the Shadowy Body of this Natural Man, and the First Creation fitted for them only, to sacrifice themselves in these to the Eternal Truth, that thus they may return on high into That.

All Shadows are under the Law. The Law hath Shadows only of Good things to come. All Sacrifices are under the Law. The Gospel is a Feast, Spirit, and Life.

How wise, how blessed is he, who gathereth himself up entirely out of Nature and Flesh into the Invisible Glory of the Spirit? In which, while Flesh is suffering, as a Sacrifice by Fire, he seeth all Flesh, Suffering, and Sacrifices to be Shadows only, Shadows of Immortal Joys, and Himself already in those Joys, triumphing over, and comprehending those Shadows in the Beautiful, and Blessed Truth, These are the *Lessons* from the *First Principle*; which was, that this World in its pure Naturals falleth as a Shadow from the Glorified Person of our Saviour.

2. *Principle.* The Presence, and Appearance of the Person of our Lord *Jesus*, and His Glory, is withdrawn from the faln, and corrupt World. The Devil is called in the Scriptures, *The Prince of Darkness*; and *The Prince of this World. This* World, the World in this faln state is *Darkness*. Darkness is the Privation of Light. The absence of the Sun from the Earth is the Cause of Darkness. Our Saviour in Glory is the Light, the Sun of the whole Creation. While He goeth away with His Beams into a far countrey, to shine in the Invisible World; He leaveth all behind Him in the Dark. *Three Lessons* naturally flow from this *second* Principle.

1. *Lesson.* Believe not any Appearances of things in this World. Darkness in the language of the *Holy Ghost* signifieth Deceit. The Lord *Jesus* saith of Himself; *I am the Truth*, Truth hath left the World together with *Jesus Christ*. Blessed is he, who having the Possessions, or Powers of this World in his Hand; the Smile, or Frowns of it before his Eyes; the Griefs, or Joys of it in his Heart;

Heart; can with a good assurance say: Have I not a Lye in my Hand, and in my Heart? Are not the Apparitions of the Devil the Father of Lyes before me?

2. *Lesson.* Love not the things of this World, *James.* 4. 4. *Ye adulterers and Adulteresses, know ye not, that the Friendship of this World, is enmity with God.* It is not now the Seed of the Woman, which is a Divine Loveliness, and Love in the Person of our Heavenly Bridegroom, which springeth up in all the Forms, and Fruits of this World. *Yet a little while*, saith He to the World, *and ye shall see me no more.* No! It is the Seed of the Serpent in Deformity, and Enmity; in a Contrariety to all Spiritual Beauty, Goodness, and Truth, which groweth up every where. Your Love to any part of this World is Unclean, and Adulterous: By it you leave the pure, and sweet embraces of your own Glorious Husband to ly down infolded in the treacherous Twinings of the old Serpent, the Dragon.

3. *Lesson.* Walk not after the Fashion of this World, *Rom.* 12. 2. *Be not conformed to this World.* While the Lord *Jesus* was with this World, it was, His Shadow. He figured His Beauties upon it; He acted it with His Spirit; His Name was as an Ointment poured out upon it; He spake to us and conversed with us there: But now, when He is absent, the beautiful Figure is gone, the Darkness with all its confusions, and cursed Fruits remain: The Spirit of Darkness ariseth in it with all his, Hellish Forms of Deceit, Defilement, and Wrath; If thou cloath thy Spirit with any Worldly Image, thou puttest on a filthy Garment, which will pollute thee; thou puttest on a fiery garment, which hath the burning poysons of Hell hidden in it, which will cleave inseparably to thee, torturing, and consuming thee with a hidden, inward, and unquenchable flame, This is the *Second Principle.*

3. *Principle.* *Jesus Christ* hath reconciled all things, hath gathered up all things into One, hath made all things New with the Spiritual, and Eternal Glory of the Father; as the World standeth in the Resurrection of *Christ* from the Dead, and in His Glorified Person, as a New Head to it with a New Name.

Lesson. You then, that are *Christ*'s live victoriously, and triumphantly in this World. Abide in your Head. There you see all this World lying conquered, captivated, comprehended in a new, and endless World of Life, Love, and Glory, *Rom.* 5. *We rejoyce, saith* St. *Paul, v.* 2. *And not onely so, but we glory in tribulation, v.* 3. *Because the Love of God is shed abroad in our Hearts by the Holy Ghost given unto us*; *v.* 5. O Christians! live in Joy; Live in Glory; live in a perpetual Triumph. For by the Resurrection, and Ascension of your Jesus, the bitterest Enmities, the blackest Extremities are Forms, Floods of Light, and Love in that Sea of Light, and Love, the *Holy Ghost* breaking forth from the sweet, and glorious Deep of the God-Head in the Heart of the Father. *Rom.* 8. *v.* 37. *In all these things, (famine, nakedness sword* mentioned before) *we are more than conquerours through Him, that loved us v.* 58, 59. *For nothing, life, nor death, nor Angels, things present, nor things to come, nor height, nor depth shall be able to separate us from the love of god, which is in Christ Jesus.* Dear Soul! dwell for ever in this good Land of Life, and Love, thy Saviour in the Spirit. Nothing here can separate thee from the Divine Love Every thing then, that cometh to thee in life, or in death, must come in that Element of Love; it must come in a Love-dress; it must be Love itself in a Lovely Form. Every thing, that toucheth thee here, must touch thee with the Heavenly kisses, and Embraces of Divine Love. Otherwise there would be a Separation between Love, and thee.

In thy glorified *Jesus* is the Love of God, that Love, which is God, the God-Head of Love. O blessed Habitation! O Happy, and Heavenly Countrey! thine own Countrey indeed! What so much our own, what so near us, so much One with us, as Love? Here Love in its God-Head filleth all, in Spiritual Forms, in Forms of Glory, and of God. O glorious Victory! O Saints more, than Conquerours in the Resurrection of your Saviour! The World is faln before you; it is no more. The old things, of Vanity, Darkness, Sin, Sorrow Death are passed away in His Death. Thus you are conquerours. But in His Resurrection the World is raised again in a Form of Eternal Love, and Glory for you. All things are come again, and are made New, All things appear again the second time Immortal Spirits shining in the Loveliness, burning in the Love of the God-Head for you; opening all things past, present, and to come in themselves, as Beautiful, and Sacred Mysteries of Divine Love to you; which ever is Delighting it self in You, sporting with you, preparing Joys & Glories for you. Thus you are more than Conquerous through Him, who hath loved You. Live then in Him Joyfully, gloriously, Triumphantly. I have done with the *first Part* of my *last Use*, the Sweetning, and Sanctifying Life in this World.

2. *Part.* To sweeten, and sanctifie Death by the Knowledge of *Christ* in Glory, I shall lay down *three Principles* to this End.

1. *Principle.* Every Saint standeth compleat in Glory in the Glorified Person of *Christ* above, even while he is living, or dying here below, *Ye are compleat in Him, who is the Head of all Principality, and Power, Col.* 2. 10. In the *verse* before the Lord *Jesus* was described, as *in Him dwelleth all the Fulness, (or Compleatness) of the God-Head bodily.v.* 9. Then this is added; *And in Him ye are compleat, (or full,) who is the Head of all Principality and Power.* A Believer is compleat in his Saviour, as He hath the Compleatness of the God-Head in him, and the Compleatness of all the Angels beneath him. His Life then, and His Death, as they stand in *Jesus Christ*, are more than Angelical. They are Divine.

I shall endeavour to set in lively Figures before your Eyes the Beauty, and Sweetness in the Death of a Saint by *four Scriptures.*

1. Script. *And hath raised us up together, and made us, sit together in Heavenly places in Christ Jesus, Eph.* 2. *v.* 6. What is to be understood by [*together*]

ther] is plain in the verse before, *hath quickned us together with Christ*, It is God, who doth all this, as is seen, *v.* 4. *God who is rich in mercy for his great love, wherewith he hath loved us. Four Positions lye* clear in this Scripture.

1. *Pos.* A Believer is risen from the Dead. He dieth no more. He is passed from Death to Life. As Abraham is said to have received *Isaac* from the Dead *in a Figure*; So the Beloved of the Lord dieth onely *in a Figure*. Death is to him a Divine Figure standing in the Resurrection from the Dead. His Death is a Flower of Life, and Immortality growing up in the Paradise of God, which is the Glorified Person of *Jesus*. It beareth indeed the Figure of Death, but is full of a Sweetness, and Beauty, which can never fade, or dye. Let us all labour for our part in the New Birth. This is a Resurrection from the Dead. All things after it are Life; Pure Life without any mixture of Death; Perpetual Life, Endless Life without any Sting of Death in the tail of it.

2. *Pos.* A Believer is already set down in Heavenly places; nay more than Heavenly. The Word *Heavenly* is by some translated, and so it properly signifieth *Supercœlestial*, more than *Heavenly* places, *above the Heavens*. Here a Saint is made *to sit down*. He is fixed, and established; He is at rest, at home, at the end of all his journeyings, and changes. He is set as a Bride, at the Marriage-feast. He is set, as a Prince upon the Throne of his Kingdom. Thus God giveth His Beloved Sleep, Rest, a Feast, a Throne in Death, *Jesus Christ* in Glory is this Sleep, this Rest, this Feast, this Throne, which endureth for ever, and ever. O Christian! rejoyce, and glory in Death for the Hope of the Joy, and Glory of thy Bridegroom there. Thy Death hath nothing of Dust, or Darkness in it. It is a Heavenly Thing, nay more than Heavenly. It is something Supercœlestial. It is a soft Strain, and ravishing Touch in the Musick of the Divine, and Eternal Rest. It is a savoury Dish, such, as thy soul loveth, at the Feast in the Kingdom of God. Solomon had a throne of Gold. On the Steps, which were the Ascents to the Throne, on each side were Lyons of pure Gold. Thy Death, O Saint, is now no more a fierce, and devouring Lyon to affright thee. It is the figure of a Lyon in Gold, in one Glory. It is not onely an Ascent to thy Throne, O *Jedidiah*! Beloved of the Lord! It is One Piece of Eternal Glory with thy Throne. It is an Ornament, an Embellishment of Glory to thy Throne.

How good is it for those, who are born of God to keep themselves pure, that they may alwaies see God, that they may see all things to them Divine Objects in a Divine Light, sparkling Jewels of Divine Love, We are ever in the midst of these things, which are more than Heavenly, in the midst of these Supercœlestials; even in the arms of Death. While we keep our selves unspotted from this world, we see these Supercœlestials, and Death itself in the number of them. But every sin casteth a mist upon them, and covereth us with a Cloud, that we see them no more. Now the Visions of our Joy, and Glory: of Light, and Truth are hid from our Eyes. Now fear, and trembling are upon us. Life is full of Trouble, and Death full of Terrour.

3. *Pos.*

3. *Pos.* A Saint is set down in Heavenly places together with *Jesus Christ*. The sweetning, and the heightning of all the Joys, and Glories of the Gospel is the Union with thy Beloved Bridegroom. The work of Grace is a Birth, a Resurrection, a Marriage, all in one. The Death of a Saint is an Act of Spiritual Communion between Christ, and the Soul; a Marriage-Joy. The Lord *Jesus* presenteth himself to the Believer in the Form of Death, as in a Heavenly, a Supercoelestial Beauty. At this sight the Saint is immediately transformed into the same Image. *Jesus Christ* springeth up into the Believer, a Believer springeth up into his Beloved in this Heavenly Form. So both are made one in it. Thus Death becometh a Love-play between Christ, and his Spouse. He by a Spiritual Kiss breatheth forth his Spirit of Divine Loves, Immortality, and Invisible Glories into the Spouse. The Spouse ravished forth from her self again in the same moment breatheth forth her Spirit into the Bosom of her Lord. Thus they die together, they die one in another, they die one into another.

In the *first* of the *Canticles* there is a Prophetical Song, which beginneth at the Resurrection of our Saviour, and the Effusion of the Spirit, together with the Spiritual Union between *Christ*, and his Church, which was, as their Heavenly Espousals solemnized, and sealed with a Kiss, with the reiterated *Kisses of his Mouth*. Then followeth in the process of the first Chapter, and beginning of the Second, the Loveliness of the Spouse, and the Love between her, and the Heavenly Bridegroom in her Sufferings, and Death, as they are acted upon the Stage, in the glorious Scene of the Resurrection, and Ascension of *Christ*, in the State of Espousals, and in their Union in one Spirit. The dying Spouse there singeth to her Lord; *Behold! thou art fair, my Love; yea thou art pleasant; also our Bed is green*, *v.* 16. *Jesus Christ* is fair to a Saint's Eye in his Divine Loveliness being risen up into the Glory of the Father. He is pleasant to her in his Loves, which are his Loveliness in Motion, acting beautiful parts; transforming it self into delightful Shapes with endless variety; in all pouring forth it self into her Bosom, taking her up into it self with Blessed Changes of one into another. The Unity of the Spirit is the Bed of Divine Loves, which is ever green, that is, as the word importeth, ever encompassed with a Heavenly Calm, and Serenity, ever flourishing, ever fruitful. Death it self is the mutual embracing of these two Heavenly Lovers in this Bed of Spiritual Loves in the midst of a Divine calm, and clearness; while out of these embraces they spring up into innumerable Forms of Eternal Beauties, and Joys, which are the flourishing Fruits, and Blessed Children of this Marriage-Union.

It is said, that *nothing was made without Christ*, (apart from *Christ*) *that was made in the Creation*, *John* 1. 2. Remember, O Christian, that in the new Creature thou art, thou sufferest, thou doest nothing, in life, or in death, without thy *Jesus* in Glory, apart from thy *Jesus* in the Unity of his Spirit, which is the Center, and Circle of all Blessed Spirits, with all the Train, and Treasures of the Divine Nature. While thou livest, all the Body of *Christ*, Heavenly Spirits, Innumerable Angels live with thee thy life. All these, all the Lights, and Loves of the Supercœlestial State die with thee thy Death.

4. *Pos.* All this Resurrection, Ascension into the Heavenly places, Fellowship of a Believer with *Christ* is *in Christ. He hath raised us together, and hath made us sit together in Heavenly Places in Christ Jesus.* See now those places above the Heavens, those more than Heavenly Things in the midst of which a Saint is set. They are all in the glorified Person of *Christ*, who is made higher than the Heavens.

The Learned tell us, that there are three Worlds. 1. This, which is visible. 2. The Angelical World. 3. The Divine World. All things of the upper, and greater Worlds are in the lower, as in the Seed. All Things of the lower are in the Superiour, as ripe Fruit. Every thing is in each according to the nature of that place. Behold! This is the Divine World the Person of our Lord, and Love ascended up on high above all Heavens of Angels. Here in him the Fulness of the God-Head dwelleth Bodily; that is, not shadowily, or seminally; in its Shadow, or Seed; but in its Substance, and Perfection. While here thou standest fast in this thy *Jesus*, thine own proper habitation, Death itself is an Angel; nay more, it appeareth in a Divine Form, is become a Divine Glory, a rich and ravishing piece of variety in the Unity of the Divine Nature. In the World of Angels every thing is a distinct Angel. In the Divine World all things are cloathed with the form of God.

As a Child lying in its Mothers lap, a branch from the Mother bearing her Image, with its mouth at the Breast, looking upon her Face, falling asleep in her Bosom; yet not so sleeping, but that still it sucketh as it sleepeth: such is a Saint dying in *Jesus Christ*. He lieth in the lap of the Supream Glory encompassing him on every side, and bearing him, as its own Birth, and Image. His mouth is at the breast of this Glory. His Eye is upon the Face of this Glory. He sleepeth in its Bosom. But it is a Divine sleep. While he sleepeth, he is awake, and keepeth his Eye still upon the Glory, and sucketh in the Glory still in Death. We have this excellently represented in one place by the Prophet *Esay*, where the Heavenly *Hierusalem*, (which is our *Jesus* in the Spirit,) is said *to bear her Children on her sides, and to dandle them on her Knee.* In another place they are said, *to walk in the Light of the new Hierusalem* These Dandlings, and Dancings in the Arms of that Glory, which is our Mother, our Father, and our Husband, our Heavenly *Jesus*; such walks in its sweet, and living Light are all the Motions, and Changes of Life, and Death to those, that are in *Christ Jesus*.

I shall conclude my Observations from this Scripture with the difference between the Death of a Man standing in the Root of the First *Adam*, and a Christian in *Christ*. Death to one is a Poyson. In eating of the Forbidden

Fruit

Fruit he dieth out of the Earthly Paradise yet remaining in its ruines in this World into a Land of Briars, and Thorns, into a vast, and howling Wilderness, where the Light is Darkness, and where there is no Order. The Death of the other is a Cordial of dissolved Pearl. In eating of the Tree of Life he dieth out of a Land of Briars, and Thorns into a Heavenly Paradise, the Paradise of God. I have done now with the *first Scripture*.

2. *Script. Verily, verily I say unto you, except a Corn of Wheat fall into the ground, and die, it abideth alone: but if it die, it bringeth forth much Fruit* John 12. 24. These are the words of our Saviour concerning himself upon a report made to him by *Philip*, that some *Greeks* desired to see him. The design of *Jesus* is partly to raise them from a Carnal view of him on Earth to a Spiritual sight of him in a Heavenly Glory after Death, partly to signify the difference between his State of humiliation in this Life, where he is single and Barren in the Flesh; and his State of exaltation after Death, where he riseth up an Universal Person reconciling, comprehending All in the Unity of the Spirit; a Fruitful Person being a new head, and root in the Love, Life, and Glory of the Father to all Mankind, Jews, and Gentiles; to all Creatures.

Our Saviour, while he lived, was, as a single, naked grain of Wheat. But when he sprung up out of the Grave, he became a pleasant, and flourishing Plant bearing much Fruit, many grains of Wheat in one Ear; many, all Persons, all Angels, and Spirits in Glory, in that one, his own Person, and Spirit. He was in the Flesh, as one Rose, one Apple pull'd off the Tree. He is in the Spirit, as the Rose-Tree, the Apple-Tree. All Angels and Saints, all Forms of Things are glorified in his Glory; all in Heavenly, and Immortal Persons are in his Heavenly Person, as full-blown Roses growing upon the Rose-Tree, as full-ripe Apples upon the Apple-Tree.

The Death of a Saint is upon this ground made most beautiful, and pleasant; *Can.* 2. 3. *As the Apple-Tree among the Trees of the Wood; so is my Beloved among the Sons. I sat down under his Shadow with great delight, and his Fruit was sweet to my taste.* There are three distinct parts in the *Hebrew*; 1. *I desired, and sweetly delighted in his Shadow.* 2. *Then I sate down.* 3. *And his Fruit was sweet to my taste.* The *Apple* in Holy Scriptures and in the writings of Learned Authors is famous for a pleasant Cordial nourishment of Life; and for an Emblem of Love. You may see this in this *Chapter. v.* 5. *Stay me with Flagons, comfort me with Apples; for I am sick of Love. Apples* are Emblems of Love for their pleasant looks to the Eye, their fragrant smell, their delightful tast, their cordial vertue, their round form, which is a Figure of Unity, the Root and Sap, and Fruit of all Love.

In the midst of the Wood of this Life, where all Forms of things are like blasted, and barren Trees, good neither for Shade, nor Fruit, *Jesus* Christ standeth, as an Apple-Tree, a Tree of Life, and a Tree of Love, Fair, Flourishing and Fruitful.

When

When the poor Spouse of *Christ* thorow all this Life is wearied with scorching Heats, sounding Tempests, raging Storms, then her Beloved, when He seeth His Fit Time, springeth up, as a Paradisical, and Heavenly Tree. As He springeth up, He overshadoweth His Spouse; not, as a cloud overshadoweth the Sun, or as Darkness in the absence of the Sun overshadoweth the earth; but as the approaching, and rising Sun overshadoweth the Stars. So the Lord, as a Tree of Glory spreadeth His Shadow over all those Lights of the Night, the Principles, Powers, Activities; Appearances of the Natural Man; drinking them up into One Light of Glory, and Immortality with Himself, while He drowneth them, with a Sea of Love breaking in upon them, and overflowing them. How sweet is this Approaching Shadow of her Lord's Blessed Person to the Love-sick Soul? a Shadow perfumed with the Ointments of His Love; shining with the purple Lustre of His Beauties; quickened with the Life of His Glories; a Divine Shadow? With what Desire, with what Delight doth the Holy Soul go under this Shadow? How precious in the Eye of God, of all the Angels, of a Saint Himself, is This Death? This Death is no Evening to a pleasant Day; but a Lovely Morning, and glorious Sun putting out the Lights of the Moon, with all the Sars, because the Time of the Night is past, and the Day is come. Never did the softest, and sweetest Sleep steal with more pleasure upon the Senses of any Person; than this Shadow of Death cometh upon the Heavenly Bride.

Here a Saint *sitteth down*. As Hee entreth into this Shadow, he entreth into Rest, into the Unity of God, where He resteth for ever from his own Work, and Spirit, to lye down in the Eternal Spirit.

Now he eateth of his own Apple upon this Apple-Tree. He meeteth with Himself in Glory in the Glorified Person of his Beloved, as the ripe Fruit of Life and Love hanging ready upon its own Tree in Eternity. In the same moment he seeth it, he taketh it in, he rellisheth it with unexpressible sweetness, and delight, as being Great, Glorious, His own by the nearest, dearest Suitableness, and propriety; Himself in the Entirest Unity; in the same Moment he feedeth upon it, is Transubstantiated into it and becometh that Lovely Apple that full-ripe Fruit of Love upon the Tree. As he thus feedeth upon his own Apple, and is changed into it, at once he feedeth upon, is changed into all the Apples of the Tree, and the whole Tree itself. For this is the Divine Mystery of Spiritual Plants in the Heavenly Paradise; each Fruit, each part of the Plant comprehendeth the whole Plant; all the Plants stand, live, and grow together in each Plant. Every Person and Spirit in Glory hath its own Name, & all Names written upon it. It is itself an Entire Heaven, in which all the Heavenly Inhabitants shine, and sing, and dance together with their various Beauties, Musicks, and Motions cast into the most Divine Harmony by a most perfect Unity.

3. Script. *John* 14. v. 2. 3. *In my Father's house are many Mansions. If it were not so, I would have told you. I go, to prepare a place for you. And if I goe*

and prepare a place for you; I will come again, and receive you unto my self; that where I am, there ye may be also.

Three Mysteries are opened to us in these words; 1. The *Place* of Blessed Persons after this Life.

2. The *Preparation* of this Place.

3. Their *Passage* into this Place. All are full of a Joy glorious, and unspeakable.

1. The *Place* of Blessed Spirits after this Life. It is, saith *Christ*, my *Father's House*. The House of the Father is the Glorified Person of His Son. This is the Temple of God in Heaven, the Palace of the great King. *In Him the fulness of the God-Head dwelleth bodily.* All glorious Persons, Angels, Saints, and Spirits, as they are comprehended in the Person of *Christ*, and make up His Body, the Divine Body, the Body of Glories, and Eternity in Him, as they are Beautiful Members in that Body, so are they Mansions in that Temple, Apartments in that Palace: Every Apartement in this Divine Palace hath the whole Palace, with all the Persons, Prospects, Furniture, Entertainments of the whole within it self. This is the *Place*.

2. The *Preparation* of this Place. *I go to prepare a place for you.* While this Palace of Eternity with all its Apartments, which are also its Inhabitants the Glorified, and Immortal Persons of all Saints, stood in the Father, in the Divine Nature alone; it was hid from the Eye of every Creature, it was shut up, that none could enter into it; it was remote from every Creature at a very great distance. The Lord *Jesus* by His Death, and Resurrection entring with the Humane Nature into this Eternal Habitation, hath set it up in the Nature of Man, hath brought it near to us, hath set it in our view, hath set it open for us. The Gates of this Temple, of this Heavenly *Hierusalem* stand open day, and night to all quarters of the Heaven, and the Earth. All the Apartements of it with our several Names written upon them, our several Persons in Glory appearing in them, stand ready. The Lord *Jesus* Himself is the Beautiful Gate, the Living Way, the Ascent, the rich Stair-case to this Temple. The Angels are continually descending in Him as Chariots, to bring down riding upon them our glorious Saviour, and our glorious Selves into the Bosom of our Spirits here below. The Bridegroom, and the Bride ready trimm'd, and already joyned in One, come thus down out of Heaven, come thus forth from the Temple. The Angels are continually ascending by this Stair-case carrying up our Spirits beforehand on visits into this Palace, into our own Apartments, into the Bosom of our own Glorified, and Immortal Substances there. Every Grace, every Providence, every Motion of things, to him whose Eyes are opened, is such an Angel such a chariot of Angels with these Persons riding in it.

3. The *Passage* into this Place. *I will come unto you, and take you unto my self, that where I am, there ye may be also.* There are three Steps of Christ's Coming to us in Glory; 1. Into our whole Spirits by Regeneration; 2. Into our

whole

whole Souls at death. 3. Into our whole Persons, Spirit, Soul and Body at the Resurrection. By every step he maketh a mutual Union, so far as he goeth. He cometh to us; He taketh us to himself, that we may be both together in one place, in one Spirit. He letteth himself down in his Heavenly Palace into us; he taketh us up into the Heavenly Palace in himself; he maketh our Persons a Heavenly Palace like his glorified Person, and one with it.

This is our passage in Death into Glory. Of old God descended upon the Tabernacle in a Cloud, & the Glory was in the Cloud. Then *Moses* was summoned to enter into the Cloud, and so into the Glory; where God talked with him. In latter times the most excellent Majesty in a white Cloud overshadowed the Lord Jesus, and in overshadowing him transfigured him, then in the transfiguration talked to him of his Sonship to the Father, and of Love. In like manner at the set time the Lord *Jesus*, as a living Temple of Heavenly Glory, cometh down upon thee in a white Cloud of some Love-storm, or Love-sickness. I call it a *Love-sickness*, because it ariseth at once from the Love of the Spirit of the Bride in thee, and from the Love of thy Bridegroom to thee; from the longings, and burning desires of both after the immediate, perpetual, and full enjoyments of each other: As thou entrest into this Cloud, and art overshadowed by it, thou art in a moment, at the same time taken into that Palace of Glory, and transfigured into the Glory of that Pallace. There thou appearest to be the Son of God, the Spouse of the Immortal King. God speaketh to thee, converseth with thee, as a Son, and Spouse in one. He seeth the Figure of his own Beauties in thy Face; and his Heart resteth in thy Bosom. He seeth, and enjoyeth thy Person, as springing up eternally with incomprehensible Pleasures out of the Root of his own Divine Loveliness; he feeleth, and rellisheth thy Spirit, as the flowing of his own sweetnesses from their own Fountain in himself; he poureth forth himself in a flood of Beauties, and Sweetnesses into thee, All his Loves rest in thy Love, and he in thee.

4. *Script.* I am now come to the *last Scripture. For we know, that if our Earthly House of this Tabernacle be dissolved, we have a Building of God, an House not made with hands, Eternal in the Heavens. For in this we groan, earnestly desiring to be cloathed upon with our House, which is from Heaven. If so be, that being cloathed, we shall not be found naked. For we, that are in this Tabernacle do groan, being burthened; not that we would be uncloathed, but cloathed upon, that Mortality might be swallowed up of Life. Now he, that hath wrought us for this self-same thing is God, who hath also given us the Earnest of the Spirit.* 2 *Cor.* 5, 1, 2, 3, 4, 5.

This is a rich, and deep Scripture. What expressions of Death are those? How full of Joy? *Not to be found naked?* Naked of any support, or comfort? Of any cloathing of Being, or Beauty; Essence, or Substance; Form, or Fulness, in Person, or Relations? *Not to be uncloathed?* Of any Garment of Light, or Life? *To be cloathed upon with an House from Heaven?* To have the

the Lord *Jesus*, as a circling Glory coming down upon this Image, in which we now dwell, neither taking away the Nature, nor Form of any thing, that here we are, or have, but taking up all as sacred Mysteries into a Temple of Glory, giving them a place for ever in this Temple, penetrating, filling, and cloathing them the Glory? *To have Mortality swallowed up of Life*? To lose none of the things, or entertainments, which here we enjoy in this mortal state, but the mortality of them only, and that not by Death breaking them down with violence, but by the sweet breakings in of Life, and Immortality upon them; not by a blackness of Darkness dreadfully over-spreading them, but a brightness of Eternal Glory delightfully rising upon them, like the Sun upon the beautiful Forms of Heaven, and Earth, after they have weakly appeared in the melancholy Beams of the Moon shining faintly in the shade of the Night. *And He that hath wrought us for the Self-same Thing, is God.* It is a Divine Hand, and Skill, which hath framed, and fashioned us to this capacity. It is God, who by his own operations in us, not mediately, as in the works of Nature, but immediately, as in all works of Grace, and Glory, hath wrought out this Spiritual, and Divine Being, this Spiritual, and Divine Nature in us, which never dyeth, but is changed from Glory to Glory; which in Death putteth off nothing, but putteth on a greater, and purer Light upon its weaker Lights, and Shades; piercing thorow, and breaking up delusive Shapes formed out of the Darkness of remaining night by stronger Beams of Glory falling from above. *Who hath also given us the Earnest of his Spirit.* An *Earnest* is part of the Sum in present, and an assurance of the rest. God doth not only frame a Spiritual work, like a new Heaven in us, but giveth us the Person of his Spirit himself, in which the Persons of the Father, and the Son are seen together unvailed in their Union, and Communion of Beauties, and Loves; in the unity of which all Angels and Blessed Spirits dwell together, as their proper Center, and Circle. This Spirit God giveth to be in the Spiritual Nature framed by himself in us, as a new Sun in the new Heaven. This Spirit in us is the *Earnest* of our Death; a foretast of its Sweetness, and Delights; a vision in part beforehand of the manner of our dying; and an assurance of the compleating of its season after the same Beautiful, and pleasant Image. As at the first Effusion of the Spirit upon us, or any new Effusion; as at any Act of the Spirit, when he shineth out freshly in us; this Natural Image of Things is no more; a Light of Glory, Forms of Glory Immortal Spirits full of a Divine Beauty, and Majesty appear every where. They are alone, and there is nothing besides in the whole space of Things above, or below, past, present, or to come. As they are, so are we. All Things are one Vision of Divine Glory. Neither do we perceive, how one Image of Things goeth, and another cometh. Both are done; one is come, the other is gone in the same moment, in the twinkling, or cast of an Eye. So is Death. This is the Earnest of our Death. This is a step of Death; a foretast of it. So shall Death be perfected us.

I have three Observations to make upon this Scripture besides that, which I have already said in order to my present purpose; to shew how the knowledge of Christ in Glory sanctifieth, and sweetneth Death.

1. *Obser.* Here are three distinct Frames. 1. *A Building.* v. 1. 2. *A Tabernacle.* v. 1. v. 4. Where take notice, that in both places it is translated *this Tabernacle*; but is in Greek, *the Tabernacle.* 3. *The Earthly House.* v. 1.

This seemeth to allude to *the Temple*, which was a standing, stately Building set up by *Solomon* in the Kingdom of the Jews; to *the Tabernacle* in the Wilderness, which was less, and moveable but rich and fine for the Workmanship, and for the Materials; to *the Tent* of course stuff, a covering for the Tabernacle. All these were Figures of *Christ*, and his Church, to which they are also applied.

1. The Heavenly Person of *Christ*, as it standeth in the high and holy place of Eternity; as it springeth up out of the Bosom of the Father, and abideth in his Bosom; as it is one Spirit, and one Glory with the Father, is the *Temple*, the *Building*. For the *Building* hath this Three-fold Character; 1. It is *of God*, in Greek *out of God*, as Gold is *out of* a Mine of Gold. 2. It is *Eternal*; 3. It is *in the Heavens.*

The Glorified Person of every Saint, as it is comprehended in this Glorious Head of all Saints, is a *Temple*, a *Building* in Heaven, in Eternity, of the same manner, and fashion.

2. The *Tabernacle* made of Sky-colour, of Scarlet, of Purple, of fine Linnen, with Silver, and Gold, and all manner of precious stones, wrought with Cherubims, and all curious Workmanship, is the Image of God in *Christ*, and a Saint here below in the Wilderness of this World. *John* 1. 14. *And the Word was made Flesh, and dwelt* (in Greek *Tabernacled*) *among us, and we beheld his Glory, the Glory, as of the onely Begotten Son of God; full of Grace, and Truth.* Here you have the *Temple*, which is higher, greater in compass, and more glorious than the Heavens, contracting itself into a *Tabernacle*, and residing in that Tabernacle, filling it with its own Sweetnesses and Glories, which are *Grace*, opposed to Wrath, *Truth* opposed to Shadows. *The Word was made Flesh.* The Eternal, and Substantial Image of God, which is the *Temple*, the true *Heaven* brought forth itself into a Temporary, and Shadowy Image, which is the *Tabernacle*, and the *Paradise* of the whole Creation. As it is in the Lord *Jesus*, so is it in his Spouse, who is *the Fulness of him that filleth All in All.* This *vile Body* in which a Saint is here; this dark, and course Form, with which our Souls, and Bodies are cloathed here, is the *Tent*, that covereth the Tabernacle; the *Earthly House of the Tabernacle.*

2. *Obser.* The Effect of Death is different in these Three.

1. The *Tent*, the *Earthly House* onely is *dissolved.* It is dissolved, and no more. It is taken to pieces. The Word belongeth to the taking down of a house; or the taking of Horses out of the Coach, and setting them up in a stable at an Inn, when

when the day, and the Journey are ended. The Dark, and Narrow Form, which made it a *Vile Body*, a *Body of Death*, is lost. The Materials are laid up in the Tabernacle.

2. The *Tabernacle* is taken into the Temple. This is that, which shall *be cloathed upon from Heaven*, *v.* 2. *If so be, that being cloathed*, (or, as it is in Greek, if having been cloathed, namely with the Tabernacle) *we shall not be found naked* (of the Tabernacle in Death,) *v.* 3. So it is explained in the words following; *For we, that are in the Tabernacle do groan being burthened: not that we should be uncloathed* (of the Tabernacle;) *but cloathed upon, that Mortality might be swallowed up of Life*; (that the Form of Mortality might be lost for ever in Immortality, and the Mortal Things continue being now become Immortal.)

When thou puttest on *Jesus Christ*, thou puttest on that Image of Grace, and Nature, in which Paradise is revived, and heightned, in which is contained all that is good, fair, and pleasant thorow the whole Creation quickned with a new Sun-shine from on high. This thou puttest on in thy Natural Man. This thou shalt never put off, after that thou hast once been cloathed with it. It is still cloathed upon with a higher and higher Glory from Heaven; until in Death the Glorified Body of *Christ* come down entirely upon it in the fulness of all its Divine Beauties.

3. The Eternal Building in Heaven, thy Glorified Person, which was hither to hid in God, with, and in the Glorified Person of thy Saviour now cometh down, cloatheth thee entirely, resteth openly upon thee, never to go off from thy Tabernacle more.

3. *Observ.* See the beautiful, and sweet manner of Dying. Death is expressed in Two Representations; 1. *A Dissolution*; 2. *A Deluge*; a *Swallowing up*.

4. *Death is a Dissolution. If our earthly house of this Tabernacle be dissolved*; *v.* 1. A Troop of everblessed Spirits united by Eternal Love into one Form of Glory make the Heavenly Body of thy Beloved. In the same Form, and yet another, they make thy Heavenly Body, and Person in the Bosom of thy Bridegroom, O Believer! These descending are by the sacred knot of this dark, and narrow Form in Nature tied together into One Mortal Person; in which they are the Shadow of themselves; and tied down to the Earth to stand their Tryal in the midst of all sorts of Temptations.

Thus they continue, till they have finished the Mystery of God, and compleated the Figure of Divine Things in their Persons here below. Then, when the set Time is come according to the Laws of that Eternal Harmony in the Nature of God, which is the Supream Love, Beauty, and Wisdom, all in One; they dye after this manner.

That Troop of glorious Spirits, which is Thy Self above come down upon Themselves, Thy Self imprisoned in their Shadow below. As the Fire of God, they touch with some Mysterious Stroak of Providence the knot of this Earthly Form; Immediately it untieth, and is dissolved. Now all these Spirits thus set free retaining the Unchangeable Unity of thy Person return, Each to Itself in the Liberty, Beauty, Joy, and Glorious Majesty of its proper Substance, and Its own, Its First Heavenly State. Yea, they are already there in their Building Eternal in the Heavens. This Eternal Building, these Heavens come down upon them, to cloath them from above; that in no one moment they may be found naked, At once they spring up out of the Earth, they come down out of Heaven, and meet, and kiss each other, and fall into One with a Wonderful Shout, a Triumphant Concurrence of all Blessed Spirits in the Perfect Freedom of all their Joys, and Glories. They fall into One, because they are One, and this One is Thy self. In an Instant, the Twinkling of an Eye, the Living Word cometh to them, the knot of Nature is dissolved, all fly, this knot, the Figure itself, the Shadow, like Doves to their Windows, like a Court to their several Mansions in the same Palace; So they fly into the Bosom of their proper Substances, where Thou art the same Person in Truth, at Liberty, and awake which thou wert in Show, in Captivity, in a Dream here below. Thou art the Unity, in which all these Spirits with the unsearchable Riches of their several Varieties ever centred, and dwelt together, as One, once shut up in darkness, and in a narrow place; but now displaying all their Beauties, unfolding all their Joys to the full. O how are the Beauties, and Pleasures of thy Death, O Saint, far beyond all those of Marriage, and of Children. How doest thou in that moment meet, and marry thy self in all the flourishing Glories, with all the warm and fresh Loves of the Divine Nature? How doest thou bring forth a Troop of Divine Spirits in thine own Form, and Person to be ever before thee, bred up, and Living with thee, rejoycing in thee, the Delight of thine Eyes, and the Jewels of thy Bosom, the pleasure of thine Embraces day by day!

This is the *first Representation of Death* by a *Dissolution.*

2. *Death* is a *Deluge*; *that Mortality might be swallowed up of Life*, 2. Cor. 5. *v.* 4. It is in *Greek*; *that the*, or, *this Mortal may be swallowed up of Life. Life* in the Abstract, in its Purity, and Perfection without any Mixture, or Allay is Immortality, Eternity, Christ, and God. As God is Light, in which there is no Darkness: so God is Light, in which there is nothing of its contrary, neither in act, nor in possibility; no Death, nor Shadow of Death. *The Mortal* is that, which is capable of Dying in a Saint with the Principles of Corruption, and Power of Death adhering to it.

See the Glory, the Might of this Glory, the Extent of it in the Death of a Saint. *Life* Itself in its own Divine Essence, as a Divine Substance, no more an Accident, in the Purity of all Its Sweetnesses, in the Perfection of all Its Powers, as it reigneth upon the Throne of Eternity, breaketh forth upon the Person of a Saint, upon all His Powers, and Parts, the lowest, the darkest, the most Mortal. As It breaketh forth, It drinketh up all together with the Shadow of Death Itself encompassing them into itself.

Mortal

Mortal Things are Shadows of Immortal; that is, Figures in the Dark. But the Darkneſs alſo is Part of the Figure. The Life of pure Nature is an Image-Life, a Shadowy Life. The Darkneſs ſwallowing up the Figure, and defacing the Shadow is a Natural Death. The Devil lurking in the Dark Part, as in His Den, from thence coming forth into the Figure is the *Life of Sin*. When a Sinner dieth, the Devil in the Darkneſs of the Shadow, Divine Wrath thorow the Devil ſwallow up the Darkneſs, Image, and all into themſelves.

But at the new Birth of a Saint, the Eternal Life, and Subſtance awakeneth itſelf in the Shadow, liveth, and weareth that Darkneſs, as a Divine Vail upon Its Beauties too bright to appear nakedly on Earth. It acteth that Figure, as a Picture with the Life in it; looking forth through, and ſpringing through it, as a Flower thorow the Lattices and the Windows. Then when the time of Harveſt, and the Singing of Birds is come; this Eternal Life drinketh up All into its own unmixt, unfading Light. Thus a Saint dieth.

As ſometimes the Sea ſendeth forth an Iſland, which after ſometimes it again ſwalloweth up: ſo is the Life, and Death of a good Man in His Mortal Part. He riſeth up like an Iſland from the unfathomable, and glorious Depths of a Divine Sea, the Sea of Eternal Life and Love. He ſtandeth rooted in this Sea, and encompaſſed with It on every ſide. So He lives. Again He ſinketh down into the Bleſſed Depths, out of which He aroſe. So He dieth.

Elijah laid His Sacrifice with a pile of wood upon the Altar. He digged Trenches round about the Altar, which he filled with Water, till it ran over. Then he called upon the Name of the God of *Iſrael*. Immediately a Fire deſcended from Heaven, which licked up all the Water, conſumed the Sacrifice with the Wood upon the Altar.

The Altar is our *Jeſus* filling the Earth, as well as the Heavens. The Saint in his Divine Part is the Sacrifice upon the Altar, in Union with *Chriſt*. The Wood is the Mortal Part of a Saint, which alſo lyeth upon the Altar of Chriſt's glorified Perſon, The low eſtate of a Saint in Fleſh with all his Sufferings, and Sorrows, all the Powers of Darkneſs, and Death, make the Trenches full of Waters round about Him: At length the Divine Sea from below, when It hath fulfilled the Days of Its Pilgrimage, and Impriſonment, calleth to Its Father above. Then in a moment the Lord *Jeſus* in His Glorified Body, as a Flame of Immortal Love and Life cometh down from Heaven upon this Saint, drinketh up at once the Sacrifice; the Wood, the Waters, and All into One Flame with itſelf. Nothing remaineth, but the Altar, and the Trenches; the Place, where they had been; the Double Image in which they had appeared; a Light-Image Beautiful, and Pleaſant in the Spirits of Light; a Dark-Image in Dark Spirits. Both theſe by degrees vaniſh into their ſeveral Elements of Light, and Darkneſs.

I have done with my *firſt Principle* in the *ſecond Part* of my preſent *uſe* which is to *ſweeten*, and *ſanctify Death* by the *Spiritual Knowledge* of our Lord, *Jeſus*,

Jesus. The *first Principle* was this: *A Saint is compleat above in the Glorified Body of Jesus Christ; while he is living, or dying here below.*

2. *Principle: The Glorified Person of our Saviour with all its Divine Fulness dwelleth Spiritually in the Natural Body of each Saint on Earth.* Our fleshly Members are the *Members of Christ* in Heaven, 1 *Corin.* 6. 15. *The riches of the Glory of this Mystery among the Gentiles, which is Christ in you, the Hope of Glory, Col.* 1. 27. As the Essential Form of a Plant with all its proportions, and perfections lieth inclosed in the Seed, which by the breaking of the Seed, displayeth itself upon it, and transfigureth the Seed; so is the Natural Body of each Believer a Seed; so is *Jesus Christ* the *Hope of Glory*, a Body of Glory to that Seed, and dwelleth inclosed in it, until the Spring of Death.

The Natural Body is called a *Body of Death*, Rom. 7. 24. *We are said to wait for the Adoption, or Sonship, the Redemption of the Body, Rom.* 8. 23. These two Bodies cannot be the same. One is a *Redeemed* Body; a Body of *Adoption*, or *Sonship*. This is, as *St. Paul* speaketh before, a Body brought forth into the *Liberty of the Glory of a Son of God.* The other is a Body of *Death*. *St. Paul* cryeth out against one: *Who shall deliver me from this Body of Death? St. Paul groaneth*, and *waiteth* for the *Redemption* of the other, as a Son of God. One is the Oppressour; the other is oppressed. One is a Grave, and Death; the other is a Divine Life, a Form of Glory, a Son of God in the Valley of the shadow of Death in the Grave.

As a Sun at night casting up its Cloud, and foretelling a fair day: so is the Death of a Saint; the Glorified Body of a Saint being one Spirit with the Glorified Body of his Beloved, casteth up the Cloud of this Natural Body, which had lien, as the Cloud of Death upon it, and now immediately maketh a fair, and Heavenly Day without the interposal, or succession of any Night. The Glorified Body of *Christ*, and his Bride are hid under this Body of Flesh, like the Sun under a thick Mist. It is long glowing, and casting glympses of itself thorow the Mist. The Mist groweth thinner. The heat and light of Divine Love, Beauty, and Joy groweth stronger. At last the Mist is quite gone, drunk up into the Sun. The Sun shineth out with open Face, and the Freedom of all its Beams.

3. *Princ. That which this Body is to a Saint here, that his Glorified Jesus is to him in Death. We take pleasure rather to be absent from the Body, and present with the Lord*, saith St. *Paul* 2 *Corin.* 5. 8. These words *Absent, Present*, relate in *Greek*, to a *Country*, a *People*. Such a presence as the Soul hath with the *Body* in Life: it hath with its *Lord*, and Love in Death. Here thy Body is the Country, the Region of thy Soul. Thy Body is the Image, into which thy Soul is formed, in which alone it appeareth to itself, or others. All thy Relations, Companions, Contentments are Images presented unto thee in this Glass, and Impressions made upon thee by the Images appearing in this Glass. All this World is nothing to thee, but as it is an Appearance rising up in thy Body, which by

vertue

vertue of the Personal Union raiseth a suitable Act of Life in thy Soul. All this World to thee is only a diversity of Forms, into which it is varied, and a diversity of Impressions made upon thy Soul by this variety of Forms.

In Death this Glass is broken, this Image vanisheth, this Country disappeareth like an Enchantment. Thy Glorified *Jesus* cometh in the place of this Body, and is a Heavenly, a Divine Body to thee. Thy Glorified Jesus is that Beautiful, Pure, and Immortal Form, in which thou appearest to thy self, and to all. Thy Relations, Companions, Entertainments are the Glorified Person of thy Jesus varied into Innumerable Forms of Love, Light, and Loveliness. All thy Motions, Affections, and Pleasures are in Sympathy, and Consort with thy *Jesus* by vertue of the mystical, and unexpressible Union between thee, and him. All acts of Life in thee, all Touches upon thy Spirit are the kisses of his Divine Mouth, Myrrhe dropping from those Lillies of the Heavenly Paradise, his Lips. This is thy Country, thy People, thy World, *the Fulness of the God-Head dwelling bodily in Christ*. Spring for joy O dying Saint! The World, thy Country, thine own People, the Body into which thou now comest, is the Fulness of all Divine Light, Divine Life, the Fulness of all Divine Forms, Loves, Joys, and Glories dwelling together with the Fulness of a Divine Harmony in the Glorified Body of thy Beloved. This hath drunk up into itself thy former Body with all its acquaintances, and entertainments, the former world with all its furniture.

PART II.

Psal. 45. 2. Thou art fairer than the Children of Men; Grace is poured forth in thy lips.; Therefore God hath blessed thee for ever.

I divided these words into three parts.

1. THe *Loveliness* of our Lord *Jesus*; *Thou art fairer than the Children of Men.*

2. The *Love* of *Christ*; The Love of this Lovely One; *Grace is poured forth in thy lips.*

3. The *Seal* of the God-Head, of a Divine Blessedness, and of Eternity upon both these, the *Loveliness*, and the *Love* in this Glorified Person of our Saviour; *Therefore God hath blessed thee for ever.*

I have finished my discourse on the *first part*. I now take in hand the *second part*. I have spoken something of the *Loveliness* of our Beloved One, as I have

by

by any Beam from his Beauties been enlightned to some glimmering vision of them, and quickned to a weak expression of that, which I have seen.

Now I am to speak of his Love, as the Grace, and Sweetness of it shall pour forth itself from his Lips into mine by a Spiritual kiss from the Mouth of this Heavenly Bridegroom.

Grace is poured forth in his Lips. The rich composition of this Heavenly-sweet Sentence is made up of three rich Materials; 1. *Grace*; 2. *Effusion*, or the pouring forth of this Grace; 3. The *Lips* of the Lord *Jesus*. These are to be explained.

1. *Grace.* This in the Language of the Scripture signifieth three Things. 1. *Grace* is *Love*. *For the Grace of God, which bringeth salvation to all Men, hath appeared*; Tit. 2. 11. *But after that the kindness, and love of God our Saviour toward Men hath appeared. Tit.* 3. 4. That which in one place the Apostle calleth *Grace*, in the other he expresseth by *kindness*, and *love*. *Grace* is *love* in its Fountain, *freest*, and *sweetest*. 2. *Grace* is *Loveliness*, or Beauty. *Prov.* 31. 30. *Favour is deceitful, and Beauty is vain. Favour* there is *Grace*. It is the same word in *Hebrew* with this in my Text. Grace is Beauty with its most powerful charms, as it toucheth every Spirit, answereth every desire, maketh all things answer it, and dance to its Musick. So the Hebrew word imports. 3. *Grace* is *Joy*, or pleasure a fair, and smiling Child begotten between these two amiable, and ever-pleasant Parents *Love*, and *Beauty*. *St. Paul* commandeth the Saints to sing, *making melody to God with Grace in their hearts*; that is, with Divine Joy kindled into a Heavenly Flame from the Love, and Loveliness of the Lord *Jesus* shining forth there unitedly, and concentring their joint Beams in the Beloved Spirit.

Thus *Grace* is all three, Love, Loveliness, and Joy; all these with a peculiar, and most eminent heightning; as the Sunshine is the Grace of a Garden, and the Flowers in it: So Grace in the sense of the Gospel is Love, Beauty, Delight with the God-Head the Sun of Spirits peculiarly, and nakedly shining in them.

But principally, and primitively *Grace* is *Love*. Then it is Loveliness, as that is the first Birth, and lively Image of Love, in which it bringeth forth itself to its own Eye, and embraces, then sporteth with it as its Spouse. It is Pleasure, as that springeth from the Union of these two, and is their mutual Life, and Perfection each in other.

Grace is a Tree, where *Love* is the *Root*, and *Sap*; *Loveliness* the fair Tree with its Body, and Branches rising out of this Root, whose Sap formeth itself into this Beautiful Figure. *Joy* is the Fruit, into which the sweet Sap of Love from its Root, thorow the Body, and Branches of its shining Beauties digesteth itself unto a perfect, admirable, and Divine Maturity to be the Food, and Feast of all Lives, all Spirits in Time, and Eternity. It is Love smiling in the face of every Beauty, which is the Grace of it, as the Water, and Sparklings of Light

in

in a Diamond are the Grace of that. It is the Tast, and Rellish of Love in every Joy, is as the Wine, which is the Grace of the Feast.

It is the *Love* of *Jesus Christ* at its height, which is the Grace intended here.

2. The *Effusion*, or *Pouring forth* of this *Grace* is next to be opened. Three, things are signified in this Effusion, 1. A *Fulness* of Grace is discovered. Natural Agents work to the utmost of their Power. God is in nothing so Natural, as in His Love. His work of wrath is his strange work, præternatural to Him, and a Disguise upon Him. Love is His Right Hand; the Sheep are set at his Right Hand. Love flows forth from the Person of the Father unveiled, & naked, as Light from the Sun; Millions of fresh Beams each moment from each point. 2. Freedom of Grace is manifested in Its Pouring forth itself. It is its own First Mover. It puts itself into Motion. It is a fluid thing. It cannot contain itself within its own Bound, the Heart of God. It is ever pouring forth itself all abroad into every Heart. Divine Love is the most universal and importunate Beggar. It cometh to the door of every Spirit. It Knocketh. It presseth in. 3. A *Force* of Love putteth forth itself in this Expression. When the Rain cometh with a Tempest, and falleth with a great force, we say; It poureth down. Love from above stormeth Hearts most fortified against it. It rusheth forth like a mighty flood. If any banks, or dams oppose it, it riseth so much the higher, it gathereth so much the more strength, till it bear down all before it, carry away all with it, overflow all, swallow up all into itself, that all things become One Sea of Love.

3 The *Lips* of *Christ* into which this Grace is poured forth, may be understood four ways. 1. The Word of the Scriptures, and the Outward Ministery are the *Lips* of *Christ*, in which Grace is poured forth. All the Scriptures are Love-letters from *Christ* in Heaven; all the Ministeries of the Gospel are Love-Embassages, Love-tokens. 2. All Outward Providences, all Inward Discoveries of the Lord *Jesus* are His *Lips*, with which He kisseth us, and poureth forth the Divine Sweetness, and Strength of His Love into our Spirits; 3. The *Spirit* Himself is the Mouth, and Lips of the Heavenly Bridegroom. By this He uniteth Himself most immediately to us in the closest, and Divinest Love-union. By this He transmitteth Himself, and His Love most warmly into us. 4. The naked Person of *Christ* in Glory is to be understood by these *Lips*. The *Holy Ghost* composeth this Psalm, as a Marriage-song to celebrate the Union, State, and Joys of the Heavenly Bridegroom, and Bride in the Resurrection, and Ascension of our Blessed Lord. Here the Person of our Beloved is all a Divine Mouth, with which He breatheth forth all the Sweetnesses of His glorious Nature, and Love, as He sucketh in ours. It is all One Divine Eye from which He poureth forth upon us continual Floods of Light, Beauty, and Grace; by which also He taketh us in continually in all Blessed Forms of an Immortal Loveliness, and Love; Thus we see our selves continually in Him; He seeth Himself continually in us; Eye to Eye, each a Living Glass of glorious Love to the other.

The *Spirit*, and the Lord *Jesus* in Glory are *Both One*. A Bee in a Garden sitteth upon every flower, and plant, sucking the vertue forth from it. This it formeth into One Sweetness in itself, which is Honey. Full of this Honey it flyeth to its Hive, and there layeth up its pleasant Treasures. So this Spirit resteth upon every Excellency in the God-Head, every Life, and Image of things in the Creature. It extracteth the several virtues from all. It turneth all within itself into One Divine, and unexpressible Sweetness, which is Love. With this Treasure of Love it maketh haste to some broken, and forlorn Heart: There in this Heart, in thine Heart, if thou wilt believe, that thou mayest tast, and see it, it layeth down its precious Burthen, it layeth up the inestimable Riches of glorious Grace.

We read in the building of the Temple that there was a great Sea of Brass, which stood upon twelve Oxen the figures of the Cherubims. Our Saviour's glorified Person is a vast Sea of Love. All the Angels of God support this Sea, serve this Love. The God-Head itself in a bright, and sweet flood of Love is poured abroad in this Sea, in this Bosom, and Person. Here every Believing Soul batheth itself in, and taketh its Fill of Loves.

Doct. The Doctrine which I intend to insist upon according to the Grace of God given unto me is this. *The Love of God is poured forth in the Glorified Person of our Lord Jesus. Thy Name is an Ointment poured forth, Cant.* 1. 2. The *Name* of our Beloved, which His Spouse Knoweth Him by, and calleth Him by, is That *Name above every Name* in this World, or the World of Angels, which the Father hath given Him at His Resurrection, and Ascension; *Ephes.* 1. 21. This *Name* is His Person itself in Glory, which is the onely Expression of itself. This is an *Ointment poured forth*. O Blessed Ointment of Divine Love, which hath all the Cordial Spices, and Sweets of the God-Head itself in it, which perfumeth all things thorow Heaven, and Earth; which maketh all Faces to shine with a Divine Lustre, and all Hearts to spring with a Divine Joy! This costly Ointment was before shut up, and kept in an Alabaster Box, in the Glorious Secret of the Father's Bosom. But now that Box is broken in the Death of our King. That Bosom is opened in His Resurrection. That sweet Treasure of all Life, and Delight, the Eternal Love of the Father is poured forth at the Root of the Creation, upon the Head of every Creature in the Glorified Person of *Jesus Christ*. Its sweet Savour is gone forth into the Nostrils of every Spirit, to revive it, and allure it to its Everlasting Embraces.

1 *John* 5. 11. *This is the Record*; (namely of God Himself,) *that God hath given us Eternal Life, and this Life is in His Son. Eternity* is defined to be The Possession of all Good at once, and in One. There are Three things, which go to make up Eternity 1. A *Perfection of Excellency*. 2. A *Collection of all Excellencies* 3. A *Station* of all these with their several Distinctions in One Top-point of Spirituality above all Division, or Change. Love is the Union of Lovely Things. The most Perfect Love is the most Perfect Union, which

bindeth

bindeth up all Lovelinesses in their several Perfections into the streightest Unity. Eternal Life then is the Life of Love in its Purity, and Perfection. Eternity is Love itself; the firmest, and Fullest Union of all Graces, and Graceful Things in the height of Glory, and the height of Unity.

This Eternal Life, this Eternal Love; this Life of Love, which is the Life of Eternity is diffused, is given to us by the Father in the Glorified Person of *Christ*. This is the Glorifying of His Person, the Pouring forth of this Love, which is the Gold of the Temple, the Glory of Eternity, in Him, as in a Common Person, in which the whole Creation lyeth.

Before I leave this Scripture, which I have brought for the Proof of my Doctrine; ye who hear, and ye who read, stand still a while, and together with me gaze upon, admire the riches of the glory of the *Grace*, and Love of God in the Gospel. *This*, saith *St. John*, *is the Record, that He hath given us Eternal Life, and this Life is in His Son.* You have here the whole Substance of the Gospel, the Record of God, the Glad Tydings from Heaven summ'd up. It is *Love*. This Love lyeth in Three Parts; 1. *Free Grace* in these words, *God hath given us.* 2. The *Gift* of Free Grace, *Eternal Life*. You have heard already, that the Eternity, the Perfection, and Crown of Life is Love. 3. The Lovely *Seat* of this Gift; *and this Life*, this Love, *is in His Son.*

Behold, how the *Love* of the Gospel is no other, than the *Divine Nature*, and the 3 *Parts* of this *Love* the 3 *Persons* in that *Divine Nature*.

1, *Free Grace* is the *Fountain* of Love, the Fountain of the God-Head, the *Father* the *Giver*.

2. The *Gift* is the Holy Spirit, Love itself, the Eternity of Life, and Love, the Collection of all Loves and Lives in Eternity, the Gathering together of all the pure, and sweet Waters of Love, and Life into One Place.

3. The *Seat* of this Gift; the *Son*. The Person of our Bridegroom is that vast, bright, and Beautiful Deep prepared, as a place for those pleasant Waters, those Treasures of Love.

How are the Windows of the God-Head here set wide open to pour down Showers of Love! How are the great Deeps of the God-Head broken up to send forth Floods of Love! What a Blessed Deluge of Love is here, enough to drown ten thousand Worlds of Sins, and Souls after a Lovely manner; so that the Sins shall never live, nor appear more; the Souls shall never dye, nor be at all darkened any more!

Come now ye unbelieving Hearts; be subdued to the Faith of the Gospel by the Strength of this Love. Come ye hard Hearts; bee softned by the Sweetness of this Love. Come ye unclean Hearts; be refined, be Spiritualised, be raised above Sense, Flesh, by the Purity of this Love. All the Strength, all the Sweetness, all the Purity, and Pure Beauties of the Divine Nature are concurrent in this Love. The Three Glorious Persons in the Trinity are no other, than Love itself in so many Forms of Beauty, and Blessedness acting those Heavenly Parts, which may make all the Joys, and Glories of Love compleat in them, and in you.

I shall prosecute my *Doctrine* under *three Heads.*

1. The *Nature* of Divine Love. 2. The *Effusion*, or pouring forth of this Love. 3. The Person of our Lord *Jesus*, as this Love is poured forth into him.

1. *Head.* The *Nature* of Divine Love. I shall endeavour to explain this to you by *three Descriptions.*

1. *Descript.* Divine Love is a *Union* between God, as a Lover, and the Soul, as his Love, 1 *Cor.* 6. 16, 17. *It is said, they two shall be one Flesh. But he that is joyned to the Lord is one Spirit.* Marriage is the Solemnity, Festival, and Crown of Love. The Marriage-Union is the perfection of the Love-Union. The Spirit speaketh here of a Marriage in the Flesh, as a Figure, and Foil only; but of the Marriage in the Spirit as Love-Union in its Lustre, and its Life.

This *Love-Union* hath *three Parts.*

1. There is a *Unity*, which is the ground of Love. All Love springeth from this Divine Seed sown throughout all things; a Primitive, and Original Unity.

2. There is a *Distinction* in the Unity, which is the Life of Love. This maketh the Lovers. The Unity springeth up within itself into a Distinct, and Beautiful Image of itself, that it may be both its Lover, and its Love.

3. There is a *Union* of these two, the Original, and its own Life-Image, as they stand distinct in the Unity. This is Love consummate. This is the Marriage-bed of Divine Love, ever flourishing and fruitful. Here it multiplieth itself into innumerable Loves, Beauties, and Joys, which flow endlesly fresh every moment out of this sacred Fountain.

Thus Love is the Circle of Eternity, hath its beginning in itself, springeth up out of itself, returneth again into itself without beginning or end.

Thus in Heavenly Love first one is made two, then two are made one again, So is it all four in one, a Birth, a Marriage, a Death, a Resurrection in a continual Circle; while they are ever bringing forth one another; dying into each other; rising again one out of the other; and in all united. This is the Divine sport, or play of Spiritual Love.

You shall see these *three parts* of the Heavenly Love-union in three *Images*; in *Heaven*; in *Paradise*; in the *Soul.*

1. *Love-Union* in *Heaven.* The *first Person* in the Trinity is the God-Head in the *Unity*, which is the Center, and Spring of all Love. The *Second Person* is the God-Head distinguishing itself into a variety of Persons in the Unity. The God-Head in the glorious, and deep center of its Unity springeth up into an express Image of itself, shining forth from the Unity, and shining back upon it in the brightness of all its own Glories within its own Divine deep,

and Center. This is to the Father perfectly *Himself, his Son,* and *his Spouse,* all in one. The *Spirit* is the *Third Person.* This is the *Union* of the other two. Divines therefore peculiarly appropriate the name of *Love* to this Person. The manner of his Production is express'd by a *Procession* from the Father, and the Son joyntly, by way of breathing, as the sweets of two Flowers mingling in the same Air, or as the Divine Kiss of two Spirits, by which they breath forth themselves each into other, and become two Spirits in one.

This is the *first Image* of the *Love-Union* in Heaven; where the Mystery of the Trinity is the high, and Holy Mystery of Love in its Original. Here first of all one is made two, and those two are made one again.

2. *Love-Union* in *Paradise. Adam,* and *Eve* together with the race of *all Living,* to which *Eve* was Mother, stood at first in *Adam,* all in one. *Male, and Female made He him, Gen.* 1. *v.* This was Humane Nature in its Unity, the figure of the Divine Unity, the Father in the Trinity. *Then Eve* was taken out of *Adam.* The Unity was distinguished into two Persons, and Sexes within itself. For *Adam* saith of *Eve* after the distinction; *This is Flesh of my Flesh, and Bone of my Bone.* The Unity of the Nature continued in the two Sexes. Now the Woman was the *Image,* and the *Glory* of the Man in Paradise, as the Son is the *Image* of the Father, and the Brightness of his Glory in Heaven. Now there is no Solitude in the Unity, which maketh Paradise a Wilderness, the Unity is the true Paradise within itself springing up into variety, then marrying itself to it, and so flourishing from this Union with all manner of Beautiful, and pleasant Fruits. By this Birth and Distinction in the Unity, *Adam* and *Eve* are capable of enjoying themselves each in other, and of multiplying themselves. *Thirdly, Eve* is brought to *Adam* again, and these *two* are made *one Flesh.* This is the making of *two one* again, which were first made *two* of *one.* This Unity in the Distinction, and Distinction in the Unity is that Marriage in Paradise, which is the Type of that Incomprehensible Marriage above all Heavens, which is the Third Person in the Trinity. In him the Father, and the Son spend Eternity in mutual Embraces, and multiply themselves into an Infiniteness of Blessed Lives, Blessed Loves.

You that are Married Persons, see your selves in this double Glass of Paradise, and the Trinity. By these Glasses dress your selves in your Loveliness, and Loves one for another. *St. Paul* saith, that *Marriage is Honourable among all, or in all things.*

A Type hath a double Honour; the Figure, which is Shadowy, the Truth, which is a substantial Glory. Husbands, and Wives preserve the Honour of your state at least in the shadowy part. Bear the Figure of the Ever-glorious Trinity, whose Type you are, by a moral Beauty, Truth, Purity, Sweetness, which are the Gold, and precious Mettal in the Ring of this Love-union. This will make Marriage an Earthly Paradise. But rest not in this. You will find a Serpent here, that will quickly poyson all your Sweets, and change your

Flowers

Flowers into Thorns; if you pass not thorow the Earthly into the Heavenly Paradise. Then you wear the Marriage-Crown in Truth, when that Spirit, which is the Band of Love between the Father, and the Son, is the Eternal Band of Divine Love between you also; when you also make your Marriage-Bed in the Bosom of the *Holy Ghost*.

What Joys, what an Immortal Off-spring is born of those Lovers, where the Love-fellowship of these below, and the sacred Love-fellowship of the Blessed Trinity above descend, and ascend one into another, where they mingle themselves Universally?

3. *Love-Union* in the *Soul, Joh. 3. 6. That which is born of the Spirit, is Spirit*

The Divine Being, Life, and Form of the Soul, in which it is a Spirit, lie first wrapt up in the Unity of the Eternal Spirit its Heavenly Mother above.

The Eternal Spirit out of this Love-Center, and within the Love-Circle of its own Unity by the New-birth in the Soul bringeth forth at once a Daughter-Spirit, a Sister, and Spouse to itself.

This Divine Spirit, like the Paradisical *Eve*, so soon as it is born of its Heavenly *Adam*, is brought to him again, and *they Two are made one Spirit*, *1 Cor. 6. 17*. As a New-born Babe, so soon as it is sprung out of the Womb, seeketh the Breast of the Mother, that it may suck forth a continued stream of Life from the Fountain of its Life: so is it in the Spiritual Birth. So soon, as the New-born Spirit ariseth up out of this Unity, which is the Womb of the God-Head; it is immediately received into the Arms of this Unity; it desireth after, it hunteth for, it returneth to, it fastneth upon this Unity, which is the Breast of the God-Head. By this it draweth in the sincere, and pure Milk of the living Word; it taketh in by plentiful streams the Light, Life, Glory, Substance of the Divine Nature to grow by them. O you, who indeed are born of this Unity, lie continually in the Bosom of it, hang continually upon this Breast. But thus, as in the Eternal Generation in Heaven; as in the Creation in Paradise; as in the Regeneration, which is the opening of Paradise, and Heaven both a second time in the Soul; all are *Love-Births, Love-Unions*. The Unity distinguisheth itself within itself into another self, which is yet still the same, that there may be a variety in the Unity without the breach of the Unity. The Virgin above bringeth forth a Son, which is also her Lord, and continueth a Virgin still. The Beautiful variety, which is the Effulgency of the Unity, rejoyneth itself again to it, and still remaineth a variety in its distinction from it. Thus the Love-Marriage is every where solemnized, and every where maketh a Paradise, and a Heaven above, and below. This is the *first Description* of Divine Love, a Divine Union, where one Glorious Spirit is made two, and these two make themselves one again.

Use. Learn from the Beauty, and Sweetness of Divine Love, the Evil of this Worlds Love by their contrariety to it. *Ye Adulterers, and Adulteresses,*

know

Know ye not, that the Friendship of this World is Enmity to the Father. Who therefore is this World's Friend. is an Enemy to God: James. 4. 4. See the Evil of this World's Love in 3. *Steps.*

1. *Step.* By loving this World you ſeparate your ſelves from the Love of God. You eſtrange your ſelves from all true Joy, Peace, and Reſt. For theſe are the Attendants, and Companions of Divine Love.

Cant. 3.7,8. You read of *Solomon's Bed. which hath fourſcore valiant men of the valiant men of Iſrael round about it, with their ſwords girt upon their thigh for the fear of the night.* How great, how Divine is the Sweetneſs, the Safety, the Security of Spiritual Love. He, that abideth in this Love enjoyeth an Uninterrupted Reſt, and untroubled pleaſures, in a Night of the greateſt Darkneſs, Dangers, Tumults, and Storms. He hath ever round about Him a Troop of Holy Angels for his Guard, armed with the Glorious Power of the Spirit. This is the Sword upon their Thigh. In the midſt of theſe he lyeth upon a Royal Marriage-bed. Here he is encircled with the Spiritual Embraces of King *Solomon,* the Lord Jeſus in Glory, the King of all Peace, Perfections, and Pleaſures, This is the Love of God, that Love, by which God, and the Soul live, and dwell together in One Spirit.

You now, who prefer the blackneſs of darkneſs before the Beauty of *Chriſt's* Face, reſtleſs cares, endleſs fears, continual dangers, and deaths before the Reſt, and Joys of *Chriſt's* boſom, love this world, and let the love of *Jeſus Chriſt* go.

2. *Step.* By the Love of this World you make your ſelves Adulterers with a Witch, and a Common Whore. Poor Soul! thou forſakeſt the Arms of thine own Love, thy Loving Roe, and pleaſant Hind, the Wife of thy Youth, of Eternal Youth, the Heavenly Image in the Perſon of the Lord *Jeſus.* Thou giveſt thy ſelf up to the Embraces of the ſtrange Woman, the Strumpet, this World the Fleſhly Image of Things.

The Love of your Saviour is all Truth, Purity, Peace, Immortality. The Love of this World beginneth in Deceit, hath its Power in Enchantments, its Effect Pollutions, its End Deſtruction. She giveth thee Drink indeed in a Golden Cup. But ſhe maketh thee to drink in firſt a Wine of Sorceries, then of Fornications. Her End is to have her Fleſh burnt with Fire; and into the ſame bed of flames will God caſt all thoſe, that commit fornication with her.

3. *Step.* By loving this world thou makeſt thy ſelf an Adultereſs with the Devil. This World, as it ſtealeth thine Heart from God is a Compoſure of Lyes. The Devil, who is the Father of Lyes, maketh thy Soul his Strumpet, upon which he begetteth theſe falſe Forms of things. Thou breedeſt theſe young Devils upon thy Knee, and as thou ſporteſt thy ſelf with them, thou ſuckeſt in by their Kiſſes the poyſon, and fire of Hell into all thy veins.

The Devil firſt wooes thee in a Counterfeit ſhape of falſe Beauty, Glory, Power, Joys. When he hath gained thee, he breaketh forth upon thee in his own ſhape of endleſs Terror, and Horrours.

There

There is nothing truer, than that the Love of this World is a Spiritual Adultery with the Devil, and the Head of all Adulteries, of all Defilements. There is nothing more sure, than that Carnal Adultery in all the degrees of it, the Similitude of this, most powerfully calleth up into us, and upon us the Spirit of this World, the Prince of Darkness, the Devil with all His Dark, Deforming, and Destroying Powers. O ye sons, and Daughters of men, who dwell in the midst of the snares, and nets of this great, painted Adulteress, be aware of your danger. Abide in your first Principle your Root, your first Husband, the Eternal Love of the Father in *Christ*. Abide in your own Habitation, the Bosom of your own Bride, the Eternal Beauty, the Essential, and Immortal Image of the God-Head in *Christ*. These Loves shall be a Fountain of Life to you above to preserve you from the snares of Death below.

4. *Step*. By the Love of this World you turn the Love of God into Wrath, and fury *If you be the Friends of this World, you are the Enemies of God*; saith St. *James*. Why do you provoke the Love of God? Will you contend with Almighty Love? Are you greater, than that? Love is the Right Hand of God's Strength; His God-Head lieth in His *Love*. *God is Love*. This Love is strong, as Death; cruel, as the Grave. What art thou, O Worm, to stand before it, to bear its rage? O choose rather to lye down, as a Bride, in these everlasting Burnings, and Devouring Fires of Love to be cherished, changed refined, and glorified by their tender, and divine Embraces; than to set thy self, as Bryars, and Thorns against them, to be consumed by them.

Thus I have done with the First Description of Divine Love; A Union between God, and the Soul, as the Beloved, and His Love in One Spirit of Purity, Immortality, Joy, and Glory.

2 Descrip. *The Love of God is the Will of God.*

This is a Universal Truth that in every Spirit *Love*, and the *Will* are *One*. This appeareth in their *Nature*, their *Object*, their *Operation*.

1, The *Nature* of the *Will*, and *Love* are One. The Will is defined to be the *Inclination* of the Spirit as it tendeth, and bendeth itself to this or that, this way, or that way. *Love* is stiled The *Weight* of the Soul. As heavy things by their Weight; so Souls by their *Love* are carried to their proper Center.

2. The *Object* of the *Will*, and of *Love* is the same. It is a rule, that The Powers, and Habits in Spirits are distinguished by their Objects. Every Principle, and Faculty is the Object in its Seed. The Object is the Form, and Perfection of the Principle. The Object of the Will is *Goodness Appearing*. The Object of Love is *Loveliness*. Loveliness, and Goodness both consist in Suitableness, which hath its Ground in Unity. If there be any Difference between Goodness, and Loveliness, it is this, that as the Flower of Light is the Sun-shine; and as *Jesus Christ* is the Effulgency, the Shine of the God-Head, the Brightness of the Glory of God; so Loveliness, or Beauty is Goodness shining out to attract all Hearts to it. Thus *Loveliness* the Object of Love, and *Goodness Appearing* the Object of the Will agree entirely in One.

3. All

3. All their *Operations* are the ſame. The Affections, and Paſſions are the Motions of the Will; All theſe are Love's Summer, or Winter; Love in the Seed is Deſire. Love budding, and bloſſoming is Hope, Love in the ripe Fruit is Joy. Anger, Fear, Grief, and Hatred are Love in its Oppoſition to its Enemy, which is Enmity alone; Love flying from, or contending with that, which ſtandeth in its way to, or would rob it of its Beloved Object.

But this is ſpoken in General onely concerning the *Will*, and *Love*.

In Particular let us ſee, how the *Divine Will*, and the *Divine Love* appear to be the ſame in the Holy Scriptures. The Will of God is diſtinguiſhed by Divines into the *Revealed*, and the *Secret* Will of God. One is the Divine Will in *Outward Signs* onely, The Other is the Good-Pleaſure of God in His Heart, and in Eternity.

1. The *Revealed Will* of God is *Love*, 1. *Tim.* 2. *v.* 1. &c. In the *firſt v.* of this *Chapter* you have a Divine *Rule*; that *All* manner of Prayers, be made for *All Men*. This Rule is preſſed by a particular Application of it to *Kings*, and *all in Authority*; *v.* 2. *All* in Authority; what ever their Perſons are, or their Right, *v.* 3. The *Reaſon* of this Rule is laid down. *For this is Good, and Acceptable to God our Saviour.* This *Univerſal Love* wound up to the Higheſt ſtrain of Spirituality, and Divinity in us is a Vein of the Supreme, and Divine Good let forth from the Heart of God, where the Fountain of Good is, and circling thorow our Hearts into his Heart again by Prayer. Therefore is it *acceptable to God*. Our Wills are never ſo in tune to the Divine Will, and in conſort with it, as when the Spiritual motions of our Hearts in the Boſom of the Father are ſtrains of Univerſal Love.

The *Root* of this Reaſon is diſcovered. *v.* 4. *God will have all Men to be ſaved, and come to the knowledge of the Truth. Love* is ſaid to conſiſt in this; *To Will good to any one.* If this be love to Will good to any; Then is it the beſt, and higheſt love to Will the beſt, and higheſt good. Behold then! The *revealed Will* of God is a *Revelation of love* to the height. *God will have all Men to be ſaved.* God willeth the higheſt end, which is the beſt good to the loweſt, and worſt of Men, to *all* Men. That this end may not fail, he alſo willeth the means to the end; that *all Men ſhould come to the knowledge of the Truth.*

The *Ground*, in which this *root* of love liveth, is the *Unity* of *God*, and *Chriſt*. *For there is one God and one Mediatour between God, and Man, the Man Chriſt Jeſus.* The higheſt Unity Is the largeſt Univerſality. It is in Spirits, as in theſe Heavens, which we ſee, the higheſt are the wideſt. All beneath them lie in their Boſoms. The whole nature of things is love. For the Divine Nature the Original is love. This love throughout the whole nature of things is as a Pyramid made up by degrees of different Unions, till it end in the higheſt, and moſt indiviſible point of Unity.

The Unity of God is that Fountain of love, out of which all things proceed. The ſecret force of this Unity is that ſtream of love, which runneth

 thorow

thorow the Heart, and Veins of Every Creature in the Person of *Christ*, whic is the golden Pipe with its several branches laid thorow the whole Creatio from the Beginning to the End. *There is one God, and one Mediator betwee God and Man, the Man Christ Jesus.*

Thus the *revealed Will* of God is *love*.

2. The *secret Will* of God is *love. Fury is not in me. Who would set th bryars, and thorns in Battel aray against me? I would go thorow them, I would con sume them.* Wrath is not *in* God. It is without him only, as a Cloud upon the Sun The heart of God is Love. Wrath is but the work of his Hand, and that hi *strange Work*, like nothing within, a disguise only. The *Face* of God, and th proper light of it is love. Wrath is vizor, a mist before his Face, and no more

Fury in God is love by the opposition heightned to a flame to consume al vanity, and enmity, that setteth itself before it, or against it.

O that I had a voice powerful enough to reach all the Souls wandring tho row the whole Creation, and to call them together, to take this Cup of Salva tion into the hand of their Faith, to set it to the mouth of their Faith, an drink deeply of it!. As the Wine of this Cup goeth down into your Spirits you will find it to go down right. How sweetly, and how fully will it touch satisfy, and fill every faculty, every desire, every Seed of life with its prope good. The Cup of Salvation, which I hold forth to you is this Divine Truth the Sum of the Gospel Preached by Angels in their Songs at the Birth of ou Jesus; *The Will of God is love.*

Hear this, and believe it, O ye Souls, the Inclination of God, the supream Spirit, and Fountain of Spirits is to you. The tendency, and the bent of th Divine Nature is to make your joys full by the possession of all good in it self; and to fulfil his own joys in you. For the Will is the Inclination of eve ry Spirit; and the Will of God is love. Hear this, and believe it, O ye Souls God is carried with the whole weight of his God-Head to you, as to his Cen ter, to rest eternally in you, and to rejoyce over you. For love is the weigh of every Spirit, and the Will of God is love. The. Will of God in th Freedom, Absoluteness, Infiniteness of it is love.

Now I live, saith *St. Paul, if ye stand fast in the Faith*, 1 Thes. 3. 8. St *Paul* speaketh not this in his own Spirit, but in the Spirit of God. God in hi own Spirit speaketh it with a greater force, and fuller sense to every one o you, if you believe me, and take in my love, which is my life, now have I a new Love, a new Life, a new Joy, and Heaven in you. As you grow in thi Faith, my Life, and Joy increaseth in you. If you stand fast in it, my Joy, and Glory is as firm in your hearts, as in Heaven itself.

If you will believe all the Declarations of God from Heaven; the revea led Will of God is Love. If you have any Inward, and Divine Touch of the secret Will of God; all the breathings of his Heart are Love. O take in the Love of God, that his Love may become a Divine, Immortal Seed of al Love, and Loveliness in you.

Bu

But now let us hearken to the groans of some poor ones among these multitudes of Souls, who parched and burnt up with their Sins, Sorrows, who benighted in the Darkness of their unbeleief; yet among all these Millions of streams of Love, which flow forth upon their Spirits from the heart of God, among thoseMillions of Beams of Love, which fall from the Eye of God upon their hearts dare not take in any one. No, though they thirst for DivineLove more than for Life,yet shut up their Spirits against all Approaches, orAppearances of it, as delusions.

Obj. These Souls sigh forth this great *Objection* against the Love of God: You say, the Will of God is love; the object of every Will is some good; the object of all love is some loveliness. What loveliness can there be in me to draw the heart of God to me, to be in love with me, who am only loathsom by my lusts,and deformed by my passions? What good can be found in me to attract the Divine Will to center itself in me by love, when no good, but all evil dwelleth in me?

Answ. 1. Dear Soul, who thus reasonest for thine own sufferings against the love of God, I shall give thee three Answers in the behalf, and in the name of Divine love. O that love itself from the heart of God would drop its Sweetness from its own mouth upon thee, and seal it upon thy Spirit, while I am speaking for it to thee!

First, Thou wert made in the *Image*, and *Likeness* of God, *Gen.* 1. All *Loveliness* consisteth in *Suitableness*; *Suitableness* in *Similitude*, and Likeness. There is nothing, which draweth Hearts and Love,which attracteth all things so powerfully, as Similitude doth. Similitude is a kind of Unity, and Likeness Oneness. Similitude is described to be one Form in two matters, or subjects. Let this, O drooping Soul; raise thee to look upward to that Heaven of Eternal Love, which ever holdeth thee in its Embraces, and shineth round about thee. The Divine Image, and Similitude is thy proper Person, thine Nature, thine Essence, it lyeth indeed captivated in chains of Darkness, dishonoured, and defiled by thy lusts, wounded, and mangled by thy passions, oppressed with guilt, slain by unbelief in thee. Yet this Divine Image is in thee. It is thy *true self* according to the first Creation.

Dost thou ask now, what that good is, which attracteth the Divine Will to thee by the love of it? God is in love with his own *Likeness* in thee. He seeketh his own Birth, His Spouse in thee, sprung forth from himself to be his Joy in the midst of all the Creatures, to be Queen, where ever he is King in the whole Creation. This Divine Image in thee, this thy Divine self is that Pearl in the Field, for which God giveth himself, that he may purchase the Fields. This is that good, to which the heart of God is carried with all its weight of love, to redeem it, to revive it, to raise it out of the Dust, that it may shine again in his Glory, and sing of his loves.

The Lord *Jesus* telleth us, *Mat.* 24. 28. *Where the Carkass is, there the*

Eagles will be gathered together. The Scriptures represent the Spirit of God in its low estate, in the Flesh of *Christ*, and his Members by a *Dove*, a *Groaning Dove.* The *Dove* is in the clefts of the Rock, and the holes of the Stairs, *Cant.* 2. The Spirit descended upon Jesus at his Baptism before his Temptations in the form of a *Dove*.

The Spirit in his Heavenly strength, and Glory is set forth by an *Eagle.* *I have born them upon Eagles Wings*, saith God. *They shall mount up on high like an Eagle*; saith the Prophet *Esay*. The *Spirit* is often expressed in the plural number, because he is that Unity, which is the Spring, the Center, the Circle, and Band of all blessed Spirits. He hath in himself an endless variety of Spiritual Glories, which are all glorious Spirits in him, as he is, and one with him. whithersoever his Will is to go, they all go together with him. He is therefore expressed by *seven Lamps*, *seven Spirits*, and *Eagles* here. Where the Carcass is, *there the Eagles will be gathered together* The end of all this is to make way for the letting in of a flood of Heavenly Balsom, of Divine love upon every heart, upon the broken heart, to heal it; upon the hardest heart to soften it.

Eagles from afar, and from on high are drawn to slaughter'd Carcasses, as to their proper Prey So when the Divine Image lyeth in thee as a loathsome Carcass at the bottom of a dark and deep Dungeon, now is it the most proper Bait, and most powerful Attractive of Divine love. Now the Lord Jesus, the Eternal Spirit with all the Troop of Spiritual Powers, and Glories resort to this Carcass, descend upon it, hunger after it. Now they feed, and feast upon it, until they have eaten it up, until they have converted it into one pure nature, and glorious Spirit with themselves.

When *Ignatius* was to be devoured by wild Beasts; *now* saith he, *shall the Teeth of the Lyons grind me into fine Flower, to make fine Manchet of me for the Table of God.* So do thou say concerning all thy Sufferings within, and without: These are the Divine Teeth of the Spirit of Heavenly love. Now doth my God feed upon me. If my God feed upon me, if he nourish, and enlarge his own Life, Joys, and Glory by me, then shall he also change me, take me up into himself, diffuse his own Life, Joys, and Glory into me.

This is the *first Answer*.

Ans. 2. Dear Soul, whoever, whatever thou art, thou art the *Off-spring of God. St. Paul* citeth this from a Poet, confirmeth it by a Divine Testimony, applyeth it Universally to *all*, maketh it the ground of Evangelical Truths, and Loves; *Acts* 17. 28. *As some of your own Poets have said*; *We are his Off-spring.*

St. Paul hath something very like this, *Ephes.* 3. 9. *The Gospel was hid in God from the Foundation of the World, who made all things by Jesus Christ.* God had the love of the Gospel in his Heart, and sowed it as a secret Seed in the Foundations of the whole Creation, when he made all things by *Jesus*

Christ.

Christ. Jesus Christ is the Seed of Nature, as well as of Grace, and so lyeth hid in the Bosom of every Creature, as the true Pearl in the Field. That Divine Image, of which we spake before, was the similitude only, the Mother of Pearl; This is the Substance, the Pearl itself. In the Off-spring of God is the Seed of God. Where the Seed of God is, there is God himself in the Vertue, Power, and fulness of his Divine Nature. For so the Seed of every Plant hath that Plant Virtually, and Spiritually in it.

Be now no more unbelieving; but believe. Believe the love, which God hath to thee. Believe, that all the Inclinations of the Divine Will are to thee; that the Eye, and heart of God are turned toward thee in every place, fixt upon thee with all that intention, and force of Sweetness in the Divine Nature. For why? He is drawn irresistibly to his own Seed, his own Son, his own self in thee. *Thou art his Off-spring.*

When *Micah* was reproved for crying after the Company, he replied: *Ye have carried away my Gods, and ye say; why criest thou after us?*

No more now doubt, and say; why should the most high God with an Eye of love from Heaven, thus follow me into every state of life, into all the corners of my heart? Why should he by a voice of love from Heaven in the Word, in Providences, in the motions of his Spirit thus cry, and call after me? Thou hast his Seed, his Son, himself in thee.

Do thou answer him again, and say: Thou seekest thy self, thy Seed, thy Sheep crucified, buried, lost in me. O seek, and find it; find it, and take it up into thine Arms; keep it in thine Arms, till thou bring it home to its own self, to its lost Life, Joys, and Glories again. But I also seek my Life, my Original, my true self hid with Christ in thee in the brightness of thy Glory. O take thy crucified self in me home to thee into thy Bosom. O give me my Glorified self with thee home to me into my Bosom. Thus much for the *second Answer.*

Ans. 3. Still the wounded Spirit sigheth, and saith: Can God take pleasure in any thing common, or unclean? Dear Souls, ever dear to the Divine Will, when you have a sense of Sin or, Love; and when you have none, understand the Mystery of the Divine Will in the order, and method of Divine love. When you understand this, you will have a deep, and kindly sense of Sin indeed, but so, as to have a righter, and sweeter sense of love by it.

There is a *Twofold Love* in God; a *Love of Complacency*, or Delight; a *Love* of *Benevolence*, or good Will. The *first* is that, by which he taketh pleasure in thee, as a Bridegroom in his beautiful Bride. The second is that, by which his Will is set on work to make thee beautiful, and a Bride to himself. The love of Complacency is the first, and the last love. The love of benevolence is a middle-love, which ariseth out of this, and endeth in it; as Springs, and Rivers come from the Sea, and run into it.

This is the *Order* of Divine love. *First* thou art beloved with a love of

Com-

Complacency from Eternity, as thou art seen in that Glass of Eternity, the Word, the Lord *Jesus*. *Secondly*, Thou art for this love's sake beloved with a love of benevolence in time in thine own Person, by which love, God willeth all good to thee, and worketh all good in thee. *Lastly*, Thou art beloved with a love of Complacency to Eternity in thine own Person, as thou art decked with all the Ornaments of the Divine Nature. This is the *order* of Divine love. Its Musick is made up of these *three Parts*.

1. *Part*. Divine love in the *first Part* is a love of *Complacency*, or Delight in thee, as thou art seen Eternally in the Person of *Christ*. Dear Soul, while thou art complaining here below, and fixest thine Eye upon thy shame, thy God seeth thee all-glorious within, and without in the glorified Person of the Lord *Jesus*. There he taketh his first view of thee. There his Eye, and his Heart are fixt Eternally to thee. Here he maketh choice of thee, here he falleth in love with thee, and his Soul resteth with perfect delight in thee. For he beholdeth thee, as a spectacle of all Divine loveliness lying in the Bosom of him, who is the brightness of all Divine Glory. As a Vessel in the Sea is filled with the Waters, and overflown with the same Waters: so art thou before the World was in the Person of thy *Jesus*, as in a Sea of Spiritual, Heavenly Beauties; all full within, all covered without with these Glories; quite thorow transparent with the riches of their lustre; entirely swallowed up into the Sea of these pure, and bright Glories. This is *Electing Love*, of which St. *Paul* speaketh; *Ephes.* 1. *He hath made us acceptable in the beloved one*. It is a significant expression which no language can answer for the Sweetness, and Fulness of it; *ἐχαρίτωσεν, made acceptable*. The phrase hath this force in it. God embraceth thee with the Arms of the dearest, and tenderest loves, finding thee entirely cloathed, and encircled with the height of all loveliness in the object of all loves, and the first seat, the essence itself of all lovelinesses the Lord *Jesus*. His Soul is well-pleased with thee to the utmost of all Content; he hath his fill of Pleasures in thee, enjoying thee in the Center of all Pleasantnesses, his own Son.

2. *Part*. Divine love in the *second Part* is a love of *Benevolence*. While thou art a desolate Wilderness, where nothing appeareth but Dearth, and Drouth, but Bush, and Brake, the love of Eternity descendeth, and soweth itself, as a Heavenly Seed in thee. It cometh down in Heavenly Showers. It breaketh forth in Heavenly Sun-shines upon thee. The same love springeth up into all manner of Spiritual loveliness in thee. Now the Grass groweth, the Roes, and the Hinds play, where the Dragon lay. The Bramble bringeth forth Roses. The Stony Heart is now made the Garden of God. The Soul which wallowed in the filth of the Devil is washed by Eternal love in its own Blood, redeemed by its own life, made to bear the Fruit of its own loveliness, and ready trimmed for a Bride to itself.

3. *Part*. Divine love in the *third Part* is a love of Complacency, and delight

light in thee in thine own Perſon: Now Heaven is opened to thee. God with all his holy Angels are continually deſcending, and aſcending between Heaven, and thine Heart, which is become as it were another Heaven on Earth, *God reſteth in his Love to thee, and rejoyceth with ſinging over thee.* The Marriage-feaſt of the Lamb, and his Bride is kept in thee, and thou art that Bride. God with all his loves reſteth in thy Boſom. All his deſires, who is Infinite, are terminated in thee. All his delights are conſummated in thee. All the Quires of Angels round about ſing of his love to thee. All his Excellencies, and Glories, all his works on every ſide ſing for his Joy in thee.

Ah! Dear Souls! When God ſhall thus bring back your Captivity, how will your Mouths be filled with laughter! How will you be, as thoſe that Dream? But why ſhould theſe glad Tydings ſeem to you too good, too great to be true. God is able to do all this for you, and in you. For his Power is Infinite. God is as willing, as he is able. For his Power lyeth in his Will, and his Will is Love. Only wait thou for him; and keep thine Eye upon the firſt Link in the Golden Chain of Divine love, which is faſtned to the Throne of God, the Perſon of *Chriſt* in Heaven, above all thy frailties, folly, and filths, before thy Being in Fleſh. This Link is that, which draweth after it the other two inſeparably, and infallibly.

This is the Circle of Heavenly love. *Firſt*, God loveth thee in Eternity with that love, with which he loveth the Lord *Jeſus*. For he beholdeth thee in the light of the ſame lovelineſs, in which he beholdeth *Jeſus* Chriſt. *Then* he bringeth down the Treaſure of this love, and lovelineſs, which is his beloved Son into thee, ſoweth him, as a Seed of the Divine Nature, and Sonſhip. He ſpringeth up in thee, transformeth thee into his own likeneſs, groweth up in an inſeparable Union, and Fellowſhip with thee. Now God hath another Son, in which he ſeeth his Son in conjunction on Earth, as he ſaw them before in conjunction in Heaven. *Laſtly*, God embraceth this Son on Earth, in whom he ſeeth his Son. He giveth him the kiſs of a Father, with all the Joys of a Father. He taketh him into his Arms, carrieth him up into Heaven changing him ſtill, as he carrieth him up, till this Union begun below, be at laſt made perfect in, and ſwallowed up into that Union, which was at firſt in Eternity. Then ſhall the Lord *Jeſus* ſee himſelf in a Saint after the ſame manner, in which a Saint is ſeen in the Lord Jeſus; both being made perfect in Each, and all made perfect in one. Follow on to know the Lord, and his love, and ye ſhall know this love of the Lord.

1. *Uſe.* See the Evil of *ſin* upon two Accounts. *Firſt* Sin is an *Aberration* from the Will of God. *Secondly* Sin is an *Oppoſition* to that Will.

1. The firſt Evil of Sin is, that is it an *Aberration* from the Will of God. The Will of God is love. In every Sinful path thou loſeſt the *Love-Preſence* of thy God. What is this *Love-Preſence* and what is thy loſs in being deprived of it? In the Love-Preſence of God are theſe Things.

1. A

1. A *Light of Glory* shining round about thee. This Light of Glory cloatheth thy Person all over with its living lustre, as with a Garment of pure Gold, of Divine Loveliness. This Light layeth all things open, and naked to thee in their Heavenly Beauties, in their Eternal Truths, and Substances. This light is a mutual Union, and Fellowship between thee, and all things in the light, all the Children of light, all Spirits, and Forms of light. This light is a Spiritual Paradise, in which thou springest up, and flourishest, as a Plant, and Flower of light. This Divine Light is a new Wine, which thou continually drinkest in, and art filled with pure Spirits of all Life, Excellency, Loves and Joys. Lastly, This pleasant, and triumphant Light chaseth away all the shadows, all the darkness, deceits, melancholy, and fears of the Night.

2. In the *Love-Presence* is the Face of God unvailed, naked, and smiling. God is as a King, and a Bridegroom, in his Ivory Palace. Thou art, as his Queen, and Bride at his Right hand in Garments of Needle-work wrought by the Eternal Spirit with all manner of Beautiful, and Delightful Flowers, and Figures. Here they make these two glad with all manner of Pleasures, as on their Marriage-day.

3. An *innumerable company of Angels* make up this *Love-Presence*. These are thy guard. They continually encircle thee, and encamp round about thee in every place by night, and by day. Which way soever thou goest, they bear thee in their arms. They go before thee, to make smooth paths for thy Feet, and to prepare a resting place for thee. They contend with all the Powers of Darkness in thy behalf, for thy Body itself, even in Death. They make Peace for thee with the Beasts of the Field, and a Covenant for thee with the Stones of the Earth in the name of the Lord *Jesus*, and by the Mystery of the Gospel. The darkest Appearances of things have the face of Pleasure itself, and put on Immortal Beauties for thee. The hardest things soften into Spirits of Life, and Love, flow with Springs of love, and delights for thee.

4. The God-Head itself encompasseth thee with a Ring of unapproachable Powers, and Incomprehensible Glories, like the Mountains round about *Hierusalem*. Himself becometh unto thee the Habitation of a Rock, the Rock of Eternity, and Glory. Himself is thy King, thy Kingdom, thy Palace, thy strong Tower; thy safety, thy rest, and thy pleasure. In this Divine strength, in this Divine secret no evil can come near thee, no good can ever fail thee, neither the Bread of thy strength, and life, nor the living Waters of thy Loves, Beauties and Joys.

This is the *Love-Presence* of God. This is drawn in, and withdraweth itself from thee in the same degrees, as sin is entertained in thy Spirit and Life.

• Evil is a Privation of Good. How great an Evil then is the least sin, which depriveth thee of the best, and greatest good the *Love-Presence* of thy God? *Blessed are the pure in Heart*, saith our Saviour, *they shall see God. Mat.* 5. How cursed are the Impure? Wo to the filthy, and unclean. They are condemned

demned to the loſs of the ſight of this God, and the ſenſe of his Love, which ſight, which ſenſe alone enlighten, alone ſweeten Heaven.

This is the Will of God, your Sanctification. The *Will*, and the *Love* of God are one. While you ſtand in a holy Temper, and State, you ſtand in the Will of God, you ſtand in the Love-viſions, and Love-embraces of God. What a horrour ſhould you have for every Sin, which cometh to ſnatch theſe bleſſed viſions of Love from before your Eyes, and you from the midſt of theſe embraces of love?

When the Lord *Jeſus* died, the Sun was entirely darkned beſides the courſe of Nature, the Rocks were rent aſunder, the Earth ſhook, and trembled, the Graves were opened, and the Dead came forth. How dreadful, and diſmal a thing would Sin appear, if we met with ſo unnatural, affrighting a Change as this, upon the act, or meditation of every Sin? But the change is far more tragical, and mournful, if we ſaw it with the Eyes of our mind, as indeed it is.

Upon the ariſing of each Luſt in thee to gain thy Will from the Boſom of thy Will, *Jeſus Chriſt* is ſpiritually ſlain in thee, who hath a Twin-life with thy life, while thou liveſt in the Divine Will. This is a Death far more deadly, than that in his Fleſh. Now that light of Glory is extinguiſhed in thy Spirit, which ſhineth ten thouſand times brighter, and ſweeter, than the Summer-Sun. Now the Rocks the Divine Powers round about thee, rend aſunder, and remove out of their places. Hell is opened. All things round about thee are Apparitions from beneath; evil Spirits walking in all Forms of things. The whole frame, and face of Nature is full of Darkneſs, and uncertainty, Tremblings, and Horrour. The whole Image of things within thee, and without is changed from a *Love-Preſence* to a ſpectacle of Wrath, and Vengeance.

O that Men underſtood, and would believe the Evil of Sin, of a departure from the Divine Will, which is a Sea of Love, to their own Will, which is a dark fire of Luſt burning up into an open Hell. But though they neither underſtand, nor believe it; yet is it true, and they feel it to be ſo.

2. *The Second Evil of Sin* is an *oppoſition* to the Divine Will, that is, to the Divine Love. But can any oppoſe unclean Luſts to ſo pure a Love? Earthly, Helliſh Luſts to ſo Heavenly a Love? Fleſhly Luſts to a ſpiritual Love, a Love, which is the Life, and Immortality of all Bleſſed Spirits? Can any oppoſe raging paſſions to the meekneſs, and ſweet Calm of Divine *Love*? Can any ſet themſelves againſt that Love which wooeth them continually, till it win them, which doth all things for them? Can any ſo caſt ſhame upon that Love, which poureth forth itſelf, as a ſweet-ſmelling Ointment of all Grace, and Beauty upon their Heads, and Perſons? Are any hearts to be found ſo hard, that they will wound Eternal Love itſelf, while it is pouring forth the Life-Blood of its own heart, partly for a Divine Bath to waſh us white in, partly as a precious Balſom to heal thoſe wounds, which Sin, and Sorrow make in them? All this we do, while by Sin we walk contrary to the Divine Will, which is all Love, Love framing all contrivances,

caſting

casting itself into all Forms in Heaven, on the Earth, under the Earth, acting all parts of Life, and Death for us, to gain us, and to crown us with all its Joys, and Beauties. O how uningenuous, how unnatural a thing is Sin? O take heed of trusting the comforts of your lives, the life of your Souls, the sweetness of your Relations to it.

The foundations of Heaven, and Earth are not so firm, as that of this Truth: *The greatest Evil of Suffering is to be chosen a thousand times, rather than the least Evil of Sin.* In the midst of all other Evils thy Will may stand in a Love-Union with the Divine Will, which is the only Paradise of Delights, and Beauties, that never fade. In every Evil of Sin thy Will standeth in opposition, and enmity to the Divine Will, which enmity alone is the Center of Hell, where all its blackness of darkness, all its unquenchable fires, all its innumerable furies, forms of torment rise up into it.

Our Lord *Jesus* in his Agony, on the Cross, in all his Sufferings had a Joy set before him. The Wrath of his Father with all its Tempests, which shook Heaven, and Earth was a spectacle of Divine Love, and Joy set before him. For in all this his Fathers Will was done by him. His Will was tuned to his Fathers Will. So the Harmony, and Musick of Divine Love plaid in the Ear of his Spirit thorow all. His Will was an excellent Lute, the more it was broken, the more sweetly it returned all that Musick.

On the other side all the pleasures of Sin, all the Glories of the Creature to a sinful Soul are only a scene of Heaven in Hell. For the Will standeth in a Contrariety to the Divine Will, which is the Supream *Love*, and Joy. What can the Contrariety to the Supream *Love*; and Joy be, but the deplorable extreams of Wrath, and Torment?

Use 2. The Will of God declareth itself to be *Love*, to this end, that you may not sin by departing from it.: but if any man do sin, that he may presently return. *Saul* was softned, and melted, when he heard the language of love from *David*, who had watched over him to preserve him, while he slept in the midst of that Army, with which he made War upon him: *Is this thy voice my Son David*? said he then. Open thine Eyes, see the Divine Will with innumerable Eyes of love watching over thee in the midst of thy rebellions. Open thine Ears, hear the Divine Will wooing thee with the sweetest language of love in the midst of thy pollutions. This will turn thee again to the Will of God to melt thy self into its Bosom, when once this thought ariseth in thee, that thou returnest to a Bosom of love ever open to thee.

Use. 3. Be in love with Holiness. Holiness is a Conformity to the Will of God. This Will is Love. How easy is that Yoak? How light is the Burthen? How pleasant is the *Law* of *Love*? *Keep my Commandment, and abide ye in my Love, even as I abide in my Fathers Love*, saith *Jesus Christ*. To abide in the Divine Will, to keep the Commandments of that, is to abide in the Paradise of Divine love, to dress it, and keep it. *David* saith of the *Law* of the *Lord*;

Lord, *Psal.* 19. *It is more to be desired, than thousands of Gold, and Silver. It is sweeter than the Honey, and the Honey-comb. In keeping it is exceeding great reward.* Hear, O beloved Souls. and be wise, and be in love with Holiness. In every command to Holiness God cometh to you in the Light, and Purity of all his Divine Beauties, in the Strength, and Sweetness of all his Divine loves, to make thee like himself, to marry thee to himself. In every act of obedience to this law of Holiness, thy Person shineth with a Heavenly lustre by the shining forth of the unvailed Person of God upon thee: thou receivest a kiss of Heavenly love immediately from the Mouth of God, and returnest it again. O tast, and see. Then you will say, that this Heavenly Traffick is beyond that of all precious, of all pleasant things. No where such loveliness, as this; no where such love. Holiness is a Conformity to the Will of God. The Will of God is Love, the Fountain, and the Life of all Incorruptible Beauties, of all pure, and ever-flourishing Pleasures.

I have done with the *second Description* of *Divine Love*, which defineth it to be the same with the *Divine Will.*

3. *Descrip. God is Love.* He, who was the Disciple of Love, who lay in the Bosom of Love, and so best knew what Love is, declareth Divine Love to be the *Nature*, and *Essence* of God. *God*, saith he, *is Love. He that dwelleth in Love, dwelleth in God, and God dwelleth in him*, 1 *Joh.* 3. 16. As the Sea is a heap of Waters: *The gathering together of the Waters God called the Sea, Gen.* 1. As the Body of the Sun is a pure, and simple Light: so is God a Collection of Loves: a gathering together of all Loves into one Spirit. This is the Divine Nature an Unity, a Purity, a Simplicity of Love.

I shall endeavour to shew you by four Arguments, that there is no name, which doth so properly, so fitly express the nature of God, as this of *Love.*

1. *Argum. The first, the principal Thing, the beginning of all Things in God is Love, Psal.* 136. I intend a short Paraphrase upon this whole *Psalm*; because it maketh so clearly, and fully for my purpose, being taken altogether from the beginning to the end of it.

If you would hear the Musick of Angels, of Heaven; if you would hear the living Harmony of the Divine Nature, as it is *all Love*: listen with a Spiritual Ear to this Psalm, which is a Song composed entirely of this Subject of *Divine Love.* If the Spirit of God assist me to sound forth aright the Heavenly Musick of this *Psalm*, I do not doubt to make your hearts in your Bosoms to leap, and dance to it, by that time I have done.

First, Take *two general Observations* concerning *this Psalm.*

1. *Gener. Observ.* This is a *Psalm* of *Praises*, and Thanksgivings; the Work of Heaven, a Heavenly Work. But all the Praises here are attributed to, all the Thanksgivings are terminated in Love, and the Eternity of Love. This is the burthen of the Song repeated in every verse; this is that, into which all the Strength, and Sweetness of the sense is still resolved; this maketh one

half of every *verse* quite thorow the whole Psalm: *For his Mercy endureth for ever.* The *Word* in *Hebrew* signifieth alike, *Mercy, Kindness*, Love. That word, *endureth*, is added by the Translatours. You may read the words with as full an agreement with the Original, as I humbly conceive, *For his Love is Eternal.*

But however this be, if we adhere to the Translation; *Mercy* is one of the sweetest, tenderest, largest names of Divine love.

1. *Mercy* is *Love* condescending, and descending from the heights of all Heavens above to the nethermost parts of the Earth, to the nethermost Hell.

2. *Mercy* is *Love* uniting itself to the vilest, and most miserable Creatures, which lie below, which stick in the Mire, and Clay in the bottom of the Pit. There love sympathizeth with them, maketh itself entirely one with them in their low estate.

3. *Mercy* is *Love* making a mutual and strange exchange with those loathsome, and lost Souls. It taketh to itself their guilt, shame, weakness, and woes. It giveth to them its own Righteousness, Strength, Beauties, Joys, and Glories.

Thus *Mercy* is the circle of Divine love, as it cometh forth from Heaven, and Eternity; goeth down to the lowest depths of Time, and the Creation; then ascendeth again, till like the Sun it return thither, where it first arose. Poor, and broken Spirits, who lie at the utmost ends of the Earth mourning as outcasts; hope evermore in Eternal love, wait for it. The love of God will find you out, it will meet with you, and take you in its way. For Divine love is Eternal. It encompasseth Heaven, and Earth; Time and Eterty. *His Mercy endureth for ever.*

2. *Gener. Observ.* This *Psalm* comprehendeth all things in it, *Created*, or *Uncreated*; the *Nature* of God; the *Persons* of *God*, and of *Christ*; the *Wonders* of God; the *Works* of God; the *Works* of *Nature, Grace*, and *Glory*. It comprehendeth all things. Then it maketh the *ground*, and Crown of all to be *Love*; this is brought in to every particular in each verse, as the *Reason, Rule, Result* of all: *For his Mercy endureth for ever; for his love is Eternal.*

It is a maxime in Nature, that *all motion is founded upon something unmoveable.* This is the Divine Maxime, upon which Heaven, and Earth standeth; all motions in the heart of God, and in the Creature; of Grace, and Nature are founded upon the unmoveableness, the unchangeableness of eternal Love.

O blessed Love! O blessed God, who is this love! O blessed Soul, which with a spiritual Eye created by this love seeth this all, this whole frame of things to be a structure, a composure of Divine Love! Eternal Love rising up into a Temple, which itself filleth with its All-powerful presence and God-Head, figuring itself in all Forms; acting all Parts; dwelling, and conversing with us, with itself in us, and in all things.

Wandring Souls, take what wings you will to your selves, you can never

fly

fly from the Face, from the Bosom of this Love. The Face of Divine Love shineth thorow all things. The Bosom of Love is the Nest, in which all things, lie. He that hath an Eye to see this Love; he that hath a Palate to rellish it, feeleth and feedeth upon a Heavenly Sweetness dropping from the Divine Nature thorow all Objects, thorow all his Senses, as that Honey from the Rock of Eternity.

1. These are the *two general observations.* I come now to the parts of the *Psalm* which are *three*; 1. *God.* 2. The *Wonders.* 3. *The Works of God.*

1. *Part*; *God.* This *Part* hath *three Particulars.* 1. The *Nature* of *God.* 2. The *Person* of the *Father.* 3. The *Person* of *Christ.*

1. *Partic.* The *Nature* of *God is Love. O give thanks unto the Lord, for he is good; for his Mercy endureth for ever. v.* 1. *Goodness* is the *Nature* of God. All the *Goodness* of God consisteth in his *Love,* and the unchangeableness, the Eternity of that. The Lord *Jesus* teacheth us in the Gospel, that *there is none good, but one, that is God.* God alone is *good essentially,* and so primitively, and so perfectly, infinitely good. For nothing can limit, or confine itself. Goodness is in each Creature, as an *accident* only. In God it is his *essence.* The *essence* of God is *goodness,* The *essence of goodness* is *Love, Eternal Love. O give thanks unto the Lord, for he is good, for his Mercy endureth for ever, his Love is Eternal.* The *Reason,* or *Object* in God of all Thanksgivings is his *goodness,* The *Formal Reason,* the *Essence* of his *goodness* is his *Love.*

As we pass, let us make four short *Notes* upon this *Particular.* 1. Faith in the Soul is to be the Counterpart of Love in God. How large then should our Faith be, which is to answer so great a Love? All the goodness of God lyeth in his Love. The Essence of God, which is so incomprehensible, so infinite is Love. The Heart of God, the Divine Nature is all Love. O that our Hearts, our Souls, our whole Being were all one Mouth of Faith, and that Mouth opening itself still wider and wider to take in these Seas of Divine Love. 2. The goodness of the Divine Nature is Love. The Seed then of all goodness in us is Divine Love. Let us never say; the Evil of my Heart, and Life keep me from the Fountain of Love in the Heart of God. If I were good, with what Freedom should I come to it? With what desire, delight should I drink of it? Take in this Love, that thou mayst be good. This is the beautiful Flower, and ripe Fruit of the Divine Nature in the Creator. This is the Immortal, and precious Seed of the Divine Nature in the Creature.

2. *Partic.* The *Person* of the *Father is Love. O give thanks unto the God of Gods; for his Mercy endureth for ever, v.* 2. The ground upon which I Interpret the *God of Gods* in this *verse* to be the *Father,* the *Lord of Lords,* in the following verse to be *Jesus Christ,* is the Authority of the *Holy Ghost* in the *New Testament,* who often distinguisheth these two ever-blessed Persons by these several Titles of *God,* and *Lord. St. Peter* saith of *Jesus Christ* in the

Acts

Acts; *Him hath God made both Lord, and King. St. Paul* saith; *There is one God the Father, of whom are all things, and we of him. There is one Lord Jesus, by whom are all things, and we by him.* The Holy Apostle seemeth here by the name of *God* to understand the *Fountain* of things; by that of *Lord*, the *Channel.* In another place he speaketh in like manner: *There are differences of Administrations, but the same Lord. There are diversities of operations, but the same God, who worketh all in all:* God is the Original of all Power; *Jesus Christ*, the great, and universal Administrator, the supream Minister in all the Affairs of the God-Head, and so the Lord.

But to return; the excellency by which God the Father infinitely surmounteth all the Gods, all Powers, Greatnesses, and Glories is Eternal Love. The Soveraignty, by which he reigneth over, ruleth, rideth forth upon all the Gods, all Powers, Greatnesses, and Glories is Eternal Love. The Fountain of the Father, from which he bringeth forth the highest Spirits, Angels, and Saints into the Heavenly Image, and Form of God, that they all become, as Sons of God, as Gods round about the Throne of the God of Gods, the Father of them all; this Fountain is Eternal Love. O ye Saints! O ye Souls, whom God hath created, and brought forth from a Seed of Love in Eternity, lay your Mouth to this breast of Love, suck in abundantly the pure Milk of Eternal Love, that you may nourish the Divine Nature, and grow up into the Form of God by it. What do we make our selves, when we cast off Divine Love, when we cease to love? We cast off the Divine Nature, and become Devils. The God of Gods, the Fountain of the Divine Nature, the Father of the Divine Life, and Image in Angels, and men hath all his Praises for his Love, he hath his vertue, perfections, and preheminence all consisting in his Love, and the Eternity of that. O *give thanks unto the God of Gods: for his Mercy endureth for ever: for his Love is Eternal, v.* 3.

3. *Part. The Person of Christ is Love. O give thanks unto the Lord of Lords: for his Mercy endureth for ever.* The Kingdom of *Christ* is a Kingdom of Love. All the Praises of his Reign are terminated in everlasting mercies, the kindnesses of Eternity. As *Jesus Christ* is the *Lord of Life*, and *Prince of Glory*; so is he also the *Lord*, and *Prince* of *Love.*

The Headship of the Lord *Jesus* over all Principalities, and Powers is the Well-head of love. Our Saviour, as he is the *Wisdom* of the Father, by which he conducteth all things, is a love-channel, the way of love, a contrivance, design, and mystery of love. As he is the *Power* of God, which carrieth on all, so he is a flood of love pouring forth itself into this channel, and running along thorow it, filling all the windings, and turnings of the Creation, and of Providence.

Who would not worship thee, O thou King of Saints! O thou King of loves! Who would not kiss this Son with a kiss of Allegiance, and be a Subject in this Kingdom; where the King, and the Kingdom both are love. The sharpest

sharpest reproof here is a kiss of love. The deepest wounding is an anointing of love. The Lord *Jesus* in this sense also is the King of Kings, the Lord of Lords. All his Subjects are Fellow-Lord, Fellow-King together with himself, sitting together upon one Throne, which is a *Throne of Grace*, Throne of love, love findeth, or maketh an equality.

I have passed thorow the *first part* of the *Psalm*, which is the *God of love*

2. *Part. The Wonders of love. To him, who alone doth great Wonders: for his Mercy endureth for ever, or his love is Eternal, v.* 4. All the wonders of God are wonders of love. God is in nothing so to be admired, as in his love.

Admiration is imperfect knowledge. Those things are wonders to us, which are incomprehensible, the causes, and natures of which we cannot search out, or reach to. What Joy is this to understand, that all that, which we cannot understand in the nature of things, which is, as a thick darkness round about us, is a glorious mystery of Divine love? That all that every where, of every Creature, of every Providence of the Creator himself, in which ourSpirits are swallowed up, and lost is an abyss of love, a great, and shining deep of Divine love?

He who thinketh, he knoweth any thing, saith *St. Paul, knoweth nothing, as he ought to know.* How wise, how right, how pleasant is this, to know, that we have a perfect, a right knowledge of nothing, that all things may become wonders of love to us; that the less we see, the more we may feel of a Divine pleasure in the admirations, and raptures of Divine love transcending our highest faculties; that where we cannot comprehend things, we may give up our selves to be comprehended by an incomprehensible love?

The Body of the Sun cannot be seen, but dazleth, and darkneth our sight, when we fix our Eyes upon it. The Stars are said to be vast Bodies of Light, and Glory. Yet we see nothing of them, but little twinklings, and sparks. The reason in one is the excess of Light; in the other the excess of Height. Believe it; all things round about us are Stars, and Suns of Divine love; love in Divine Forms of a transcendent magnitude, and lustre. But we see them generally in a dusky, and shadowy Appearance, like the Sky at a great distance; or at best as little sparks, and twinklings of love. Our sight faileth by reason of the greatness of the Glory, and its height above us.

I come now from the *second* to the *third part* of the *Psalm.*

3. *Part. The works of love.* All the *works* of God are *works* of *love.* The works of God, and of love are of *three sorts*; *works of Nature*; *works of Grace*; *works of Glory.*

1. *Works of Nature.* These are summed up in the Principal, and Universal parts, which comprehend all the rest, *v.* 5. 6, 7, 8, 9. The *Heaven*, the *Earth*, the *Day*, the *Night*, the *Sun*, the *Moon*, the *Stars* are mentioned. To every one of these distinctly is annexed that close, and Crown of love; for *His Mercy endureth for ever; or his love is Eternal.* The

The whole frame of things is a Creation of love. All the Creatures are ſo many Forms, and Shapes, which love putteth on to appear to us in, to converſe, to ſport itſelf with us. If it take to itſelf the Glory of a King in the diſcovery of itſelf by the light of the *day*: it taketh to itſelf a greater Glory, and affordeth a greater pleaſure by ſurmounting all our Powers, and being incomprehenſible, when it hideth itſelf in the darkneſs of the *Night*.

Love is the Center of the *Earth* beneath, on which the whole Creation reſteth and moveth. Love is the Circle of Heaven above, which encompaſſeth all.

It is Divine love, which rideth upon the Circuit of the Heavens, of all the Heavenly Spirits, and Heavenly Bodies, ruling all things by its bleſſed, and ſweet influences from thence. It is Divine love, which ſoweth itſelf, as a Seed in every duſt of the Earth, to ſpring up from thence into a Divine Form and Fruit. The Sun is a Figure of Eternal love ſhining forth with its naked Beauties in their full Glory. In the Moon we ſee love ſhadowed, and coming forth with its Night-dreſs to rule, and enlighten every night, the blackeſt, the moſt tempeſtuous. The Stars are innumerable Eyes of Love looking forth upon us, watching over us, attracting our Spirits, and drawing them up to Heaven, to the Fountain of love. They are ſo many ſparks of love flying forth from the Heart of God, and glowing continually round about us to warm, and melt our Hearts.

Can we now keep dark, blind, cold, unkind, unclean, dead hearts in our Boſoms in the midſt of a Creation of love, where ſo many Eyes of love ſhine ſo ſweetly upon us, ſo many ſparks of love lie glowing round about us, ſo many Seeds of love are ſown in our Earth, ſo many influences of love are continually falling from the Heavens on every ſide.

The heat of the Sun warmeth ſtone-walls, quickneth ſlime to a living Creature. You that have hearts of ſtone in your Boſoms, lay them open to the Beams of his love, they will be warmed with a Heavenly heat, they will live the life of Angels, of God.

The *work* of *Providence* is to be annexed to the *Creation* among the works of *Nature*. The work of *Providence* is painted out to us in the Nation of the *Jews*, as in a Figure from the *tenth verſe* to the *twenty third*, as the Soul formeth, animateth, and inhabiteth the Body; as the Soul is all in the whole Body, and all in every part of it: ſo is Eternal love the Spring, the Life, the Sweetneſs, the Beauty reſiding in the whole work of Providence, and reſting entirely on each line, each motion of it. Every particular in *each verſe* is ſet off with this love, as the ground, the glory, and the reliſh of all: *For his Mercy endureth for ever: or, his love is Eternal.*

As a Silkworm ſpinneth a ſoft, and ſhining piece of work out of its Bowels, in the midſt of which itſelf liveth, and dyeth to live again with Wings, and multiply itſelf: ſo is the whole piece of Nature, and Providence a rich, and delicate

delicate contexture of the tenderest Love. Eternal Love spinneth it out of its own Bowels, liveth with us, and dyeth for us in the midst of it. Then it riseth again with Wings of Spirituality, and Glory. In this Divine Form it cometh again to generate a Divine Seed to itself.

A Painter, who is drawing a Beautiful Person, keepeth his Eye ever upon the Life. Whether he lay dark or bright Colours, whether he make Shade, or Light, crooked lines, straight or circular: still he is acted by that Idea of Beauty, which he taketh into his Spirit by his Eye from the Life itself; still he is forming that lovely Face in every stroke, and colour. Thus Divine Love in the whole Age of the World, in the life of a particular Saint, in the general Affairs of the Church sometimes maketh a Land of *Ægypt*, sometimes a Passage out of it; here a red Sea, there a way thorow it; now a Wilderness, then a Land of *Canaan*. But in all these it ever hath its Eye upon that Divine Glory, which Eternal Love bringeth forth to itself, within itself, as its own Essential Form and Image. This Glory, this *Life-Image of Love*, is that, which it is forming in every *Ægypt*, Sea, Wilderness, and Canaan.

The Heathen represented the *Nature* of this thing by *Venus*, the Mother of Love; the Seeds, and Life springing by a *Cupid*, Love the Child of this Mother, *Gen.* 1. 2. It is said that the Spirit of God moved upon the Waters. The Paraphrase upon that Scripture maketh it to be an allusion to a *Dove*, which is the Bird of love sitting upon her Eggs, and hatching her young ones. The *Holy Spirit* is often in Scriptures represented by a *Dove*. Eternal Love is of a Truth, that Almighty Spirit, which at first sate upon the whole Creation to form it, and moveth upon it thorow all times to cherish, and govern it. *Love* is the Mother of all above. All things are the Off-spring of Love, a Race of Seminal, and Springing Loves. Mercy, Love runneth along with the whole, with each particular of the whole thorow the length of Eternity itself. This is still the Burthen of the Song: *For his Mercy endureth for ever.*

2. *The Works of Grace.* These are the *second sort of Divine Works*; and these also are the Works of *Love*.

These are divided into *three Ranks.*

1. *The constant abode of the Soul in the Heart of God. Who remembred us in our low estate. v.* 23. Thou, O broken Heart! Art sinking by ignorance, by unbelief, by thy fall from God, thou art sinking still deeper into the Darkness, and Filth of this World, and thy Lusts. Still thou sinkest into the Power, and Horrours of the Devil. Now thou sayest; the Lord hath forgotten me, he hath cast me off for ever. Yet he *remembreth thee in thy low estate.* Still thou art in his Thoughts, thou art in his Heart, as a Pillar in the Temple of the Divine Nature, which is Love, never to go forth. Thy Person is ever before him with a Sweet, and deep Impression upon his Spirit never to be rased out. What hath done this? It is Eternal Love. This is the Light of the Divine Mind, which continually presenteth thee to it in the dress of its own Beauties.

This is the ſweet force of the Divine Will, which holdeth thee faſt in itſelf, which beareth thee in its Arms thorow all conditions, and will not let thee go for ever. This is the Reaſon, why *He remembreth thee in thy low eſtate: For his Mercy endureth for ever.*

2. *The bringing us back into the Boſom of God.* This is the *ſecond Rank* in the *Works of Grace. And hath redeemed us from our Enemies: For his Mercy endureth for ever. v.* 24.

It is Eternal Love in the Boſom of the Father, which hath ſent *Jeſus* Chriſt forth from thence for us, and to us; that he may be our Sacrifice, our Ranſom, and our Redeemer.

It is Eternal Love in the Perſon of *Chriſt*, which cometh down from Heaven to make itſelf a Sacrifice for us to the Juſtice, and Wrath of God.

It is Eternal Love in the Perſon of our *Jeſus*, which deſcendeth upon the Earth, as a Field of Blood to undertake the Fight with the Powers of Darkneſs, that he may reskue us, and redeem us from all our Enemies on Earth, and in Hell.

It is Eternal Love in the Perſon of *Jeſus Chriſt*, that giveth itſelf a Price for us, that one Pearl, in which Heaven, and Earth, with all the treaſures of the Creature, and Creator lie to purchaſe us to itſelf.

It is Eternal Love in the Perſon of our Heavenly Bridegroom, that giveth itſelf to us, to cloath us, to form us, to act us, to be a Crown of Divine Glory upon us; to be a Fountain of all Spiritual Lovelineſs, Life, Grace, Purity, and Joys in the midſt of us. Thus it redeemeth us from our Captivity, and Shame. Thus it maketh us a Bride fit for itſelf coming forth ready trim'd out of the Heaven of its own Embraces.

3. *The nouriſhing of us in the Boſom of God.* This *Work of Grace* cometh in the *third Rank*: *Who giveth food to all Fleſh: For His Mercy endureth for ever.* Mark, how theſe anſwer one another: *Mercy*; *Food*: *All Fleſh*; *For ever.*

Eternal Love is both the Feeder, and the Food. If God give Food; If everlaſting Mercy, Eternal Love in the Divine Nature, and Form give Food: This is Food indeed, not the Flood of a Shadow, or a lie. *My Fleſh is Meat indeed, my Blood is Drink indeed*; ſaith our Lord *Jeſus.* The Lord ſpeaketh not this of his Humane Nature. For of this he ſaith in another place: *The Fleſh profiteth not: but the Spirit quickneth.* It is Eternal Love, which is the *Fleſh* of *Chriſt*, the ſtrength, and ſubſtance of the Divine Nature. It is Eternal Love, which is the Blood of *Chriſt*, the Life and Sweetneſs of the Divine Nature. This is that *Meat indeed*, and *Drink indeed*, which Love giveth for *Food to all Fleſh* in its Boſom to nouriſh it to Eternal Life.

I have paſſed thorow the *ſecond Sort* of *Divine Works*, the *Works of Grace.*

3. *Works of Glory. O give thanks unto the God of Heaven*: *For his Mercy endureth for ever. v.* 26. *and laſt.* The Pſalm begun with *Goodneſs*, as its

ground

ground of Love, *v.* 1. It closeth its Musick with *Heaven*, as the Crown of Love. The natural Heavens, the Heavens of the first Creation are not intended here, These were mentioned in the body of the Song, and pass away. These are the last and highest Heavens; the Heavens of Glory: the high and holy places of Eternity. These Heavens are all made of Love. All the precious, and incorruptible Substance; all the unexpressible, and pure Sweetnesses: All the Divine and unfading Beauties of these Heavens are Eternal Love. All the Praises given to God, as he appeareth in these Heavens with all his Saints, and Angels; all his Joys, and Glories round about him, are attributed to Eternal Love, the Root, the Flower, the Fruit, the only reason, and rellish of all. *O give thanks to the God of Heaven: For his Mercy endureth for ever: For his Love is Eternal. The midst of Solomons Chariot is paved, or flameth with Love, Cant.* 3. The Center of Heaven is a Love-fire. All the Spirits, and Spiritual Glories of it are Immortal flames of Divine Love.

2. *Argum. Love is the end of all Things with God.* This is the second Argument to prove *Love* to be the proper Name of God, and full expression of the Divine Nature. *Love* appeareth to be the *last end* of all things *three ways.* 1, *All the Works of God end in Love.* 2. *All the Attributes, and Excellencies of God serve his Love.* 3. *God resteth in his Love.*

1. *All the Works of God end in Love.* Psal. 145. *v.* 9. *His tender Mercies are over all his Works.* The word *Mercies* cometh from the *Belly*; *the inward parts*; the *Womb.* It signifieth the very heart of Love, where it first liveth, and never dieth. where it lyeth warmest, and hath the strongest pulse. It signifieth Love in its Center, and Fountain, where its operations are tenderest, liveliest, and highest. It signifieth that the dearest of all Loves, the love of a Mother to the Child of her Womb. *This Love is over all the Works of God. Over* in Hebrew hath also the sense of *Above.* It is the *end* alone, which is *over* all, and *above* all. In these two respects Love appeareth to be the end of all the Works of God.

1. *Love is over all the Works of God.* As a Bird spreadeth itself over its Nest to hatch, and cherish its young ones: So the end spreadeth itself over all the means, and ways to it. The end fashioneth, and formeth them. The end directeth and moveth them. The end putteth a Beauty upon them, and a pleasantness into them. The end terminateth, and perfecteth them in itself. Thus Divine Love, as the Heavenly Dove, maketh the whole compass of things its Nest, and sitteth upon it. Love giveth Being, Form, Motion, Light, Life, Loveliness, Perfection to all the Works of God. Love is the consummation, and Crown of all. Thus love is the last end.

2. *Love is above all the Works of God.* Nothing can be above all besides the end of all. The end of all boundeth all things and confineth them. Every thing, which hath an end is finite. The end itself is infinite, because it hath nothing above it to give bounds to it, nothing beyond it to terminate and

confine it. Divine Love is the end of all good, the measure of all good, an infinite good. For the love of God is above all the Works of God. O the transcendent Sweetness, Suitableness, Goodness of Divine Love! When you have extracted all that is sweet, all that is agreeable, all that is good out of every Creature, every Divine Work; the Love of God is sweeter, and better than all this. Yea, there is in this Love a sweetness, which so much excelleth; which is so quite of another kind;that by all this you can take no measure of it, you can make no conjecture of it. For all this is finite, and that is infinite. Now it is a firm and sure Rule: there is no proportion between a finite,and an infinite Being. You must tast this Love itself to know how precious it is. All the delights here, when they are highest, truest, and purest are dreams only of this Love. Awake, O Soul, and dress thy self to be a Bride to this Love. Stir up all those infinite desires, which are sown in thee to meet, embrace, and take in the infinite excellency, the infinite Sweetness of this Love.

2. *All the Attributes, and Excellencies of God serve his Love*; This proveth *Love* to be the *end* of all. We read thus, *Ephes.* 1. 5, 6. *Who hath predestinated us to the adoption of Sons by Jesus Christ in himself according to the good pleasure of his will to the praise of the Glory of his Grace.* Grace is Love with these three Graces adorning it, Freedom, Sweetness, Fulness. See if this Love be not God himself, to which the Praise and Glory is given. Can this be any other, than God in his last, and naked Appearance, the end of all, to which the Praise, and Glory of all is ascribed? Behold, with what Pomp Divine Love is brought in. A long order of Divine Glories go before it. Love followeth them, as King, and God. 1. The Counsels of God in Eternity comprehended in the head of them all predestination; *Who hath predestinated us.* 2. The Adoption, the Sonship, all the Sons of God. 3. *Jesus Christ* himself, the brightness of the Glory of God, by whom all the worlds Visible, Invisible; of Nature, Grace, and Glory are made; in whom all the Fulness of the God-Head dwelleth Bodily. 4. The Will of God, which is the unsearchable Treasure of all Sweetness, Goodness, Power, and Joy; the Seed, and Fruit of all Desires thorow Earth, and Heaven. Yea the good pleasure of his Will, which the Will of God, like the Sun shining in its strength, or a full Sea. All these in their Order serve to the Praise of the Glory of Divine Love. *Who hath predestinated us to the Adoption of Sonship by Jesus Christ in Himself according to the good pleasure of his Will, to the Praise of the Glory of his Grace.* All the most Spiritual, and highest Images of God in his Sons; all the most beautiful, purest, and sweetest Idea's of Eternity within himself; Jesus Christ the Supream Image, the Universal Idea, which comprehendeth them all, and surmounteth them all, give up all their Glories to Love, as Stars do their light to the Sun. Love is the first, and the last, the most high Father, and end of all. This is that last opening of the God-Head, in which

all other lights of Nature, Grace and Glory terminate, as in their proper, and beatifical end.

Let us apply this two ways. Let it be a *Caution*, a *quickning* to us.

1. *A Caution.* Take heed of provoking the Love of God to Jealousy. The greatest Sea rageth with the highest, and most dreadful Waves in a Tempest, when the Wind's upon it. The Jealousy of this Love is the rage of a God in the greatness of his Power, Glory, and Majesty, at the height of his God-Head. For this Love is God in the full and final Glory of his Divine Nature, after which we are to expect no other, no further Discovery.

There are *two things*, of which the love of God is most Jealous, its *Glory*, and its *Bride*.

1. *Love is most jealous of its Glory.* The Glory of Divine Love consisteth in its Purity, its Spirituality, its Heavenliness. It is a pure Spirit, the first and purest of all Spirits. It is itself the highest Heaven, the Heaven of Heavens. If you impute to this Love any thing impure, fleshly, or earthly; if you make this Love, a pretence to the flesh, and to filth, you stain its Glory, you put it to open shame, you blow up its jealousy to a flame, which will burn to the nethermost Hell.

2. *The Love of God is most jealous of its Bride.* Thy Soul, O Man, is the Daughter, the Sister, the Bride to this Love. Take heed of dishonouring the Marriage-bed of Divine Love in thy Soul, and defiling its Spouse. If thou pollute thy self with any fleshly lust, with any worldly love, with any Idol without thee, or within thee: this most high, and holy Love will be an everlasting flame, and a devouring fire burning npon thee, until it have burnt up, and consumed every Idol of thine Eyes, or Heart, every Lust, every other Love.

2. *A quickning.* Direct the Eye of your Spirits thorow all things, thorow all the Attributes, and Excellencies of God to his Love. Terminate your desires by all Divine Actings, and Discoveries beyond them all upon the Love of God. For this is the end of all; this is God.

Divine Love is the great, and rich Diamond of the Divine Nature. All other operations, and excellencies of the Divine Nature are the Sparklings, the Lustre, the Water of this Diamond. Let all the Sparklings, and Streams of sweet light from this precious Stone draw your Eyes, and Hearts to the Diamond itself, to the naked Bosom of Love. There is the abundance of Glory. There you shall milk forth the Divine Life, Delights, and Glory in abundance,

As the Wood was of old laid upon the Altar, and the Sacrifice upon the Wood in order to the descent of fire from Heaven, which turning the Wood, and the Sacrifice into one flame with it self, returned thither from whence it came: so let your life, and religion be a continual Sacrifice to Eternal Love. Let the Lord Jesus be thine Altar, which is Love rising up out of the Earth.

Lay

Lay all Duties, Graces, Truths, Spiritual Discoveries, as Wood upon this Altar. Bring thy Soul, thy Heart, thy whole Person for the Sacrifice. Now wait, look upward, pray for Love, as the pure flame of the God-Head to come down, to change all, to unite all unto itself in one *Love*, and so ascend again with all unto its own place above the Heavens.

I have shewed in general, how the Divine Attributes all serve *Love*, as their end. I will explain it yet more by three instances of the three chief excellencies in the Divine Nature. *Wisdom, Power, Righteousness.*

1. *Instance; The Wisdom of God serveth his Love. According to the riches of his grace, in which he hath abounded towards us in all Wisdom, and Prudence.* As a plentiful Spring by the abundance of its Waters maketh a bed, and channel to itself, in which it runs along: so is the Divine Wisdom a manifold, and deep channel, which the full Spring of free Grace, of Eternal *Love* maketh to itself by the force of its endless streams, as they flow thorow all things, and play with themselves in various courses, and forms, until they meet again in the Sea of *Love*, the Bosom of God. Divine Wisdom is the richness of Divine *Love* spreading itself into an infinite variety; sporting itself with itself in all diversity of Forms, and Shapes; thorow innumerable Changes, innumerable Windings, and Turnings bringing forth itself into a most ravishing Harmony of all Divine Beauties, and Joys. Divine Wisdom is *Love* forming itself into rich designs, most beautiful contrivances, full of unexpected, and surprizing turns, full of depths past the search of every created Eye: that in the close it may display its blessed Treasures more fully, that it may raise, and enlarge every Spirit to take in its Joys. Thus *the riches of Grace have abounded towards us in all Wisdom and Prudence.*

The Wisdom of God is the Divine art of *Love*. The Divine Prudence and Providence is the Net of *Love* to catch Hearts, and Souls in, spread thorow the Sea of the Creation.

O blessed Fisher of Souls, Divine *Love*! O blessed Net of love, the Divine Wisdom, and Providence! Thrice-blessed Souls, that are caught in this Net, by this Fisher! These are taken only to be removed out of the Salt, and troubled Sea of this World, into the sweet, clear, and calm Sea of *Love*.

But wretched are those Spirits, who like Carps in a Pond sink themselves down deep into the mud of flesh, and fleshly lusts, that they may escape this Divine net of *Love*,

The Wisdom of God is the Musick of *Love*, by which it charmeth Spirits, to attract them to itself, to compose them unto a Heavenly Harmony of Peace, and Purity. Those are indeed Adders, the Seed of the Serpent, who love not the sound of this Musick, who stop their Ears, that they may not hear this Charmer the Divine Love, though he charm with so much skill.

2. *Instance. The Power of God serveth his Love, Rom.* 1. 16. *I am not ashamed of the Gospel of Christ: for it is the Power of God unto every one that*

believet

believeth. The Gospel is the Minstry of Grace, or *Love*. The Divine Power then acting in the Gospel is the Minister, and Servant of *Love*.

This will appear more by laying together *three Scriptures* in the *Canticles*, which opening one another will send forth a sweet light of Divine Grace shining in them.

1. *Scrip. Cant.* 5. 10. It is said of the Lord *Jesus*; *He is the Chief among ten thousand.* The *Hebrew* word for *Chief* is *Standard-bearer.* I humbly conceive, that we are not to understand here the Person, that beareth the Standard, or Banner, who ever is inferiour to many Persons in the Army; but the Prince, whose the Standard, or Banner is, which is carried, unto which all the Army is gathered together, and under which it moveth. The sense seemeth to be the same with that; *Joshu.* 1. *Jesus Christ* appeared in the form of a man with a drawn Sword in his hand. Being asked by *Joshua*, who he was, he answered: *The Captain of the Lord's Hosts.*

2. *Scrip. Can.* 6. 10. The Spouse of *Christ*, which is the Church in general, and every believing Soul in particular is described to be; *Terrible, as an Army with Banners.* This relateth to the *Army*, and *Banners* mentioned before; *Cant.* 5. 10. *Psal.* 34. 7. we read, that *the Angel of the Lord pitcheth his Camp round about those that fear the Lord.* It is in the Original Tongue; the Angel *Jehovah.* The Lord *Jesus* is God with God the Father above all Angels, and Men. He is God setting up his Pavilion in the midst of the holy Angels. He is God setting up his Pavilion with Men in the midst of their Spirits. This is the Captain of the *Lords* Hosts, the Prince of Glory, who as a great Prince at the head of an Army placeth things dearest to him, his Treasure, his Princess in the midst of the Army, as in a place of Strength and Honour.

3. *Scrip. Cant.* 2. 4. *The King brought me into his Banquetting House, and his Banner over me was Love.* You will say now; what hath *Love*, or a Banquetting House to do with a Banner of War? You shall now see, how these Scriptures come home to my end, and declare the *Power* of God to be the Servant, and the Soldier of his *Love.*

The proper intent of a Banner is to bear the Cause of the War wrought upon it, either by Image, or Inscription, or both. It is frequent, when the War is ended, for the Conquerors in the rooms, in which they feast for joy of the Victory, to have hanging over their Heads the Banners, under which they are fought. These are Tropheys, marks of the Victory, and Ornaments of the Triumph. Silken flags at solemn Shows, at publick Feasts, at Funerals are Imitations, and Images of this.

If a King make a War for his Bride, or *Love*, he may very well have *Love* in a rich Figure, and in Golden *Letters* displayed upon his Banners. Neither can any thing be more pertinent, when he returneth home, and feasteth publickly with his Queen, than to have these Banners with *Love* inscribed upon them.

them in golden Letters, and figured upon them in glorious Images waving over their Heads to encrease their Joys by this Declaration; Love was that, for which the King fought; Love was the force, by which he conquered; Love is the end of the Victory, the Joy, and Crown of the Feast.

I know you prevent me in your thoughts, you, who love the Lord *Jesus*, by applying this to your Prince, your Beloved, and his Love, his Bride, your own Souls.

I shall bring down all to my purpose, and to your practice in the exercise of those Principal, and Triumphant Graces, Faith, Love, Heavenly Joy by *three Conclusions*, or *Spiritual Maxims*.

1. *Conclu.* All the Armies of God, all the Powers of the God-Head, the innumerable Companies of holy Angels, and blessed Spirits, all the Hosts of Heaven, and Earth with their Captain the Lord Jesus at the head of them move, and fight in their courses under the Banner of *Love*. Thy Person in a glorious Image of all Divine Beauties is figured upon the Banner, as this Eternal Princes *Love*. *Love* to thee is wrought upon the Banner in Characters of Glory. This is the Cause of all motions in Heaven, and Earth. To this Banner all *Powers* every where resort, unto this they are united, under this they march, and fight.

2. *Conclu.* The Lord *Jesus*, as Captain of the *Lord's* Hosts, with all his Heavenly Armies, his ten thousands of Angels, his Chariots of fire, and Horses of fire continually encompasseth thee, marcheth, encampeth round about thee, as his chiefest Treasure, his *Love*, with Banners of *Love* spred, and displaid over thee; on every side of thee round about. Every step thou takest in thy way to Heaven is in the midst of these Warriours. All Divine Powers continually circle thee in. The Invisible, and Invincible Hosts of God under the conduct of thy Beloved *Jesus* are thy perpetual Guard, and Convoy. In the midst of these thou walkest, sittest, and lyest down; thou wakest, and sleepest, *Psal.* 91. 11. The Angels have a charge of thee from their Prince, and thy Bridegroom, that they *keep thee in all thy ways*, that they *bear thee in their hands, lest at any time thou strike thy foot against a stone*; that thou never stumble. The Angels of God are thy Chariots of War: thy Chariots of State, thy Chariots of *Love*, thy Chariots for Travel, in which thou journiest thorow this Wilderness to thy Kingdom, the Kingdom of *Love* and Glory. All this they are in one. They make thy way thy Palace in the midst of thy Kingdom for Strength, for Glory, for Delights, for Rest in thy *Love*. They bear thee up above in the light of *Life*, in the *Life* of Divine *Love*. This is the way high, and lifted up above all the Powers of Darkness, and Death, in which they carry thee along, that thou mayst never strike thy foot against any stone of offence, against any hard and hurtful Form of Darkness, Enmity, or Death. Thy *Jesus*, the Bosom of thy Beloved is this way.

3. *Conclu.* These Banners of *Love*, which are spred over thee in thy

mar-

marches here, the same hang streaming over thy head to Eternity, and over the Head of thy King, as thou sittest at the Feast with him in Heaven. The Fights about thee here, are the Trophies, and Triumphs at the Feast there. The same Love is figured on all, which maketh all precious Stones, and Jewels in thy Marriage-Crown, and Crown of Glory, to shine there, and adorn it for ever.

Use. The *Use*, which we make of this is to see the difference between the two states of a Saint, and a Sinner; a Believer, and him, who believeth not.

1. See the blessedness of a Believer. *Heb.* 1. 2. *Jesus Christ* is said to be *the Brightness of the Glory of God*, that is *of Love*; *the express Image of the Substance, or Person of God*, that is, of *Love*. For *God is Love*. *v.* 6, 7. *When God bringeth his Son again*, that is, after his Resurrection, in his Spiritual, and Heavenly Appearance, *into the world*; *he saith*: *Let all the Angels of God worship him. He hath made all his Ministers Spirits, and his Angels a flame of Fire.* This concerneth thee O Believer, and is spoken of thee.

O the blessedness of that Soul, which indeed receiveth Jesus Christ, and his Love by Faith, if only thou didst know thine own happiness! God hath brought his Son in his second Appearance, in his Spirit, into thine Heart. He is in thee the brightness of the Glory of Love, that is, of the Divine Nature shining in the midst of thee. This is that Eternal Sun, from which all blessed Spirits continually drink in the Light, Influences, Joys of Life, and Immortality. He is in thee the express Image of Love, which is the Substance, and Person of God. This setteth itself thorow him, as a Seal upon thine Heart. Now the Power of God is a Servant to his Love in thee. Now God saith; Let all the Angels of God worship, bow down to, serve my Love in this Soul. God himself maketh his Angels Flames of Love enfolding thee, penetrating thy Body, and Spirit, shining within thee, round about thee continually in the darkest night. He maketh his Angels Ministring Spirits to thee. Spirits of Glory Minister Love to thee after an Invisible manner in all visible Things. Every moment of time, every Circumstance, or Accident in time, are the Wings of Angels, a Chariot of Angels, carrying thee above the snares of Death below into Heaven. This is thy Portion, who believest in the Lord Jesus and his Love.

2. See the misery of Unbelievers. How wretched art thou, who believest not, who sayest to the Love of God, and the Tydings of it from Heaven: Depart from me, I have no pleasure in you.

Those Powers of Darkness, that are ever ready to raise up *Leviathan* from his Stormy deep below, curse thee. All evil Spirits are Flames of Wrath burning within thee, burning from without upon thee alwaies, in the midst of thy Jollities, at thy Feasts, on thy Beds of pleasure. Evil Spirits are ever Ministring Wrath to thee after an Invisible manner thorow all Visible Things. Devils are thy Chariots. These wrap thee up in a thick Cloud, in the blackness of Darkness, and hurry thee to Hell. O be not unbelievers, but believe, that you may inherit the Land of *Love*, and dwell in it for ever. Love inviteth, wooeth you to believe, that is, to receive itself into your Hearts. Love will bring its own entertainment, and make the Feast for itself; if you for your parts will but take it in, as a guest.

3. *Instance. The Righteousness of God serveth his Love. Rom. 5. l. Grace reigneth by Righteousness unto Eternal Life thorow Jesus Christ our Lord.* Grace is *Love* in its Fountain, Love upon the Throne. Love is brought in here by the Apostle under the name of Grace, as a King. Eternal Life, Heaven is the Kingdom of Love. Jesus Christ is the chief Minister of State to this great King. God is *Love* sitting upon the Throne. The *Lord* Jesus is the same, supream *Love* descending from the Throne to be the Universal Servant, and General Officer throughout all this Kingdom of Love. Righteousness is the Scepter of the King. *Thy Scepter is a Scepter of Righteousness, Psal.* 45. Love *reigneth by Righteousness unto Eternal Life thorow Jesus Christ our Lord.*

There are three Ways, in which the Righteousness of God serveth his *Love*.

1. Righteousness is the Royal-Garment, and the Wedding-Garment for Love itself, and its Bride on the Coronation, and the Wedding day, which are both one, the day of the Spirit, the day of Grace, the day of Eternity. The Bridegroom himself is said to be *fairer than the Sons of Men*, in my Text; *Psal.* 45. 2. He is cloathed with the Righteousness of God, which is the Comeliness, the Beauty of Holiness, or the Holy, the Pure, the unstained, unmixt Beauty of the Divine Nature. Two things make Beauty; Features; Colours. The Features in the Face of the God-Head are the variety of all Excellencies in a Harmony. The Colours are the Glory shining in all these. This is the Righteousness of God. *Jesus Christ* hath both these. He is the *express Image of the Person* of God. There are the Divine Features. He is the *brightness of the Glory* of God. There are the Divine Colours, and Lustre. Both these make up the Garment of Righteousness, which is the Divine *Love*-liness of Love himself. In this he appeareth fairer, than the Sons of Men on his Marriage-Day in the day of the Gospel. For Behold! He cometh forth in the Righteousness of God.

This also is the Garment, with which *Love* cloatheth, and adorneth his Spouse, the Believing Soul to make her fairer, than all the Daughters of Men, than all the Daughters of *Hierusalem*, than all Angelical Beauties. The Queen is said to be brought to the King, *all Glorious within, in Garments of beaten Gold, in Garments of Needle-work: Psal.* 45. The Glory quite thorow, the beaten Gold, the Needle-work is all comprehended in the Righteousness of God. *He was made Sin for us, that we might be made the Righteousness of God in him,* 2 *Cor.* 5. 21. This is the Garment, with which Divine Love adorneth his Queen to make her fit for his Throne, and his Embraces. This Garment

ment of Divine Righteousness hath a mysterious vertue in it. It is at once a Bath of Divine Blood, which taketh off all the blackest, deepest stains of deformity from the most loathed Souls. It is a Tincture of Divine Beauty, which giveth in a moment Youth, Immortality, a loveliness quite thorow its whole Essence, a Substantial, Essential loveliness, a loveliness resembling, and answering that of love himself, of God. This is the beaten Gold, all Glory within.

A learned Interpreter teacheth us, that the *Needle-work* in the Garment signifieth properly *Oes* wrought in Gold, like so many Suns, all over the Garment. How rich, how Beautiful is that Garment of Righteousness, with which the Lord *Jesus* decketh the Soul of every Saint, in which it fully pleaseth the Eye of God, and dazleth the Eyes of Angels! It is set all over with Golden *Oes* of an Eternal Glory, with Invisible, and Eternal Suns, the unvailed Face, the entire Person of the Lord Jesus set in every part, and shining from every point of it. This is the *first Service* of the Divine Righteousness to the Divine Love, to make itself, and its Bride, the Beloved Soul Infinitely, Unchangeably Lovely, and Pleasant one to another. This is the *Righteousness* of our *Justification*.

2. Eternal love soweth the Righteousness of God, as a Divine, a Spiritual Seed in our Hearts. This Seed changeth the ground into its own Nature. It draweth the vertue and strength of it to itself. It groweth up in it, together with it to a Tree, which is an entire Paradise in itself. The body of this Tree is the Lord Jesus in the Power, Glory, Fulness of his Spirit. The Branches are all the Spirits of God, of Angels, and Saints spread thorow all times, and things. All moral Excellencies, all the Beauties, and Perfections of the Divine Image in the first, and universal frame of Nature are the leaves of this Tree, which here never fade. All Divine Righteousness, all Evangelical Perfections, and Spiritual Graces are the Fruit, which is fitted for every Season, and ever ripe in its Season. On this Fruit love itself, which is God, the Son of love *Jesus Christ*, all the Angels of love, the Soul herself feed, are refreshed, and raised to a Divine Joy. This is the *Righteousness* of our *Sanctification*.

3. *The Righteousness of God is the Scepter in the Hand of Love, by which it ruleth all things.* As *Moses* commanded all the Elements, the Air, the Water, the Earth by stretching forth the Rod in his hand: so the Love of God swayeth all things every where by the Scepter of his Righteousness. The Harmony and Motions of the Divine Righteousness from the hand of Divine Love are felt, and obeyed by all things to the utmost end of the Creation. Righteousness is the Musick of Divine Love, by which all things are charmed.

Use. See the distinction between the *liberty* of *Spiritual Love*, and the *licentiousness* of *Fleshly Lusts*.

1. Divine Love is free, but Divinely fair, and pure. *St. James* calleth the Gospel, which is the Ministery of Love from Heaven; the perfect Law of

Liberty; and in another place, the *Royal Law*. Love is free, but it is perfect. Love is a Liberty: but it is a Law to itself in its Liberty. Love is a King: but it reigneth in Righteousness. It is itself, both King and Law to itself. *Love*, saith St. *Paul*, is the fulfilling of the whole *Law*. *Jesus Christ* said to *John the Baptist*; *It behoveth me to fulfil all Righteousness*. This is the Language of Heavenly Love in every Holy Heart: It behoveth me to fulfil all Righteousness. Love is an obligation of Righteousness to itself. Righteousness is the decency, the comliness of Love. Love is the Divine Unity, and Righteousness the Heavenly Harmony, in which this Unity of Love diffuseth itself thorow all things. True liberty is only found in Harmony. All Bondage ariseth from Discord, which hath its Root in Contrariety, and Enmity. Righteousness is the Harmony, and Beauty of Love.

It is the liberty of the Sun to shine; of a Tree to flourish with Leaves, Flowers, and Fruits. Righteousness is the liberty, the Sun-shine, the Beauty, and fruitfulness of Divine Love.

As the Sun by its light: so the love of God by its Spiritual Beauty, which is Holiness, attracteth Spirits to it; maketh them in love with it; maketh them lovely by Assimilation, making them like itself; filleth them with all delights: maketh them fruitful with all Beautiful, and Divine Births of Grace, and Glory.

Love and Righteousness are, as the Father and the Son in the Blessed Trinity. Love bringeth forth Righteousness, as its proper brightness, its lovely light, its essential Image, the express Image of its Substance, and all its Sweetnesses, or vertues. As the Father is at liberty only in the Son, his own Image; as the Son is no where at liberty, but in the Bosom of the Father, his own Principle, and Original: so is love no where truly free, but where it springeth up, and flourisheth in the Fruits of Righteousness. Righteousness is then only Free, Kindly, Evangelical, and Divine, when it springeth from the Womb of love, lyeth in the Bosom of love, hangeth at the Breasts of that love, which is God; of God, as he is in his own Eternal Form of love.

He that hath the Son, hath the Father also. He that hath the Father, hath the Son: saith St. *John*. Let us not be deceived. He that worketh Righteousness, hath the love of God in him; and he that hath the love of God, hath also the Righteousness of God. Love is the fulfilling of the Law, of every Law; Natural, Moral, Evangelical; of the Letter, and of the Spirit. Love doth nothing uncomely; offendeth no Principle, Humane, or Divine; of Sense, Reason, or Grace. Thus Divine Love is free, but Divinely fair and pure.

2. So is not Lust. The Lust of the Flesh is licentious, without Law, Light, Harmony, Order. All Disorder, Deformity, Shame, Bondage, Anguish, and Death are there, where Lust is. Can there be any Freedom, Beauty, or Peace in the midst of Confusion, and Contrarieties?

Every Lust maketh thy Spirit a narrow, and deep Pit of Darkness, and

Horrour.

Horrour. Thou lyest *sunk to* the bottom of it in the midst of loathsom Toads, and poysonous Serpents *twining* about all thy parts, crawling upon thy naked Bosom, and naked Heart.

3. Cast out every flesh Lust. A Lust is the spawn of the Devil. If thou suffer it to lie in thy Soul, innumerable Devils will spring up out of it, and make thee a Hell in thy self, a Habitation of Devils. The Devil was a Beautiful, and Blessed Angel, until Lust came. Lust made him a Devil. Lust is the Nature, and Essence of the Devil. It maketh thee the Child of the Devil.

4. Take in, cherish the Love of God in thine Heart. Pray for, wait for, receive gladly the Blessed Sower, the Lord *Jesus*, when he cometh forth to sow the Seed of Love in thy Soul. Cherish it, when it is sown. Give it depth of Earth; let it take root deep enough in thee. Suffer no cares of this world to choak it. Love is the Seed of God in thee: The Image of God with all the Graces, and Joys of it; the Divine Nature with all its Purities, Powers, and Perfection; God himself will grow up out of it to dwell and walk in thee; to fill thee with the presence of his Glory; to make thy Spirit, and Person another Heaven to him. The God-Head of God; the Guilding, Sweetning, and warming of Heaven; the life of Eternity is Love.

I have now shewen, how all *the Attributes of God serve his Love*, in *general*, and in *three particular Instances* of the *Wisdom, Power, Righteousness* of God. This is the *Second Proof*, that *Love* is the *end* of all.

3. *God resteth in his Love*; This is the *third Proof*, that *Love is the end of all.* Zephan. 3. 17. *He will rejoyce over thee with singing; he will rest in his Love.* Like the Joy of Harvest, when the Countryman bringeth in the last shocks of ripe Corn out of the Field with Songs and Garlands; because this is the end of all his labours for the whole year: so God rejoyceth, when his Love is come to the ripe Corn in the Ear, when it is cut off from its Earthly stalk, when in the full declaration of it, in the riches of its Glory, in the Simplicity, and Spirituality of its Divine Nature, it is brought home into his Bosom again, for this is the end of all the Circuit of his labours thorow the whole Creation. This is his Noah; his rest.

No man resteth, till he come to his last end. The Love of God is his last end. For he resteth in his love. All motion tendeth to, and endeth in rest. All the Motions, Works, and Ways of God tend to, and end in Love. For this is his rest.

God in all other Appearances, and Forms of things is *in transitu*, passing thorow them, as a way-fairing man, till he cometh to the full expression of his Love. This is his Mount *Sion*, his resting place for ever. Upon this Mount of Love God casteth off every disguise, layeth aside every vail. Here God is seen naked, in the simplicity, and brightness of his own Beautiful Person. Love is the Chrystal Glass of the Divine Essence in its own light, and purity. Here all the Saints see God, themselves, all things in their Eternal Forms of Divine love-

Loveliness with a beatifical vision. Here time is no more. The mystery of God, which is the mystery of Love is made perfect, is finished and ended.

A wise man, so far as lieth in his Power, maketh all his desires, and designs, all his works, all things within his Sphear to meet in his end; that his rest in his end may be sweet and full. God is infinitely Wise, and Almighty. All his Counsels, and Contrivances; all his Works, and Ways in Heaven above, on the Earth below; all his Attributes, and Perfections; all things, that ever were, meet in his Love; as in their end. So he resteth in his Love. His Soul, and all that is within him is well-pleased in his Love. His Joy is full. He lieth down upon the Bed of love with the perfection of all contentment; with the sweetest and highest Complacency of all those infinite Powers in him. Love is an end every way proportioned to him. For it is himself. God is Love.

Use. 1. How happy a thing were it, if Men were like to God in this, to have their rest in love? This would be a Heaven upon Earth. What a Divine Calm should we be continually in? Divine Love would be a Bed of rest to us, while the Storms only made Musick to the Heavenly Dances of things round about us. O the blessed, and unknown force of this Wine of Heaven, Eternal Love, where it is drunk deeply, down into any Soul by large draughts!

Beware of the Corruption of Love. The Corruption of the best things produceth the worst of all things. Lust is the Corruption of Love. Beware of the Contrarieties to Love. All Passions are Contrarieties to Love. There can be no Peace, no Rest, no Comfort of Love, while our Lusts, and Passions prevail. Seek God, seek the Rest, and Joy of the Lord in his Love. *Behold he giveth his Beloved to sleep.* It is Divine Love alone, which singeth us into a Divine sleep of sweetest rest, and delight in its own Arms, in the midst of every Tempest of Sickness, Sorrows, or Death.

I have finished the *second Argument* for the confirmation, and explication of the *description of Love* taken from *St. John*; that *God is Love*; in as much as *Love is the end of all.*

3. *Argum. The Unity of God is the highest, and purest love.* This is the third Argument to shew, that *God is Love* that the first and Supream Love is the most high God over all Blessed for ever. The highest, purest, and most Spiritual Union of all things in the highest, purest, and most Spiritual Forms in one Eternal Spirit; this is the Love; this is God.

I will unfold to you this sweet, and glorious *Unity*, which is the *Divine Nature*; and which is *Divine Love* by *three Principles* of our common Orthodox Divinity rightly founded upon the *Scriptures.*

1. *Prin.* God beholdeth All things in himself. He goeth not forth out of himself to converse with any Thing. He receiveth not any Impression from things without himself. *Rom.* 11. *v.* 35. 36. *Who hath been his Counsellour? or, who hath given to the Lord first that he should repay him?* God is Simple, ever Perfect, uncompounded. He seeth all things in the Glass of his own Essence He is Himself All to himself, his own Center, and Circumference.

2. *Prin.*

2. *Princ. Every thing which God seeth in himself, he seeth as himself.* All ’orms of things, as they appear in God, appear cloathed with the Form of iod. *James.* 1. 5. *every good, and perfect Gift cometh from above, from the ’ather of Lights, with whom there is no variableness, nor shadow of Turning.* All ppearances of things in the Father of Lights, the *Sun* of Eternity, are Lights; ood, and Perfect Lights, not Beams, but so many entire Suns; Springs, and eas of Light, the Light of Life, and Love in the Bosom of that Sun, the Faer of them All. For there is no Variableness in God, although there be ’ariety. God is the Same in every season, and Appearance without any Shadow f Turning.

3. *Princ. God, as he seeth all things in himself, in one Divine Form with himlf, comprehendeth them unchangeably in the closest, and sweetest Embraces, conerseth with them Eternally in the highest degree of all mutual Suitableness, weetness, Satisfaction and Delight. Pythagoras* said; Friendship, the best .ind of Love on Earth was One Soul in several Bodies, as in so many Images, id Reflections of itself. Such is God, such is Love, One Incomprehensible pirit multiplying itself into Innumerable Representations, and Reflections of self; that it may contemplate itself, possess itself, delight it Self Infinitely r the Divine Form compleat in every One, endlesly for the Variety ever lew.

This is the sacred, Unsearchable Unity of the Divine Majesty. Thus this nity is the most Sacred, and Supreme Love.

Quest. Now you may perhaps say within your selves, some one of you: This ove, of which you speak, is the Love of God within himself, the Love of God himself. What is all this Love to me?

Answ. My answers to this Question shall be so many Applications of this ’ruth.

Use. 1. All this Love is nothing to thee, who separatest thy self from the ivine Unity by sin: *Your Sins separate between me, and you*; saith the Lord by e mouth of his holy Prophet. You have accounted your selves unworthy Spiritual Loves, in that you have divided your selves from the Unity, the eavenly Body, and Spirit of the Lord *Jesus*. You stand in the strength of ur own Spirits, and walk after your own Imaginations; Principles, and nages, which you have found out and chosen to your selves to stand in the ower, and walk in the Light of them. Matth. 23. 37. *Jesus Christ mourn- over* Jerusalem in these words: O Jerusalem, Jerusalem, *who stonest the Proets, and killest those that are sent unto thee; how often would I have gathered e, as a Hen gathereth her chickens under her Wings? But ye would not. There- e now shall thy house be left unto thee desolate. I say unto you; Ye shall see me no re, until ye shall say; Blessed is he, that cometh in the name of the Lord,*

Wretched Soul, who art still in thy Sins, hear thy Saviour after this man- mourning over thee with tears of blood falling from those Wounds which Love

Love in him, Sin, and Unbelief in thee have made; with Words of Pity, and tender Compassions falling from his Lips: O wretched, wretched Soul, which by sin woundest that Unity of Divine Love; which first sent thee forth from its Blessed Womb; which by Unbelief continually killest in thy Self that Unity of the Eternal Spirit, which springeth up in thee, which sendeth forth sweet glances, maketh strong Impressions of itself upon thee, to draw thee into its Blessed Bosom. O sinful, O Unbelieving soul, how often within thee, without thee, in thoughts of thine Heart, in touches upon thy affections, in the ministery of my Word, in the works of my Providence have I spread over thee the Shadowing wings of the Divine Unity, the wings of Divine Love, of the Heavenly dove, my Spirit? How often would I have gathered thee under these wings; to have lien safe from every Bird of Prey, every Evil, and Unclean Spirit; to have lien warm under that Divine Heat, which would have cherished the Divine Life in thee with all the Graces and Joys of it. But thou wouldest not Therefore is thy Spirit, and Person left to thee desolate, without Spiritual Life, Spiritual Comfort, Spiritual Company; which all as Plants of Immortality grow, and flourish together in the Unity of the Eternal Spirit, as in their Root. But, poor, forlorn Soul, when thou shalt see thy Saviour come again, in his Spirit, into thy Spirit; then shalt thou fall down at his feet, fly into his Arms, and say; Blessed is my Jesus coming in the Heavenly Evidence of the Divine Unity, which is the Supream Love, that subdueth all things to itself. Now I believe. This Unity, this Love is the Ground and Root of Faith.

Use. 2. All this Love is nothing to thee, who livest in the enmity of the Serpent. Thou hast no lot, nor portion in that Divine Unity, which is the Fountain of Love, who livest in Wrath, Malice, and a bitter Zeal. The Spouse of Christ, the Soul, on which he hath set his Love, is a Dove, hath Hony and Milk under her Tongue. Divine Love, Heavenly Peace, and Joy are a Fountain of Milk, and Hony in her Heart. Gentle Language, Words of Meekness, Healing, Peace-making works are streams of Milk, and Hony under her Tongue flowing from the Fountain of Divine Love in her heart.

We read in the Book of *Job*; that the Wicked Man shall *never see the Land of Brooks, of Fountains, and of Rivers of Waters: but the Serpent shall bite him*; These expressions seem to allude to the Land of *Canaan*, and the fiery Serpents in the Wilderness; which things themselves were Types of the Paradise of Love in the Divine Unity, and the Enmity of the old Serpent in the Wilderness of Sin.

As thou likest not to retain Love in thine Heart, language, and life; but art a fiery, biting Serpent by deadly hate, bitter Speeches, works of wrath and malice formed in Hell: so thou shalt never see the pleasant Land flowing with Brooks, with Fountains, and Rivers of Love. The crooked Serpent shall wrap thee up in his cursed folds, to draw thee into his hideous Den, there bite, and devour thee.

Use 3. Believe. So shall all this Love be thine, in thee, and to thee. I shall make good this to thee by 3 *Arguments*, which are so many Motives, to perswade thee to believe, to stand fast in the Faith, to grow in Faith.

1. Argum. Believe, and by believing thou shalt be transplanted into the Divine Unity. *He, that is joyned unto the Lord, is One Sp rit.* 1. *Corin.* 6. 17. Faith, which joyneth us to Christ, by his Approach to us, by our Reception of him, and Adherence to him, ingrafteth us into the Unity of the Eternal Spirit.

The Unity of God is a Golden Chain, which fastned to the Throne of the Divine Essence above all Heavens, letteth itself down to the lowest parts of the Earth by several rich, and curious Links, that It may draw us up to itself. The first and Highest Link of this Golden chain is the Union of the ever-blessed Persons in the most Holy Trinity in One, Glorious, and Incomprehensible Essence.

The second Link in this Mystical Chain is the Union of the Divine, and Humane Nature in One Divine, and Heavenly Person by the Incarnation of our Lord *Jesus*.

The Third is the Mysterious Union of Two Persons, a Saint, and his Saviour in One Spirit by Regeneration thorow Faith. While thou believest, the Divine Unity by these degrees, like the Steps of Gold to Solomon's Throne of Gold, descendeth into thee, that thou mayst ascend to that by the same Steps. By believing thou art One with God in the Fountain of the Divine Nature. The Father himself, the Fountain of *Israel*, is now thy Fountain and thy Father, Believe, and thou shalt be One with God in his Son, His Image, His Glory. God giveth His Son for thee, that thou mayst believe. God giveth his Son to thee in Believing. Believe, and thou shalt be One with God in his Spirit. *Believing ye received the Spirit of Promise*; saith *St Paul Ephes.* 1. The Spirit is the Great Promise. The Spirit is All the Promises in a Knot, living, and flourishing upon the Root of eternity, like the Sun with his Beams. The Spirit is the Unity Unvailed. *Jesus Christ* in his Flesh is the Sun of the Divine Nature, under a Cloud. *Jesus* in his Spirit is the same Sun shining out clear, and shedding abroad all his Glorious Beams, which are all the Great, and Precious Promises in their Accomplishment.

If thou believe, whoever, how vile, how deep in sin, how black soever thou art with Guilt, thou art now One with God in his Righteousness. *Christ is made Sin for thee, that thou mayst be made the Righteousness of God in him*; *according* to St *Paul*. If thou believest, thou art One with God in his Rest. *he, that believeth, entreth into Rest, as God also rested*: *Hebr*. 4.

Finally believe, and thou shalt be One, as the *Father*, and *Christ* are One. *Jesus Christ* prayeth not onely for his Apostles; but for all, that shall believe on him thorow their word. He maketh this Petition expresly for them to his Father: *That they may be One, as we are One*. John 17. 22. *If two lye together,*

gether, they shall be warm; saith *Solomon* in *Ecclesiastes*. What warmth of Divine Life, Love, Joy, and Pleasure is there, where these Three, the Father, Christ and a Believer ly together wrapt up in One? See how Faith placeth the Soul in the warm Bosom, upon the Golden Throne of the Divine Unity together with *Jesus Christ*. This Divine Unity in *Christ* is become now thy Center, and thy Circle, O Believing Soul; thy Center, out of which and in which thou doest at once both rise, and rest; thy Circle, unto which thou enlargest thy self, with which thou art encompassed.

Qu. Perhaps some souls are so far touched with the Sweet sense of this Blessed Unity, that they say within themselves; We see indeed a glorious Rest and Joy, in being implanted into the Unity of the Eternal Spirit by Believing: But what shall we do that we may believe, and be set in this Root of Eternity?

Ans. This Root of Eternity, this Glorious Unity eternally comprehendeth and holdeth thee. Look then up to this Unity, fix thine Eye unmoveably upon it, as thy first Principle and Habitation. So wait, until by a Virtue coming down from thence, thou apprehend by faith this Heavenly Unity of the Spirit, in which thou art comprehended.

Arg. 2. Believe, and thou shalt partake of the Divine Love, by being planted into this Divine Unity. The Unity, in which the Sons of God dwell together, as Brethren, is compared by the *Psalmist* to the holy Oyntment which was poured forth upon the Head of the High Priest, and ran down to the skirts of his Garment. Thus by Faith the Unity of God in Christ poureth forth it self as a rich Oyntment of Divine Love, which spreadeth itself in its precious Substance and Sweetness over thy whole Person to the lowest border of thy Garment. Thus art thou anointed to be a King and Priest to God the Father together with the Lord *Jesus*. When this Unity openeth itself upon thee to the Eye of thy Faith, and taketh thee into itself; then shalt thou see thy self, and be ravished to see thy self in the midst of all the Loves of God and embraced most closely by them all.

1. In this Unity the Eye of Faith discovereth to thee *Electing Love*, Now thou rellisheth the Sweetness, now thou receivest upon thy Spirit the Seal of Electing Love, which was before the World was, and then had thee with it in its Bosom. Now thou seest by the Light of the Glory of this Unity shining upon the Eye of thy Faith the Father in the Height of Eternity looking upon thee in One Loveliness, loving thee with One Love together with himself in the Beautiful, and Blessed Person of his Son.

2. Faith sheweth the *Justifying Love* in this Unity. What peace, what Joy is there in this Sight, when a poor Believer taken out of the Dungeon where he lay in chains of guilt, and filth, a Prisoner to the Wrath of God, seeth himself set in the Court of the great King before his Throne, acceptable, and amiable in the Beloved One? Thou now appearest washed in the same precious Blood of God. Thou shinest in the same Beauty, and Righteousness of

God

God together with *Jesus Christ*. Yea, he is thy *Loveliness*, who is Height and Sealed Sum of all Loveliness; of all Loves. For *thou art made acceptable in the Beloved One*; *Eph.* 1. *v.* Thou art not only Righteous, but Righteousness itself; the Righteousness of God. Thy Person is a Solid Glory, a Transparent Glory, a Pure, unmixt Glory of Divine Righteousness. For thou art *the Righteousness of God in him*. Faith maketh thee *One Spirit* with him, who is *the Brightness of the Glory of God*.

3. Believing thou meetest in this Unity with the *Sanctifying Love* of God. That Seed of God, which is One, soweth itself in thy Soul, and springeth up into the Fruits of Holiness, and Immortality. Now say to thy Soul upon a good account: Return unto thy Rest, O my Soul: The Lord hath dealt bountifully with thee. The Goods of Heaven, and Eternity are sure to thee. For this Seed of All Good, of Grace, and Glory, which is now sown in thee, will grow up by day, or by night, whether thou sleep, or wake; though thou know not, how it grow.

4. The Believing Soul seeth, and smelleth the Heavenly Flower of *Comforting Love* living, and flourishing in this Root of Eternity, the Divine Unity. The Spirit himself, whose Unity is the Band of all Peace, and Joys, is now *with thee*, and *in thee*, a Comforter, the Fountain of all Living Comforts.

5. Believe, and Faith will set in thine Eye this Glorious Unity, as the Crown of *Glorifying Love*. *Jesus Christ* saith expresly among his last Words, *John.* 17. 22. *That Glory, which thou hast given to me, I have given to them: that they may be One, as we are One.* This is the concluding, and crowning Glory; This is the Glorifying Love, Love in Glory; the *Unity* made Perfect. The Father hath given Glory to *Christ* by giving him the Being of his Heavenly Person, which is the Glory, and himself in that Being a Glory, in that Glory. *Jesus* giveth the same Glory to us, himself, and his Father, to make us One Glory with themselves; that the Unity may be the Glory, and each in the same Spirit may be a Unity of Glories. O! believe. Can any thing be desired sweeter, surer, greater by any Soul, than to be one Love, one Glory with *Jesus Christ*, and his Father? Faith planteth thee into this Love, into this Unity.

3. *Argum.* Faith by planting thee into the Unity of God bringeth thee to the Light of God. The Eye of Faith seeth the Truth of Things, as it is *Jesus*, and *Jesus*, as He is in the Unity of the Spirit. *Ephes.* 4. 21. *If ye have been taught in Him, as the Truth is in Christ.* *Ephes.* 4. 3, 4, 5. *Keep the Unity of the Spirit in the Band of Peace; One Body; One Spirit, One Lord.* The Light of Faith, is the Light of the Divine Unity; as the Light of Sense is the Brightness, and Glory of the Corporeal Unity, which is One Sun. This Light discovereth the Truth of things in the Secret of the most sacred Unity, the Lord *Jesus*, as He is One in the Unity of the Spirit. How different the Appearance of things to Sense, and to Faith? What different Lights shine in the Diversity of flesh, and in the Unity of the Spirit? In the latter of these

are seen all beautiful, and pleasant things; all things in Beauty, Pleasantness, in Heavenly, Immortal Forms. And this Sight alone is the Truth. Believe, so shalt thou see thy self in *Christ* in One Glory. Thou shalt know, that this which thou now seest is the Truth, thy True Person, and Form. Now thou shalt cry out with Joy, and Wonder. *Behold I am fair; I am altogether fair. It is easie for me now to believe that I am my Beloved's, and that His desire is toward me; while I see my self in this Glass of Christ's Glorified Person, in this Circle of Glory, the Unity of the Spirit.* Believe; So shalt thou see all the Saints in One Glory with *Christ*, and shalt know, that this is the Truth of every Saint. Then shalt thou stretch forth thine arms to them, and say; *How is my heart enlarged towards you! Ye are, as I am, all look like Princes, the Sons of the great King. My joy is fulfilled in You all.* Believe: For, when thou believest, thou shalt see all the Works of God in a Vision of Truth and Glory. Thou shalt see them in *Christ*, as Christ is One in the Unity of the Spirit. All shall appear to thee like *the Joynts*, or white Circles *of the Thighs of the Spouse* Cant. 7. 1. *Jewels, the Work of a curious Artificer*; Master-pieces of Divine Love; they shall be all to thee, as the hands, and fingers of thy Beloved; Rings of Gold with a precious stone set in them; Circles of Divine Light, and Life; figures of the Supreme Unity, with that Glorious Unity it self set in them to enrich them.

Believe. O what a Paradise in the third Heavens is a Believer caught up into, when first the Eye of Faith is opened in him? Yea, as often, as it openeth it self in him; He beholdeth all Forms of Things, as they are in Truth, this Truth, as it is in *Christ*, this *Christ*, as he is in the Unity of the Spirit. With what pleasure like that of a Resurrection from the Dead, when all things, that ever we conversed with, rise together with us into the same Glory, doth a man now look round about him, and say. *O all ye Appearances of Things, that ever were, or are to be! Are these your Forms, your true Forms? Is this sight of you, which I have now in the Divine Unity, the only Truth?*

Then the Believing Soul stretcheth forth her hands to them all, and cryeth out with wonder, and delight: my Father, my Mother, my Husband, my Wife, my Brethren, my Sisters, my Children, all the delights of my Eyes; all the Sweetness, and Joy of all Relations are ye all.

Use 4. You who are planted by Faith into the Divine Unity, shew the Fruits of this blessed Root in *Purity* and Love.

1. Let a Divine Purity shine in thy Life, O Christian. The Unity of God is his Simplicity. The Simplicity of God is his Purity. The Purity of the most excellent things is their freedom from mixture. The more they are themselves, the more they shine, the more pure, and precious they are.

Live, and walk in the Unity of the Spirit, Galat. 5. 25. Behold thy self, and all things; converse with all, as they appear, as thou meetest them in thy walks in this circle of the Divine Unity. Sleep not the sleep of Sense, or Flesh, lest thou be hurried in Dreams into the Land of Darkness, where the Light is Darkness, where there is no Order, no Unity.

Awake

Awake into the Light of this Blessed Unity. So shalt thou be ever with God. So shalt be ever like God.

2. Be unmoveable in Love. God is Love, because he converseth with all things in the Light of his own Spirit alone, which is the Light of Loveliness, and Love. Be thou a Child of God, a Child of this Light, and so a Child of Love. Be a Priest of Divine Love. Be ever within in thine own Spirit, as a Temple of Holy Loves, filled with the Glory of that God, which is Love. Know nothing any more in any Appearance besides that, which sheweth itself to thee in this Temple by the Light of this Glory.

Object. Here an Objection cometh in our way, which may arise in every understanding against all this discourse, which we have had concerning the Divine Unity, and Divine Love. Doth not God see Sin, and hate Sinners? Ought not we to do so?

Ans. I answer affirmatively; the Divine Nature both in God, and in the Children of God discovereth the deformity of Sin by a most clear Light; and hateth it with a most perfect hatred.

I shall confirm, and explain this *Answer* by *four particular Answers.*

1. *Ans.* Sin is a privation of Holiness, which is the Beauty of Spirits, as Darkness is a privation of Light; and every Evil of some Good. Privations are known only by their contrary habits. God, and all Holy Spirits see the Evil and Ugliness of Sin in the Light, and Glass of their own Heavenly purity.

2. *Ans.* Hatred is an intellectual contrariety. The Unity and Love of the Divine Nature, in the King of Saints, and all his Holy Ones is essentially and formally in itself an irreconcilable opposition, an active contrariety to Enmity, and Sin, as Light, Day, and Immortality are to Darkness, Night, and Death.

3. *Ans.* God seeth Sin in order to his Wrath. God seeth his Wrath in order to his Glory; his Glory as the full object of his *Love*, order is the Chain, and Band of Unity. Thus God beholdeth all at once, as they lie comprehended in the Unity of Eternal *Light*, and *Love* by their several *Subordinations.*

God beholdeth Sin, as it is swallowed up into a flame of wrath; the flame of wrath, as it is heightned to a *Light* of Glory; the Light of Glory, as it shineth, and liveth in the Eye of his *Love*, the Fountain of all *Lights*, *Life*, and Joys. *Love* is the Eternal, and rich Root of all. Glory is the Tree, that springeth up out of this Root, the perfect, and full Image of *Love*, in which it liveth, diffuseth, and delighteth itself within itself.

This Tree of Glory spreadeth itself into many flourishing Branches, among which are Holiness, Justice, Wrath against Sin. Wrath by the force of the contrariety raiseth up Sin, as a mark to shoot its burning Arrows, and cast his fiery Darts at. Love thorow these Attributes letteth in Sin by the *Law*, that it may display itself more fully in its War with its Enemy, in it Conquest, and Triumph over it; that it may break forth, and rise up thorow it more power-

powerfully, purely, and sweetly; like a flame going up to Heaven from a great pile of Wood perfectly subdued to it.

The Unity of God is now the Glass of *Love*, in which alone God seeth all Things; and the Diamond, which he seeth set, and shining in every Ring of Operative, or Permissive Providences.

Sin appeareth to him in the Glass of his Wrath and Justice. These shew eth themselves to him by their reflections, and Images in the Glass of his Glory. His Glory shineth forth from the Arms, and Bosom of his Love, which is the inmost Center, and outmost Circle of the Divine Unity. Here all things lie, here all things present themselves to God, as Mysteries of Divinity, and Love in the Unity of the Divine Nature.

God beholdeth with a fulness of Joy his Love the reflection of himself, his own Fountain, the Fountain of his blessed Unity, in which he lyeth Eternally bathing himself in pure floods of Incomprehensible Pleasures; this Love, this Unity, this Fountain he beholdeth in all his Glory. His Glory is the Object of his Eye in the Severity of his Justice, and Wrath. He contemplateth his Justice, and Wrath alone in Sin. Thus God seeth every where the Mystery of his Divine Unity, as the great and bright deep of Eternity. He seeth every where the Seal, the express Image of his Divine Unity, where all the riches of his Glory, and Sweetnesses of his *Love* unfold themselves, and sport together.

Thus, O Saint, learn to look upon every Sin. See it in this Glass of Truth, the mystery of the Divine Unity. See this secret and invisible Jewel, the mystery of the Divine Unity sealed upon it, sealed up in it. Thus shalt thou see Sin so, as to preserve thy Purity, and thy Love both in one. Thou shalt see Sin so, as to be at once a flame of Wrath to it, and a *Light* of Glory, a flame of Love in that flame of Wrath, comprehending both, Wrath and Sin in the Wrath. So shalt thou see Sin, Hate, and dwell for ever with God, who is the Beauty of Holiness, and Love.

4. *Ans.* God looketh upon a Sinner, as upon a Prison and a Grave, where the Truth, the Divine Seed, the *Light* and Life of the Divine Image lyeth detained, captivated, slain by a Lie; the Prince of Life, and Light by the Powers of Darkness. His Wrath and Hatred against the Sinner is a zeal of *Love*. He cometh forth with Thunders, *Lightnings*, Tempests and Earthquakes in his Wrath to break down the Prison-walls, to break open the Grave, that the Prince of Glory may come forth into the Light of Life, and the liberty of the Glory of a Son of God.

God, as a Sun, breaketh forth with power, and in his Strength, to dissolve by the force of his Beams the Inchantment, and Light; that the Sons of *Light*, and the Truth may be set free.

Thus God hateth Sinners; thus do thou hate them with a perfect Hatred. *Let* thy fire be no bitter zeal, but a zeal of *Love*. Let thy woundings be Divine Anointings.

I have

I have hitherto passed thorow only one half of my discourse upon the escription of Spiritual *Love* by the supream Unity in the Divine Nature.

I shall take my ground for the other half; *Galat.* 3. 20. This shall be my enter for a time, from which my Motions shall arise, and whither they shall eturn to end there.

The words are these: *Now a Mediatour is not of one; but God is one.* This Scripture hath a sweet, and clear depth of Love in it, but unfathomable. This depth is the Unity of God.

St. Paul stateth here the most essential difference between the Law, the Ministery of Wrath; and the Gospel the Ministery of Love. One is *established in the hands of a Mediatour*; in the other God is one. The Love-union in he Gospel is too near, too sure, too sweet to need, or admit a Mediator.

The Fountain of all Evangelical Grace, and Love is the Unity of God. *The Unity of the Spirit* is *the Band of Peace* between the Uncreated, and all Created Spirits, *Ephes.* 4. 6.

But we shall more clearly see the Riches Treasured up in this *Scripture*, if we look upon it by the light of another *Scripture* in the same Chapter; *v.* 16. *Now the Promise was made to Abraham, and his Seed, he saith not to Seeds, as of many, but as to one. And to thy Seed, which is Christ.*

The Holy *Apostle* in this *Chapter* maketh it his work to prove, that Righteousness is not by the works of the *Law*; but by Faith in *Jesus Christ* according to the Gospel.

God descending into Christ, and taking up Christ into himself; *Jesus Christ* in this fulness, and Glory of the God-Head entring into the Soul, and taking the Soul into himself, by the free Revelation, and immediate Union of Faith: This is the Righteousness of God, and of his Saints in the Gospel.

One Argument, by which St. *Paul* maintaineth Righteousness to be of Grace, and not by Works is laid down. *v.* 15. the Covenant of Grace was long before the Law. He confirmeth that here *v.* 16. *The Promises were made to Abraham, and to his Seed,* &c.

The *Holy Ghost* in this verse establisheth the Heavenly Building of the Gospel upon three beautiful, and firm Pillars.

1. *Pillar*; The Gospel is a meer, simple, pure Promise. That, which was called in the verse before, the *Testament*, or *Covenant*, is here expressed by *Promises*. The Law is compounded of *Precepts*, and Promises dependant upon those Precepts, as condition of the Covenant to be performed mutually on both sides; of prohibitions and threatnings annexed. But, as the Sun is a body streaming forth freely by a knot of Beams. So is the Gospel a knot of Promises, which are all *Love* in so many clear, unmixt Beams shooting themselves freely forth from the fulness, and force of Love alone in its Head-spring, the heart of God.

Obj. But you will say; Are there not Precepts set down; Conditions imposed;

posed; Duties required; high, and hard things to be performed in an Evangelical State?

Ans. It is most true. The Gospel hath its Precepts, Conditions, Duties; and these all high, hard, raised to a pitch of Spirituality, and Heavenliness beyond the reach and sight of any natural Spirit. But these all depend upon the Promise, and not the Promise on them. All Evangelical Graces, and Duties are Children of the Promise. The Promise is, as the *Hierusalem* above, free, the mother of all living Principles, and Performances.

We read; 2 *Pet.* 1. 4. That *we have given to us, great and precious promises, by which we are made partakers of the Divine Nature.*

You, who believe not, hear, and believe. You who believe but faintly, and weakly; hear, that your Faith may be encreased. You, who are strong in Faith; hear, and believe yet more. Hear, how all the difficulties in believing, in the whole life of Faith from the Beginning to the end; the Promises are Pipes of pure Gold laid into your Hearts from the Heart of Christ in Glory. By these from that flourishing Olive Tree, the Divine Nature, as the best Oil, floweth in upon you freely, and perpetually.

When a Gardiner would set choice Plants, Flowers in a barren, sandy Soil; he first bringeth in fresh, and fertile Soil to lay upon it. Then he planteth in this good ground, which he hath made, his Flowers, and Trees, which now flourish, and make that barren Earth a rich, and pleasant Garden. So God findeth thy Spirit, O Man, barren, and sandy, a Rock. No Spiritual Plant, no Truth, or Grace of the Gospel can take root, or live here. But be not thou discouraged by all this, by the hardness of thine Heart, the barrenness, and enmity of thy Spirit to the Heavenly Seed, which it killeth, as often, as it is sown in it. Look to the Promises, God by these will bring in the Divine Nature. With this, as a good, and Heavenly ground he will overlay, and enrich thy Spirit. Now God will plant every pleasant Truth, every Evangelical Grace in thy Spirit. Now they shall all prosper, they shall unfold their several Beauties, send forth their sweet smell, and bring forth much fruit in thee. For this new Earth of the Divine Nature shall send forth its Fatness and Sweetness into them, and make them to grow.

When a Prince goeth his progress, his Gests are set down before he leaveth his Court; which way, and how far he shall Travel every day; where he shall lodge at night. His Servants with Furniture, and Provisions from his Court wait upon him all along.

A Promise is a Declaration, and Obligation of Divine Love, which it maketh of itself, which it layeth upon itself, free, and immutable.

Whoever thou art, that hearest this, believe in the Promise: Believe freely, in a free Promise. This Faith will make thee the Prince, of which I speak. Thou art now a Prince come forth from Heaven to take thy Progress thorow this world, and so return home to Heaven again. All thy Gests by day, and

Rests

Rests by night are set down Eternally in Heaven in the Book of Love there, which is the Heart of God, and from thence in a Promise, which is Eternal Love, or the Heart of God transcribed, to be read by thee. The day of a Saint is the Light shining from the Face of God. The night is the drawing in, and darkning of this Light. All thy motions by day with every Circumstance, O Believer, O Heavenly Prince, are described exactly in the draught of Divine Love, the Promise. Thou goest, as it is written of thee there.

The Holy Angels, thine own Servants from thy Court in Heaven attend thee in all thy way with Heavenly Provisions, and Minister unto thee, as is appointed there. Thy resting-place every Night is ordered in the Promise. The Blessed Angels go before thee. They take up thy lodging for thee. They make it ready with Heavenly Furniture. They make thy Bed for thee. They are a Guard round about thee for the fear of the night. All things are done, as was set down before in the Bosom of Eternal Love opened in the Promise. Thus the Gospel is All a Promise. The Promises are Love shining forth by its own Brightnesses, and Beams. Love is that name of God, which is an Ointment poured forth. Love is the Divine Nature freely flowing, and diffusing itself, like Live-Honey. As a Bottom of Silk is unwound, and wrought out into divers beautiful Figures in a Garment of Needle-work: such is thy Life, thy whole Story, O Saint, Divine Love spun forth from the glorious Heart of God, as Silk from the curious Worm, is wound up into a Bottom in the Promise. This rich Bottom worketh out itself into all thy motions, and Acts, into all thy Changes, and Chances thorow thy whole course, as into so many exact, and shining Figures of Eternal Glories. Thus Love maketh itself the entire History of thy Life; of that History, and Life it maketh for thee a Garment to wear in Heaven, becoming the Bride of the great King.

You may see something by my description of this first Pillar, on which the Gospel standeth, how God is one in the Covenant of Grace, and that high, Heavenly Unity the sweet Spring of all the Grace, and love of the Covenant. You will see this breaking forth more, like the day dawning by degrees upon you, as I shall set before you the other two Pillars of Evangelical Truth.

2. *Pillar. The Promise of the Gospel is to the Seed, and to that Seed, as to One. To* Abraham, *and to his Seed were the Promises made. He saith not, to Seeds, as to many; but to his Seed, as to One. v.* 16.

The Seal of the Promise upon the Seed is the Unity. God will not give his Glory to another. The Love, and Grace of God in the Gospel is his chief Glory. Therefore is Evangelical Love to the Evangelical Seed; and that for the Unity sake. The Seed every where in the Father, in all the Offspring is one with itself. Love, and Unity are ever inseparable. The Strength and Sweetness of the Relation between the Father, and the Child is the Unity. Love is at its height in a Father, because there is the Head of the Unity. The Unity here is the Spring of Love. From hence its streams run along into all relations with the sweeter, and stronger force, as they are nearer to this Spring. *God is Love. God is one.*

3. *Pillar. That one Seed, to which the Promises are made, is Christ. To* Abraham, *and to his Seed: as to One; and that one, Christ. Isaac* was the Seed of *Abraham. Isaac* stood only, as a Figure of the Lord *Jesus. Isaac* signifieth *Laughter.* The Lord *Jesus* is the true Seed of Mirth and Joy. When he cometh to us by his Spirit, which is his proper, his eternal Presence, and Appearance; he bringeth back our Captivity from the Powers of Sin, Sorrow, and Death; he filleth our Mouths with laughter; he maketh us, as those that Dream; he placeth us in the midst of such glorious Persons, and Things, he cloatheth our Persons with so much Glory; and all this by so easy, so sweet, so sudden, so universal, so unexpected a change; that it seemeth for the greatness of the Glory more like a Dream, than Truth.

But if *Isaac* here typifie the Son of God; then doth *Abraham* stand in the place of God the Father. The name signifieth *The high Father of a Multitude*; or, *The Father of a high Multitude.*

God the Father maketh the Promises to himself, and to his Son *Christ. Jesus Christ* is the Seed, to which the Promises are made, and the Promised Seed, the Pearl in the Casket of every Promise. Thus God is one in the Gospel; the Gracious Maker of the Promise; the Rich Matter of the Promise; the Glorious Heir of the Promise. This Unity is the Love of the Gospel, in which the Seed is one in the Father, in Christ, in all the Saints; and this one Seed is the Lover, the Love, and the Beloved.

God loveth himself in his Son; his Son in his Saints. God, Christ; and the Saints lie all wrapt up in one Seed. This is the Unity; and this Unity the Love of the Gospel. One Seed shining out, and springing up thorow all into the Fellowship of all Beauties, and delights with itself, within itself.

We have set up some Lights in this verse to shew the Glories of Divine Love the more advantageously, as they are presented to us *v.* 20. in those words; *God is One.*

Now let us draw nearer to the verse itself, the Center of our discourse.

St *Paul* raiseth an *Objection*, and answereth it. *v* 19.

Object. This is the *Objection*: If the Gospel were before the Law of Eternal Force, the only dispensation of Love, Life, and Righteousness: why then was the Law added.

Ans. St. *Paul* answereth this *Objection*, by *Defining*, and *Confining* the *Use*, and *Times* of the Law.

1. St *Paul* defineth the end,& *Use* of the Law. *The Law was added because of Transgression.* There was a fourfold use of the Law, until *Christ* came; to *discover*, to *restrain*, to *heighten Sin*, to *bring Condemnation*, and *Death* upon *Sinners.*

2. The *Times* of the Law are *confined* to the coming of *Christ*: *Until the Seed should come.*

The

Then the *Holy Apostle* giveth us *two Arguments* to make it plain, that the Law can be no more of force, or have any place, when *Jesus Christ* appeareth. These *two Arguments* are taken from *two Essential differences* between the *Law*, and the *Gospel*.

1. *Argum. The Law was ordained by Angels.* God appeared not under the Law in his own Person, nor in that sweet, and supream brightness, which floweth immediately from his Face. He cloathed himself with the created Light of the Angelical Nature, and Glory, as with a Garment. In the Persons of Angels, and their Beauties, as under a vail, he was seen, and conversed with Man. But when the Seed cometh, which is *Jesus Christ*; this is God in Person, God in his own Essential Form, and Image.

Now the Scene, the Appearance is changed from the diversities of Angels, and their Glories to the Divine Unity. Now the Angels, thorow which, as multitudes of little Stars in the night, the Light of the God-Head scattered faint glimmerings of it self, vanished out of sight. They resigned their weak Beams, Beauties, and Beings to one Sun, that one Seed their Fountain, the Unity of God in Christ. Here they are New-born, they are made perfect, they shine again in one Glory. The Son of Man cometh now in the Glory of his Father, in his own Glory, in the Glory of all his Angels. When Christ is seen in his Heavenly shape, which alone is the Light of the Gospel, Angels appear no more singly, all Glories are seen united in their Center, the Person of God in Christ. Now hear, O *Israel*; come forth; and O ye Daughters of *Sion*; the Lord your God, your Jesus is one. This is the *first Argument*, and the first essential difference between the Law, and the Gospel.

2. *Argum.* The Law was ordained by Angels; *in the hand of a Mediator. Now a Mediator is not of One; but God is One. v.* 19. 20. Thus we are come home to the verse it self, where you shall see all this discourse come home to our mark, at which we aim; the Fountain of all Evangelical Graces, and Loves in the Unity of God.

We shall best understand these words by a distinction of Mediators.

There is a Mediator of Distance, and of Unity. This latter the Mediator of Unity is one with both the Parties, between which he mediateth, comprehendeth them both, maketh both one in himself. Such a Mediator *Jesus Christ* is in the Gospel. Such a Mediator the Law hath not; this place intendeth not. This hath some shadow of it self in the *Medium Participationis*, which Philosophy treateth of.

The *Mediator of Distance* is one, who standeth between two to keep them apart, because they cannot approach one to the other. This is here meant. The People of *Israel* said to *Moses*; *Let God speak to thee, and we will hear thee. But let not God speak to us any more, least we die.* God approved of their words: *They have said well.* Thus the Law was ordained in the hand of *Moses*, as a Mediator. This we may express by the *Medium Abnegationis*; a Mediator of Distance.

 When

When the Seed cometh, this Mediation, this Administration, the Distance, and so the Law ceaseth. Now *God is One. Christ* is the *Seed, Christ* is come *Christ* hath *two Natures* in him, but he is One Person in both Natures, and that One Person, the One only God. God is the Person, the Subsistency, the Root, out of which the whole Tree with all its Arms and Branches of both Natures, Humane, and Divine springeth; in which it subsisteth; from which all operations, and fruits proceed; to which all denominations belong, which is the name to be named in all, and to which every name belongeth. This is Christ. The one Seed, the one Spirit in all the Saints, in all the Graces, and Comforts of the Gospel is this *Christ*, that one Person, which is the only true God. Thus God is one in all.

The Lord *Jesus* in his Heavenly Spirit, and Body is the Glorious Circle of the Divine Unity, in which God, Christ, and all the Elect, Saints, or Angels lie so close, so enfolded, and wrapt up mutually one in another; that no Mediator can come between them; that they need no Mediator; save as this Unity itself, the *one Seed* is the Mediator.

There are two Promises made to *Abraham* concerning his Seed; one, that they shall be, as the Stars of Heaven for number; the other, that they shall be, as the Dust of the Earth for Multitude.

The *Seed* is *Christ*. The Lord *Jesus* one *Seed* in all the uncreated Glories, which are fixed, as innumerable Stars in the Heaven of the Divine Nature. The Lord *Jesus* is the same Seed in the Dust here below, sown in the form of Flesh, and Dust.

When the Lord *Jesus* cometh in the Power of the Gospel into any Heart, this one Seed at once shineth down from all those Glories of the God-Head above, and springeth up out of the Dust here below. It awakeneth itself from above and below. It meeteth with, receiveth itself, and twisteth into one with itself, the Glory from on high, and the Dust from beneath. It continually ascendeth, and descendeth into its own Bosom, and feasteth itself eternally upon itself with all Divine Substance, and Sweetness.

I have endeavoured to draw aside the Curtain from this Scripture, to shew you the Joy, and Glory of the Lord in the Gospel, the *Unity* of God, and the Fountain of Love with him in that *Unity*.

Let me add one Scripture to this to bring in more Spiritual Light into a Room so rich in, so full of Heavenly Beauties. It is that *Rom.* 4. 16. *It is of Grace that it may be sure to the Seed.* You, whose hearts the Love of God in Christ hath touched from Heaven, that you pant after the Water-brooks, and Fountain of this Love opened in the Bosom of the Lord *Jesus*; why come ye not to your Saviour, that you may drink abundantly of the Divine Love? Are you discouraged, and driven away by the sense of your own unworthiness, and weakness, by unbelief? Hear, and believe, and come with boldness to the Fountain of Love. Love is made sure, and tyed fast from the Throne

of

of Love in Heaven to the Hearts of Believers on Earth by a three-fold Cord.

1. *Cord.* The *first Cord* is the *Promise.* By the immutable tie of a Promise, in which it is impossible for God to lie, hath he assured, and secured his Love to thee. The two chief Attributes of God, on which all the rest wait, in which they are comprehended are *Goodness*, and *Truth.* Both these must fade, and pass away, before one tittle of the Promise can fail of its accomplishment. For *Goodness* maketh the Promise: but *Goodness*, and *Truth* both are obliged to the keeping of it.

2. *Cord. The second Cord is Grace. The Promise is of Grace, that it may be sure.* You, who are apt to despair of Love, and Blessedness let down from Heaven into your Souls by the Golden Line of a Promise, because your hearts are unfit Mansions to entertain such Heavenly Guests, hear, and consider this: As the Beams of the Sun descend upon the Earth, infuse a precious vertue into it, quicken, and call up the vertue, and Seeds of the Sun there, make it green flourishing, and fruitful; yet lean not, depend not at all upon the Earth; but have their root in the Bosom of the Sun above, from which they shoot themselves down into the lap of the Earth: so the Promises of the Gospel, as Beams of Eternal Love, are fixed in the Sun of the Divine Nature, as their Heavenly root. From that they are bred, by that they are nourished, and maintained. This Sun poureth them down upon thee to enlighten, enliven, and transform thy earthly, carnal heart into a Spiritual, and Heavenly Garden. But these Beams, that come to warm, and beautify thee, lean not at all upon any thing in thee. They depend singly, and entirely upon their proper Sun, which is Love, the heart of God.

3. *Cord.* The *third Cord* is the *Seed. That the Promise may be sure to the Seed.* Lawyers say, that no gift by any deed is good without a consideration: They say also, that there is no consideration, which bindeth more, than that of Fatherly affection; when a deed runneth in those words: *I out of my Fatherly affection give to my Son, &c.*

This is the consideration in the New Testament the Love of a Father. All the Promises of Grace, and Glory, of Heaven, and Earth, Time, and Eternity are made to the *Seed.*

The ground of a Fathers Love is the Unity. A Father loveth himself in his Seed. His Seed is one with himself. The Seed lay first in the Father. It cometh forth from the Father. It is one Nature with the Father, and beareth the Image of the Father before him. The same Seed in the Father is the Father, and the Son in the Son. All Relations, the Loves, and Sweetnesses of all Relations are Unions, that is, Participations, and branches of Unity. Paternity, the Relations, and Love of a Father is Unity, the Root, and Head of all Unions, Relations, and Loves.

The Philosopher teacheth us, that the reason of a Fathers Love to his Children is *Self-love*, and the Love of Immortality. He seeth *himself* ever-fresh,

fresh, and flourishing, propagated to Immortality in his Off-spring. All numbers are said to be the first Unity multiplied. Each number springeth from Unity, is made up of Unities, consisteth in an Unity. Thus God is one in his Seed. The Seed is the Unity of God multiplying itself into many Self-Images in the same Divine Nature, in the same Essential, and Eternal Image, the Lord *Jesus*. Is not the Promise now sure, when it is to the Seed, in which the Unity of God, the Love-spring of Eternity, is the Band of Love?

I have not yet sounded the Sea of Sweetness opening itself to us in this Scripture: *Now a Mediator is between Two: but God is One.*

God is said to have created all things by *Jesus Christ*; *Ephes.* 1. 9. *To have made all things by him, and in him*, *Colos.* 1. 16. God then is *One* in Nature, and in Grace, in the new Creature, and in the first Creation. There is *one Seed* of both, the Lord *Jesus*. *All things were made by him, and without him was nothing made, that was made*, *John* 1. 2. As no Wheat springeth without a grain of Wheat cast into the ground, as no Rose groweth without the Seed of a Rose: so no Flower of Divinity, no Divine Work, no Divine Image cometh forth any where, in this World, or that which is to come without the Divine Word, the Seed of God, which was in the Beginning with God, and was God.

Acts 17. 24. *St. Paul* maketh this his great Argument to convince the *Athenians*, and to persuade them to Faith in *Jesus Christ*, the *Unity* of the *Divine Seed*. *They feel after him*, saith he, *if so be they may find him*; *although he be not far from every one of us. In him we live, and move, and have our Being*; as in our proper Seed and Element. *For as one of your own Poets hath said*: *We also are his Off-spring*. The *Apostle* in the Authority, and with the Seal of the *Holy Ghost* confirmeth the Testimony of Nature to this Truth; the *Unity of the Divine Seed* in *Nature*. *God is One* not in *Regeneration* only, but in the *Creation* also. *We also are his Off-spring.*

Thou, who art hitherto Earthly, and Natural, an outcast of Nature, cast down to the nethermost parts of the Earth in Lusts, Unbelief, Blindness of Mind, Hardness of Heart, Profaneness, Enmity, seek thou also after God, feel after him. Thou also mayest see him, and feel, and find him in every motion, in every act, and part of thy Life, in every point of thy whole Being. Every Motion, Act, and Part of thy Life, every Point in thy whole Being is that Field, in which is hid the Treasure of the Divine Being, Beauty, and Blessedness. *Thou livest, and movest, and hast thy Being in him* He liveth, and moveth and hath his Being in thee. He is thy *Seed* in thee. *For thou also art his Off-spring.*

Believe the Love of God, open all the parts of thy Being, and Powers of thy Soul to take in this Love. Thou hast in thee the Band of the Love-union, the Divine Love-spring, the Unity of the Divine Seed. For thou also art his Off-spring.

Blessed is he, who believes, and seeks for this Pearl more than Silve an d

digge th

diggeth for it more, than for hidden Treasures. Blessed is he, who findeth it, and goeth, and selleth all that he hath to purchase it. Thou hast this Pearl in thine own Field, the Divine Seed in thine own Soul, and Being.

Let this be the only Seed in thy Soul. Then hast thou sold all for it. Then will it spring up into a living Palace of one Immortal Pearl in thee, which God himself, and all Glorious Spirits will inhabit together with thee, filling it with the sweet Lights of their Divine Beauty, with the Eternal Flames of their Divine Loves, and Joys.

Obj. But you may say; if this be so, why are not all saved? If all be of *one Seed*, which is *Christ*, why doth not one Life of Grace, and Glory spring up in all from that one Seed?

Ans. My *Answer* to this *Objection* shall be a threefold use; a *Reproof* to *Sinners*; a *Root of Comfort*; a *Reason for Holiness*.

Use. 1. A *Reproof to Sinners.* The Sin of the Devil was the first, and Fountain Sin: In that therefore the evil Nature of Sin in the whole Kind, and in every individual Act is most manifest. St. *Jude* painteth it out in its black, and bloody colours after a most lively manner, *Jude* 6. *The Angels not keeping their first Principle* (ἀρχὴν) *and forsaking their proper Habitation* οἰκητήριον. O Man! Thy God is thy *first Principle.* Thou didst stand in him, as in thy Root. Thou wert filled with Sap from him. Thou didst partake of the Fatness, and Sweetness of the Divine Nature. Thou wert a flourishing and fruitful Tree. All the Birds of Heaven; the Holy Spirit, the Blessed Angels delighted to sit, and Sing in thy Branches. All visible things rested under thy Shadow. How art thou fallen to the ground? How dost thou lie withered, and dead upon the face of the Earth? No good thing cometh near thee. Sin hath done this. *Thou hast not kept thy first Principle.*

O Man! The Divine Image was thy *proper Habitation.* This Image in thy Person was a *Sun* of Beauty shining in every part of it; and a Shield of Power defending it on every side. In this Image all Blessed things were united to make a Paradise for thee, which thou didst carry about in thine own Person, as thy proper Form, thine inseparable Habitation, like to God, who carryeth his own Heaven into every place with him. Alas! Thou art now naked in the Eye of God, and all the Creatures. Thou art exposed to shame, to every storm of Rage, Malice, and Wrath from all. Sin hath done this. By Sin thou hast forsaken thine own, thy proper Habitation.

Beware, O Men! Of the Evil of Sin. You cast out anew the Divine Seed out of your Garden by every new act of Sin. You cut off anew the Divine Form, Flower, and Fruit from every Plant in your Garden by every new Act of Sin. As oft as you Sin; so oft you make a fresh wound upon the Divine Unity, you make it to bleed afresh, and dye in your Persons.

But besides this there is yet a greater Evil in Sin. The Seed of God is one, the Divine Unity, the Love-spring of Eternity. The Seed of the Serpent

the

the Devil is Enmity, the Hellish Spring of Hate and Death. Every Sin is this Seed of the Serpent in thee, Enmity to the Heavenly Seed, the Unity of God.

In the Law the Jews were forbidden to seethe a Kid in his Mothers Milk for the Cruelty, and Unnaturalness. O the cruelty of every Sinner in every act of Sin! O the unnaturalness! Thou makest a Fire of the Kid, that thou mayst burn its Mother in it. Thou changest the natural Image, the natural Life in thee into a fire of Wrath, and Lust, to burn up, and consume in it the Heavenly Seed, out of which it springeth.

Solomon in his *Proverbs* telleth us, that he, who curseth his Father, and despiseth his Mother; the Ravens of the Valleys, and the young Eagles shall pick out his Eyes. This hath its highest truth here: go on in Sin. But know, that now in each Act of Lust, of Wrath, of Profaneness, of Unbelief, thou offerest despight to, thou cursest, thou killest the Seed of God in thy self, the Divine Unity, the purest, and perfectest Love, thy Father, which hath begotten thee, and thy Mother, which bare thee, which brought thee forth. What will thine End be? The Ravens of the Vallies, and the young Eagles; Unclean, and devouring Spirits from Hell below, Spirits of blood, of death, of horrour, and slaughter shall eat thy Flesh, consume all the Light of Life, and Beauty in thee, shall swallow up thy Spirit into the Bottomless Pits of Darkness, Dread, and Death within themselves.

Use. 2. The Root of Comforts in Believing; the Root of Faith, that we may believe, and have Comfort is the *Divine Unity*. The *Unity* of God is thy *Seed* in thee. The *Seed* is *one*, and that one *Christ*. The *Unity* of God is the highest, and purest Love. The Unity of God, Divine Love is the Seed of all Things, thy Seed. Believe this Love, believe in this Unity, that is in Christ, who is this one Seed of Love. Let these *Arguments* persuade thee to believe.

1. *Argu.* The Unity of God is the Fountain of Love. The Unity is the Simplicity, the Purity of the Divine Nature. God in the nakedness and simplicity of his Divine Essence is Love. Lean, stay thy self upon this Rock of Eternity, the Divine Unity, Simplicity, Purity of Love.

2. *Argu.* The Unity of God is Love; How strong is this Love? All the Attributes, Powers, Excellencies, Vertues of the God-Head are united, and centred in Love. How great is the force of Divine Love? What is its Vertue, its Excellency, its Sweetness? O Almighty, O Supream, O Soveraign Love! All Things Good, Great, and Divine are joyned, and raised to the highest point of Unity in Love. God assembled all the Powers, and properties of the Creation, all the Angels, the Persons in the Trinity to form a shadow of the Divine Nature in the first Man; saying; *Let us make Man.* O Man! All the Beauties, Blessedness, and Treasures of the Divine Nature are gathered together into one Sun of Divine Love to make thee new, no more a Shadow, but a Sun in this Sun, a Light in this Light of Eternal Love. Open thine Eye, and thine Heart to this Love by believing it.

3. *Argu.*

3. *Argu.* *Power* consisteth in Unity. The Supreme Unity, which is *Love*, is then Almighty, the Supreme, and Soveraign Power. Is any thing impossible to Almighty Love? Is any thing too hard for it? What change is there, from Darkness to Light, from pollution to Purity, from profaneness to Piety, from the hardness of a Stone to the softness, and sweetness of a Dove, from a Devil to a Blessed Angel, from a Hell to a Heaven, which Almighty Love cannot make in thine Heart, in a moment, with one cast of its Eye upon thee?

4. *Argu.* A simple Unity is *Infinite*: It is ever, every where the same. Nothing boundeth it, because it is itself alone, and there is no other thing besides itself together with it, to give an allay to it, or confine it. This is the Infiniteness of the Divine Unity. This Unity thus Infinite is Divine Love.

Come, whoever thou art; Believe, and cast thy self, thy Hopes, thy Fears; thy Griefs, thy Joys; thy Sins, thy Graces into this Abyss, this Sea of *Love*, which hath no Bottom, nor Shore. This will receive them all. This will swallow them all up into its sweet, and shining Depths. This will cover them all with its own rich, and glorious Floods, as Waters cover the Sea.

Come, Believe, and cast thy self, all thy Relations, the delights of thine Eyes, the dear, and pleasant things of thine Heart, thy whole Spirit, Soul, and Body into this Infiniteness of Divine Love. Thou shalt find them after many days, to day, immediately, eternally sporting themselves in this great and wide Sea of Love.

Love in the Person of the Lord *Jesus* descended to the nethermost parts of the Earth, and ascended above all Heavens, that it might fill all. Behold ow a Deluge of Divine Love in the Resurrection of thy *Jesus*. Love, as a manifold Fountain of a great Deep from below breaketh up, and breaketh open itself. *Love* poureth down itself thorow all the Windows of Heaven opened pon thee. Thus the Floods of *Love* increase, rise higher, and higher till they cover the tops of the highest Mountains of Guilt, or Despair, of Desire, or ope in thy Spirit: Only do not thou stop these Fountains of Love from beow, shut not these Windows of Heaven above to thy self by thy unbelief. ove in the Person of the *Holy Ghost* by the mouth of the *Psalmist* cryeth nto thee; *Open thy Mouth wide, and I will fill it.* Open all thine outward, and nward senses; open all the Powers, and Faculties of thy whole Man to take n this Love. Open them yet wider, wider still. Take in still more of this ove. When thou art full of Love to thine utmost Capacity; still that Love, hich remaineth is infinitely more, infinitely sweeter, than all that, which thou ast taken in.

5. *Argu.* That *one Seed*, the *Divine* Unity is thy Seed in thee, that is, Love tself, the first, the highest Love. *Thou also art his Off-spring. No Man ever ated his own Flesh. Can a Mother forget her Child?* saith the *Holy Ghost*. Diine Love is the Seed, out of which thou springest. Divine Love is thy Father,

 which

which hath begotten thee; thy Mother, which hath brought thee forth. Can Love itself hate its own Birth, and Branch? Can *Love* itself forget its own Child, the Child of Love?

The Prodigal returned first to himself; then he thinketh of his Father, and of Heaven; then his Father, meeteth him, kisseth him, bringeth him home, entertaineth him with the best Garment, with Feasts, with Musick, with an Universal Joy.

O Prodigal! Thou hast wasted thy Beauty, thy Strength, thy Parts, thy Comforts, thy flourishing hopes among Harlots, in lewd Company, and Conversation. Thou feedest among Swine upon Husks, and thou starvest in the midst of the Swine, for want of Husks. O Prodigal! The Divine Unity, the Seed of God, Eternal Love is still thy true self, which lyeth below all these disguises of Darkness, and Deformity; as *Jesus Christ* lay sleeping at the bottom of the Ship, which was ready to sink by the violence of the Storm. Thou art the Seed of God. *For thou also art his Off-spring.* Thou art the Seed of Love. For *God is Love.*

O Prodigal! Open the Eye of thy Spirit. Believe, and see Divine Love awakening, and appearing in thee, as thy true self to thy self. Feel it drawing thee by a sweet and irresistible force to itself, that is, to thy self, from whence thou hast so long wandered in a strange Form by the Sorcery of Sin, and the Devil. Believe, and see Divine Love, in the true Forms of thy Father, and of Heaven opening their Bosom again to thee, sending forth a vertue of Heavenly Love from themselves, with which they touch thy Heart, soften it, melt it into kindly repentings, a lovely shame, and tears of Love; kindling sweet desires, lively hopes, and ardent longings in thee after thy Father, and Heaven thine own Country.

Believe, and see Divine Love, thy Father coming into the midst of the Swine to thee, carrying thee in a rich Chariot made of his own Bosom, and Embraces, heaping kisses upon thee, as he carryeth thee. So Love bringeth thee home to its own House, the Heavenly Palace of Love. There Divine *Love* cloatheth thee with the best Garment, its own Native, and Divine *Loveliness:* Love feasteth thee with its own Joys, as they have sprung up thorow a Death for thee into a Resurrection for thee also. Love sweetneth, heightneth all thy entertainment with its own Musick resounding with a Divine Harmony from all Heavenly Hearts, all Glorified Spirits round about thee, yea, from all things in Heaven, and Earth tuned by the Eternal Spirit of Love itself, and plaid upon in a most exact, and charming Consort.

Return then to thy true self, thy Father, and to Heaven: Heavenly Love is all these. It is also thy way to these; thy Light, and thy Life in the way. Believe: Say not now; O that I could believe, and repent! Heavenly Love will form itself into inward Divine Meltings, Repentings, Acts of Faith, and of all Grace in thee. Look to this *Love*, and live Eternally in the Bosom of

Love.

Love. The Unity of God, which is Love is thy Root, which will rise up unto a Divine sap, and form itself into all Divine Fruit in thee if thou wait for it. *For thou art the Off-spring of God.*

Use. 3. *The Unity of God is the Root, and Reason of Holiness.* The Unity of God is the Fountain of Love, of all Grace, and Comfort in the Gospel The Promises are all made to this one Seed, which is *Christ* in the Unity of the Spirit, in the Unity of the Divine Nature. Thou hast then no further any part, or portion in the promises of the Gospel, or the Comforts of Love, than thou abidest in the Unity of Christ, and of the Spirit. It is the Seed of Love, which is a Holy, and Divine Seed; it is the Life, and Fruit of this Seed, on which, as on the Fleece of *Gideon*, all the Dew of Divine Blessings falleth. Every other Seed with its Life, and Fruit is, as the Mountains of *Gilboah*, on which no Rain, or Dew of any Divine Grace, or Promise descendeth. Abide then in this Love, which is the Holy Seed in thee; bring forth the Fruits of this *Love* in thy whole *Life*. So shalt thou be Blessed in thy Seed, and in thy Deed. I have now finished the *third Argument* for the confirmation, and explication of the *third Description* of Divine Love which was this; *The Love of God is the God of Love.* For *the Unity of God is the most high, and holy Love.* I pass now to the *fourth*, and last *Argument.*

4. *Argu. The Mystery of the Trinity is a Mystery of Divine Love.* This is the fourth Argument to prove, that *God is Love.*

The Divine Philosopher defineth *Love* to be *a Birth in a Beautiful Subject.* As the *New Hierusalem* is said to come down out of Heaven, a Bride ready trimmed: so out of the Bosom of Divine *Love* opening itself, as a Heaven cometh forth the Divine Loveliness, the Garden of Heaven, the Heavenly Paradise. This is the Heavenly Bride. In this Garden *Love* planteth, and maketh to grow all Beautiful, and Divine Images, all Heavenly Pleasures, and Joys.

Divine Love, and the Holy Trinity agree in this, that they are a *Birth*, and a *Marriage* both in one. This Mystery is figured in Paradise in the first Man. *Adam* bringeth *Eve* forth from himself. Then *Adam* bringeth forth *all Living* in and by *Eve*. *Adam* first bringeth forth *Eve*, the Beautiful Image of himself, and of that Paradise, which he then comprehended, and carryed about with him in his own Person. Then he brought forth all Beautiful Images of Humane Life, and Humane Nature in this Beautiful Subject by the *Love*-union of a Paradisical Marriage.

In like manner the Supream *Love* first bringeth forth the Supream *Loveliness*, the Image of itself. Then it marryeth itself to this Beautiful Image, and bringeth forth in the Bosom of it all *Lives*, *Loves*, *Lovelinesses*. Delights, and Glories.

Thus Divine *Love* is a Trinity. There are *three* in Divine *Love*. 1. The *Love-spring*, or the Divine Fountain of *Love*. 2. The *Love-Birth*, or the Divine Birth, and Image of *Love*, the Supream *Loveliness*. 3. The *Love-union*, the Divine Union between these two, the Sacred Fountain, and the Beautiful Image. These are the *three Properties* in Divine Love, which are all *one Love*; as there are *three Persons* in the Divine Nature, which *three* are *one God*. In *Love*, and in *God* these *three* are the same Divine Love, the same Divine Nature standing in distinct and opposite Relations to itself, within itself, infinitely above all things without itself. These Relations are in both the same.

1. The *God-Head* in the *Father* is Divine *Love* in the *Fountain*, the *Love-spring* of Eternity.

2. The *God-Head* in the *Son* is Divine *Love* in the *Birth*, or *Image*, the *Love-Birth* of Eternity.

3. The *God-Head* in the *Holy Ghost* is Divine *Love* in its *Marriage-Union* between the *Love-Spring*, and the *Love-Birth*, the *Love-Union* in Eternity.

See, how *God* being *Love* is compleat in Eternity by being within himself a *Birth*, and a *Marriage*, which Two include all Beauties, Sweetnesses, and Blessednesses, all the Beautiful, Sweet, and Blessed Fruits of Love.

Learn here, how Honourable Marriage is, and to keep the Bed of Love undefiled. God hath Sealed upon it the Image of the most Holy, and Blessed Trinity, the Trinity of Divine Love, the Trinity in the Divine Nature.

Marriage in Paradise was the fairest, and fullest Figure of the highest and sweetest Mystery in Heaven, the Ever-Blessed Trinity. The *Jews*, and *Gentiles* before the coming of the *Lord* Jesus were for the most part strangers to the Doctrine of the Trinity. They were therefore loose, and dissolute in the rites of Marriage. They made nothing of Fornication, and very little of Adultery. The Lord in the Revelation of the Gospel at once unvaileth the glorious face of the God-Head in the most Blessed Trinity; and discovereth the sweet, and beautiful Figure of it in the Holy State of Marriage.

Our Saviour by the Appearance of the Divine Nature in its numbeless Glories shining thorow every Created Form in his own Mysterious Person, as thorow their proper Figures, and Images hath restored all things. He hath restored Marriage not only to its primitive institution in Paradise, but to its Eternal Pattern, and Original in Heaven, the high, and holy Trinity. Preserve carefully this Marriage-Glory pure from Lusts, untroubled by passions: So shall you see with the Joy of Paradise the sacred Impression of that supream Mystery of all Divine Loves, Lovelinesses, and Delights the Trinity in the Divine Nature set, as the Seal of Eternity upon it. So shall you draw down the Trinity itself with all its secret, and sacred Treasures of Blessedness to inhabit with you in it. Blessed are they, who hold the Band of Marriage undefiled, unbroken in the sweet, and beautiful Type, in the Glorious Truth of the Heavenly Unity in the most Blessed Trinity.

We have said something in general to shew, how the Mystery of the Trinity is a Mystery of Divine Love. Let us launch a little further into this Sea of unexpressible Sweetnesses, and Beauties by contemplating this God-Head of pure loves in the several Persons of the Trinity.

1. The

1. The God-Head in the first Person; the Father is Divine Love in its Fountain. The *Father* in the Trinity is the *Love-spring* in Eternity: A Divine plenitude, or fulness, an unfathomable deep of Divine, and Unexpressible Sweetness ever rising up, ever flowing, overflowing all things; this is the Sacred Person of the *Father* in the Trinity, this is the Sacred Spring of *Divine Love* in Eternity; and this is that Fountain so dear to you, O ye Saints! out of which you all are made to drink that Sacred Fountain of *Free-Grace*.

I shall endeavour to open this beloved Fountain, the streams of which are the Life, Love, and Joy of all things in Heaven above, and on the Earth below by three precious inlets into it.

1. *Inlet. The Person of the Father is Divine Love in its Glory.* St. *Paul* speaking of the *Father* terminateth all the mysteries of the Gospel in the *Glory of his Grace*, as the Beginning, and the end of them all, the sweet, and shining Sea, from which they come, into which they all run again.

Grace is the name of *Love* in its *Freedom*, *Sweetness*, and *Fulness*. Every thing is in its Glory, in its Fountain. For there it is fairest, freshest, sweetest, and fullest. Love is in its Fountain in the Person of the Father. For there Love is in its Glory. There is a *Three-fold* Crown; the Marriage-Crown; the Crown of a King; the Crown of a Conqueror. There is accordingly a Three-fold Glory. 1. There is the Glory of *Beauty*. This is that of the Sun which sendeth forth his Beams thorow all things, and outshineth all things among the Earthly, and Heavenly Bodies. 2. There is the Glory of Soveraignty, which ruleth over all. 3. There is the Glory of Victory, which subdueth all things to itself, and maketh every thing an Ornament to its Triumph.

This Three-fold Crown doth *Love* wear, this Three-fold Glory is it cloathed with in the Person of the Father. It is the Eternal Sun, which enlightneth, enliveneth, sweetneth, cheareth all things by its Beams sent forth thorow all from the heights of the Heavens above to the depths of the Sea, and the center of the Earth below. It also infinitely surmounteth all things in Beauty, and Sweetness; as it shineth Eternally. It is the great King, that swayeth, and ruleth all every where by its Golden Scepter. It is the Glorious Conqueror, which pierceth deep into the hearts of all, which subdueth all to itself by its flaming Sword of Paradise turning every way. By this Sword it cutteth off, and consumeth all Flesh, and Earth, to keep that out of Paradise, and from the Tree of Life. By this Sword it refineth, and converteth all into a pure, and Heavenly Flame, into Spirit. So it bringeth them into Paradise, to the Tree of Life in the midst of it. Every thing every where doth Victorious Love make the Subject of its Conquests, and the Ornament of its Triumphs.

This is *Divine Love* in its *Glory*, in its *Fountain*. This is the *Divine Nature* in the *Person* of the *Father*. This is the *Glory* of *Free-Grace*.

2. *Inlet* into the Fountain of Divine Love. *All the Riches of Love are*

seated

seated in the Person of the Father. The *Apostle* applyeth the Riches of Grace to the Father, *Ephes.* 1. 7. *According to the Riches of his Grace. Three* things meet in Riches, Preciousness, Plenty, Power. Every thing is purest, and so most precious; every thing is most united, and so most plentiful, and so most powerful; every thing thus is richest in its Fountain. The first Person is the Fountain of Divine Love. For in him are the riches of Grace. Love is Richest in the Father. The heart of the Father is the Treasury of Love. No where is Love so pure, so unallayed, so precious, as in the heart of the Father. Traffick, O Man, for the Treasure of this Love with all thy faculties, with all that thou hast, and art. This Merchandise is beyond that of Gold, and Rubies: Traffick to this Coast of Spices, to this Land of rich, and precious Cordials, the Land of the purest Love, the heart of the Father. No where is Love so plentiful, in such abundance, as in the heart of the Father: The heart of the Father is infinitely larger than the Sea: yet doth *Love* cover it, as waters do the Sea, where it is deepest, when it is fullest. Cast thy world of Sins, O guilty Soul, with all thy Mountains of guilt into this Sea of *Love*. Love shall cover them, that they shall never appear more. If thou seek for them, thou shalt not find them. Come, drink thy fill of *Loves*, O dry, and thirsty Soul, from this rich, and full Spring in the heart of the Father. Come, thou most insatiate Soul, cast thy self into this full Sea of *Loves* in the Bosom of the Father, bath thy self, roul thy self in the midst of its rich Billows, which rise as high as Heaven. No where is Love so powerful, so irresistible, so full of vertue, as in the heart of the Father. Wash thy heart in this Fountain, and it shall be healed of the Leprosy of every Lust. Lay thy heart down in this Spring in the Bosom of the Father, and all its hardnesses shall be dissolved. Drink in these waters of Love fresh from the heart of the Father, and it shall be a powerful Cordial in thine heart. It shall restore thy Life, thy Strength, the complexion of thy Soul, thy Beauty, thy Spirits, thy Joys as at first, as in Paradise, as in Heaven, as in thine Eternal Original.

3. *Inlet. The Father in the Trinity is the Fountain of all Relations, and so the Fountain of Love. Father* is the sweetest of all Names, the Name of the highest, tenderest, purest, and most perfect sweetness. A Father is the first Relation, and the Fountain of all Relations. *Adam* was first a Father, then a Husband. So the Humane Nature from him streamed forth into Husband, and Wives, Sons, and Daughters, Brethren, and Sisters, into all Degrees of Kindred, Allyances, and Friendships.

Ephes. 3. 15. *St. Paul* saith, that from the *Father the whole Family in Heaven, and Earth is named.* Some render that word *Family*, the *Fatherhood*, or *Paternity*, Πατριά. All Fathers in that Relation, all the Fatherhoods, and Paternities of every Father in Heaven, and Earth lyeth first in that first Father, the first Person in the Trinity, as in their Fountain.

What comfort is this to every tender, careful grieved Father of every *sick*

sinful

ſinful, or loſt Child. The true Father to thy Child, which acteth the part of the Father behind the vail of the ſhadowy Father in thee, is the Father in the Trinity. He is the ſtrength, ſweetneſs, and truth of the Relation every where. The Paternity, the Fatherhood every where is named from him.

But if we take the word according to our Tranſlation, it affordeth us the ſame ſweet ſenſe more fully. *The whole Family in Heaven, and Earth is named from him*, from the Father of our Lord *Jeſus*. A Family is a chain of Relations, which are as ſo many Links in the chain faſtned one to another, Father, Mother, Husband, Wife, Brother, Siſter, Children, Friends. All theſe are named from the Eternal Father. All theſe ſweet, dear names of Union, of Love, agree firſt, moſt properly, moſt truly to him, who is the Supream Unity, the Original, and Fountain of all Unions, of all Love. All theſe are named from him. He is the true Parent in the Parents, the true Child, Husband, Wife, Brother, Siſter, Friend in thy Child, thy Husband, thy Wife, thy Brother, thy Siſter, thy Friends. He is deſcended into all theſe, ſhadoweth himſelf under them, ſubſiſteth, as the truth, and ſubſtance in them. It is this deſcent of his in them, this Preſence, and Appearance of his, which giveth theſe names to them. Love is either the Relation itſelf, or the Blood, which runneth along in the vein of every Relation. Every Relation is a Union. Every Union is Love in its proper kind, and degree. The Original, the Fountain of all Unions, of all Loves, of all Relations is the Supream Unity, which is the Father, the firſt Perſon in the Trinity. All Relations in Heaven, and Earth, all Unions are broken pieces of the great Diamond of Divine *Love*. The Father is this great Diamond of Divine Love, Entire, Eternal, the firſt, and higheſt Unity, in which all Unions lie together undivided, compleat, making up one Sweetneſs, which hath the names, and relliſhes of all ſweetneſſes, which giveth name, and relliſh to every ſweetneſs, which is above all names, and relliſhes, unexpreſſible, incomprehenſible. This is the Love-ſpring in the Trinity of Divine Love. This is the Father in the Trinity of the Divine Nature.

Uſe. I. Give all Glory to *Free-Grace*. Aſcribe all Riches to it. Set your Love upon it. This is the Fountain of Divine Love in the Boſom of the Father. This is the Fountain of *Iſrael*. This is the Fountain of the God Head. This is your own, your only Fountain, O Saints! All your ſtreams of Life, Grace, Comfort, Glory ariſe out of this Love-ſpring in Eternity, which is the heart of the Father. This is the Fountain, this is the Father of *Jeſus Chriſt*, your Fountain, and Father in him.

He that hath drunk the Waters of Life, and Love from this Well, will never thirſt more after any other Waters, or drink of any other Spring. We read in *Numbers* of a *Well* in the Wilderneſs, which the *Princes digged with their Staves, and ſung to it*; *Spring O Well.* O wandring Souls, behold your Well, which is before you in every Wilderneſs. The Prince of Life, your *Jeſus* hath dig'd, and opened it for you from the depths of the God-Head

with

with the Staff, the Scepter of his Spirit. Look to no other Fountain. But ſing continually to this; Spring O Well; Spring O thou heart of the Father; Spring in mine heart; Spring with ſtreams of Divine Truth; Spring with ſtreams of Divine Strength; Spring with ſtreams of Divine Joy; Send forth thy ſtreams over all my Soul, and Body; Make all my powers, and parts to ſing like the Garden of *Eden*! O thou Fountain of Gardens, My Prince hath dig'd, and opened thee in my heart, O thou heart of the Father, with the Staff of his Spirit. Open mine Eyes, O Bleſſed Spirit, that by thee I may ſee this Fountain, which by thee is opened in me!

It was at the Fountain, that Jacob, and his beloved *Rachel* firſt met. The Daughters of *Laban* came thither to water their Flocks. But the Well had a great ſtone upon it, which they could not move. *Jacob* rolled away the Stone, and watered their Flocks for them: From thence they brought *Jacob* to their Fathers Houſe, knew him for their neer Kinſman, and were marryed to him. It is at this Fountain of Free-Grace, that the Lord *Jeſus*, and the elect Soul firſt meet. Sin, Death, and Wrath make the Stone, which cover this Spring. The Lord *Jeſus* rolleth away this Stone, that thou, and all thy Fathers Flocks with thee, all the Principles, and Powers of Life in thee may drink of this Well. Here the Lord *Jeſus* looketh upon thee, and loveth thee. Here he maketh himſelf known to thee, to be thy Brother, and taketh thee to be his Bride: From this Well he goeth home with thee unto thy Fathers Houſe, into thine heart, into thy natural Spirit, and thine Earthly Image, in theſe to marry thee to himſelf, to make the fruitful to Eternal Glory, to encloſe this door of thy natural Spirit with Boards of *Cedar*, a Divine Beauty, Sweetneſs, and Incorruptibility, to build upon the wall of thine Earthly Image, a Palace of Silver, into which he will invite his Father, the Holy Angels, all glorified Spirits to feaſt, and inhabit with himſelf, and thee.

There was often contention for Wells between the Servants of *Abimelech*, and the Servants of *Iſaac*. Theſe digged them, and the others ſtopped them up. Contend, O Believers, for this your Well of Free-Grace: Suffer no *Ægyptians*, or *Philiſtines*, to ſtop it up by caſting in the Earth, or Stones, and Rubbiſh of *Free-Will*, of any Wiſdom, Work, or Worth in the Creature. As Earth caſt into a Spring defileth it: ſo by every thing of the Creature mingled with the Waters of this Fountain, they loſe their clearneſs, their ſweetneſs, their vertue.

Keep this Spring of the Fathers heart, of Free-Grace pure. So ſhalt thou ſee a clear, ſhining deep of Divine Sweetneſſes without any Bottom, the Glorious Deep of Eternity itſelf. In the clearneſs of this Spring ſhalt thou ſee thine own Face. From the freſhneſs of this Spring thou ſhalt drink in perpetually new Floods of all living Sweetneſſes. With the pure Waters of this Spring thou ſhalt preſerve thine heart ever new, ever ſoft, ever flouriſhing with all Joys, ever fruitful in all Graces. O Saints! Keep this Love-Spring, the Fountain of Free-Grace open, keep it pure in your Spirits. *Uſe.* 2.

Use. 2. Learn this Divine skill, O Christians, which comprehendeth all the rich mysteries of the Gospel in it. Rise up now every moment with all things round about you out of this Fountain of Love in Eternity, the Bosom of the Father. Return again every moment with all your troops into this Fountain of Love, the Bosom of the Father. Lay your selves down for ever here. Here alone is *Jesus Christ* in his naked Beauties, nakedly embraced.

Seek, see, and enjoy all your pleasant Relations, all pleasant Unions in this Unity of Divine Love, the heart of the Father, as in their proper Fountain. Here is the Truth, here is the Life of them all, in their Original. Here they are unchangeable. Here they are, as Sun-beams, before they come forth, descend, divide, grow shadowy, and fading.

As we keep Flowers fresh by setting their stalks in Water: So say of all your Relations in their shadows on Earth, of all your sweet things with their Sweetnesses; *Who is their Father?* Answer thy self; *The Fountain of Love.* Then keep them with their stalks in this Fountain. So shall they be ever fresh, ever sweet to thee.

2. *Person. The Love-Birth. God is Love.* The *three Persons* in the Trinity are *Love* in a *three-fold Form, and Property,* or in a *threefold Distinct,* and *opposite Relation* to itself, within itself, for the enjoyment of itself in the secret of Eternity, abstracted from all Creatures, infinitely before them, and above them. I have spoken of the *first Person* in this *Trinity* of Divine *Love,* the *Father,* the *Fountain of Love* in Eternity. I come now to speak of the *second Person.*

The *God-Head* in the *second Person* is *Divine Love in its Eternal Birth, and Image,* The Fountain of Divine Love, which is the *Father,* bringeth forth from itself, within itself an Eternal Birth, the compleat Image of itself, the Supreme Loveliness, and Beauty. This is our *Jesus* in the Bosom of the Father.

I shall endeavour to draw the Curtain from before this Blessed, and Glorious Birth of Divine Love, the Beloved, the only one of all Holy, and Heavenly Spirits. I shall endeavour to set this most desired, and most pleasant Person our Lord *Jesus* before the Eyes of your mind by *five Characters,* or *Marks.* The second Person in the Trinity is. 1. The *Birth,* or Image of Divine Love. 2. The *First.* 3. The *Fairest.* 4. The *Freshest.* 5. The *Fullest* Birth, and Image of Divine Love.

1. *Character.* The Lord *Jesus* is the *Birth,* or Image of Divine Love. The Heathen in their Divinity tell us of two *Twin-Loves* in Heaven, which exactly answer one the other. Thus Love, which is the Divine Nature, subsisteth in two Forms, two Persons, the *Father,* and the *Son,* which are *two Loves,* and the *same,* equally compleat, equally loving, equally lovely, equally beloved. *Adam* in Paradise brought forth *Eve* to be ever *before him, a meet help for him.* So the Father, and Fountain of Love bringeth forth in its own Bosom this Son of Love, this Divine Image of Love, to be ever before it, a meet help

to it, that Love in this entire Image of itself may perfectly behold, possess, enjoy, and multiply itself to Eternity.

Mat. 3. 17. The Father speaketh to *Jesus Christ* from Heaven: *This is my Beloved Son, in whom I am well pleased. Jesus Christ* is the Supreme object of Divine Love, the Supreme Loveliness, and so the Birth, or Image of Divine Love, the Son of *Loves*. In Divine things every faculty, or power brinketh forth its proper object, which is its perfection from itself, within itself, that it may be independent, and undivided in all its Joys, in all its Glories. The Divine understanding is the Sun, and Spring of Divine Truth, which is the light of its Life, its Object, and its Beauty. The Divine Will is the center of all Divine goodness, which is its proper Object, and Crown. There it Eternally riseth up. There it Eternally resteth. So *Divine Love* in the Person of the *Father* is the *Parent*, and the *Bridegroom* of the *Divine Loveliness* in the Person of the Son. *This is my Beloved Son*, saith the Father from Heaven, *in whom I am well pleased*. All the Joys of the Father are full; all his pleasures compleat here. All Seeds of Love in the heart of the Father are here sprung up into the fair Flowers of all Beauty, into the ripe Fruit of all delights within his own Bosom in the Person of *Christ*. This is the only Birth, Image, and Object of the Father, the Love-Spring; its *Birth*, and its Bride within itself. The Father, the Love-Spring bringeth forth this Love-Birth, and lovely Image, the Son of Love; that Love may be both, a Bridegroom, and a Bride to itself.

The *Persian* Prince called *Alcibiades* his *Garden of Pleasure*. The Father in the Trinity is the Fountain of Love: The Son is the Garden of Love rising up within this Fountain. Here the Father of Love soweth all the precious Seeds of Divine Love. Here so soon, as they are sown, they spring up into ripe Fruits, of which the Father eateth, and with which he delighteth himself in his Garden. This is the Circle of Eternity; Love Eternally sowing the rich Seeds, Eternally feasting upon the ripe Fruits of Divine Love in his Garden of Love.

Use. 1. Christians, seek your selves, your Love-Birth in this Eternal Love-Birth of the Son. Seek the Original, and true Image of your selves in this Eternal Image of Divine Love. See your-selves, seeds of Love sown in this Garden of Love from Eternity; ripe Fruits of Love flourishing in it Eternally. This is the dearest Jewel of a Saint; that Jewel, which the Saints wear in their Bosom, next their heart, with the sight of which they renew their vigour, and their beauty, recreate all their spiritual senses; I mean the rich Jewel of *Electing Love*, the *Love of Election*. In this Jewel a Believer seeth with the Eye of his Faith God the Father, the Fountain of Love in Eternity, God the Son an Eternal Birth of Divine Love from this Fountain, an Eternal Image, an Eternal Garden of Divine Love in this Fountain; himself born in this birth of Love, himself a lovely Image in this Image of Love, himself a

Tree of Love in this Garden of Love. Blessed is he, who hath this Testimony in his heart, and from Heaven; that *he was born here*; that here he rose up first out of the heart of the Father; that here he first appeared to the Eye of the Father; that here the Father set his Love upon him, and took pleasure in him. *He hath saved us*, saith *St. Paul* of the Father, *Not according to works which we have done, but according to his own purpose, and Grace given to us in Jesus Christ before the World was*, 2 Tim. 1. 9. *Grace given to us in Christ before the World was.* See your Love-birth in the Eternal Love-birth of the Lord Jesus, O Believers. *His purpose, and Grace given to us in Jesus Christ before the World was.* See the Fountain of Divine Love in the heart of the Father *his purpose*, and all the Births, all the Images, all the Gardens of Divine Love rising up from the sweet, and blessed depths of that Fountain, all comprehended in that only Birth, that only Image, that only Garden of Divine Love, the Lord *Jesus*.

Use. 2. Seek this Love-Birth in your selves. *When it pleased the Father to reveal his Son in me*; saith St. *Paul* speaking of the new Birth in himself. When the Father openeth himself, as a Fountain of Divine Love in your Spirits; when the Lord *Jesus* ariseth up, and appeareth to you, as the Birth, and Image of Divine Love within this Fountain; when your selves appear in him one Love-Birth in this Fountain of Love together with him; then may you rejoice, and say; now I live; now I am new-born from the Love-spring on high, in the highest Glory. You that have the mystery of this Divine Birth revealed in you, who see the Garden of Love flourishing in the midst of the Fountain of Love within you; retire into this Fountain, into the Garden in the Fountain, the Lord *Jesus* in the Bosom of the Father. Walk there, solace your selves there, hide your selves among the Trees of Divine Loveliness, and Love from the strife of Spirits. Here you shall be fed with the Fruit from these Trees, until the storm of Wrath be over past.

2. *Character. The Son of God is the first Birth of Divine Love.* It is said of him, *Mic.* 5. 3. *His goings forth are from everlasting.* The goings forth of the Lord *Jesus* the first Birth, and Image of Divine Love from the Bosom of the Father, the Fountain of Love are Eternal, without Beginning. The goings forth of the Light, which is the first, the beautiful Birth, and Image of the Sun, were from the beginning of the Creation. So soon, as the Sun had being, it had Beams. There was no moment, in which the Sun was without its circle of Beams, no more, than the Beams were without the Sun. In like manner the Lord *Jesus*, who is the Light, the Brightness, the Beautiful Image of Divine Love had his Birth from Eternity together with the Being of the Father. This Fountain in Eternity was no more without this Image the circle of all its Beauties shining in the midst of it, than this living, and lovely Image of all Glories was without its Fountain, from the unsearchable depth of whose Divine sweetnesses it riseth up continually. The Father is no more

without the Son, than the Son without the Father. Both are from Eternity, both equally Eternal in this sacred Mystery, and Trinity of the Divine Nature, of Divine Love.

Prov. 8. This Son of Love is brought in speaking of himself, and his Father: *Before the Mountains were formed, ere yet the foundations of the Earth were laid, I was before him, as one brought up with him, his delight day by day.* Before all the Creatures in Eternity, the Lord *Jesus* alone was with the Father, and none other besides him. He was bred up together with him, the Lamb, the lovely, the beloved Birth, and Object of all his Loves, the delight of his Eyes, that fed at his Table, and lay in his Bosom. If you ask now, what the Father did, before he made the World; the answer is full, and sweet; the Father in the infiniteness of Eternity brought forth *Jesus Christ*, delighted himself in *Jesus Christ*, the only Birth of all his Love, and Desires, the entire Image of all his Loves, and Joys.

Use. If you would be Holy, Heavenly, and Happy, if you would be perfect in all Graces, Joys, and Glories, as your Heavenly Father is perfect: be like him in this. He is taken up with his Son *Jesus* alone before, above a[ll] Creatures in Eternity. Let this *Jesus* as he is the Birth, and Image of all Divine Loves in the Father the Fountain of Love be your only one, the only Birth, and beautiful Image of your Spirits, continually before you, bred up with you into every Age, Form, and State, your only delight day by day. This is the first Birth of Love, the Birth of Love in Eternity. All those Birth[s] of Love, and lovely Images, which are in the Creature Shadowy, Finite, Fading, are here Substantial, a Spiritual, and Heavenly Substance, Infinite, Endless, Ever-flourishing.

3. *Character. The Lord Jesus, as he is the second Person in the Trinity is the fair[est] Birth of Divine Love.* We read, 1 *Cor.* 13. 5. *Love behaveth not itself unseemly, doth nothing uncomely.* The word *uncomely*, signifieth a want of Proportion, Harmony, Order, Figure, which make all Beauty, and Musick every where. Lo[ve] can conceive, can form nothing within itself, can bring forth nothing fro[m] itself, but its proper Object, its proper effect, which is suitable to it. Th[is] is Loveliness, and Beauty. As the Trees of Paradise had their Seed in them so every Birth of Love is in every part full of the Seeds of Love, by which [it] begetteth Love again; full of the Beams of Love, which kindle the swe[et] heat, and fire of Love. This is loveliness, which soweth the Seeds of Lov[e] and sendeth forth the Beams of Love into Spirits round about it. As the Su[n] the Supreme Eye of the visible World is to the Light: so is Love, the Ey[e] and heart of Eternity to loveliness. Loveliness is the proper Emanation, a[nd] Image of Love, by which it planteth itself in all Eyes, and Hearts, attract[ing] all things into the Golden Circle, and Center, into the Glorious Palace of t[he] Blessed, and Eternal Unity in itself, which is itself.

Love then bringeth forth Loveliness, and Beauty; the Divine Love, a

y

ne Loveliness, and Beauty; the Supreme Love, the Supreme Loveliness, and
auty. So the Lord *Jesus* is Beauty itself, a Divine Beauty, the Supream
auty, the fairest Birth of Love, being the first, the only Birth of the Father,
e Fountain of Divine Love, Love at the highest, Love in its first Sweetness.
John 1. 14. *We*, saith the Holy Apostle speaking of *Jesus Christ*, *saw his
lory, the Glory, as of the Only-begotten Son of God.* The Son of God is the
ly Birth of Love from the Father the Fountain of Love, in two respects;
mparatively; *Comprehensively*. *First*, The Lord *Jesus* is the only Birth, and
nage of Divine Love *Comparatively* for his excelling loveliness. *We saw his
lory, as the Glory of the Only-begotten of the Father.* So great a Glory shineth
his Person, as darkneth all other Beauties, all other Births, and Images of
ove, maketh them quite to disappear, and seem none at all. *Secondly*, Our Be-
ved *Jesus* is the only Birth, and Image of Divine Love *Comprehensively*. *All
Saints are in thine hand.* All Holy Births, and Images of the Father, the
ring of Love in Eternity; all Divine Lovelinesses the works of this curious
orkman; all the Jewels of Beauty framed by the skill of the first, and Su-
eme Love in the heart of the Father, all are comprehended in this Birth, and
age, all adorn the Person of Jesus Christ, are there in their highest lustre,
d take their Beauty from him. Thus is the Son of God the fairest Birth,
d Image of Divine Love.

Use. 1. O Sinners! This is that *Jesus*, who wooeth you, the fairest of all
ings, Beauty itself, the Divine, the Supreme Beauty. Object no more against
m, and your union with him. *Obj.* 1. Say not, you are unworthy of him, it
nnot be, that he should love Creatures so unlovely as you are. *Ans.* He, who
ould be your Bridegroom, will be your Beauty. What Bosom of the High-
t, and Divinest Love are you not fit for, when he, who is the Highest, and
ivinest Beauty is your Loveliness? What stains can appear in you, when
e fairest Image from the Fountain of Love comprehending in itself innume-
ble Glories, all Divine, all Supreme, descendeth upon you, and wrappeth you
entirely in itself? *Obj.* 2. Say not, you are unfit, you cannot believe his
ove, you cannot love him again, you shall never be pure, and lovely like him,
please him, to honour him. *Ans.* He, who offereth himself to be your
eauty, and Loveliness, will be your Lover, your Bridegroom. This Glorious
irit the Life of all Divine Loveliness will be the Husband of your Spirits.
ll your Fruit shall be from him. He, who is the fairest Birth, and Image from
e Fountain of Love, will be the Birth of all Spiritual, and Heavenly Beau-
es in you, of all Graces, Comforts, and Glories. He will be the lovely Image
ringing up, the root of Love, the heart of the Father into your whole Spirit,
ul, and Body. Object then no more. Make plain his way. Lay open your
arts to this *Jesus*, who cometh to be a Divine Beauty to thy Person, a Divine
idegroom to thy Spirit, the Divine Birth of Faith, of Love, of all Graces,
lories, Joys, and Immortality in thee. He will be better to thee than all thy

Righte-

Righteousness; sweeter to thee than all thy Lusts; Lovelier than all the Idols of thine Eyes, and Heart; Fruitfuller than all thine hopes.

Use. 2. O Saints! Behold another of your rich Jewels. See here that Jewel, which when you wear, filleth Heaven, and Earth with the brightness, and sweetness of its light round about you; dazleth, blindeth, and confoundeth the Devils, that they cannot come near you to hurt you; attracteth, and draweth down the Angels from Heaven to gaze upon you, to admire you, to attend round about you, to encompass you, whithersoever you go; yea, allureth, ravisheth the heart of the Father himself, to come, and inhabit in you, saying in his Songs of Love: *This is my Beloved Birth, my Beloved Bride, in whom my Soul is well pleased.* What is this Jewel of the Saints? It is the Righteousness of thy *Justification.* What is the Righteousness of a Saints *Justification?* It is this *Jesus* the fairest Birth of Divine Love, the fairest Image of all Loveliness in the Eternal Fountain of Love, the Bosom of the Father uniting himself to thee, and making himself thy Loveliness, making thee one fair Image of Divine Love, one Divine, and Supreme Beauty with himself. By vertue of this union thorow Faith; wherever he is seen, thy Person is seen together with that fairest Image of Divine Love in the Fountain of Love. Wherever thou art seen rightly, there together with thee, and in thy Person is seen this fairest Image of Divine Love in the open Fountain of Love, the Fathers Bosom. Thou art *the Righteousness of God in Jesus Christ*; Thou art the Birth, and Image of Divine Love in the fairest Birth, and Image of Divine Love in the midst of the Fountain of Love.

This is thy Beauty, thy Beloved, thy *Jesus*, O Believer. Trust thy self to the perfection, and covering Glory of his Loveliness. Lie down in the Bosom of his Beauties. Seek all Births, and Images of *Love*, which ever have been, are, or can be dear to thy Soul in his Face the immortal Seat, and Eternal Spring-season of thy self, and them.

4. *Character. The Lord Jesus is the freshest Birth, and Image of Divine Love,* that is, *of the Divine Nature.* The *Father*, the *Love-Spring* in Eternity speaketh to the *Son*, his *Love-Birth* thus: *To day have I begotten thee, Psal.* 2. The principal, and terminating sense of these words is the *Eternal Generation* of the Son in the Trinity. Eternity is one continued day, ever present, never past, never to come, above all Succession. So is the Generation of this *Love-Birth* ever perfect, ever present, never past. This is true from one end of Eternity to the other, if we may so speak of that, which hath neither Beginning, nor End, *to day* hath the Father begotten the Son. *Eternity is Indivisible. All Acts, all Joys, all Things* of *Eternity* are *together at once, in one.*

There are *three Rules*, which our Divines lay down concerning this Act of the Generation of the Son by the Father in the Trinity.

1. *Rule.* This Birth of Divine Love is perfect from Eternity, perfectly

ſpring up, perfectly brought forth from the Fountain of Love, the Boſom of the Father. The reaſon of this is the Unity of the Divine Eſſence. The Divine Nature, the Eſſence of Love, the God-head is one, equally Eternal in the *Father*, and the *Son*.

2. *Rule*. The Lord *Jeſus* the lovely Image of Divine Love is ever in the Birth, ever newly riſing up out of the Fountain of Love to Eternity. For the Act of Divine Generation, of the Divine Birth in the Myſtery, and Trinity of Divine Love is Eternal, one continued Act from Eternity to Eternity.

3. *Rule*. This Birth, and Image of Divine Love, the Son ever lyeth in its Fountain, the Boſom of the Father. This ariſeth from the *Unity* of the *Eſſence*, and the *Union* of the *Perſons* in this glorious ſecret of Eternal Love. Theſe Love-Perſons in the ſame Love-Subſtance are ever diſtinct, never divided.

Hoſe. 6. 3. *The coming forth of Chriſt*, as the anointed, and anointing of Divine Love, is ſaid to be, *as the Morning*. The Love-Birth of our *Jeſus* is in this ſenſe, as the Morning. It is ever new, ever freſh, ever pleaſant, as the lovely Summer-Morning in its firſt Sweetneſſes, and Light, in its Virgin-Purities, and Pleaſures. It was a Divine Sentence of a Holy, and learned Biſhop in the primitive times: *All that God doth from Eternity to Eternity, is the bringing forth of Jeſus Chriſt*. The Lord *Jeſus* is at once a lovely morning for new, and freſh Sweetneſſes; ever a glorious noon for the height of his Beauties, and the brightneſs of his light. He is a lovely Roſe ever in the Bud, ever full-blown.

Uſe. 1. Chuſe *Chriſt*: Refuſe the Creature. Take into your Boſom this Love-Birth of the Father. Caſt out of your Boſom your own Love-Births in the Creature. All theſe are Flowers, which wither, and dye away, either upon their ſtalk, or in your hand. Every thing of the Creature declineth ſo ſoon, as it cometh to its height. The Lord *Jeſus* is ever the ſame, ever full, ever freſh, a fruitful Autumn, and a floury Spring both in one continually. This is your *Inheritance Incorruptible, Undefiled, that paſſeth not away*, 1 *Pet*. 1.

Uſe. 2. Ever believe, as freſhly, as freely, as at the firſt moment of your Converſion, as in the firſt Act of Believing. the Lord *Jeſus* the ground and object of your Faith is ever freſh, ever new. All thy Sins againſt the Spiritual Marriage-Bed of thine Heavenly Bridegroom in thine heart can make no impreſſion upon him. He is New-born to thee from the unſearchable depths of Divine ſweetneſs in the heart of the Father every moment. He ſpringeth up a new Love-Birth in the Fountain of Love every moment with all his lovelineſſes freſh, fair, and full, like a Roſe new-blown; as if now alone they had firſt appeared.

5. *Character*. *Jeſus Chriſt in the ſacred Trinity is the fulleſt Birth, and Image of Divine Love from the Father, the Fountain of Love*. Our Saviour is called *The Power of God*, 1 *Corin*. 1. Whatever the Father hath brought forth from the Eternal ſpring of Love, of the God-Head; whatever he doth, whatever he

shall

ſhall, or can bring forth to Eternity; all is comprehended in this *Love-Birth*, in this Glorious, and full Image of Love, of God, *Jeſus Chriſt*.

The Father, the Fountain of Love, the Supream Unity bringeth forth itſelf into all variety in this full Image of himſelf, his Son, that he may reſt in his Son, that his Joy may be full in him.

As the Father is the firſt Unity: ſo the Son is the firſt diſtinction, or variety. The firſt is the higheſt diſtinction, and variety, the fulleſt diſtinction, and variety; the Fountain of all diſtinctions and varieties. As the Father is the Unity of Love, the Love-ſpring; ſo the Son is the variety of Love, the entire Image of all *Loves*, and *Lovelineſſes*. All things in Heaven, in Earth, and under the Earth lie together here in this Image, in the perfect Harmony of the Supreme Love, and Beauty, according to their proper diſtinctions, as Branches of the firſt, the faireſt, and the fulleſt variety.

Uſe. 1. With all thy ſtock of Life, and abilities, Traffick for this great, and rich Pearl the Lord *Jeſus*. His price is beyond that of Rubies. All thy deſires cannot equal him. All Prices are comprehended in his Price. All precious things are in this Pearl. O that we underſtood with Spiritual Hearts, that we ſaw with Spiritual Eyes, that we relliſhed with a Spiritual taſt this Love-Birth, this Image of Love, this variety of Love, the firſt, the full diſtinction, and variety, the Fountain of all diſtinctions, and varieties in the Perſon of *Chriſt*, we ſhould then rejoice to ſee each dear, or diſpleaſing object, each ſtate, and circumſtance of Life in its proper, and diſtinct Form, a diſtinct Form, a diſtinct Spirit of Divine Love, and Beauty, immortal ſhining in this Eternal Spirit; in this Heavenly Image; Love, and Lovelineſs itſelf; the firſt, the fulleſt variety, all variety in one entire, and All-glorious Form, the Fountain of variety, which is our *Jeſus*. *Ignatius* being to die, ſaid: *Let Sword, Fire, wild Beaſts, the Croſs, breakings of all my bones, tortures thorow all my body; ſo I may find Chriſt, ſo I may gain Chriſt*. If thou haſt *Jeſus Chriſt*, he is thy Garland; and all theſe are ſweet-ſmelling, Immortal Flowers in thy Garland; he is thy Crown, all theſe are precious Stones, and Jewels in thy Crown. A *Sword* in *Chriſt* is a living Form, and penetrating power of Divine Love, dividing between Fleſh, and Spirit, the Bone, and the Marrow in thee; piercing to the Bottom of thine heart, to open the Fountain of Eternal Life, and Joys in thee. The fire ſpringing up in this Love-Birth is a flame of Love working thee into one Heavenly flame with itſelf, and to this end embracing thee, winding itſelf into all the ſecrets of thy Body, and Soul. The Teeth of wild Beaſts appearing in this Image of Divine Love are the Eternal Spirit, the Spirit of Love feaſting upon thee, and then feaſting thee upon itſelf. The Croſs in this Garden of Love is a Tree of Eternal Love, thou art the fair, and ſweet Fruit upon this Tree. The breakings of Bones looked upon in this myſterious Glaſs of all varieties, the Eternal Word, the Eternal Image of Love are no Wounds, but Divine Anointings. The tortures of the whole

Body

Body are the costly perfume of Love poured forth upon the head of the Sacrificer, and running down all along to the hem of his Garments.

Use. 2. Hast thou *Jesus Christ*? Care for nothing more In him are all things given thee richly to enjoy. If he be come to thee, look for no other thing. There is nothing can come after him. He is the full Birth, and Image of Divine Love. The vanity, and emptiness of the Creature is expressed by *Solomon* after this manner: *What is that, which hath been? It is that, which is; and what is that, which is to come? It is that, which hath been, It is named already It is man.* So do thou express the variety, and fulness of *Jesus Christ*. So quench all other Loves in thee. What is that, which hath been? It is that, which is. What is that, which shall be? It is that, which hath been. It is all named in *Jesus Christ*. If thou hast *Jesus Christ*, thou art rich to God, thou hast all his Treasure. Now sing thy Soul to a Divine sleep, and rest in the Bosom of Divine Love with these words: go to rest, O my Soul. Thou hast all good things laid up for thee in the Person of thy *Jesus* to Eternity. The Bosom of the Father, the Fountain of Love is opened in thee. The Lord *Jesus*, the full Birth, the full Image, the full variety of Love springeth forth from this Fountain for thee.

Poets say, that every Spring hath at the bottom of it a palace of Pearl, in which the Divinity, the God of this Spring dwelleth. God the Father is the Fountain of Love. The Lord *Jesus* riseth up in the rich depths of this Fountain, as the Palace of Eternity, composed of all variety in most precious Forms, and Figures; furnished with, inhabited by all variety in all Beautiful, and Heavenly Images; in the dress of all Divine entertainments; in the form of all Glorious, and Eternal Spirits flowing continually with all manner of Sweetnesses. O Saint! O Believer! Thou hast this Fountain, this Palace continually open in thee. Open thou the Eye of thy Faith. Look upon the Treasures of it; if thou canst number them, if thou canst comprehend them. Separate thy self through desire kindled in thee by the strength of thy Faith, and thy Love. Descend into this Fountain. Dwell for ever in this Palace, and intermeddle with, enjoy all substance.

I have spoken of the *two first Persons* in the *Trinity*, I come now to the *third*.

3. *Person. The Holy Spirit, the third Person in the Trinity is the Love-union between the Love-Spring, and the Love-Birth; the Father, and the Son.* The *Holy Ghost* hath his name from *Breathing*. Eternal Love distinguishing itself into two Persons, the Father, and the Son, from both these by a conspiration of Love doth breath forth itself into one third person, the Holy Spirit, in which they both stand two distinct Persons in one third Person, which is the Love-union, the golden Marriage-knot of them both. The *Holy Spirit* is frequently expressed in Scriptures by an *Ointment*. Several rich Spices breath forth themselves into one costly ointment. The Spices all meet in one precious Form, in which they still retain their own distinct forms; the sweetnesses, and vertues of

the ſeveral Spices breath forth themſelves into one pleaſant perfume, in which all the ſeveral ſweetneſſes remain diſtinct, mutual penetrating, and infuſing each the other in that one ſweetneſs diſtinct from them all. So the Father, and the Son by the force, and myſtery of Divine Love, breath forth themſelves into one diſtinct Perſon, the Holy Ghoſt, in which they alſo remain diſtinct, diſtinctly, and mutually, penetrating, poſſeſſing, enjoying the Perſons of each other, with their Properties, Powers, Sweetneſſes, and Beauties in that one. This one is diſtinct from both, becauſe it comprehendeth both diſtinctly in one. This is the *Love-union* between the *Fountain*, and the *Birth*, or *Image* of *Divine Love*.

It is a ſaying, which *Thomas Aquinas* citeth from St. *Auſtin*: *Whatever there is of Sweetneſs, of Pleaſantneſs, of Complacency, of Delight, of Joy, of Love, of Loveline ſs, of Agreeableneſs, of Suitableneſs, of Harmony any where; it is the Holy Ghoſt.* The reaſon is this: All Colours with their ſeveral Beauties are the mixtures of ſhade, and light. Children are the Parents united. So every thing of Love, or Beauty; every Divine Work, and Operation thorow Heaven, and Earth is the Love-union between the Father, the Fountain of Love, and this lovely Image, which is both the Birth, and the Bride of Love, of the Father. All Pleaſantneſs, all Divine Acts of Creation, and Providence with their ſeveral Lights, Lives, Loves, and Vertues are this Love-union in its lovely extent, and vaſt variety. The *Pſalmiſt* ſaith of God: *Thou haſt ſtretched out the Heavens by thy Breath, by thy Spirit.* The *Heavens* are the Beauty, the Pleaſantneſs, and Joy of the Divine Appearance, and the Divine Operation, which is the *Love-Image*, and the *Love-Birth* every where.

Uſe. 1. Pray, O Chriſtians, for the Heavenly Eye-ſalve of the *Holy Ghoſt* to anoint the *Eyes* of your minds. What Bleſſed ſights ſhall you then ſee every where? What Heavenly Viſions of Divine Love, and Beauty upon the Spiritual Bed of Eternal Love ſhall you meet with in every object? In every work of God, in every act of Providence you will ſee the high, and glorious Trinity; the adored, and amiable myſtery of Eternal Love; the three Beautiful, and Bleſſed Perſons of this Trinity, of this myſtery; the Father, the Fountain of Love, the Son the Fathers Lovely Birth, Bride, in their Love-union, on their Heavenly Marriage-Bed figuring themſelves, and ſhining with the naked, ſubſtantial *Glory* thorow the *Figure.* You will *ſay to the ſweetneſs* of every Flower, to the Beauty of every proſpect in your walks: this is the Love-union between the Father, and the *Son; this is the fruit of the Marriage-Bed*, on which the Father of Loves, and his Lovely Image his Son, and his Bride lie eternally embracing each other. This is the perfume, this is the luſtre of the holy Spirit. You will ſay of every Sickneſs, Sorrow, and Death Here alſo is the *Love-union.* Theſe alſo are Love-Births, Love-Images from the Marriage-Bed of Love in Eternity. Theſe alſo are Doves with Wings of Silver, and Feathers of Gold from that Mother-Dove, the Holy Spirit, the

Love,

Love-Marriage between the Father, and the Son in the most holy Trinity.

Use. 2. Give Glory to the Persons of this blessed Trinity, to this mystery of Divine Love continually. Dost thou perceive any good principle in Grace, or nature putting forth itself in thee. Give thanks, and say: This is the Father, the Fountain of Divine Love opening himself, and springing in me. Dost thou feel any sweet Appearance of Truth, or Goodness, Light or Love in thy Spirit? Rejoyce, and say, this is the Son, the Love-Birth, the *Love-Image*, the *Lord* Jesus rising up from his Fountain, the Bosom of the Father in me. *If* there be any Vertue, any Power, any Pleasantness, any Joy, any *Life* of *Love*: lift up thine heart, and hands on high, say: This is the *Love*-union, the *Love*-knot in the most high, and Holy Trinity; this is the Holy Spirit, the Marriage Bed of the Eternal Bridegroom, and Bride, the Father of all *Loves*, the Image of all *Lovelinesses*. This is thy high, and Heavenly Marriage-Bed, which is now Green, flourishing, and fruitful in me.

Use. 3. *Let* this be the mark, at which thou aimest, O Believer, to be taken up into this *Love* union, into this Eternal Marriage-Bed; to be one with he *Father*, and the *Son*, as they are one in the Unity of the *Spirit*.

I have now finished the *last Argument* for the confirmation of that propo-ition, *God is Love*. The *Argument* was this; *The mystery of the Trinity is a ystery of Divine Love*. Let me conclude this *Argument* with one general se.

Use. Hold fast the Doctrine of the Holy Trinity. Study it with humble, pure, piritual understandings, with the Scriptures in your Eye, as your mark to uide you in your way, with the Holy Ghost in your heart, as your *Light* of ife, to discern your mark, your way, and your end.

It is a deep, and Divine contemplation, that of a *Learned*, Acute, and Hea-enly Person: God hath two Boxes, in which he hath laid up his Jewels; the carnation, and the Trinity. God hath opened one Box, the Incarnation. here we have seen rich, and sparkling Jewels in the union between the Di-ne and Humane Nature here below, God manifested in Flesh. But O! What wels shall we see, what *Loves*, what Glories, what Unions, when God shall pen his other Box of the Trinity, when we shall see God justified in the irit?

The *Trinity* is the Supream, the Soveraign mystery of the Gospel; the undation of fair Colours, upon which all evangelical mysteries are built; e Fountain in Eternity, from which they flow. Then shall we understand l mysteries, when God shall take the vail from before this, which is the entire, d clear-shining Face of the God-Head. Here is the *Supream Unity*, the Foun-in of all *Love*, *Life*, and *Light*. Here is the variety of *Love*, and of Life, its fairest Light, in its first, and fullest Image. Here is the *Love-union*, the h Treasury, the curious Spring, the golden Band of all Unions, Motions, easures, and Joys. Blessed is he, who with Eyes washed in this Fountain looketh into it, seeth himself, and all Divine Mysteries there Unvailed. St. *Austin* wished to have seen *Christ in the Flesh*. O how much more Divine, and Blessed a Spectacle is it to see *Christ in the Spirit*, that is, in the Glory of the Trinity, the *Three Persons* in One with all their Eternal Beauty, fully, and freely displayed. Pray for, Wait for, Look up continually into the Heights, and Lights of the Spirit for this sight.

I have now brought to an End my *last Description of Divine Love*, which is the *Divine Nature. God is Love*. I will seal up this Sweet, and Soveraign Truth of the Gospel with *One Use*.

Use. *If you will be Children of God, be Children of Love. God is Love. Love* is the Divine Nature in God, and in all His Holy Ones. 1. *Beware of Lust, the Corruption of Love.* 2. *Beware of Passion the Contrariety to Love.*

1. *Beware of Lust the Corruption of Love.* The Corruption of the best Thing is the Worst. All Lust is Love degenerated, Love Corrupted. Love is the Best of all things. Love in its purity, at its Height, is the Godhead in God. Lust is the Formality, and Essence of the Devil, as he is a Devil. St. *Jude* teacheth us; that fleshly Lusts are the similitude of that First sin of the Faln Spirits, which made them of Angels Devils.

Ixion in the Poets loved a Goddess, in the place of whom he embraced a Cloud formed into the Shape of a Divine Beauty. Thus he became the Father of the *Centaures*, half Men, half Beasts. Then he was cast into hell where he is fastened to a Wheel turning continually round, on which he is tormented day, and night. This Parable is meant of thee, O Lustful Spirit: Thou wert made for Divine Love, for the Love of the Divine Beauty. Thus hast changed, this Love into various Lusts. Thou defilest thy self with Shadows, Clouds of Darkness formed into the Empty Shapes of Beauty. Instead of the Divine, and Humane Nature in the Blessed Harmony of an Immortal Union, all thy Births, all thy Production are Horrid hateful monsters; Man, Beast, and Devil all in One Spirit, in One Person. Thy end is the Endless Circle of thy Lusts, and of the Divine wrath, as the Wheel of Eternity, a Wheel of Fire, holding thee fast tied to it, and torturing thee without any Rest, or Period.

2 *Beware of Passion the Contrariety to Love. Sampson* tied Foxes together by their Tails with Firebrands between them. So he sent them forth to burn up the standing Corn of the *Philistines* in the Fields. O men! when ye fall from the Wisdom of God into the Subtlety of the Serpent, you become Foxes, not Men. Your Lusts, your Carnal Interests are your Tayls, by which you are tied together in all your Unions, and Commerce; your Passions are Fire-brands fastned to your Tayls. Thus the Devil sendeth you forth to deface, and consume the Beauties, the Peace, the Comforts each of other, of the whole Creation round about you. Behold the true Figure of Passionate Persons, whose Wrath, Envy, Hatred, Malice are Fire-brands Kindled from Hell,

and

and fastned to their Lusts, as to their tails, in which they carry them burning about thorow all things.

In the Holy of Holies was placed a Mercy-Seat all of Beaten Gold, the Throne of Grace, the Throne of Love. Out of this Throne of one piece with it, rose up two Cherubims of Beaten Gold. They stretched forth their Wings they set their faces one to the other. They together looked down to the Mercy-Seat. This is the Heavenly Figure of your Christ, and you, O ye Children of Love, in your Love-Union, and Spiritual Communion. God in *Christ*; Christ in the Glory of the Father is the Golden Mercy-Seat, the Throne of Love. The Saints are the Cherubims, the Children of Love rising up from the Throne of Love, of one piece of Gold, of one Love-Spirit with it. With their Faces, their Divine part they look one to another, and maintain a mutual society. *They spread their Hearts, their Spiritual understandings*, their Spiritual affections to each other, and so meet, so embrace. With united Spirits they look down to the Throne of Love in the midst of them, out of which they grow up together, from which they continually draw fresh Beams, fresh Love, Life, and Joy.

O Saints, O Holy Souls be rooted in Love, grow up out of this Throne of Love, Shine forth with Faces of Love, spread forth wings of Love. Be in all things one piece, one pure Gold of Divine Love with the Throne of Love, the Divine Nature. For God is Love.

I am now come to the period of my discourse upon the *first part* of my Doctrine; *The Love of God.*

The *second part* is *the Effusion*, or *pouring forth of Divine Love.*

I shall express this to you by *six Properties.* The Love of God is poured forth in *Jesus Christ.* 1. *Freely.* 2. *Purely.* 3. *Plentifully.* 4. *Powerfully.* 5. *Essentially.* 6. *Eternally.*

1. *Property The Love of God is poured forth in Jesus Christ freely.* 2 Sam. 7. 21. *David* is brought in, as a Type of *Jesus Christ.* He sitteth in the Temple before the Lord, when he was setled in his Kingdom, and at the height of his Kingly Glory. Thus Jesus Christ sitteth upon his Throne in the highest Heavens before his Father. He discourseth to his Father of the wonders of his Fathers Love, and his own Glory. *What is my Fathers House, that thou hast brought me hitherto? v.* 18. I was a Man, a poor Creature, a Worm of the Earth, Earthy, as the Dust of the Earth, as low, as the neathermost parts of the Earth, as low, and naked, as the first principle of the first Creation, when the Earth was empty, and void, when darkness covered the face of it: This was my Fathers House. Yet thou hast brought me hitherto, thou hast brought me to thy right Hand, far above all Principalities, and Powers, all Heavens to thy Throne. Thou hast given me a new Name above every Name, a Name, that eminently comprehendeth all Names in it; a Name, that infinitely transcendeth all Names. Thus Love is poured forth in Christ.

Jesus

Jesus Christ goeth on in the Person of *David. And this was yet a small thing in thy sight; O Lord God; thou hast spoken of thy Servants House for a great while to come, v.* 19. This, O my Father, which thou hast wrought so wonderfully; these mighty Works, these Miracles of Divine Love, and Glory in my Person seem a small thing to thee. Thou hast spoken of my House, my Church, my Members, my Seed to reign with me in the same Kingdom of Glory to Eternity.

Then *Jesus Christ* raiseth this Love to the highest point of Admiration, to a state of transcendency above the capacity, and comprehension of all Humane Hearts, of all Created understandings. Is this the manner of Man, O Lord God! Is there any thing among Men, in the compass of the Creation, to which this Love can be likened, or with which it can be compared? Is there any where any Image, Figure, or Resemblance of such a design, such a work of Love, and Glory?

Thus Love is poured forth in the Person of the Lord Jesus. See now, how freely it is poured forth. *According to thine own heart hast thou done all this, v.* 21. Indeed he bringeth in first; *For thy Words sake*; for thy Promise; for thy Sons sake, thine Eternal Word, thine Essential Image, the Ground of thy Promise; the Subject of thy Love, and Design; the Pattern, and Model of thy Work. But this word springeth from that Root, to which all is ultimately referred; the Heart of God; *According to thine own Heart hast thou done all this.*

The Heart of God is the Fountain of living Loves, which springeth up *freely* of its own accord to Eternal Joys, and Glories in the Person of Christ.

The Love of God in Christ receiveth its Beginning, Force, Form, Fashion, and Finishing from the Heart of the Father. *All the Works of God* are said in the *Epistle* to the *Hebrews*, to have been *Finished from the Beginning of the World.* All the Loves of God, all the Works of Divine Love manifested, and wrought in the Blessed Person of our Lord *Jesus* were finished from Eternity in the heart of his Father.

All Tides are from the Æstuation of the Sea. The Sea boyling up from its Bottom, as it riseth, and dilateth itself, poureth forth floods of Waters into all Rivers which run along in the Bosom of the Earth. The Heart of God is the great Sea of Love. This from its own Divine Heat, Height, and Fulness filleth all Spirits with its Heavenly Floods in the Bosom of *Jesus Christ.*

The Will in the Soul is said by a learned Man to be *Amplitudo Intellectûs*, the understanding in its full extent.

The Love of God poured forth upon the Person of Christ, and upon all the Saints, upon all things in him, is *Amplitudo Cordis Divini*, the largeness of Gods Heart, the Heart of God in its full extent, and latitude. So *David* addeth in the same place, that God doth all this *to shew his Greatness*, the *Greatness of his Heart*; for he saith; This is to make thy Servant know; *v.* 21.

To

To display thy self, to draw a perfect draught of thy self in the Person of Christ. In what? The next *verse* expresseth it. *Wherefore thou art Great.* v. 22.

James 1. 5. God is said *to give to all men liberally, and to upbraid none.* Love is implyed in the gift; Freedom in the liberality, and gentleness without reproach. The Person of *Christ* is signified in the universality; *All Men.* Christ is one among the rest of Men, *Christ* is the Fulness of Mankind. He took not upon him the Person, but the nature of man, unrestrained to any particular Person. His Humane Nature was not a Branch, or an Apple, but the Apple-Tree.

There are two expressions, which St. *James* maketh use of here to set forth the Freedom of Divine Love in the effusions of it.

1. He giveth *Liberally.* The Word in Greek is *Simply,* without any Reserve; without any Division of the Heart. Simplicity is Unity; The Intentness of the Mind upon One Thing. The heart of God, All the Thoughts of his heart, All the Powers of the Godhead, All the Divine Attributes are united, and intended upon This One Thing alone; Love poured forth on the Person of the Lord *Jesus.*

Simplicity is without Alteration, or Composition. The heart of God is single in this, Natural, unchangeable. This is the One Thing, the Onely Thing of God's heart. This is the Simplicity of the Divine Operations from Eternity to Eternity; The Effusion of Love in the Person of Christ There may be many Shadows, many Vails; many Windings: But this is the Simplicity, the naked Face of the Divine Design, of the Divine Work from the Beginning to the End; as it lieth in the heart of God.

2. Upbraiding none To upbraid, is to object some Evil, as an Argument of withholding some Act of Love, or exercising some Act of Wrath. *John.* 1. 29. Jesus Christ is called the *Lamb,* which taketh away (*αἴρων, tollit,* taketh up, beareth) the Sins of the World. When the Father was to pour forth his *Love* upon *Christ* he did not reproach him saying; Thou hast the Sins of all the World upon thee. Thou hast upon thee Millions of Whoredomes, Adulteries, Incests, Treasons, Witchcrafts, Murthers, Idolatries, Rebellious Blasphemies, Horrid Profanenesses, Apostasies, Spiritual wickednesses in Heavenly, Angelical, Divine Forms, the proper Sins of Devils. Thou hast many *Davids, Amnons, Absaloms, Manassehs, Mary Magdalens,* many *Peters,* many *Judas's* in thee; and comest thou to me for Love? How can I give thee my Love? Instead of this, when he is Baptized into that publick Ministry, in which he professedly beareth the Sins of all the World before Men and Angels, in which he beareth the Person of the greatest Sinners, that ever were in the open Eye of Heaven; Heaven openeth upon him, the God-Head descendeth upon him visibly in a living Form of Love, in the Form of a Dove; a voice cometh to him from the Father: *This is my Beloved Son, in whom I am well pleased.*

St. *Paul* saith; *Love thinketh no Evil. Solomon* saith; *Love covereth All sin.* When the Father should express Love to *Christ* in the Person of a Sinner

ner; he doth not object thy Unloveliness, thy Filth, thy want of Love, thy enmity; neither to deny Love, nor to make the manner of expressing love less sweet, less lovely. No. As the Sea, when it floweth covereth all the Sand on the Shore round about, with Multitudes of deep Waters, so God, when he poureth forth his love in *Jesus* Christ drowneth Eternally the innumerable multitudes of thy Sins with mighty, and unfathomable Seas of *Love*, which never return to leave them naked, or bare to any Eye any more for ever.

God poureth forth his Love in *Jesus Christ freely*; that is. 1. *Naturally*. 2. *Nakedly*. 3. *Indifferently*.

1. God poureth forth his *Love* in *Christ Naturally*, Mat. 3. 17. ***This is my Beloved Son; in whom I am well pleased.*** Every Faculty, or Power is carried forth naturally to its proper object. *Jesus Christ* is the proper object of the Fathers *Love*.

The most perfect work of Nature in every thing is to bring forth its like. Then nothing so Naturally, so Powerfully attracteth love, so delighteth, as this similitude doth. The most perfect, and perpetual Act of the Divine Nature in the Father is to bring forth the most perfect Image of himself in the Person of Christ; then to pour forth himself in all Divine Loves, and Pleasures into his Bosom.

Pleasure accompanieth all natural operations. Pleasure naturally draweth every Spirit. *Jesus Christ* draweth the Heart of the Father, all his love entirely to himself; because the Father is pleased in him. He is the Rest, and Joy of his Father.

Three Things follow upon This *Naturalness* of the Father's Love in Christ; 1. *Sweetness*; 2. *Force*; 3. *Duration*.

1. *Sweetness*. That is ever Sweetest, which is most Natural. Live Honey is most esteemed; because it droppeth Naturally of its own accord from the Honey-Comb. Thou, who hungrest after the Love of God, lye down in the arms of thy *Jesus*. There Love will drop and fall from the Heart of the Father into the Mouth of thy Spirit, as Freely, as Naturally, as Sweetly, as the Live Honey from the Hony-Comb.

2. *Force*. That, which is Natural, hath the Greatest Force in it. Every Natural Agent worketh to the utmost of its Power. Thou, who wantest Love, be found in *Jesus Christ*. As the Sun every moment poureth forth All his Beams from every part of him because he shineth Naturally: so will the Father pour forth himself in Millions of Loves from every Point of his Heart, of his Godhead; he will pour forth himself in All his Loves; he will pour forth himself All in Loves upon Thee in *Jesus Christ*. For the Father, as Naturally loveth in *Jesus Christ*; as the Sun shineth.

3. *Duration*. Nothing violent, unnatural continueth. Psal. 30. 5. ***His anger endureth but a moment. In his favour there is Life.*** Clouds, and Storms last not long. They are a violence upon the Air, and Præternatural to it. Calms

sere-

Serenities and Clear Sunshines, are its Natural State. Clouds, and Storms of wrath are a Force upon the Divine Nature, Strange to it, a Disguise upon it. The Blessed Calms, Serenities, and Sun-shines of Loves of Love are its proper State. Comfort thy self then, O afflicted Soul! The rain will be over; the storm will be pass't away. The sweet, and clear, the Golden, the Glorious smiles of Love will return after the Storm, and Rain. These will rest the last in the Face of God, and upon thy Spirit. Wrath is but for a moment; at longest the moment of this Life, this Shadow, this short Dream of Lifes. The Truth of Life, the Perpetuity of Life, Eternity is for Love.

2 God poureth forth his Love in *Christ Nakedly*. John. 3. 34 *God giveth im his Spirit without Measure*. The Spirit is Love in a Living Person, in its ternal Substance, in its Native Seat, in its Unlimited Freedom; as Light in e Sun. God saith to the Lord *Jesus*; I will not stand to measure out my Love thee. Take it All. I will not give thee a Jewel out of my Cabinet; but my ibinet of Jewels. I will not give thee an Apple of Love off from the Tree; t the Tree of Love, with all ripe, and pleasant Fruits of Love, hang- g upon it. I will not give thee some Spice from the Island; but the Island of ices, the Land of Loves, where they grow, and increase eternally. I will give e the Infinite, Eternal Spirit of Love himself, where all the Treasures of Love without number, measure, or End.

The Face of Divine Love in *Jesus Christ* hath no Vail upon it, though 'er so thin; no Cloud upon it though never so fine: No. Its Love shineth th in Jesus Christ with a naked face; in its Strength, with all its Beauties, its Sweetnesses.

Thou, who art weary, who art heavy laden with any Debt, any Burthen Guilt, Sin, or Sorrow; come lay thy head upon this Pillow, the Naked t of God in the Naked Bosom of Jesus Christ. Here thou wilt sleep, and thy will be sweet to thee; thou wilt forget thy Debts, and Cares; thou wilt no weight, no burthen upon thee any more.

. The Love of God poureth forth itself in *Christ Indifferently*, that is, 1. *hout Distinction*; 2. *Without Condition*.

. The Love of God poureth forth itself in *Christ without Distinction*. John. 6. *God so loved the World, that he gave his onely-begotten Son; that whoso- believeth in him, should not perish; but should have everlasting Life*. Let inners, let all the Souls of all Mankind hear this. All Persons, all States, Degrees; the Persons of all Sinners, All States, and Degrees of Sin are A- to the Love of God in *Jesus Christ*. It findeth no Distinctions. It maketh Distinctions by its own Election, Descent, and Operation. It taketh away Distinctions by putting the greatest Comeliness upon the most uncomely ; by pouring forth itself in the greatest Loveliness upon the unloveliest ; by being Infinite in the Effusion of itself upon Every Part of Christs Bo- The First Matter is said by learned men to be a Deep of Emptiness, and

Ddd Darkness,

Darkneſs, a meer Poſſibility, a Pure Paſſiveneſs to all Forms of Things. Such Matter, ſuch a Subject is every Soul to the Divine Love in Chriſt. Every Soul is in itſelf a great Deep covered with the Blackneſs of a Darkneſs. But it is to This Love a meer Poſſibility, a Pure Paſſiveneſs. It cannot actuate itſelf to a Complyance, or a Reſiſtance. Love cometh to it, as its Form, infuſeth itſelf into it, penetrateth thorow the whole Subſtance of it, filleth it in every Part. Love reigneth Powerfully over it, reigneth gloriouſly in it; maketh it a Kingdom of Love; maketh it a Lovely Queen to itſelf ſtanding at its own right hand, reigning, and ruling together with itſelf in this New Kingdom of Love.

Rom. 5. 20. *Where Sin abounded, there Grace hath abounded much more.* Seas, and rivers have their High-Water Marks. Thus far their Waters come, when they are higheſt, but no further. The Sea of Divine Love in the Boſom of Chriſt hath no High-Water Mark, no Bound; Thus far Love ſhall flow, thus high its pure and ſweet Waves ſhall riſe, to waſh, to make white, to make new, to overflow, Sinners of ſuch Circumſtances; But beyond this no Love ſhall paſs, to Sins of ſuch aggravations, of ſo deep, and foul a Dye; to Sins againſt ſo much Light, ſo much Love; to Sins ſo often repeated after ſo many new Repentances, new Reſolutions; to Sins ſo black, ſo bloody, No; The Love of God is without Diſtinction; to all Sins, and over all Sinners in Jeſus Chriſt. If It maketh any Difference; It floweth firſt, It riſeth higheſt there, where Sin hath moſt abounded; that there It may be moſt Glorified. The Love of God in *Jeſus Chriſt* maketh the greateſt Sinners its Patterns to all the World of Men, and Angels; Its Maſter-pieces to Eternity.

1 Tim. 1. 15. *God had mercy on me the Chiefeſt of Sinners; that I might be an Enſample to all that ſhall believe in ages to come*; ſaith St. *Paul.* The holy Apoſtle doth not ſpeak vainly, when he calleth himſelf *The Chief of Sinners*, he ſpeaketh the truth in the Holy Ghoſt, and lyeth not. He ſetteth himſelf, as a Light on a high Watch-Tower, to all thorow all ages, that ſhall ſail upon Seas of Luſt, in a dark Night of Ignorance, and Unbelief, expoſed to Storms of Wrath. He inviteth them to make thither, there they ſhall be ſafe, they ſhall find reſt, they ſhall find a Haven of Divine Love in the Boſom of *Jeſus Chriſt* defended by the Rocks of Eternity, the Divine Attributes from every wind.

No Veſſel will fear want of water there, where it ſeeth the greateſt Ship of the greateſt burthen, deepeſt loaden which draweth the greateſt depth of waters, to ſail ſafely. St. *Paul* being dead yet ſpeaketh to the greateſt Sinner in every age after this manner. Behold a Sea of Love, a Channel of Love th[e] Love of God poured forth in the Boſom of *Jeſus Chriſt*. My ſelf the greateſt Sinner deepeſt loaden with Sin, and Guilt, who draw the greateſt depth of Love, have here found Love enough, unfathomable Love, on which I hav[e] bin carried ſafely, triumphantly unto that Flouriſhing Land of Glory, whe[re] now I feaſt continually with all Bleſſed Spirits in the midſt of all Incorrupt

b

ble Beauties, and Joyes. Let no sinner ever after me doubt to trust himself to this Channel, to put himself upon this Sea of Love in the Bosom of the Lord Jesus. Thus the Love of God poureth forth itself without Distinction in the Glorified Person of our Blessed Saviour.

2. The Father poureth forth his Love in *Christ Indifferently*, that is, *Without Condition.*

1. The Love of the Father dependeth upon no Conditions between himself, and his Son; the Father doth not say to *Christ* ; I will pour forth my Love in thee for Sinners; but upon this Condition, that thou make thy Soul an offering for Sin ; that thou satisfie my Justice and my Wrath ; that thou take upon thee to make them capable of my Love, suitable to me in Holiness, and Spirituality. All, that the Lord Jesus hath done, or suffered is no Condition, but Consequent of the Father's Love. Love is the Sea : These are the many Springs, by which it variously boileth up, the many Streams, and Windings, in which it playeth with itself, as it runneth along in this Earthly Image, until it return into the Sea, itself again, from whence it came.

The Lord *Jesus* testifieth ; *The Words, which I speak, are not mine, but the Father's. He doth the Works.*

It is the First, the Supreme Love itself, which shut up itself in Flesh, which was made Flesh ; It is That Love, which weepeth bleedeth, dyeth ; which hangeth upon the Cross, lieth in the Grave. It is that Love, which riseth again, maketh itself a Spirit, ascendeth up on high, taketh to itself Its First, and great Glory. It is that Love, which, as a Spirit, cometh to thee Invisibly, by day, and by Night; which is now with thee Invisibly, wooing thee in all Forms, in Its Blood, in Its Beauties, by all means working itself into thine heart. It is The Love of the Father, That Love, which is the Onely Father, which doth all the Works, which speaketh all the Words in the Person of the Lord *Jesus.*

It is the same Gold which is stampt in several pieces, with several Images, to make Crowns Angels, Twenty shilling Pieces. Coin, and Currant Money for Traffick. The Incarnation, Active Obedience, Sufferings, Resurrection, Intercession of the Lord Jesus ; his Presence, his Powers, his Operations in the Spirit are All The same Gold, The same Divine Love in several Forms bearing several Figures, for Traffick, and Commerce between God, and the Creature. When thou presentest to God the Blood, the Glory, the Intercession, the Spiritual Operations. the Graces of the Lord Jesus ; thou settest before him, his Love, himself in various Manners, in various Mysteries. The Onely Coin, the Onely Currant Money, the Onely Means of Commerce in the Kingdom of Heaven, is Love, the First Supreme, Eternal Love, the Gold of Eternity, the most high, and most Glorious Unity in all varieties, stampt with all Figures.

2. *The Father in giving his Love maketh no Condition with Sinners.* He doth not say ; I give thee my Love for that Sinner upon Condition that he be hum-

bled, that he accept of my Love, that he believe in thee. The Gospel is a Covenant of Grace. The Covenant is All Love. The Covenant is Compleat in the Person of Christ, who is The Divine Love, Eternal Love in a Divine, Infinite, Eternal Person. *I have given him*, saith the Lord by the Prophet *Esa'ah, for a Covenant to the Nations.*

All Preparations, Qualifications, Acceptations are not Conditions of This Love, but Infallible Consequents; not Causes, *without which* the Covenant hath no Force; but Irresistible, Immutable Effects of it.

By Grace ye are saved: Ephes. 2. The whole Work of our Salvation from the Begining to the End, from the first Design in Eternity to the last Act in Eternity is Pure Love.

Divine Love shineth in upon a Dark Spirit, Enlightneth, Awakneth, Convinceth it by Its own Heavenly Brightness. Divine Love burneth up, flameth in a Defiled, Dead heart, raiseth a Divine Life, and Sense in it, melteth it, consumeth its Dross, maketh it new.

The Love of the Father in the Bosom of the Lord Jesus is the Golden Mine, out of which a Saint is first taken: the Flaming Mint, where he is Melted, refined, made pure Gold, and stamp't with the Divine Image.

Rev. 1. 5. 6. *He*, saith St *John* of our Lord *Jesus, hath loved us, and washed us in his own blood, and made us Kings, and Priests to God his Father.* The Love of the Father in the heart of Christ is our onely Fountain. All the Blood, which streameth from the Wounds of Christ to wash us, runneth down from this Fountain. This Love is the Costly Ointment running down upon all our Persons, anointing us for Priests, and Kings.

Poor Soul, which lyest in thy Sins, which lyest a Slave in Chains, at the bottom of a Dark, Deep, and Miry Dungeon. The Love of the Father in the Person of the Lord Jesus cometh to thee; It taketh thee into itself, as a Bath of most pretious Blood, in which It cleanseth thee from all thy filth, cherisheth all thy parts, bringeth thee to thy self, to a Divine Beauty, to a Divine Warmth, sense, and Life. This Love setteth itself, as a Priestly, and Kingly Crown upon thy Head. It infuseth itself, as a Priestly, and Kingly Spirit, into thee. It changeth itself in thine Iron Chains into Bracelets of Gold upon thee; in thy Dungeon into a Temple, and Palace: It filleth thee, this Temple, this Palace, round about thee with Its own clear, and Proper Appearance in the Glory of God. Thus it dwelleth with thee Eternally. Thus the Love of the Father in the heart of Christ, softneth, enliveneth, washeth thee with Its own Blood, maketh thee by itself, a Priest, and King to itself Eternally.

I have done with the First *Property* in the Effusion of Divine Love; *Freedom*.

Use. 1. The Gospel is compared to a Marriage-Feast for a King's Son. God the Father is The King: His Son is the Bridegroom: Eternal Love attended with all The Lovelinesses, and Joys of That Love are The Feast. Thou, Man, O Sinner, Thy Soul is invited to this Feast of Love, not onely to be Guest, but The Beautiful, Blessed Bride.

Th

The Ministers, the Angels, The Spirit of Love himself are sent forth, as Embassadours, to bring thee to This Marriage.

1. *Obj.* Say not, I am Unworthy, Unlovely, in my Sins, and shame.

Answ. This Love is free. It seeketh not, but bringeth Loveliness along with it. This Love is itself The Wedding-Garment, and the Marriage-Crown. This Feast, as thou eatest, giveth thee strength, Beauty, and a Right to it. This Feast of Love maketh Its Guest. This Marriage of Love maketh a Bride.

Obj. 2. How can I leave my precious, and pleasant Things for This Love?

Answ. Canst thou not part with a single, dying Flower in thy hand for a Root of Flowers to set in thine heart, in thy Garden? The Love of God is The Root of all Precious and Pleasant Things in Eternity.

Canst thou not part with a Shadow for the Substance, a Picture for the Life, a Counterfeit for the Truth, a glass Diamond, or Pearl, for a right Diamond, the true Pearl? All thy Pleasant Things here are *Shadows*, Pictures, counterfeits; This Love is All Pleasantnesses, all Preciousnesses in their *Substance*, Life, Truth.

Obj. 3. I am weak. I shall dishonour This Love; I shall be disloyal to It. I shall return to my Lusts.

Ans. This Love requireth no Qualifications, but worketh all. Give up thy self to be the Creature of This Love. This Love will make Thee a Heavenly Bride to itself out of Nothing, out of Contrariety, Enmity, This Love will be both a new, a Divine Creation of Thee; and a Continual Preservation. This Preservation shall be a Continued Creation of Love. Resign thy self to This Love, which is the onely Fountain of Life, and of all Loveliness.

Use 2. Love again. Who planteth a Vine, and drinketh not of the Wine? The Father planteth Jesus Christ, his Love, his Vine in thy Soul. Let him drink of the Wine of thy Loves. Love thy God with the same Freedom, Simplicity, and Sweetness, with the Same Naturalness, Nakedness, and Force, with which he loveth Thee.

Use 3. Love one another, as God loveth you. Pour forth all your Love into the Bosom of *Christ*. There let it run into the Bosom of every Saint, of every Creature. There love one another without Distinction, without Condition, Freely receive one another into, embrace one another in the Riches of the Grace, and Glory of *Jesus Christ*, as the Father receiveth, and embraceth you.

Use 4. Abide in the Love of the Father.

1. Abide in the Father's Love by Faith in the Lord *Jesus*. The Glorified Person of Christ is the Land of Life, the Land of Love; the Love of the Father is the Sweetness, and Fatness of this Land. Faith is the root of thy Soul in this Pleasant Land. By Faith thy Soul is vitally fixed in this Divine Soil, in the midst of all the Sweetnesses, and Pretious Sap of Divine Love. By Faith thou drawest the rich heart of this Glorious Earth the Love of

of The Father to thy self. Thou feedest upon It, nourishest thy self by It, and growest up to an Entire Tree of Love.

2. Abide in this Love by holiness. Holiness is the lovely Fruit, which springeth up out of the Love of the Father, and is Its Food. Holiness, is the Purity of the Spirit, by which the flame of heavenly Love liveth, and spreaded itself there. Holiness is the Spiritual Chastity of the Soul to her heavenly Bridegroom.

3. Abide in the Father's Love by keeping his Commandments. The Commands of the Father are Beams of Love, which he shooteth into our Bosoms. Obedience to them is the Reception of these Beams, and the Reflection of them back again into the Bosom of God.

Obedience is the Activity of Divine Love enlarging itself freely in our Souls. If it be contracted, or shut up, it goeth out.

4. Abide in the Father's Love by the Peace of your Spirits. Peace of Spirit is a Heavenly Calms, and Serenity, which freely receiveth, and preserveth entire the Beams, and Sunshine of Divine Love. Passions are Clouds and Storms, which cut off, and darken the Beams of Love. The Spirit of Love resteth not upon an Angry, or Melancholy Man.

5. Abide in the Father's Love by Spiritual Joy. Joy is Love flaming. One saith; that Laughter is the Dance of the Spirits, their freest Motion in Harmony; and that the Light of the Heavens, is the Laughter of Angels. Spiritual Joy is the Laughter of Divine Love, of the Eternal Spirit, which is Love, in our Spirits. True Joy is Eternal Love, the Eternal Spirit in Its Freest Motions, in Its fullest Harmony, and Complacency in our Spirits.

6. Abide in the *Love* of the Father by Heavenliness. The Presence of God in his Wrath is hell. The Presence of God in his *Love* is Heaven. *Love* is the Sunshine of the Godhead sweetning, and guilding all things round about It after a Divine Manner; as this Sun doth these Skies. So far, as thou abidest in a Heavenly Image of Things, where every Object is covered with an Immortal Pleasantness, and Glory; thou abidest in the Love of God.

7. Abide in the Father's *Love* by Spirituality. *Love* is an Union. The highest Love is the highest Unity, the Unity of the highest Spirit. In the Unity of this Spirit all things are Spirit of this Spirit. All Varieties in this Unity of the Spirit are Spirits, Divine, Eternal Spirits of this Supreme Spirit, in this Supreme Spirit; Supreme, Eternal *Loves* from the womb, in the Bosom of this Supreme *Love*. Abide in This Palace of *Love*, The Unity of the Spirit. *Let* this be thine Eternal habitation. Be continually here in the Sweet, and Blessed Society of Beautiful, Pure, Eternal Spirits; *Living*, Immortal *Loves*. Behold, Converse with all things within Thee, without Thee in these Forms. So shalt thou abide in the *Love* of the Father, as It is poured forth in the Glorified Person of the Lord *Jesus*. So This *Love* shall guide Thee, as thou walkest, into Fields of *Light*, and Divine Pleasures, into the Gardens of the Divine Nature. This *Love* shall talk with Thee, when Thou wakest, as *Moses*, and *Elias* talked with *Jesus Christ*,

Christ, in the Transfiguration, of the Departure out of every other Image of things, into this Paradise of *Love* flowing with all the Joyes of *Life*, and *Love* in the heavenly Form of Christ. So This *Love* shall keep thee, when thou sleepest, as a Rich Canopy of Divine Substance over thy head; as a Guard of Immortal Sweetnesses round about Thee, as a heavenly Consort of Divine Spirit, Divine *Loves*, by their Musical Harmony continuing, and crowning thy sleep. I have done with the *First Property* of Divine Love, as It is poured forth in *Christ*, *Freedom*. I come to the *Second*, which is Purity.

2. *Property* in the Effusion of Divine Love, *Purity*. *The Love of God is poured forth in Jesus Christ Purely.* The Lord *Jesus* is said to be, *the Brightness of the Glory of God*; *Hebr.* 1. *v.* 2. Brightness is the Purest Light of Glory. The Prime Glory in God is his Grace, his Love. He doth all *for the Praise of the Glory of his Grace*; *Ephes.* 1. *Jesus Christ* in heaven, in thine heart, O Believer, is the purest Stream, the richest Flood of Divine Love; the Love of the Divine Nature in the Brightness of Its Glory.

We are taught; that this Light of the Sun, which we enjoy here below, is only a Shadow of that Light, which shineth in the Body of the Sun itself. The Sun in its highest Lustre is the Shadow of an Angel. The Highest, and Brightest Angel in his Purest Glories is no more, than a Shadow of our Glorified Jesus. He alone is the Brightness of Divine Glory without any Shade; the Purity of Divine Love without any Allay.

Love is Loveliness in Motion. As fine Gold melted into a Pure, and shining Stream: so is the Person of our Lord Jesus in Glory; the Godhead in the Purity & Perfection of all Its Lovelinesses melting itself into a most Pure & Precious Stream of Love, in which it runneth along, winding, turning, meeting, & sporting with itself from Bosom to Bosom, in the Father, the Son, and all the Saints.

O Broken-hearted Sinner, who sittest in the Shadow of Death, who wanderest in a Wilderness, where there is no water, ready to dye for thirst; open thine Eyes, see this Pure Light of Divine Love, which shineth round about Thee, in the midst of Thee; see this Pure Stream of Divine Love, which runneth along before Thee, in that Wilderness thine heart; the Blessed Person of thy Saviour, which is this Pure Light, this Pure Stream of Divine Love which filleth All. Take in the Waters of this Stream; drink freely of it. Cast thy self into this Stream; let it cover Thee; let it roul Thee along with it; sport thy self in it.

There are *Two Arguments* of the Pure Effusion of Divine Love in *Christ*;

1 *The heighth of Its Sweetness.*

2 *The Greatness of Its Virtue.*

1 The *Love* of God in *Christ* sheweth Its *Purity* by *The heighth of Its Sweetness*. The Purest things are Sweetest. The Love of God in *Christ* is the Rose upon its Stalk, New-blown, in its Virgin-Freshness, and Sweetness. *To be Carnally-minded is Death*; *to be Spiritually-minded is Life*; saith St. *Paul*; *Rom.* 8.

Impurity

Impurity, Carnality is the Death of Love; dulleth, embaseth, embittereth it by Corrupting it. Purity, Spirituality is the Life of Love, heighteneth, and immortaliseth all its Sweetnesses, all its Pleasures.

The *Sweetness* of the Love of God in *Christ* is made up of *Three Parts*; 1. *The Nearness of the Union*; 2. *The Firmness of the Union*, 3 *The Efficacy of the Union.*

1 *The Nearness of the Union* is the *First Part* of the *Sweetness* in the Love of God poured forth in the Glorified Person of our Saviour. Love is an Union. Where Love is Sweetest; the Love-Union is Nearest. The Love of God in *Christ* bindeth up God, *Christ*, all the Saints immediately in the most naked, most warm Embraces of each other. It maketh them All up into One Beautiful Body; It melteth them All into One Blessed-Spirit of Divine Love.

The Bridegroom in the *last* of the *Canticles* expresseth his Love to his Bride after this manner: *If she be a Door, we will inclose her with Cedar.* Cedar Wood is Eminent for three Things: It is sweet, Beautiful, Incorruptible. Blessed art Thou, O Believer, the meanest of all Believers; who art a Door onely in this heavenly Temple, *Christ* risen from the Dead; a Door, by which the Glories of the Godhead go in, and out between the Visible, and Invisible World. Thy *Jesus* by the Immediate Embraces of Divine Love incloseth, comprehendeth thy Person entirely with the Sweetness, Beauty, Immortality of his own Glorified Person.

The Soul in the Bosom of Christ lieth, as a Pleasant Island in a Sea of Love. The Sea bringeth to an Island Pleasure by its prospect, and by sayling upon it; Safety by inclosing it; Riches by Traffick unto all parts. Thus thou, O Saint, art seated in the midst of a vast Ocean of heavenly Love. This Ocean of Love is thy Prospect on every side. Which way soever thou lookest, thou seest Waves of Love rolling, and tumbling one upon the neck of another; sometimes rising up, as high, as heaven, sometimes again falling, as low as Hell. All Storms are The Workings of this Lovely Sea of Love, and Delightful Entertainments to Thee, thou lanchest forth and sailest round about thy Island, which is thy self, upon this Sea of Love. These are thy Pleasures.

How safe art thou? How great, and impregnable is thy Strength? Nothing can come to thee but by a Sea of Love, Divine, Almighty, Eternal Love. Thou art inaccessible, but this way, by the Sea of Love. No vessels can pass upon this Sea, nothing can pass thorow it, but Divine Forms of Love; heavenly Angels, and Ministers of Love. Whatever other Form of things attempteth, This Blessed Ocean of the Father's Love poureth forth in *Jesus Christ*, is swallowed up by it, and never seen more.

Thou hast Traffick, and Commerce by this Sea of Love with all things holy, heavenly, Beautiful, and Blessed every where; with all Lands of Life, and Joy. Thou sendest forth thy Spirit, thoughts and Affections into all Parts. Thou bringest home all the Precious, and Pleasant things of Heaven, and Earth; of Time, and Eternity: of God, and the Creature. Thou hast a Love-Union, and by this Love-Union, a Communion of Love with all the Treasures of the Godhead in the Sun, and in the Moon; in the Heavens above, and the Deep, which lieth below.

This is the Purity, the Sweetness of the Father's Love in *Christ*; the nearness of the Love-Union.

2. The Sweetness of the Love of God in *Christ* sheweth itself in the *Firmness of the Union.* What the Spouse of *Christ* saith of her self in the *Canticles*, that is the Language of this Love to the Soul in *Jesus Christ*; *I took hold of him, I will not let him go.* The Love of the Father hath taken hold of Thee, & will never let Thee go. St. *Paul*; Rom. 8. *v.* 35. maketh a Challenge; What shall separate us from the *Love* of Christ? Affliction? Danger? Sword? the Love-Union between God, and the Soul in *Jesus Christ* is so close, so fast; that the Point of the sharpest Sword cannot pierce between them; the subtilest Flame cannot divide between them. If it wound, or burn one, it must wound, and burn the other also. There is no Vein of Blood in the Body of Man, which hath not running along beneath it an Artery, a Vein of Spirits to preserve the Warmth, Motion, and Life of the Blood. There is no Vein of Divine Providence in the whole Life of a Saint; there is no Vein of Life or Death in the whole Person of a Saint, which hath not a Vein of Divine Love running along inseparably with it, to sweeten it, to give a Spiritual, a heavenly Tincture, of Life, Joy, and Glory to it.

To me to live is Christ, to dye is *Gain*; saith St. *Paul*; Philip 1. *v.* 21. There is nothing so Dividing, as Death. The Life of a Man is the Union between Soul, and Body. Death dissolveth this Union. The Life of a Saint is the Love-Union between his God, and Spirit in *Christ*, who is the Glorious head, and the Golden knot of this Union. Death maketh this Love-Union faster, and sweeter; more close, more clear, more compleat. Death is a Gain here.

The Death of a Saint is like the Tabernacle in the Wilderness. Without was a course Tent of *Badgers* Skin, exposed to the Injuries of all Weathers. This was seen by the Common Eye. But this was not the Tabernacle. This was onely the Tent, the Covering upon the Tabernacle. The Tabernacle within, as it appeared to the Priest's Eye, which entred into it, was Silk, Silver, Gold, and Precious Stone; Fine Linnen, Scarlet, Crimson, Sky-Colour; Cherubims richly wrought. Be not deceived. That is not the Death of a Saint, that is not a Saint in Death, which appeareth outwardly to the Eye of Sense, so affrightful, so mournful, so dark, so deformed, so Dividing from all the Joyes of Life: No. This is the Covering onely upon Death, to hide the sacred Mystery from common Eyes.

That, which is within, which presenteth itself all along to the Eye of a Saint, that entreth into this Death is indeed a Tabernacle of Immortal, of Divine Love with all rich, and pleasant Appearances wonderfully heightened; the Love-Union between God, and the Soul in Christ opening itself, taking the Soul entirely into itself, as into the true Heavens, where all things, which are seen are the highest Forms of Beauty in the highest Lights of Divine Glory; all things, that are heard, tasted or felt, the highest Joyes of the Divine Life with the most heightned Sweetnesses of Divine Love.

3 The Sweetness of Divine Love is manifested in its *Efficacy*, in its *Sweetning Operations*, as it is poured forth in the Lord *Jesus*. St. *Paul* saith; *Philip* : 3. *l. We have our Conversation in Heaven, from whence we look for the Lord Jesus, who shall change these Vile Bodies (these Bodies of our humiliation, and make them like his own Glorious Body, according to that Power, by which he is able to subdue all things to himself.* As the Flowers put forth, unfold all their Beauties, send forth their several Sweetnesses to the Sun: so do all the Excellencies, Joyes and Glories of the Godhead display themselves to the Divine Love. God in the Presence of his Love is the highest, the Truest Heaven. This is the Heaven, which containeth, and hideth *Jesus Christ*. *Jesus Christ* cometh forth from this Heaven, as a Bridegroom from his Chamber he cometh forth in this Heaven, with this Heaven round about him; he maketh this Heaven, every where, as he cometh forth; as the Sun maketh a Glorious Sky. He boweth this Heaven, and cometh down upon It into the broken heart. To this broken heart he changeth the vilest, the Bitterest Image of things, the Body of its humiliation, the Body of this Darkness, and Death, in which it dwelleth here into the Likeness of his own most Glorious Body, the Body of the highest Heaven in its Brightness; the Pure, and clear Body of Divine Love. This Love of the Father is that *Power, by which our Jesus subdueth all things to himself*, that is, to the Brightness, and Sweetness of the Glory of this Love; to the Express, to the Naked Image of this Love in its own Divine Substance, in its own most Lovely Person. This is the transfiguring Efficacy of the Love of the God-Head poured forth in the Glorious Person of Christ, and making for him a Body of Divine Loves above all Heavens.

Rom. 8. 28, 29. St. *Paul* triumpheth after this manner: *I am perswaded, that neither Death, nor Life; neither Angels, Principalities, Powers, nor things present, nor things to come; nor heighth, nor Depth; nor any other Creature shall be able to separate us from the Love of God, which is in Jesus Christ our Lord.* The Love God in *Jesus Christ* lineth, covereth all things transubstantiateth all things into the same Divine Love. St. *Paul* mentioneth the nearest things to us, the most intimate, the most Potent, the most Penetrating, the most Universal, the most comprehending, the most Transforming; Death, Life, Angels, things Present to come, Depth, Heighth. What cometh nearer, what toucheth every Point o our whole Substance, and Being, than Death, Life, Angels? What more i timate to our hearts, and Spirits? If none of these can come between the Lov of God in *Jesus Christ*, and our Persons: then all these by the Touch of thi Love must be Tinctured, and changed into new Forms, into Essences Love.

A

As Sugar is dissolved in a Glass of Wine ; so Death Life, Angels, things Present, things to come, heighths, Depths, every other Creature in this Golden Cup of Divine Love, the Glorified Person of Christ, is dissolved into Love, becometh a Rich Love-Cordial to a fainting Spirit, making it to dance, and sing for Joy, when it was intended a deadly Poyson to it. The holy Apostle had said upon this Ground a little before : *In all these things, Sword, Famine, Persecution, wee are more, than Conquerours.* It is plain, how we are *Conquerours.* Captivity is carried Captive. Those Forms, and Powers of Darkness, of Death, which thought to captivate us, are themselves Captives to Eternal Life, and Love in the Lord *Jesus.* As Saul among the Prophets : so the Bitterest, the Blackest things, which assault the Spirit of a Saint, encompassed with this Love of the Father poured forth in Christ, uncloath themselves, and put on Amiable Shapes of Love, sing songs of *Love*, breath forth from every part of them the most Delightful Sweetness of Divine Love.

Thus this Love maketh us Conquerours. But what meaneth this ; to be more, than Conquerours? Is there a Joy, or Glory above this of a Conquerour? Grace coming into Glory ; Love Reigning after Suffering ?

Is there any thing sweeter, any thing greater, than this Victory of Love ?

Yes. St. *Paul* saith ; when he was caught up into the Third heavens, into the Paradise there, he heard Words, which it is impossible to utter. This is *The Paradise in the Third Heavens,* the *Love* of God in the Glorified Person of *Christ.* This Love transformeth every thing, every Creature to this heavenly Paradise. Those blessed Souls, which by believing enter into this Paradise, hear Words of Love, Words of Joy, Words of Pleasure, of Glory from this Love, which it is impossible to utter, which are too sweet, too high, too ravishing to be exprest.

A holy Soul in This Paradise of Love feeleth a Joy far beyond that of Marriage, of Conquest, of Reigning, of Children, of any thing named in this World, or in that, which is to come.

Thus the *Sweetness* of Divine *Love* expresseth itself in its Sweet *Efficacy.*

Thus the *Purity* of Divine *Love* in Christ is manifest in its *Sweetness.*

2. *The Love of God in Christ is most Pure, because it hath the greatest Virtue.* Our Divines express hell after this manner. All Diseases, Pains, Griefs here are Evils by a Tincture onely of Divine Wrath, a little Drop of Divine Wrath mingling itself with them. Hell is Pure Wrath. Hell is the Abstract of Wrath; the Evil of all Diseases, Pains, and Griefs abstracted from them, and heightned to the utmost. So *Jesus Christ* bare all our Infirmities, and took our Griefs ; though he was never sick.

On the Contrary, all the Good, all the Joyes in the Creature are a Weak Tincture of Divine Love. The Shadow of St. *Peter* as he passed along, healed the sick. All the Sweetness and Pleasure in things here, is the Shadow onely

 of

of Divine Love falling upon them. All the Joy in any heart here, is the Shadow onely of Divine Love cast over it.

The *Love* of God is poured forth *Purely* in the Person of *Christ*. There *Love* is a Substance, no Accident. There *Love* is Infinite, being allayed, or limited by no mixture. Our Saviour in Glory is Divine *Love* in the Abstract.

It is a Weak Glance of Divine Love, like the Sunshine here below cast upon the Water, or a Looking-Glass, which maketh the Beauty, the Sweetness of all Colours, Figures, Motions in the Creature.

It is a remote Touch of Divine Love, like the Ends of the Sun-beams, reflected in a Burning-Glass, which maketh the Pleasantness, and Pleasant Properties of all Plants; the *Lustre*, Gracefulness, Virtue of all Precious Stones, and Pearls; the Joy of all Relations.

The Beauty, the Sweetness of all Colours, Features, Motions; the Pleasantness, the Pleasant Properties of all Plants; the *Lustre*, Gracefulness, Virtue, Life of all Precious Stones, Pearls, heavenly Bodies, heavenly *Spirits*; the Joyes of all Relations are contained Eminently, with an Infinite Enlargement, an Infinite heightning in this Divine Face, This Tree, Pearl, this Union, the Unity, the Purity of Eternal *Love* in our Glorified *Jesus*.

O Sinner; come, cast thy self freely into the Bosom of thy Saviour. Here thou fallest immediately into a Sea of Pure *Love*. Open thy Mouth wide, enlarge all thy Faculties to drink in the Sweetness of Pure *Love* pouring itself by Floods and Seas into thee. Feel the Transcendent virtue of Pure *Love* transforming thee, thy heart, thy Person into a rich, clear, and heavenly Pearl in this Sea,

O Saints! swim continually in this Sea of Pure Love, the Bosom of your Glorified Saviour. Feel the Transcendent Virtue of Pure *Love* dissolving you also into a Sea of pure Love, a Sea of Glass, and Fire; a Sea of Pure Chrystal, Divine Beauty without any Spot of Flesh, or Earth, Darkness, or Death; a Sea of Pure Chrystal shining, and burning with a Pure Flame of heavenly Joyes without any Smoak of *Lusts*, or Passions.

Obj. how is the *Love* of God *Pure* in Christ? Is there not in the Lord *Jesus* a mixture of Love, and Wrath? He saith of himself in one place; *All Judgment is given to the Son of Man.* He adjudgeth to Hell, and to Torments, as well as to Heaven, and to Joys.

Matt. 25. *Jesus Christ* is represented, as a King, upon the Throne, in Glory, in the Judgment of the last day, *v* 31. He maketh Separation between the *Sheep*, and *Goats*; *v.* 32. He setteth the Sheep at his Right hand, in the Place of Power, Honour, and Love. He setteth the Goats at his *Left* hand, on his Wrath-side, *v.* 33. He passeth the Sentence of Love upon One, inviting them, as Blessed Ones, to the Kingdom of Love prepared for them of the Father in Eternity; *v.* 34. He passeth a Sentence of Wrath upon the other,

sending

ſending , them away with a Curſe into the Hell fire with the Devils *v.* 40:
How is the Love of God poured forth *Purely* without mixture in *Chriſt*?

I ſhall give 3 *Anſwers* to this *Objection*; 1. *A Conceſſion*; 2. *A Diſtinction*; 3. *An Application.*

1. *Anſw. A Conceſſion.* It is true Contrary things are ſpoken of *Jeſus Chriſt* in this point.

We read; *I judge no man; Moſes, in whom you truſt, he judgeth you*; *The Son of Man came not to deſtroy Men's* Lives. *but to ſave them.*

The Work, for which *Chriſt* came, is a Work of Love, of Light, of Life; not a Work of Wrath, and Death. *Jeſus Chriſt came to deſtroy the Works of the Devil.* The Devil Is a *Lyar*, and a Murtherer from the Beginning. He is the Serpent, the Seed of Enmity. The Deceit of Sin, Death, Wrath are the Devil's Work. *Jeſus* cometh full of Grace, and Truth; like the Sun full of ſweet Light, and influences of Life to deſtroy the Deceits, to ſcatter into Nothing the Clouds, and black Shades of Sin, of Death, of Wrath; to make all a clear, and Lovely Sky over our heads, a Green, and Flowry Earth under our Feet. O the Delightfulneſs of Chriſt's Perſon, and of his Appearance!

We read again; *I came not to ſend Peace, but a Sword, I came to Kindle a Fire. The Lord Jeſus ſhall come in a Flame of Fire to render vengeance to all thoſe, who know not God, and who have not believed our Goſpel,* 2 *Theſſal. v.* 8. O the Dreadfulneſs of the Lord Jeſus, and of his Appearance.

2. *Anſw. A Diſtinction.* 2 *Corin.* 3. 13. You have *Moſes* brought in with *a Vail upon his Face* You have the Effect of this Vail. There is a Blindneſs upon the Minds, upon the Notions, (νοήματα) of the Jews. The Children of Iſrael cannot ſee to the End of that, which is to be done. away. They cannot ſee thorow; beyond the Shadowy Glory of the *Vail* to be taken off, to the Naked Glory of the Heavenly Face, which liveth, and is the ſame for ever. *v.* 13. 14.

There is the Interpetation of the Vail. The Vail upon the Face of Moſes is a Vail upon the Hearts of the Iſraelites, *v.* 15.

The Vail is removed by the Turning of the heart to the Perſon of *Chriſt*, *v.* 16. The Perſon of Chriſt, and the Removal of the Vail are Both deſcribed, *v.* 17. *Now the Lord is that Spirit, and where the Spirit of the Lord is, there is Liberty.* The Lord *Jeſus* in Glory is a Spirit, the Eternal Spirit. The Perſon of *Chriſt* was ever a Spirit, the Spirit, the ſame Yeſterday, to Day, and for ever; even in that Day, when he was made Fleſh in his humane Nature, this Spirit carrieth Liberty along with It; as the Sun doth the Light of the Day.

This Liberty of the Spirit anſwereth to that Removal of the Vail in the *verſe* before. *The Vail ſhall be taken away.* It is a ſignificant Word, περιαιρεῖται, ſhall be taken away quite, all round about, on every ſide; from off the Whole Image of things, from off the Whole Perſon of *Chriſt*, from off the Whole Heart; the Compleat Perſon of the Lord *Jeſus* in his Supream Glory, as the

Supreme Spirit ſhall ſhine entirely in the whole Image of things, in the whole heart, in every Part, in every Point of Both.

The Cloſe of all is the Bleſſed Effect of the Removal of the Vail, of the Free, and full Appearance of this Spirit, the Lord *Jeſus*; A Liberty of Sight; A Liberty of Growth; a Liberty of Union, and Divine Communion. A Saint looketh forth with Open Face with an Open Eye in the Naked Glory of the Spiritual Man, having caſt the Vail entirely off. He ſeeth the Glory of the Lord in the Naked Beauties of the Spirit himſelf compleatly unvailed. He ſeeth this Glory in the Unity of the ſame Spirit, as in a Looking-Glaſs; where Face anſwereth Face, where one is ſeen, as the Dear Image, and Reflection of the other. A Saint in the ſame moment ſeeth, and is changed into the Image which he ſeeth, as by one Spirit at once working Both. The Lord, the ſame Spirit in its Unity is the Root, the Eye, the Life, the Light, the Looking-Glaſs, the Glorious Face in the Looking-Glaſs to a Saint. Where this Spirit is, there is Liberty in that Heart. The Vail is taken off from it, when the Spirit exiſteth, and appeareth in it. There the Lord *Jeſus*, and a Saint ſee each other; grow up together, in one Glory. *We all, with open face, as in a Glaſs, beholding the Glory of the Lord, are changed into the ſame Image, from Glory to Glory; even as by the Spirit of the Lord, or, by the Lord, the Spirit.* By this time, I believe, you ſee the Diſtinction, which I aim at. *Jeſus Chriſt* with the Vail upon his Face is *Moſes*. *Moſes* unvailed is *Jeſus Chriſt*. Jeſus Chriſt to the Vailed heart is *Moſes* ſtill. *Moſes* to the Naked heart is the ſame *Jeſus* from the Beginning. The Appearance of Jeſus Chriſt according to the Letter, after the Fleſh, is Chriſt with a Vail upon his Face, caſting a Vail upon the heart. The Appearance of *Jeſus Chriſt*, as the Spirit, the Lord of Glory, is Chriſt with his Vail caſt off, taking the Vail off from the Heart; that Both may meet, ſee, embrace each other Nakedly, Immediately, at Liberty; in the Open Light of their Eternal Loves, and Beauties.

3. *Anſw. Applications.*

1. *Application Fear the Wrath of the Lamb.* There is a Day, in which the Kings of the Earth, Great Men, Captains of Thouſands ſhall cry to the Rocks, and to the Mountains to fall upon them, and hide them from the Wrath of the Lamb. When the Great Day of his Wrath cometh, who is able to ſtand? *Rev.* 6. *v.* 16, 17, 18.

Revel. 5. 6. 8. You read of *a Lamb, who had bin ſlain, ſtanding in the midſt of the Throne of God, of the Four Living Creatures, of the* 24 *Elders, having ſeven Eyes, and ſeven Horns, which were the ſeven Spirits of God ſent forth into all the Earth.* Behold the Lord *Jeſus* riſen from the Dead. He ſtandeth in the midſt of the Throne of God, of the Four Living Creatures, of the four, and Twenty Elders. He is the Center of All Glories; He filleth All; He uniteth All, and Compleateth All in his own Perſon; the Uncreated Glories of the God-Head; the Four-fold Fountain Glories of the Uncreated, and Created

Created Natures in Union; The Manifold, and Multiplyed Glories of Those Fountains in the Person of every Saint from the Beginning to the End of *things*, having his Crown upon his Head; the Universal Kingdom of all Glories in himself; with which Kingdom he standeth out of the Person, and in the Person of the Lord *Jesus*, which Mysteriously, and Divinely involveth, and unfoldeth all in itself. For this reason they cast down their Crowns at his Feet.

This *Jesus* uniteth all States in himself, from the highest, the Sweetest Light of Life, to the Darkest, most Dismal Deep of Death. For he standeth in the midst of these Glories; *as having bin slain*, shewing all the Bloody, Baleful Forms of Death in the Triumph of Eternal Life.

This *Lamb* hath *seven Eyes, and seven Horns, which are the seven Spirits of God sent forth into all the Earth. Seven* is a Perfect Number, the Power of all Numbers, which multiply themselves endlesly by the Marriage of the Two First Numbers, Three, and Four, the Numbers of the Trinity upon the Throne, and the Four Living Creatures, most immediately to the Throne, and from thence spreading themselves thorow all things; being *in the midst of the Throne, and round about the Throne on every side, Revel.* 4. 6.

The seven Spirits of God sent forth into all the Earth, are *the Holy Ghost*, that one, Manifold, Infinite Spirit, which divideth Itself into Innumerable, flaming Tongues, Eyes, Horns; into all Forms of things according to it's own Good Pleasure; ever Containing all within itself; ever filling all with itself.

See now *the Lamb with seven Eyes, and seven Horns, seven Spirits sent forth into all the Earth.* The Lamb is *Jesus* risen from the Dead; *The Lord, the* Spirit, who hath Innumerable, Living Lights of Glory in himself; Innumerable Living Springs of Light, and Glory; with which as with so many ever-waking Eyes he shineth, and seeth thorow all things; who hath innumerable Powers, Almighty Powers, Fountains of Power, as so many Horns, with which he ruleth, and reigneth in the midst of all things.

A Poet in a bright Night taken in a Wood by Robbers, which would kill him, said to them: As many stars, as shine in the Sky; so many Eyes now look upon you, and will be witnesses of this Murther.

O Sinner, who art hatching, who art practising any lust in the most secret corner of thine heart, or Closet; be awake, be aware. See the Lord *Jesus* with ten thousand, with a Numberless Number of Eyes; Shining, Flaming Eyes of Pure Glory looking forth full upon thee, from every point of the Walls, the Roof, the Floor, all things round about thee; from every point of thine own Heart, and all, that is within Thee. See the Lord *Jesus* with as many Horns of Divine Power from every Point of things running upon thee, to break Thee off from thy Lusts, or to break Thee in pieces.

O Saint, who mournest sitting in Darkness, Lying in Prison, encompassed with black thoughts, with Enemies Invisible, or Visible; be awake, be aware: See thy Jesus, thy King, thy Beloved with ten thousand, a Numberless Number

of

of Eyes; ſweetly-ſhining, ſweetly-Flaming, Eyes of Pure Love, from every Point of the blackeſt Darkneſs, of the darkeſt Priſon, of thy Darkeſt thoughts themſelves looking forth upon Thee.

See him with as many Golden Horns of Divine Power from every part, from every ſide running upon thine Enemies, to ruine them to caſt them down to the Ground, down to the bottom of the Pit, until they riſe no more, whether they be things Viſible, or Inviſible.

See him with the ſame Innumerable Golden Horns from every part of things, from the thickeſt Darkneſs, round about thee running to Thee to raiſe Thee up, to ſet Thee on high upon the Rock of Eternity in the midſt of the Throne of God.

Revel. 1. 14, The *Eyes* of the Lord *Jeſus* are compared to a *Flame of Fire.*

A Spirit is all one Entire Eye, and full of Eyes. The *Lord Jeſus* is the Supreme Spirit ſpreading himſelf thorow all things from the height of Heaven above to the Depth of Death, and Hell beneath.

The Firmament is not ſet ſo thick with Stars; as the Whole Earth, the whole Creation, all things are ſet with the Eyes of the Lord *Jeſus*. Theſe Eyes are ſo many Suns of Love to the Flowers, the Wheat, the Gold, the Diamonds, to increaſe their Beauty, draw forth their Sweetneſs, ripen their Fruit, make them ſparkle, and ſhine more pleaſantly. But to Stubble, and Thorns; to Vanity, or Enmity, they are a flame of Fire, burning upon it, until it be conſumed. O *Fear the Wrath of the Lamb.*

2. *Application. Fear to look with a Vailed Heart upon the Vailed Face of the Lord Jeſus.* If thou ſeeſt the Shadow, the Letter of the Goſpel; if thou ſeeſt the Vail, the Fleſh of Chriſt; if thou ſeeſt not to the End of theſe, as things to be done away, if thou ſeeſt not thorow theſe, beyond theſe, the Lord, the Spirit, which is the Heavenly Body, and Subſtance to the Shadow; the Naked Face, the Naked, Unchangeable, Eternal Perſon of *Chriſt*, hid under the Vail: it is not *Jeſus Chriſt*, but *Moſes*, in whom thou truſteſt. Thou art not in the Arms of a Lovely, pleaſant Bridegroom; but at the feet of a ſevere Judge.

This is the *Law* from Mount *Sinai*, which engendreth bondage, which trembleth, and ſhaketh for fear, where Thunders roar, and Lightnings fly abroad from the midſt of a thick Darkneſs. This is not the Lord *Jeſus* full of Grace, that Perfect Love, which caſteth out fear; the Perfection of Beauty, on Mount Sion; which ſtandeth firm for ever; which may be touched, kiſſed, and embraced. Take heed to thy ſelf, O Temporary Believer; Thou Jew, thou *Chriſtian* outwardly, in the Letter onely. This is not the *Sun of Righteouſneſs*, on which thou lookeſt; but the Cloud, which covereth the Sun. If the Eye of thy Spirit ſtay here, and pierce no further: out of this Cloud will come down upon thy head, a tempeſt, a Whirlwind, and Flames of Fire. The Vail is upon your Hearts, while the Goſpel is read, even to this day.

3 *Appli-*

3 *Application. Blessed art thou, who lookest with a Naked Heart upon the Naked Person of Christ.* He who is fixed in the Letter, the Outward Form, the Flesh of the Eternal Word, is One of the People of the *Jews*, who stood below at the Foot of the Mountain, having in their Eye the Outside onely of things. These saw nothing, but the Blackness of Darkness, and the Flashes of Lightning; these heard nothing, but the dreadful claps of Thunder.

He, who ascendeth, and entreth into the Truth the Spirit, is with *Moses*, within, upon the Top of the Mount. He talketh with God face to face, as a man talketh with his Friend. He seeth the Divine Light, and Calm of Eternity in the naked Person of the Lord Jesus. He receiveth the Language of Divine Love, the Musick of Eternity, with kisses of Love, immediately, from the Lips of the Lord Jesus. He feeleth the Fountain of Life, & all Joys flowing from the Heart of the Lord Jesus, running nakedly thorow his whole Body, and Spirit; being a better Feast, than that of all meats, and Drinks; filling him with Spirit, and Pleasantness; cloathing him with a fresh Lustre, Beauty in a more excellent way.

The Lord *Jesus* saith of himself in the Gospel; *I have a Baptism to be baptised with, and how am I streightned, till it be over.* The Loves, the Lovelinesses, the Divine Life, the Delights, the Glories, the Lord *Jesus*, all the Treasures of the Eternal Word are streightned in the flesh of *Christ*; as the Beauties, and Sweetnesses of a Flower; the Fruits of a Tree are shut up, and imprisoned in the Seed. When the Lord *Jesus* by Death is baptised into a Divine Form and Glory, when he cometh forth, as A Spirit, as the Eternal Spirit having married the Humane Nature into One Heavenly Form, and Spirit, with itself: Now all the Treasures of Righteousness, Life, Immortality, Love, Joy; all the Treasures of the God-Head display themselves over the whole Person of Christ, entirely, nakedly, richly, to the Height of all their Beauties, and Sweetnesses, as Flowers full-blown in Spring; as Fruit-trees laden with ripe fruit in Autumn.

Who now can express the Joys, when a Naked Heart meeteth with its Naked Jesus? when both have cast off their Vails; One from his Face; The other from his Heart. It is the same Blessed hand of the Eternal Spirit, which taketh off the Vails, from Both, dropping Myrrhe, a heavenly Sweetness, Purity, and Immortality, as It taketh them off.

The Reflection of the Face of God upon the Face of *Moses* on the Mount cast a Divine Lustre, and Beauty, which remained upon it.

He came down into the midst of the People, bringing a Heaven in his Face along with him. But they could not bear the Brightness of this Naked Beauty. He therefore casteth a Vail upon his Face. So they remain in Darkness, their Minds are blinded; until Wrath cometh upon them to the uttermost.

This is an Example unto us; upon whom the Ends of all Fore-going Times, and Actions are come. Behold the Lord *Jesus* is gone up to the top of the Mount. He is ascended. He is Glorified with the Father, with that Glory, which he had with the Father before the World was. As a Spirit he cometh down again to us in the Shining Form of this Spiritual, Uncreated, Eternal Glory.

Wo to you, who cannot bear the Brightneſs of this Appearance, who cannot look ſtedfaſtly upon the Naked Face, the Naked Form of the Lord *Jeſus*, this Spirit. To you he caſteth a Vail over his Face ; and as he caſteth a Vail over his own Face ; he caſteth a Vail over your Hearts. To you now he cometh, as a Thief in the Night, bringing Darkneſs, and Doubt ; Trouble, and Terrours ; Confuſion, Deſolation, and Deſpair ; ſpoiling you of all your Counterfeit Jewels, falſe hopes, falſe Joys, falſe Graces, falſe *Chriſt*.

But you, who love, and wait for this Appearance of your Lord, and Saviour, like Lightning ſhining from Heaven into your Hearts ; you who with the ſingle Eye of a Chaſt Spouſe look to the Beloved Perſon of your *Jeſus* in the ſimplicity of his Spiritual, and Divine Form ; Bleſſed are you of the Lord *Jeſus*. To you he cometh, as a Sun of Righteouſneſs with healing in his Wings ; Overſpreading you with his warm, and Naked Beauties ; Covering your Deformities ; Curing your Maladies ; Infuſing new Cordials of Immortal Life, and Joy into your Hearts ; Hatching you to Spirituality ; raiſing you upon Silver Wings, and Golden Feathers to Heavenly Flights with himſelf.

To you he cometh Enlightning, enlivening, Transforming, Glorifying, Gathering you up into One Spirit, One Glory with himſelf.

Where this Spirit, the Lord *Jeſus* is, there is Liberty of beholding, of enjoying the Lord *Jeſus* nakedly, immediately, entirely, eternally ; without any chain, clog, cloud, interpoſal, or interruption. There is Liberty of growing up into a Spirit out of All the Vails of Fleſh : into One Spirit with him. O the Joys of a Naked Heart, when it meeteth with its Naked Saviour.

But, as it was with the Painter, who called to remove the Vail, that he might ſee the Picture ; when their was a Vail onely painted there. The Vail was all the Picture : ſo is it with the hypocrite, with the Temporary Believer. His Jeſus, his Heaven is a Vail onely ; a Vail, like that of the Tabernacle, finely wrought with Pictures of Angels, of Heaven, of Jeſus ; but Keeping him for ever from the Face, the Boſom of Jeſus the ſociety of Angels, the Joys of Heaven, in the Outermoſt Darkneſs. His hope is a Spiders Web. The Poiſon of Death, and Hell are bred there.

I hear a Voice frequently in my Spirit ſaying to me ; Cry. What ſhall I cry ?

1. Cry ; There was an Ark in which *Noah*, and his Family were ſafe from the Flood, which drowned the World. The onely Ark in which *Noah*, the Believer, the Child of Reſt ſhall be ſafe from the Flames, which are now ready to devour the World, is the Naked Perſon of Chriſt in the Inviſibility, and Spirituality of his Divine, *Eternal* Form.

2. Cry ; The Sound, and noiſe of the Hammers framing the Ark for *Noah*, preached

preached the Righteousness of God, the Ruin of the World, very near. The Sound, and noise of the Lord *Jesus*, the Spirit of Life, the Spirit of Love, in his Naked Person, in his Naked Loves, and Lovelinesses growing up, forming himself in the Spirit of his Saints preaches now a Deluge of Destruction, Death, and Hell at the Door, ready to enter in; The Rest, and Righteousness of God in his Bosom alone, the Rest of God in his Loves; the Righteousness of God in his Loveliness.

3. Cry; As it was in the Days of *Noah*; so it will be now. The whole World will go on to eat, and Drink, to marry, and give in Marriage; to mock at this Preparation of an Ark; at these Discourses of, these Endeavours for the Spiritual Person of Christ in the Heavenly Image: for the Revelation of him in our Spirits; for the Retirement of our Persons into him. The whole World will go on in Sensuality, and Carnality, mocking at the Lord, this Spirit, the Ark; till the day that God open the Windows of Heaven from above, and break up the great Deep of Hell from below to cover them with, and swallow them up in Unquenchable Flames.

They say; that *Seth* foreseeing Two Destructions of the World prepared Two Pillars, upon which he engraved all Mysteries of Humane, and Divine Knowledge; One of Marble. to endure the Flood; the other of Brick, to continue in the Flames.

St *Peter* speaking of the Flood and the Ark addeth; *The Like Figure, whereunto now saveth us, Baptism; not the washing away of the filth of the Flesh, but the Answer of a Good Conscience by the Resurrection of Jesus Christ from the Dead.*

The Lord *Jesus* counselleth the last Church, *Laodicea*, *to buy of him Gold tried in the Fire.* Gold tried in the Fire no more loseth any thing, or receiveth any harm in the Fire; but shineth more gloriously.

The Lord *Jesus* risen from the Dead, and become a Spirit, the Fountain of Life, is the Gold tried in the Fire of Death, and the Divine Wrath. An Ark of Wood saved *Noah* from the Waters.

Behold an Ark of pure Gold, a Spirit of Immortality, and Glory, which shineth with greatest Glory in the midst of the Everlasting Burnings. This is our *Jesus*, who saveth us from the Fire, which is already Kindled, and burneth upon the World, which will immediately raise itself to a Mighty, Irresistible Flame. Blessed are you, who enter into this Ark of Gold, and shut your selves up into It. Here you shall lie upon beds of Love, as in the Marriage-Chamber, in the Bosom of your Bridegroom, encompassed with Songs of Joy; while the Fire dreadfully devoureth all without, round about you. Then shall Worldly Christians, Hypocrites, Temporary Believers, all who have lived in the Lusts of the Flesh, or the Letter onely of the Gospel take hold of, climb up upon the outside of the Ark, the outward Fleshly Form, and Appearances of the Eternal Word, the Lord Jesus. Then shall they too late cry to be taken into the Spirit, which alone is Truth, which alone hath Immortality. But they shall be rejected. They shall lose their hold, drop off into the flames, and perish there. I will conclude all with that Scripture; *John*, 14. *v*. 30. 31. When *Jesus Christ* perceived, that the hour, and Power of Darkness were now come upon him, he saith; *The Prince of this World cometh*; *Arise, let us go hence.* Thus saith the same *Jesus* now in the Hearts of his Beloved Ones, to his Spouse: The Prince of Darkness; The hour, and Power of Darkness, of dread, of Destruction, of the Devouring Fire cometh; Arise, let us go hence; out of the visible things of the Flesh, into the Invisibility of the Spirit; The Ark of Pure Gold, Paved with Loves.

3 *Property*; *Plenty*. This is the Third Property in the Effusion of Divine Love upon the Glorified Person of Christ. It is poured forth *plentifully*.

I will divide this Head by Streams flowing from it.

1. *The Fulness of all Love is poured forth in Jesus Christ.*

2. *The Person of Christ is all Full of* Love.

1. *The Fulness of all Love is poured forth in Jesus Christ*. We read; *Colos.* 1. 19. *It pleased the Father, that all Fulness should dwell in him*; that is, in *Jesus Christ*. All Fulness and so the Fulness of All Love had its Seat, its Bed in the Bosom of our Saviour. But the Pleasure, the Will of the Father, which is the Highest Pleasure, Pleasure in one, Substantial, most Perfect, Eternal Act, is the Well Spring which sendeth forth this Plenitude of Divine Love into Christ.

The Words lye so in Greek, that they may be properly rendred according to the rules of Grammar after this manner: *All Fulness was well pleased to dwell in him*. God is the Fulness, which filleth all in all. He alone is in any Place, in any Spirit, in any Creature *Repletivè*, so as to fill it. *God is* Love. God then is the Fulness of all Love.

Nothing attracteth, and draweth so powerfully, as Pleasure doth. God, who is that Love, which is all Fulness, the Fulness of all; God, who is the Fulness of all Love poureth forth himself to the Full, to the last drop, if we may so speak of that Love, which hath neither First, nor last; Beginning, nor End; in the Lord Jesus. For in Christ he poureth forth himself with Pleasure, which is the highest of all Pleasures. The Effusion of Love is itself a Pleasure. Then the Beautiful and Blessed Person of the Lord *Jesus* is the most pleasant Channel, the most pleasant Seat, and Palace of Divine Love.

This Fulness of Divine Love in *Christ* shooteth forth itself into Three Branches;

1. *Love in all States*. 2. *Love of all Kinds*. 3. *Love in all Degrees*.

1. There is in *Jesus Christ* flowing forth from the Father *a Fulness of Love in all States*. There are *Three States* of Divine Love in our Blessed Saviour. There is 1. *Preventing Love*; 2. *Assisting Love*; 3. *Finishing Love*. Divine

Love

Love *in Jesus Christ* hath these Three States, and a glorious, transcendent, triumphant Fulness in every State.

1. There is in the Lord *Jesus* poured forth from the Father *A Fulness of all Preventing* Love. 2. *Tim.* 1. 9. St. *Paul* teacheth us that *God hath saved us, not according to works, which we have done, but according to his own Purpose, and Grace given us in Christ, before the World was.* Before thou hadst any thoughts of Love to *Jesus Christ*, before thou hadst any Being in This World, before the World was; there was a Love from the Father in Jesus Christ to Thee; to Thee, whoever thou art, that liftest up the Eye of thy Spirit, the Eye of Faith, to see thy true Self, thine own Person in this Dwelling-Place, this Palace of Divine Love, where thou hast bin hid, where thou hast had thine abode thorow all generations, from Eternity: *Christ* in the Glory of the Father, the heart of the Father in *Christ.*

This Preventing Love well understood, removeth *Two Objections* out of the way of many hearts to the Bosom of their Jesus.

Object. 1. Broken-hearted Sinners, distressed Souls frequently plead thus against themselves: We cannot think, that *Jesus Christ* hath any Love for us: because we cannot believe his Love.

Answ. Hear, O broken-hearted Sinners, O Distressed Souls, Hear, and believe. *Jesus Christ* hath in himself from his Father the Fulness of all Preventing Love. He beginneth to you in Love. He beginneth with you. He giveth you Faith to believe his Love. *To you it is given to believe.*

The Son of Man cometh, and giveth you an understanding to know the True God by his Proper Name of Love; 1. *John.* 5. 20. The Preventing Love of God in the Bosom of Christ cometh to Thee, poureth forth itself in thy Bosom, giveth Thee a new Eye to see the Divine Beauty; a new Ear to hear the heavenly Melody; a new heart to take in, rellish, and understand the Spiritual Sweetnesses, Fulnesses, Joys of this First Love, Love in its Fountain, in the Fountain of Eternity.

This New Wine of the Everlasting Kingdom giveth itself to Thee with a New Bottle, a New Spirit, which will take in, and hold this precious Liquour. Not one drop, of it shall ever fall besides this Bottle, or be spilt out of it.

Object. 2. But still thou poor, troubled, trembling Soul thinkest the glad Tydings of the Gospel, of Pure, Preventing Love too good to be true. Thus thou arguest against thy self, If I were but moderately evil, or morally good; if I could in any degree comply or close with *Jesus Christ*, when he offereth his Love, and himself to me: then might I have some hope, that I had some place in his heart. But, if the Lord Jesus himself should shine forth with the Sweetest Vision of Preventing Love in the midst of my Fleshlinesses, Filthinesses, hardnesses, Enmities; and should say to me, as the Angel to Mary; hail thou, that are greatly Beloved; Hail thou, that are freely Beloved: I should not onely wonder at this Salutation; but believe it all to be a vain Dream of my deluded Fancy.

Answ.

Answ. Let me tell Thee a Story. A beautiful *Ægyptian* Youth, when his Friends desired to take his Picture, desired them to take him up seven daies after his death, and then to take his Picture. Thou, the most defiled, the most deformed Sinner, wert once beautiful, once in the freshness, and flower of thy Youth, in Paradise. It is true; thou art now dead, dead of the most loathsom disease, dead by the most killing, and corrupting Death, dead in sin; Yet now, after that thou hast bin many years dead, Jesus Christ in his Glorified Person cometh like a Bridegroom from heaven, not onely to take thy Picture but to take thy Person into the Arms of his Preventing Loves, to breath his Preventing Loves into Thee, as a New Life, the Spring of a New Beauty, excelling that, which was lost by Thee in Paradise, incorruptible, that never fadeth, nor passeth away.

Ladies and Queens have sometimes hatched Eggs in their Bosoms. Thy dead, deformed Person will thy Saviour hatch in the warm and naked Bosom of his Preventing Loves unto a Divine Life, that shall answer Love with Love, and flourish in the Loveliness of every Grace, every Glory, through thy New-born Soul, and body, according to their proper seasons.

Having known the Love of the Lord my Spirit laboureth, yet not my Spirit, but the *Love* of the Lord Jesus in my Spirit laboureth by all means to bring forth itself in the fresh, and full Sense of its First, its Free, its Preventing Sweetnesses, in your hearts; as a Spring of Living Waters in a dry, and barren Wilderness. But, as a tender Mother taketh a beloved Child, weak, and peevish; laieth it in her lap; poureth a Cordial down into its stomack: so will your Jesus do with you, O Grieved Spirits, who are weak, without strength; froward, & will not take in his Love. He will take you, lay you upon his knees, and pour this precious Cordial of his Preventing Loves into your Mouths. Then will it go right, and sweet down to the bottom of your heart; There it will become a Well springing up with pure, sweet, and plentiful Streams of every Spiritual Truth, Grace, Comfort, or Joy unto Eternal Life. This is The First State of Love in the Lord *Jesus*; *Preventing Love.*

2. There is in the Lord *Jesus* poured forth from the Father *a Fulness of all Assisting Love.* 2. *Cor.* 14. *v.* 7. 8. 9. St. *Paul* had a thorn in his Flesh, messengers of Satan sent to buffet him. He prayed thrice, that he might be delivered from them. He had this answer from the Lord: *My Grace is sufficient for Thee.* Many tender-hearted Saints, who feel their Lusts, as Thorns in their Flesh; who feel their Passions, as the Messengers of Satan, the Angels of the Dragon buffeting them; cry out frequently in the Agonies of Fear, and Grief; O this Lust! O this Thorn in my Flesh! Sure at last it will wound me so deeply to the heart, that it will let out the Life-blood of all faith, hope, grace, and comfort. O this Passion! O this Messenger of Satan! It will one day carry me back again into those Chains of Darkness, and that Bottomless Pit, out of which I seem to my self sometimes to have escaped. But, O Believer! tossed

with

with the Tempests, be comforted. Fear none of these things. Look up continually to the Blessed Person of your dear Saviour lifted up into Glory in the midst of your Spirits. See the Father pouring forth himself into the Fulness, the Glorious Fulness of all Assisting Loves in his Bosom. Pray continually; and hear this Blessed voice from the Mouth of your Saviour continually sounding in your ears; *My Assisting Loves are sufficient for Thee.*

Obj. But some Soul, that wanteth Comfort, will say, When the Lord Jesus hath once by his Preventing Love planted a New Principle, and Habits of Grace in me, he now expecteth; that I should improve this Principle, and act these Graces. If I do this, and make use of that, which I have: I may comfortably look for his Assisting Love, and that more Grace should be still given me. But what New Loves can I promise my self to accompany me, and carry me on in my way; while I so ill requite the Lord Jesus for his First Loves, that I suffer his Gifts to lye unimproved, his Graces to lye unactive in me, hid in the Earth by my Sloth, or Sensuality?

Answ. I shall proceed in my answer to this *Objection* by *Three Steps.*

1 *Step.* This *Objection* wrappeth up together in it something *True*, something *False*.

1. This is *False*; That the Assisting Love of the Lord *Jesus* dependeth upon our Emprovement of Grace already received from him. This is not True; No; by no means. Assisting Love is as free, as full, as absolute, as much all, as much alone in Carrying on the Work of Grace in us: as Preventing Love is in Beginning it. God hath poured forth in *Christ* the Fulness of all Assisting Love.

I am the Truth, the way, and the Life; saith our Saviour. *Jesus Christ* is the *Truth*, and the *Life* of all Grace in the *way*, as much, as in the Beginning, or End. *Without me ye can do Nothing*. Every Act of Grace, every thing in every Act of Grace, which distinguisheth it from a meer Non-Entity, from an Absolute Nothing; Every Degree of Spiritual Being in the whole Life of Grace with all the Exercises of it through the whole way from the Beginning to the End; is all alike, Immediately from *Jesus Christ.*

That, which is True in the *Objection* is this; the Emprovement of Spiritual Principles, the Exercise of our Graces are attended with Clearer Illuminations. Sweeter Enlargements, more Divine heighthnings of all heavenly Truths, Graces, and Consolations in us. On the other side, when Faith is not acted, when holiness is neglected: Darkness, Decay, Distress, and Death dwell upon us. But these things are all entirely Consequences, and Effects; not Causes, or Attractives of Assisting Love The Assisting Love of our Lord *Jesus* is as the Sun, which by its Presence bringeth Light, Warmth, Fruitfulness, Life, Beauty, Pleasure along with it. When it withdraweth itself, leaveth the Cold, hardness, Storms, Desolation of Winter behind it.

The Bridegroom chargeth the Virgins of *Jerusalem*, by the Roes, and Hinds of of the Field, that they ſtir not up, nor awake his Love, until She pleaſe. *Cant.* 2. 7. The Angels of heaven, which are the Inviſible Miniſters, by whom all things move in the whole Order of Second Cauſes; are here underſtood according to the ſenſe of ſome learned Divines, By the Virgins of *Jeruſalem*. The Roes, and hinds of the Field are the Pleaſant Loves, and Lovelineſſes of the Eternal Spirit in the heavenly Perſon of *Chriſt*. The Law of the Eternal Beauties, and Loves of the Divine Nature lieth upon all things, upon all the Miniſters, and Armies of God; that the Spouſe of Chriſt be never laid to ſleep, or awakened; but according to its own good pleaſure, as it is One Spirit with the Lord Jeſus by a knot of Everlaſting Love, as a Queen at the Right hand of her King, ſet down in Heavenly Places with him, in him, upon the ſame Throne. When the Divine Principle, which is the *Bride*, and the *Spiritual Man* in a Saint retireth itſelf, and goeth to its reſt: in this Night the Wild Beaſts, Bruitiſh Luſts, Raging Paſſions come forth to prey upon the Natural Man covering it with filth, & wounds. But, when the Day ſpring ariſeth from on high when the ſeaſon cometh for this Man, this Heavenly Seed, & Bride to awake, to ſtir up her ſelf, and come forth again; in this New Morning the Beaſts return to their Den; Luſts, and Paſſions ſink down into their own Principle, the Bottomleſs Pit, out of which they aroſe. But the Muſick, to which the Spiritual Spouſe moveth in theſe Retirements, and Returns, is the Love of the Spiritual Bridegroom, like the Silver Trumpets of the Sanctuary in the Wilderneſs to the Children of *Iſrael*, ſounding a Retreat, and a Reſt, or a March, and a Progreſs.

Obj. But you will ſay; If there be nothing to be done by us, to what purpoſe are all Duties, Prayers, Attendances on the Word? If nothing can be done by us in the Acting, and Improvement of Spiritual Principles, to what end are all Admonitions, Exhortations, Inſtructions, Promiſes, in the Holy Scriptures?

Anſ. Theſe are all Aſſiſting Love deſcending from the Boſom of the Bridegroom above, into the Lap of his Bride below in various forms, like the Sunſhine, & Showers from Heaven falling upon the Boſom of the Earth. They are the ſame Aſſiſting Love aſcending again by various degrees, in various Shapes, or Growths, like the Flowers, & the Corn ſhooting up out of the Ground. *Hoſ.* 2. 22. It is promiſed; *that God will hear the Heavens, the Heavens ſhall hear the Earth, the Earth ſhall hear the Corn and Wine; and the Corn and Wine ſhall hear Jezreel. Jezreel* is the *Seed of God.* All the Ordinances, all Forms, all Motions not of *Grace* alone but of *Nature* alſo, are the Commerce, and Traffick of the Divine *Nature* with itſelf, as it is the head of Fine Gold above all; and the Hidden Pearl, the Precious Seed at the bottom of all. In every Step of things, in every Form, in every Language of Heaven, and Earth, of Grace, and Nature, in every Ordinance, God ſeeth the face, heareth the Voice, anſwereth the Cry of *Jezreel*, his own Seed, his own Son; *Jezreel* ſeeth the Face, heareth the Voice, anſwereth the Call of God, of its Father. *Jezreel* is the Dove whoſe

whose Face is Lovely, whose Voice is Sweet to the Heavenly Bridegroom, although it be from the Holes of the Rock, and the Hollow places of the Stairs; from the lowest, the darkest Dispensations, from the nethermost parts of the Earth; from the meanest Ordinances; from an Inward, an Outward Prison, or Grave. The Heaven, the Earth, the Corn, the Wine, Duties performed, Ordinances enjoyed, Graces Acted, the Word published; All are the Green Flourishing, Fruitful Bed of Preventing, or Assisting Loves, on which the Lord Jesus, and his Spouse embrace each other.

In Ordinances the heavenly Bridegroom pipeth, or mourneth to *Jezreel*, the Divine Seed, his Sister-Spouse. In Duties, or Graces *Jezreel* danceth, or mourneth to him again. Thorow all these Assisting Love sweetly shineth, or soundeth from above; sweetly again reflecteth and Ecchoeth back from the Spirit of a Saint below. This is the *Answer* in its *First Step*.

2 *Step*. The Reason given by the Philosopher, why the Heavens, which we see over our heads move so regularly, so harmoniously, so constantly, from the begining of the world hitherto, is this; They have Assisting Forms, Intelligences, Angels, which move them, which turn them round. Many Souls sweetly touched with the Allurements of Divine Love in *Christ*, fear to come to him, to cast themselves into His Bosom by Believing. They distrust their own strength, and constancy for their continuance in a holy temper. They doubt they shall fall back with greater guilt and shame to themselves; with greater reproach to the name of the Lord *Jesus*. Many weak Christians are day and night tormented with like fears, and doubts; that they shall fall away at last by the force of some Corruption, or the Difficulties in the waies of Holiness. Dear Souls! be not discouraged from believing, or in believing; be not kept off from the Bosom of Christ, be not disquieted in His Bosom by any fears or doubts. You have a Good Angel for an Assisting Form, you have an Assisting Form brighter and more glorious, than the highest and brightest Angel; more powerful, than all the Angels in Heaven. You have the Assisting Love of the Lord *Jesus* present with you, in your Spirits, by day, and by night. This doth move, this will move, and turn about your Hearts, your lives regularly, harmoniously, constantly, in all the Circles of Divine Graces, Truths, Joys, Glories, according to the *Laws*, and Patterns in the Supreme Mind, in the Heart of God, thorow all times Eternally.

Preventing Love is the Golden Chain, which draweth thee to the Embraces of *Christ*. O run when thou feelest thy self so drawn. Assisting Love is the Golden Chain, that tyeth thee fast, and close, immediately, inseparably, for ever in these embraces. Rest with Confidence, and full Assurance in these embraces; feed with desire and delight among the Lillies here; lye down to sleep in these embraces. Thy sleep will be sweet to thee.

3 *Step*. Learned men and Divines teach us; that the Preservation of the world is *continuata Creatio*, a continued Creation. In every moment of Time

G g g from

from the Begiuning of the world to the end, the Divine Act of Preserving, and Governing the world according to the Present form proper to it for that Season is entirely the same with the Act of Creation. In every moment from the Begining of the world to the end, the whole world with all things in it rise up into the form designed for that moment in the Eternal Law of the Divine Wisdom, out of the nothingness of the Creature out of the Omnipotency of the Creator, as freely, as freshly, as fully, as Absolutely, as in the first Moment of Its Being.

So is it, and much more clearly, sweetly gloriously so in this Creation of God, the Creation of *Grace*. Assisting Love is no other than Preventing Love Continued: A continuation of Preventing Love. They say; A line is One Individual Point in motion. This is most true; All Assisting Love; the whole Life of Grace, and Glory in a Saint is One, Individual, Unchangeable Point of Preventing *Love* Eternal Love in Motion, spreading itself, within Itself to an Infinite Circle.

In every moment of a Saint's spiritual Being from his first Conversion to Eternity the Act of Assisting Love in Preserving, in Governing thee is the same with that first Act of Preventing Love in Regenerating thee.

In every moment of thy Spiritual Being from thy first Conversion to thy Glorification in Eternity, thy Spiritual Man the Divine Nature in thee riseth up into the form of that Moment answering Its Pattern in the Heavenly Image, the Glorified Person of *Christ*, out of thine own Nothingness; out of the glorious fulness of the God-head in *Christ*, as freely, as freshly, as sweetly, as absolutely, as entirely; as in the first moment of the New-Birth in thee.

I will conclude this Second State of Divine Love in *Christ*, *Assisting Love* with that of the Greek Epigram thus translated: *fer Fatum*; *sin ferre recuses*; *non minus te feret Fatum.* Bear thy Destiny. If thou refuse to bear it; thy Destiny will nevertheless bear thee, and carry thee along. Cast thy self, (O believer into the Bosom of the Assisting Love of thy God in *Christ*, to be born up, and carried along in it. But if thou refuse, and murmure; nevertheless this Assisting Love will take thee into Its Bosom, and bear thee and carry thee along with It in Its own Way laid out and lifted up in Heaven in the Spirit into Eternal Joys.

If we believe not; *yet is He faithful, and cannot deny Himself.* God is Love He cannot deny Himself in the unchangeablness of His Divine Essence which is Love. He is True and faithful to the unity and simplicity of his own naked Being which is Love in the midst of all our changes, unbeliefs, unfaithnesses.

3. There is poured forth from the Heart of the Father in the Bosom of our Glorified Saviour *The fulness of all finishing Love.* I know no Scripture, which displayeth the finishing Love of God in *Christ* with more sweetness, riches and fulness; than that; *Ephes.* 2. *v.* 4, 5, 6, 7, 8. You have here *Love* under several names in five verses repeated six times; *Mercy*; *Love*; *Grace*; *Grace*;

Kindness

Kindneſs; *Grace.* You have it brought in with Magnifying Titles; *Rich in Mercy*; *Great Love*; *Exceeding Riches of Grace.* The Salvation of a Saint is here preſented to us, as a rich Piece of fine Enamelling. Firſt the Ground on which the Enamelling lieth, is Gold. Then you have the rich Enamel upon the Gold. Laſtly ſome beautiful Picture is formed in the Enamel. Such a piece of Divine Work is a Saint. 1. The Ground of the Work is Pure Gold, Pure Love, Preventing Love. God doth all from Rich Mercy, for the Great Love wherewith he hath loved us, *v.* 2. 2. The rich Enamelling upon this rich Ground of Love is Love too. All the Work is a curious, cloſe, and fine Enamelling of Divine Love upon a glorious Ground of Love. You have this brought in and doubled, *v.* 3, 8. *By Grace ye are ſaved.* 3. The Beautiful Picture formed in this Enamel of Love upon a Ground of Love is, the Heavenly Face of Divine Love, naked, entire in all its Lovelineſſes and Glories, to raviſh all Spirits into a delightful Admiration: *That to the Ages to come might be ſhown the Exceeding Riches of his Grace, v.* 7. This is the End of God in *Chriſt*. He draweth upon the whole Perſon of a Saint, the Heavenly Form, the Divine Figure of Love, as Love is God; of Himſelf, as God is Love. He draweth this Divine Figure of Love in all its Riches, in thoſe Riches of Sweetneſs, Lovelineſs, Glory, which exceed, which tranſcend all Degrees, all Capacities, all Underſtandings in the Creature. He doth it to this end, that the Father, the Lord *Jeſus*, all Angels, and Spirits, all Creatures, *in Ages to come*, that is, in Eternity may ſee with Extaſies of Joy and Wonder, the Entire Form of Divine Love in its moſt naked, moſt lively, richeſt Beauties, figured upon, and ſhining in the whole Perſon of a Saint from one end of his Story unto the Other. Do you not diſcern the *Finiſhing Love* of God in *Chriſt* making All perfect in Eternity?

The Ground of the Work of God in a Saint is Love. It is all inlaid in every point of it with Love. It is All Overlaid with Love. When St. *Paul* had gone through the Particulars, and ſeveral times declared All to be *Grace, Pure Love*: after all that he wrappeth up all over again in *Grace*, in *Pure Love*. By *Grace ye are ſaved*; *v.* 8. A Saint is like a Gold-Watch in a Gold-Caſe; A Work of Love in a Covering of Love, as rich, as the Work. If you go never ſo low all thorow a Saint to the Nethermoſt parts of the Earth to his loweſt Foundations; All is Love. If you ſearch into the Heighths of Eternity above him, round about him; All is Love, Comprehending, Crowning Love.

You will ſee the Fulneſs of the *Finiſhing* Love of God in *Chriſt* yet, more clearly: if you conſider *Three Things* ſet before you in *this Scripture.*

1. It is Love, which is the Supream Sun of Eternity, which generateth us to a Divine Birth, which infuſeth a Divine Principle of Life into us, and awakeneth it in us. *For his greateſt Love, wherewith he hath loved us, he hath quickened us, v.* 4. 5. This is *Pre-venting Love.*

It is Love, which maintaineth, carrieth on, floweth forth into the Stream

 of

of Divine Life in us from the Beginning to the End. *By Grace ye are saved; He hath raised you.* v. 5. 6. The Way of a Saint is a Continued Resurrection Every Moment is a New Resurrection, every Resurrection supposeth a Death.

The whole Way o a Saint from the First Incarnation of Christ in him is a Contexture of Deaths and Resurrections, Divine Lights of Life and Shades. This whole Way of a Saint;, the Deaths, as well, as the Resurrections the Shades, as well, as the Lights, are Divine Grace, Pure Love. Love putteth on the form of Death, and shineth thorow it. Death putteth on the Form of Love, and shineth in it. This is *Assisting Love.*

It is Love, which setteth us down in Heavenly places. Love maketh itself a Heaven of glory and bliss; a Kingdom of Joy, a Throne of pure Gold; a Crown of Immortality. This is Finishing Love. They are the same Riches of Mercy, the same Greatnesses of Love, which shine forth in our hearts at our Regeneration, at every Resurrection; and in Heaven at our Glorification. God rich in Mercy, for his great Love hath quickened us, raised us, set us down in Heavenly Places. All is the Same Love, the *Seed*, the *Tree*, the *Blossom*, the *Fruit.*

2 All the Steps in the whole Way of a Saint from the Beginning to the End are so many *Love-Unions. He hath quickened us together with Christ*; v. 5. *He hath raised us together* with him; *He hath set us down together*; v. 6 Every new Step in Grace, or Glory is a New Love-Union.

Every Act of Divine Life is composed of a Blessed, and Beautiful Trinity of Divine Loves. 1. There is the Lord Jesus, That Spirit, which is the Supream Love, the Essential Image, the Eternal Son of That God which is Love; the Bridegroom, and Beloved of a Holy Soul. 2. There is the Spirit of a Saint, the Sister, the Spouse, the Love of this Love, this Bridegroom; Spirit of the same Spirit; Love of the same Love; sprung from the same Root, formed into the same Image, and Tree, bearing the same Fruits of Divine Love. 3. There is the Holy Spirit, the Marriage-Dove, the Marriage-knot, the Love-Union between these Two Divine Loves. Thus every Act, every Moment of a Saint's Life is a Divine Trinity of Heavenly, Eternal Loves coming forth in a New Dress suitable to each New Moment.

3. All the Parts of a Gracious, or Glorious Life are acted; all the Forms, and Moments of the State of a Saint; His Beginning, Progress, End are acted, and comprehended in the Pure Element of Heavenly Love; in the Divine World of Spiritual Love; in that Great, and Glorious Deep, into which all the Fountains of Love in the whole God-Head, in the Heart of the Father are broken up, and pour forth themselves, in the Glorified Person of the Lord Jesus. *He hath quickened us together in Christ*; v. 5. *He hath raised, us together, made us to sit together in Heavenly Places in him*; v. 6. Thus you see the Absoluteness, the Compleatness of Finishing Love, as well, as of *Preventing*, and *Assisting Love.* You see the Finishing Love of the Father poured forth with all Fulness in our Blessed Saviour: You see Divine Love in the Bosom of your Beloved

loved, Alone Beginning Alone Continuing the Work of Grace, Alone in the Purity, Power, Simplicity of Free Grace Finishing, Perfecting All in Glory.

I will make this clear to you by *One Scripture* more; 2 *Tim.* 1. 9. *he hath saved us not according to works, which we have done, but according to his own Purpose, and Grace given to us in Christ, before the World was; Who hath abolished Death, and brought Life, and Immortality to Light by his Appearance in the Gospel.* Behold this Heavenly Sight! Believe, rejoyce, and wonder. A Saint is a Spiritual Building of all Heavenly Graces, and Glories. It is entirely composed thorowout of Free Grace, of Pure Love. The Foundation of it is laid in the Fair Colours of Divine Love, all the Rooms, the several Stories, the Furniture, the Riches, the Entertainment is of Pure Love. The Roof is laid with the Precious stones of Pure Love. The whole Work of a Saint's Salvation, the Materials, the Form the Proportions. the Measures of the Whole, and of every Part are Free Grace, Pure Love *He hath saved us according to his Purpose, and Grace given us in Christ before the World was.*

That Word *Purpose* signifieth properly the *Fore-laying* of a thing.

This Divine Building of Love, this Heavenly Frame of Life, and Immortality, which is the True Form of a Saint, was set up in the Glorious Person of our Jesus from Eternity. All, that is done in time is the unvailing, and Discovery of this Heavenly, and Eternal Building by Degrees, according to the Measure of the Appearance of the Lord Jesus in us, in whose Person, and Spirit this Frame standeth, as a Living, Precious Corner-stone, out of which it is grown up; as a most pleasant Situation, which encompasseth it on every part.

This Palace, this Temple of Divine Love, of Light, of Life, of Immortality is Eternal in the Heavens, in *Christ*. Time, Flesh, Sin, the whole Work of this Creation are a Vail of Darkness, and Death cast upon It. As *Jesus Christ* shineth forth upon the Soul in the Gospel, he casteth off this Vail, he abolisheth this Death, he discovereth, and bringeth forth into the Clearness, and Sweetness of Its own Divine Light this Divine Frame of Life, and Immortality, which is the True Saint, the New *Jerusalem*, the Bride, the Lamb's wife coming down out of Heaven with her Beloved ready trim'd.

How manifest, how full is the Finishing Love of God in Christ? The whole Being of a Saint is a Building, where all the Materials, the Work, the Finishing is Pure Love. Pure Love finished all its Works in this Building, before it began the World, from Eternity; and set it up in the Person of *Christ*. Pure Love cleanseth it from the Dust of Time, the Filth of Flesh, and bringeth it forth into the clear Lights of Grace, of Glory, which are the Brightness of its own Spiritual Beauties, in the Evangelical Appearances, and Out-Shinings of *Jesus Christ*.

Use 1. Receive the Love of God in *Christ*. 2. Resign your selves to the Love of God in Christ.

1. Receive

1. Receive the Love of God in *Christ*. It is a ſweet, and eaſy work. For this Love giveth reception to itſelf in the Soul. When the Sugar taketh in the Wine; In truth the Wine into which the Sugar is caſt, or which is poured upon it, worketh itſelf into the Sugar, then melteth, and diſſolveth it into One Body with itſelf; until you can no more diſtinguiſh between the Sugar, and the Wine. So the Soul lieth in the midſt of Divine Love. Love in its own way, by its own force worketh and melteth itſelf into the Soul, until it have melted and wrought the Soul into One Spirit, One Love with itſelf.

Divine Love is received into thy Soul, as thy Soul is received into thy Body; by Bringing it forth New out of its own Boſom; by Comprehending it in itſelf; by Forming it unto a Divine Image of Itſelf; by Inhabiting, Filling, Acting it; by Delighting in it, as its Daughter, Siſter, Spouſe, as its ſelf multiplyed. Receive this Love, which thus receiveth you, giveth reception to itſelf in you.

2. Reſign your ſelves to Divine Love. This Love worketh all your works, all its own works in you, and for you; all Works of Love and of Lovelineſs. Philoſophy teacheth us, that all Colours are Light mingled with Shade in various degrees, and manners; until it break up thorow the Shades, and drink up the Shades into One Pure Brightneſs. The Goſpel teacheth us; that all Graces are Divine Love ſhining variouſly, and gradually forth, thorow the Darkneſſes of our Spirits; until by a ſweet and Heavenly Force, as the Fire of the Divine Life kindled from the Throne of God, it burn out, and burn up all thoſe Darkneſſes, Diſtances, Defilements, Enmities, into One Eternal Flame of Pure Love, of Perfect Joy.

St *James* teacheth us; *c.* 1. 4. *If Patience have its perfect work, it ſhall make us perfect, wanting nothing.* This is the ſame thing, as if he had ſaid; Let Divine Love, Preventing, Aſſiſting Finiſhing Love have their Perfect work. Theſe will make you Perfect, wanting nothing. This is the Grace of Patience; the Love of God in *Chriſt* by its own force inſinuating itſelf into our Souls; by its own Charms alluring our Souls, tempering them to a harmonious Repoſe in it, a ſweet, entire Reſignation to it; until it have wrought out, and finiſhed its own Glories upon it.

Patience hath its Perfect Work; when Love hath its Perfect work. Love hath its Perfect Work in us; when we oppoſe nothing of the Devil to it; when we mingle nothing of our own with it.

O that I were indeed a Miniſter of the Goſpel! Then I ſhould miniſter the Spirit to you, which is Love; The Fountain, and the Sea of Love. Then while I ſpeak of Love, you would feel the *Holy Ghoſt* in his own proper Form, in the Form, and Fulneſs of Divine Love coming down upon you, entering into you, forming himſelf in you unto a Free Reception of himſelf, a Full Reſignation to himſelf, until he had Finiſhed his own moſt Lovely Form of Heavenly Love in you.

Uſe 3.

Use 3. Be aware, that you must receive the Love of God in *Christ* thorow eath. St *Paul* admonisheth us, that *as many, as are baptised into Christ, are* *ptised into the Similitude of his Death. Rom.*6.3. If we will be baptised into e Love, we must be baptised into the Death of the Lord *Jesus*. When *Moses* son was circumcised, *Zipporah* his wife said to him; *A bloody husband st thou been to me.* Some interpret the Words, as they run in the Hebrew; *ou hast been to me a Husband in Blood.* So they are the Solemn words of at Sacrament pointing out the Truth figured in that Type. The Lord *Jesus* a Husband to Thee in his own Blood. Thou must also be a Spouse to him thine own Blood,

St *Paul* saith; *Ye are dead to your first Husband by the Dead Body of Christ, t ye may be married to another, to him, who is risen from the Dead. Rom.*7. 4. ou must come thorow the Death of *Christ* into his Marriage-Bed. You nnot lye down in the Embraces of his Love in Glory; except ye be first rried to his Crucified Body, and united to that in the Embraces of Death. *sh, and Blood* saith St *Paul* *cannot enter into the Kingdom of God*; into the ngdom of Spiritual Love.

If a Fleshly, a Natural Spirit striveth to enter into the Love of God in the orified Person of our Lord *Jesus*: it falleth short of the Truth, the Life; it aineth to a Similitude only. The Love and Glory of the Father, of *Christ*, of aven to the most raised Spirit of this Creation is an Enchantment, Delusion, ream. This Grace of God in the Figure, this Divine Love in a Dream is for most part turned into Wantonness, & Lust. So men become in the heighth he Purest Notions, of the Sweetest Images no more than *Filthy Dreamers.*

The Death of *Christ* in the New Birth, in Purity, and Power of the holy ost is the Angel with a Flaming Sword turning every way, which keepeth Entrance into the True Paradise, the Way to the Tree of Divine Love, ell, as of Divine Life. The Eternal Spirit is the Flaming Sword. Death here s outward form is an Angel ministring to this Spirit. He, that dieth by Sword, and Flame in the hand of this Angel, cutteth off, burneth up all hly Forms, and Lives; is in the same moment new-born into a Divine, ortal Spirit. In this Spirit he entereth into the Paradise of Love in the rd Heavens, above the Heaven of Sense, or all things Visible, above the ven of Reason, Angels, all things Invisible, Intellectual, of the First Creation; e Glorified Person of Christ. Here nothing entereth, which hurteth, or eth.

t be not discouraged, when ye hear of a Baptism in Death, before the ens open and the Dove, Divine Love descend to rest upon you, to give rest in itself. It is Love itself, which is the Baptiser, which leadeth you, goeth down with you into Death. It is a River of Love, which is the *an*, the Death, into which you go down, and are baptised.

e are baptised, St. *Paul* saith in the forementioned place, *into the Similitude* of *of Christ's Death.* The Death of *Christ* was Death in Truth; a Substantial, Real Death. The Death of *Christ* in a Saint is Eternal Love, Eternal Life in the Likness, and Form of Death; a Similitude onely of Death in a Substance of Immortal Love, and Glory, in the Person of our *Jesus* ascended.

Use. 4. Take heed of mingling the Lusts of the Flesh with Spiritual Loves. Jealousy is the Rage of God, as well, as of Man. It burneth to the Foundations of the Earth. A Fly bred out of Dung so infested the Eagle, that it forced him to lay his Eggs for safety in the Lap of *Jupiter*, the Heathen-God. The Fly mounteth up aloft, carrieth up some Dung with it, letteth it fall into *Jupiter*'s lap. He arising, and shaking the Dung out of his Lap, shaketh out the Eagle's Eggs with it, which fall broken to pieces upon the ground.

This is a Fable. The Moral is good. Thou art a Saint. Thou layest the Births of the Divine Spirit in Thee, thy Graces, Hopes, Joyes with thy self in the Bosom of Divine Love. O take heed, that thy Flesh, that Dung-Fly, mingle nothing of its Filth with these Births of the Spirit in the Pure Bosom of Heavenly Love. If it do; assure thy self, that Love will cast all the Filth, all Flesh out of its Chast, and Spiritual Embraces, As that falleth to the Ground, thou also wilt fall with it, and have many a broken bone, many a broken heart.

We read in the *Revelation* of the Dragon, and his Angels in Heaven together with Michael, and his Angels. But they fought there, till the Dragon, and his Angels were cast out. Thou, O Believer, art a Heaven in which God dwelleth as Love, where all the Angels, as Angels of Love; where all Forms of things are, as Heavenly Angels of Pure Love round about him ministring to him. Shall there be now seen in this Heaven, in thy Person, O Believer, filthy Lusts, furious Passions; the Dragon, and his Angels together with the Lord *Jesus*, Divine Love, and its holy Angels. How hateful, how horrid a Wonder! What a Prodigy is this?

If it be so, let there be no rest in the Heaven of thy Spirit; let there be a continual Fight, until the Dragon with his Angels, the Fleshly Spirit with its Lusts, and Passions be cast out. When the Unclean Dog, and the fiery Dragon are no more; Thy Lamb will feed, and lye down to rest; thy Turtle will make its Nest, and enjoy its Mate, its Beloved in quiet. Nothing shall disturb, or make them afraid in all the Paradise of Divine Love.

Use. 5. Comfort your selves, O Believers. You travel thorough the Valley of *Baca*: *Baca* signifieth a Mulberry Tree, and Weeping. You travel thorow a Valley of Tears, a Mournful Valley; where all the Trees, that grow, are Mulberry Trees, Emblems of Grief, and Wo.

You are frequently overspread with the black Shades of Fear, Unbelief, Doubt, Distrust, Despair. You often fall into the hands of violent Robbers, Evil Spirits in the forms of various Temptations, Corruptions, Passions. These spoil you, leave you naked, wounded, desolate. You dig up pits in Duties,

Ordinances

Ordinances. But many times no Rain, no Descent of the Spirit from Heaven filleth these Pits.

Yet be not discouraged, all you, who believe the Love of God in *Jesus Christ*. Strengthen the feeble Knees. You shall go on from Strength to Strength, from Light to Light; so you shall come every one of you at last to a Clear Sight, to a Compleat Fruition of the God of Gods on Mount Sion, of God in his Supreme Glory, in the Nakedness, Purity, Simplicity, Unity of the Eternal Spirit. Lift up the feeble hands. These weak Graces of yours mixt, interrupted with so much Corruption; These weak Persons; Bodies, and Spirits wearied, wounded, stained with so many Sufferings, Sins, and Sorrows shall be crowned with perfect Glory.

For why? Pure Love, Almighty Love, That Love, which is itself God over all Blessed for ever; This Love comes forth casting off all vails, pouring forth itself from all its Eternal Springs, in all its Infinite Fulnesses in the Glorified Person of *Christ*; This Love hath begun, and shall it not make an End?

As Certainly, as it hath laid the Foundation, and you have cried to it; *Grace, Grace*; *Pure Love*; *Preventing Love*; as Certainly, as it hath gone on to build you up thus far; and still you have cried to it; *Grace, Grace*; *Pure Love*; *Assisting Love*: so certainly will it lay the Top-stone. Your Eyes shall see it. You shall in like manner cry to it, with a Shout of Angels, and Blessed Spirits all round about you; *Grace, Grace*; *Pure Love*; *Finishing Love.*

There are *Three Sorts of Comforts*, which the *Finishing Love* of God in *Christ* ministreth to us; 1. *Against the Difficulties of Life*;

2. *Against the Darkness of Death*; 3. *Against the Dreadfulness of the Great and Last Day*.

1. *Comfort*; *against the Difficulties of Life*. St. *Paul* had prayed thrice against the *Thorn in his Flesh*, and the *Buffetings of Satan*. He receiveth this Answer; *My Grace is sufficient for thee*: *My Strength is perfected in Weakness*; *I rejoyce therefore gladly in my Infirmities. For, when I am weak, the Power of Christ resteth upon me. My Grace.* You have there the *Father*, the Fountain of Love, the Fountain of Free Grace. You have at the end of the *verse*, the Lord *Jesus* Glorified, into whom this Fountain floweth continually, covering his Person all over without, filling it all within with the Glories, Immortalities and Joys of Divine Love. This *Jesus* resteth upon St *Paul* in the Power, in the Perfection of All his Loves; He maketh Perfect, he finisheth his Loves, the Pure, and heavenly Work of his Loves upon him; when he is weakest.

The *Holy Ghost* discovereth a *Mystery* here. A *Mystery* is a *Divine Secret*: A Divine Glory with a Divine Vail cast over it; a Divine Light surrounded with a Divine Darkness; The Head of *Christ* all Pure, Fine Gold covered with Locks, and Curles black, as a Raven. The *Mystery*, which the Holy Ghost here unvaileth to us is, One of the richest, and sweetest among all the Mysteries of the Gospel. It is the Mystery of Love, of *Finishing Love.* Blessed are those Eyes, that see the Glory; Blessed are those Hearts, that understand, and rellish the Sweetness of This Mystery. It is This: When Divine Love would put forth itself in Greatest Power, and Glory; when it would finish, make Perfect the general, or any Particular Work of Love in us: it chooseth that Season, when we are weakest, lowest, have least of Loveliness, Life, Love, or Suitableness to Love; when we are in the greatest unlikelyhood for it; when we seem to be at the greatest Distance from it.

Cant. 6. *v.* 12. The Spouse is brought in speaking thus: *Ere I was aware, my Soul made me, as the Chariots of* Amminadib. I have not Learning enough to understand, why *Amminadib* is set here, as One Proper name, whenas in the Hebrew there are Two distinct Words, which have their common signification, and are rendered in the Margint of the Bible; *My Willing People.* Moreover that word *As* is put in by the Translatours; and where we read *Made me,* the Original properly is expressed by *Set me.*

The words then run thus in the *Hebrew Text*; Ere I was aware, (or, I knew not, I knew not how, I knew nothing of it) my Soul set me the Chariots of my Willing People; or by the Addition of One Preposition understood; *My Soul set me in the Chariots of my willing people.* It will be worth our time, and pains; if we stay a little upon the opening of this verse. We shall find a Spiritual, a heavenly Treasure in it; and bring the Application home to our hearts more Clearly, more Comfortably.

There are *Four Questions,* which may be made here: 1. *Qu.* Who this *People* are, which the heavenly Bride calleth; *My People.* 2 *Qu.* What the *Willing People* are. 3 *Qu.* What the *Chariots* are. 4. How the Soul of the Bride setteth her *In* these Chariots or maketh her *As* these Chariots.

1. Qu. *Who the heavenly Bride's own People are.*

Answ. These whom the Spiritual Bride calleth *Her own People* are *Heavenly Spirits in Glory.* It was said of *Jacob,* when he died; *He was gathered to his People.* While a holy Soul is in this World, she is, as an unknown Princess under a Disguise, in a strange land, the language whereof she understandeth not. In Death this Princess-Bride returneth home to her own People, to her own Kindred, her own Relations, and Acquaintances. There all understand the languages, Faces, and hearts of Each other. There they mutually drink in the Spirits of Each Other, and in the Spirits of Each other all Pure, Immortal Loves, Beauties, Joys.

There is another *Scripture,* which commenteth upon this, and confirmeth our Explication of it: It is *Eccles.* 12. 7. *The Dust returneth to the Earth, as it was: The Spirit to God, who gave it.* That which is translated *God,* is in the Plural Number *Gods,* often applyed to the *Angels.* The *Jews* say it signifieth God *cum Indumentis suis*; as he cloatheth himself with the Forms of Angels, and appeareth in them. The Soul of a Saint cometh forth from the Land of Angels, and Glorious Spirits, in the midst of which God reigneth, into this World,

World, as into an Exile or Banishment. When it dieth, then it goeth home to its own Countrey, and People; to its own City, and Fellow-Citizens; The Inhabitants of the heavenly *Jerusalem*, the Mother of us all.

I shall add one *Text* more, which will make all the rest Clear; *Hebr.* 11. 14,15,16. The Saints there are said to seek *a Countrey*. The Word is πατρίδα; Their Native Countrey. Then to prevent a mistake you are told; that this *Native Countrey* was not that, from which they came on Earth. It is distinguished from that, and plainly called; *A heavenly Country*; Their Native Land, which is a heavenly Countrey. Behold those whom the Spouse of Christ calleth *My People*; The Inhabitants of the City of the Living God; her heavenly Countrey, her Native Land above the Heavens, as the word beareth. These are described in the *Epistle* to the *Hebrews*, *The Assembly of the First-born*. all Forms of things, all the Saints, in Spiritual Beings, and Beauties, in the Likeness of *Christ*, as he is the first-born of every Creature, before they descend from their Thrones of Pure Glory, from their Virgin-Lustre, and Sweetness in the Bosom of *Christ*, into Flesh, upon the Earth; *The Innumerable Company of Angels* the Glorious Attendants of the Saints in their higher, and First-born Glory; *The Spirits of just men made Perfect*; either in the Body, or out of the Body, come to this heavenly Land; Living, walking, and conversing there among the Inhabitants of this Land, in the Spirit: These are *Thy People, Thine own People*, O Believer, O thou Blessed Bride of thy Glorified *Jesus*. You have the *Answer* to the *First Question*.

2 Qu. *What are the Willing People?*

Answ. Again I am ignorant, why the same word is rendred in the Margin of this *Scripture*; *Willing*; when as immediately after, *Cant.* 7. 1. The same word *Nadib* is translated *Prince*; O *Prince's Daughter*; or O *Princely Daughter*. If I mistake not, the Church is spoken of in that *Chapter*, as being now in Glory, upon the Throne. You have this word *Nadib* used to the same sense, of the same Subject; *Psal.* 110. 3. *Thy People shall be Willing in the day of thy Power, in the Beauties of holiness, from the womb of the morning; thou hast the dew of thy Birth*. The words lie thus in *Hebrew*: *Thy willing People in the Day of thy Power, or, thy Armies, in the Beauties, or Excellencies or Majesties of holiness, or in thy holy, Pure Beauties, from the Womb of the Morning, to thee the Dew of thy Youth.*

You have here the Lord *Jesus* in Glory, in his Kingdom; in the Day of his Power with his Armies of Angels round about him; in the Beauties of holiness, in his Freshest Beauties, in the heighth of Excellency, and Majesty in the Glory of his God-Head filling, shining thorow, overspreading his humane Nature. You have him here in the Brightness Sweetness, and Newness of his Eternal Sonship, as he cometh forth Immediately from the Womb of the Morning, the Bosom of the Father, who is the Morning, the Day-Spring of the God-Head. Thus is *Jesus Christ* with the Dew of his Youth upon him as Fair, as Fresh, as unfading as a New-blown Rose in the Morning, while the

Pearly Dew lieth yet upon it. *Jesus Christ* is now, as a Bridegroom upon his Coronation Day, or as a King upon his Marriage-Day. Now his People are a Princely People, all Fellow-Kings together with him. Now the holy Soul is That Princess, and Daughter which is his Queen all *in Beaten Gold at his* right hand.

The Willing People are Princes, heavenly Spirits in Glory. This is the *Answer* to the *Second Question.*

3.Qu. *What are the Chariots of the Princely People ?*

Answ. 1. The *Chariots* are the *holy Angels*, Psal. 68. 17. *The Chariots of the Lord are Thousands ; Ten Thousands of Angels. God is in the midst of them, as on Sinai, in the holy Place* You may observe in your *Bibles* that word *Place* not to be printed with the same letter, as *holy*, to signifie, that it is not in the *Hebrew* but added by the Translatours.

The Holy may be here any of these, or rather all of these in their Subordinations; the *Sanctuary*, or *Temple*, the *Holy Place*, the *Figure*; the *Lord Jesus*, the *Substance*, & *Life* to this *Figure*, the *holy One* the *Saints*, the *holy Ones*, the *members* of *Christ*, *Christ Mystical*, the *Spiritual Temples*; *Heaven*, the *Everlasting Glory* of the *God-Head*, in which Christ resideth.

Sinai was a Type to all these. These in their several degrees are *Sinai* heightned to *Sion*, to the Perfection of the Divine Presence in the Beauty of Holiness, and Love. You may see too, that *As* before *Sinai* is added. The Hebrew lieth thus ; *Sinai in the holy.*

The Thousands, and Ten thousands of holy Angels make all One Chariot in which God rideth. Each Angel is also a Distinct Chariot The Chariots of the Lord are according to the number of the Angels. But Each Angel comprehendeth in himself the whole Millions, of Angels. They are distinguished in their Essential Forms; but undivided. As the same Colours, and Lines varied make all Beauties: So all Angelical Forms in distinct Relations make up the Essence, and Glory of Every Particular Angel. God with the Thousands of his Chariots rested on Mount *Sinai*. *Sinai*, or *Sion* rather is in the Lord *Jesus*; in the Assemblies of the Saints ; in the Person, and Spirit of every Saint ; in Heaven ; in the Spirit thorow all the Heavens, and the Earth, in the Lord *Jesus*, and every Saint.

The Chariot of *Solomon* is the Chariot of his Queen also. The Bridegroom, and the Bride ride together in the same Chariot ; *Jesus Christ* and his Spouse ; *Jesus Christ*, and his *Brethren*, his *Fellow Kings.*

Behold then the Chariots of the Princely People of the Immortal Kings, of Saints in Glory, in the Glory of Christ, and of the Spirit, whether in the Body, or out of the Body. They are the Chariots of God ; The Thousands, and Ten Thousands of the holy Angels.

These are in a double sense the Chariots of these Divine Princes ; 1. These Princes ride in them ; 2. God rideth, upon them in these Princes, as on *Sinai*, as on *Sion*, as in Heaven.

Answ.

Answ. 2. The Chariot is the Divine Presence in the Light, and Evidence f its own Appearance, with all its Train of Glories, and Angels, as in Heaen with the Universal Form of things comprehended in it, enlivened, and nlightned by it; as in the Glorious Person of *Christ*, at the last day. This Diine Presence descending and ascending; resting upon, and shining forth in e Prophets and Holy men of old in their Visions; is described Mystically; *zek. c.* 1. and called by the *Jews*, *The Chariot*.

There are *Wheels*, Living, High, Dreadful, Glorious, Shining, as a Pretious one, full of Eyes, that is, of Angels, of heavenly Spirits. I humbly offer it be considered; whether these *Wheels* be not the Elements, these Globes of e Visible Earth, and Heavens, made New, made Spiritual, filled with Angeal Lives, cloathed with Angelical Forms, and Glories in the Kingdom of e Spirit, and Mystical Person of *Christ*.

Then the *Horses*, which draw these *Wheels* are the *Living Creatures, full Eyes*. If the Wheels may be understood to be the visible Part; these Living Creatures may present the Invisible Part of the Creation in its Renovati-, by a Spiritual Glory flowing forth from the Fountain of The God-Head in e Glorified Person of the Lord *Jesus*.

These Wheels, and Horses together may perhaps not improbably be thought be *the New Earth*.

Above the *Wheels*, and the *Living Creatures* is the *Chariot* itself, a *Firmant*. If I may pursue my former Apprehension with Submission to the Spirit Truth in every Spirit; I shall call this the *New Heaven*; The *heavenly age*, the God-Head unvailing itself, appearing in a New Glory. This is e Firmament, the Heaven, born up, and carried along by the Innumerable ompany of Angels; while *Jesus Christ* sitteth in it, as in his Chariot.

Above this Firmament is the Similitude of a Man; as Fire, from his Loins ward, and as Fire from his Loins downward. This is our Blessed Saviour the Union of his Divine, and Humane Nature. The Glory of the Divinity, the Eternal Spirit cloatheth both with the same Similitude of Fire, which neth with the Sweetest Light burneth with the greatest force of Love, nsformeth all things with an Almighty Power into One Pure, Immortal, vine Flame with itself.

The Lord *Jesus* himself speaketh of his own Coming, and Appearance in Kingdom after this manner; *The Son of Man shall come in his own Glory, the Glory of his Father, and in the Glory of all His holy Angels.*

Our Saviour seemeth to have had the same Vision in the Eye of his Spirit ich *Ezekiel* had. The Jews distinguish the Angels into Angels of the *rone*, nearer to the Divine Majesty; Angels of *Service*, at a greater Distance. The Glory of the holy Angels make the New Earth; the Horses, and the heels in the Chariot of the great King. The Wheels, the Visible Part of Creation, the Wheels are made of Angelical Glory: But they are the Angels

Angels of *Service* in a New, Spiritual Glory. The Invisible Things of the Creation, the Living Creatures in the Chariot are the Angels of the Throne in the Glory of the Kingdom ; of the Coronation, , and Marriage-Day.

The *Firmament*, the *New Heaven* is the *Glory of the Father* ; The Chariot itself which containeth him, in which he descendeth, bowing down the Heavens, as he descendeth. The Lord *Jesus* himself in his own Glory is Distinct from all these Glories, comprehendeth them ; and rideth forth in them.

This is that Image, in which he shall appear at the last Day, as a New Creator and a New Creation, making all things New; as the most Entire, most Naked Image of the Invisible God, in all his most Pure, and most Invisible Glories ; as the First-born of the whole Creation in general, and of every Creature in Particular ; as the Whole Creation in its Virgin-State, in its Ideal Glory, while yet it sprung up out of the Bosom of God, and stood onely in the Bosom of God, and was a Sister-Spouse to the uncreated Beauty.

This is that Testimony of Jesus, which is the Spirit of Prophesy ; That Divine Presence, that Word of God, which came to all the Holy Men of old, in the Light of which, as in the Glass of Eternity, the First, and Supreme Truth, they saw Visions, dreamed dreams, and spake of him. This is the Chariot of the Princes ; of the Saints in the Glory of the Spirit.

4 Qu. *How doth the Soul of the Spouse make her, as this Chariot of her Princely People, or set her in it?*

Answ. The *Soul* of the heavenly Bride is her Lord, her Life, her Love, her heart, her True Self, her Beloved, her *Jesus*. He descendeth in his Chariot, and taketh her up into it. He appearing in his heavenly Image composed of the Glory of his Father, his own Glory, the Glory of all his holy Angels, which is his Chariot, as he appeareth in her, translateth and transfigureth her into the same heavenly Image. She also is now become a Chariot made up all of the same Glories, with the same *Jesus*, the same Queen, the same Company of Princes riding together in it. The *Soul* of the Bride is also *Faith*, the *Seed of God*, the *Divine Nature*, the *Spirit* in a Saint.

This Divine Life in a Saint by a Descent of the Lord *Jesus* upon it, in a moment, ere a Saint is aware, he knoweth not how, both taketh him up to set him in this Chariot, and Transformeth him into it.

I have onely prepared you by all this for the Application of the Scripture opened by us to our present purpose ; that we may take in with a greater Sense, with a Deeper Impression the Comfort, and Joys of Finishing Love making Perfect its most Beautiful Works, and Displaying its most pleasant Strengths in our Weaknesses.

Ere I was aware, my Soul made me, as the Chariots of my Princely People; or set me in them.

Hearken to me, my Brethren. Is there not among you a Poor Believer, a Mournful Saint, which hath long prayed, long sighed for a Clear Sight of

Jesus

esus Christ, a Sense, and Seal of his Love, Sweet, and Constant Communion ith him? To this Soul I now speak. Perhaps after all this thou art embracing e Dunghil of Distrust, and Despair. Perhaps thou art sitting upon the unghil of some Fleshly Lust, or Earthly Care; of Covetousness, or Lascivisness; Vanity, or vexation. Now, in a moment, which thou thinkest not , ere thou art aware, Jesus Christ in the Divine Brightness of some heavenly ruth flashing, like Lightning, in upon thy Spirit, may descend, may discover mself in his Heavenly Image, with his naked Glories, naked Loves to thee. ow, are thou art aware, he may make this heavenly Image, at once a Laver Precious Blood, in which he washeth Thee white, as the Light itself, from ery Spot; a Chariot of heavenly Princes, in which he cometh down to Thee on thy Dunghil, taketh Thee off from thy Dunghil to ride with him in the llowship of all Immortal Spirits, while all the holy Angels bear Thee up, l carry Thee on upon the Firmament of the Father's Glory at the side of r Beloved, whither the Mind of the Spirit is for Thee to go.

Ere thou art aware, the Lord Jesus can change thy Dunghil, can change ee, into a Divine Chariot of Eternal Spirits, in which he will ride forth h Thee; thou shalt ride forth together with him having his Loveliness in ne Eye, his Love in thine heart, thorow all Forms of things, Light, and kness, Life, and Death, as thorow various Fields, differing Regions of Spiial Beauties, and Delights in the Vast Continent, the Vast World of the ine Nature.

Thus comfort thy self against the Discouragements of Life with the Fulness Divine Love, Finishing Love in the Glorified Person of *Christ*; which maketh fect its Strength and Sweetness in Weakness, and Enmity; which giveth ee the Desire of thy Soul, thy *Jesus*, most clearly, most dearly into thy Bo-, when thou lyest locked up fastest in the Bosom of the Strange Woman; This Strumpet, and this Witch, the Hellish Darkness cloathed with Figures fleshly Softnesses, Sweetnesses, Lights, and Treasures.

Gen. 28. 11, 12. *Jacob* had pursued the Spiritual Blessing, the heavenly h-right, and had obtained the Promise, the Purchase. After all this he fly- alone, as a Banished Person, from his Father's house. He is benighted in open field. He lieth upon the naked ground. He hath under his head for llow, a Cold, Hard Stone. Now Finishing Love maketh Perfect its ngth in this Weakness, giving him now the Evidence, the Pledge, the -fruits of that Spiritual Blessing, that heavenly Birth-right, which he had omise of, and a Title to.

ow Heaven is opened to the Eye of his Spirit in a Dream. A Ladder ch from Heaven to Earth. One End of it resteth on the Bosom of God e. The other End standeth upon the Ground at his head below. Angels nd, and ascend upon the Ladder. He awaketh, and saith; This is none , than the Gate of Heaven, the house of God; and I was not aware of of it. The Stone on which he lay, is now anointed, and becometh a Pillar, and Altar, a Figure of *Jesus Christ* in all his Divine Loves, and Lovelinesses.

Jacob is in every holy One. Hear this you broken hearts. You complain We have tasted something of the Sweetness of *Preventing* Love, if this be Preventing Love to cast in upon our Spirits gracious hints, and hopes of Spiritual Blessings, and heavenly things, when we sate in the Shadow of Death, and did not so much, as know, or Believe, that there was a *Spirit*, a *Heaven*.

We have also tasted something of the Sweetness of *Assisting Love*, if this be assisting Love to help us, to carry us on for a wearisome length of time with sighs, and groans, unutterable, to cry for the Revelation, the Possession, the Fruition of these Spiritual Blessings, and heavenly things, in the Foretast of them.

But, O! where is *Finishing Love*? Now instead of this, behold, we are benighted with Darkness of Spirit surrounding us, far from our Father's house, from the Bosom of our *Jesus*, in the wide, solitary, naked field of this Fleshly Image. We lie upon the Cold Ground of our own Natural, Earthly, Comfortless Spirits. Under our head is the hard Stone of unbelief, Distrust, Care, and Fear. Where is now *Finishing Love*?

Finishing Love is now nearer to you, than you are aware. This is the Season for Finishing Love. this is the Time, in which the Work of Finishing Love is most Beautiful. What it now doth, will be for Ever, for an Eternal Joy, and Glory; a Work of Eternity.

It will be now Pure Love, Perfect Love; It will now work with All Freedom, with all Fulness in your Weaknesses.

Ere you are aware, Finishing Love will open itself, as the Heaven of Heavens round about you. You shall see the Lord *Jesus*, as a Mystical Ladder of Divine Loves reaching from Heaven, to Earth, filling with the Fulness of Divine Loves poured forth in his Glorified Person all the Space between Heaven, and Earth; while One End of this Ladder toucheth the Heart of God in the Glories of Heaven, and Eternity; the other End toucheth thine Heart, thou liest covered with darkness below on the Desolate Earth. Divine Love in all Angelical forms stand upon every Round of this Ladder, every Degree and State of Things between heaven, and Earth, in great Troops. These at once descend, and ascend; bring down the Heart of the Father into thy Bosom and carry up thy Heart into the Bosom of the Father.

Now thou saiest; This Open Field was the House of God, of Divine Love This Darkness was the Gate of Heaven; the Gate of Finishing Love; and I was not aware. By this Gate Divine Love cometh forth from Its Spiritual Palace unto me. By this Gate Divine Love bringeth me into its Palace. It is enough I have received the Spirit of Promise; I am Sealed by it with the Eternal Image of Divine Loves, and Glories, with the Heart of my *Jesus*, my God, set upon my Heart. O my *Jesus*, it is true, it is True. This was the Sea-

son

ſon of thy Finiſhing Love, and I was not aware. Thy Finiſhing Love maketh Perfect its Strength, Light, Sweetneſs, in Weakneſs, Darkneſs, Enmity.

Thus comfort your ſelves againſt the Difficulties of Life in the *Freedom*, the *Fulneſs* of the Finiſhing Love of God treaſured up in the Glorified Perſon of *Chriſt* for you.

2. *Comfort*; *Againſt the Darkneſs of Death. Gladly therefore will I rejoyce in mine Infirmities. For, when I am weak, the Power of Chriſt reſteth upon me*; ſaith St *Paul*; 2 *Corin*. 12. 10. in the place cited before. It is the Power of *Finiſhing Love* in *Chriſt* which is here intended. For that was the Subject of the former part of the *verſe*: My Grace is ſufficient for Thee. Behold Free Grace, Pure Love! *For my Strength is made perfect in Weakneſs.* The Strength of Grace, of Love is made Perfect in Weakneſs. Behold *Finiſhing Love*! This maketh the Infirmities not of old Age onely, but of our dying hour Pleaſant to us; that, when we are weakeſt, the Power of Divine Love reſteth upon us in its Finiſhing Sweetneſſes, and Glories.

When the Lord *Jeſus* hung upon the Croſs, he cried out; *My God, my God! why haſt thou forſaken me*? A Darkneſs covereth the face of the whole Earth round about Him. The next words, which we hear from him, juſt as he giveth up the Ghoſt, are theſe: *It is Finiſhed*; A Declaration of Victory; A Triumph. The Myſtery of my Sufferings, of Divine Wrath are finiſhed in my Perſon. The Glory of the God Head, of Heaven, of Eternity; All Beauty, all Joyes; The Myſtery of Divine Love are finiſhed, and compleated in my Perſon. Both theſe Myſteries are now finiſhed, Both Compleated in One Glory, in this One Moment of my Death.

This is the Pattern of a Saint, and of Finiſhing Love in the Pangs of Death. You have a Saint ſick on his Death-bed; a ſenſe of Sin, of Wrath; Doubt, Deſpair ſpreading their black Wings over his Spirit; pains, faintings, deadly pangs ſeizing upon his Body. In a Moment, in the midſt of theſe Weakneſſes the Lord *Jeſus* in a Chariot of Angels, and Inviſible Glories, with the full Power of all Finiſhing Loves reſteth upon him from without; raiſeth himſelf and ſhineth from within. Now in this Moment is the Whole Scene changed. The black, and baleful Image of Things is changed into a Heaven. The fainting, dying Perſon into a Glorified Spirit triumphing in his Chariot of Angels, and aſcending with the Lord *Jeſus* into the Heighths of Eternity.

He crieth one moment; The Joys of Life, the Light of the Sun, the Delights of mine Eyes, My Deareſt Relations, and ſweeteſt Friends, *Life* itſelf forſake me. My hope, my Faith, my Spiritual Comforts; my God, my God, why do ye, why doeſt thou forſake me?

The Next moment with a Shout of Angels, with the Sound of the Silver Trumpets in Heaven, he crieth out; *It is finiſhed.* The Sufferings of *Chriſt* are finiſhed in me. Divine Love hath finiſhed upon me all its Myſteries, and made the Joys of Eternity full in me.

A modest Person was sick, and in want: A Friend sensible of his want, and modesty conveyed a Bag of money under his head, and pillow, while he slept. He waketh, findeth it, smileth, and saith: *This is the Stealth of my Friend.*

Our *Jesus* frequently casteth a deep Darkness, the Shadow of Death over us then, when he purposeth under the covert of this Darkness to convey some finished Piece of Glory, some Compleat Work of Finishing Love, Heaven itself into our Bosom; our Persons into a Heaven of Immortalities, and Glories unsought, unexpected, unperceived by us, until we are possessed of them, until we are in the midst of Them. These are the *Stealths* of our Beloved. These are the *Stealths* of *Finishing Love.*

The Power of *Christ* with all the Fulness of *Finishing Loves* resting upon a Saint in his Death is excellently described, 2 *Corin.* 5. *v.* 1, 2, 3, 4.

Observe there *Four things*; 1. *A Glorious Building.* 2. *The Groans of Burthened Saints.* 3. *The Workmanship of God*, 4. *The Earnest of the Spirit.*

1. *A Glorious Building.* This is *A building of God*; ἐκ Θεοῦ; *out of God.* The Materials, as well as the Builder, and the Form, are all of a Divine Nature. It is a Pallace hewn out of the Rock, and standing in the Rock of Eternity. Gold, precious Stones, Pearls, the Body of the Sun, Angelical Substances are, as Dung to the Materials, of which this Building consisteth.

It is *Eternal*; above Time; and so without Beginning, or End; above Succession and change.

It is *in the Heavens*, in the Highest Heavens, the Heavens of Eternity, the Heavens of Heavens, in the Eternal and Supream Spirit.

It is situate in the most Divine Heighths, in the midst of the most Divine Lights, Loves, Purities, Powers, and Pleasures; in the midst of the most Divine Lives, and Immortalities.

2. *The Groans of burthened Saints. We groan* being burthened. The Burthen is the Earthy Tabernacle; This Life; The Weight of vanity, and Corruption. These burthened Spirits groan for the Dissolution of this Tabernacle. But how? *Not, that we would be uncloathed, but cloathed upon with our house from Heaven*; not to be *found naked*, but to have *Mortality swallowed up of Life.*

St. *Paul* expresseth the meaning of the Unutterable Groans, with which the Spirit of Supplications maketh Intercession in the Saints. They would not be uncloathed of the Spiritual Image, which they put on at the New Birth. They would not be uncloathed of the Natural Image, which they put on at their First Birth. They would never, no, not for a moment be found naked of any thing of that Life Light, or Sweetness, Heavenly, or Earthly, which belong to either of these. No; they groan to have these cloathed upon with that their Building from above; to have not onely their Immortal, and Inward, but their Outward, and Mortal Part itself swallowed up into *Life*; Life itself, in its Purity, in its Perfection, in its Spring, which is Eternity.

3. The Workmanship of God in a Saint is wonderful, and indeed Divine

in this. *Now he that hath made us for this, or, he that hath wrought us unto this, is God.* St *Paul* assureth every Saint, that his Groans are heard, and answered ; from the Workmanship, and the Workman. We read in the *Canticles* ; that the *Thighs* of the Princess, and Bride are, *as Jewels, the Work of the hands of a Curious, and Faithful Workman.* So the *Word* in *Hebrew* signifieth.

The Spiritual, and Natural Life ; the Whole Frame, and Composure of a Saint, Inward and Outward ; all are Mysterious Jewels, wrought by the Divine hands of God himself, as a most Curious, and Faithful Workman, as a most Skilful, and Firm Piece of Work. They are by an Unexpressible Wisdom, and Love framed unto this ; that the Substance of these Jewels should never fail, the Vertue never decay, the Lustre never fade ; no, not in Death itself ; but then most of all grow bigger, and brighter ; more Pure, more, Perfect more Powerful by being drunk up into Eternity ; as the Waters of a fine Spring, are drawn, and drunk up by the Sun.

4. *The Earnest of the Spirit.* Who hath also given us *the Earnest of the Spirit.* The Eternal Spirit in the Immortal Soul, and Mortal Body of a Saint ; The Eternal Spirit, in which a Saint possesseth Soul, Body ; things of Faith, of Reason, of Sense ; This Spirit is to a Saint an Earnest ; both a foretast, and a seal of this truth ; that both the Soul, and the Body of a Saint in Death, are like the Spice in the Golden Censor, or upon the Golden Altar in the Temple, which is the Glorified Bosom of *Christ*. Both lose nothing of themselves, but change into a more Spiritual, and Divine Form, in which they ascend, and carry up all their Preciousness, all their Pleasantness with them, like the Pillar of Smoak from the Altar perfumed with all the Spices of the Apothecary, in which those Spices themselves with all their Sweetness, and Vertue go up refining, and enlarging themelves, till they rest and spread themselves, in the Bosom of Heaven.

How Curious, and Sure a Workman is *Jesus Christ*, is the Love of the Father in the Death of a Saint ? O the Freedom, O the Fulness ; O the Skill, O the Faithfulness of Finishing Love in the Death of a Saint !

O Believers ! *Preventing Love* hath brought you out of *Ægypt*, out of the Servitude to your Lusts, and the God, the Spirit of this World. *Assisting Love* hath carried you along thorough this Weary Wilderness, your Conformity, and Fellowship with the Lord *Jesus* in his Sufferings. Be of good Courage. Your Cloaths shall not wax old. Nothing of you shall fall in this Wilderness. You shall certainly come into the Good Land, the Land of Promise, the Land of Rest, the Land flowing with Milk, and Honey ; with Life, and Peace ; Immortality, and Immortal Pleasures.

Finishing Love in the Glorious, and Immortal Person of your Beloved like the Ark before the *Israelites*, shall lead you thorow this *Jordan*, thorow Death, on the Dry, Firm, and Pleasant Land of Life itself. Not so much, as any single Drops of any Dark Waters shall sprinkle themselves upon any Parts of your

Garment. The clear Streams of this Beloved River ſhall ſtand on heaps, on each ſide of you; as Chriſtal, or Diamond Rocks; as Lights, Proſpects, and Guards of Angels, while you paſs.

When You are weakeſt under the Pangs of Death, the Finiſhing Love of Chriſt in Power, your Glorified *Jeſus* in the Power of his Finiſhing Love ſhall reſt upon you, ſhall ſpring up in you; at once to comprehend you, and enlarge you; to Cloath you upon, and to transform you within.

Nothing of the Graces, and Joys of your *Inward Man*; Nothing of the Beauties, and Delights of your *Outward Man* ſhall be divorced from you, or darkened in you. Like a Heaven of Stars, they may paſs under many Clouds; But under all Clouds, they ſhall go on ſhining ſtill, and increaſing their Luſtre. When they ſeem to be extinguiſhed in Death, they ſhall be only drunk up into that Pure Light of Life, which is Inviſible to all Mortal Eyes by its Fineneſs, and Fulneſs of Glory. They ſhall diſappear onely by the Degree of heightning.

He, who hath wrought us unto this, is God. The Sweet Colours of a fair Summer-Morning in the Sky are ſo made, that they fade not, but go on changing to fair and freſher Colours ſtill, until they all vaniſh into Pure Light. For Theſe Colours are all the Light of the Approaching Sun figuring itſelf in divers degrees into Different Forms of Beauty; till at laſt It Break up into the Full Glory of unmixt Light by the immediate Preſence of the Sun appearing with the unclouded Brightneſs of his heavenly Body.

In like manner all the Excellencies, Entertainments, and Joys of a Saint, in his Immortal, and Mortal Part; The Immortal, and Mortal Parts themſelves of a Saint thorowout are ſo framed by the Father of Lights, and Loves; that they can never fade, nor paſs away; but in the moment of Death itſelf, are cloathed upon from above with a Brighter, a Diviner Form, and are ſwallowed up into the Abyſses, the Incomprehenſibleneſſes of Eternity.

For God is Love. A Saint is a Birth of Love; A Seed of Divine Love ſpringing up in his Outward, and Inward Man, Forming itſelf into a Body and Spirit, into all the Powers, Pleaſures, Objects, Relations of Both. Divine Love is the Subſtance, and the Sap; The Matter, and the Form in all. A Saint in his Eſſence, and Operations, all Entirely is a Plant of Divine Love. Death is the Ripening of the whole Plant all over into the Perfect Fruit of Pure Love, of Finiſhing Love. In this Form It can be ſeen, felt, taſted no more but by the Pure Eyes, Embraces, and Mouth of Divine Love. God hath *alſo given us the Earneſt of his Spirit* for this. Tell me now you, who have received the Spirit; What do you ſee, what do you feel, when you are bleſſed from on high with any freſh Anointing, any freſh Effuſion of the Spirit upon you? When the Activity of Grace, when the Operations of the Divine Life are heightned in you by any peculiar Appearances, and Outſhinings of the Lord Jeſus in you; what do you Find? Do you not find *all things made New*? Do you not find

find the Invisible Image of things within, the Image of all Visible things without; Your self your Life, Your Soul, your Body, Your Graces, your Comforts; Husband, Wife, Children, all Objects of Life, the whole World itself renewing its Light, its Sweetness, its Lustre; All heightened, Spiritualised Immortalized, transfigured into Divine Forms Invisible to all other Eyes, and this without any Darkening, without any Eclipse, or Cloudy moment interposing.

This is the Earnest of the Spirit given unto Thee for a Figure, a Forecast, and a Seal of Thy change in Death.

Thou shalt not be uncloathed of any Garment of Life, or Light; Spiritual, or Natural, which thou hast ever put on. Thou shalt never be found naked of any Forms of Light, Life, or Love, which have ever accompanyed, and encompassed Thee.

Thy Faith shall be swallowed up into Vision; Clear, Full Immediate Vision, Eye to Eye; Thy Hope into Entire Possession, and Compleat Fruition; hy Soul itself into a Simple Divinity and Eternity.

Thy Body; thy Dear Relations; the Delights of thine Eyes; the Precious, nd Pleasant things of thy Senses shall All be cloathed upon from above with hose Immortal Substances, of which here they are the Shadows; with their wn Original Forms, of which here they bear the Figure; with their Flourishing 'atterns upon the Mount of Glory, in that First, and Pure Spirit, the Founain of Life, the shining Fountain of Good; in the Glorified Person of the ord *Jesus*; in Eternity.

The Movable Tabernacle with its Tent, both are Dissolv'd, and fall in- the Eternal Building of Glory in the Heavens; where they become, as Myerious Figures of Divinity, in that Temple; or Rich Furniture, & Delightl Apartments of that Palace; where every Part beareth the Figure; possesth the Life, and Beauty of the Whole.

This is the Freedom, the Sweetness, the Fulness of the Finishing Love of od in *Christ*. Death itself is made at once A Consummation of the Marage Love between the Heavenly Bridegroom, & his Bride; A Bed of Loves; e Divine Embraces of Eternal Love; and the Divine Fruitfulness of these nbraces.

Jesus in his Invisible, and Eternal Form descendeth, overshadoweth emaceth his Bride; transfigureth her into a Form of Eternal Beauties perfectanswering his own; maketh her to spring with, to bring forth in the mont of those embraces, in the moment of her own Transfiguration all Forms Things above, and below in Immortal, Divine Images, and Essences of re, Perfect Love.

The Dark, aud Dreadful Appearances which surround Death, are onely Cloud, which hide these Delightful, these sacred Mysteries and changes m all Natural Eyes; while the Saint himself in the Spirit seeth its own uties, feeleth its own Joys in these Transfiguring, and Impregnating Embraces:

braces: So *Christ* himself, was taken by a Cloud out of the sight of the Apostles while he ascended.

Death beginneth to the whole Saint in all parts that Coming down of the Lord *Jesus* in a Flame of Glory; that Rapture of a Saint caught up into the Bosom of the Lord *Jesus*, with the Sound of the Heavenly Trumpet: The Universal Shout of Divine Lives, Loves, Glories, thorow all things. The Resurrection finisheth them. O the Absoluteness of *Finishing Love!* All work of Glory is made perfect in a Saint: *Jesus* in all these Powers and Treasures of the God-Head resteth upon a Saint then, when he is weakest, when he seemeth nearest, likest to Darkness, Dust and Dung, in the Agonies of Death.

3. *Comfort*; *Against the last Day*. There are peculiar Terrours accompany the *Day of Judgment*. It is indeed the most Dreadful of all Dreadful things.

The Last Day is twofold; 1. *Universal*, the *Day* of the *Lord* upon the whole Earth. 2. *Particular*; the day of the *Lord* upon a City or Nation.

Both these are spoken of mixtly. The same dreadful things are attributed to both; *properly*, or *figuratively*. We know not how near the *Universal Day* of the *Great Judgment* of the Lord upon the whole Earth may be. The Lord *Jesus* may be now at the Door, and ready to enter. He shall come as a Thief in the Night, in Clouds, unperceived, unexpected. All things shall be in the moment of his Appearance, as from the Beginning: Some at the Mill, some in the Field, some in the Market, some at Church to be married, others in the Marriage bed, others Eating and Drinking. All the signs which are to fore-run that Great Day of the Lord's Last Appearance from Heaven, may be come to pass in the midst of us in another manner and form, differing from that, which we figure to our selves, and we not aware of it: As *Elijah* the great fore-runner of our Lord *Jesus* in his first Appearance was come and gone in the Person of *John the Baptist*, not understood either by the *Jews* in general, or by the *Disciples*. Watch and pray; have your Loyns ever girt, your Lamps burning; go forth from the things of Sense into the Spirit, to meet the Lord, who cometh in that Air of Heaven, and Eternity. So shall you be caught up to meet him, as he cometh, and enter with him into the Bride-chamber.

I shall give you my Reasons, which make me to believe, that the *Particular Day of the Lord* upon this Land and City approacheth, and cometh like a Traveller, like an Armed Man upon us.

1. *Jerusalem* and the *Jews* seem to be set up for a *Type* to every City and Land, which beareth the Name of God. St. *Paul* at large in the 11th to the *Romans* describeth the Succession of the Gentiles by Christianity into the place of the *Jews*, the Progress and Way of God with the External Professors of the Gospel, as with *Israel*. He representeth this by Natural Branches cut off from an Olive Tree, by wild Branches ingrafted in their place, standing upon the same Terms, in the same danger of being cut off.

2. Are

2. Are not we, as *Hierusalem*, ripe for the Harvest? Have we not had the Ministry of the Law, of the Gospel, of the Letter, of the Spirit, in great power, and glory? Have not all varieties of chastisements, and judgments inferiour to, preparatory for the great, and last Judgment, already passed upon us? Have not our Sins among all sorts, of all kinds, grown up to maturity to be ready for the Sickle?

3. We have seen *signs* in Heaven above, and on the Earth beneath, and in the Waters; which *Jesus* Christ foretelleth, as *Joel* before, and St. *Peter* afterwards from him, to precede immediately the great and dreadful day of the Lord upon *Hierusalem*. *Hierusalem* is in *London*.

But, O what comforts flow from the *finishing love* of God in *Jesus Christ* to make this day of the Lord not only supportable; but lovely to us, and longed for by us.

Lift up your heads, for your redemption is at hand; your Redeemer cometh. This is the day of *finishing love*. *Jesus Christ* cometh in this day to thee, O Believer, to consummate the Marriage, and so all thy joys, thy graces, thy glories in thy compleat Marriage to himself. The *day of the Lord* is said to be; *The Revelation of the Lord from Heaven*. As the natural day chaseth away the shadows of the night; but is the brightness of the Suns beautiful, and glorious Body, making all things new in the pleasantness of his light to those Eyes, that watch for the morning: so is this *day of the Lord* a day of Clouds, and Darkness to the Children of the night. But it is to thee, who lovest, and waitest for the appearance of our Lord *Jesus*, the breathing forth of all finishing loves, the breaking forth of all finished Beauties from the beloved Person of thy *Jesus*, appearing nakedly in all the glories of the God-Head *from Heaven*, in thy Person, in all things round about thee; as the Sun of Eternity at once shining in every point of things, making a new day of immortality, and glory every where.

The Lord *Jesus* cometh indeed *in flames of Fire*. But these *flames* are the Almighty powers, and Supream glories of the eternal spirit, of eternal love in its purity, in its simplicity. These are of a truth *flames of fire* to the enmity, to the enemies, to all flesh: but they are to thee, who livest in the spirit, *flames* of *finishing love*, of finished beauties presenting themselves to thee in all forms of things; feasting themselves upon thee; feasting themselves with thee; making themselves a feast to thee.

I will conclude with that History of *Elijah*, 1 *Kings* 19. 11. There passed before him a *Whirlewind* rending the Rocks, removing the Mountains; a *Fire*, and *Earthquake*. After these came a *still voice*. The learned *Jews* say; That all this was acted before the Prophet in a divine vision; that the Whirlwind, the Mountains, the Rocks torn in pieces; the Fire, the Earthquake were Angels presenting themselves in those Forms, as so many Divine Scenes that the still voice were all the Angels in a Quire, making a heavenly melody;

Thy

Thy Royal Bridegroom cometh in every day of Judgment to make more than this, true to thee, O thou Dove, thou Bride of the *Lamb*. He cometh in the weakness of all flesh round about thee, to rest upon thee, upon all things round about thee in the power of his finishing loves. This is the great day of love, and of the spirit, in which he will make perfect the strength of his love, and spirit, while thou art trembling, while all things are falling with a great noise round about thee, as dreadful ruines in a devouring flame.

Now lift up thy head into that living, and glorious light of the eternal spirit; now lift up thine Eyes, and thine heart unto that living, and glorious light of divine love, which breaketh forth from the face of thy *Jesus* within thee, without thee, on every side of thee.

This is the day of the anointing of thine Eyes with the heavenly Eye-salve; of changing thee, and the whole world to thee into fine Gold, Gold tryed in the fire.

All things now appear to thee, as indeed they are, a divine vision in a light of Glory. The whirlewinds, Earthquakes, Fires, Deaths, Ruines are all Angelical Scenes in the Spirit. In them all thou seest the Dances, thou hearest the still voice, the calm, charming, soft Musick of all the Angels, all the Spirits, all the loves of God; as on his, and thy Marriage-day.

Thus finishing love maketh perfect the light, the life, the strength of the spirit, and of love in thee in thy personal weakness, in the universal weakness, decay, and ruines of all flesh, of the whole Creation round about thee.

A skilful Painter is most discerned in laying his shadows. By these he maketh his work softer, sweeter, more full of life, and more taking. Thus comfort thy self in all thy weaknesses, darknesses, and deaths. Say thou; now is my *Jesus* exercising his divine wisdom, and skill in laying, and placing his shadows. Now upon these sad grounds will he curiously lay his rich and pleasant colours. Now will he form and finish the glorious face of his divine beauties, of his divine loves upon me.

Finishing love then appears, then displayeth itself with greatest freedom, fulness, and sweetness: when it maketh perfect its strength, its beauties, its joys, its eternal light in our weakness, deformity, despair, darkness, death.

These are the rellishes to the Musick; the shadows to the beauty of finishing *love*. These are the times for *finishing love*; when it is most beautiful.

I have now made an end of my discourse upon the *first* rich *branch* of this divine *fulness of love* in *Christ*; the *fulness of love* in *all States*. I come now to the *second branch*; the *fulness of love in all kinds*.

2. *There is poured forth from the Father in the glorified Person of the Lord Jesus a fulness of love of all kinds.* St. *Paul* saith; that God *the Father hath abounded in Grace towards us in all wisdom, and prudence in Christ. Ephes*, 1.6,7. There are *three parts of wisdom*, where it is compleat. 1. There is in *wisdom* a *variety* of things. 2. *A contrivance of this variety into one piece.* 3. *A concurrence*,

currence, and meeting in one of all the ſeveral varieties in each part, and point of the whole piece by the force of the Harmony. The Father aboundeth in his Grace, his love *to us in all wiſdom, in Chriſt.* here is fulneſs upon *fulneſs. He aboundeth.* He aboundeth in all wiſdom. Nay you have a *threefold fulneſs* ; an *abundance* ; an abundance *in wiſdom,* which itſelf expreſſeth a fulneſs, a riches of *variety.* but then there is ſuperadded *all wiſdom* ; *all variety.*

The Father is a plenitude of love tof *all kinds*, in *all varieties* pouring forth himſelf inceſſantly, endleſly, eternally in *Chriſt*. God is in *Chriſt*, in his *electing love*, in his *creating love*, in his *preſerving love*, in his *redeeming, regenerating, juſtifying, adopting, ſanctifying, comforting, glorifying love.* God aboundeth with a fulneſs, with a filling, an overflowing fulneſs in all theſe, in each of theſe ſeveral kinds of love in *Jeſus Chriſt*. Enlightning, enlivening, ſoftning, ſweetning, healing, cleanſing, defending, delighting, heightning, crowning loves, all are here, and all are full here to infiniteneſs.

Come all ye Souls, who want a ſenſe of ſin, or mourn under a ſenſe of ſin for want of a ſenſe of love ; come hither to *Jeſus Chriſt*, and have love, love of every kind, love ſuitable to your longings, or wants ; and have it in abundance. The glorified Perſon of *Chriſt* is a ſpiritual Garden. Indeed it is a Garden inviſible, ſealed up from the outward ſenſes. But by how much the more inviſible it is ; it is ſo much the more real, glorious, and divine. This Garden is ever preſent before thee. It flouriſheth in the midſt of thee. It is continually open to every humble, believing Spirit.

In this Garden all kinds of divine love grow, as ſo many flowers, which are ever full-blown, ever in their full beauty, and ſweetneſs, ever freſh, never fading, never failing. As faſt as one is gathered, another ſpringeth up in its room. Theſe Immortal flowers of divine love grow here for thee. They have thy name written upon them. They bend and bow themſelves towards thee. They invite thy hand to gather them. They are ripe in every ſeaſon, and gathered with the leaſt touch of thy ſpirit. Thou, who haſt a Spirit black, and burning with the deepeſt guilt, take the flower of juſtifying love, ſtick it in thy boſom. This will take out all the heat of pain, and take away all the deformity, and ſtain from thy ſpirit.

Thou who laboureſt under the diſeaſe of any corruption. See here the flower of ſanctifying love. Carry this in thine hand, in thine heart. It is a powerful, a pleaſent remedy againſt every luſt, or paſſion. Doth the Inſtability of thy ſpirit, the uncertainty of thy ſpiritual condition afflict thee? The flower of electing love hath a ſoveraign vertue in it to eſtabliſh, and fix thine heart in a triumphant peace and joy above all changes or fears. Art thou melancholy is thine heart caſt down within thee for ſome apparent reaſon, or thou knoweſt not, why? look upon this pleaſant flower of comforting love ſmell to it, wear it in thy boſom. It ſhineth with a heavenly luſtre, which re-

 createth

createth the Eyes, and infuseth strange joy into the heart. It breatheth forth a sweetness from it, which will make you think your self in Paradise, or kissing those blessed *Cheeks* of your heavenly lover, your *Jesus*, which are *Beds of Spices*. It hath a *spirit* in it, which is the extract of all Cordials, which hath all comforting vertues in it, which is the soveraign Comforter of hearts, and spirits, the only causer of delight, and pleasure on Earth, or in Heaven.

If any one be dejected with a sense of shame, let him make himself a Nose-gay of these three Flowers, regenerating, adopting, glorifying love. Every one of these casteth a wonderful light from it, which will make thee to see thy self in the unity of the eternal Spirit, in the form of the Son of God. Thou wilt see the whole face of things, as a glorious Heaven round about thee, all full of bright, and shining Angels encompassing thee, guarding thee, attending upon thee, as the heir of God; Jesus in glory walking with thee hand in hand, as his Brother, God himself beholding thee with an unmoved, and full Eye of esteem, wonder, and complacency, as his onely one, the Object of all his love, the Ground of all his joy.

The State of a Saints Soul and Body in Death.

THE peculiar consolations, and joys of Death to a Saint, pour forth themselves, into ten distinct channels, or streams.

1. Death is no dissolution to the Soul, or Body of a Saint, but a restitution and return of both to liberty, peace, and perfection.

2. Both descend no more, but ascend in Death.

3. Death hath in it no melancholy overcast, or unpleasant darkning to the Soul or Body; but a sweet, unexpected, surprising, and ravishing increase of a pure, divine, and triumphant light, circling in, and shining through all.

4. Death casts no deformity upon either part of a Saint, but cloaths both with an heavenliness, amiableness, and beauty.

5. Death is no streightning, or imprisonment to Body, or Soul, but a blessed enlarging of both to a divine state, and freedom.

6. The Death of a Saint hath nothing bitter in it; but is a spring of pure sweetnesses, and pleasures dividing itself into every part, and making all the garden of God.

7. There is nothing of the Devil in the Death of a Saint; but Christ risen, and glorified is all, fills all, and shines thorow all.

8. Death hath nothing of wrath in it; but is all divine love unvailing itself.

9. There is nothing of Death in the Death of a Saint; but life, and immortality unclouded, and shining forth clearly.

10. Death is no other thing to a Saint than a heightning of his spirituali-

ty, making him all thorough-out ſpiritual, purely ſpiritual, without any mixture u ichangeably ſpiritual without any interruptions, inconſtancies, or dark intervals.

1. Death is no diſſolution to the Soul, or Body of a Saint, but a reſtitution and return of both to liberty, peace, and perfection. 2 *Corinth.* 5. 1. St. *Paul* expreſſeth this ground of confidence, and joy in Death: For we know, that if our earthly houſe of this Tabernacle be diſſolved, we have a building of God, an houſe not made with hands eternal in the Heavens. It is the obſervation of learned Divines, that the Greek word here καταλύεσθαι, which we render to be diſſolved, ſignifieth to take up our Inn, from that circumſtance of unlooſing the Horſes, and taking them out of the Waggon, or Chariot to bring them into the Inn, and Stable, that there they may be at their liberty to reſt, and feed, and lie down. From this word upon this ground, an Inn, or Houſe of reception, & refreſhing for Travellers, hath its name in Greek, καταλύμα.

At our Birth, which is the morning of this life, and our entrance upon our Journy through this weary world, our Souls and Bodies are joyned to this fleſhly Image by the natural ſpirit, the ſpirit of this world, as Horſes put into a Waggon, to which they are faſtned by their Harnes, and Traces. The Body is as the fore-horſe, but the Soul as the filler, which draws moſt, and bears the chief weight, All the day long of this life we draw this Waggon heavy laden with all ſorts of temptations, and troubles thorow deep ways of mire, and ſand. This only is our comfort, that the divine will, which is love itſelf in its perfection, as a hand put forth from Heaven thorow a Cloud, at our Birth put us into this Waggon, and governs us all the day. In the evening of our life, at the end of our Journey Death is the ſame divine will, as a naked hand of pure love ſhining forth from an open heaven of clear light, and glory, taking our Souls, and both Bodies out of the Waggon, and Traces of this fleſhly Image, and Spirit, and leading them immediately into their Inn, into a place of freedom, reſt, and refreſhing into the unity of the eternal ſpirit into the Boſom of our Lord Jeſus.

Obj. But before I proceed any farther, I will indeavour to make my whole way more clear by anſwering an objection, which perhaps already ariſeth in moſt of your thoughts. You may be ready to ſay; Is this your meaning, as you ſeem clearly to expreſs it, that the Bodies alſo of the Saints ſuffer no diſſolution in Death, but return immediately to a ſtate of purity, and perfection? This ſeemeth to contradict the common ſenſe of all, the faith of the Saints, and the plain letter of the Scriptures. Do we not with our Eyes ſee every day the dead Bodies of the beſt Perſons thrown into the Grave, turning to Corruption, and Putrefaction, either before, or in the Grave, diſſolved to Worms, and Duſt, their bones ſcattered, and caſt up and down Church-yards? The bleſſed Body of our Lord Jeſus was taken off from the Croſs, a bloody, liveleſs, mangled Corps, a ſad, and ruthful ſpectacle. So he was laid in the Grave, the ſame Body, which after three days roſe again, and was taken up into Glory.

ry. The Scripture plainly testifieth, that in Death, as the Spirit returns to God who gave it, so the dust returns to the Earth as it was, God passeth this sentence of death upon *Adam* for his transgression: Dust thou art, and to dust thou shalt return. Do not we by faith, grounded upon the clear letter of the Scripture expect the Resurrection of our Bodies, at the sound of the last Trumpet?

Ans. I answer to these objections first in general. I fully assent to all these testimonies of sense, of the letter of the Scriptures, & of the common faith of all the Saints concerning the Resurrection of the Body. Yet is it true that I mean this, I believe this, in this meaning and belief my Soul, and Body rejoice, and triumph together; that not the Soul alone, but also the Body of a Saint in the very first moment of Death, meeteth with no dissolution, but a restitution, and most delightful return to liberty, peace, and perfection: This is that sweet, and comfortable sense of Death, which the holy Spirit seemeth to have sealed upon my Soul, from all principles of reason, of Faith, and from the letter of the *Scriptures*. In this sense I wish, that all were, as I am, to behold with the same spiritual Eye in the same light of the Spirit, the beauty, and loveliness of Death in the Body of a Saint, the beauty, loveliness, and pleasant life of the Body of a Saint in Death.

I come now to give a more particular answer fitted to the several objections by four distinctions.

The four distinctions are these. 1. Of a two-fold body in a Saint. 2. Of a two fold Dust. 3. Of a two-fold Sense. 4. Of a two-fold Resurrection.

1 *Dist.* There is a twofold Body, which the Scripture in its language attributes to a Saint: There is a Body, from which a Saint is to be delivered. You read of this, *Rom. 7. l. Wretched Man that I am, who shall deliver me from the Body of this Death.* There is a body in a Saint, which is to be delivered. St. *Paul* speaks of this in the name of all the Saints. *Rom.* 8. *We also, who have the first-fruits of the Spirit, wait for the adoption, the redemption of the Body.* There is a Body, which is the seat of Death, a Body of Death, as in the forementioned place; who shall deliver me from the Body of this Death? In all the members of this Body sin reigneth, as a King, establishing his Law. For so, in the same place, a little before, it is written: *With my Members I serve the Law of Sin.* This is the Body of Flesh, in which there dwelleth no good, as St. *Paul* speaks in the same Chapter. There is again in a Saint a holy, living, immortal Body, the seat of a holy, heavenly, and immortal Life, in as much as it is the Temple of the Holy Ghost For so St. *Paul* testifieth, as to an unquestionable, and known truth, granted of all the Saints in the primitive times, 1 *Corin.* 6. 19. *What? know you not, that your Body is the Temple of the Holy Ghost?* Again, a Saint carryeth about with him thorow his life a Body, which is a partition-wall between him, and his Beloved, which divides between Christ and him, which he must break

forth from, and cast off, before he can be taken into the Bosom of Jesus Christ, and be with him, 1 *Corin.* 5, 6. 8. St. *Paul* complains that while he is present in the Body, he is absent from the Lord, and breaths forth passionate longings to be absent from the Body, that he may be present with the Lord. But a Saint hath a Body, which is so far from dividing him, and Jesus Christ, that these two divine lovers are entirely united, and both one in it. It is Christs own Body, as well as a Saints. All the Members of it are the Members of Christ, as they are of a Saint, 1 *Corin* 6. 15. *Know ye not, that your Bodies are the Members of Christ*? shall I then take the Members of Christ, and make them the Members of a Harlot? God forbid. Yea he carryeth this union so high, that he maketh the Lord Jesus, and a Saint in this Body of his, of which alone he speaketh, to be one Spirit, and makes that the principal ground, upon which he builds his arguments against Fornication, *v.* 16. 17, 18. *What? know ye not, that he, which is joyned to a Harlot, is one body, for two,* saith he, *shall be one flesh, but he that is joyned unto the Lord is one Spirit.* Flee Fornication, he that committeth Fornication, sinneth against his own Body. How manifestly here are a fleshly Body, and a spiritual Body distinguished one from another? A Body, in which Fornication makes the Man one flesh with the Harlot? a Body, in which a Saint is one Spirit with Jesus Christ?

These two are one Body, which standeth in two mixed Principles, and Images. The Body of a Saint, while this life lasteth, standeth partly in a carnal, or fleshly principle, and Image. This is the Body of Death, in which no good dwels, which is subject to the Law of Sin. While a Saint is present in this Body, he is absent from Christ. This is that, from which a Saint groaneth to be delivered. The Body of a Saint standeth in part, and imperfectly, while we live here, in a Spiritual Principle, and Image. Thus the Body of a Saint is the Temple of the Holy Ghost, the Body, and Member of Christ, one Spirit with Christ, by which one Spirit it is Baptized into his Spiritual, and heavenly body. This is that body of a Saint, which groaneth to be redeemed, and delivered from the Body of Death, as from its Captivity, Prison, and Grave.

The Death of a Saint finisheth this Captivity, breaketh open the Prison, and the Grave, and setteth free the Body of a Saint into the liberty of its Adoption or *Sonship*; that is, into its Spiritual, and divine form of a Son of God. As fire is said to separate things of different kind, and to gather into one things of the same nature: so is the Death of a Saint the flame of God, the fire of Divine Love, Jesus Christ coming in the invisible flame of this Heavenly fire to separate the fleshly Principle, and Image from the spiritual Principle, and Image, both in the Soul, and Body of a Believer. The fleshly Principle, and Image, which is in the Body of a Saint, as a foreign, and strange thing, as rust upon Gold, is entirely cast off to the Spirit, and Image of this world,

world, and of the Devil, to which it belongeth. The Body of the Saints in its Spiritual Principle, and Image, which are truly, and properly its own, in which it is truly, and properly itself, is intirely for ever gathered up into the unity of the Eternal Spirit, the heavenly Body, and Bosom of our Lord Jesus.

In the Epistle to the *Hebrews*, *ch.* 9. 23. The Blood of Lambs, and Goats were said to cleanse the figures of heavenly things in the Tabernacle, but the Blood of Christ the heavenly things themselves. The Soul, and Body of a Believer are the heavenly things themselves. For these are that true Temple of the Holy Ghost, of which the first Tabernacle, and Temple were figures. As the death of a Saint is a conformity to Christ, and a fellowship to Christ on his death: so doth the Blood of Christ, that is, the divine virtue, and the life of the God-Head in the death of Christ, cleanse these heavenly things, the Soul and Body of a Saint at his death from all their dust, rubbish, and filth, from all mixture with the fleshly Principle, and Image.

Thus now the Body of a Saint, as well as his Soul, is made compleatly a pure, and heavenly Temple of the Holy Ghost. It subsists alone in an immediate, entire, and mutual union with this blessed Spirit. It lyeth wholly in it, as in the Fountain of life, immortality, love, peace, and joy. It is filled with it, as the Temple with the smoak of the sweet incense, and with the Glory of God.

How unhappy are you? How bitter is death, how full of deformity, how dreadful, how dark, how dismal to you, who leave this life before the Fountain of Eternal Life hath opened itself in you? Death to you is a devouring fire from below, which burns upon your Spirit, and flesh, consuming the order, the beauty, the sweetness of both, and changing them into a ruinous heap of utter darkness, desolation and confusion.

But blessed are you, thrice blessed are you, whose Souls, and Bodies are both married by one Spirit unto Jesus Christ, before Death comes to separate them one from another; whose *Souls*, and Bodies are become Temples of the Holy Ghost, and are inhabited by the Holy Ghost, before Death comes to demolish the fleshly frame, and building. Death to you is a lovely form, in which your Jesus himself comes into your whole Person, both Soul, and Body, as into his Garden or Vine-yard, to drive out the wild Beasts, all the powers of darkness, to pluck up by the roots, and to cast out the Weeds, every thing of this worlds, of a fleshly Spirit, and Image, that the Divine Shades, the Spiritual Plants, the fruitful Vine of his own Life, and Love, and of his own heavenly Image may alone flourish here, and himself alone may delight himself in the midst of these, as i a Garden shut up. *Jesus Christ comes by Death to your Bodies, and Spirits,* to a Beloved fountain, to cast out of it every thing of filth, of earth, and fle which polluteth it, that he may see his own face clearly all over it, that he alo

ma

ay drink of it, that he may lye in the midst of these waters for ever bathing
them, that you in both may be a fountain sealed up to himself. Death is to
ou, who believe, a rich Marriage-bed of Gold and Purple, into which your
ked Souls and Bodies quite stripped in the twinkling of an eye, of all their
ggs, are taken to lye in the naked bosom and imbraces of your beloved
idegroom the Lord Jesus.

Thus much for the twofold Body.

2 Dist. The 2. Distinction next to this of the twofold Body in a Saint, is that of
e twofold dust in Death. In the last chapter of *Ecclesiastes*, *v.* 7. we read
hat *in Death the dust shall return to the earth as it was, and the Spirit to God*
ho gave it. Gen. ch. 3.17. God passeth this Sentence of Death upon *Adam*
ter the Fall: *Thou shalt return to the Ground. For out of it thou wert taken,*
ust thou art, and to Dust thou shalt return.

There was a Dust before the Fall, out of which the Body of Man was made,
n. 2.7. *God formed man of the dust of the ground.* First observe here by the
ay, that the ground from which the dust was taken, of which the Body of
an was formed, was the ground of Paradise. For so we read immediately af-
at the 9th *v.* That out of the ground God had made to grow every Plant
at was pleasant to the eye, and good for food, with the Tree of Life in the
idst of them.

The Jewish Doctors teach us, that the dust, of which the Body of Man was
ide, was a fine and precious powder, in which all the excellencies of the
iole Creation were exactly tempered, and mingled together in one Body.
he Scripture seemeth to give us a foundation for this belief. When *Moses*
th, That God made out of the ground to grow every Plant pleasant to the
e, good for food, and the Tree of Life in the midst of them; he seemeth to
nifie that this was a divine ground, in which God from the beginning had
vn the divine seeds of all the beauties, pleasantnesses, sweetnesses, and of all
e beautiful and pleasant Lives of Paradise it self, and of the whole Creation,
it was in a Paradisical state. The dust then of this ground, which com-
seth the Body of Man, was the manifold beauty, sweetness, virtue and life
Paradise, of the whole Paradisical state of things gathered together, con-
cting themselves into one, and shading themselves, like the beauties,
eetnesses, and virtues of a flower in its precious seed. But that which is chief-
to be considered here, is the state of all things before the Fall. Sin was not
entred, which brought in Death. The Unity of the Creature among
mselves, between God and the Creatures, was yet entire. The divine life
l Image flourished thorow the whole Creation. All the Creatures stood up
their divine root, and were filled with a divine Sap, like flowers upon their
ks, and trees at the height of the Spring.

St. *John* gives us a sweet, and beautiful Image of the whole Creation in
irst state before it lost its life, sweetness, and unity by Sin, *Joh.* 1. 3. 4.
All

All things were made by him, that is, Jesus Christ, and without him nothing was made that was made. In him was life, and that life was the light of Men. There are two things obſervable in this Scripture. 1. That which we read, without him was nothing made, ϗ χωρὶς αὐτοῦ, ſignifieth properly nothing was made apart, or ſeparate from him. The Holy Spirit ſeemeth here to point out the primitive union of the whole Creation, and all the diſtinct parts of it with the Lord Jeſus, the living Root, the glorious Head of all, and in all. 2. Where we read; *Without him nothing was made, that was made*, this latter clauſe, that was made, addeth nothing to the ſenſe, and looketh like a vain repetition. Some therefore place it at the beginning of the following verſe, and read it thus; that, which was made, in him was life. This deſcribeth to us the effect of that union. Jeſus Chriſt put a life, a divine life into every Creature by his union with it. St. *Paul* ſeemeth to relate to this Scripture, and to confirm this living, beautiful, and Divine State of all the Creatures, as they came forth from God, *Coloſ.* 1. 16. *All things were made in him, all things were made thorow him, unto him, and into him.* v. 18. *All things ſtood together in him.*

Well then the Duſt, the Ground, the Earth, the Darkneſs in the pure ſtate of the Creation were made in Chriſt, were life in him, were made in union with Chriſt. They were made thorow Chriſt, as their mould, and channel. They were made by Chriſt, as their Original pattern, as the immediate power putting forth itſelf in them. They ſtood together with the reſt of the Creatures in the Divine Unity in Chriſt. Thus had this Duſt, of which we ſpeak, a Divine life in it, a Divine Beauty upon it, a Divine Seed in it; this life was the life of Chriſt, and ſo comprehended according to its kind, all the lives and vertues of all the Creatures, and of Paradiſe. Its beauty was the beauty of Chriſt, in which after the like manner all created beauties centred, and met in one. Chriſt himſelf was the Seed in this Duſt, and ſo not only the excellencies, and virtues of the whole Creation, but all the uncreated Treaſures of Life, and Glory lay together ſhaded, and vailed within this Duſt. But their vail, and their ſhade was a living, beautiful, and pleaſant Picture of themſelves, all filled with the ſweet Odour of thoſe hidden Ointments.

I have one thing more to ſay to deſcribe this Duſt. Man, who was the laſt days work, the comprehenſion, and perfection of the whole Creation, was made in a ſhadowy Image of God. For ſo the word Image in the firſt of *Geneſis* ſignifieth, and the Scriptures in their whole courſe teſtify. In the beginning all things came forth from God in an univerſal Darkneſs before the Light of the firſt day.

This Darkneſs is remarkable in ſeveral eminent circumſtances. 1. *It* was caſt forth immediately *from* the Divine Nature, and from the glorious Perſon of Chriſt to be a vail round about upon the Eternal Glory itſelf, and to be a ground of the whole Creation. 2. It ſtood in an immediate union with e Divine Nature, and the glorious Person of Christ, springing forth immediely from it, and depending immediately upon it. 3. The unsearchable riches f the God-Head, and of Christ, with all the various Excellencies of the creatures they were in their eternal patterns and principles, lay hid together within is shade. 4. Out of this ground did God make to spring all the creatures in eir primitive paradisical purity and pleasantness, being wrapt up here, as in eir first matter, and having their proper seeds sown here.

Thus was this Darkness a shade indeed, but pure, indued with a Divine Life, eathed with a Divine beauty and lustre, bearing a Divine figure, breathing rth a Divine sweetness, spread forth every moment fresh with a new lustre, d sweetness from the Divine Nature, vailing within it self all the Joys and lories of God, Christ, Heaven and Paradise, and as it hides all these in its Bosom, lying it self in the Bosom of Christ.

Such is the Ground, such is the Dust of the Ground, and the Earth, out of hich the Body of Man was first taken, and into which the Body of a dying int returns. Such is the Darkness of Death, that overshadows a Saints bo-, like the Nights in Paradise. But there is this advantage now, that this pure, imitive Dust and Darkness are heightened, have a new, and greater beau-, and sweetness by the Resurrection of Christ from the Dead. This is the st Dust, the Dust before the Fall.

2. The second Dust is that after the Fall understood in that sentence; *Dust u art, and to Dust thou shalt return.* This is the Dust of that Death which sin ings forth, a cursed Dust, the Dust of the cursed Earth, which bringeth forth yars and Thorns. That former beautiful and blessed Dust lies captivated in is, as in a Prison, or Grave of contrariety and enmity. This Dust is comsed of three things; 1. A Separation, Dissolution, and Desolation, from the ce and power of Enmity. 2. A Blackness of Darkness from a cloud and rm of wrath. 3. The seeds of shame, pain, anguish, horrour and torment dden in it.

This Dust is that which the Body of a Saint casts off in Death, upon this rldly Image and Spirit, together with the Spirit and Image of this world. is is that which suffereth dissolution, which representeth deformity, and iketh the horrour in Death. All which are now of the Image of this world, d to the Image of this World, in the Spirit of this World, and to the Spiof this World, within the Kingdom of the Devil, having no more relation a Saint in Death, than the filthy raggs of a Prince in a Dungeon, to the ince at Liberty, and in his Pallace.

Death rubbing off the Rust of this cursed Dust from the Body of a Saint, ves it all a shining, rich, incorruptible Dust of pure Gold. His Body is w entirely with Christ, a precious, pleasant, and living Dust in the Gar-Beds, the Beds of Spices or perfumed Flowers in Paradise. This is the ond Distinction of the two Dusts.

L l 1 3. Di-

3 *Dist.* The third distinction is of a twofold sense, *Rom.* 8. 6. St. *Paul* teacheth us, *That to be carnally minded is Death, but to be spiritually minded is Life, and Peace.* The Greek runs thus: the mind of the flesh, and the mind of the spirit. The word mind is φρόνημα, which signifieth a practical understanding, and comprehendeth a twofold act; one of the understanding to discern, and judge; another of the will to tast, and rellish. So the mind is here a sense, and a savour both in one. Thus you have here a twofold sense, Spiritual, and Carnal or Fleshly.

1. The Spiritual sense is set forth three ways. 1. By the Principle. 2. By two effects of this Principle. 3. By two companions of these effects.

1. The Principle of a Spiritual sense is the Spirit; this holy, and blessed Spirit is the only, and proper Principle of a Saint, and Saintship, of a Son of God, and a Sonship to God. Art thou indeed a Saint? then thou art in the Spirit of Glory, and of God, as in thy Root, and Element, as a Tree of Life in the Root of Eternal Life, and Love, as Fishes in the water of Life, as Birds in the pure air of Divine Love, as Angels in Heaven, *Rom.* 8. 9. *You are not,* (saith St. *Paul* to the Saints) *in the Flesh, but in the Spirit.* Art thou indeed a Son of God? Then is this Spirit of Grace, and Immortality in thee, as thy natural Principle, as the power of Nature according to the new, and Divine Nature which acteth thee. *Rom.* 8. 16. *As many as are led by the Spirit of God, are the Sons of God.* The word led is ἄγονται acted. As the Soul acts the Body, as the principle of reason the Soul of Man, as the nature of the Sun acts the Sun in its shinings, in its motions; thou also art acted by the Divine Spirit, to which the Sun, the Soul of Man, the principle of reason are empty, and weak shadows, so far as thou in truth art a Child of Light, and a Son of God the Father of Lights.

Let me here by the way touch a three-fold string in your Souls. 1. A mournful string. 2. A string of desire. 3. The string of praise.

1. Is the Spirit the principle of a Saint? how then should we mourn, that this Spirit of Grace, this Comforter is grieved, that this Spirit of Light, and Life is quenched by unbelief, sensuality, unkindness, and neglect? how should we mourn that this Holy Spirit, this Spirit of Truth is slighted, and spoken evil of, as a Spirit of licentiousness, or as a fancy, and delusion, and all this among Saints, at least in profession, when as this Spirit is the only principle of Saintship? St. *Jude* in his Epistle, speaketh of this as the Sin of Devils, for which they are cast down to Hell, and bound in Chains of Darkness, that they did forsake their first state, and their own habitation. It is in Greek not their first state, but their first principle, ἀρχὴν. O Saints is not this a Sin, greater than that of Devils, not only to forsake, but to grieve, and cast shame upon this first, and most blessed Spirit, which is your only principle, a principle of Divine Life, Light, and Purity; your own habitation, a habitation of Divine Rest, and Glory?

2. O

2. O all you, who desire to be Saints, or to grow in the new, and Divine Nature of a Saint; let your hearts burn by day, and by night with continual longings for the Spirit. This alone is that of which a Saint is bred, by which he is nourished. This alone is the Heavenly Root, the Sap, the sweet Dew, Showers, and Influences, the warm, and cherishing Sun-shine to every Spiritual Plant. Cry therefore, and wait for this Spirit; wait upon it; minister to it; seek it; suck it in by all means, thorow all its own manifestations, and ordinances, of Nature, or of Grace. When this world was first made a beautiful frame out of a dark Deep, the Spirit moved upon the face of the waters. When Jesus was conceived in the womb of the Virgin, the Holy Ghost overshadowed her, and rested upon her. In both places the expressions seem to allude to a Bird, or a Dove spreading itself over its Nest to hatch its young Ones. When the Lord Jesus was Baptized, the Holy Ghost descended, and rested upon him in the form of a Dove. Dost thou indeed desire to have thy dark, defiled, dead heart made a new Creature, to have Jesus Christ to be born, or to grow within thee, and to be Baptized yet more, into Jesus Christ the Sea of all Heavenly Beauties, Loves, and Joys? O then pray to the blessed Spirit to make thy Soul his Nest, to move upon the face of thy Spirit, to overshadow thee, to descend and rest upon thee in his Dovelike form.

3. O all ye Saints, sing the praises of the holy Spirit; let the high praises of the holy Spirit be ever in your mouths. Say to the Spirit; this is the womb of Divine Life and Power, which hath born us, and brought us forth to be Children, and Heirs to God; these are the Breasts of Divine Life, and sweetness, which give us suck; this is itself, the Heavenly Milk of the Eternal word, by which we live, and grow. Do you see any glympse of Evangelical Light, and Truth, do you feel any workings of Grace, any sweet springings of Love and Joy? Give Glory to the Spirit, it is this blessed Spirit, which now shines in you, enlivens you, and acts you. The Children of *Israel* in the Wilderness, in a great want of water, met with a Well, then they sang to it in these words, *Spring O Well, the Princes have digged it with their Staves.* When ever thou meetest with any fresh stream, any sweet drop of the water of Life rising up within thee in this parched Land, and weary Wilderness, sing to thy Well, sing to the blessed Spirit, and say in thy Song: my Well springeth, my Jesus hath digged it in my heart with the Golden Scepter of his Grace, and Love. Thus let every gracious thought, gracious moving of thy mind, will, or affections put into thy mouth a new Song of joyful praises to the Spirit, as the dear, and inseparable principle of Life, of Heaven, of Eternity within thee, thine own principle. Thus much of the Principle.

2. The two effects of this Principle are a Spiritual sense, & savour both comprehended in that expression: to be heavenly minded. How often doth my Spirit labour in the Bosom, and power of the Eternal Spirit for these two things, 1. That all Men were brought forth into this Spiritual Principle. 2.

 That

That all, who have the Spiritual Principle within them, were continually acted by it! How sweet would life be to them, for the sight of their Eyes, and rellish of their Spirit? They that live in the Spirit, see all things by a Spiritual Light, It is indeed a pleasant thing to behold this Light. Every glympse of it insuseth a heavenly joy into the Heart, and scattereth all Clouds of grief, or melancholy. These see all things in a Spiritual Image, that is in a Divine, and Immortal Glory. They tast the sweetness of a Heavenly, and Divine Love in every thing. Every thing presenteth itself to them in an Heavenly Appearance, and every appearance of things entreth into their Souls with a heavenly taste, and rellish, far sweeter than Hony to the Palate.

All our converse with things of every kind of Nature, or Grace; of Sense, or reason proceedeth from a union with those things in one Principle, and is a communion with them in that Principle. Such as the Principle is, such are the Appearances, and rellishes of things to us, such is our converse with them. All Appearances of things to Men, or to Angels in every natural Principle, to our senses, or to our understandings are no more than shadows, or dreams. The Spirit alone is Truth. When melancholy forms, and Images of things in this world afflict our Spirits; when the pleasant things here lift them up to vain joys, and glories; if the holy Spirit awaken himself, and arise in us: all these fly away, all other appearances of things break up into an appearance of Eternal Beauty, and Blessedness springing forth from this Spirit like the shadows of the night, when the Sun is seen, and a dream, when a Man awaketh.

We are taught by natural Philosopy, that the Images of things are seen thorow a Christalline humour in the Eye, as a fine Glass. If this Christal be dyed with any colour: all things, which we see, appear to us in that colour. In like manner there is a native moisture upon our Palates, and Tongues, by which we tast things. If this moisture have any tast of its own, every thing tasteth of it. Blessed art thou, who livest the life of a Saint. Thou livest the life of Heaven upon Earth. The Spirit is the Christal in the Eye of thy Soul, thorow which thou seest all things. This Christal hath a heavenly colour of Glory ever upon it. Thou then seest all things in this ravishing colour, in a Heavenly Glory. The Spirit is the Divine moisture, and water of life upon the pallate of thy Soul, by which thou tastest all things. This water of the Spirit hath ever the heavenly rellish, the unexpressible sweetness of the Divine Nature, of the Divine Love, of the pleasures of the God-Head. Thus thou savourest all things. This Love, and Sweetness thou rellishest in every thing.

3. The two companions of these two effects of a Spiritual Principle are Life, and Peace. *To be spiritually minded is Life, and Peace.*

1. Life The Spirit, and Life are inseparable one from another. The words that I speak, they are Spirit, and they are life, saith Jesus Christ, *Joh.6. The Spirit is the Fountain of Life. For he is called the Spirit of Life,* Rom. 8.

The

The Quickening Spirit. 1 *Cor.* 15. The Power of an Endless Life. *Heb.* Let us ever pray, that we may ever live in the Spirit: For now we live, if we stand fast in our spiritual Principle. The Life which we now live, is first, pure. It hath nothing of any Mixture, of any Defilement, or of any shadow of Death. Secondly, It is perfect. It hath all the Sweetnesses, Virtues, Joys, and Beauties of Life in it. Thirdly, It is perpetual, It never ceaseth, It never endeth, but springeth to Eternity. Fourthly, It is a powerful Life. It maintains itself against all the Powers of Darkness, and Death. It maintains itself in the midst of them, as a sweet Light of Glory, shining in a dark place, and triumphing over the darkness. In a word, this Life is the purest, sweetest, aud most lasting Life: For it flows immediately, and springs up continually from the Fountain of Life itself. Nay, which is far sweeter, and more glorious, it is Life, as it lies in the Fountain of Life. It is Life not only from the Spirit, but in the Spirit. So St. *Paul* speaks in this Chapter: *They that are in the Spirit*; and to the *Galatians*; *if ye live in the Spirit.*

2. The other Companion of a Spiritual Sense is Peace, Peace in the Language of the Scripture, signifieth a perfection of Happiness. It is distinguished into, 1. Peace above with God. 2. Peace within, in your own Consciences and Spirits. 3. Peace with all Creatures round about you. O how true is it, that they keep the Feast continually, a Royal and Divine Feast in white Garments, who live in a spiritual sense of things! Every day to them is a Holy Day, a Festival Day. All things are festival round about them. All things are in a Covenant of Peace with them, in a Covenant of Grace, and Divine Peace. All appearances of things in every State shine upon them from the glorified Person of Christ, as heavenly Beauties smiling upon them. All Providences, Changings, and Motions of things, are a Heavenly Musick, springing up to them, and sounding round about them, in the Unity of the Spirit. All Impressions made upon their Souls from every passage of Providence, or Change, is a most delicious sweetness upon their Spirits, an unexpressible taste of Heaven and Eternity.

But the manner of St. *Paul's* Expression is very observable, and hath a great force in it: *To be spiritually minded is Life and Peace.* The sense and savour of the Spirit is itself Life and Peace universally, absolutely, in the abstract, in perfection, without any Confinement or Allay. The spiritual sense of a Saint, is the pure, and compleat Essence of Life and Peace in its highest Activity. How true is it, that a good man is satisfied from himself? How Holy, how High, how Happy, how Heavenly a thing is it to be a Saint, to be spiritual, to live as a Saint, to live spiritually? Thou now comprehendest all things in an uncorruptible Beauty, Love, and Joy in thy self, in Heaven: For all things are to thee thine own spiritual Principle, thine own spiritual Sence, springing up and diffusing itself into all blessed Forms of Glory, Delight, and Immortality within thee. Jesus Christ tells his Spouse

in

in the *Canticles*, That she is a Fountain of Living Waters flowing from *Lebanon*; That she is a Fountain of Gardens; That all her Plants are Plants of *Paradise*. O blessed Spirit, who livest in the Eternal Spirit, as thy Principle, by which thou art inwardly acted! This Principle of thine is the Fountain, the ground of Paradise within thee. All forms of things are Paradisical Plants, at once pleasant to the Eye, good for Food, desirable, to fill thee with all the most glorious Treasures of the Divine Wisdom. Thy Spiritual Principle is the Divine Ground, out of which all these Plants of Paradise grow up within thee, as thine own Plants. Thy spiritual Sense and Savour, is a perpetual Feeding and Feasting upon the Fruits of Paradise, which these Plants continually bring forth.

2. The Fleshly or Carnal Sense is also illustrated by three Circumstances. 1. The Principle. 2. The Effect of that Principle. 3. The Companion of that Effect.

1. The Principle of a Carnal Sense is the Flesh. It is expresly called the Mind or Sense of the Flesh. The Flesh, the Natural Man, the Earthly Man, the Spirit of man, the natural Soul in the Language of the *Gospel*, and most of them in this present Chapter signifie the same *Principle* of a *carnal Sense* of Sin, and of Death. Happy is he that is not here deceived. Every Earthly, Heavenly, Humane, Angelical Spirit, or Principle, however enlightened, sanctified, heightened by the work of the Spirit, below that Spirit which is immediately born of the eternal Spirit, which is one Spirit with it, and liveth in it, is Flesh, and this Principle of a fleshly Mind, or *Sense*, or of Death.

2. The Effect of this Fleshly Principle is Twofold: 1. A Carnal, or Fleshly Sense. 2. A Fleshly, or Carnal, Savour. How unpleasant is thy Life who livest in this Principle for the sight of thine Eyes? The Light of the World, which alone thou seest, is Darkness, and the shadow of Death: For the Prince of this World is the Prince of Darkness. Thou measurest Heavenly and Spiritual things by Earthly and Carnal.

When Jesus Christ in the Gospel was reproved by *Peter*, for the mention of his Sufferings and Death, the Lord replies to *Peter*, *Get thee behind me Satan*; *For thou savourest not the things of God, but the things of man.* There are Three things remarkable in these words. 1. There is a Humane, and there is a Divine Sense of the same things, and these two are contrary one to another. 2. Those things that are the things of man, and dreadful to man in an humane Sense, as Death, are Divine, have a Divine Beauty, and sweetness in them, to a Divine Sense and Savour. 3. The Humane sense, the Humane Image, and rellish of things, springs from the Devil, as he is Satan, that is, the Hater, the Enemy to all things Divine, to Love, to Light, to Truth to Immortality, and Blessedness.

3. The Companion of a Carnal Sense, and Savour, is Death: *To be Carnally minded is Death.* 'Tis Death in all the black Properties and Powers of Death. 1. That Divine Image of things, which alone is the Truth, is Spiri-

nd Life, both the Paradises, the Heavenly, and the Earthly, as it is new orn, and united unto the Heavenly, lie captivated in a Carnal Mind, or ense, as in a Prison or Grave. 2. A Carnal Sense is that outermost Darkness, which is without the new, and Heavenly *Jerusalem*. 3. In a Carnal Sense re disorder, confusion, and desolation, the dissolutions of all the ban:s of 'eace, Beauty, and Life. For these all consist in that order alone, which hath for s band the Unity of the Spirit. 4. A Carnal Sense hath ever the sting of earh in it. Fears, Cares, Grie', Pains, Anguishes, Torments never cease here. 'hey are the Worm which never dyes, the Fire, which never goes out, in iis region of the shadow of Death, a Carnal Mind, or Fleshly Sense.

Naturalists tell us, that some Candles may be so made, that all the Persons seen, y those lights shall appear as Ghosts one to another, or the whole place seem ill of Snakes, and dreadful Serpents. Such are those lights of a Carnal :nse, by which all things are seen of thee, who art in a Carnal, Fleshly :ate. Every thing of Truth, as it appears to thee, is an apparition from be-:w, bearing Paleness, Terrour, Death, and Hell in the face of it. Thou canst o where walk, sit, lie down in peace. All places, all States to thee are full of :rpents, hissing, shooting out their forked stings, casting their poyson at thee.

Wo to you, O ye Inhabitants of the Earth, ye, who dwell in a fleshly nse of things. The Devil is ever in the midst of you with great rage; here : is known by his name Satan, the Enemy, the Hater. But ye, O ye Inhabi-nts of Heaven who live in a Spiritual Principle, why are you ever found a-'oad? Why are not all your walks within in the Spirit, the heavenly Para-se, which God hath planted, and set you in to dress it, and to keep it, and eat of the fruits of it without any exception within your own Spirits? Be-old! not a single Cherubim, but the whole Army of glorious Angels, with ie Presence, and Power of the Eternal Spirit, as a flaming Sword turning 'ery way, keeps the entrance into this Paradise, not to keep you out, but to :fend you in it by suffering no evil thing, none of the Powers of Darkness, ' Death, of Wrath, to enter here. While you are without in a Carnal Mind, id Worldly Spirit, you are among the holes of the Foxes, the Dens of the yo:s, and the Mountains of Leopards. All things, with which you converse, :cend from below, from the Earth, from the natural Soul, and from the De-l, as St. *James* teacheth us. All these three the Earth, the Natural Soul, and the :evil are Links in the same chain of Darkness immediately fastned one to a-other. The light, and breath of your life in the Spirit of this world is the ioak from the Bottomless Pit. Your Beauties, your Joys, your pleasant ings are those Locusts sent forth from thence, mentioned in the Revelation, ith Faces, and Hair like Women, with Crowns upon their Heads, false ows of Sweetness, Softness, Greatness, and Glory, but stings, invenomed ngs, the stings of Death are in their tails. O! Retire into your own enclo-l Gardens, there within your own enclosed Grounds, your own Souls, sit un-

der

der your own Fig-Tree, your own Vine, which are your own Spiritual Principle, out of which the universal Image of things both Heavenly, and Earthly springeth up into the perfection of all pure Beauties, and Joys with immortality. Delight your selves under their shadows, where you are safe from all Evil, and at rest for ever. I again testify unto you, as I have often, and alwaies testified in all my Sermons, and Discourses, that there is no Salvation to the flesh, or in the flesh. O then ye, who are yet found walking after the flesh, give no rest to your selves here. Cry night and day without ceasing to the Holy Spirit to take you up upon his Wings, and to translate you suddenly, in a moment, out of this Wilderness of fiery Serpents into the promised, and good Land flowing with Rivers of Milk, and Hony, the Milk of the Eternal Word, and the Hony of the Divine Wisdom, which both are Jesus Christ, the Fulness, Sweetness, and Glory of the God-Head. O that these words, as now you read, or hear them, in this very moment, thorow the power of the blessed Spirit might be as the hands of Angels laid upon *Lot*, to hasten you out of this Sodom of the flesh, while you linger here, into a place of safety, the City of the living God in the secret of the Spirit, before the Lord rain down fire from the Lord upon all Flesh.

The profit, the pleasure, the seasonableness of this discourse hath carryed me farther, & stayed me longer upon it than my method seemed to require. Let us now return to apply this distinction of a twofold sense, Carnal, and Spiritual to our present purpose, which is to set forth the Beautiful, and Blessed State of a Saints Soul and Body in Death. We have heard that a Spiritual sense is Life, and Peace absolutely, universally, eternally, without mixture, confinement or change; that all things here are in the purity, and perfection of Divine Life, Beauty, and Joy. We have also heard, that the Carnal Sense is Death, as it reigns entirely here, so it it is confined hither, shut up in this Pit, and without this fleshly Principle hath no where any place.

I shall bring this Distinction home to my purpose of making Death all over, in every part lovely, and pleasant to a Saint, by two Propositions.

1. Propos. This is the first. A Saint by dying is taken entirely in his whole Person, Soul, and Body out of the Carnal, or Fleshly Principle, out of the Fleshly Sense, and so out of Death.

2. Propos. A Saint by dying is in his whole Person, Soul, and Body gathered up entirely into a Spiritual Principle, and so into the Immortality of a Divine Life, Peace, and Delight.

1. Propos. A Saint by dying is taken entirely in his whole Person, Soul, and Body out of the Carnal, or Fleshly Sense, and so out of Death. I shall open, and confirm this Proposition to you by two Scriptures.

1. The first Scripture is the 1 Epistle of St. *Peter*, 4. 1. Wherefore seeing Christ hath suffered in the Flesh, let us also arm our selves with the same mind. For he that hath suffered in the Flesh, hath ceased from Sin. The Holy Ghost

clearly

clearly relates to the death of the Lord Jesus, and of a Saint. He speaks of the time perfectly past; he that hath suffered in the Flesh, that is, he that by dying hath compleated, and finished his sufferings in the flesh, he hath ceased from sin. He that dyeth in union with Christ in the vertue of his death, and in a conformity to it, in the first moment of death ceaseth from all the Evils of Sin, the Guilt, the Power, the Pollution, the Punishment, and so from Death itself.

See the inseparable connexion between the Flesh, Sufferings, Sin, and Death. All these continue together, and cease together. O you, that hear or read, understand these things, and lay them to heart! This Flesh, which is so dear to us, which we are so loath, and unwilling to part with, which we tender as our nearest, and dearest self, is our only division from our self, a bed of Snakes, and Enmity. It is the root, the seat, the food, the fewel, the fruit of Sin, and suffering, and death. This Fleshly Principle, and Sense, this worldly Light, and Image, which we account Life, and the Sweetness of Life, in which we think all the dear Treasures and Joys of Life are comprehended, is no other, than a deep, dark, and miery Dungeon, where we lie in the midst of the hissings, stings, and poysons of innumerable Toads, and Serpents. This Sin, which so easily besetteth us, and winds itself into our bosoms, is that weight, which presseth us, and sinketh us down, that chain of Darkness, which tyeth us down, and fastneth us here below in the horrible Pit, and Dungeon of this Fleshly Principle, and Sense, this Fleshly, this worldly Spirit, and Image. This Death which seemeth so dreadful to us, which we so tremble at, and fly from, is that dearest Friend come down from Heaven, from the bosom of God, that beautiful hand put forth from the secret of Eternal Life, Love, and Glory, which taketh off this weight, which knocketh off this chain of Darkness, and restoreth to us our silver Wings, and golden Feathers, by which in a moment we fly forth from this Cage of unclean Spirits, this Dungeon of the Fleshly Principle, and Sense never to return into them any more.

O Believers, fear not, fly not from Sufferings! Be willing to sacrifice and offer up this Flesh, as a whole Burnt-Offering in the Flame of Sufferings unto Death. Kiss Death as a lovely Bride, as those perfumed Flowers, those Beds of Spices, the Cheeks of the Heavenly Bride-groom, mentioned in the *Canticles*: For the Flesh, the fleshly Principle, and Sense, the Spirit and Image of this Flesh, of this World, together with the Sufferings, Sin, and Death, end all at once in the Death of a Saint, in the very first moment of his Death.

A Holy Divine, when he was dying, lay upon his Death-Bed, singing this often over; *Now I shall sin no more.* We read *Isaiah* 59. 2. *That our Iniquities separate between us and our God, our Sins hide his face from us.* Death is indeed a separation, but it is not the separation of the Soul from the Body. The separation of the Soul or the Body from God, this is Death indeed, this alone is Death. This world, this worldly Spirit, and Image is the Curtain, or Vail, the Partition wall between us and the Face, or Bosom of our Heavenly Bridegroom our Lord Jesus. So saith St. *Paul*: *Our Gospel is hid to those, whose Eyes the God of this world hath blinded, that they should not behold the Light of the Knowledge of the Glory of God in the Face, or Person of Christ.* The Fleshly Principle, or Sense is the unpassable gulf between us, and the unsearchable Treasures of the Divine Nature, of the Blessed Persons in the Divine Nature, the Father, the Eternal Word, the Holy Spirit. Sin digs up, and keeps open this Gulf, sin builds up this *Partition* wall. Sin draws this Curtain between us, and the Divine Beauties, the Divine Blessedness. O dying Saints, break forth into singings! O all ye Saints rejoice, and triumph at every thought, at every approach of Death! *Abraham* saw the day of Christ, and rejoyced to see it, saith our Lord Jesus in the Gospel. The word rejoyce in Greek is ἠγαλλιάσατο, that is, he danced a Galliard. When the Virgin Mary, with Christ in her Womb, came to the Mother of *John* the Baptist, the Babe within her sprung for joy. Thus O Believers let your hearts spring for joy within you at the approach, and presence of Death. So Death coming to you as a beautiful, and a heavenly Virgin with Jesus Christ in its Womb, not after the Flesh, but in the Glory of the Spirit, to be delivered of him immediately into your Bosoms, as a Bridegroom that at once in the same moment appears to you in Glory, makes you worthy of himself, by being like himself, and one Glory with himself, makes all things Life, Immortality, & Glory round about you. Behold the day of your Death both afar off, & near at hand as the day of Christ, as a day, which the Lord Jesus makes, rising himself, as the true Sun upon you, & so turning this Sun into Darkness, before the brightness of his own appearance, enlightning all within you, and, without you with another Light infinitely greater, infinitely sweeter. At the sight of this day, as *Abraham* did, so let your hearts spring with a pleasant lightness, and dance Galliards in your Bosom. Now sing of Death, and say in your songs every one of you, as you lie upon your Death-beds: I shall sin no more, I shall be in Flesh no more, no more for ever in this Fleshly Principle, and sense, which hath so long bewitched me, and held me by their sorceries in the House of Whoredoms, and of Death. I shall be in this world so loathsome, and so hateful to me, I shall see this world, and this Image of things, which hath been so long so tempting, and tormenting to me, no more for ever. Farewel for ever all distances, all divisions between me, and my Jesus, my God. Henceforth shall I with open face in my Soul, and my Body behold the open, and unvailed Face of God. Henceforth shall I with my naked Soul, and Body lie for ever in the naked Bosom of my Glorified Saviour, my King, and Husband, giving him of my Loves, drinking in abundantly his Loves, and bringing forth continually by him all the Spiritual, and Heavenly fruits of Life, and Immortality.

The morning is called Rosy-fingred, because the morning Beams, as Rosy-fingers seem to open the Curtains of the night, and let in day upon us. Death is to a Saint of a truth this Rosy fingered morning, which by sweet beams breaking forth from on high, draws aside the Curtains of this night of Flesh, and lets in upon us the Eternal day, which at once in a moment overspreads our Souls, and Bodies, and fills all things to us with its blessed Light, making us, and all things new in the newness of its own Heavenly, and Immortal Beauties.

The second Scripture is, 2 *Corin.* 5.6,8. *Therefore we are alwaies confident, knowing, that whilst we are at home in the Body, we are absent from the Lord.* We are confident I say being willing rather to be absent from the Body, and present with the Lord. Of what Body speaketh the Apostle here? What Body is this, which thus divideth between the Spiritual Bride, and her Heavenly Bridegroom, that a Saint cannot be present with both at once? If he be at home in this Body, he must be absent from Christ, and a banished Person from his Bosom. If he will be present with Christ, and enjoy him, he must cast off this Body, and be absent from it.

Is this the true, and proper Body of a Saint? How can that be? The true Body of a Saint is as much himself, as his Soul is himself. He can be no more absent from his own Body, than he can be absent from his Soul, or from himself.

We read in the same Chapter, 1 *Corin.* 6. Towards the latter end, that the Body of a Saint is the Member of Christ, and the Temple of the Holy Ghost. When St. *Paul* speaketh of a Body, from which we must be absent, that we may be present with the Lord Jesus; sure he cannot mean this Body, which is a Member of Christ, which is united to Christ, and implanted into him. Can I be absent from Christ by being present with that Body, which is a Member of him, a Member in him? Can I be absent from this Body, which is a Member of Christ, while I am present with Christ? O Believers, be not weary of living in the Body, only know your true selves, and your own Bodies! while you live in these, you live in Heaven, and are ever with the Lord Jesus. For your Bodies are his Members, and so the fulness of him, who filleth all in all. O Believers fear not to die, you part not with any thing, that is truly your selves, truly your own. You part not with your Bodies, nor with any thing, in which they have any true propriety, or which hath any dear Relation to them. For your Bodies are the Members of Christ, Baptized into one Body with him by that one, and the same Spirit, which gathereth up all things together unto him, and into one in him.

Thy Body, O Believer, is the Temple of the Holy Ghost. When the Spirit of God, and of Glory rests upon this Temple, he never removeth off from it any more. When he enters into this Temple of his, he never goeth forth, nor leaves it empty. This is his true Temple upon the true Mount *Sion*, the Soul, and Body of a Saint, which he hath chosen for a resting place

 for

for ever. O Saints have patience, and peace in life. For by being at home in your Bodies, you are in the Temple of the Holy Ghost, which he fills with his Glory, where every thing utters Glory. O Saints have pleasure in Death. For Death cannot divide your Bodies from you, nor the Holy Ghost from your Bodies, which are his Temple. Can you ever be absent from Christ, while you are present in your own proper Bodies, which are the Temples of the Spirit of Christ? Can you by being present with the Lord Jesus be absent from these Bodies of yours, which are the Temple of the Holy Spirit, which is the highest band of Unity; the dwelling place of that Spirit, which is one with the Lord Jesus? No certainly, this can never be. Thy Body O Saint is ever, in life, and in death, filled, and overshadowed by the Holy Ghost. When it seems to fall into the Dust, and Darkness of Death according to the Carnal sense; then doth thy Heavenly Dove give to it according to the Spiritual sense its own silver Wings, and golden Feathers.

What then is this Body of which St. *Paul* speaks to the *Corinthians*, which gives him a triumphant confidence in the face of Death, while it is his greatest desire to be absent from this Body, that he may be present with Christ? Is it not that Body of Death against which he cryeth out, *Rom.* 8. *l.* O *wretched Man that I am, who shall deliver me from this Body of Death*? This he calls also a little before in the same Chapter that flesh of his, that self, in which there dwels no good. This is the Fleshly Principle, and Sense, the Spirit, and Image of this world, which is sprung up out of the Fall, which lies as a disguise, and a cloud upon the true Person, the Soul and Body of a Saint. What is not this the Body, which is the partition-wall between these two Spiritual Lovers, Christ, and a Saint, while he lives here, which being cast off in Death, they find themselves in the pure, beautiful, and naked Arms of each other. What is Death now to a Saint? Is it not the power of the Divine life, and love in a Saint breaking forth, and as it breaks forth, tearing off, and burning up this disguise of Flesh? Is it not the power of a Divine Light, and Glory breaking forth, and as it breaks forth, scattering, and blotting out the cloud of this Body of Death for ever? How beautifully does the Body of a Believer shine forth now in Death, as a naked Member of our glorified Jesus cleansed from all its dust, and defilement, when it is taken up entirely out of the fleshly Principle, and Sense? How beautiful, and glorious a Temple on every side of it doth the Body of a Believer now appear in Death, when it cometh entirely out of its Cloud by being entirely taken out of the Spirit, and Image of this world? The true Body of a Saint lieth while this life lasteth, as in a Dungeon, or Grave. It stands here like the glorious Tabernacle composed of the most precious materials, Silks, Silver, Gold, the choicest Woods; wrought with all the richest colours, and the most curious Figures in Needle-work, and Carvings of a Divine Workmanship, which stood in a vast, and howling Wilderness, covered with a Tent of Badgers Skins. O! how

pure,

pure, how precious, how beautiful, how divine a thing is the Body of a Saint in Death, when it casts off this Body of Death, the corrupt, the carnal Image, and Principle entirely, and is seen now no more for ever in any appearance, besides that alone of a naked Member in the most lovely, & shining Body of the Lord Jesus? With what sweetness, and beauty doth it break forth now as a most amiable, and admirable Tabernacle of the Eternal Spirit, when by death it casts off the Tent of Badgers Skins, with all the darkning, and deforming impressions of Dust, and heat, and at once passeth out of the Wilderness of this worldly Spirit, and form of things unto the good Land of rest, and promise, by passing in a dry, and flowry path thorow the River *Jordan*, that sweet, and blessed bound of Death, between the dreadful desart, and heavenly *Canaan*.

Give me leave here to drop upon your hearts four brief exhortations.

1. O that all Men would love the King of Saints, the Lord Jesus. It is he alone, who subdues the King of Terror, that is, Death, and is more, than a conqueror over him, making him the King of delights. He changeth the Region, and Kingdom of Death, which is the Principality of the Devil, into the Kingdom of God, which is Righteousness, Peace, and Joy in the Holy Ghost.

2. Set a value upon the union with the Lord Jesus by faith. Ask, seek, [knock]ing for this by day, and by night, in Prayer, in the Word, in the Society of the Saints, in every ordinance, in every creature, that you may believe in the Lord Jesus, and that you may be united to him by believing. Let nothing discourage you in this pursuit, and expectation. The Lord Jesus hath given himself for you, even unto Death, that you may be his in the sweetest, and most intimate union. He giveth himself to you in his life of Glory, that he may be yours by an immediate, and entire union. He giveth his Spirit to you, to be the Maker, and the band of this union, to work faith in you, and make you Believers. He is now with you, now in you in the fulness of his merits, righteousness, glory, love, and Spirit. Now this moment open the eyes of your minds, and behold him in the midst of you, open your hearts, and take him in, cast your selves into his open arms, and heart, cleave to him by believing. So even this moment shall your Souls, and Bodies both, which are naturally the Members of this Harlot, the Flesh, and the World; which are naturally Dens of Thieves, and Devils, become the Members of the Lord Jesus, and the Temples of the Holy Ghost. The Lord Jesus shall be in your Body it self, as in a Member of himself, a Fountain of living waters even in Death, and in the Grave, making it there a Paradise, a Garden for God, and all blessed Spirits. The Holy Ghost shall be, not only in your Souls, but your Bodies also as in his Holy Temple, even in the darkness of Death it self, filling it with his Glory, and moving over it with his Doves Wings, the Wings of Eternal Love.

3. Make it your chief work, and end to grow in the knowledge of the Lord

Lord Jesus. What care, and pains do we take to grow in riches? yet riches profit not in the day of Wrath. To know him is eternal life. With what diligence do we pursue the wisdom of this world? Yet saith *Solomon*, as dyeth the Fool, so dyeth the wise Man. If thou gain, and grow in the knowledge of the Lord Jesus, this is a wisdom, which will make thy Soul, and Body both shine with a Light of Glory, and Immortality, even in Death it-self. *Solomon* saith, that when understanding enters into our Souls, wisdom will be sweeter, than hony to our tast. O what new tast, and rellishes of new, and unexpressible sweetnesses doth the Soul still meet with, which is still growing in the knowledge of our Lord Jesus? What a sweet tast, and rellish of Death beyond all the delights of Life doth the knowledge of Jesus Christ give unto us, representing it as a Feast of pleasant things to our Bodies also, as well as to our Souls? When thou understandest the fellowship, and vertue of Christs Death in thy Death, thou shalt see Death in thy Soul, and in thy Body, as the Carkass of a dead Lyon torn in pieces by that true *Samson*, the Lord Jesus, whither the Father himself, and Christ, and the Holy Spirit, with all the blessed Angels resort, as Bees to their Hive; laying there their Hony, and their Hony-comb for thee to eat.

4. O you, that are Christs, love Death, Death is now become but a shadow of Death. True life with all the joys of life, vails itself beneath that shadow. If you knew the love of the Father, the Glory of the Lord Jesus, the joys of the Holy Ghost in Death; if you knew what the Death of a Saint were, how precious, you would ask it continually of God, that he would hasten it in the time thereof. You would cry out continually, as *Sisera's* Mother did, why doth his Chariot stay? Death is not now a shadow of Death, but a living, delightful, and divine shadow cast from the glorious face of our Lord Jesus, under which our Souls, and Bodies lie together, as in a sweet, and divine sleep in his Bosom, in which sleep all the joys, and glories of Heaven, and Eternity are present with us, as a divine Dream, out of which we wake at the Resurrection, finding all to be true, eternally true, and the sweet shadow, and dream themselves swallowed up into a bright, clear, and full enjoyment. Thus, according to St. *Pauls* Language, doth the very Body of a Saint, when he dies, sleep in the Lord. Thus is death to the Soul, and Body of a Saint, as the Curtains of Purple round about *Solomons* Bed, where the Saint lies now in the embraces of the true *Solomon* himself, the King of Righteousness, and King of Peace, or round about the Chariot of *Solomon*, which had within it a Throne of Gold, and was paved with Love. As the Sun by its influence forms a precious Mine of Gold in the bowels of the Earth, which afterward being taken out, and separated from its dross, becomes pure and incorruptible, and is made a Crown for the Head of a great King: so the Lord Jesus by his Spirit frames a new, a heavenly Soul, and Body in a Saint, which are both his precious Members, his Temples of Gold. But while this life lasts, they

are

are in this Body of Sin, and Death, as Gold in the Oar. In the moment of Death the Lord Jesus takes them both out, separates them entirely from the dross of all earthliness, and carnality, makes them pure, and shining Diadems in the hand of God.

2. Propos. The whole Person of a Saint in Soul and Body at the moment of Death, is gathered up entirely into a Spiritual Principle, and so into a Spiritual Sense, and so into a Divine *Life*, and Peace. This followeth of necessity upon the former Proposition, which I have already proved by the Scripture. For, if a Saint in Death be gathered up entirely out of a Carnal Principle; he is gathered up entirely into a Spiritual Principle. There is now no middle between these two.

We read in Scripture of the divided state of a Saint between freedom, and bondage, liberty, and captivity; the War between the Spirit, and the Flesh, while he lives on Earth. Accordingly we meet with exhortations to abide in Christ, to walk in the Spirit, if we live in the Spirit. But, when a Saint dies, we read of him, and that with a peculiar relation to his Body, that he sleeps in the Lord, that he sleeps in Christ. O sweet, and full expression! O beautiful and blessed State! Now is a Saint with his Body, as well as his Soul alone in Christ, entirely in Christ, for ever in Christ, in Christ risen from the Dead, a quickning Spirit, in the Glory of the Father, with the fulness of the God-Head, and all fulness dwelling in him. Now is the Body also of a Saint at rest in a sweet rest, in a living rest. For such is the rest of sleep. It is in an immortal, and glorious rest, in a rest of Divine Love, and Joys, which, though it bears the similitude of Death to Carnal Sense, yet in truth is above all the degrees, and delights of life here. For such is the sleep in Christ.

But I will open this Proposition to you more clearly, and fully by that twofold relation, which the Scriptures attribute to the Body of a Believer. 1. Of a Member of Christ. 2. The Temple of the Holy Ghost. Both these are affirmed by the Holy Apostle, and the Blessed Spirit, with an assured confidence, as truths known to all, and undeniable by any, *1 Corin. 6. 15. Know ye not, that your Bodies are the Members of Christ? 19. Know ye not, that your Bodies are the Temples of the Holy Ghost?*

1. The Body of a Saint is the Member of Christ. This relation of Membership implyeth three things. 1. Union. 2. Communion. 3. Proportion, or Suitableness.

1. There is an union between the Body of a Believer, and Jesus Christ, an Union of Membership. But to what Christ is the Body of a Believer united? To Christ risen from the Dead, to Christ in Glory. So you shall read, *Rom. 7. 4. You are dead by the dead Body of Christ, that you might be Married to another, to him who is risen from the Dead.* Marriage, and Membership are two distinct expressions of the same union between Christ and a Saint, which for its dearness, nearness, entireness, and inseparableness is unexpressible, in as

much

much as it comprehends the sweetness, and vertue of all unions among the Creatures, either Men, or Angels, and transcendeth them all. But you have these two unions of Membership, and Marriage between the Body of a Saint singly and expresly, and the Lord Jesus, joyned together by St. *Paul*, who founds that of Membership, upon that of Marriage, 1 *Corin.* 6. 15. *Know ye not, that your Bodies are the Members of Christ* Then he makes good that, thus, *v.* 16. 17. *It is said those two shall be one Flesh; But he that is joyned to the Lord is one Spirit.* The days of Christs life on Earth are called the days of his Flesh. He hath the name of a Spirit given to him, as he is risen from the Dead, as he is in the Heavenly Image, and in Glory. So St. *Paul* calls him in one place the Lord that Spirit, in another place, the quickning Spirit. St. *Peter* saith of him; he was put to death in the Flesh, and quickned in the Spirit. Thus the Body of a Saint is married to Christ, is a Member of Christ. By this union it becomes a Spiritual Body, a Spirit, one Spirit with Christ.

There is a threefold band of this union of Membership, the same Spirit, the same Life, the same Image.

1. The first band of Union in this Membership between the Body of a Believer, and Jesus Christ, is the same Spirit, St. *Paul* saith, 1 *Corin.* 12. 13. *We all by one Spirit are Baptized into one Body.* The Unity of the ever-blessed Spirit is the sure, and sweet band which tyeth one to another, the glorious Head, and all the blessed Members in the Body of Christ. But what sweetness lies in the universality of that expression; we all are Baptized by one Spirit into one Body? As the Soul of Man is all in the whole Body, and all in every part of it; so is that ever-blessed Spirit, which is in the whole Heavenly Body, of which the Holy Angels, Glorified Saints, Christ, and the Father are Fellow-members, one and the same, whole, and entire in every part of this Body of thine, O Believer, which in its lowest, and most broken State is a Member of Christ. This union is so much more close, full, and sweet between the Members, by how much more Spiritual the Body is; by how much the more high, and divine the Unity is in this Body; by how much the more high, and divine the unity of that blessed Spirit is, in which the Father of Lights, the Heavenly Bride-groom, Glorified Saints, all the Elect Angels dwell together in one,

2. The same Life flowing from this one Spirit is the second band of this Union. We read from St. *Paul*, *Rom.* 8. 11. *If the Spirit of him which raised Christ from the Dead, dwell in you, he that raised up Christ from the Dead, shall also quicken your mortal Bodies by his Spirit dwelling in you.* This expression, shall quicken, signifieth not only an effect at a distance, at the last day, but a present effect immediately flowing from the indwelling of the Spirit in us. For the union between the Spirit, and our Bodies, by which he dwelleth in them also, as well, as in our Souls, is a vital union, an union,

from

from which Membership springs. This expression then, shall quicken your mortal Bodies, is like that of St. *Paul* in the same Epistle; Sin shall not have dominion over you, if you be not under the Law, but under Grace. *Shall*, there expresseth an effect immediately, and inseparably flowing from its cause, a freedom from the dominion of Sin by being under Grace, not under the Law. The Spirit of Christ findeth our Bodies Natural, and Mortal; but by its enterance into them, and inhabitation in them, maketh them, immediately Spiritual, and Immortal by their union with Christ, and by the pouring forth of his *Life*, and *Immortality* into them.

3. The band of union in this Membership is the same Image. All the Members of every Body make up one Image, in which each several Member bears a part. As we have born the Image of the Earthly Man, so shall we also bear the Image of the Heavenly. So far, O Saint, as thy Body is a Member of the Heavenly Body of Christ, it bears the same Heavenly Image. This is the first thing in Membership, the union.

2. There is in Membership a Communion. We read the 1 *Corin.* 12. 24, 25, 26. God hath tempered the Body together, having given the more abundant honour to that part, which lacked, that there should be no Schism in the Body, but that the Members should have the same care one for another, and whether one Member suffer, all the Members suffer with it, or one Member be honoured, all the Members rejoice with it. There is a threefold Communion in the Body of Christ. A Communion of Cares, a Communion of Sufferings, a Communion of Joy and Glory.

1. There is a Communion of Cares. All the Members have the same care one for another. As it is in the Natural Body, the Head, the Heart, the Eye, the Hand, all are set on work for every other part, for the little Toes, as for themselves, to defend, or cherish it upon every occasion: so is it in the Body of Christ. O Saint! with what quietness, and security mayest thou lye down to rest, and sleep in the midst of all wants, enemies, and dangers? Thy Body itself is a Fellow-Member in the Body of Christ with all the glorious Angels, and Blessed Spirits, with Christ the head of all, and the Father the Head of Christ. All these have the same care of thy Body for every part of it in every State, as for themselves. For it is themselves, a Member, and part of themselves. They all are present with it, they encompass it, they minister unto it all things seasonable for its defence, and comfort.

2. There is a Communion of sufferings. Whether one Member suffer, all the Members suffer with it. O Christians! what a sweetning is this to the bitterest affliction? How doth this take away the solitude, the sadness, the sting from Poverty, a Prison, a Sickness, the Grave? You are in the heart of all Angels, and Saints of Christ, and of the Father to suffer, to live, and to die together with you. All the Heavenly company, that are by one Spirit gathered together into that one glorious Body of Christ, lye down with you in

the Dust, in a Dungeon, on a sick Bed, in the Grave. How is the Spouse of Christ now in its most solitary, and afflicted State indeed, as two Heavenly Companies, according to the expression in the *Canticles*?

3. The Fellow-members in the Body of Christ have a Communion of Joy, and Glory. Whether one Member be honoured, all the Members rejoice with it. A Believer is ever glorious, ever blessed. St. *Peter* saith, that when we suffer for the name of Christ, the Spirit of Glory, and of God resteth upon us. Every suffering of a Saint, so far as he is a Saint, is for Christ. Why art thou ever melancholy, why is thy Heart heavy within thee, O Believer? Open thine Eyes to see them, open thine Heart to take them in. Behold the Joys, and Glories of all the blessed in Heaven are thine, are present with thee, and ever rest upon thee. I will conclude this Communion with that most remarkable expression: God hath tempered the Body together. The word is hath mingled the Body together. How full an expression is this? How doth this mixture sweeten all our sufferings, and make all our Joys far more pleasant? Thou, O Believer, with all thy shame, and sufferings art tempered, and mingled together with all the Saints, and Angels above, with Christ, and the Father, with all their Joys, and Glories. All the same Heavenly Company, with all the same Joys, and Glories, are tempered, and mingled together with thee, with thy shames, and sufferings here below. Thus are all one piece, and that one piece whole, and entire in every one. Thus is the greater, the greatest comeliness put upon the most indigent. Thus is there no Schism in the Body. As in many Spirits tempered into one Spirit, many Liquors tempered into one Liquor, many Spices beaten into the smallest Powder, mingled into one costly Ointment, every portion of this Spirit, this Liquor, this Ointment hath all the Spirits, all the Liquors, all the Ointments of the whole in it: so is the Body of Christ in general, and every Member in particular.

3. The proportion, or suitableness. There is no Schism in the Body of Christ. If this be pure, precious, living, immortal, heavenly, and glorious; then is thy Body also, O Believer, so far as it is a Member of this Body, pure, precious, living, immortal, heavenly, & glorious. How living, how immortal, how beautiful, how glorious, how divine a thing is that Body of a Saint, which is a Member of Christ in Glory? What Life, what Joys are those of this Body, which is in so dear, so inseparable, so intimate an Union, and Communion of the same Life, Joys, Beauties, and Spirit with all the glorious Angels, blessed Spirits, Christ himself, the Head of all, & the Father in Christ? This is the State of the Body of a Saint, as it is a Member of Christ. But while a Saint lives in this world, his Body is partly the Member of this Heavenly Husband, the Lord Jesus, and partly the Member of a Harlot, this World, and the Flesh; in as much as a Saint here below hath his life, and conversation divided between the pure Spirit of Christ, and the Whorish Spirit of this world. O sweet, O beautiful, O precious, and blessed Death! By Death is the joyful, and glorious separation

separation made in the Body of a Saint, between the precious, and the vile, between the heavenly Bridegroom, the Lord Jesus, and the Hellish Adulterer, this World. Now it ceaseth for ever to be in any degree any more the Member of the Harlot, to be in a Carnal, or worldly Spirit. Now it's for ever singly, entirely gathered up into the Spirit, Body, and Bosom of Jesus Christ. O! how pure, how shining, in what Angelical, in what Spiritual, in what Divine a form, and fulness of unexpressible rest, beauty, and delight is the Body of a Saint in the very moment of Death, when, like fine Gold purged from its dross, or a Heavenly Sun, that hath cast up its cloud, it now comes forth out of the Whorish Spirit of the Flesh, and this World, a single, and pure Member in the pure, and divine Body of our Lord Jesus? These are the three things contained in this Membership of the Body of a Believer in Christ; Union, Communion, and proportion.

From this I shall raise a threefold short exhortation.

1. Set a value upon the new Birth, upon the Regeneration. Content not your selves with being once born. By your first Birth you have Souls, and Bodies Members of this world. By the Spirit of this world they are Baptized into the Body, and Society of Darkness, Corruption, Death, Wrath, the whole Company of wicked Spirits, and Devils. Give your selves no rest till you are born again. By the new Birth, which is from above, you have new Souls, and new Bodies, which are Members one of another, Fellow-members of Christ. Your Souls, and your Bodies both are by that one, Eternal Spirit Baptized into one Spiritual, Immortal, and glorious Body with the Spirits of all just men made evangelically perfect by the Blood, and Spirit of Christ; with all the Holy Angels, with Christ, and the Father. Press into the Fellowship of this mystery. Here you shall see it indeed to be true, that Grace is Glory begun in your Souls, and Bodies both; that when you believe, a Spirit of Glory rests upon your whole Person by your Union with Christ.

2. Possess this Vessel of your Bodies in holiness. For so you shall possess it in honour. Possess it, converse with it in a Spiritual Principle. So you shall enjoy it, and your selves in it, as a Member of Christ. You shall see, feel, enjoy within your selves in this Body, the Spirit, the Life, the Immortality, the Joy, the Glory of the whole Body of Christ, the society of all things Heavenly, Blessed and Eternal, to wake, and to sleep, to walk, and lie down, to live, and to dye with you. This is the true Church-fellowship, a Fellowship in our Souls, and in our Bodies by a Spiritual Principle, and Life with the Church, and Assembly of the first-born, with all things in their first born State, in one Spiritual, and Heavenly Body in Christ.

3. How amiable, and lovely doth this make death to the Saints? This is the chief end I aim at in my discourse, and the point to which I bring it. With what a beautiful, and smiling Face doth Death now look forth even in the Body of a Saint, in which he hath been wont generally to appear so grim to the

the holiest Persons? Thy Body, O Believer, so far as thou standest in a Spiritual Principle, is a Fellow-member with thy Soul in the Body of Christ: It is a Jewel, the work of a faithful, and curious workman the most holy Spirit; as *Solomon* in the *Canticles* speaketh of the Spouse of Christ. But here the mixture of the fleshly, and carnal Principle is as Dust, and Dirt, which covereth, and sullyeth this costly Jewel. With what a sweet, pure lustre of Immortality, and of Heavenly Glory doth it sparkle, and shine forth, ravishing thine own, and all spiritual Eyes, and Hearts in the moment of Death, when the blessed hand of Death clean wipes off the dust, and stain of the carnal Principle, and brings it forth entirely into its Spiritual Principle, that now it stands singly, as a Spiritual Member in the Spiritual Body of Christ?

The Lord Jesus saith; if thine Eye be single, thine whole Body shall be light, as when a Candle enlightens a Room. In this life O Saints, we have a double Eye, and have a double sight. The mixture of the Spiritual, and Carnal Principle is the double, and divided Eye. O welcome Death, receive it with open embraces. Now is your Eye single. Now is the carnal Principle cast out for ever. Now you look forth with the open, and single Eye of the single Principle of the Eternal Spirit. Now is your whole Body, nay, now is the whole body of things filled to you with a Heavenly light of Immortality, &c Glory. This single Eye pours forth from the Unity of the Spirit, as from the Fountain of blessed Light thorow your whole Souls, and Bodies, thorow all things round about them a Light of Glory, as when a Candle enlightneth a Room.

A way of cleansing Pearls, when t hey have any spot, or cloud upon them is to thrust them down the throat of a Pigeon into its Crop, where the heat of the Pigeon takes off the stain, and makes them perfectly white. This is the mystery of a Saints Death. The Heavenly Dove, the Holy Spirit in the same moment takes a Saint entirely in Soul, and Body out of this Life, out of the Carnal Principle into himself, into his Bosom of Love, by the Divine heat of that Love takes off every spot, or cloud of the flesh by consuming it both in the Soul, and in the Body, and makes them both purely white, and shining Pearls in the Heavenly Body of that one great, and only Pearl the Lord Jesus.

2. The second relation, into which the Body of a Believer is taken at the new birth, is that of a Temple to the Holy Ghost. There are 4 things proper to a Temple. 1. The Figure. 2. The Glory. 3. The Communion. 4. The Defence.

1. *Every thing* in the Tabernacle, and so in the Temple to the least things, and lowest actions were divine Types of Spiritual Truths, and Heavenly Excellencies *in the Person of the Lord Jesus.* So it is said, that all things were made, and ordered according to the pattern in the Mount, which pattern in the *Mount* was *Christ in Glory. O Saints!* This Tabernacle, and Temple were Types first of Christ, then of you, whose Souls, and Bodies both are the true, and living Temples of *God.* The *Body of a Saint* is a

more

nore excellent Temple, in as much as *Solomons* Temple was a ſhadow only of this. It is a Living, Divine, and Immortal Temple. It is therefore in the whole a far more excellent, more rich, more glorious, and delightful Image of the God-Head in its entire form. It is in every part, and point of it a moſt lively, a moſt beautiful, a moſt pleaſant figure of ſome particular Myſtery, and Glory in the God-Head.

All the parts of your Bodies themſelves, the loweſt, and leaſt, even to a hair of your Heads, every thing that befals you in every part of your Body in the meaneſt, and ſlighteſt circumſtance, is formed exactly by the Divine Wiſdom, and Power, according to the Divine Will, to anſwer the Pattern in the Mount, to be the holy figure of an eternal Glory in Chriſt. We read *Pſal.* 29. 9. *Every thing in his Temple ſpeaks Glory.* Every thing in thy Body, O Believer, so far as thou art a Believer, ſpeaks Glory. For this is his Temple. O live alwaies in the Spirit, that thou maiſt alwaies be in thy Body, as in the Temple, that there thou maiſt ſee, underſtand, and enjoy the Glory in every thing!

2. The Temple of God is filled with the Glory of God. There is a prophesy in *Malachy*, concerning the times of the Goſpel, that he ſhall come into his Temple. You, O Saints are the Temple, which is here Propheſied of. Jeſus Chriſt, as God in the Glory of the Father, in the Third Perſon, the Holy Ghoſt, comes into you, into your Bodies alſo, and fills them with his Glory. The ſame word in Hebrew ſignifieth a Temple, and a Pallace. The name of a Temple in Greek, ſignifieth an Habitation, or dwelling place. It is a note of a learned Divine, that the Temple had Tables, and a Throne, and a ...ate in it, which was the Golden Mercy Seat called in the Goſpel, the Throne of Grace, to ſignifie that the Temple of God was his Pallace, as he is the great King. The Eternal Spirit is preſent in the Body of a Believer, as in his Pallace. He keeps his Court there. There is his Throne, with all the bleſſed Angels, and all the Heavenly Company, waiting round about it.

It is called his reſting-place. Ariſe, ſaith *David* to God, thou, and the ...k of thy ſtrength into thy reſting-place. God ſhineth forth in his Temple, ...eth it with his Glory within, reſting upon it, and overſhadowing it with ... Glory without. In the 50 *Pſal.* at the beginning the Pſalmiſt ſpeaking of the Temple ſaith; God ſhineth from *Sion*, the perfection of Beauty. What perfection of Beauty then, what a Divine Pallace, how full of Glory within, how encompaſſed with a clear, & ſhining Glory round about is that Body of a Saint, which is the living, eternal Temple of the Holy Ghoſt? In ...at Majeſty doth this Eternal Spirit appear here upon its Throne of Love? ...he midſt of what Divine Pleaſures, and Delights doth it reſt for ever? What a Court does it keep here with all its Train of Angels, and heavenly Attendants, waiting round about its Throne, as in another Heaven? O Believers, honor your Bodies. For theſe, ſo far as you ſtand in a Spiritual Principle, ...as another Heaven, the Heaven of Heavens, the Pallace of the great King, ...ch he fills with his Glory, where he heeps his Court, & ſits upon his Throne.

3. The

3. The Saints have communion with God in his Temple. In the Temple was the Golden Mercy-Seat. There, saith God, will I commune with thee. This was overspread with Cherubims of Glory, as St. *Paul* calls them. These Cherubims covered this Golden Mercy-Seat with their Wings, and so made the State, or Glory about the Throne. This is therefore called the secret of the most high, and the shadow of the Almighty, where a Saint is said to dwell, and to lodge. Hear, O ye Saints, what glorious things are spoken of your Bodies; be Spiritual, and behold in these Temples the Golden Mercy-Seat, which is the glorified Person of Christ, and the Cherubims of Glory covering it with their Wings, and God here upon this Golden Mercy-Seat, the glorified Bosom of Christ from between the Wings of the Cherubims, ready alwaies to commune with you, yea taking you up upon this Golden Mercy-Seat, within the Wings of the Cherubims, to commune freely with him at all seasons in this secret of eternal safety, rest, love, joy, and glory.

This Temple is the Body of a Saint while he liveth below; but now it is in too great a degree covered with a cloud of Flesh, filled with the smoak of the Spirit of this world, that a Saint too rarely enters into this Temple of the holy Ghost in his own Body, and more rarely seeth with any degree of clearness the Glory, or heareth the voice of the blessed Spirit there. What joy is it to think, in what a purely sacred, and Divine Temple, in what a clear, and shining Pallace of the eternal King, in what open, and unstained, unvailed visions of Divine Glory, in what a secret, in what a presence of glorious Angels, and Eternal Spirits, in the midst of what sweet overshadowings, dear encompassings, naked outshinings of the Eternal Spirit, in what most blessed, most ravishing Communion of Eternal Light, Life, and Love with this Spirit, in what sight, and embraces, with what kisses of incomprehensible Beauties; in the sound of what words, what salutations, what wooings, what expressions of the highest Loves, and Joys from the Eternal Spirit a Saint finds himself even in his own proper Body in the very moment of his Death, when departing out of this Life at once he departs for ever out of the Fleshly Image, and the Spirit of this World ?

4. The Divine Presence, and Glory was the defence of the Temple, *Esa.* 4. 5. There is a Prophesy concerning the times of the Gospel expressed by figures taken from the state of things under the Law: And the Lord will create upon every dwelling place of Mount *Sion*, and upon her Assemblies a Cloud, and smoak by day, and the shining of a flaming fire by night. For upon all the Glory shall be a defence, or a covering. When the first Temple was to be destroyed, the Prophet *Ezekiel* saw the Glory removing off from it; afterwards, when the second Temple was near its end, a voice was heard in it saying; Let us be gone from hence, which was understood to be the voice of God, and of his holy Angels with all those invisible companies, and Ministers, which made up the Glory of the Divine Presence, as Nobles, Officers, and Guards make up the Court of a King.

O Saints

O Saints! why do you fear for your Bodies hidden *Conspiracies*, or open force, diseases, the fury of the Elements, the malice of Men, or *Devils*? These Bodies of yours are the Temples of the Holy Ghost. Here are the Holy Assemblies of all the Heavenly Company in the unity of the Spirit, whose Temples your Bodies are. Of these it is Prophesied, to these it is promised, that God will create upon them a cloud, and a smoak by day, the shining of a flaming fire by night. Upon these the Glory is a defence, or a covering. God himself with all his holy Ones, his Angels, his Watchmen, his ministring Spirits is this Cloud, this Glory, which is the defence, and covering upon your whole Persons your Bodies, as well as your Souls: both have together with Christ a hidden Life, a secure Life, in this secret of God within this covering of this Divine Cloud, Flame, and Glory. From off these Temples of your Bodies this Glory never removes. From within these Temples of your Bodies this heavenly Company never departs; for as much as the union in the Spirit of Grace under the Gospel is Eternal.

Thus the Bodies also of Believers in this Life are the Temples of the Holy Ghost. All things in them here are divine Figures of a divine Glory. They are filled and covered with the Glory it self. They are the seats of the freest Communion with this Glory, being the Temples of the God of Gods, and so the Pallaces of the King of Kings. All this is true of them here, as they stand in a Spiritual Principle, and in union with Christ by the new birth.

But this Life is a mixt State. We stand partly in a Spiritual, partly in a Fleshly Principle. These Temples of our Bodies are covered with a corrupt Flesh, that we can hardly discern their Spiritual Beauties. They are too frequently in too great a part filled with a smoak of Hell, the smoak of the Spirit of this world, that a Believer can rarely enter into this Temple of his Body to behold, and converse with the Glory there.

This is the precious, the blessed work of Death in a Believer. It breaketh the union, it maketh a separation not between Christ, and a Believer, not between the Soul, and Body of a Believer, as they are joyned together in Christ by the band, and unity of the Eternal Spirit, and make one Spiritual Man, or Person in Christ; but between the precious, and the vile, between the Carnal and Spiritual Principle of a Saint both in Soul and Body.

Now in the moment of Death the Soul, and Body of a Saint come forth immediately, clear, and shining Temples of the Spirit; the smoak, and clouds of the Fleshly Principles, and of this worldly Image being for ever driven away from within them, and from without.

Thus you understand St. *Pauls* sweet, and blessed sense of Death, when he speaketh of the Body, and saith, 1 *Corin.* 5. 1. 2. That, *we shall not be found naked, but be cloathed upon from above with a building of God Eternal in the Heavens, which shall swallow up mortality in life.* Our Spiritual Body, which we have in this life by our new Birth, as we stand in our Spiritual Principle is this Divine Building sprung from a Divine Root, of a Divine Nature, or Sub-

stance

ſtance, of a Divine Form, and Workmanſhip. This is ever in Heaven, being inſeparably united to Chriſt, and being ever in the Spirit. This is Eternal, when we die, this caſts off the Cloud of corrupt, and curſed Fleſh. This ſprings forth out of its Spiritual Principle, as out of Heaven, and the Boſom of God. This reſts upon us, takes us in, cloaths us entirely, univerſally with itſelf. Thus we are never found naked not for any one the leaſt moment. All that life, all thoſe objects, entertainments, and joys, which we poſſeſſed before in the Cloud, in the Captivity of a mortal Image, yea the very Image of mortality itſelf, beſides innumerable new and unconceivable Glories, are all the very ſame things preſent with us in this Heavenly Building; this Heavenly Body; but after a new, and more excellent manner. We have our pleaſant things a hundred-fold more pleaſant. We have our unpleaſant things with an unmixed, pure, and perfect pleaſantneſs, as they ſtand within in the Divine Myſtery, and Love. Thus deſirable, and delightful is death to a Saint, which now indeed is no more Death, but the flood, the Fountain of pure Light, Eternal Life, the Divine Love breaking forth in his Soul, and Body, and ſwallowing up every thing of Mortality into itſelf.

Give me leave here to take occaſion to ſtir you up to the love, and purſuit of Spirituality in Religion, by a ſhort exhortation.

1. Underſtand your loſs. How many precious, and glorious truths of the Goſpel? What Heavenly, and Divine growths in Grace? How many ſweet, unexpreſſible conſolations, and joys in life, and in death are we unacquainted with, are we uncapable of for want of the Spirit, and Spirituality? I have many things to ſpeak unto you, ſaith our Lord Jeſus to his Diſciples before his Death; but ye cannot bear them now. Why? Hitherto they knew Chriſt after the Fleſh only. The Spirit was not come, which was to lead them into all truths, and to be their eminent comforter. I could not ſpeak unto you, as to Spiritual, but as to Carnal, ſaith St. *Paul* to the *Corinthians*, who yet were puffed up with a conceit of their knowledge.

2. Conſider the danger from the want of Spirituality. St. *Paul* ſaith in one place, that what the Law ſpeaketh, it ſpeaketh to thoſe that are under the Law. The Law in Scripture is called the Letter, which is the Figure, and Image only: The Goſpel the Spirit, which is the Life, and Truth. This then is the dreadful curſe, which the Law pronounceth upon thoſe, who live, and worſhip God in the oldneſs of the Letter; not in the newneſs of the Spirit: that their Eyes, their Ears, their Hearts ſhall be cloſed, made fat, and hardned, that ſeeing they ſhall not ſee, hearing they ſhall not underſtand, that they ſhall be taught line upon line, precept upon precept, here a little, and there a little, that they may fall backward, and periſh, and never riſe more; becauſe, when Chriſt was preſented to them in the Spirit of Life, and Glory to be their reſt, and refreſhing for ever, they would not obey the heavenly Call. O dreadful danger! O deadly curſe! Hear this O Profeſſors; O Believers,

vers, who are Carnal, and not Spiritual! Tremble and fear to be eternally imprisoned in the dark Image, and killing Letter, being for ever excluded from the marvellous light of God, from the Eternal Life, and from the most glorious truth it self of all Heavenly, and Divine Things, to wander perpetually in a barren Wilderness of Graves, and of fiery Serpents, never to enter into the rest of God, nor the refreshing of the Eternal Spirit. O Silly Men, and silly Women, that are ever learning, ever hearing Sermons, ever praying, ever reading the Scriptures, ever sounding forth the name of Christ, and God; yet at the end of one, ten, or twenty years, still laden with the same diversity of Lusts, and Passions, still moving forward, and backward upon the same Carnal, and literal sense of things, never coming to the knowledge of the Truth, as the Truth is in Jesus, as the Spirit is Truth!

3. See the advantages of Spirituality, as they are laid together, 2 *Corin.* 3. At the latter end.

1. Liberty, *Where the Spirit of the Lord is, there is Liberty*; a pure freedom from the servitude of hellish Lusts, and passions; a pleasant freedom from fears, cares, confinements; from the Law, Death, and Wrath; a Divine Freedom from the vale of the Flesh, the Law, the Letter of things, from every Earthly, Created, Darkning, Dividing Principle, Life, and Image; the liberty of a free access into the purity, power, rest, joys, glories, immortality, infiniteness of the Spirit, and of the Divine Nature.

2. A clear discovery, evidence, and seal of the new Birth in you. *We with open Face behold the Glory of the Lord.* The open face there (as appears clearly by the context of the words) is the Spiritual, and Heavenly Man within us unvailed, appearing evidently with the Seal of his own Spiritual Beauties, and Glories upon it, in the openness, and freedom of a Spiritual, and Divine Light. Where are doubts, where are fears now concerning our condition? they are fled away, and vanish, as the shadows of the night before the Sun rising, and shining forth with open face.

3. A clear vision of the Lord Jesus in Glory within thy self. *We all with open face, as in a glass, beholding the Glory of the Lord*, saith St. *Paul.* It is in Greek beholding, as in a Looking-glass, where the Face, that is seen, is the Face of him who sees, reflected upon it self. O blessed State of a Spiritual Saint! The Spiritual Man in him is a Divine, and living Looking-glass, in which, while he beholds the face of the Lord Jesus in Glory, he sees his own Face, and the glorious form of his own Heavenly Person reflected upon it self. The Person which sees, the Heavenly Person which is seen, and the Glass, are all one Spirit. All these dwell together, see, possess, and enjoy one another in the same Life, and Image.

4. Spirituality brings a lively, and lovely growth in all Grace. We are changed, saith St. *Paul*, into the likeness of the same Image from Glory to Glory. These words import three excellencies in the growth of a Spiri-

tual Person. 1. It is continual, which is implied in that expression *from Glory to Glory*. One degree of growth immediately follows another. The Kingdom of Heaven, which is the State of Spirituality, and in the Holy Ghost, is compared to Corn, which grows by day, and by night, in Winter, and in Summer. *It is growing every moment,* till it be ripe for the Harvest. 2. Spirituality groweth by great increases. Here the name of Glory is put upon the growths of Grace in a Spiritual State from Glory to Glory. In another place St. *Paul* expresseth it by *the increases of God*, that is, swift, great, glorious, divine increases, as by the immediate springings of the Godhead, and bearing the likeness of God in Glory. 3. Spirituality makes the Glorified Person of Christ the Pattern, the Measure, the Mark, and End of its growth. So saith St. *Paul*, *Beholding the Glory of the Lord, we are changed into the likeness of the same Image.* A Spiritual Person hath the Lord Jesus cloathed with a Spiritual Glory ever in his eye; is continually taking him into his Heart, continually bringing him forth into his whole Person and Life, with an increasing clearness and fulness. As the Object is to the Faculty, and to the Soul; so is Jesus Christ to a Spiritual Person, his Pattern, his Object, his Food, his Feast, which spreads itself quite thorow his Person and Life, which all throughout turns into Life, Strength, Beauty, Cheerfulness, and Joy to him.

5. A spiritual person in a sweet and sealing manner sees the Spirit himself presenting the Lord Jesus to him within himself in a spiritual Glory; feels the Spirit himself springing up immediately within him in all sights of Christ, in all his changes, and growths into Christ. He sees, and feels this Spirit to be Jesus Christ himself. He sees and feels this Spirit, and this Jesus to be in himself, and one Spirit with himself. So the verse forementioned runs; *We all with open face, beholding, as in a Looking-glass, the Glory of the Lord, are changed into the likeness of the same Image, from Glory to Glory, as by the Spirit of the Lord*; or, according to the Greek, *by the Lord that Spirit.*

These are the sweet and blessed Advantages of a Spiritual State. I will add some few and short Directions to this State.

1. Look to the New Birth in You. See that you be born again, that you be born from above, that you be born of the Spirit; that this which is born in you, be Spirit. Jesus Christ saith, *That which is born of the Spirit, is Spirit.* This only is the New Birth. Newness is only in the Eternal Spring, the Spirit.

2. Take care of your Union with Christ, that it be a Spiritual Union; that you be united to Christ, as he is risen from the Dead, and in Glory, as he is a Spirit, the King and Bridegroom of Spirits; that you be united to Christ in the Spiritual Man; that your Union be a Spiritual Marriage; that you be one Spirit in the Unity of the Eternal Spirit, which is Love.

3. Pray for the Spirit, for a Spiritual Understanding, for the Knowledge of things in the Spirit, as they are Spirit and Life, and so alone Truth. Suck in the Spirit by day, and by night, from the lips of Christ, from the kisses of his mouth.

4. Die to every thing of the Flesh, that you may live in the Spirit. Bear about in your Bodies the dying of the Lord Jesus, that the Life also of the Lord Jesus, according to the Spirit, may be manifested in your mortal Bodies. As the young Phœnix is said to spring new and fresh out of the Ashes of the Old One; so doth the Spirit in the newness of an Heavenly and Immortal Glory spring out of the Grave of Christ.

5. Live purely, live in Love. These two, Purity and Love, are the principal fruits of the Spirit, by which the Spirit himself is drawn down, and held in our Hearts, being fed, and delighted with them. Every kind and degree of impurity and enmity quencheth the Spirit and maketh him to withdraw himself into Heaven again. The Scripture saith, *The Flesh lusteth against the Spirit*, to bring forth its own Beauties, Delights and Fruits all over the Spirit of Man in the place of the Eternal Spirit. The Scripture saith also, That *the Flesh envyeth against the Spirit*: The Flesh hath an envy, and an envious malice to see the Spirit with its Eternal Glories, Joys and Fruits to flourish in the Soul.

6. Lastly; Take heed of thinking that you know enough. *He that thinks he knows any thing, knows nothing as he ought to know it*, saith St. *Paul*. He that thinks he knows any thing, knows things only after the Letter, which is a knowledge of shadows only, and a shadow of knowledge. This is that knowledge, which puffeth up, which swels a man with a windy conceit of knowledge. But that knowledge which is from the Spirit, as its Fountain, and in the Spirit, as its air, and element, and of the Spirit, as its only object, this makes a man at the highest degree of his knowledge on Earth to be sensible, that all his knowledge is, but as the light of the night, a light shining in a dark place, not the day-star, and the Sun itself risen upon him. This man thinks himself at best, as a door-keeper only, or (as the Hebrew word signifieth) one standing at the threshold of the House of God, who looketh in at a distance, and hath only a weak glimmering prospect of the Glories there, but is not yet entered into the Light of those Glories to behold them, as they are, to know them, as he ought to know them, and is to know them. He therefore, as a new born Babe from the Womb of the Spirit, keeps his Eye ever fixed with wonder, and pleasure upon the light of the Spirit, and ever thirsts to drink in more, and more the sweet milk of this Light.

The Subject of our discourse hath been the passage of a Saint by Death, not only in his Soul, but in his Body also, into a State of purity, pleasure, perfection, and immortality. One of the objections against this was taken from common sense, to which Death presents the Bodies of the holiest Persons liveless, ghastly, dissolving to dust. We have answered this objection by a distinction between a twofold sense, Carnal, and Spiritual. But this objection was enforced from the Body of Christ, which was a rueful, and bloody spectacle in Death, which lay three days in the silence, darkness, and restraint of the Grave. It is necessary therefore to say something, particularly to the State of

O o o 2 Christs

Christs Body in Death, by the application of this distinction to that also.

I shall ground this discourse upon that Scripture, *Luke* 12. 50. They are the words of Christ: *I have a Baptism to be Baptized with, and how am I streightned till it be over.* This Baptism is generally, and as I humbly conceive, rightly, interpreted to be the sufferings of Christ at his Death. The Baptism of Christ, and the accomplishment of that Baptism were both at the time of his Death. The sense of this Baptism before it came, was an unexpressible streightning, or affliction, and oppression to the Soul of Christ. He cries out, how am I streightned?

The words thus opened, afford this observation: The Lord Jesus had his greatest trouble, and his greatest Triumph at the time of his Death. Then was this bloody Baptism; and then was the blessed accomplishment of this Baptism. I shall open this in seven Propositions, whereof 5 set forth the trouble, the other two the Triumph of Christ at his Death.

1. Propos. It was the most glorious, and eternal Person of God himself in two Natures, Divine, and Humane, which was our Jesus.

2. Propos. God in his own Person, as the Divine Nature lived in our Nature here on Earth, stood at once in a twofold Principle, one Natural, and Temporary; the other Supernatural, and Eternal.

3. Propos. As this Eternal Person our Jesus with his God-Head in the Humane Nature, stood in a Natural, and Temporary Principle, he stood under the curse, receiving, and feeling all the stings, and bitterness of the curse to the utmost extremity.

4. Propos. This our Jesus, as he at the same time with his Divine Nature in his Humanity, stood in a Supernatural, and Eternal Principle, he in his Humanity comprehended his Humanity itself, in its natural Principle, together with the natural Principle itself, the Curse, all the stings, and bitterness of the Curse, in a light of Divine Glory, in a life of Divine Love, as so many varieties of pure Love, Joy, and Glory with Immortality.

5. Propos. The Curse with the stings, and sense of it upon the Natural, and Temporary Principle, as also the conflict between the Natural, and Temporary, the Supernatural, and Eternal Principle in the Lord Jesus through his whole Person, as it lived in a Humane Soul, and Body, were highest at his Death.

These are the five Propositions, which set forth the trouble of Christ at his Death. In the other two followeth his Triumph.

6. Propos. This Eternal Person our Jesus with his God-Head in his whole Humanity both Soul, and Body, in the moment of Death by dying, went entirely forth from the Natural, or Temporary Principle, and so from under the Curse.

7. Propos. This same Jesus in his whole Person with his whole Soul, and Body, in the moment of Death by dying went forth entirely into the simpli-

city, and singleness of his Supernatural, the Eternal Principle, and so into a State of pure Eternity, unmixt Joy, and Glory.

I shall briefly open these Propositions in their order.

1. Propos. It was the most glorious, and eternal Person of God himself in two Natures, Divine, and Humane, which was our Jesus, *John* 1. 14. *The Word was made Flesh.* The second Person in the Trinity, from which the other two Persons, the Father and the Spirit are inseparable; the eternal, and essential Son of God, which hath the fulness of the God-Head in himself, in its most express Image, and greatest Glory, he in his own Person, in this Eternal Person, and Sonship, was made Flesh. This Eternal Person, this Essential Son of God was that Flesh. This Flesh was that Person, that Son, which had the Father, and the Spirit inseparably with himself, and was essentially one with them.

O Christians, study this union of the two Natures Divine, and Humane in one only Divine, Unchangeable, and Eternal Person, which is the most glorious, and Ever-blessed God. This is the deep and rich ground of the Christian Religion, out of which, as the true ground of the Heavenly Paradise, the God-Head itself makes to spring all the precious mysteries of the Gospel, all Evangelical Truths, Graces, and Joys in their most Spiritual Beauty, Sweetness, and Life. Understand this: Pray for the understanding of this, for a sight, sense, and feeling of it within your own Spirits, that it is God, God himself in his own only Divine, unchangeable, undivided Person, in your own Form, in your own Nature, in your own Persons, and Spirits, which is your Jesus, your Saviour, Redeemer, Husband, and King, your Ransom, Atonement, and Righteousness, your Beauty, your Life, your Joy, your Root, Branch, Flower, and Fruit. This union between the Divine, and Humane Nature in one Person in our Lord Jesus, is the Original, and Reason of the union between you, and this Jesus, which is God in Person, to which Person, thorow his union, you also are immediately, eternally united in one Spirit, in one mystical Person, which is Christ, as St. *Paul* speaketh, as there is one Body, and many Members, so is Christ.

A Spiritual knowledge of this union of two Natures in one Person, and that God himself is this Person, will sweeten all sufferings of life to you, and perfume the Grave. Open the Eyes of your Spirits, and behold with joy, and wonder the goings of your God, and King in the Sanctuary of this Earthly Body. It was the ever-glorious, and immutable Person of God in the most high, and holy Trinity, which made itself Flesh in the Womb of the Virgin, which was that Flesh, which in that Flesh eat, drank, slept, talked, and walked upon the Face of this Earth, which passed under all the clouds, thorow all the storms of life here, which hung upon the Cross, dyed, and lay down in the Grave. O with what a Divine, and delightful Glory hath this Divine presence, and Person filled, and cloathed this Flesh, this Earth, all the

natu-

natural actions, and passions of this Flesh, on this Earth, Clouds, Storms, the Cross, Death, and the Grave to the Spiritual Eyes of Believers? What living Plants of Paradise; how beautiful, how laden with most pleasant, and Immortal Fruits are all these springing up out of this Root, this Divine, and Eternal Person? What Jewels are they of incomprehensible virtue; sweetness, and lustre, hanging upon this Person?

See your selves O all ye Saints, even the lowest, and the least, conformed to this Image. It is the immortal Seed, and Son of God *in you*, *it is your* Jesus, the most glorious Person of God himself in this Seed in you, which is made partaker of Flesh, and Blood, which walks on Earth, and acts all the parts of the natural Life here, which passeth thorow all the Clouds, and Storms of life, which suffers, dies, and lies in the Grave. The Spouse saith of Christ, He is a bundle of Myrrh; he shall lye all night between my Breasts. Thus the Humane Nature of Christ saith to the Divine Nature. Thus the Earthly Nature saith to the Heavenly Nature, to the Divine Seed, to the Lord Jesus, to the Divine Nature in the Lord Jesus: thou art my bundle of Myrrh, thou liest all the night of this life, and death between my naked Breasts. What corruption can I see in the Grave it self? What Divine Sweetness breaths forth it self in all States? What Divine Treasures of Life, and Immortality, fill, and overflow all; while we thus lye most intimately united, entirely wrapt up in each other, in the most sweet, and glorious Unity of one Divine, and Eternal Spirit, one Mystical, Divine, and Eternal Person?

2. Propos. God in his own Person, as the Divine Nature lived in our Nature here on Earth, stood at once in a twofold Principle; the one Natural, and Temporary; the other Spiritual, and Eternal.

The Lord Jesus was truly, and really a man in every point like unto us, sin only excepted, as the Scripture speaketh in the Epistle to the *Hebrews*. Thus he did bear in himself the Earthly, and Natural Image, he stood in an earthly, and natural Principle. He came forth from the Father into the World. So was he made a Servant, and made under the Law.

But the Lord Jesus was in Person the Eternal Son of God. In this Person alone did the Humane Nature of Christ, with its Natural Principle, and Fleshly Form in this world subsist. The second Person in the Trinity was the Glorious, and Invisible Root, which, through the Divine Nature sent forth, sustained, lived, and appeared in the spotless Flesh of the Lord Jesus. Thus the Manhood of Christ in its Earthly State stood in a natural Principle, according to its proper essence, and created Form; but in a Supernatural, and Eternal Principle according to its Personal subsistence in the Eternal Word.

How patient should we be of Life; nay with what delight, and wonder should we pass the time of our Pilgrimage here, if with a Spiritual Eye we beheld the Lord Jesus in Flesh, and saw our life in flesh a conformity to his? What a Divine Spectacle, what a mystery of Divinity, how full of Sweetness,

ness, Beauty, and Glory doth the Life of Christ in Flesh appear, when it is rightly seen? The Natural Spirit of this world with its natural Image in its full compass stood in the midst of the Lights, Immortalities, Glories of that Divine Person which is the Brightness of Glory, the Sea of all Sweetnesses, and Loves, Eternity itself, God himself. This was the Eternal Principle, which brought it forth from itself, which bears it up in its own *Bosom*, which acts it, fills it, comprehends it, as itself, one Person with itself, itself Personally in a Divine, and Mysterious Figure, in the midst of all its Divine, and Substantial Glories.

3. Propos. As this Eternal Person our Jesus with his God-Head in the Humane Nature, stood in a Natural, and Temporary Principle, he stood under the Curse, receiving, and feeling all the stings, and bitterness of the Curse to the utmost extremity. The Scripture saith he was made a Curse for us. Although together with the Natural Principle, he took not the Corruption, yet he took the Curse. You that read, or hear this, prepare your selves to receive a Relation of Divine Love, which will at once break your hearts, and make them whole again: That God, who is Blessedness itself, the purest Light of Life, Joy, and Glory in Person, cloaths himself with Flesh, even with the Fleshly Spirit, and Principle, that he may make himself a Curse for your sakes, in your stead. Thus he receives immediately into his own Person, into his own Breast, and Heart, all the stings of the Curse, of Separation, of Loss, of Shame, of Pain, of Guilt, of Grief, of Horrour, Amazement, Death. All these stings he receives into himself, as they are dipt all over in the most unmixt, and fiercest Poison of the Divine Wrath. All these stings he felt at once, envenomed with Wrath in the tenderest, and most sensible manner, with the quickest, and sharpest sense. Never was, never can there be such a sting, such a sense of any sting in the Spirit of Man, or Devil, or any Creature. Do we hear all this, and that all this was from love to us, and are we not by a sympathy of love wounded with a sense of those stings, which thus stuck in our Saviours Heart? Do we not feel our hearts wounded with a sense of those Sins of ours, which fixed those stings there? But doth not this sense also fall like drops of precious Balsom upon our Hearts to heal those wounds immediately, or to turn them into Fountains of Love, and Joy, when we hear, that it was Love, and infinite Love in the Heart of God himself, which took these stings out of our low, and wretched Persons, to fix them in that most High, and Glorious Person, which is Eternal Love, and Life itself? He was made Sin for us, that is, a Sacrifice for Sin in a flame of Wrath in our stead, that we might be made the Righteousness of God in him, to ascend in the Bosom of his glorified Person in a pure flame of Love, Delight, and Glory above all Heavens.

4. Propos. This our Jesus, as he at the same time with his Divine Nature in his Humanity, stood in a supernatural, and eternal Principle, he in his Humanity comprehended his Humanity itself in its natural Principle, toge-

ther with the natural Principle itself, the Curse, all the stings, and bitterness of the Curse in a Light of Divine Glory, in a Life of Divine Love, as so many varieties of pure Love, Joy, and Glory with immortality. Our Jesus, at the same time in his natural Principle, and in his Flesh was encompassed with a blackness of darkness, and was filled with the bitterness of the Curse; at the same time in his supernatural Principle, the Eternal Spirit, even in the natural Principle in the Flesh, in the midst of the darknesses, & bitternesses he saw them all, he conversed with them, he tasted them, feasted upon them, enjoyed them, and himself in them, as the Light, and Sweetness of Heavenly Love, as Roses, and Lillies, the Hony, and the Hony-comb in the Paradise of God, as the delicacies of Eternity, and a banquet of Wine in the Kingdom of God. For he received, he saw, he rellished them in the will of his Father, and the will of his Father in them. Thus he speaketh of them, when he cometh first into the World, *I come to do thy Will, O God.* All things, which he met with in the World, and in Flesh were to him the pure, and entire Will of God alone presenting itself in so many various Forms, where the Substance, and the Forms both were the same Will, like a Feast in several Dishes, where the Meat, and the Dishes too are alike delicate food. So Christ himself expressed it, *John* 4. It is my Meat, and Drink (a Divine Meat, and a Divine Drink) to do the Will of my Father. All the sufferings, and passions of Christ, were an active accomplishment; an active entertainment of the Will of the Father, of that Will, of that supream Will, which is the pure Fountain, Measure, Essence, perfection of all Good, Loveliness, Love, Sweetness, and Joy.

The sufferings of our Lord Jesus appeared to him in a Spiritual Light, as Heavenly Beauties cloathing his Person, making it so much the more lovely in the Eye of his Father the truest Judge of loveliness, and Beauty. *My Father loves me*, saith Jesus Christ, *because I lay down my Life for my Sheep.* How sweet, and dear a sense hath the Lord Jesus of the Curse, and of Death, when he had this sense of them, that they made him lovely to his Father, attracted his Fathers Heart to him, and made him more in love with him.

The blackest Cloud, that resteth upon Christ, discovered itself to his Spiritual Eye to be in truth a Glory surrounding him. All the griefs of his Heart appeared to be Jewels of Glory, and Immortality hanging in his Bosom. For, saith Christ, when he was now to suffer; now is the Son of Man Glorified; and again, he saith, the Father is Glorified in the Son. O! how different is the truth of things in the Spirit from the outward appearance in the Flesh? When Jesus Christ was spit upon, Scourged, Crucified, as this World gives, forms, and names of things, then in the sense, and language of Heaven of Eternity, of the Eternal, and Spiritual Principle in himself, he was glorified; all these were as so many fresh *Lights of Glory*, in which his Person shines forth to itself, and to the Father, in which the Fathers Person shines forth in his Person, as in a new Heaven with new, and increasing Beauties.

O you,

O you, that are Followers of Christ, what a mystery of Spiritual Joy, and Heavenly Glory is there in the life of a Saint, if this be to be a Saint, to walk on Earth, as Christ walked, that is, in a Spiritual Principle, in the midst of the Natural Principle, and Fleshly Image of things governing, comprehending, seeing, handling, rellishing all in the Divine Light, Beauty, and Sweetness of the Eternal Spirit? When the blackest Cloud of melancholy rests upon thy Spirit, when the sharpest Sword of Grief pierceth thy Heart, retire into thy Spiritual Principle, there thou shalt be, as on Mount *Tabor*, the Mount of Transfiguration, where the Face of thy God shall be as a pleasant Sun of Joy, and Glory shining forth in its strength within thee, and the whole Image of things in thee, and round about thee, as a Garment of Light all weaved, and wrought with the freshest, and purest Beams of this Sun in all living, and immortal Figures of the highest Joys, and Glories.

5. Propos. The Curse with the stings, and sense of it upon the Natural, and Temporary Principle, as also the conflict between the Natural, and Temporary; the Supernatural, and Eternal Principle in the Lord Jesus thorow his whole Person, as it lived in a Humane Soul, and Body, were highest at his Death. The Lord Jesus saith, the Prince of this World cometh: This is your hour, and the power, or principality of Darkness. The Devil came now to make his two last, and most furious assaults upon the Lord Jesus in the Garden, and upon the Cross. He therefore comes with all the powers of Darkness, and Legions of Devils, with all the blackest, and most dreadful Furniture, and force of Wrath from Hell below, from Earth, and Heaven above, as the Prince of this World, and the Prince of Darkness. The Battel was so sore against the Lord Jesus, that he himself, who was the Wisdom, and Power of God was amazed. He, who was the eternal delights of his Father day by day, cries out, *My Soul is very sorrowful even unto Death*; The word in Greek is περίλυπος which signifieth an excess of sorrow, and a surrounding sorrow. All things round about the Lord Jesus were hung with a blackness of Darkness, and amazing horrours, that he himself, who bears up the weight of all things, could hardly sustain the weight of his own fears, and sorrows, or sustain himself in Life under them. He falls beneath them to the ground. His whole Person is so prest, and opprest with them, that through the agony of his Spirits, the boiling blood is strained forth through all the parts of his Body. He cries to his Father thrice: Angels are sent from Heaven to strengthen him, and comfort him.

But after this, the conflict upon the Cross was yet sharper. Now the Prince of Darkness grows desperate, knowing that this is his last effort, and that now at once he fights for his Kingdom, Liberty, and Life, that his whole Kingdom of Darkness, and his Person too depend upon this one Fight. The Earth-quake, the rending of the Rocks, the total Eclipse of the Sun, and the Universal Darkness upon the face of the whole Earth were Types of what Christ the

Prince of Glory, and the Devil the Prince of Darkneſs ſuffered in this laſt Conflict; the like to which never was before, nor ſhall ever be. The whole frame of things ſhook, and trembled under the Feet of the Lord Jeſus, and round about him. The Rocks, all the ſupports of his Soul, all the Foundations, and Pillars of his ſtrength, and life were rent in pieces, and diſſolved. The face of the Creature, the face of Heaven, the face of his Father were all covered with a thick, a threatning, and an amazing Darkneſs, as in a dreadful Tempeſt above the courſe, and force of nature. The Lord of Life, in whom all things ſubſiſt, is now ſinking, and ready to give up all for loſt. How deeply was his Heart pierced, how cruelly wounded, how were every glympſe of Light, every drop of Comfort intercepted and with-held, when he cried out; *My God, my God, why haſt thou forſaken me?* What potent inchantment from Hell was this, what power of Darkneſs, what infuſion of Wrath, what ſeparation ten thouſand times more bitter than Death, which ſo wrought, that he, who is God himſelf, ſeems divided from himſelf, and totally deſerted by all the power, and ſweet lights of the God-Head?

Thus you ſee in this 5th Propoſition the trouble of Chriſt at its height: In the two following Propoſitions, you ſhall ſee, that notwithſtanding this dreadful ſtorm in the evening, and lateſt hour of his life, this beautiful Sun in his dying moment, as in the cloſe itſelf of the day; caſts up its cloud, comes forth Triumphantly, and no night follows.

Before we paſs to the other Propoſitions, let us make a few ſhort obſervations upon theſe.

1. See how dreadful, and hateful an evil Sin is by the effects of it in the Perſon of God himſelf, our Lord Jeſus. Let not that be a light thing to us, which lay with ſo great weight upon him, neither let us be ſecure in our Luſts, Vanities, Covetouſneſs, Sloath, playing with theſe, which were ſo many Serpents in the Boſom of Chriſt, and ſhot deadly ſtings into his Heart. Can we ſtand under thoſe things, which had almoſt ſunk the Son of God into deſpair, and Eternal Darkneſs? It is true God brings good out of the evil of Sin, order out of its diſorder, and reconciles all into a beautiful Harmony of Divine Love, and Joy. But how? by how dear a price? by how precious an atonement? by how coſtly, how cruel, how bloody a Sacrifice? by how violent a conflict between all the powers of light, and darkneſs at once? by how dreadful a diſſolution of the whole frame of things, with the blackeſt Tempeſt of Divine Wrath from above? by what horrours of Death in its uglieſt ſhape, with its moſt venemous ſtings; and all this in the Perſon of God himſelf, our Jeſus?

2. Be good Soldiers of the Lord Jeſus. Endure hardſhips. Endure the fight of Sufferings. Think not ſtrange to have the Clouds blackeſt, and the Storm greateſt with Thunders, and Lightnings round about you in your lateſt hour, in old age, and death. Thus you bear the Croſs of Chriſt. Thus

you fight under the Banner of Love. A Husband in Bloods art thou to me, saith the Wife of *Moses* to him, *concerning the Circumcision.* Jesus Christ hath been a Husband in Blood to thee, O suffering Saint. Now art thou also indeed a Sister, and a Spouse to him in Blood. This Life is the Season of suffering. Christ suffered here. Can you not suffer with Christ one hour, the short Season of this fleeting Life? Think how glorious in the Eyes of all the Holy Angels, and of the Blessed Saints of Christ, and the Father you shall come into Heaven? How dear to the Bosom, and Embraces of them all, when you come most covered with Dust, and Blood, when you come immediately out of the greatest sufferings; when you come so much the lovelier, by how much the liker you are to Christ; when Christ, and the Father have been so much the more glorified in you; when they in their Glories have so much the more clearly, eminently shined forth in your Persons, and rested upon them, by how much the more extream your sufferings have been? When the Father hath thus accomplished his will in you, what a Feast of Eternal Pleasures, what a Crown of Eternal Glories will he make this will of his to you, how will he accomplish your will in himself to the utmost height of all delights, & blessedness?

3. See here a threefold comfort against sufferings, and Death.

1. He, who hath conquered them is your Captain the Lord Jesus. We read *Heb.* 2. That the Captain of our Salvation, being to bring many Sons to Glory, was made perfect through Sufferings. There are four things in that word *Perfect.* 1. There was a perfection of sufferings in all kinds, and degrees. Nothing of any evil of sufferings in the evil of it was absent, or could be added. 2. Jesus Christ perfectly endured these sufferings in the sense of them, in the continuance under them, in pressures, and oppressions by them. 3. He was a perfect Conqueror over them. 4. To be made perfect, signifieth an initiation in Sufferings, as in Sacred, and Divine Mysteries. So Christ was at once in his Sufferings the Priest, the Altar, the Fire, the Sacrifice, the Temple, the God. This Jesus, thus a perfect, and a Divine Conqueror over all Sufferings, who holdeth all evil of Sin, and Sorrow, as Captives, in Chains of Eternal Goodness, pure Love, Light, and Joy, He leads you upon Sufferings; he goes before you into them; he turns them all into Holy, and Heavenly Mysteries of Divine Life, and Love, and makes you in the midst of them, as Priests, like *Aaron* in his Priestly Robes, and Ornaments, and Anointings in the Temple of the Eternal Spirit.

2. You, O Saints, have nothing to do in your greatest Sufferings, that you may be Conquerors over them, but to abide in the Lord Jesus. He himself in his dying discourses, thus comforts his Disciples in the Gospel of St. *John*; *In the World you shall have trouble, but in me you shall have peace, be of good chear, I have overcome the World.* Stand still, be stedfast, and unmoved in the Lord Jesus; so shall you never have any other sight of your Enemies, or Troubles, but such as the Children of *Israel* had on this side of the Red Sea,

 when

when they came forth with their Timbrels, and Dances. You ſhall ſee them drown'd in the Sea of your Saviours Blood, in a Sea of Glory in his Victory, never to appear more in any melancholy ſhape. When thine Enemies encompaſs thee on every ſide, like mighty Floods, with greateſt force and fury, lie down upon thy glorified Saviours Boſom, as the Bed of Love, have his high praiſes in thy mouth, ſing aloud of his Love, his Lovelineſs, his Victory in his Death, his Reſurrection, and return in the Spirit. So ſhalt thou ſee all the powers of Darkneſs, Death, and Hell under thy Feet, bound in Golden Chains of Love, Immortality, and Glory.

3. Look forth now with a Spiritual Eye, and ſee, that Sufferings, and Death are a name only, and empty ſhadows without any ſubſtance. The things themſelves are for ever deſtroyed by the Death of Chriſt, and buryed in his Grave, never to riſe more. A good Woman, a Martyr, being reproved for going with joy to the Fire, when Chriſt was ſad at the approach of Death, anſwered ; *My Saviour was ſad, that I might be joyful.* Sufferings, and Death are now to Saints, like Snakes, out of whom the Lord Jeſus hath taken the Sting, that we may take them into our Boſoms, and make them our ſoft, and ſhining Play-fellows. They are become now in the Blood, and Spirit of Chriſt like Vipers in Wine, which have loſt their Poyſon, and are high Cordials ; like Bees they have ſhot their ſtings into the Lord Jeſus, and loſt them there. They have Hony now without any ſting for thee to ſuck forth, and feed upon.

6. Propoſ. This Eternal Perſon, our Jeſus with his God-Head in his whole Humanity both Soul, and Body in the moment of Death by dying, went entirely forth from the Natural, or Temporary Principle, and ſo from under the Curſe. I ſhall open this by four Scriptures.

1. Scrip. *Heb.* 10. 19, 20. The Lord Jeſus is ſaid to have conſecrated a new, and living way for us to enter into the holieſt through the Vail, that is, his Fleſh, *Math.* 27. 50, 51. You ſhall ſee, that as Jeſus Chriſt yielded up the Ghoſt, immediately the Vail of the Temple was rent in twain from the top to the bottom. The Temple was a Figure of the Perſon of Chriſt, as the Vail was of this Fleſh. How particularly, and emphatically is it expreſſed, that the Vail was rent from the top to the bottom, to its utmoſt extent in the Perſon of Chriſt? The Fleſh was as a Vail lying upon the Divine Beauties upon the Eternal Perſon, and the Heavenly Image in the Soul, & Body of Chriſt. The Fleſh of Chriſt was a dividing Vail, ſeparating between the Lord Jeſus, & the naked Beauties, the naked Boſom of his Father keeping his Soul, and Body, his bleſſed Perſon, and Divine Nature, as they ſubſiſted in his Soul, and Body out of the holieſt, out of the pure, and open Glories of the God-Head. As the Lord Jeſus dies, in that ſame moment this Vail is rent from the top to the bottom, from the the higheſt part of his Soul, and Spirit to the loweſt part, and appearance in the Body. Now the Holieſt, the Heavenly Image, the pure, and naked Glories

ies of the Eternal Perſon, of the God-Head were opened, and diſcovered horow his whole Soul, and Body. His Soul, and Body both entered into the Ioliest, into this Heavenly Image, into theſe pure Glories in the unity of the ternal Spirit.

2. Scrip. *John* 19. 30. When the Lord Jeſus was now breathing his iſt, he formed his laſt breath into theſe words, *it is finiſhed.* As he ſpake thoſe ords, he bowed his Head, and gave up the Ghoſt. What was that, which as finiſhed with the life of Chriſt? Not the work of our redemption. Ma y great, and principal parts of that remained ſtill behind, the Reſurrection the Lord Jeſus, his Aſcenſion, his Interceſſion, his return in the Spirit at e pouring forth of that his laſt Appearance, his Judgment, and Kingdom. hat then was that which was finiſhed with the finiſhing of the life of hriſt? The days of his abode in the Fleſh without the Vail; his Humiliation, s Sufferings, the State of Nature, the Curſe, the Wrath of the Father ere now finiſhed; the Spirit, and Image of this world, the hour, and power f Darkneſs, the bloody Fight with the Prince of Darkneſs, the Prince of is World were now at an end, as the life of Chriſt ended.

O you, who are followers of Chriſt, and predeſtinated to be conformed to m in your Lives, and in your Deaths; meet Death with Joy, with the ſhout thoſe, who cry out for victory. Now is your Warfare accompliſhed; now your Captivity in the Fleſhly Spirit, and Image at an end. You ſhall dwell w no more in *Meſhek*, at a diſtance from the Divine Glory, nor ſojourn in Tents of *Kedar*, in the Land of Darkneſs. The Vail of the Fleſh is now t from the top to the bottom thorow your whole Soul, and Body. In both, you ſeem to fleſhly ſenſes to enter into the ſhade of Death, you in that mo nt enter into the Kingdom of Light, the Glorious Pallace of your Fa r, the Divine Beauties, and Joys of the Heavenly Image. You have now ght the good Fight, and finiſhed it. Henceforth from this moment it is, t the Crown of Righteouſneſs, the Crown of Life, and Immortality hath n laid up for you to be ſet upon your Heads, and worn by you, which d ſhall now give you from his own preſence, from his own hand, in this of Glory, which now breaketh, and riſeth upon you.

3. Scrip. *Coloſ.* 2. 15. The Apoſtle ſpeaking of Chriſt ſaith thus; and ing ſpoiled Principalities, and Powers, he made a ſhow of them openly, triumphed over them in it, that is, his Croſs, which was mentioned in the er end of the foregoing verſe.

There are three parts in this Scripture, which is a glorious deſcription of Victory of our Lord Jeſus. 1. The Subject of his Victory. 2. The Victo tſelf. 3. The Seat of his Victory.

. The Subject of Chriſts Victory are Principalities, and Powers. The word ἀρχαὶ ſignifieth Principles. The ſecond word ἐξουσίαι, ſignifieth Do ions, Principalities, and a power of ruling. By theſe names the Angels

are

are expressed, as they are the Invisible Springs, out of which all visible things continually flow; as they are the Supream Glories, Virtues, Powers, among things created, to which this present world is subjected, by which it is enlivened, enlightned, formed, acted, and ruled. Thus the Victory of Christ extendeth itself over the whole Creation, the whole frame of Nature in its Heavenly, Angelical, and unseen part; in that which is Earthly, and visible; in the Fountain-Glories, and flowing Streams; in the Princes on high, and their Principalities beneath.

2. The Victory itself is exprest in three steps. 1. The Spoil. 2. The Show. 3. The Triumph.

1. The Spoil. He spoiled Principalities, and Powers. The word signifieth to uncloath. The Lord Jesus, as a conquering Prince, uncloathed the Invisible Princes of this World of all Power, Principality, and Appearance, by which means the whole Creation, and the frame of Nature, which stood by these Powers, in these Appearances, according to their first, and natural State, were dissolved, fell into the depths of Darkness, and confusion, disappearing for ever.

2. The Show. Our Victorious Saviour brought forth all the Principles, Powers, and Appearances of Nature, into the open light of the Eternal Spirit. There he led them as Captives through the Streets of the Heavenly *Jerusalem*, showing them, as the subjects, and marks of his Victory to all the Innumerable, and Glorious Inhabitants of that Blessed City of the great King.

3. The Triumph. He Triumphed over them. All natural Powers, Glories, Lives, and Images lay beneath the Feet of the Lord Jesus, as his Footstool, while he sat down upon a Throne of Glory, cloathed all over with Garments of Glory, and wearing a Crown of Glory upon his Head. These are the three Parts of Christs Victory.

3. The Seat of Christs Victory was his Cross. He Triumphed on it. Hear this all ye, that are one Seed, one Spirit with the Lord Jesus, that are made conformable to his Death in your Lives, and Deaths. Hear this; let it be written upon your Hearts in Characters of Glory with a living Beam from that bright Sun, the Face of our Lord Jesus, as he shines in the Eternal Glory of his most Blessed Victory, and Triumph. It was upon his Cross, it was upon his Cross, that the Lord Jesus spoiled, made a Show of, Triumphed over the Principalities, and Powers of this World.

Our Blessed Saviour, in dying, by dying, in that very moment, by that very act, dissolves, and defaceth at once the whole frame of Nature, and of the first Creation. He taketh away from it all Power of being, subsisting, acting, or appearing. He blotteth out every natural Image, and form of Light, or Darkness; Life or Death, Beauty, or Deformity; Shame, or Glory; Grief, or Joy for ever. You have this excellently painted out in a clear Prophesy, *Psalm.* 73. 20. *As a Dream, when one awaketh; O Lord, when thou*

thou awakest, thou shalt despise their Image. The word Image signifieth a Shadow. The Eternal Word, the Heavenly Image, our Lord Jesus was in this Creation, as under the Vail of Darkness, and Night; as in a sleep. He bringeth forth, and beareth up all the Powers, and Forms of Nature, as a Dream in this sleep, and as shadowy Images in this Dream. By dying he awakes out of this sleep, he sets an end to this Dream. The whole frame of Nature with all Forms, and Images of things within the vast compass of it either Visible, or Invisible, break up, fly away, and vanish, as a Dream, as the shadowy Images in a Dream, when a Man awaketh.

But neither are they quite lost. They only change their Principle, and Appearance. In the same dying moment doth the Lord Jesus, who is that Eternal, and Essential Image, in whom they all subsist, appear, and pass thorow their several changes, carry them with himself into the Divine Light, and Life of the Eternal Spirit. There are they seen again, as the Fruits of his Conquest, spoiled of all their own Life, Light, and Form, having put on a new Life, Light, and Form according to the Will of the Conqueror, to show forth his Power and Glory, to make them pleasant, and Eternal Spectacles of his Divine Triumph to all the Inhabitants of Heaven, and Eternity.

Now, before he is taken down from the Cross, even upon the Cross it self, the Lord Jesus, as he gives up his Spirit with his last breath, Triumphs in his Soul, and Body too, whose proper Seat the Cross was: In both, cloathed with Triumphal Robes of an immortal Beauty, and Blessedness, he rides forth in the Glorious Chariot of the Heavenly Image, and of the Eternal Spirit. All the Powers, and Forms of Nature, of Life, and Death, the Cross it self, and the Crucifiers, as Captives follow his Chariot, bound in the Golden Chains of Divine Light, and Love, making up the delight, and Glory of his Triumph.

This also doth the *Psalmist* clearly Prophesy of, *Psal.* 68. 18. *Thou hast ascended up on high, thou hast led Captivity Captive.* The descent of our Lord Jesus was finished with his Life. He begins his ascent upon his Cross the first moment of his Death. This World, with all its Powers, and Principalities, the life of this World, the Cross it self, and Death, which had so long captivated the Lord Jesus with all the Powers, Beauties, Joys, and Glories of his Heavenly Image, binding them in Chains of Darkness within the Dungeon of his Earthly Image, whose light is darkness, are now themselves in the Person of our Lord Jesus, in his Soul, and Body, together with his Captivity it self, carryed up, as he ascends, and made Captives to that Heavenly Image, which they held Captive. Here, in this Pallace of the Spirit, and of Eternity, where Darkness it self shines, as the Light, they are seen, as the Captives of the Lord Jesus, bound in Chains of Glory, spectacles to all the Holy Angels, and Blessed Spirits, in which the Beauties of Christs Victory, and Triumph, as so many ravishing Wonders of an Incomprehensible, of a Mysteri-

ous

ous Power, Wisdom, Love, Glory, Divinity, subduing all things entirely to themselves, eternally shine.

This honour have all the Saints in their Deaths, by the vertue of their Saviours Death, by vertue of their fellowship with him, and his fellowship with them mutually in their several Deaths, all in each Death dying together. Where now is the Melancholy of Death, and of the Grave? It is swallowed up into the Divine Pomp, and Pleasure of a most Glorious Victory, and Triumph. O Saint! What fearest thou in Death? Or thou, who fearest not to be dead why fearest thou to die? If thou rejoicest in the Glory of thy departed Soul, why mournest thou over thy Body, as left behind in a naked, and loathsome Prison? The act of dying to both is the gaining of a Glorious Victory over the Life, and Death; the Powers, and Principalities of this whole World. The passage itself out of this *Life is a Glorious Triumph to* thy Soul, and Body both, which, with all the Triumphal Ornaments of the *Light of Life, and Immortality, ride forth in the* Chariot of the Heavenly Image, and the Eternal Spirit over the Spirit, and all the forms of this Creation, which lie conquered under your Feet.

In the very moment of your dying, all the Powers, and Appearances of Nature, which rule in the Kingdoms of Sense, and Reason, are lost for ever; so that their place, where once they reigned in your Persons, knows them no more. You sit down upon the Throne of Christ, and the Father together with them. All the Births, Images, and changes of time are swallowed up into the bright, the beautiful, the most delightful depths of Eternity, the unfathomable depths of purest Light, Love, and Joy immediately; as Triumphant Conquerors, and Kings, you are encompassed with the ravishing applauses, and shouts of innumerable Angels, of Immortal, and Glorious Spirits, springing up, and shining forth in all the places of this World, where its Light, or Darkness Life, or Death seemed before to stand. You see all these with a Heavenly Musick, and Songs of Triumph, setting Garlands, and Crowns of Victory on your Heads immediately, as you pass out of the Light of this Life, you see your selves received, your Souls, and your Bodies both, with the most delicious kisses into the Eternal Embraces of the Father, and of Christ, in that Unity of the Spirit, which is the unfathomable center of all Lights, Loves, and Joys, of all beautiful, and blissful Spirits created, and uncreated. All now for ever are filling full your Joys in themselves, and fulfilling their Joys in you.

4. Scrip. *Heb.* 2. 14. That he by dying might destroy him, who had the power of Death, that is, the Devil, and set them free, who all their life time were subject to bondage by the fear of Death. The word Power, in this place signifieth properly a Prince with a Principality, or Dominion. This whole world is the Principality of the Devil. For the Devil is called in Scripture the Prince of this world. All Flesh, every thing of Nature, and of

this

this Creation is comprehended under that name, as it is distinguished from, and opposed to the Spirit, and the new Creation in the Spirit, the Kingdom of God in the Holy Ghost, and is the Principality of the Devil. All Darkness every shadow, every evil of Sin, or Suffering; of Corruption, and the Curse; of Shame, Deformity, Pain, Grief, and Wrath, as all these are expressed in the Scripture, and in common Language, with every other kind, or degree of Evil, by Darkness, are the Principality of the Devil. For the Devil is called the Prince of Darkness. Death is the Devils Principality, who in this Scripture is called the Power, or Prince of Death. All this then hath Jesus Christ by dying destroyed in his own Person, this World; the Principles, and Forms of Nature; the Life, and Images of Flesh; every Darkness inward, or outward, of mind, or sense; Death itself. For all these lie within the Principality of the Devil, and are his Region, his Kingdom; without the bounds of this Dominion all things are Light, Life, Love, Joy, Immortality, Spirit, and Truth.

As it is Jesus, who dies again in the Death of every Saint; as the Death of every Saint is the Death of Christ acted over again in the similitude, by the vertue of his Death: so doth every Saint, as he is one Spirit with Christ, after the like manner, by dying destroy the Principality, the Kingdom of the Devil in his Person also. For this is said to be the end of Christ in his Death, that he might free all the Saints from the fear of Death. O Believers! Let your Saviour gain his end upon you, an end of most tender Love. Be no more in bondage to the fear of Death. Let the Lord Jesus see the seed of his Death springing up in your Deaths, a Glorious, and Divine Seed of Life, and Immortality springing up in the place of Death, and swallowing it up into Victory. Lay aside now for ever those melancholy, and delusive Imaginations of Death, as a separation of those tenderest Bosom-Friends, Soul, and Body; a separation from your dearest Relations, and entertainments, the delights of your Eyes; an extinguishing of the sweet Light of Life; a dismal solitude, a perpetual Darkness; the Confinement of the Body to the nakedness, coldness, streightness, and horrour of the Grave; Dust, Stones, and Bones covering it, and ratling over it; Worms feeding upon it; the Soul naked, and alone taking its flight through a vast distance of empty air, and space to another place. These are the Forms, and Appearances of Death to the Dead only. Those, who follow Jesus Christ in that living, and shining way, in which he went thorow Death, meet with none of these appalling, and affrightful Apparitions. *Let the Dead bury their Dead*, saith Jesus Christ to his Disciples, *but follow thou me.*

Understand this, O Believers, that all Shadows, all Forms of Darkness, and of Death are from below, Earthly, Sensual, Devilish, from the Earth, from the Natural Soul, and from the Devil, as St. *James* speaks. All this Image, and sense of things is that Kingdom of the Devil, which together with the

King himſelf, which the Lord Jeſus by dying, in himſelf, in thee, hath everlaſtingly deſtroyed in his own Perſon, in his own Death, and in thine by the vertue of his own. As an Inchantment, ſo is this whole Frame, and Form of things diſſolved, ſo doth it vaniſh at the going forth of thy laſt breath. If thou ſeek now for the region of Shadows, and the Land of Darkneſs thou findeſt it no more for ever, as he that would ſeek for the Night, the Nightly Shades, and Forms of things when the Sun is once riſen. Let thy Soul, and Body both then rejoice together, and reſt in this aſſurance, that in their departure out of this Life, in the paſſage of Death they ſhall meet with nothing of loſs, nothing uncouth, nothing unpleaſant, nothing of Darkneſs, of Diviſion, of Death, of the Devil; but the moſt beautiful, and bleſſed Face, the moſt dear, and delightful Embraces of the Lord Jeſus, as a Glorious Lover, as a Heavenly Bridegroom immediately preſenting himſelf, immediately receiving them. In the ſame moment do all things here diſappear, and all things appear again, as they are reconciled into a moſt raviſhing Harmony of Divine Beauty, and Love: As they are gathered up into their Head, into their firſt Glory, their Eternal Unity in the Glorified Perſon of Chriſt.

7. Propoſ. This ſame Jeſus in his whole Perſon, with his whole Soul, and Body, in the moment of Death, by dying went forth entirely into the ſimplicity, and ſingleneſs of his Supernatural, and Eternal Principle, and ſo into a State of pure Eternity, unmixt Joy, and Glory.

I ſhall endeavour to explain, and confirm this Propoſition by the fuller opening of a Scripture, which I have often touched.

Pſalm. 16. 9, 10. 11. Thus we read: *Therefore my heart is glad, my Glory rejoiceth, my Fleſh alſo ſhall reſt in hope. For thou wilt not leave my Soul in Hell; neither wilt thou ſuffer thy Holy One to ſee corruption. Thou wilt ſhew me the path of Life; in thy preſence is the fulneſs of Joy, at thy Right Hand are Pleaſures for evermore.* This is a Propheſy of Chriſt in his Death. *David*, as a Prophet, ſpeaketh concerning Chriſt, and in the Perſon of Chriſt. So St. *Peter* interpreteth, and applieth this Scripture. *Acts* 2. 25.

This then is the Triumph of Chriſt in Death, over Death, which Triumph conſiſteth of four Parts. 1. The Subject. 2. The Triumph. 3. The Ground. 4. The manner of the Triumph.

1. The Subject of Chriſts Triumph. This is threefold. 1. The Soul. 2. The Glory. 3. The Fleſh of the Lord Jeſus.

1. The Soul. This ſeemeth to be that unſeen, and principal part of the Natural Man, which in our common language is oppoſed to the Body, as the Viſible and inferiour part.

2. The Glory hath a twofold acception. *Davids* Harp, and his Tongue, were his Glory upon two accounts; both, as he was a ſweet Singer, a moſt skilful Muſitian; and alſo as he was the ſweet Singer of *Iſrael*, as his Harp, and Tongue recorded the Praiſes of God, and made all things

round

round about him to resound the perfections and loves of the Lord Jesus. Thus the Tongue of Christ was his Glory, as he is the sweet Preacher in *Jerusalem*, the Heavenly Interpreter, one of a thousand, who sheweth to Man his Righteousness, and his rest. But again this Glory in *David* was the Spiritual Man, the birth of the Spirit, the Seed of God, the Life of Christ, Christ in *David*. This Glory in Christ was the Spiritual Man, the Heavenly Image, the Divine Nature, the God-Head. For so *Heb.* 1. 1. Jesus Christ is said to be the brightness of the Glory of God, as he is the express Image of his Person, and Substance.

3. The Flesh of Christ is his Body, as it is distinguished from the Soul, and is covered with a Vail of Flesh, under which Vail it contains within it-self those other two, the Soul, and the Glory. This is the threefold Subject of the Triumph; the Natural Body, the Natural Soul, the Eternal Spirit, as it inhabiteth in these.

2. The Triumph itself is exprest in those four words; Gladness, Joy, Rest, and Hope. Gladness is the same with Joy. The State of Blessedness in Heaven, and Eternity is expressed by Joy. The Lord Jesus saith to the Good, and Faithful Servant; *Enter thou into thy Masters Joy*. St. *Peter* calls the Blessedness which we have here in believing, and loving the Lord Jesus, which is Heaven upon Earth; a Joy Glorious, and unspeakable. As our Lord Jesus dyed, the Humane Soul of Christ before imprisoned in a Fleshly Body, went forth to be comprehended, and swallowed up in that Joy, which it could not take in, nor comprehend, because it was boundless, and infinite. His Divine Nature, which in this Humane Soul, together with it, had been vailed by an Earthly Body now breaks forth and shines out into the freedom, and full liberty of its own unconfined delights, and unvailed Glories. My Soul, saith Christ, is glad, and my Glory rejoiceth.

The Triumph of Christ in his Body, and his Flesh is set forth by Rest, and Hope. which two words import Life, Sense, a Sweetness, and fulness of Life, and Sense with Immortality.

The Sabbath in the beginning of the Creation, as it figureth the perfection of a Sanctified, and blessed State in Christ, and in Heaven, is expressed by Rest, the name Sabbath signifieth Rest.

The Land of *Canaan*, as it was a Land of Rivers, and Springs, and floods of Water; as it was a Land flowing with Milk, and Hony, and so a Type of that good Land, that flourishing Land of the Spirit, and of Eternity, where the Fountains, and full floods are of all Divine Goodness, and Truth, is expressed by Rest. *Joshua*, who gave the Land of *Canaan* to the *Jews*, is said to give them Rest.

That perfect Cessation from all trouble, that perfect Consummation of our Happiness in the quieting of all our desires by the full accomplishment of them, that terminating of all our motions to good in their most wished for end, the chief good, which the Lord Jeſus, which the Goſpel, which Faith bringeth us to in an immediate, entire, eternal Union with God; all this the Holy Ghoſt expreſſeth by Reſt. *Come to me, and I will give you Reſt*, ſaith the Lord Jeſus. *He that believeth, entereth into Reſt*, ſaith the Epiſtle to the *Hebrews*. Thus the Body, and Fleſh of Chriſt reſt in Death. Theſe are the words, as he dies, in his Song of Death; *My Fleſh alſo doth reſt in hope.*

The Hebrew word for Hope, ſignifieth two things, Confidence, and Hope.

Confidence implies a double certainty. 1. A certainty in the object, which is the good in proſpect, or in poſſeſſion; hoped for, or already enjoyed. 2. The certainty of the Subject, which is a ſweet, a deep, a clear Senſe, and Seal upon the Soul of the certainty of the object, of the certainty of that Good, which it hath in fruition, or expectation. This twofold Certainty maketh that confidence, or aſſurance which compleateth, or crowneth the Souls Reſt.

In this confidence doth the Fleſh of the Lord Jeſus reſt in Death. It hath no more for ever any Conflicts, or Allarms. It is overſpread with a ſweet, and clear Heaven. It breaths in a gentle, and delicious air, where there is no ſtorm, no rain, nor cloud. It is in a State of immutable joys, where there is no Death, no Shadow of Death, no trouble, no tear, no ſhadow of fear, or any ſuch thing. All things ſing an eternal *requiem*, and reſt to it.

As the Fleſh of the Lord Jeſus reſteth in Confidence; ſo it reſteth alſo in Hope. Hope is good in proſpect, or in progreſs, At our firſt converſion the Eternal day breaketh upon us. While we live on Earth in a State of Grace we have ſweet, and clear ſtreaks of the Light of Life appearing thorow our Spirits, which ſtill grow clearer, and brighter unto a perfect day. But all this while there are dark, and black ſhades of the Night, Sins, and Sufferings every where mingled with the pure Light of this bleſſed Day. At Death it is perfect Day. The ſhadows of the Night are perfectly drunk up into the riſing Light, that now they appear no more in dark Forms, but are ſeen only, as by a lovely temperature with the Light, they make beautiful, and pleaſant colours of Saffron, and of Roſes. In the Reſurrection the body of the Sun, the Eternal Sun, the Lord Jeſus, in the Glory of his God-Head ariſeth upon Soul, and Body both, and is nakedly ſeen, nakedly enjoyed, without the Vail of any dark, and nightly ſhade, or any Floury, Spicy, or morning ſhade. From the Reſurrection to the utmoſt point of the aſcention, this Divine Sun is riſing higher, and higher in Glory upon us, till he comes to that Noon-ſted of Eternity, and of the God-Head, where there is no more any aſcent, or deſcent, where the Unity is entire, where God is one, and that one God is all in all. In the Confidence, and full aſſurance of this Hope doth the Fleſh of our dying Saviour, and of every dying Saint reſt.

Object. But you may ſay, we have formerly ſeemed to affirm according to the Language of the Scripture, that the days of Chriſt on Earth before his Death, were alone the days of his Fleſh; that the Fleſh of Chriſt was a Vail

upon

upon his Body, which was rent in Death; that it was not the substance of his Body, nor its true, proper, and natural Form; but a darkning, and dividing Form, in which the *Body* of Christ appeared, and with which it was cloathed in the State of fallen Nature, in the *State* of his Humiliation, in his Earthly State. This State ended, this Form was put off in Death. How then had the Flesh of Christ a part in his Triumph? How did the Flesh of Christ rest in Hope?

Ans. In a Garden of Flowers by night, the Flowers are seen in dusky, and dark Forms, while the shades of the night lie upon them, as Vails upon their Beauties. When the bright day riseth upon this Garden, the Flowers appear in their naked, and shining Beauties, in their proper and lovely Figures; their dark appearances, together with their darkning vails the shades of the night, are drunk up, and transformed into the brightness of the Rosy morning. The Body of the Lord Jesus, and of all his holy Ones, are the immortal Flowers, Flowers of the Heavenly Paradise. Their Fleshly Form is the shadow of the night upon them, their dim, and dusky appearance thorow this Shadow. Death s the lovely, and rosy Morning of the Eternal Day rising upon them. The Spirit of Glory, and of God is the brightness of this Day. The Flesh is now changed into Spirit, the dusky appearance thorow the Vail of Flesh into a spiritual, and Heavenly brightness. In this brightness these bodies, of which ve spake, shine forth in their naked, native shapes, and Beauties, from all arts they shed a Divine Lustre, they breath a pure sweetness of Divine Joys, ke the Flowers of the Spring in a fair morning. Thus the Flesh of Christ esteth in Death.

3. The ground of this Triumph is the inseparable union between the God-Head, and the whole Humanity of Christ living, or dying, These are e words of the Lord Jesus by his Spirit in the mouth of *David*: *Thou ilt not leave my Soul in Hell.* Expositors agree, that the word Hell signifi h not a place of torments according to the common acception, but the ate of Soul, and Body in Death. The Greek word, by which it is rende d in the New Testament is ᾅδης, which by its notation signifieth the State of ings Invisible, or the Invisible State of things.

It is also well known that the Soul in the language of the Old Testament not used to express only one part of a Man, but the whole Person.

It is a Maxim in Divinity laid down by all learned, and holy Men, that hen the Natural Union between the Soul, and Body of our Lord Jesus cea- d in Death, the Supernatural, and Hypostatical, or Personal Union between e Divine, or Humane Nature in both parts of it remained inviolable, and tire. Thus it is frequently said, that although the Soul of Christ was sepa- ed from his Body in the Grave, yet the God-Head was never separated m either. O sweet and sure truth! A Spring of Holy, Heavenly, and Im- rtal Joys in Life, and in Death. This Truth rightly understood is a bles-

sed

sed Light, which discovereth to us a Divinity in our Life here, Immortality in Death, and Heaven in the Grave. This Divine Truth is the rich ground of our dear Saviours Glorious Triumph over Death in Death.

There was a twofold band of Union between the Soul, and Body of Christ while he lived in Flesh, one Natural, the other Supernatural.

1. The Natural Union was that composition of Soul, and Body, by which he became a Natural Man, and had the true Forms, Substance, and Essence of a Man, sprung from the first *Adam*. This band of union was broken in Death, by which means the Natural Man now was no more for ever according to its Natural State, and Principle, but vanished like a shadow, breaking up into the Light of a Spiritual Glory.

2. The Supernatural Union is that of the second Person in the Trinity, which is the Eternal God; who at the Incarnation of Christ made himself Flesh, that is, a compleat Man, himself subsisting, as the single, and undivided Person in this Man, in both parts of this Man, in Soul, and in Body, giving in like manner a personal subsistence to them in himself, that the Divinity, and the Humanity in its Soul, and in its Body both were all one simple individual, indivisible Person. This is that, which Divines call the Hypostatical, or Personal Union in Christ, which remained firm, and altogether unimpaired in Death itself.

See now the beautiful, and delightful consequences of this Union. The Soul, and Body of Christ continued immediately, intimately, sweetly, triumphantly united upon the Cross, in the Grave, were both one Immortal, Glorious Person, by the Heavenly, and Personal Union in, and with the Eternal Word. Soul, and Body were separated in respect to their Natural Union, and Composition. All the Relations, and Delights of both; all the precious Treasures, all the clear Images, and Lights of Life with the sweet life itself vanished, and fled away, so far as they were founded upon the Natural Union, the band being broken, which tyed them all together in one, at the dissolution of this Union. But all these still dwelt together undivided, still possessed, and enjoyed one another after the most intimate manner without allay, or interruption in the Unexpressible, and Glorious Unity of the Eternal Word the Second Person in the Trinity. This Unity was a Divine Band, an undivided Center, a living Spring, an unfathomable depth of Loves, and Glories, where they lay perpetually enfolded in the warm embraces each of other, covered with all the sweetest Lights, and Beauties even upon the bitter Cross, and in the cold Grave never to be divorced from each other. Separation itself was here only a various, and delightful form of embracing in the Unity of this Eternal Person.

4. In the fourth, and last place follows the manner of the Triumph. This hath three parts.

1. The Triumph over Corruption, exprest in these words; *Thou shalt not suffer thy holy One to see Corruption.*

2. The

2. The Triumph of Life, *Thou wilt shew me the path of Life.*

3, A Triumph in the Pleasures of Life, *In thy Presence is fulness of Joy, at thy Right Hand Pleasures for evermore.*

1. The first part in the manner of the Triumph is the Triumph over Corruption. *Thou wilt not suffer thy Holy One to see Corruption.* The Triumphant Person here is the holy one of God, the holy Son of God, the pure Seed, Birth, and Image of God, Jesus Christ in his Divine, and Humane Nature, as he is in both the Holy One of God, the Holy Birth, and Son of God, Jesus Christ in himself; Jesus Christ in *David, David* in Jesus Christ, Jesus Christ in the Holy Soul, and Holy Body of every Member of Christ, as they are the Spiritual Births, and Spiritual Temples of the Holy Spirit. This is the Person, which Triumphs in Death.

That which he Triumphs over is Corruption. There is a complication of four Evils in Corruption. 1. Division, or Dissolution, which is the chief, and the Root of the other Evils. 2. Darkness increasing. 3. Deformity overspreading. 4. Decay, which is a tendency to a destruction of Being, or to a contrariety in Being, to all the good of Being. Over all these Evils of Corruption Jesus Christ Triumpheth, as he dyeth.

1. Jesus Christ Triumpheth over Division, or Dissolution in Death. The Eternal Unity of his Divine Person was at once, as a Root, and a Band to both his Natures, to both parts of his Humane Nature, to all the Powers, and parts of his Soul, and Body, to the several Elements in his Body, to all Perfections of Glory, Grace, and Nature in all Powers, and Parts of the Humane Soul, and Body. All were, as an Immortal Nosegay, or a Mysterious Knot of Divine Flowers ever inseparably united in this Band, ever unfadingly flourishing in this Root of the Hypostatical Union, or the Divine Unity of the Eternal Person, which was indissoluble in Death itself. Yea those Separations, which are Natural, and necessary in Death, were themselves Flowers of the Heavenly, and Earthly Paradise bound up with this Heavenly Band in this ever-fair, ever-fragrant Nosegay.

2. JesusChrist dying, Triumpheth over the gloomy horrours of the increasing darkness, which ariseth from the hateful Womb of Darkness in the dreaded vaults of Death. The Divine Nature, which is inseparable from the Humane Nature, the Personal Unity, which is really, and substantially one with the Divine Nature, which gives a subsistence in itself to the Humane Nature, and makes it in its Personal subsistence one with the Divine; this is a brightness of Glory shining in the Grave, this is a Golden Candlestick, in which all the seven Lamps of God burn continually by day, and by night before the Throne of God, and make the vaults of Death themselves a Temple of Gold, and Christal filled with the sweet Beams of the Heavenly, Eternal Sun. All things, even Death, and the darkness of Death are as precious Stones set together in the rich Jewel of this Person, or Hypostatical Union,

where

where no one Stone contracts the least degree of dimness, but all in the midnight of Death itself ever sparkle with the sweetest, and clearest water of Eternal Life.

3. The deformity of Death, as it springs up out of the Corruption in Death, is the subject of our dying, and dead Saviours Triumph. The Heavenly Image of the God-Head, which is the supream Beauty the Arche-type, and first Pattern of all Beauties upon the Mount of Eternity, is the Person of Christ, in which the Divine, and Humane Nature with all its changes of Life, and Death stand, and subsist together. Can any thing be deformed in Beauty itself? Can any thing be Unlovely, where the highest, and purest Loveliness shines thorow all, and over all? What must the Harmony, what must the amiableness, and agreeableness be; how exact, and ravishing, as in Heaven itself there, where the Supream Unity, the most Sacred Unity of one of the most blessed Persons in the All-glorious Trinity, diffuseth itself thorow all the *variety* of things, Divine, and Humane, of Soul, and of Body, binding up all by itself immediately into the most perfect, and Divine Order, and gathering up all into one most perfect, and Divine Person in itself? How High, and Glorious is the Triumph of Divine Beauty over the deformity of Death, when thus the Eternal Beauty itself dies, dressing itself up in the Forms of Death, and giving to Death its own most lovely Face, which enflames the highest Angels, and God himself with Eternal, and Infinite Loves? In the place of Deformity, what potent, what attractive charms of Loveliness hath this Death to ravish Souls into the bosom of it, which are thus to die by a Fellowship with the Lord Jesus, as he dies?

4. The last Evil in the Corruption of Death is the decay, which is a Tendency to a Nothingness, a Privation, the destruction of the being of things, or to a contrariety to all good in Being. This is that dark Cave, that bottomless Pit, out of which, like the smoak of Hell, like gastly, black, and flaming apparitions from Hell, the deepest, and darkest Melancholy, the most dismal Horrours, and the most horrid Imaginations from the sense, and fear of Death issue forth, and cover the face of the Soul, as pitchy, and stormy Clouds cover the Face of Heaven. How does the dying Soul dread to be cast forth into the uttermost Darkness to be dispossest of itself together with all things? To be endlesly sinking in an abyss, or bottomless deep of a vast emptiness, and a cheerless, formless shade? to be no more? or to be in the midst of all the wounds, and torments that Being is capable of? to be consuming so, as ever to wish it as the only medicine of ones evil, and ever to fear it, as the greatest of all Evils, as the most incomprehensible Evil, to be no more?

How sweet, and delightful was the Triumph of our *Lord Jesus* over this Monster, which stands with so grim, and frightful a look in the Gate of Death? O Corruption! O Decay! O Destructions! where is your Victory? Jesus Christ comes into the empty, and obscure shades of Death with the fulness

of

of the Godhead with all the Lights of the Divine Nature, of Angelical, and created Glories, of Heaven, and Eternity, with their full splendours shining together all at once in the Unity of his Divine Person. This Person, which is the Fulness, that filleth all in all, which is the Brightness that shineth eternally in the Divine Essence, now filleth the whole space of Death, now enlighteneth it thorough-out, now becometh the stage, and Scene of Death, supporting it on his delicious Bosom, bounding it with his bright, and blissful Beams. Where is the emptiness, where is the shade, where is the bottomless Pit of Dread, & decay in Death? They are all swallowed up into shining, full, & substantial Glorys in this Triumph of our Saviour over Death. These are the Evils of Corruption in Death, over which Christ triumphs.

See now the height of this Triumph. *Thou wilt not suffer thy Holy One to see Corruption.* Jesus Christ passeth so triumphantly through the Regions of Death, that Corruption loseth not onely its force, but its appearance at his presence. Jesus Christ seeks for the place of Corruption, and finds it no more. Thou, O God, wilt not suffer thy Holy One to see Corruption. The Godhead itself, the Divine Person of Christ, the Divine Nature inseparable from that Person goes before the Lord Jesus, as a Guide, when he passeth through this waste Wilderness. It cometh behind him, as a Rearward of Glory. It encompasseth him on every side with its highest Brightnesses, and Blessednesses. It suffereth him to see nothing but Itself on every side of him. The living, & shining Glorys of his God-head are Light, and Eyes to his dead Body in the Grave. With these, and with these alone his Divine Person now looketh forth thorough his Body in the Grave, thorough the Grave, to the utmost bounds of the Regions of Death. In this Light, to these Eyes all things near at hand, and afar off throughout, are a shining Prospect of Living Beauties to Eternity. This Divine Light, and these Divine Eyes are a Divine Flame, which in a moment, in the twinkling of an Eye break up all Shades of obscurity, fill all space with their own Brightnesses, transform all Shapes even Corruption, and Death into the same Divine Forms with themselves to the utmost bound of things. Thus God suffereth not his Holy One to see Corruption.

2. The second part is the manner of the Triumph: the Triumph of Life is expressed in those words; *Thou shalt shew me the Path of Life.* There are here two remarkable Triumphs over Death, 1 Life in Death; 2. The sight, and Triumphant sense of this Life.

1. Life in Death is declared by the Path of Life, which is made for the Lord Jesus thorough Death. *Noah* with his dear Relations, and all kinds of Creatures kept dry, and safe in the Ark, while the fountains of the great Deep were broken up from below, and the windows of heaven were opened from above to cover all things with a Flood of Waters; the Children of *Israel* in the Land of *Goshen*, where there was Light, and Rivers of Water, while darkness was upon the whole Land of *Egypt*, and the Rivers in it were turned into

Blood; the Children of *Israel* passing in a dry path thorough the Red *Sea*, which overwhelmed the *Egyptian* King with his whole Army; the Three Children with the similitude of the son of God walking in the midst of the fiery furnace, which burnt their bands only, and devoured their enemies, which cast them in; all these were Figures of Jesus Christ passing in a Path of life thorow Death. The Lord Jesus himself in his Heavenly, & divine form, as he is the Essential Image of his Father is his own Way, and Life thorough Death. This is the Fountain of Life, and Eternity itself. This hath all Lives bound up in one, like those innumerable Beams, which pour forth themselves through all things in Heaven, and on Earth, united in the sun. Here Life riseth up in its greatest Fulness, in its freshest, purest, and sweetest Streams, where all the strengths, Beauties, and Joys of Life are at their greatest heighth. Thus the Godhead in its Essential Image stands in every part, and point of the Humane Nature of Christ dying, or dead. Thus it stands in every step, and point of its Way through Death. Thus it makes it all, as a Fountain and Flood of Life. As the Milky way in Heaven, where innumerable Stars mingle their Beams into one Path of Light: Such is the Way of Christ in Death, which is all a mixture, or contexture of the innumerable Beauties, and sweetnesses of Life rising up fresh from the innumerable springs of Life in the Bosom of this Heavenly Image, which is Eternity, and the Divine Essence it self in its own substantial Form.

2. The Triumphant sight, and sense of Life acompanys the Lord Jesus in this Path of Life thorow Death; as is signified by those words, Thou shalt shew me, or make me to know the Path of Life. As a Princely Bridegroom leading his Royal Bride in his hand thorough delightful walks, when the spring is in its prime, makes her to observe all the delights in the Walks, saying to her; see, how pleasantly all things look; how sweetly Heaven and Earth smile one upon another; how lovely the leaves, and blossoms are upon the Trees, the grass, and the Flowers upon the ground; how pleasantly the birds sing in every bush; how pure, and sweet the air is; how beautiful the year is now: Thus God the Father leads Jesus Christ; thus the Divine Nature in the brightness of its Glory leads the Humane Nature thorough the Path of Life in Death, as a heavenly Bridegroom its dearest Bride. He looks forth upon him with a flaming eye of Love, he saith to him; behold a new and large prospect of Divine Lights, and all the Beauties of Life in Death; with what spicy sweetness, and immortal perfumes the Spirit of Life, and Love, as the Air of Paradise, and Heaven itself breaths upon all things here! How do Heaven, and Earth, the uncreated and the created Image of things reflect the same Beauties, and sweetnesses one upon another, like the Living Face, and the Face in a Chrystal Mirrour? How do all glories in their lovelyest Forms, & richest Varieties, looking down from above, sprouting forth, and blossoming from beneath, meet and kiss each other? How do Angels, how do Immortal, and shining Spirits spring, and sing every where? How doth the Shade of Death

itself, mingling itself with all these, surrounding this Divine Light, & at the same time surrounded by it, *give a solemn sweetning*, and heightning to all, like the Base string to the Musick of a Lute, making Death it self another Heaven distinct from the Heaven after Death, and contending with it for delightfulness? Thus God the Father maketh Christ to see the Path of Light in Death.

3. The third part in the manner of the Triumph, the Pleasure; In thy presence are all pleasantnesses, and at thy right hand Pleasures for evermore. Three pleasant things are here presented in one: 1. The Seat of Pleasure: 2. The Perfection; 3. The Perpetuity of Pleasures.

1. The Seat of Pleasure is the Presence, and right hand of God. The Presence in Hebrew is the Face of God. The Son of God, The Eternal Word, the Essential Form of God, and the Brightness of his Glory, is the Face of God. *Behold thou art fair, my Beloved, yea thou art Pleasant, our Bed is green*; saith the spouse in the Canticles to Jesus Christ. He is that Eternal Form, and naked face of the Godhead where all the Pleasantnesses of the purest Beauties, Loves, and Joys, first spring, flourish and seat themselves. His Cheeks therefore in the same Book are said to be the Garden-beds of the most fragrant Spices, and perfumed Flowers, where the highest Beauties, and the highest sweetnesses are born, and married one to another, and bring forth an endless race of Loves, and Delights. This Face of God, in which all Loveliness, and Loves thus shine, and flame together is also set with so many eyes, which continually behold, and rejoyce in their own Beauties and Pleasantnesses. This Face, this Form of God is the Person, which subsists in the Human Nature of Christ both Soul & Body, which in it self gives a subsistence to the whole Humanity of Christ living, and dying. Thus is it in the Grave and in the dead Body of Christ, the seat of all Pleasantnesses, the Throne of divine Beauty, & of Love in Death. It is also as a thousand never sleeping, never slumbring eyes, in this blessed Body, with which it uninterruptedly contemplates in it self this Eternal face, and Form of God, this seat of Pleasantnesses, which is its own Person, its own self in its personal Unity, and subsistence.

The right hand of God is the Godhead in the strength, at the heighth of Love, Power, Majesty, and Glory, as it is above all heavens. Here are Pleasures in their proper seat, in their greatest force, and fulness, as they transcend the joys themselves of all created Heavens. At this right hand of God is Jesus in the Grave. By this right hand of God, which hath all pleasures ever attending it, was he pleasantly led thorough the Shadow of Death: In the Bed of Death this right hand of the most High embraced him, that he might sweetly rest there in the midst of all the Pleasures of this Right Hand of his.

2. The Perfection of Pleasures is exprest by these two names of Pleasantnesses, and Pleasures. Pleasantnesses are the Objects of delight, or Pleasures in the object. Pleasures are the Delights themselves in the fruition, and enjoyment of those objects, or Pleasures in their Subject. The Subject, and the Object

 uniting,

uniting, and mingling, and transforming themselves variously by their various mixtures in their union into one mutual life, and Form of Beauty, and Love, make Pleasure, and delight. You have here all Pleasantnesses in the Face of God, and so all Pleasures at the Right Hand of God.

The Lord Jesus dying, and in death beholds the Face of God. In this Face he at once beholds all pleasant forms and Forms of Pleasantness, the pleasantness of all Forms among Men, & Angels in their first & highest Patterns, to which the most Glorious spectacles, and spirits of Men, or Angels, are obscure Shadows and faint imitations. In this face he beholdeth pleasant Forms, incomprehensible for variety, and Glory, which never cast any the least shadow of themselves, nor were capable of being in the least degree imitated in the highest of created excellencies. Death itself is a divine Marriage-bed, in which Jesus Christ receives all these pleasant Forms into his Bosom, as Lights of Glory shining thick thorow the Cristal Temple of his pure, and sacred Body in this Night of his Divine Death. He beareth in his dead Body the impressions, and Figures of them all with the Heavenly substances themselves in these Impressions, and Figures like a seal of Gold fixed on Virgin-wax; his dying, and dead Body is transformed into one Life, and Form with those Original Forms of Pleasantnesses, being embraced by them, as by a Divine flame, which makes it one pure flame of Pleasantness, and Pleasure with itself.

3. The Perpetuity of the Pleasure; *At thy right hand are Pleasures for evermore.* Two things are here signified. 1. The continuation of Pleasures in the Person of Christ without any interruption: 2. The endlesness of those Pleasures. Jesus Christ saith to his Father in one Place, thou leadest me by thy right hand. The Lord Jesus was ever led by the right hand of the Father out of Heaven into the Virgins Womb, out of the Womb into the gloomy Light of this World, thorow this World, thorow Death, and the Grave into Heaven again. Thus was this blessed Person ever at the right hand of his Father, that is, at the right hand and Fountain of Power, Majesty, Love, Life, and Pleasures, in the Womb, on the earth, on the Cross, in the Grave. So was the Path of this righteous one a shining Light of divine Pleasures uninterrupted thorow all these thick shades of the blackest darkness.

There is one thing more in the duration of Christs Pleasures signified in the last Verse of this Psalm above all this. The Lord saith to his Father, all Pleasantnesses are in thy Face. Behold here in one undivided point the full circle of Eternity, and that an Eternity of Pleasures; The Face of God with all Pleasantnesses in it. Eternity impyes three things; 1. the Fulness of all Being, 2. the utmost heighth of being; 3. the undividedness. In this Time falls below Eternity, that it is a contracted, successive Shadow.

The Face of God, which is his Essential Image, and substantial Form, the God Head itself in the second Person in the Trinity, which is our Lord Jesus, is this Eternity. This is that Person, which was Man, was Flesh, hung on

the

the Cross, and lay dead in the Grave. No more could the Lord Jesus be separated from the Face of his Father in any part of his Soul, or Body in any season, either of Life, or of Death, than a person can be separated from itself, or the Lord Jesus be divided from the Second Person in the Trinity. Thorow every state, thorow the most cloudy days, and the most tempestuous Nights the Face of God, the Son of Eternity went along with the Lord Jesus shining upon every Cloud, and Storm, shining thorough all, gilding all with the Joys, and Glories of Heaven itself. In this Face, as in the undivided Circle of Eternity always, at once, in every moment, and cast of his eye he saw, possest, and enjoyed all pleasantnesses. In this Face of his Father, which is the Light of Eternity, he saw his own Face as he passed thorow all changes: Even then when he cried out, that he was forsaken by his Father, he beheld this forsaking of him, himself thus forsaken in this Glass the face of his Father in the midst of all Pleasantnesses, one of the Pleasantnesses, one with all the Pleasantnesses there. The Angels that take care of Children here below in the midst of this their work on Earth, ever behold the Face of the Father in Heaven. How much more is it true of that Person who is the Face of the Father, who is one Essence and Substance with the Father, who unites the Humane Nature, to the Divine Nature in the Unity of this Person? Shall not he much more see the face of his Father in Heaven, while he is on Earth, or in the Grave, serving the little Children of his Father, his younger Brethren, as their good Angel? This Face, in which all Pleasantnesses are at their fulness, at their heighth, was that Joy set before Jesus Christ upon the Cross, for which he endured the Cross, and despised the shame.

I shall now conclude this discourse of our dying, and dead Saviour, of his sacred Body living, and immortal in Death with those four things which were too wonderful for Solomon; the way of a Ship upon the Sea; of an Eagle in the Air; of a Serpent upon a stone, or a rock; of a man with a maid, or, as it is in Hebrew, in a maid. The most learned Jews teach us to understand this, as the Mystery of the Messiah. The most learned of the Christian Divines give us such a Gloss as this upon it, while they make this place from the authority of the Jews themselves to prove against them, that the Messiah was to be born of a Virgin. 1. The Man in the Maid is the Heavenly Man in Womb of the Virgin. 2. The Ship upon the Sea is the Humane Nature in its Union with the Divine Nature, Sailing along in its course of time, and life here below upon the Sea of Eternity. 3. The serpent upon the Stone or the Rock, is the deep, and Glorious wonder of Death in the Person of Christ, who is the Rock of Eternal Life, and God himself, who lives for ever. 4. The Eagle in the Air is the Humane Nature risen, and ascending in the Spirit to the right hand of the father above all Heaven to the utmost heighths of all Joys, and Glories of the Divine Nature, and Eternity.

Before

Before I leave this Subject, I will point out one Use and Application of it. When a Voice came with Thunder to the Lord Jesus, declaring Love and Glory from on high upon him; Jesus Christ saith to his Disciples, *This Voice came not for my sake, but for yours.* In like manner these glorious things are spoken of Christ in his life, and in his death, not for himself only, but for all his Saints. Christ, and all the Saints, are one seed. To that one seed, to all the Saints in Christ, to Christ in himself, and in all his Saints, are all the Promises made.

All those pleasant things which we have spoken of Jesus Christ, and of his holy Body, in Death, are true of him, as his Humane Nature is joyned to the Divine Nature in one Divine and Eternal Person, which is the most High God. The same things are true in us also, who believe in him, by that Mystical Union, which joyneth us to the Lord Jesus in one mystical Person and in the Unity of that Spirit, which is also the most high God, one with the Father, and the Son.

While we live, as Saints by the Faith of the Lord Jesus, we live not, but Christ liveth in us, we live, and we are Spiritual only, as we are Spirits, the Birth of the Eternal Spirit, and one Spirit with the Lord Jesus in his Resurrection from the Dead: All things in Heaven and on Earth, of Soul, and of Body, of Life, and of Death are Spirit, and Life to us.

It is true, that while we live on Earth, a fleshly Spirit, a fleshly Image, in which Satan hath his Throne, have a part in us, not as our true selves, but as our disguises, our diseases, our enemy, as evil Dreams in our sleep. These often prevail over the Spiritual Man in us, and captivate us to many sinful Lusts, fears, and Griefs. But still the Spiritual man in itself, which is our true self, puts them under its feet, and makes them Captives to the Light, Love, and Immortality of the Spirit. The Spirit in us is like the Sun, which, when we think it under a Cloud, or eclipsed by the Moon, is so only to our Earthly Light, but in truth, and to itself it is upon its own Throne of Light triumphantly above the Clouds, and the Moon, comprehending them in the brightness of its own Glory.

But besides this, in the moment of Death this fleshly Spirit, and Image is for ever cast out of all power, and rule in a Saint, and is entirely subdued to that pure, and Heavenly Spirit, which is the true Saint, which now without any interposing vail or interrupting interval perpetually sees the glorious Face of Jesus Christ in it self, which is one Spirit with him, and the Glorious Face of the Father in Jesus Christ.

Yea one advantage of unexpressible Joy, and Glory hath the death of a [illegible] h of Christ. The Death of Christ had all the stings of [illegible] any creature ever felt, or can feel, the guilt of Sin, [illegible] Wrath of the Father; all the Powers of Hell in [illegible] All these stings are taken out of the death of a Saint.

Saint. Christ is risen, all the Powers of evil subdued, captivated, and changed into mysteries of eternal Light, and Love in the Glorified Person of Christ, by the Virtue of his Resurrection. A Believer living, and dying stands in the Resurrection of Christ, is risen with him, in him. A Believer is married to Christ as he is risen from the Dead. His Life, his Death throughout all things of them both, are Divine Fruits of this marriage-bed, brought forth in the Bosom of God, to God.

Break forth then, O ye Saints, into singing, both living, and dying, tune your last breath to this song of the Lamb, and say like him; *I have set my glorified Jesus, my Heavenly Bridegroom and the Father in him before me. My glorified Jesus, my Heavenly Bridegroom, and the Father in him is at my right hand; therefore shall I not be greatly moved.* Therefore doth my Soul rejoyce in Death, my Body also sweetly rests in the Grave, as in a Marriage-bed, in the midst of all Divine delights, as Flowers of Paradise strewed upon it. It rests in the Bosom of my glorified Jesus my hope. This sweet, and sure hope is he, that will never leave my Soul in the state of Death; nor suffer his Holy One, his spouse, this Soul, or this Body, which he hath espoused, as chast Virgins to himself, to see Corruption. No, no; my Bride-groom, with all his Lights of Glory, and the Father of lights in him, will accompany this Darling-Soul, and Darling-Body, his pair of Doves, which are to him as his two eyes, through Death, and the Grave. There will he, filling all things round about me with his shining Beauties, make me to see the Path of Life, & Immortality, all composed of innumerable Angels of Glory, or the innumerable Glories of the Godhead, as the Milky way in Heaven is said to be composed with innumerable Stars thick set. Thorow all the shades of Death shall I behold all pleasantnesses in his Face shining forth upon me with a fresh Glory, as a new Sun turning those Shades into a flowry, and perfumed Arbour in the Heavenly Paradise, I shall be continually at his right hand, where pleasures are for evermore without mixture, interruption, or end. Thus is his right hand, which is the heighth and Fountain of Life, and Pleasures, the beginning of my Life, my strength, and guide in my way, my end in Death.

We have finished the answers to the objection against the Immortality and Glory of the Body of a Saint together with the Soul in Death, which was taken from the Body it self, and strengthened by the particular consideration of the Body of Christ in Death, and in the Grave. We have finished the distinction between the two Bodies, the Body of Death in a Saint, and the proper Body of a Saint, which is an inseparable Member in the Spiritual, and Heavenly Body of Christ, and the Temple of the Holy Ghost, as the Soul is.

We come now to the last objection, taken from the resurrection of the Body at the last day, which seems to be without any sense, if our Bodies become Glorious and Immortal at our Death. This

This Objection is answered by the distinction of three eminent steps, or degrees in the resurrection from the Dead. I shall take my ground, upon which I shall build this answer, and distinction from St. *John Chap.* 11. *v.* 25. these are the words of our Lord Jesus in that place; *I am the Resurrection, and the Life. He, that lives, and believes in me, shall never die. He that believes in me, though he were dead, yet shall he live.* The Lord Jesus is here comforting *Martha* mourning over her dead Brother: He propounds to her the comfort, and Joy of his Resurrection. *Thy Brother*, saith he, *shall rise again.* That, which would have been a present, and powerful Joy looked upon with a Spiritual eye in a Light of Glory, becomes to *Martha* a faint, and far distant Joy, while she looks upon the Resurrection a great way off, at the end of the World. So she answereth the Lord Jesus: *Yea, Lord I know, that my Brother shall rise again at the last Day.* The Lord Jesus scattereth this Cloud of Flesh by shining out upon *Martha* in the Brightness and Glory of his Heavenly, and Divine Person, as that Invisible and Eternal Sun, which is at once the Fountain, and Treasury of all Lights, Lives, and Forms of things in a state of Perfection, and unchangeableness. The Lord, as he shineth out upon her annointeth the eyes of her mind with his Spirit, and the Light of his appearance, to see him, as he is in the fulness of Glory, as the fulness of the Glory of God, and of all things dwelleth in him, as he is the same, and all things in him are the same yesterday, to day, and for ever. *I*, saith he, *am the Resurrection and the Life.* The latter of these is the cause, and demonstration of the former. It will not seem strange to him, who seeth the Lord Jesus to be the Life of all things, & all things in their most exact distinction to be living perfectly, and Eternally in him, in the vast, and unbounded Circle of the Unity of his Person, and Spirit, as in a secret Paradise, a Field of Light, and bliss above the Heavens, and yet invisibly present every where; that he should at his Pleasure bring forth things, which have disappeared here by Death, into new appearances, as Resurrections from the Dead, and present them again to our eye in the same Forms, in which they before conversed with them, not as Phantasms, or as empty Apparitions, but real, and Substantial. Thus to *Martha* inlightned by this Spiritual Vision of Christ, it was easie to understand, that Jesus Christ could give her Brother *Lazarus* again out of his Grave, living, into her Arms even at that present time.

Having thus cleared my ground for my ensuing discourse by the opening of the words, I proceed to my distinction of a threefold eminent degree in the Resurrection from the Dead.

1. The first eminent step, or degree in the Resurrection from the dead is Regeneration, which signifieth a new birth, a second birth, to be born again of God, after the Death of that Life which we receive from him by our first Generation, as Sons of God by the Creation.

2. The Second eminent step, or degree in the Resurrection from the Dead is the Natural Death.

3. The

3. The last eminent step, and degree is the Resurrection of the Dead at the last day.

1. I shall begin with the first of these, that the difference between these three Resurrections may more clearly appear. I shall lay it down in the form of a Doctrine.

Doct. Regeneration is a Resurrection from the Dead. St Paul clearly so expresseth it *Eph.* 5. *v.* 14. *wherefore*, he saith, *Awake thou, that sleepest, and arise from the Dead, and Christ shall give thee Light.* Behold three things here. 1. A Sleep. 2. The Awakening from this Sleep. 3. The cause of Awakening.

1. Here is a sleep; *Thou that sleepest.* Every man in his Natural state is a divine Spirit, an Immortal Soul, an Image of God, a Son of God in a deep Sleep. The Natural Sleep is defined to be a perfect ligation, or binding up of all the senses outward, or inward. But this is an unnatural Sleep, into which we are cast by the Enchantments, and Power of the Devil. It is the Sleep of Sin. O man, all thy senses and faculties, outward and inward, which were true, pure, and divine, in the Similitude of God, whilst they were awake, and at liberty, were continually feasted with divine Objects, they possessed, and enjoyed a Paradise in themselves. But how are they now fallen asleep, how are they bound up? Thou now no more seest, hearest, tastest, feelest, understandest, enjoyest any sweet beam of truth, any thing of the Harmonious Musick, of the delicate Relish, of the soft Embraces, of the immutable, all-satisfying Reality, and Substance of pure Love, pure Light, pure Beauty, pure Joy, pure Goodness, Every thing pleasant. every thing Real, every thing Divine is to thee, as if it were not at all: Yet is not thy sleep quiet. All this, which thou seemest to thy self, to hear, to see, to understand, to converse with by any of thy senses, or faculties, is a Dream in thy sleep, a delusive, a defiling, a melancholy Dream, where false, and filthy showes of Pleasures are mingled with tumultuous disquiets, confusions, torments fears, and Horrours.

This Sleep is the Sleep of Death, not a Natural, and momentany Death, which is a meer cessation of Life with a rest from all its troubles, but a living Death, the second Death, a Hellish Death, the Death of damned Spirits. Thus are Sleep and Death joyned here; *Awake thou that sleepest, and stand up from the Dead.* This Sleep is a true Death, and this Death is truely a Sleep, a living Death, or an unquiet Sleep full of evil Dreams.

2. The second thing is the Awakening. The Awakening out of this Sleep is also a Resurrection from the Dead. *Awake thou that sleepest, and stand up from the Dead.* This is the Regeneration, or new Birth, by which the soul is raised up from the Sleep, and Death of Sin into the Light of Life, and Immortality.

3. The third thing is the cause of this Awakening; *And Christ shall give*

thee Light. And, here signifies, as much as, For, by a common Hebraism. Thus you are to read it, Awake thou that sleepest, and stand up from the Dead, for Christ shall give thee Light. This will be plain, if you look to that Scripture, from which this is taken *Isaia.* 60. 1. *v. Arise, shine; for thy Light is come, and the Glory of the Lord is risen upon thee.* St. *Paul* applies this to the Lord Jesus, and a Sinner in the work of Conversion, or Regeneration. Poor Sinner, thou sleepest in a dark and miry Dungeon, of Sensuality, Lust, Passion, Ignorance, Unbelief, Despair, like *Peter* sleeping in Prison, bound with two Souldiers on each side him: so thou sleepest in the dark Prison of the flesh, and this World, in the midst of Devils, with whom thou art chained, and bound. Thou liest dead in this dead Image of things, as in a Grave of Corruption, and Rottenness. Behold the Lord Jesus full of the Beauties of Holiness, full of the unsearchable Riches of Divine Love shineth upon thee with a Light of Glory. He, who is the Light and Glory of God, of Heaven, of Eternity, as he shineth upon thee, giveth thee Light, infuseth this Light of Glory into thee, by giving himself to thee, by infusing himself into thee, by springing up himself within thee, as he shineth from without upon thee. Thus he awakens thee. Thus awakened, stand up from the Dead. For Christ giveth thee Light.

The work of Regeneration, which is a true Resurrection from Death to Life, will be more clearly understood by considering it in these four Circumstances; 1. The Life, which is raised again; 2. The Death, out of which this Life is raised; 3. The Resurrection itself; 4. The way of this Resurrection.

1. The life which is raised again is twofold; 1. One Life is that of Paradise at the beginning of Time. We had an earthly head in Paradise, in whom we all stood, and subsisted together in the Garden of *Eden*, or of Divine Pleasures. There we were clothed with a Divine Image, and enjoyed a Divine Life. We were made in the similitude of God, and lived a life like to that of God himself. St. *Paul* speaks of this Life, *Rom.* 7. 9. *v. For I was alive without the Law once.* I know that this Scripture, is generally applied to the convincing, and the condemning Power of the Law. So St. *Paul* is understood here to speak of that Life of Pleasure, and satisfaction to his own deceived mind, and senses, which he enjoyed in sin before he felt the work of the Law upon his Heart convincing him of the Evil of Sin. But whoever well considers this Scripture will very plainly see, that it cannot bear this sense. For 1. The scope of this place is to shew that which is expressed at the 5th. Verse, *That the Motions of Sin are by the Law* which work in our Members to bring forth fruit unto Death. 2. The objection which is made at the 7th. verse, *what shall we say then, is the Law sin?* can have no ground in any other sense than this, that Sin itself takes life from the Law. 3. St. *Paul* expresly proceeds in his reasoning by these steps verse 8th. 9th. *Sin taking*

ing occasion by the Commandment, wrought in me all manner of concupiscence. He proves that by this Argument; *for without the Law sin was dead.* The force of the connection makes it clear, that the death of sin here meant, is not the death in Sin with stupidity and security, but a Life free from the power and pollution of Sin. This is explained and illustrated by another Argument; *For I was alive without the Law once.* While all things stood in the simplicity and unity of the Divine Image undivided, the Light, and the Darkness no where appearing as two, but as one in one Divine Spirit, in one Divine Harmony. There was nothing from which sin could take life. Now St. *Paul* lived, now as he, so we lived, and all Mankind, according to our several properties, and distinct Persons in Paradise, together with *Adam* & in *Adam*, who was the Earthly Head, and collective Body of us all, like Christ in Heaven. 2. The other Life, which is raised again in the Regeneration, is the Life of Heaven in Eternity. Before, and above our Earthly Head, we had a Head in Heaven, in Eternity, the Lord Jesus, in whose Image and Similitude *Adam* was Created to be a Figure of him. In this heavenly and eternal Head had we a Heavenly and Eternal Life. Our Heavenly Life in Eternity is as the Light. Our Earthly Life in Paradise as the Shadow to this Light. O thou, who art now as a Dunghil covered with, and composed of the most loathsom pollutions and defilements of Sin, who art withered in all thy Beauties, Hopes and Comforts; who art sunk deepest into despair; who art now no more a Man, but a Worm, the worst of Worms, the seed of the Serpent; See from whence thou art fallen, what once thou wert; what Lives, what Joys, what Glories lie buried in thee? Thou wert once a beautiful Prince, like the Morning Star: Thou wert once the Perfection of Beauty, and Pleasantness in the Figure, in Paradise, in *Adam*: Thou wert once the Perfection of Beauty in the Life it self, in Heaven, in Eternity, in the Lord Jesus. Whither are these Beauties now fled? How do these Beautiful Lives now lie as in the Grave covered with the Darkness of Death? The Psalmist saith to the Lord, *That the Saints pity the Dust of Sion, and take Pleasure in the Stones thereof.* O all you, who hear, and read this; In your selves, in each other see, pity, take Pleasure in the Ruins of the Divine Life, of the Divine Image, of Paradise, of Heaven with all their Beauties, Joys, and Glories. See the Lord Jesus from Heaven looking upon them with an eye of pity, and delight. Let this be a Beam of hope to you shining from his face into the midst of the Darkness of your Guilt, Defilements, and despair that by him these beautiful, and blessed Lives may rise again.

2. The Death out of which this Life is raised, is that of Sin, and of the Curse for Sin. *Eph.* 2. 1. *v.* St. *Paul* saith, we were dead in Sin. Hear, and read this, O man, with sighs, and tears, with trembling, and terrour. Thy Life it self is now a Death, and a cursed Death such a Death, as makes the difference between an Angel in Glory, and a Devil in Hell. The corruption of

the best things is worst. The fall of the highest and greatest things makes the greatest, and most dreadful Ruine. The Divine Life is dead; the Divine Image is fallen in thee. Thou art dead in Sin. *Sin* lived, and I died, saith St. *Paul* in the forementioned place. A *Life* of Darkness, shame, Disorder, deformity, enmity, the Life and Image of Hell, and Devils are sprung up in thee, and are become a Grave of hate and horrour which hath swallowed up the Life, the Image of Love, Beauty, and Joy, of Heaven, of Angels, of God into a cursed Victory in thee. All the stings and terrours of the first death in the separation of the Soul, and Body, are all the secret burnings of this Hellish fire of the Death in Sin now quite consuming the broken Relicks of the Divine Light, and sweetness in the Flesh, and enlarging itself into the second Death, as into an eternal Flame of Wrath, and torment.

Look up, oh man! see this whole World of these Heavens, and this Earth, as a Charnel-house, or a dark Vault for the Dead. See thy self in this Body, as a melancholy Coffin in the midst of this Vault, where thine own Divine Life and Image, with ten thousand blessed Lives, the Life of Christ, of Paradise, of Heaven, lie dead and buried. See this place in which now thou art, the smoaky porch, and gloomy entrance into Hell, like a cloudy Evening to that dismal Night. See thy self walking here as a wretched Ghost and Shade in the midst of the Dead, in the midst of cursed Apparitions from below, and thy self together with all these, ready every moment to vanish into everlasting Darkness, and Flames. This is the Death, out of which the Divine Life is raised in the first Resurrection or the Regeneration.

3. The Resurrection of this Life, out of this Death, is to be declared in its first step, which is the Regeneration, or New-birth. The Divine Nature, which lies hid at the bottom, and in the center of the Soul, lives there to itself with its Heavenly, and Earthly Image, as in the Secret of its own twofold Paradise, whereof one was never yet revealed in any Creature until Christ; the other with drew itself hither from the sight of the Soul at the Fall. This Divine Nature, as to the Soul itself, whose Root it is, of whose Being it is the only Life, and Truth, lies slain by the Life of Sin, and buried in its own Ruines beneath the Darkness, and Confusion of the Corrupt, the Fleshly, and the Hellish Image.

This Divine Nature in the moment of Regeneration, or Conversion is new-born in the Soul, or, which is the same, the Soul is new-born into the Divine Nature, and comes forth with a new, and Divine Being, into a new, and Divine World.

This change is called a Birth, because the Divine Nature, as the Seed of God sown in the Soul, diffuseth itself thorough the Soul, changeth the Soul into one Nature, and Life with itself, so bringeth forth itself in the soul, and the Soul together with itself, in its own Divine Life, and Likeness.

The Eternal Spirit is the Father of this Birth, which sendeth forth this holy

Seed,

Seed. This Spirit is also the Mother. For in the naked Bosom of the Eternal Spirit, at once the Seed of God is sown in the soul, and the Soul is sown, as a new Seed sent forth immediately from God, wrapt up in the Seed of God: The Spirit also itself is this Seed. For so the Lord Jesus saith, *John* 3. *That which is born of the Spirit is Spirit.*

This New birth is said to be from above ; because it is immediately from God ; the Birth of God, as he is in the Simplicity of his Godhead uncloathed of every Vail, infinitely transcending all created powers, and perfections. This Birth is expressed by being born again, as a second Birth. For man was first born unto a Divine Light, and Image in Paradise, where he also dyed to this Life, and Image, unto which he is now born a second time, That was a Shadow onely : This the Shadow, and the Substance both in Union.

This Birth is also called a Resurrection, and is truely so upon this account. That same Divine Person, in his own proper, and individual Existency, which died in Paradise, which ever since hath lien slain, and buried in the corrupt, sinful Person sprung up in its place, as in a Grave, now riseth again. As it riseth, it casteth off this cursed, and Hellish person as a Body rising to Glory casteth off the form of a dead Carcass, of Rottenness, and dust, recovering its own proper place, and right.

But there is a threefold difference, between this Divine Nature in its first Life in Paradise, and its first Resurrection in its Regeneration, or New-birth.

1. In Paradise the Divine Nature sprung up, and appeared in a Earthy Image and in an Earthy Person, only as in a lovely shadow of itself. The Heavenly Person, the Heavenly Image, although it were the Root, the Truth, the Life, the Fulness of this Shadow, yet it lay concealed beneath it, as a Vail, or as the Fruit lies hid in the Blossom. By Sin the Blossom falls to make way for this Fruit. In the new birth, out of the Ruins of the Earthy Person, and the Earthy Image, as the rending of the Vail, the Divine Nature springs up, and shines forth in its own Heavenly Person, and Image. Thus that which was sown by the Fall a Heavenly and Divine Shadow riseth again by the new birth a Heavenly, and Divine Substance, which is the Shadow in its Life, and Truth.

The Holy Scriptures declare this Glorious Mystery ; 1 Epist. *John* 5. c. there we read, *That there are three which bear record in Heaven, the Father, the Word, and the Spirit,* A little after we read, *That he, who believeth hath the record in himself.* If a Believer hath the Record within himself, he hath also within himself those who bear the Record, For a Record, or Testimony hath all its authority, and force from the Persons of the Witnesses, as it is given by them, and cometh forth out of their mouths. Behold then here in the moment of believing, God himself in the three Persons in their Heavenly Image, which is the Heaven of Heavens, bringing forth the Divine Nature, as their own proper Birth, and Child in an Heavenly Person, and in their

their own Heavenly Image, in which they themselves dwell together with him, giving their Testimony to him, in which he believes.

2. That which was the Beauty, and the beautiful Inhabitant of Paradise, was the Divine Nature in the Earthly Image, and in an Earthy Person, which stood singly in a shadowy Joy, and Glory, The Heavenly Person, and the Heavenly Image, which were the Life it self were hidden, and Vailed beneath this Shadow ; like the Glory of a Flower in its seed beneath the Earth, when the Plant begins first to appear ; or like the ripe fruit hid in the Blossom.

In the New birth that Divine Person, and Form, which died in the Shadow, riseth again in the blessed life, and most beautiful Truth of the Eternal Substance. As the Accorn, which was first an Oak, being sown in the Ground, and dying, springs up again into a fair, and flourishing tree. But there is this difference the Accorn is not the same Oak which at first it was, but only another of the same kind. But here the Shadow in its new birth riseth again in that Individual Person, and proper Essence of Glory, out of which it first descended. As Jesus Christ saith, *I came forth from God into the world ; again, I leave the world, and go to the Father.* So Saith this new-born Child of God, I was before the World, with my Elder Brother in the bosom of the Father, I was with the Father in the bosom of my Elder Brother, one Spirit, one Heavenly Image, one Brightness of Glory together with him. I came forth from this Glory into a Shadowy similitude of it, into an Earthly Paradise. From thence I fell by sin into that Death which is my Life in this present evil World. Again through the Death of Christ by the Resurrection of the new Birth I leave both this living Death in the World, & that Shadowy Life of Paradise, & return to my first Glory with Jesus Christ in the bosom of the Father.

Moreover that Earthly Image, and shadowy Paradise are not lost. These also rise again in their Regeneration. They arise again the same Individuals, but in a far different Form, and in a far differing manner of subsisting. The Earthly man of the first Paradise is born anew, subsisting in the Person of the Heavenly Man, as the Humanity of Christ subsisted in his Divine, and Eternal Person. The Earthy Man springs up in the bosom of the Heavenly Man. It is no more now, as at the first, a vail on the Sun-like Face and Spiritual Beauties of the Heavenly Pattern, and Original. But it is to it, as the freshest Beams, and the most Flowry Light of the Sunshine is to the Sun. It Flows immediately from the naaked Form, and fulness of the Heavenly Glory, it, is transparent to it, filled and covered with it. The Earthly Paradise now flourisheth in the midst of the Heavenly Paradise, which shineth all through it, bringing it forth, as one Person, and one Spirit with it self.

This is the new Heaven, and the new Earth, the Heavenly Man, and the Heavenly Paradise newly, and nakedly discovered, so as it never before was in this Creation ; The earthly man also, and the earthly Paradise, brought forth into a new state, and Glory by their Union, and fellowship with the

Heavenly Man, and the Heavenly Paradise, as a Bride adorned by the presence of her Bridegroom coming forth like the Sun. Thus Jesus Christ makes all things new in the new Creature; and brings forth the new Creature together with himself in himself, as St. *Paul* speaks 2 *Corin. c. 5. v. If any man be in Christ he is a new Creature*, or a new Creation. For behold, saith Christ, I make all things new.

This new birth, and Resurrection of the Heavenly, and earthly Glories united in one Person in a Saint is excellently represented in that forementioned place of St. *John.* 1 *Epist. c. 5. v.* Having said, *There are three that bear record in Heaven, the Father, the Word, and the Spirit*; he adds, *There are three that bear record on Earth*; and saith he, *these three agree in one.* The first three were one Heavenly Spirit, and Image. The last three agree in the Earthly Image with themselves, and in one Heavenly Spirit with the Heavenly Image and the Heavenly three. A Believer, as is before noted, is said to have the Record, or Testimony of these Witnesses in himself. He hath then also the Witnesses in himself; for these Witnesses testifying of themselves to the Soul are in their own unvailed persons, and Divine presence, the Testimony, the Truth of the Testimony, the Authority, the Witnesses all in one.

The second Trinity of Witnesses is 1. the Water. 2. The Blood. 3. The Spirit.

1. The Water is the natural or Earthly Image washt as by a Baptism of Water from its filth, like a piece of Gold fallen into the dirt. The first Creation is exprest by Water. It was a pure, and clear Sea of finest Christal. The Face of God shining forth upon this Sea of Chrystal at once filled it with the sweet Light of his Beams, and figured his Beauties upon it, which Light and Figure, were the Light of Paradise, and the Life of the first man in ... Sin by a mixture of Earth with this pure Water polluteth it, troubleth it, changeth the Light into Darkness, and the Beautiful Figure of the Divine Glory into Confusion. The clear, and sweet calm is now changed into a black and foul Tempest. The new birth separating the dark, & defiling Earth from the clear, & pure Flood, gives a Resurrection to the Divine Light, the Divine Form, the Earthly man in its purities, and the first Paradise in its Beauties.

2. The Blood is the second Witness joyned together with the Water. This is the Earthly Image heightened with a more excellent washing than that of Water, which is this of the precious Blood of God himself. This Blood taketh away by the vertue of Christs Death the darkness of the vail, which interposeth between the naked Glories of the Heavenly Image, and the Earthly Image, keeping it in the state of a shadow only. Now this most precious Blood as a rich Flood of Divine Light, and Life breaks in freely, and ...y upon the Earthly Image in its new birth, that it is no more the shadow of that Heavenly substance, but the face in the Glass answering to the living face of the supream, and Eternal Beauty. Thus the Earthly Man and the

the Earthly Paradise returneth, and riseth again in the Regeneration not by Water only, but by Blood, not as the shadowy Similitude of a concealed Beauty, but the shining brightness of a present, and unclouded Glory. This is the second Witness on Earth. The Spirit is the last of the three Witnesses in the Earthly Image. This giveth his Testimony joyntly in both Images, the Heavenly and the Earthly. This Spirit is the same in both; the Mother, which bringeth both forth from its own Eternal Womb; the Life, which dwells in both; the Glory, which fits, and cloaths them both; the Love which Eternally sports in both, which fills both with purest, & perpetual Pleasures in themselves, & in each other. This Spirit is that band of perfection, which by its Heavenly, & entire Unity maks the heavenly & the earthly Image both one Spirit, one Life, one Glory, one Divine Person, one new man in Christ Jesus, in whose bosom they lie, mutually infolding each other in most beautiful, and most delightful Embraces. Thus now is the Earthly man, and the Earthly Paradise risen again in the Regeneration, not single, but as a glorious Bride to the Heavenly Image, & the Heavenly Paradise, having her Bridegroom in her arms, and being clasped fast in his. This is the second difference between the Soul in its Earthly Paradise, and in the first Resurrection, when it is new born to a life of Grace in the place of that Life of pure nature.

3. You have seen two differences between the *Life* in the state of pure nature in Paradise, and the Resurrection of this Life unto a state of Grace in the Regeneration, or new birth. In these two differences this Life, as it is risen again excelleth itself, as it was in its pure, and primitive state for the kind, and nature of it, after a wonderful manner, by an accession of the most Heavenly, and highest Glory together with Immortality.

But this third difference will shew us this Life in the Resurrection as it is a *Life of Grace* for its present state and degrees on Earth far inferiour unto itself as it was purely natural in the first Paradise.

1. The *Life of Grace* in the Regeneration, or Resurrection is imperfect in degree, while it is on Earth, it is in its Infancy, in its Childhood, under age, under Guardians, under the Tutorship of Angels, as St. Paul speaks. It is a Life of Faith, not of clear, and compleat Fruition. It is a dying Life, a Life bearing the Image of Christ's Death, and not yet brought forth entirely into the Resurrection from the Dead. It is a Life subject to many weaknesses by reason of its Infant-state, and Childhood. It is a Life in Growth, and so not arrived to its perfect Stature.

2. The *Life of Grace in this first Resurrection is imperfect for its state.* The Spiritual or Heavenly Man in a Believer is joyned in the same Person with the Old Man, which is cursed, aud corrupt with the Child of the Curse, and Corruption. The Heavenly Image, and the Earthly Image new-born, Heaven itself, and the first Paradise risen again, are truly in a Saint on Earth, do compose the true Nature, Essence, and Person of a Saint. But there are

joyned

joyned together with these in the same outward Person the Earthly Image, as it is corrupt, and the Hellish Image, the Earthly or fleshly Image, as it is fallen, and the Hellish Image, in which inseparably do reside the universal Corruption, and Curse, all the powers of Darkness, Death and Hell. Thus are all the Purities, Sweetnesses, Glories of Paradise or Heaven in a Saint mixed, and Vailed, that they can never appear intire or in their own proper Form, but imperfectly, darkly, and Enigmatically, as St *Paul* speaks, or, as those men, that were seen walking in the forms of Trees, by him, whose eyes Jesus Christ had touched the first time only. Thus the Spiritual Man in a Saint, though it have Heaven, and Paradise united in itself, yet in this first step of its resurrection, it hath within the same outward person a continual interchangeable War, and Fight with the Earth, and with Hell, the Flesh, and the Devil. Sometimes it is made a Captive cast into Chains of darkness laid low with all its Glories in a deep, and miery dungeon, where no spark of Divine Light appears; when it is a Conquerour it is in the field still where its sweetness, and Glory are vailed, and stained, as with the dust of the Earth, as with the smoke of the Fight and of Hell, as with the Blood of its Wounds. In the midst of these it is ever alarmed to new Fights. This is the state of a Saint in the first step of the Resurrection, which is the new Birth or the Life of Grace on Earth.

Objection. Some that are truly Saints, may now say to us, Alas how are we excluded from the new birth, if they, who are new born, have Heaven, and Paradise in an Heavenly Form brought forth within them, and they themselves, are after an Heavenly manner brought forth into these, as by a Resurrection from the dead? How far are we from discerning any thing so sweet, so great, so Glorious in our selves?

Ans. I shall give five answers to this Objection to comfort the lowest of the Saints, who least of all seem to themselves to be such.

1. The Lord Jesus lay in the Womb, was laid an Infant in the Manger, slept as a man, had all the Light of Heaven, Visible, or invisible withdrawn from him, being deserted by the God-head itself in respect to any sensible presence, assistance, or enjoyment of it, died on the Cross, was shut up a dead Corps in the Grave. Yet in the Womb, in the Manger, in his sleep, in his Desertion, on the Cross, in the Grave, had he Heaven, and Paradise with their divinest sweetnesses, and fulnesses in himself, he himself was after the sweetest, fullest, and Divinest manner in Paradise, and Heaven. For he himself in his own Person is the Light, the Life, and Truth of both. All this was unchangeably true of him even in his Flesh, and in his natural man, when to

him in his Flesh, and in his natural man nothing of this appeared, or seemed to be at all. Thus may it be with thee, O doubting, and mourning Christian, who weepest for that life of the Spirit, which hath Heaven, and Paradise in it by having Jesus Christ risen from the dead in it. Thou refusest to be comforted, because these are not, or rather appear not in thee. But consider this, and be comforted. Cast thy eye upon thy Pattern the Lord Jesus, and then say; Christ with Heaven and Paradise may be in me. I may be in Heaven, and in Paradise by being in Christ, though this appear not to me. Christ may be in me, I may be in Christ in the Womb, or in the Manger, in a deep sleep, or a desertion upon the Cross, or in the Grave. But in Truth by all these, Heaven and Paradise with all their Divine store, and furniture, rise up in me so much the more Gloriously, by how much the more Christ is formed in me, and I am conformed to Christ.

2. *Ans.* Jesus Christ in the Gospel compareth the Kingdom of Heaven, or of God, to a seed of wheat sown in the field, which cometh up first in the Blade, then in the Stalk, then in the Ear, and lastly in the Ripe Corn in the Ear. Why dost thou sigh, O Believer, and say, that thou hast nothing of Christ, of Heaven, of Paradise risen from the dead, and new-born in thee, because they shine not forth in thee, and they take not thee in to see them, to be seen by them, to converse with them in their Spiritual, proper, eternal Forms, and Glories? It may be true, that they may not yet be sprung up in thee like the ripe corn in the ear in the Ripeness, and maturity of their own Spirituality, and of the Heavenly Image. Yet may they flourish in the Ear, that is, in a high and sweet Figure of Spirituality according to the purest letter of the Gospel, which may have the Spirit itself for a hidden life in it, and ready to reveal itself, as the perfect Fruit. But suppose thou hast not attained to this, yet sing for Joy; the Spring and the Summer Season are come; Harvest is not far off; if the Kingdom of God, which is Christ, Heaven, Paradise all in one, and all in a Heavenly Glory be come up in thee into a Green and Living stalk. Perhaps thou art yet subject to the Ministry of the Law. Rejoyce in this, if it Spring from the Seed of Promise, if it flourish by the Virtue, and Life of this Seed forming itself into this stalk, although it lie vailed there. This living Stalk, this living Ministry of the Law, hath not only an outward Glory, and Lustre upon it, but the inward Glory of the Spiritual Kingdom within it, which sends forth this outward Life, and Lustre, which will itself also in its proper season sprout forth from it.

Dost thou fall short of this also, dost thou see nothing in thy self of Letter or Spirit, of Law or Gospel, in any clearness of Life, or Power, by which thou canst make any comfortable Judgment of thy self; Are not these mournings of thine, that sence, those impressions, those desires, affections, endea-

vours,

vours, the causes and companions of these mournings, which come up so thick in the ground of thy Spirit by day, and by night; are not these that Kingdom of God, that Jesus, with Heaven, and Paradise in the midst of thee, before thine eyes, as in the Blade, or the Herb, which can hardly be discerned, or distinguished from common grass, by common eyes? In the mean time thou like *Mary* complainest, that Christ is taken away from thee, when he standeth before thee risen from the dead, and talketh with thee though vailed under the form of a Gardener.

But let it be that no green thing appears in the field of thy Soul, it is naked, cold, and hard, like the Earth in Winter. Yet mourn not as one without hope. This naked ground may be a flourishing field of Corn in the Summer time. This naked and hard heart of thine may in its proper Season soften, and flourish into an Heavenly Paradise by the springing up of Christ in it. For even now in this disconsolate & desolate state, may God the Father, and the Holy Angels from on high have their eye with Love, and delight upon it from one end of the year to the other, as seeing Heaven and Paradise with all their own Joys and Excellencies treasured up there in their seed, which is Christ, sown in thee.

3. *Ans.* The Heavenly Image in thee, who art born again, while thou livest on Earth, is subject to various Clouds, and Storms. It is always in a conjunction with the fleshly Image and the Spirit of the Devil. These never suffer it to shine forth clearly, and purely. These often so cloud it, and captivate it, that it can send forth no one sweet beam or spark to enlighten thee to any sensible discovery of it, or warm thee with any sensible comfort in it. The Law of God, which is the Law of the Spirit of Life, in which Spirit the Heaven, and Paradise of a Saint are seated, is within in the inward man, in the mind. But the Law of Sin, which is the Spirit of this World, where Death, Hell and the Devil, have their place, and their Throne, is still manifest and Powerful in thy Members, in thy outward man. What wonder then, if thine inward Man, like the Face of Heaven, and of an Heavenly Paradise with the Lord Jesus in his Spiritual Glory shining in them, as the Sun in its purity and strength, be discerned by thee very weakly, and uncertainly, when they are to be seen thorough so thick, so polluted, so troubled an Air of the natural Spirit in thy Members? Nay what wonder is it, if from the Morning of thy Life to the Evening of it, such blackness of darkness cover the whole Face, of these beautiful, and Heavenly things in thee, that they appear not at all to thee, although they constantly shine in the same Glory, and move in the same order in themselves, to themselves within thee; when as such Powers of Darkness have their seat in thine outward Man, thorough which they are to appear.

4. *Anſ.* Thou perhaps, O afflicted Soul, with the eye of Senſe, and of Reaſon, by the Light of thine own Spirit, lookeſt to ſee the Kingdom of God with its Joys, and Glories, and Glorious Inhabitants in thee. But theſe are Spiritual things, and to be diſcerned Spiritually. They are Spiritual Senſes, which alone can take in the Divine ſweetneſſes, and Beauties of this Spiritual Paradiſe, and Heaven. It is the Light of the Spirit alone, in which they ſhine forth and appear. It is the Breath of the Spirit alone, which makes their Spices to flow forth, and give their ſmells. Thou O dejected Soul! mayeſt have thy Spiritual ſenſes yet weak: Like a new-born Child thou mayeſt behold, and gaze upon the Light of the Heavenly Sun, and yet not underſtand, what that is, which thou ſeeſt, or that thou ſeeſt any thing at all. Again, the Spirit is free, he breaths, and gives his Light, where he pleaſeth, when he pleaſeth, and in what degree he pleaſeth. The Garden of God may be in thee, thou mayeſt be in the midſt of this Garden, and yet not aware of it, becauſe it is either a dark Seaſon, where nothing appears, or a twilight of the Spirit only, where the Flowers, and Plants of this Garden appear, like little Clouds, or dark ſpots undiſtinguiſhed.

5 *Anſ.* There are three ways, by which the new Birth or the Reſurrection from the dead evidenceth itſelf to the Soul. 1. The Seal of the Spirit. 2. The Witneſs of the Spirit. 3. A Spiritual Inſtinct.

1. The Seal of the Spirit is the cleareſt, and compleateſt evidence. Of this you read *Eph.* 1. *v* 13. *You are ſealed with that Holy Spirit of Promiſe.* The Spirit himſelf, in his own perſon was the Promiſe, and is the Seal. St. *John* 14. *v.* 20. Jeſus Chriſt in that Chapter promiſeth the Spirit, which he would ſend down, when he was aſcended, to be in them. He calleth this Spirit the Spirit of Truth, and the Comforter. Together with the promiſe of the Spirit he promiſeth them, that he would come again to them, and that they ſhould ſee him, and have Joy, and that none ſhould take this Joy from them; becauſe they ſhould never more loſe the ſight of him. He promiſeth likewiſe that at that day of the Spirit his Father, and himſelf would come together, and ſup with them, and lodge with them. The rich, and glorious ground of all this ſweet myſtery of the Divine Love, and Fellowſhip between the Father, and Chriſt, and the Spirit, and the Saints in the Spirit, at the coming of the Spirit is this: 1. The bleſſed Perſon of the Holy Spirit in the Trinity is the beautiful band of that ſweet, and ſacred Union, in which the two other Perſons the Father, and the Son moſt nakedly, moſt entirely at the utmoſt heighth of their Beauties, and Loves, poſſeſs and enjoy each other. The ſame Perſon of the Spirit in the myſtical, and Marriage Union between Chriſt, and the Soul, is that ſweet, and ſacred Unity, by the Virtue

of

of which the Father, Christ, and a Saint in the Purity, and Perfection of all Heavenly sweetnesses, and excellencies behold, love, and take Pleasure in each other, as one Spirit. By this you may see how the Spirit is the Promise, and the Seal and what this Seal of the Spirit means.

The Lord Jesus fully expresseth it in the verse mentioned: *At that day ye shall know that I am in my Father, and you in me, and I in you.* This day is the day of the Spirit, the day of the Spirits coming into the Soul, and appearing there. In the Revelation of this third Person the Holy Spirit, when he shines forth in the Spirit of a Saint; the Father, Christ, and a Saint are all seen together in one Glory, the Glory of the Father; in the Fellowship, and Unity of this Spirit, which is the Spirit of Glory. This Union, and this Vision takes the Saint up into itself, fixeth itself in a Saint, displayeth itself there by the immediate Brightness, and Glory of that Heavenly Person, the Spirit himself which is the Spirit of Truth. This is the Seal of the Spirit; this is the Banner of Love. Thus he sets himself as a Seal upon the Heart of his spouse, thus he spreads himself, as a Banner of Love over her head in his Banqueting-house. How clearly in this Day, in this Vision, and Unity of the Spirit doth the Beloved Spouse of Christ see Heaven and Paradise, ten thousand Heavens and Paradises, new-born, and risen within herself; herself new-born, and risen into the midst of them, and enjoying them all?

Dost thou mourn, O dejected Soul, that thou hast not received this Seal of the Spirit? Alas! how few have? How hath this Seal been withdrawn, since the Nations of the World received the mark of Anti-Christ? Mourn thou together with all the Saints, for the absence of the Heavenly Bridegroom in this Vision of his Glory, and Seal of his Love. But mourn not as without Hope. Press forward to this Day of the Spirit, and to the Brightness of the rising of the Lord Jesus together with the Father upon thy Soul in the Person of the Spirit, which is the Union of all Loves, Joys, and Glories, as all Lights are United in the Sun. This Day hath already dawned, some few have seen the dawnings of it, and rejoyced to see it, when it hath shone forth upon the tops of their Spirits, as the Sun in the pleasant morning of a Summers-day gilds the Tops of the Mountains.

2. The Second Evidence is the Witness of the Spirit. Of this *Paul* speaketh *Rom.* 8. *v.* 16. *The Spirit itself beareth Witness in our Spirit, that we are the Children of God.* This Witness of the Spirit may be more interrupted, and be accompanied in the Soul with less Glory, and a less triumphant Joy; yet is it clear, and sweet, and sure; although the clear-

clearneſs, and the ſweetneſs have their different degrees. The Witneſs of the Spirit is as the Voice of God in the Soul received, and ecchoed to by the Soul. The Seal of the Spirit is the Glorious Face of God unvailed in the Soul, and by the kiſs of its mouth Uniting it to the Soul, ſo that it ſtamps its own Heavenly Image upon the Soul, and Raviſhing the Soul into one Life, and Form of Glory with itſelf becomes its own Reflection there, equally embracing, and embraced, enjoying, and enjoyed in the Unity of the Spirit.

Thou, who ſeeſt not the Seal of the Spirit upon thy heart, open thy Spiritual Ear, hearken unto the voice of the Spirit, hearken to the voice of thine own Spirit. Theſe two by a ſweet Conſent, and Harmony may teſtifie together the Love of God in thee. Their voice may be low, and not to be heard in the Tumult, and noiſe of thy Fears, and Doubts. In the calmneſs, quietneſs, and reſt of a meek, and reſigned Spirit, hearken diligently, and thou mayeſt hear this low voice. Though this voice be low, yet is it clear and ſweet. The Love, and Peace, and Joy of the Spirit, the Spirit of Love, Peace, and Joy himſelf are in this low voice.

3. The third Evidence is the Inſtinct of the Spirit, which ſeems to be mentioned by St. *Paul*, as a leſs degree of Evidence going before that of the Witneſs of the Spirit. *Rom.* 8. 15. *Ye have received the Spirit of Adoption whereby ye Cry Abba Father.* The little Lamb newly yeaned, and come forth from the Dam in a great flock amongſt many Lambs, and Ews knoweth its own Dam, diſcerneth its call from all others, runneth to it, keepeth by its ſide, when it is in any fear, ſeeketh and ſucketh its Milk, and the nouriſhment of its Life from it. This is the Inſtinct of Nature, which faileth not the Births of Nature. Thus every Child of God hath much more a Spiritual, and Divine Inſtinct, which is inſeparable from the Divine Nature in it. The Spirit of God in it, when the Light of the Divine Nature is moſt obſcured, is a Spirit of Son-ſhip, or Childhood in the Soul by ſecret Impreſſions leading it, inclining, and carrying it to God, as its Father, giving it a ſecret ſenſe, and diſcerning of the Voice of God, and of its Relation to God, as by the inſtinct of the Divine Nature. Conſider this, ye doubting, fearful, and diſtreſſed Saints; conſider this, and be comforted. Thou haſt no clear ſight of the Face of God. Thou haſt no clear Teſtimony of the Love of God in thy Spirit. Thou haſt no diſtinct underſtanding of thy Union with God, or of the Nature of God, or of the things of God. Thou haſt no Evidences, by which thou canſt ſatisfy thy own Reaſon, thorow any diſcourſe of Reaſon. But thou art inwardly carryed in thy deſires, and inclinations to God, to pleaſe him, to be with him. Thy Soul ſecretly hangs upon God, and clea-

cleaveth to him. Thou inwardly longest, and thirstest to suck in from his Breasts the milk of Spiritual Life, Comfort, and Light. In the day of thy fears, and distress thine Eye looketh to God, thine Heart cryeth, and hasteth to him. The call, the voice of God in his Providences, his Word, and the inward motions of his Spirit touch thine Heart, and turn thy Bowels within thee. How often in the greatest doubts, and distresses of thy Spirit dost thou sigh forth to God the name of Father? Behold this is the instinct of the Divine Nature in thee. This is the Spirit of Adoption, by which thou art acted, and by which thou cryest *Abba* Father. Although thou understandest it no more, than the Lamb understandeth how, or why it is carryed to its Dam, and drawn by its bleatings. Go thy way then, and be no more troubled, give thy self up to the instinct, and leadings of this holy Spirit within thee. Thou shalt certainly see the time, when the obscure smoak of the Spiritual Instinct in thee will break up into a clear Light, and flame of a Joy unspeakable, and Glorious, both in the Testimony of the Spirit heard within thee, and the Seal of the Spirit seen upon thee, either in this Life, or in Eternity.

We read in the 2 of *Chron*. That *Solomons* Throne had a Foot-stool of Gold, and six steps up to the Throne. On each side of these steps *were two Lyons*, that supported every step. Thou, who hast the Throne of the Divine Nature in the midst of the Spiritual Paradise, and Heaven set up within thee in its obscurest, and lowest state, rest in peace, and joy on the Foot-stool it self, and upon the lowest step of this Throne. For the Foot-stool it self, *the lowest state is of* Gold, of an incorruptible, and Divine Nature, which will certainly in its proper time lift thee up to the full height, and Glory of the Throne it self. The lowest step here, even at the highest, hath for its support, and guard, two Lyons. The Lord Jesus, the true Lyon of the Tribe of *Judah* in all the Varieties, and Riches of his Spiritual Glories, multiplies his Presence, and Appearance round about thee, to sustain, defend, and cherish thee in these first beginnings of Grace in thee, in the midst of thy darkness, and weakness after the same manner, in the same Heavenly Person of his, in the same fulness of Love Power, and Glory, as he is with the highest Saints.

When we began to speak of this first step of the Resurrection, or new Birth, we propounded four Heads to treat upon. 1. The Life, which is risen. 2. The Death, out of which it riseth. 3. The Resurrection it self. 4. The way of this Resurrection. We have finished our discourse upon three of these. We are now to speak briefly of the last.

4. The way of the Resurrection in the new birth is Jesus Christ. He saith

ſaith of himſelf in the Goſpel of St. *John*, *I am the Way*. Jeſus Chriſt is the way of this Reſurrection in ſix Steps. 1. He is the Price. 2. The Head. 3. The Root. 4. The Pattern. 5. The Companion. 6. The Life of this Reſurrection.

1. The Blood of Chriſt is the Price of this Reſurrection. Jeſus Chriſt by his Blood hath doubly redeemed us from Death. 1. By Purchaſe giving his Life a Ranſom for us to the Divine Juſtice. 2. By Conqueſt having by the effuſion of his Blood, and loſs of his Life gained a perfect Victory over all the Powers of Darkneſs.

2. The Lord Jeſus above in Heaven is the Head of the Reſurrection from the Dead. In the latter part of the firſt of *Eph.* we have Jeſus Chriſt glorioully preſented unto us in his Reſurrection, from the nethermoſt part of the Earth, and in his Aſcent above all Heavens. Then the Apoſtle concludes that diſcourſe and Chapter with this Bleſſed Conſolation, that God had given him in this Glory of the Reſurrection from the Dead to be the Head over all things to his Church. Thou who mourneſt over thy ſins, as the worſt of Deaths, who doubteſt, who deſpaireſt of Life, raiſe thy ſelf to a lively Hope. Look up, and ſee thy ſelf already riſen in his Reſurrection, already ſet down in Heavenly Places together with Chriſt, as a Glorious Spirit in that firſt Spirit, the Head, and Fountain of them all, from which they are as Inſeparable as the Beams in their upper ends are from the Sun. Thus St. *Paul* ſpeaks in the former part of the 2d Chap. of the *Eph.* upon that Divine Ground, which he had laid in the end of the firſt Chapter, *That Chriſt in his Reſurrection from the Dead, is the Head over all to his Church.*

3. The Lord Jeſus, as he is riſen from the Dead by his Spiritual Preſence in our Hearts, is the root of the Reſurrection, or new Birth in us. 1 *Corin.* 15. Jeſus Chriſt, as he is the ſecond *Adam*, is ſaid to be a quickning Spirit; and the living corner Stone precious, and tryed in his Death, and precious in his Reſurrection, out of which we grow up to be a Temple to God, that is, both a Spiritual Heaven, and a Spiritual Paradiſe. *Eph.* 3. *He is ſaid to dwell in our Hearts by Faith.* The Lord Jeſus is that Spirit, which is the Root of all Spirits, natural, or ſupernatural; the Root of all Life, Natural, and Spiritual; Earthly or Heavenly; Humane, Angelical, or Divine. Doſt thou feel the weight of Death heavy upon thee? haſt thou no ſenſe of any ſpark of true Life in thee to ſweeten either Death, or Life to thee? Look up to thy Root at the bottom of thy Spirit, thy Jeſus. Abide in this Root, wait for this Root. Here are all

the

the Treasures of Spiritual Life laid up. At the set time, in the proper season this Root shall spring, and bud, and blossom, and bring forth it's heavenly Fruits replenished with the Light, and sweetness of the Divine Life and spreading themselves thorow thy whole Soul. Thus shall that Life of God, which thou hast lost, which in thy death retired itself hither into its Root, rise again in thee, and thou be new-born into this Life. Thus shall Jesus Christ, as an Heavenly Root in thy Heart, bring forth himself unto the Life of Faith, which is his own Heavenly Image in thee within the Vail, the Cloud of Flesh. Thus doth he make thine heart from this Root of Eternity to be an Heavenly Habitation, and dwelling place for himself raised up new, and Eternal out of the Ruines of Death.

4. Our blessed Saviour is the Pattern of the Resurrection to us. In the 8th of the *Rom.* we are said to be predestinated to be conformed to his Image. *Eph.* 1. God is spoken of as working Faith, and so bringing forth the Spiritual Life in us according to that exceeding greatness of his Power, by which he raised Christ from the Dead. We read in the Gospel, that a mighty Angel came down from Heaven, and rolled away the Stone from the mouth of the Grave, while the Watchmen about the Grave were cast into a deep sleep, to make way for the rising of Christ. How frequently doth the Soul, which feels the horrour of the Spiritual Death, think its Resurrection to a Divine Life, to the Heavenly Graces, and sweet Peaces of that Life, impossible? Alass! the Flesh is as a Grave, in which it is shut up. Its Lusts, and Temptations are, as a mighty Stone rolled upon the mouth of this Grave. Tempters visible and invisible are, as Watchmen round about the Grave, to keep thee there. But be not discouraged at any of these things, O thou disconsolate Soul! Look to thy Pattern, the Lord Jesus; as it was with him; so shall it be with thee. A supernatural Power, a mighty Angel from Heaven shall bind up thy Tempters, thy Spiritual Enemies in chains of Darkness, as in a deep sleep; shall remove the great Stone, the most powerful Lusts, and Temptations from the mouth of thy Grave. God himself in his Power, in the greatness of his Power, as it excelleth, and transcendeth all Powers, all things, all thoughts of men, or Angels; God himself in his Almightiness, in the infiniteness of his Power, and God-head, God himself in the immediate naked, most potent, most high, most Glorious Appearances, and Operations of his God-head shall come down upon thee, shall arise, and shine in thee, and as he riseth, raise thee together with himself into the Light of Life. Whil'st thou lyest in Sin, thy true Person, or Life lie together dead in thee, as to thee, But beneath thy Soul, at the bottom of it they lie hid in God, who is the ground of every natural being, and the Treasury

sury of all Spiritual Beings. At the season of the new birth God disco covers himself in thy Soul, as a glorious ground, out of which thy Life, and thy Jesus spring up together by degrees, like Twin-lillies, Roses from the same stalk or root, which is Christ. Thus shalt thou rise from the Dead with a shout of Heavenly Joys.

5. Christ is the Companion in the Resurrection. St. *Paul* tells the *Galatians*, he travels in birth again with them, till Christ be formed in them, We read 1 *Corin.* 6. *He, that is joyned to the Lord is one Spirit.* A saint and Christ are one Spirit by a Spiritual Marriage, which makes two Spirits perfectly one, yet so, that they remain perfectly, and distinctly two in one. When thou risest from the dead in Regeneration, thy Jesus riseth together with thee out of that Grave in thy Heart, into which thou hast cast him by thy Sin at the Fall, when thou in thy true Life, and Paradise in thee fell into the same Grave together with him. Jesus Christ, and the Soul spring up together in the first Creation as Twins. For St. *John* saith in his first Chapter of his Gospel, that without him, that is, in a single state disjoyned from Christ, was nothing made, that was made; Christ and the Soul, like two Twin-lillies, flourished together in Paradise. Together they died by the Fall. Many times since thy birth into this world have Jesus Christ, and with him that Beautiful, and Blessed Life, which thou enjoyed'st in Paradise, been rising again into thy Heart into a more excelling Paradise, *that* in the Spirit, and in Heaven, which is Eternal. But alass! thou hast still thrown them back again into the same Grave in thy flesh by the new wounds, which thy renewed Lusts, and Unbelief have given them. Notwithstanding all this, when the set time is come, nothing can withstand the rising in thee. Jesus Christ, and thy Soul are together born anew in thee from the womb of Eternal Love, where they lay hid, and wrapt up together in the Grave itself. They now come up together in one Spirit into one Spiritual Life, and Heavenly Image, in which Paradise also comes up new and fresh together with them. By the same immediate, and glorious operation of the God-head they break irresistibly forth thorow the darknesses of the night, and scatters them, and breaks them up, as it shines thorow them. How blessed is this Union and Fellowship! Christ and the Soul ever undivided, grow up now together in the mutual sight, in the mutual embraces of each other thorow every state and degree of the Regeneration, or Resurrection, Light, or Darkness; Solaces or Sufferings; Life, or Death. In all by the Heavenly Union they are mutually a Crown of rejoycing one to another.

6. Christ

6. Christ is the Life of this Resurrection. So himself testifieth in the 11 of St. *John*; I am the Resurrection, and the Life. How sure, how sweet is thy Life, O Believer, who art risen from the Death of Sin, and born again to thine Heavenly Father? Thy Life is sure. It is Christ himself, the Power, God, eternal Life itself, who is thy Life, the Life of thy Graces here, the Living Hope of Glory in Heaven, the Life of God in thee which never dies in the midst of Death. Thy Life is sweet, O Believer! How unexpressible is this pleasure to feel Jesus Christ himself, the only delight of the Father in Eternity, the only Delight of all the Holy Angels, and Glorified Saints in Heaven springing up in thy Heart, flowing thorow thy whole Soul, and Person, working in all, acting all, as Life in thee?

Thus I have finished this fourth Head, the way of the Resurrection in its first step, the Regeneration, or New-birth, and the discourse itself upon this subject.

FINIS.

ERRATA'S.

PAge 15. line 22. for *word*, r. *world*, p. 19. l. 25. for *and thou*, r. *O thou*, p. 55. l. 1. for *spirit*, r. *letter*, p. 66. l. 15. for *three*, r. *four*, p. 115. l. 38. *dele by*, p. 126. l. 2. *dele* the first *have*, p. 139. l. 2. for *ni*, r. *in*, l. 14. for *an*, r. *any*, p. 151. l. 1. for *no*, r. *not*, l. 7. for *divinesss*, r. *divineness*, p. 158. l. 22. for *thee*, r. *the*, p. 175. l. *ult.* for *their*, r. *there*, p. 189. l. 16. for *because*, r. *and 3dly because*, p. 194. l. 14. for *word*, r. *words*, p. 205. l. 11. *dele* the first *1*, p. 206. l. 32. for *beautiful*, r. *beauty*, p. 208. l. 39. *dele* ? at the word *below*, p. 210. l. 17. for *of spirit*, r. *of the spirit*, p. 211. l. 20. for *creature*, r. *creatures*, p. 228. l. 35. for *forms*, r. *form*, p. 236. l. 24. for *each in*, r. *each creature in*, p. 249. l. 20. for *form*, r. *forms*, p. 252. l. 33. for *though be it*, r. *though it be*, p. 279. l. 9. for *Use 3d*, r. *Use 4th*, p. 294. l. 35. for *pants*, r. *plants*, p. 297. l. 5. for *the glory*, r. *with glory*, p. 299. l. 27. for 4, r. 1. p. 300. l. 32. for *so God is light*, r. *so God is life*, p. 301. l. 31. for *the Divine Sea*, r. *the Divine Saint*, p. 311. l. 3. for *3 steps*, r. *4 steps*, p. 314. l. 11. for *is vizor*, r. *is a vizor*, p. 315. l. 28. for *thine nature*, r. *thy nature*, l. 39. for *fields*, r. *field*, p. 319. l. 39. for *is it*, r. *it is*, p. 321. l. 16. for *thy will*, r. *thy God*, p. 325. l. 22. for *four*, r. *two*, p. 329. l. 17. for *nature of this thing*, r. *nature of things*, p. 332. l. 33. for, *which the will*, r. *which is the will*, p. 335. l. 35. for *are*, r. *have*, p. 341. l. 4. for *flesh*, r. *fleshly*, p. 342. l. 19. for *beware*, r. *2dly beware*, p. 349. l. 41. for *it conquest*, r. *its conquest*, p. 350. l. 39. *dele the Light*, p. 352. l. 14. for *to the end*, r. *to the end are removed*, p. 380. l. 25. for *thus*, r. *thou*, l. 41. for *o passionate*, r. *of passionate*, p. 392. l. 36. for *poure h*, r. *poured*, p. 423. l. 9. for *are*, r. *ere*, p. 433. l. 7. for *tof*, r. *of*, p. 448. l. 27. for *it is*, r. *it*, p. 450. l. 17. for *so*, r. *see*, p. 451. l. 21. for *same*, r. *next*, for 1 *Cor.* r. 2 *Cor.* p. 472. l. 32. for *resteth*, r. *rested*, p. 480 l. 7. r. *form.* p. 512. l. 3. r. *Look to thy Root.*

Lightning Source UK Ltd.
Milton Keynes UK
UKOW041902071211

183365UK00005B/15/P

9 781171 269366